THE ROUTLEDGE HA
EUROPEAN SECURITY

This new Handbook brings together key experts on European security from the academic and policy worlds to examine the European Union (EU) as an international security actor.

In the two decades since the end of the Cold War, the EU has gradually emerged as an autonomous actor in the field of security, aiming to safeguard European security by improving global security. However, the EU's development as a security actor has certainly not remained uncontested, either by academics or by policy-makers, some of whom see the rise of the EU as a threat to their national and/or transatlantic policy outlook.

While the focus of this volume is on the politico-military dimension, security is also put into the context of the holistic approach advocated by the EU. The book is organized into four key sections:

Part I: The EU as an international security actor
Part II: Institutions, instruments and means
Part III: Policies
Part IV: Partners.

This Handbook will be of great interest to students of European security, the EU, European politics, security studies and IR in general.

Sven Biscop is Director of the Europe in the World Programme at Egmont – Royal Institute for International Relations in Brussels, and Editor-in-Chief of its journal *Studia Diplomatica* and its *Egmont Papers*. He teaches at Ghent University and the College of Europe (Bruges).

Richard G. Whitman is Professor of Politics and International Relations in the School of Politics and International Relations at the University of Kent, and an Associate Fellow at Chatham House.

THE ROUTLEDGE HANDBOOK OF EUROPEAN SECURITY

Edited by Sven Biscop and Richard G. Whitman

Routledge
Taylor & Francis Group

LONDON AND NEW YORK

First published 2013
by Routledge
2 Park Square, Milton Park, Abingdon, Oxfordshire OX14 4RN

Simultaneously published in the USA and Canada
by Routledge
711 Third Avenue, New York, NY 10017

First issued in paperback 2014

Routledge is an imprint of the Taylor & Francis Group, an informa business

British Library Cataloguing in Publication Data
A catalogue record for this book is available from the British Library

Library of Congress Cataloging in Publication Data
The Routledge handbook of European security / edited by Sven Biscop and
Richard G. Whitman.
p. cm.
Includes bibliographical references and index.
1. Security, International--European Union countries. 2. Security, International-
-Government policy--European Union countries. 3. National security--European
Union countries. 4. Strategic culture--European Union countries. 5. European Union
countries--Foreign relations. 6. European Union countries--Military policy. I. Biscop,
Sven. II. Whitman, Richard G.
JZ6009.E94R68 2012   355'.03304--dc23
2012008308

ISBN 978–0–415–58828–7 (hbk)
ISBN 978–1–138–84087–4 (pbk)
ISBN 978–0–203–09841–7 (ebk)

Typeset in Bembo and Minion Pro
by Bookcraft Ltd, Stroud, Gloucestershire

To Sven and Aberu, husband and husband since 5 May 2012. We do not believe in matches made in heaven, but we do believe in matches made in Asia.

CONTENTS

Contents

LIST OF FIGURES,
MAPS AND TABLES

Figures

Maps

Tables

CONTRIBUTORS

Åsne Kalland Aarstad is a PhD candidate at the Department of Political Science at Aarhus University. Her research focuses on the privatization of military and security services and its implications on threat perceptions. Recent publications include the chapter 'The EU and the Private Military and Security Industry: regulatory challenges and opportunities' in *Europe and International Institutions: Performance, Policy, Power* (Routledge, 2012).

Jan Joel Andersson is Senior Research Fellow and head of the programme on Defence, Security and Development Policy at the Swedish Institute of International Affairs (UI) in Stockholm and Dragas Distinguished Visiting Professor of International Studies at Old Dominion University in Norfolk, Virginia. Dr. Andersson received his PhD from the University of California at Berkeley and has taught International Relations at Berkeley, Stockholm and Uppsala. He has been a Visiting Fellow at the EU Institute for Security Studies in Paris and served on the staff of a US Senator on Capitol Hill in Washington, DC.

Sami Andoura is Senior Research Fellow at Notre Europe, the European think tank created by Jacques Delors, where he heads research projects on EU energy policy and Europe External Actions. He is the deputy editor-in-chief of *Studia Diplomatica* and a Senior Associate Fellow at Egmont – Royal Institute for International Relations. Andoura completed his degree in Law at Paris II Panthéon-Assas University and holds LLMs in European Business Law from Paris II Panthéon-Assas, in International Economic Law from Paris I Panthéon-Sorbonne and in European Legal Studies from the College of Europe.

Javier Argomaniz is a Lecturer in International Relations at the St Andrews Centre for the Study of Terrorism and Political Violence (CSTPV). Dr Argomaniz's general interests lie in the areas of international cooperation in counter-terrorism, the application of quantitative methodologies to the study of terrorism, and EU security policies. He has recently published a monograph for Routledge on the coherence of the European response to the threat of transnational terrorism and currently co-directs an EU-funded project studying terrorism victims associations in the UK and Spain.

Sven Biscop is Director of the Europe in the World Programme at Egmont – Royal Institute for International Relations in Brussels, and editor-in-chief of its journal *Studia Diplomatica* and its *Egmont Papers*. He teaches at Ghent University and the College of Europe (Bruges), and is an Associate of the Centre for European Studies at Renmin University (Beijing) and the Geneva Centre for Security Policy. He sits on the Executive Academic Board of the European Security and Defence College, the Scientific Council of the Institut d'Etudes Stratégiques de l'Ecole Militaire (Paris), and the Strategic Advisors Group of the Atlantic Council (Washington, DC).

Malte Brosig is a Senior Lecturer in International Relations at the University of the Witwatersrand in Johannesburg. He holds a PhD from Portsmouth University and is a Senior Non-Resident Research Fellow at the European Centre for Minority Issues and Co-Chair of the Human Rights Working Group of the German Political Science Association. His research interests focus on IO interplay and security governance in Africa and minority rights and compliance research in Europe. He has recently published a special issue on IO interplay in the *South African Journal of International Affairs*.

Jo Coelmont is a Senior Associate Fellow at Egmont – Royal Institute for International Relations and a Senior Fellow at the Belgian Royal Defence College and retired from active duty in 2008 as a Brigadier-General in the Belgian Air Force. He was the Belgian Permanent Representative to the Military Committee of the EU and the WEU, and Military Advisor to the Belgian Ambassador to the Political and Security Committee of the EU, from January 2002 to October 2007. In April 2006 he was elected Dean of the EUMC.

Karen Del Biondo has a Master's in International Relations (Ghent University) and EU Studies (Université Libre de Bruxelles). She is a PhD candidate at the Centre for EU Studies at Ghent University. Her research is funded by the Flemish Fund for Scientific Research (FWO-Vlaanderen) and focuses on EU political conditionality in sub-Saharan Africa, EU development policies and EU–Africa relations.

Geoffrey Edwards is Reader in European Studies in the Department of Politics and International Studies in the University of Cambridge and Jean Monnet Chair in Political Science. He has been a Fellow of Pembroke College, Cambridge since 1993, where he has also been a Graduate Tutor. He received his PhD from the London School of Economics and thereafter worked at the Foreign and Commonwealth Office and then in various think tanks, including Chatham House, and taught for the University of Southern California and the University of Essex before taking up his post in Cambridge.

Catriona Gourlay is the Research and Knowledge Manager at PeaceNexus, a Swiss operational foundation that provides tailored expertise to organisations working on peacebuilding. Working as a consultant from 2010 to 2012 she provided research support and advice to international agencies, governments and NGOs. Previously from 2005 she was Research Fellow at the United Nations Institute for Disarmament. From 1995 to 2005 she was the founding executive director of the Brussels-based International Security Information Service, Europe. She has published on a range of crisis management and peacebuilding issues, in particular in relation to EU and UN interventions. She holds a PhD in International Relations from the University of Lancaster, a Masters in International Relations from the University of Pennsylvania and one in Politics, Philosophy and Economics from Oxford University.

Contributors

Richard Gowan is an Associate Director at New York University's Center on International Cooperation and a Senior Policy Fellow at the European Council on Foreign Relations. In 2005–6 he coordinated the first edition of the *Annual Review of Global Peace Operations*, and in 2010 he edited the first *Review of Political Missions*. He also edited *Cooperating for Peace and Security* (Cambridge University Press, 2010) with Bruce D. Jones and Shepard Forman and is working on a book about multilateral crisis management since the Iraq War.

Eva Gross is Senior Research Fellow and head of the research cluster European Foreign and Security Policy at the Institute for European Studies at the Vrije Universiteit Brussel. She is the author of *The Europeanization of National Foreign Policy: Continuity and Change in European Crisis Management* (Palgrave Macmillan, 2009 and 2011); and co-editor of *EU Conflict Prevention and Crisis Management: Roles, Institutions and Policies* (Routledge, 2011). She holds a PhD from the London School of Economics, and has been a Visiting Fellow at the Center for Transatlantic Relations, SAIS/Johns Hopkins University (Washington, DC) and the EU Institute for Security Studies (Paris).

Hiski Haukkala is a Professor of International Relations at the School of Management at the University of Tampere, Finland. He was formerly a Special Adviser at the Ministry for Foreign Affairs of Finland. He has also worked at the Finnish Institute of International Affairs and the University of Turku and held visiting positions at the EU Institute of Security Studies (Paris), the IISS (London) as well as in the Department of Politics, University of Stirling (Scotland). He is the author of *The EU–Russia Strategic Partnership: The Limits of Post-Sovereignty in International Relations* (Routledge, 2010).

Jolyon Howorth is Jean Monnet Professor of European Politics and Emeritus Professor of European Studies at the University of Bath. He has been a full-time Visiting Professor of Political Science and International Affairs at Yale University since 2002. He is a Senior Research Associate at the Institut Français des Relations Internationales (Paris), a Fellow of the Royal Society for the Arts, Chevalier dans l'Ordre des Palmes Académiques (France) and Member of the Advisory Boards of the European Institute for Public Administration (Netherlands), the Centre for the Study of Security and Diplomacy (UK), and the Institut de Recherches Stratégiques de l'Ecole Militaire (Paris).

Adrian Hyde-Price is Professor of International Politics at the University of Bath, where he lectures on international security. His main publications include *European Security in the Twenty-First Century* (2007); *Germany and European Order* (2000); *The International Politics of East Central Europe* (1996); and *European Security beyond the Cold War* (1991). He has also co-edited *British Foreign Policy and the Anglican Church* (2007); *Europe's New Security Challenges* (2001); and *Security and Identity in Europe: The New Agenda* (2000).

Knud Erik Jørgensen is Professor of International Relations at Aarhus University. He is the chair of the ECPR Standing Group on International Relations and former editor of the journal *Cooperation and Conflict*. Recent publications include *The European Union and International Organizations* (Routledge, 2009); *International Relations Theory: A New Introduction* (Palgrave, 2010); and *The European Union and International Institutions: Performance, Policy, Power* (Routledge, 2012).

Michael Merlingen is an Associate Professor at the Central European University in Budapest. He is the author of *European Union Peacebuilding and Policing: Governance and the*

European Security and Defence Policy (Routledge, 2006, with R. Ostrauskaitè) and *European Security and Defense Policy: What It Is, How It Works, Why It Matters* (Lynne Rienner, 2012), and has co-edited (with Ostrauskaitè) *European Security and Defence Policy: An Implementation Perspective* (Routledge, 2008).

Christoph O. Meyer is Professor of European and International Politics at King's College London and Director of the 'Foresight' research group on warning and preventive policy, which was originally funded by the European Research Council. He is also the Co-Chair of a Task Force on improving the EU's capacities for the prevention of mass atrocities. His most recent books are *Forecasting, Warning and Responding to Transnational Risks* (Palgrave, 2011) and *The Quest for a European Strategic Culture* (Palgrave, 2006).

Leo Michel is a Senior Research Fellow at the Institute for National Strategic Studies at the National Defense University in Washington, DC. Previously he was Director for NATO Policy within the Office of the Secretary of Defense. During more than 17 years in OSD, he has worked on a range of nuclear and non-nuclear policy issues and international negotiations involving the former Soviet Union. During 1996–9, he served as the first OSD representative on the senior faculty of the Geneva Centre for Security Policy. Mr Michel served as a US Navy officer during 1969–72.

Costanza Musu is an Associate Professor in the Graduate School of Public and International Affairs at the University of Ottawa. She obtained her PhD from the London School of Economics and Political Science. Subsequently she was Jean Monnet Fellow in the Transatlantic Programme of the Robert Schuman Centre for Advanced Studies at the European University Institute in Florence and Assistant Professor of International Relations at Richmond University (London). Her latest book on European policy towards the Arab–Israeli peace process was published by Palgrave Macmillan.

Stefan Oltsch holds a Diploma degree (master's level) in Social Sciences from the Leibniz University Hanover. With a focus on international relations, his research topics are the security–development nexus and human security in European development policy. He is a member of the Working Group European Studies at the Leibniz University Hanover and coordinated the Interdisciplinary Master's Programme in European Studies between 2004 and 2008. He currently lives in Manila, the Philippines, and consults for governmental and non-governmental development cooperation organizations in the fields of security and conflict sensitivity.

Jan Orbie is a Professor at the Department of Political Science of Ghent University, as well as the co-director of the Centre for EU Studies, and a member of the university's Research Council. He has edited two books on EU trade and development politics (with Gerrit Faber, Routledge, 2007 and 2009), one on European external policies (Ashgate, 2008), and one on Europe's global social policies (with Lisa Tortell, Routledge, 2008), and has co-edited special issues of *European Foreign Affairs Review* (2009 and 2011), *Res Publica* (2008), and the *Journal of Contemporary European Research* (forthcoming).

Oleksandr Pavlyuk has for the past ten years worked for the Organization for Security and Co-operation in Europe (OSCE), including as Head of External Cooperation at the Secretariat (Vienna) and as Senior Policy and Planning Adviser to the Secretary General. Before joining the OSCE, he was Director of the Kyiv Centre of the EastWest Institute

(1997–2001). He is author of *Ukraine's Struggle for Independence and US Policy (1917–1923)* (UKMA, 1996, in Ukrainian), and editor of *Building Security in the New States of Eurasia* (M.E. Sharpe, 2000) and *The Black Sea Region: Cooperation and Security Building* (M.E. Sharpe, 2004).

Walter Posch is a Senior Research Fellow working on Iranian domestic, foreign and security policy at the German International and Foreign Policy Institute (Berlin). He previously worked at the EU Institute for Security Studies (Paris) and at the National Defence Academy (Vienna).

Gerrard Quille works in the Policy Department of the Directorate-General for External Policies of the EU in the European Parliament. Previously, he served as Director of the International Security Information Service – Europe (Brussels), and as Deputy Director of ISIS-UK (London), where he was also a Research Associate at the Centre for Defence Studies. He has completed an Economic and Social Research Council-funded PhD at the Department of Peace Studies, University of Bradford, on the role and conduct of Defence Reviews as a mechanism in the UK's management of defence.

Wyn Rees is Professor of International Security in the School of Politics and International Relations at the University of Nottingham. His research interests are threefold. First, contemporary transatlantic security relations and European security, especially the debates surrounding institutional 'architecture'. Second, counter-terrorism and the cooperation that occurs between Western countries. Third, postwar British security policy with a particular focus on recent debates about the country's role in the world. His most recent publication is *The US–EU Security Relationship: The Tensions between a European and a Global Agenda* (Palgrave Macmillan, 2011).

Thomas Renard is a Research Fellow in the Europe in the World Programme at Egmont – Royal Institute for International Relations (Brussels) and a PhD candidate at Ghent University. His research focuses on the multipolarization of international relations, and on the relationship between the EU and emerging powers in the framework of the strategic partnerships. He is a regular Guest Lecturer at the College of Europe (Bruges), Ghent University and the Université Catholique de Louvain (UCL). He holds an MA from the Elliott School of International Affairs, the George Washington University.

James Rogers is co-editor of European Geostrategy. He is completing his PhD in European Studies at Pembroke College, Cambridge. He holds an MPhil in Contemporary European Studies from Hughes Hall, Cambridge and a BSc Econ. with first class honours in International Politics and Strategic Studies from Aberystwyth University. In 2008, he was a Visiting Fellow at the EU Institute for Security Studies.

Richard G. Whitman is Professor of Politics and International Relations in the School of Politics and International Relations at the University of Kent, and an Associate Fellow at Chatham House. He was Professor of Politics at the University of Bath 2006–11, and Senior Fellow, Europe (April 2006–April 2007) and Head of the European Programme at Chatham House (April 2004–April 2006). He is on the editorial boards of *European Security* and *Studia Diplomatica*. Professor Whitman was elected an Academician of the Academy of Social Sciences in October 2007 and currently chairs the University Association for Contemporary European Studies (UACES).

Richard Youngs is Director General of FRIDE in Madrid and Assistant Professor at the University of Warwick. Prior to joining FRIDE, he was EU Marie Curie Research Fellow at the Norwegian Institute for International Relations, Oslo (2001–4), and senior research fellow at the UK Foreign and Commonwealth Office (1995–8). He has a PhD and an MA in International Studies from the University of Warwick and a BA in Social and Political Science from the University of Cambridge. His latest work is *Europe's Decline and Fall: The Struggle against Global Irrelevance* (Profile Books, 2010).

INTRODUCTION

Sven Biscop and Richard G. Whitman

In the 20 years since the end of the Cold War, the European Union (EU) has gradually emerged as an autonomous actor in the field of security, aiming to safeguard European security by improving global security: 'A Secure Europe in a Better World', as the 2003 *European Security Strategy* (ESS) has it. A key aspect of this development has been the emergence of a defence component through the EU's European Security and Defence Policy (ESDP), rebaptized the Common Security and Defence Policy (CSDP) by the Lisbon Treaty. The EU's development as a security actor has certainly not remained uncontested, neither by academics, some of whom deny the EU the capacity to be an effective global actor, nor by policy-makers, some of whom see the rise of the EU as a threat to their national and/or transatlantic policy outlook. Yet regardless of one's normative perspective on this emerging international role for the EU, its development can definitely not be denied: in spite of all its imperfections, the EU presence as a security actor is here – and the trend is that it is here to stay.

The aim of this Handbook is to bring together the key experts on European security from the university and think-tank worlds and assess the state of play of the EU as an international security actor. While the focus is on the politico-military dimension (CSDP and CFSP – Common Foreign and Security Policy), security will be put in the context of the holistic approach advocated by the EU.

The Handbook does not shy away from taking sides: it is the conviction of the editors and contributors that the development of the EU as an autonomous actor in this area is a positive evolution, offering the best chances for effective European policies to safeguard and enhance European security in an increasingly multipolar world. Labels abound to describe the EU: civilian, normative or transformative power, *puissance tranquille* – if a label is required, perhaps 'positive power' can serve (Biscop 2005). More important than the adjective is the noun: the EU must be a *power*, an effective strategic actor. Being a model for others to emulate is not sufficient, for too many, swayed by nationalism, radicalism, fundamentalism or just cynicism, simply no longer see the EU as a model. Attractiveness alone does not generate soft power – the EU must be seen to act upon its strategy. The EU therefore cannot be a status quo power that seeks to maintain current conditions: its agenda entails a commitment to proactively shape the environment.

The idea of the EU as a power is mentioned neither in the ESS nor in the 2008 Report on the Implementation of the ESS – the former states only that because of its weight the

EU 'is inevitably a global player'. To be a power rather than a player demands a much more self-confident and voluntarist outlook. The European Council's Laeken Declaration (15 December 2001) had already put it in much more assertive terms:

> Now that the Cold War is over and we are living in a globalised, yet also highly fragmented world, Europe needs to shoulder its responsibilities in the governance of globalisation. The role it has to play is that of a power resolutely doing battle against all violence, all terror and all fanaticism, but which also does not turn a blind eye to the world's heartrending injustices. In short, a power wanting to change the course of world affairs in such a way as to benefit not just the rich countries but also the poorest. A power seeking to set globalisation within a moral framework, in other words to anchor it in solidarity and sustainable development.

The EU definitely has the means to be a power – if that is what it *wants* to be. This brings us back to the starting point: our belief that the EU must be an autonomous strategic actor. That implies the choice of a certain type of Union. An EU that is a mere market simply cannot be a grand strategic actor. This is Europe as a process: a platform for functional economic cooperation between sovereign states, which may continue to evolve in line with the technical needs of the internal market. Such a Europe does not constitute a pole of the multipolar world; it lacks the centre of gravity to be a strategic actor. But as argued above, if Europe wants to safeguard its interests vis-à-vis the other large strategic actors, it has no choice but to become one itself. That automatically entails the choice for Europe as a project: an ever deepening political union in which Member States pool sovereignty in order to pursue their common vision with maximum effect.

In that sense, this Handbook takes stock of the EU's achievements to date in the area of international security. The Handbook is organized in four parts:

- Part I sets the scene. After a historical overview of the development of European security institutions, and a theoretical perspective on this development, it analyses the holistic 'grand strategy' underlying EU policies and assesses whether a European strategic culture has emerged.
- Part II looks at the institutions that make and implement policy in the different dimensions covered by the 'grand strategy', charts the instruments and means at their disposal and assesses the extent to which 'sub-strategies' in each area are linked up with the overall objectives put forward in the ESS and the 2008 Report on the Implementation of the ESS.
- Part III then assesses the effectiveness of the actual policies and actions undertaken, focusing on CSDP, but putting the politico-military dimension in the context of the holistic approach and other EU policies towards third countries/regions.
- Part IV analyses the role of partnerships with other actors in these policies.

Each chapter critically examines EU objectives, instruments and means, in order to assess their effectiveness, identify the weaknesses and offer some recommendations for the way ahead. Thus the Handbook is not only retrospective, looking back at and evaluating what the EU has done, but also prospective, putting forward proposals to enhance the effectiveness of EU security policy. And that is exactly what political science is for.

PART I

The EU as an international security actor

1

EUROPEAN SECURITY INSTITUTIONS 1945–2010

The weaknesses and strengths of 'Brusselsization'

Jolyon Howorth

A 'security institution' can be anything from a treaty-based alliance such as NATO to a small European Council Secretariat working-group such as the Committee on the Western Balkans (COWEB). Hundreds of such institutions contribute to the management of European security. The common feature behind all of them is their underlying purpose: cooperation in the field of security between sovereign member states and/or their agents. The underlying assumption is that each institution offers a positive-sum outcome. The post-World War II history of such institutions nevertheless reveals a tension between two contrasting approaches to security: Europeanist and Atlanticist; externalized and internalized (Cleveland, 1966; Schmidt, 2001). For the greater part of the Cold War period, Atlanticism and externalization held undisputed sway through NATO. However, prior to 1954 and since the mid-1980s, attempts to create *internalized Europeanist* institutions have competed with, while nevertheless simultaneously attempting to cooperate with, the NATO model. This double dichotomy was brought into focus as early as 11 November 1944 during a meeting in Paris between Winston Churchill and Charles de Gaulle. De Gaulle suggested to Churchill that, whatever the differences in the wartime experiences of their two countries, when faced with the new reality of a bipolar world dominated by two superpowers, they henceforth shared objective strategic comparability, and probably identical interests. De Gaulle proposed a Franco-British security partnership – both to put Europe back on its feet and to help shape the contours of the emerging world order (de Gaulle, 1959: 63–4 and 367–78). Churchill listened attentively before informing de Gaulle that, unlike France, which effectively had only a European option, Great Britain also had an Atlantic option, from which the country fully intended to benefit (Churchill, 1954: 218–20). Thus were evoked, even before the war ended, the two dimensions of that double dichotomy which has divided European policy-makers ever since.

During the closing months of World War II, blueprints for the creation of a *West European security bloc* had been developed in a number of European countries – Norway, Holland, Belgium, France and Britain (Young, 1984: 5). Notwithstanding Churchill's response to de Gaulle, virtually all these different projects attributed to the UK, in association with

France, the responsibility for leading such a European security arrangement. At first, the British seemed keen. In the immediate post-war years, Britain saw closer association with the Continent as essential – albeit limited to military and security issues (Young, 1984: 7). Most 'continentals' on the other hand were already thinking in terms of economic and even political integration. The institutional process which would eventually lead to the Treaty of Lisbon in 2009 was tentatively set in motion. The Franco-British Treaty of Dunkirk (4 March 1947), essentially directed against a hypothetical resurgent Germany, was the first formal post-war agreement between two European nation-states (Greenwood, 1989). By the spring of 1948, both the launch of the Marshall Plan (5 June 1947) and the Soviet take-over of Czechoslovakia (February 1948) had transformed the European security situation. The German 'problem' had been overtaken by the Soviet 'threat'. Europe needed to close ranks. The Treaty of Brussels (17 March 1948) marked the first major step on the road to European integration, involving as it did economic, social, cultural and security dimensions. Although the term 'Brusselsization' was coined only in the 1990s (Allen, 1998) the phenomenon first appeared as early as 1948.

The Brussels Treaty was impelled by both an internal European logic (it made eminent sense for the European nation-states to put an end to their centuries-long civil war) and an external American logic (the Marshall Plan was conditional on the European recipient states coming together to cooperate on optimal spending of the US stimulus money). In this way, the externalization/internalization dichotomy was hard-wired into the very origins of the European security-institutional process. That dichotomy was reinforced by two consecutive events, one featuring externalization, the other internalization. The first was the European effort, between 1948 and 1949, to persuade the USA to enter into an entangling alliance, the result of which was the creation of NATO (Cook, 1989; Acheson, 1987). The second was the parallel effort, between 1950 and 1954, to establish a European Defence Community (EDC) (Fursdon, 1980). While European nations (including France and the UK) proved prepared to pool and indeed even to alienate sovereignty in the US-underwritten security institutions of NATO, they ultimately proved unwilling (especially France and the UK) to share sovereignty in a purely European institutional arrangement such as the EDC. Instead, they built on the 1948 Brussels commitments through the 1950 creation of the European Coal and Steel Community (ECSC), the first supranational institution of the future EU. According to its architect, Jean Monnet, the ECSC's avowed aim was, by pooling the raw materials of conflict, to 'make war not only unthinkable but materially impossible'. However, the early promise of internalized security institutions faded with the 1954 defeat of the EDC. The dynamic created by the ECSC was instead to lead to the 1957 Treaty of Rome, which prioritized integration through markets and economics. At the same time, under largely British diplomatic pressure, the security dimension of the Brussels Treaty was subsumed under the 1954 Modified Brussels Treaty, whereby West Germany and Italy joined NATO (Deighton, 1997). Throughout the remainder of the Cold War, therefore, any prospect of *internalized European* security institutions was off the agenda. The first tussle between the two contrasting approaches to European security awarded game, set and match to the externalized Atlanticist model. The internal, Europeanist efforts implicit in Dunkirk, Brussels and the EDC would have to wait until the 1990s to be offered a second chance.

Beyond the Cold War: reviving internalized European security institutions

The institutional arrangements offered by NATO were never perceived by Europeans as entirely satisfactory (Freedman, 1980). External dependency on the USA generated internal demotivation, which simply exacerbated the dependency. France, indeed, found this vicious circle so unsatisfactory as to warrant withdrawal from NATO's integrated command structures (Vaïsse *et al.*, 1996). But for as long as the Soviet threat persisted, the Europeans seemed in no position to guarantee their own security. This situation began to change in the 1980s for three reasons. First, as a result of growing recognition that dependency and demotivation constituted a potentially lethal cocktail in the context of an increasingly unilateral American administration. In his first term, Ronald Reagan seemed prepared to risk limited nuclear war in Europe. In his second term, he seemed prepared to abolish nuclear weapons (along with their perceived deterrent value) altogether (Halliday, 1986; Mann, 2009) – without consulting the European allies. Second, Europe's mood changed as a result of a renewed sense of confidence in the European project in light of the Single European Act (1986), the proposed single currency and continued EU enlargement (Keohane *et al.*, 1993). This resulted in the creation of the European Council Secretariat, a Brussels-based agency geared to harmonizing various aspects of the EU's foreign policy initiatives. Third, change came as a result of the 'Gorbachev phenomenon' which seemed to usher in a qualitatively new period of transcontinental détente (Grachev, 2008).

All these elements provided the impetus for a renewed attempt to create an *internalized, Europeanist* set of security institutions. First, between 1983 and 1987, came the 'revitalization' of the Western European Union (WEU), that semi-dormant security institutional structure dating from the 1948 Treaty of Brussels. In its 'Platform of The Hague' (October 1987), the WEU boldly declared that 'we are convinced that the construction of an integrated Europe will remain incomplete as long as it does not include security and defence' (WEU, 1988: 37). Under the terms of the Treaty of Maastricht (1991), the embryonic EU launched a *Common Foreign and Security Policy* (CFSP) which designated the WEU as the key agency for the harmonization of security policy. Alas, the WEU proved to be too limited militarily and too unwieldy and ineffectual politically and institutionally to take on the challenges of the post-Cold War world (Howorth, 2007: 160–7). WEU was quietly put out to grass at the Franco-British Summit of Saint-Malo (December 1998), a summit which gave a major boost to Europe's security-institutional arrangements by launching the *European Security and Defence Policy* (ESDP) (Howorth, 2007). A decade later, the Treaty of Lisbon 'converted' Saint-Malo by introducing the definitive institutional structures of EU security policy. After Lisbon, ESDP became the *Common Security and Defence Policy* (CSDP).[1] In what follows, I shall trace the evolution of the EU's security-institutional 'architecture' from the late 1980s to the present.

Prior to the 1998 Saint-Malo summit, there were no fewer than eight *European* institutions with inputs to EU security policy, some of which continue to this day to exert influence. At the highest level stand the three monthly *European Council* meetings of heads of state and government with ultimate decision-making and political responsibility for all policy areas, including security policy. It was agreed in the Maastricht Treaty (1991) – and was subsequently confirmed by the Treaty of Nice (2000) and the Treaty of Lisbon (2009) – that security and defence policy would be conducted by a special *intergovernmental* pillar of the EU in which the heads of state and government and appropriate ministers, voting unanimously, would take all ultimate policy decisions (De Schoutheete, 2006; Werts, 2008). Below the European Council came the *General Affairs Council* (GAC), which was renamed the *Foreign Affairs Council* (FAC) by the Lisbon Treaty. This body meets monthly and comprises the EU's 27 foreign ministers. It is, in practice, the main decision-taking body for the bulk of foreign and security policy (Hayes-Renshaw, 2006; Cross, 2011). Traditionally, the meetings of the GAC/FAC have been prepared by the *Committee of Permanent Representatives*

(COREPER), formally comprising the ambassadors (referred to in this context as permanent representatives) of the member states to the European Union. This committee, the third of our longstanding foreign and security policy institutions, meets at least once a week in Brussels, and has traditionally enjoyed considerable influence over the policy-shaping process (Lewis, 1998; Cross, 2007). Any items on which the permanent representatives agree unanimously are normally adopted by the FAC without discussion. However, as we shall see below, COREPER's influence over security policy has waned since the advent of the new post-Saint-Malo institutions of security policy, particularly the *Political and Security Committee* (PSC).

A fourth body of some significance used to be the *Political Committee* (PoCo) comprising the political directors of the member state *Ministries of Foreign Affairs* (MFAs). This agency derived from the informal process of *European Political Cooperation* (EPC) whereby, from the 1970s onwards, European foreign ministers and political directors would hold monthly meetings to discuss policy coordination (Nuttall, 1992). However, as with COREPER, much of PoCo's *security and defence* remit was, after Saint-Malo, taken over by the PSC – made up of 27 ambassadors from the member states (see below). Occasionally the PSC is still convened at the level of the political directors but the institution as such has ceased to function in its traditional guise. The fifth pre-1999 institution is the *Council Secretariat*, which dates from the Single European Act of 1985 when it was felt necessary to establish a permanent secretariat to coordinate the foreign policy implications of the EU's growing trade and economic relations with the rest of the world. The Secretariat, which involves some 2,500 officials from across the EU, supports and advises both the European Council and the FAC. The sixth institutional input traditionally came from the rotating *Presidency* of the EU, which, prior to Lisbon, assumed responsibility for galvanizing and even initiating foreign and security policy during its six-month term of office. However, although after Lisbon the rotating presidency continues to exist with respect to most policy areas, in the field of foreign and security policy its powers of initiative have been overtaken by the creation of the key Lisbon institutions we shall examine below. In addition to these six separate agencies of intergovernmentalism, there is, of course, the supranational *European Commission* (EC), which has been largely responsible for the *delivery* and *implementation* of foreign and security policy through its *Directorate General for External Relations* (Relex), which contributes to policy formulation and works closely with other DGs such as EuropeAid, Development, Trade and Humanitarian Aid; and the *European Parliament* (EP), whose specialist committees on foreign affairs (AFET) and security and defence (SEDE) have continued to play an oversight role of growing importance (Duke, 2002: 127–30). One further institution technically pre-dating Saint-Malo[2] is the post of *High Representative for the Common Foreign and Security Policy* (HR-CFSP), which from 1999 until 2009 was occupied by Javier Solana and, since Lisbon (in an upgraded form), by Catherine Ashton. We shall assess this institution below under the Lisbon institutions.

The post-Saint-Malo institutions

One might have thought, given this multi-level and already extremely cumbersome decision-making apparatus, that the advent of ESDP and the call in Saint-Malo for 'appropriate structures' would have presented a golden opportunity for wholesale institutional rationalization. However, the intergovernmental conference leading up to the Treaty of Nice (2000) was already in train and was essentially concentrating on the institutional consequences of the major EU enlargement planned for 2004. Therefore Nice simply added four key new institutional agencies to the already complex nexus we have just outlined. These new institutions have proven to be extremely important.

Political and Security Committee

The most important of these was, and still is, the *Political and Security Committee* (PSC), which was enshrined in the Treaty of Nice, modified by the Treaty of Lisbon, under Article 25:

> [A] Political and Security Committee shall monitor the international situation in the areas covered by the common foreign and security policy and contribute to the definition of policies by delivering opinions to the Council at the request of the Council or on its own initiative. It shall also monitor the implementation of agreed policies [and] shall exercise, under the responsibility of the Council and of the High Representative, the political control and strategic direction of the crisis management operations referred to in Article 28B.

The PSC as an institution was first convened on an interim basis in March 2000, becoming permanent in January 2001. It was aptly described in the first detailed scholarly studies of its activities as the 'linchpin' (Duke, 2005) and as the 'work-horse' behind ESDP decision-making (Meyer, 2006: 116). The 27 permanent representatives, with the rank of ambassador, meeting twice to three times a week in Brussels are involved in monitoring the international situation, formulating security policies and overseeing the implementation of those policies. However, an important caveat is immediately in order. Despite its centrality to the decision-shaping process, the PSC can easily be short-circuited by national capitals in the event of a real crisis which rules out member-state consensus. During the Iraq crisis of 2002–3, for instance, the Committee, notwithstanding the text of Article 25 of the Treaty, was kept entirely at arm's length from what was certainly the most significant foreign and security policy issue of the entire five-year period following Saint-Malo. This stark reality speaks volumes about the relative salience of *national* security policies as opposed to *European* policy on security when push really comes to shove.

The PSC deals with all aspects of the EU's common foreign, security and defence policy (CFSP/CSDP), although interviews with current and former ambassadors suggest that it works best in what is considered its 'core business' – the planning, preparation and oversight of operations, whether civilian or military. Some ambassadors feel that the body works less well when it ventures over-ambitiously into broad-ranging generalities about the future scope and direction of CFSP/CSDP. A representative of the Commission is present as the twenty-eighth member of the Committee in order to ensure cross-pillar consistency and coherence. Meetings are also attended by four representatives of the Council Secretariat. The work of the committee is assisted by 'European Correspondents' based in the MFAs who form a liaison between the political directors and the PSC ambassadors. The wide-ranging remit of the committee generates a vast amount of paperwork, creating an intensive workload for its members. This pressure is somewhat alleviated by the assistance of the Politico-Military Working Party, comprising officials from both MFAs and MODs and which convenes up to four times per week, dealing with both the diplomatic aspects and the technical details of planned operations, including relations with NATO. In addition, the meetings of the PSC are facilitated by a preparatory group, the 'Nicolaidis group', which fixes the most logical order for discussion of agenda items and indicates in advance where member states have concerns that they wish to raise.

How influential is this key committee? The first systematic attempt to evaluate the influence of the PSC was conducted by Ana Juncos and Christopher Reynolds (2007). They sought to assess the committee with reference to the methodological and theoretical debates between rational choice institutionalism and sociological institutionalism (Hall and Taylor, 1996; Schmidt, 2010³). The key issue here is the extent to which the members of this formally intergovernmental committee, through a process of socialization and mutual familiarity, actually reach consensus in a quasi-supranational mode. Juncos and Reynolds present their conclusions based on some 20 interviews with a variety of actors in Brussels and in the national capitals. Recognizing that rational approaches fail to grasp the significance of the permanence of the PSC in Brussels, they conclude that the PSC members, far from being bogged down in rational bargaining around pre-set national 'red lines' are involved in problem-solving and consensus-seeking. Their aim is to define what is and what is not possible under CSDP. Although the authors use the somewhat ambiguous notion of 'government in the shadow' as the sub-title of their article, the intention behind this notion is to argue that the members of the PSC do *take decisions* in the manner of governments and to some extent operate, in their words, 'outside the charmed circle of diplomacy'. The committee, they conclude 'remains a forum where informal norms and rules play an important role and in which routine interaction can make a difference, both to the representatives themselves *and to the actual substance of national foreign and security policies*' (my emphasis). My own work on the PSC (Howorth, 2010) fully corroborates these findings. The PSC has emerged as a strong *epistemic community* which, increasingly, operates as the de facto central agency for the definition and implementation of EU security policy.

That national capitals are prepared to champion this institution is so for several reasons. First, although member states formally retain their longstanding autonomy in national foreign and security policy-making, they all know that they have a strong vested interest *in making CFSP and CSDP work*. In these policy areas above all, there is recognition that, most often, the whole will prove to be greater than the sum of the parts. Second, there is a strong collective desire to achieve results. For this reason, it is rare for a proposal to come up to the PSC which is clearly going to run up against some strongly entrenched national interest on the part of one or more member states. What the PSC is in effect doing is writing on a blank sheet of paper the limits of the possible in CFSP/CSDP (and, by the same token, the profile of the impossible). It is, in a sense, *creating* an entire policy area from scratch. It is a kind of script-writer for the CSDP narrative. Debates thus tend to turn around proposals that have a realistic chance of success. Finally, the PSC is effective because, while operationalizing EU security policy, it in no way interferes with the maintenance, in the major national capitals, of a residual *national* foreign and security policy for those member states who attach fundamental importance to their individual role in the world.

Military Committee and Military Staff

Two other institutions were created in 1999 alongside the PSC. The *European Union Military Committee* (EUMC) is the highest EU military body. It is established within the Council and is formally composed of the *Chiefs of the Defence Staff* (CHODs) of the member states meeting at least biannually, but is normally attended by their military representatives (MILREPs), who, in most cases, are double-hatted with each nation's NATO representative. This Committee rapidly imposed itself as a vital mechanism in the policy-making process. Its ultimate function is to deliver to the European Council, via the PSC, the unanimous advice of the 27 CHODs on all matters with a military dimension as well as recommendations for action. Such unanimity is essential to the commitment of EU forces to any military operation. The EUMC is the designated 'forum for consultation and cooperation between the member states in the field of conflict prevention and crisis management'. Its advice and recommendations pertain to

> the development of the overall concept of crisis management in its military aspects; the ... political control and strategic direction of crisis management operations and situations; the risk assessment of potential crises; the military dimension of a crisis situation and its implications, in particular during its subsequent management; ... the elaboration, the assessment and the review of capability objectives according to agreed procedures; the EU's military relationship with non-EU European NATO Members, the other candidates for accession to the EU, other states and other organisations, including NATO; and the financial estimation for operations and exercises.
> (Rutten, 2001: 193–4)

These terms of reference are essentially drawn from those of NATO's Military Committee. The EUMC thus emerges as the key decision-shaping body in crisis-management situations, drawing up and evaluating strategic military options, overseeing the elaboration of an operational plan and monitoring operations throughout the mission. It is also responsible for giving advice on the termination of an operation. The Chairman of the EUMC is a four-star flag officer, normally a former Chief of Defence of a member state.

The most complete analysis of the impact of this institution has been conducted by Mai'a Cross (Cross, 2010, 2011), whose findings are unequivocal. This is a committee where the role of expertise, the impact of a pre-existing common recruitment pattern and common culture, the intensity and sustained periodicity of meetings (especially informal meetings), shared professional norms and the ability to persuade capitals of the wisdom of EU consensus is exceptional. Cross notes that

> despite the fact that EU military power is still a relatively new aspect of EU security integration, the impact of the military epistemic community on the trajectory of security integration has been quite[4] strong, and is likely to grow. The professional norms, culture, and worldview of the military epistemic community indicate that it is a highly cohesive transnational network of experts. In particular, their tactical expertise is for all intents and purposes the same, and this enables them to come to agreement very quickly.
> (Cross, 2011: 257–8)

There is no doubt whatever that this key military committee of experts plays a fundamental role in the shaping of policy options on CSDP. Its inter-governmental structure in no way impedes its capacity to deliberate in supra-national ways.

The third agency created by Saint-Malo is the *European Union Military Staff* (EUMS). This body comprises some 200 senior officers from the 27 member states. It provides military expertise and capacity, including during the conduct of EU-led military operations. The EUMS works under the political direction of the European Council (through the PSC) and under the military direction of the EUMC. Although the EUMS does not act as an operational HQ, it performs the operational functions of early warning, situation assessment and strategic planning and provides in-house military expertise for the High Representative. The EUMS is in fact a General Directorate within the Council General Secretariat and is the only permanent integrated military structure of the European Union. Established on 11 June 2001, the EU Military Staff has had four Directors-General, each fulfilling a three-year mandate.

The fourth post-Saint-Malo institution is the *Civilian Crisis Management Committee* (CIVCOM). This body mirrors the EUMC, providing policy options to the PSC, but on *civilian missions* – which have turned out to be the most numerous of all CSDP operations. However, it offers a somewhat different picture from the EUMC, for a number of reasons. First, the members of this committee are drawn from a wide range of civilian and diplomatic backgrounds and lack the cohesive recruitment patterns and culture which characterize the military. Second, they meet more frequently in formal settings and less frequently in informal settings and are thus less likely to 'bond' with one another than the members of PSC or the EUMC. Third, by its very nature, the work of CIVCOM is relatively new and experimental and little can be taken for granted about the outcome of committee discussions. However, Cross has demonstrated that CIVCOM representatives nevertheless succeed, just like their EUMC counterparts, in focusing on the achievement of consensus rather than on the defence of national red lines (Cross, 2010). The socialization processes work in a variety of ways. First, CIVCOM members (like the initial cohort of PSC ambassadors) are conscious that they are breaking important new politico-diplomatic ground. This helps considerably in the forging of an *esprit de corps*. Second, there is 'a common desire to move the EU forward' which contributes in important ways to the generation of a shared mindset. Third, representatives on CIVCOM tend to be younger than those on the other committees and consider it an exciting opportunity to create something new together. All in all, despite the obstacles to socialization outlined above, the workings of CIVCOM also tend to gravitate towards consensus-seeking rather than red-line defending.

One final post-1999 innovation which has become a regular institutional feature although technically still with informal status is the *Council of Defence Ministers*. In February 2002, it had been agreed that defence ministers would be authorized to meet under the aegis of the General Affairs Council (the monthly meeting of the EU foreign ministers) to discuss 'certain agenda items, limited to … military capabilities'. The very fact that member states recognized the necessity for such top-down meetings constituted a major step forward. In democratic systems, defence ministers are generally kept strictly subordinate to foreign ministers and, of course, prior to Saint-Malo there had never been any prospect of the Council of Ministers meeting in defence-minister format. Since February 2002, they have tended to meet several times a year to oversee the development of military capabilities, and they have gradually become significant security policy-shapers. They were instrumental in helping move the debate on capacity away from the raw numbers of the Headline Goal and towards a clear set of qualitative criteria. This development was taken to a new and qualitatively different level by the informal meeting of the defence ministers in Ghent in September 2010, followed by the formal meeting in December, at which firm decisions were taken on cooperative projects for the development of European military capacity (Gros-Verheyde, 2010). The defence ministers also meet regularly in another format – as the Steering Board of the *European Defence Agency* (see below).

The Lisbon institutional framework

CSDP is at the heart of the Lisbon Treaty. Of the 62 amendments to the previous treaties introduced by Lisbon no fewer than 25 concern CFSP/CSDP. Moreover, with the exception of the confusion in Ireland over that country's traditional neutrality, the national debates over these foreign and security aspects of the Treaty gave rise in no member state to any particular issues of concern. Opinion polls across Europe consistently suggest that there is considerable popular support for the view that foreign and security policy ought logically to be conducted at European level rather than exclusively at national level.[5] There were four major institutional innovations introduced by Lisbon and a number of minor institutional adjustments.

The European Defence Agency

The existence of this institution, first called for in the aborted 2004 Draft Constitutional Treaty, was formally confirmed by the 2009 Lisbon Treaty. By that time, it had already been in operation for five years. Its formal title is the *European Armaments, Research and Military Capabilities Agency* (EARMCA), but it has long been referred to for short as the EDA. Prior to its launch, armaments cooperation had taken place rigorously outside the EU framework. Two main reasons lay behind the decision to bring the business inside the EU institutions. The first was the relative failure of previous attempts to coordinate procurement and armaments cooperation. The second was the accelerating reality of ESDP and the concurrent perceived need to link capabilities to armaments production. The urgency of these drivers was reflected in the fact that, at the Thessaloniki European Council in June 2003, it was agreed not to await ratification of the Constitutional Treaty in order to launch the EDA, which was to be created immediately. Its objectives and role were narrowed down to four basic purposes:

- to work for a more comprehensive and systematic approach to defining and meeting ESDP's *capability* needs;
- to promote *equipment collaboration*, both to contribute to defence capabilities and to foster further restructuring of European defence industries;
- to encourage the widening and deepening of regulatory approaches and the achievement of a European defence *equipment market*;
- to promote defence-relevant *research and technology* (R&T), 'pursuing collaborative use of national defence R&T funds' and 'leveraging other funding sources, including those for dual use or security-related research'.

The EDA is guided by a Steering Board meeting at the level of defence ministers, nominally headed by the High Representative and managed by a Chief Executive, most recently Claude-France Arnould. However, it enjoys only a tiny budget (€25 million in 2005, rising to €30 million in 2010), a sign that governments remain uncertain about how far they can trust their own political instincts.

In a pioneering study written at the time the agency was being established, Martin Trybus (2006) contrasted the supra-national aspirations of the European Defence Community's 1950s approach to weapons procurement, with the determinedly inter-governmental approaches adopted ever since – including in the case of the EDA. Noting that defence procurement is recognized by member states as a policy area where European cooperation is essential if the EU is to avoid sub-contractor status to the US industry, and stressing that the European Commission has in recent years introduced a number of measures to facilitate Europeanization of the defence equipment market, Trybus concludes that the resolutely inter-governmental terms of reference of the EDA are likely to clash fairly constantly with the requirements of procurement rationalization. In a more recent assessment of the 'clash of institutional logics' involved in the EDA's existence and work, Jozef Bátora (2009) detects three additional clashes of institutional or functional logic within the EDA: between the logic of defence sovereignty and the logic of pooled resources; between the Europeanist and the Euro-Atlanticist logics; and between the logics of liberalization and of Europeanization of the defence market. He detects clear evidence that the EDA has been making significant efforts to transcend the logic of defence sovereignty by introducing a raft of procedures and rules into the *Code of Conduct on Defence Procurement* which will, in effect, facilitate cooperation and even integration in the procurement process. Where the appropriateness of partners is concerned, the Agency has found itself unable to resolve the tensions between the Europeanist and the Atlanticist proclivities of its member states. On the liberalization versus Europeanization conflict, the EDA has made a robust pitch to break down national monopolies and to introduce mechanisms for cross-border tendering. Yet, the logic of liberalization runs up immediately against the logic of European preference, and here the EDA has to date been unable to resolve the contradiction.

The Presidency of the European Council

Article 9B of the Lisbon Treaty introduces a long overdue and major modification by creating the position of *President of the European Council*. The six-monthly rotating presidency of the EU had long been seen as counterproductive, particularly in the area of foreign and security policy. Initially intended to give all six member states experience in 'steering the EU ship', the practice had become a symbol of internal incoherence, generalized confusion, erratic policy shifts and external incomprehension. The position of President of the Council involves a two-and-a-half-year mandate, renewable once. The President's main functions are to 'facilitate cohesion and consensus' within the Council, and to 'ensure the external representation of the Union on issues concerning its common foreign and security policy'. It is, potentially, a very powerful position. However, there was always considerable speculation as to how much turf jostling would be involved between the Presidency position and the other major institutional innovation, the post of High Representative.

The High Representative of the Union for Foreign Affairs and Security Policy

Throughout the decade-long process of Treaty review, most commentators were agreed that the key institutional innovation of what eventually became Lisbon would be the introduction of the double-hatted post of *High Representative for Foreign Affairs and Security Policy and Vice-President of the Commission* (HR-VP). There were three main reasons for this. The first was political: the need for ever greater coordination and integration of the foreign and security policies of the EU's 27 member states. The second was operational: the need for synergies, on the ground, between the main thrusts of CFSP/CSDP: trade, development aid, humanitarian assistance and crisis management. The third was institutional: the growing recognition by member states that effective international action on the part of the EU required the existence, in Brussels, of centralized decision-shaping agencies.

The Lisbon Treaty merged the posts of High Representative for CFSP (previously held by Javier Solana) and that of External Relations Commissioner. The aim was to generate far greater coordination between the two main thrusts of the EU's international activities: development aid and crisis management. The appointee enjoys a five-year term. This is the first time in the history of the EU that a position has straddled the hitherto mutually impermeable institutions of the Council and the Commission. The post-holder also has powerful responsibilities as Chair of the EDA. The ramifications of this appointment are very considerable and the office is referred to no fewer than 52 times in the Treaty text. The post-holder also contributes both to the preparation of and to the implementation of CFSP/CSDP, represents the Union in international organizations and at international conferences, and conducts 'political dialogue' on the Union's behalf. The incumbent replaces the previous six-monthly rotating Presidency of the *General Affairs Council* (which dealt with external and security policy) and takes over as Chair of the newly created *Foreign Affairs Council* (FAC), which s/he can convene in emergency session within 48 hours. Moreover, the HR-VP presides over the new *European External Action Service* (see below). The position of HR-VP has long been seen as the key institutional position in the EU's foreign and security policy.

One imponderable throughout the protracted business of Treaty revision had been the extent to which the HR-VP position would clash with the new Presidency of the Council position. In designating 'external representation' as a function of the Presidency, the Treaty took care to specify that this would be 'at the appropriate level' (meetings with heads of state) and that it would be 'without prejudice to the powers of the High Representative of the Union for Foreign Affairs and Security Policy' (who would expect to interact with foreign ministers). An analogy occasionally deployed in the commentariat is that of the relationship between the US President and the Secretary of State. This is doubly misleading. Both those office-holders exercise clear lines of authority, whereas their new EU 'counterparts' still have to coexist with powerful heads of state and government and with influential foreign ministers. Moreover, between the US President and the Secretary of State there is a hierarchical relationship entirely missing from the new EU positions.

Analysts had always agreed that the actual job descriptions for these two key posts (which remain somewhat vague and aspirational in the Treaty text) would depend heavily on the personalities of the two post-holders. There was widespread astonishment when the European Council, in November 2009, appointed former Belgian Prime Minister Herman Van Rompuy to the post of European Council President and former Trade Commissioner Catherine Ashton to that of HR-VP. Neither had any international name recognition and neither had any real experience of international or security affairs. Both appointments were greeted with generalized scepticism and not a little dismay, the general interpretation among the commentariat being that the leading heads of state and government had ensured the appointment of individuals that they would be able to micro-manage (Graw, 2009; Parker, 2009). As this volume goes to press, it is too soon to say what verdict history will record on the two initial incumbents. Van Rompuy has benefited from a relatively positive and generous media coverage, aided in large part by his dynamic *chef de cabinet* Frans van Daele, and by an agenda which has been less exhausting and less challenging than that of Ashton. He has been credited with being taken relatively seriously by his global interlocutors and with having succeeded to some degree in putting the position of EU President on the map. Ashton has had to rise above a great deal of small-minded sniping, largely to do with her lack of prior experience, her monolingualism and her choice of priorities. Her job, involving the accumulation of two major positions, has involved endless travel and a super-charged agenda, which she appears to have taken physically in her stride. Moreover, she succeeded relatively well in her first major priority: that of establishing the *European External Action Service*.

The European External Action Service (EEAS)

In effect an EU Diplomatic Service, this body, which was launched without fanfare on 1 December 2010, will work in cooperation with the diplomatic services of the member states and comprises around 3,000 officials from relevant departments of the General Secretariat of the Council and of the Commission,[6] as well as staff seconded from the national diplomatic services of the member states. It *should*, if it works as intended, help the EU to arrive at joined-up foreign policies (aid, trade, soldiers, policemen, crisis management, asylum, etc.); provide more high-quality and unified analysis to ministers; coordinate the work of member states' embassies in third countries; and eliminate the danger that a weak presidency (such as the Czech presidency in early 2009) can actually undermine EU foreign and security policy. This is, potentially, a major and highly significant development (Avery, 2007; Crowe, 2008). It reflects the well-established tendency for the EU member states to resist 'Brusselsization' for as long as possible, but eventually to recognize the inevitability and indeed the desirability of ever greater policy coordination and coherence. The service, in its initial guise, was the result of a year-long struggle between the HR-VP, the member states and the European Parliament. In a March 2010 proposal designed to attach the service directly to the Commission (rather than to the Council or to the member states), MEPs Elmar Brok and Guy Verhofstadt also proposed EP oversight over the EEAS budget, personnel, aid policy, ratification issues and hearings for top jobs. As a counterproposal, the HR-VP insisted that the service be an autonomous body under her direction, equally answerable to the Council, the Commission and the member states. She suggested a pyramidal-style hierarchy headed by a very powerful Secretary-General. While the MEPs, in response, threatened to veto the entire institution, the EU foreign ministers aligned themselves with the HR-VP. This led to an unseemly tug-o-war between the EP and the HR-VP which was resolved only by a compromise agreement in June 2010. The EEAS will indeed be an autonomous body, but will work in close coordination with the EP. The hierarchical structure was toned down by agreement on the appointment of several deputy Secretaries-General and Directors-General (Missiroli, 2010). Widely applauded were the appointments, in summer 2010, to the top positions: Secretary-General Pierre Vimont, Chief Operating Officer David O'Sullivan, Deputy Secretaries-General Maciej Popowski and Helga Schmidt, Head of Strategy Robert Cooper. Contrary to the fears of some, the leaders of the EEAS are exceptionally prominent diplomats.

Will appointment to the EEAS emerge as the most coveted career move for more junior EU diplomats? Will there continue to be a tug-o-war between the different actors over control of this service? What will be its impact on the work of the Foreign and Commonwealth Office, the Quai d'Orsay or the Auswärtiges Amt? Will the new service succeed seamlessly in absorbing the 120-odd diplomatic representations previously attached to the Commission? The quasi-revolutionary implications of the EU per se having diplomatic representation around the world, with diplomats trained to speak on behalf of the Union rather than on behalf of its member states are almost impossible to double-guess. Once again, everything will hinge on the precise modalities of its implementation and on the degree of cooperation it enjoys from the member states. The bottom line, however, is that all member states actively want the EEAS to be a success. It would thus become a fundamental institutional underpinning of the entire CFSP/CSDP nexus.

Conclusion

It was clear to certain leaders, in the wake of World War II, that Europe, if it were ever to become a significant global actor in its own right, would need its own institutional framework, centrally located in a European capital city. In the immediate aftermath of the war, such a prospect seemed too daunting for some leading European member states and refuge was taken in the US-dominated Atlanticist structures of NATO. However, dissatisfaction with those structures, as well as the eventual end of the Cold War, reignited the quest for *internalized, Europeanist* security institutions. At every juncture in this process, a similar and powerful institutional logic imposed itself. This involved some form or another of 'Brusselsization'. Iterative policy coordination, among and between the national capitals, eventually proved to be inadequate or too messy (usually both) and led to calls for a new Brussels-based institution to rationalize inputs and coordinate policy. With the creation of the *Political and Security Committee* and its sub-committees, the *European Council Presidency* and the *HR-VP*, not to mention the *EEAS*, the general thrust has been uni-directional – towards ever greater delegation of authority and responsibility away from the member states and towards the central institutions of the EU. Even when many of these institutions were specifically devised as agencies of *intergovernmentalism*, forces of socialization and policy-urgency transformed them into quasi-supranational organisms whose overwhelming objective was the quest for consensus.

The security institutions of the EU are still in their first infancy and there remains a great deal to be sorted out, refined and bedded in. But the underlying belief in the need for (European) institutions which would be greater than the sum of the (member state) parts has driven the entire process. The Treaty of Lisbon, to paraphrase Churchill, was not the beginning of the end but it certainly constituted the end of the beginning of this lengthy historical process.

Notes

1   For the sake of consistency, I shall use the abbreviation CSDP throughout this chapter.
2   The post was created by the Amsterdam Treaty (1997), but disagreements among the member states over the level and remit of the post-holder delayed its initiation until 1999.
3   The classic reference on this debate has long been the Hall and Taylor article. However, Vivien Schmidt's more recent piece massively updates the discussion and introduces a new perspective which has particular relevance in the context of the deliberations of the PSC – discursive institutionalism.
4   Note that in American English 'quite' normally denotes 'very'.
5   In a *Eurobarometer* poll (71, p. 147) published in September 2009, 81 per cent of citizens polled believed that foreign and security policy broadly understood (promotion of peace in the world and fight against terrorism) should be conducted at European rather than at national level.
6   The EEAS incorporates the former Commission DGs with responsibility for foreign and security policy which constituted RELEX. However, the Commission succeeded in retaining responsibility for enlargement, the EU neighborhood and some aspects of development aid.

2

REALISM

A dissident voice in the study of the CSDP

Adrian Hyde-Price

This chapter provides a realist analysis of the European Union's role as an emerging regional and global security actor in what remains, in its essentials, an anarchic and 'Hobbesian' international system. It draws on the rich tradition of realist international theory, from classical realists such as E. H. Carr, Reinhold Niebuhr and Hans Morgenthau, to structural realists such as Kenneth Waltz and John Mearsheimer. Realist theory emphasizes the significance of material and systemic factors as key determinants of international outcomes, and argues that a foreign and security policy that does not recognize the distribution of relative power capabilities in the international system and does not focus on the pursuit of national or (in the case of the EU) common interests is destined to be weak and ineffectual. Realists argue that security and defence policies are the product of a complex interaction of systemic and domestic level factors, along with the perceptions of decision-makers and the strategic culture within which they operate. Having reviewed classical and neorealist approaches to the CSDP, therefore, this chapter concludes by pointing to some of the interesting work being undertaken within 'neoclassical realism', an approach which offers a more fine-grained analytical framework that includes both systemic pressures and national and EU-level factors shaping the evolution of the CSDP.

At the heart of a realist analysis of the EU as an international security actor is the argument that if its member states are serious about the Union becoming an effective and coherent vehicle for collective endeavours to safeguard and enhance common European security interests in an uncertain world, they must shed some of their lingering illusions about the virtue and efficacy of an EU security strategy based primarily on 'soft power' and moral suasion, and develop the political will and military capacity to back up EU diplomacy with coercive instruments when necessary. In his remarkable treatise on political realism, *The Prince*, Niccolò Machiavelli argued that 'princes' (i.e., strategic actors) needed to learn how to act like Chiron the centaur, 'half beast and half man'. Unless they knew 'how to act according to the nature of both', they would be vulnerable to predators and ineffective as political actors.

The allegory of the centaur is one that seems particularly apposite for the EU as it evolves from being a one-dimensional 'civilian power' to a more multifaceted security provider equipped not only with the instruments of declaratory diplomacy and economic statecraft, but also with the means for military and civilian crisis management. As Robert Cooper (one of the principal draftees of the 2003 *European Security Strategy*) has argued, European 'postmodern' states need to 'get used to the idea of double standards':

Among themselves, the postmodern states operate on the basis of laws and open co-operative security. But when dealing with more old-fashioned kinds of states outside the postmodern limits, Europeans need to revert to the rougher methods of an earlier era – force, pre-emptive attack, deception, whatever is necessary for those who still live in the nineteenth-century world of every state for itself.

In the jungle, one must use the laws of the jungle. In this period of peace in Europe, there is a temptation to neglect defences, both physical and psychological. This represents one of the dangers for the postmodern state.

(Cooper, 2003: 61–2)

Realism as the dissident voice in the study of the CSDP

Realism is a multifaceted and sophisticated approach to international politics that has been highly influential in the discipline of international relations (Grieco, 1997). Indeed, for much of the Cold War, it was seen – by both its advocates and critics – as the dominant paradigm in the discipline. It is therefore something of an anomaly that it has had so little impact on the study of European foreign, security and defence policy.

There are a number of reasons why realism has been marginalized in the study of the EU as an international security actor. To begin with, realists themselves have tended to downplay the significant of institutionalized multilateral cooperation and emphasized instead the problems of achieving 'cooperation under anarchy' (Mearsheimer, 1990, 2000; Waltz, 2000). Consequently, 'realists have not produced comprehensive theory-informed empirical studies of this area' (Jorgensen, 2004: 38). At the same time, realism is widely perceived to be state-centric; overly preoccupied with hard power (particularly military power); and focused on the 'high politics' of national security and grand strategy (Keohane and Nye, 1977: 23–4). Because of this, few in the sub-field of European studies regard it as having much – if anything – to say about an atypical international actor that is not a state, possesses limited coercive power capabilities, is primarily concerned with 'low politics' and has a penchant for declaratory diplomacy (Chryssochoou, 2001: Kelstrup and Williams, 2000).

The result is that realism is much misunderstood and widely misrepresented. It is usually portrayed in highly simplistic terms and used as a 'straw man' with which to demonstrate the sophistication of other approaches and theories (White, 2004: 11). Moreover, many scholars working on the European Union tend to empathize with the object of their research, and identify with the aims and aspirations of the European integration project (Jorgensen, 2004; Bull, 1982). This has further marginalized the realist voice, which provides a more critical perspective on some of the liberal-idealist assumptions and perspectives underpinning both the official discourse of the EU and the academic study of 'European' foreign and security policy.

As the dissident voice in the study of the CSDP, the first task of the realist approach is to cast a critical – albeit sympathetic – eye on the liberal-idealist orthodoxy of European studies, and on the liberal 'common sense' that defines the contemporary European *Zeitgeist*. In particular, realists criticize both the reductionism of much liberal-idealist thinking, and the tendency to downplay or overlook the importance of power in the international system (Pijpers, 1990).

In the wake of the *annus mirabilis* of 1989, the belief that Europe – if not the world as a whole – had entered a new era of international peace and cooperation was pervasive (Hyde-Price, 1991). In Europe itself, liberal and idealist understandings of the EU as a 'civilian' power committed to 'civilizing' international relations as part of a broader transformation of international society were widespread (Maull, 1990, 1993). Armed with 'soft power' and

19

universal normative appeal, the EU was portrayed as a novel and uniquely benign entity in international politics that served as the harbinger of a Kantian *foedus pacificum*. François Duchêne's notion of Europe as 'the first of the world's civilian centres of power' (Duchêne, 1972: 43; Hill, 1990) acquired renewed currency, whilst commentators such as Mark Leonard wrote glowingly about the 'power of weakness', arguing that 'when we stop looking at the world through American eyes, we can see that each element of European "weakness" is in fact a facet of its extraordinary "transformative power"' (Leonard, 2005: 5).

More recently, Ian Manners has argued that by virtue of its historical origins, hybrid polity and political-legal constitution, the EU has emerged as something new and unprecedented – a 'normative power'. The EU is a 'normative power of an ideational nature characterised by common principles and a willingness to disregard Westphalian conventions' (Manners, 2002: 239). Its distinctive role as a 'changer of norms' reflects the fact that it is an ontologically new international actor with a 'different existence', 'different norms' and 'different policies', all of which are part of 'redefining what can be "normal" in international relations' (Manners, 2002: 253). The EU is ontologically distinct because it is 'constructed on a normative basis, and is consequently the first international actor whose role is shaped not by 'what it does or what it says, but what it is' (Manners, 2002: 252).

This is not the place to undertake a detailed critique of these arguments, a task undertaken elsewhere (Hyde-Price, 2007). However, two general points can be made. The first is epistemological: actor-based ontologies that focus on the internal structure and operation of the EU overlook the impact of external, systemic pressures on international actors that are rarely able to impose their domestically determined policy goals on external actors and the surrounding environment. Consequently, realists argue that such actor-based approaches are reductionist in that they seek to 'explain international outcomes through elements and combinations of elements located at national or subnational levels' (Waltz, 1979: 60; Waltz, 1959). Realists thus argue that seeking to understand the CSDP without analysing the nature and dynamics of the international system within which the EU is situated is to miss important influences on foreign and security policy behaviour.

The second general point is that liberal-idealist approaches to the CSDP suffer from a weakness identified by E. H. Carr in *The Twenty Years' Crisis* – 'the almost total neglect of power' (Carr, 2002). Power has a number of different sources and a number of dimensions (economic, military and the 'power to persuade'), as Carr famously argued, but actors are most likely to affect the behaviour of others and shape the international environment if they can deploy a mix of 'hard' and 'soft' power resources. As Hedley Bull noted of the notion of 'civilian power', this was a contradiction in terms because 'the power of influence exerted by the European Community and other such civilian actors was conditional upon a strategic environment provided by the military power of states, which they did not control' (Bull, 1982: 151). Similarly, to speak of the 'power of weakness' or of a 'normative power' rooted in the distinctive hybrid polity and historical origins of the EU is to overlook the extent to which the Union has been effective only when its diplomatic interventions have been backed up by hard power – either in the shape of economic carrots and sticks, or its crisis management capability (Smith, 1998).

The realist tradition

Realism itself is a broad and diverse tradition of thinking about international politics. Generally speaking, one can distinguish between the 'classical realist' tradition of Carr, Morgenthau and Niebuhr, and the 'structural realist' (or 'neorealist') approach of Waltz and Mearsheimer. More recently, the 'neoclassical realist' approach has emerged combining elements of both classical and neorealism as a tool of foreign policy analysis (Rose, 1998; Hyde-Price, 2000). This means that realists working in different traditions will have slightly different approaches to the study of the CSDP. There are, nonetheless, some broad principles that define the realist tradition, and which are relevant to understanding the realist approach to the European integration project.

To begin with, realists focus on what *is*, not what *ought to be*. 'Political realism', Hans Morgenthau argued, 'does not require, nor does it condone, indifference to political ideals and moral principles, but it requires indeed a sharp distinction between the desirable and the possible – between what is desirable everywhere and at all times and what is possible under the concrete circumstances of time and place' (Morgenthau, 1993: 7). Central to a realist analysis, therefore, is the task of identifying the underlying systemic dynamics, in order to understand both the drivers and impediments of change. By identifying the structural limitations to foreign and security policy, as well as the structural opportunities, different policy options can be determined.

Whilst this 'realist' approach to political analysis might seem largely uncontroversial to many, it does differ significantly from critical theory and the more explicitly normative liberal perspectives. Both of these approaches argue that given that 'all theory serves some one and some purpose' (as Robert Cox claimed), political analysis should serve the interests of 'emancipation' and other normative and political objectives. However, as John Vasquez has written, whenever 'empirical and normative work are closely tied together as critical theorists like to do, there is always the danger that one's idea of normative goodness (or political interests) will weigh too heavily in one's thinking about what is empirically true or theoretically adequate' (Vasquez, 1998: 384). Similarly, E. H. Carr argued that abstract normative theorizing and political advocacy reflected a preference for 'the role of the missionary to that of the scientist' (Carr, 2002: 136).

Second, realism is a social and political theory that emphasizes the role of social collectivities in history, particularly that of 'conflict groups'. Robert Gilpin notes that a core assumption is 'that the essence of social reality is the group. The building blocks and ultimate units of social and political life', he continues, 'are not the individuals of liberal thought nor the classes of Marxism'. Rather, it is 'what Ralf Dahrendorf has called "conflict groups"', which 'is another way of saying that in a world of scarce resources and conflict over the distribution of those resources, human beings confront one another ultimately as members of groups, and not as isolated individuals' (Gilpin, 1986: 305). This is an approach which has some overlap with historical materialism, and more congenially, the communitarian – rather than cosmopolitan – traditions of political theory. Realists would also argue that the most important – and successful – conflict groups since early modern Europe have been states, and that despite regular announcements of the withering away of the state, states remain key actors in international politics. As Reinhold Niebuhr argued, the modern nation-state is 'the human group of strongest social cohesion, of most undisputed central authority and of most clearly defined membership'. Since the seventeenth century, therefore, it has been 'the most absolute of all human associations' (Niebuhr, 2005: 56). Consequently, the realist approach to the CSDP is one that focuses particular attention on the interests and preferences of member states, rather than ascribing significant agential capabilities to intergovernmental institutions (Pedersen, 1998). As Waltz notes, 'states set the scene in which they, along with nonstate actors, stage their dramas or carry on their humdrum affairs. Though they may choose to interfere little in the affairs of nonstate actors for long periods of time, states nevertheless set the terms of the intercourse' (Waltz, 1979: 94).

A second key realist principle is that conflict groups operate in a context of anarchy, in the sense of an absence of a central authority able to ensure compliance. In this context, the international system may not necessarily be 'Hobbesian' in the sense of experiencing a constant 'war of all against all', but it is certainly prone to varying degrees of competition, rivalry, insecurity and fear, and exhibits a constant and ineluctable jostling for status, power and influence amongst its major units (Wolfers, 1962; Waltz, 1986, 1995). As Kenneth Waltz has argued, although the international system 'is not entirely without institutions and orderly procedures', and despite the fact that international politics are 'flecked with particles of government and alloyed with elements of community', the existence of these elements of cooperation and institutionalization 'does not alter and should not obscure that principle by which a society is ordered' (Waltz, 1979: 114–15). In the context of an international system that remains essentially anarchic, 'hierarchic elements' established within international structures (such as the EU) 'limit and restrain the exercise of sovereignty but only in ways strongly conditioned by the anarchy of the larger system' (1979: 115).

The third defining characteristic of the realist approach is its materialist ontology. Material factors such as land, resources and geography are regarded as the key determinants of the social world, and material factors such as economic resources or military capabilities are seen as the key determinants of power. Realists do not deny that ideas and values can influence behaviour, but they regard material factors as the primary determinants of social relations, and ideas as intervening variables. State behaviour (and consequently the CSDP) 'is largely shaped by the *material* structure of the international system', John Mearsheimer has argued. 'The distribution of material capabilities among states is the key factor for understanding world politics. For realists, some level of security competition between great powers is inevitable because of the material structure of the international system' (Mearsheimer, 2000: 436).

Finally, realists are wary of both power and military force. They are wary of power, especially concentrations of power, because of the temptations it produces in an anarchic international order. Realists take to heart Lord Acton's adage that 'power corrupts, absolute power corrupts absolutely'. Consequently, realists tend to focus on the balance of power in the international system as the primary determinant of peaceful relations between states – rather than international organizations and multilateral institutions. Realists are also generally sceptical about the efficacy of coercive military force, particularly as an instrument of military intervention or 'milieu shaping'. This may appear counter-intuitive to those more versed in the 'straw man' realism frequently portrayed by its detractors, who paint a caricature of realists as muscle-bound Rambos in love with the smell of napalm in the morning. However, given that many realists do give great attention to the use of military force, they also tend to be more aware of its limitations and shortcomings. It is not surprising therefore that realists like Niebuhr, Morgenthau and Waltz came out in opposition to the Vietnam War, and more recently, realists like Waltz, Mearsheimer, Walt and Gilpin opposed the 2003 Iraq War. Thus whilst realists recognize the pervasive role of coercive military power in international politics, and the need for all serious strategic actors to acquire a robust military capability, they are sceptical of the benefits of humanitarian military intervention, and dismissive of suggestions that war can ever be 'humane' (Coker, 2001).

Classical realism and the CSDP

Building on these basic tenets of the realist tradition, classical realism suggests a number of distinct perspectives on the CSDP. Given the moral and ethical preoccupations of classical realists such as Carr, Niebuhr and Morgenthau, many of these perspectives focus on the balance to be struck between power and morality, virtue and necessity.

The first is that classical realists have long been sceptical of claims made on the basis of 'universal principles'. 'Political realism', Hans Morgenthau argued, 'refuses to identify the moral aspirations of a particular nation with the moral laws that govern the universe' (Morgenthau, 1993: 13). All international actors tend to argue that their actions and policies accord with 'universal' values and principles, and are not simply the pursuit of naked self-interest. The EU is no exception in this regard, insisting that its security and defence policies are based on universal values and serve the common good of humankind (EU, 2003; Prodi, 2000; Aggestam, 2004). Liberal–idealist conceptions of the EU as a 'civilian' or 'normative' power are explicitly grounded on these sorts of cosmopolitan norms that claim to transcend the particularist claims of discrete political communities. However, as E. H. Carr noted, clothing one's 'own interest in the guise of a universal interest for the purpose of imposing it on the rest of the world' is nothing new. He quotes Dicey to the effect that 'Men come easily to believe that arrangements agreeable to themselves are beneficial to others' (Carr, 2002: 71). Pointing to the crucial role played by power relations in constructions of moral and political claims, Carr argued that 'Theories of social morality are always the product of a dominant group which identifies itself with the community as a whole, and which possesses facilities denied to subordinate groups or individuals for imposing its view of life on the community' (Carr, 2002: 74). 'The exposure of the real basis of the professedly abstract principles commonly invoked in international politics', Carr noted, 'is the most damning and most convincing part of the realist indictment of utopianism' (Carr, 2002: 80).

Following from this critique of the particularist interests lurking behind professedly 'universal principles', realists also argue that foreign and security policy should be focused explicitly on the pursuit of vital interests, and not on quixotic moral crusades. In an anarchic international system composed of a plurality of discrete political communities, there are inevitably a plethora of different national conceptions of the *summum bonum* and how to achieve it. This generates different national interests, and an ineluctable degree of security competition and rivalry. Rather than pursuing a moralistic and crusading foreign policy defined rhetorically in terms of 'universal principles' which seeks to reshape the world in a liberal, European image, realists argue that the EU should accept the existence of rival interests and seek to manage conflicts and disagreements on the basis of reciprocity, compromise and quiet diplomacy. In other words, the EU needs to eschew what Morgenthau termed 'moralism in foreign policy'. Instead, the EU should think and act as a 'calculator' not a 'crusader', to use David Clinton's striking phrase. 'Thinking in terms of national interests – of balancing power and commitments', he has written, forces policy-makers 'to be calculators rather than crusaders' (Clinton, 1994: 259).

Acting and thinking as a calculator rather than a crusader is a way of avoiding two very different dangers. On the one hand, it is a way of avoiding the danger of unintended outcomes, which is particularly prevalent given the degree of unpredictability inherent in an anarchic international system. In a strategic context in which other actors will be pursuing divergent goals, good intentions are no guarantee of good outcomes – as Tony Blair found to great cost in Iraq. 'How often', Morgenthau warned, 'have statesmen been motivated by the desire to improve the world, and ended up by making it worse? And how often have they sought one goal, and ended by achieving something they neither expected nor desired?' (Morgenthau, 1993: 6). On the other hand, it is also a way of avoiding the danger of acting as a high-minded, principled 'ethical' actor rather than focusing on the common economic and strategic interests of its member states. As Machiavelli noted, 'the fact is a man who wants to act virtuously in every way necessarily comes to grief among so many who are not virtuous' (Machiavelli, 1961: 91).

Third, classical realists do not advocate an amoral or immoral approach to security and defence policy, nor are they indifferent to human suffering and injustice. 'No political realism which emphasises the inevitability and necessity of a social struggle', Reinhold Niebuhr argued, 'can absolve individuals of the obligation to check their own egoism, to comprehend the interests of others and thus to enlarge the areas of cooperation' (Niebuhr, 2005: 180). The realist approach to international politics does not involve a brutal and self-serving *realpolitik*, but rather a hard-headed foreign and security policy based on an understanding of the structural constraints imposed on political agency in an anarchic international system. As we have seen, Morgenthau argued that political realism required a 'sharp distinction between the desirable and the possible' in order to understand 'what is possible under the concrete circumstances of time and place' (1993: 7). 'Realism', he argued, 'maintains that universal moral principles cannot be applied to the actions of states in their abstract universal formulation, but that they must be filtered through the concrete circumstances of time and place' (Morgenthau, 1993: 12).

The realist approach to international security thus involves identifying the parameters within which political agency can be effective, seeking 'to detect and understand the forces that determine political relations among nations, and to comprehend the ways in which those forces act upon each other and upon international political relations and institutions' (Morgenthau, 1993: 17). 'What Morgenthau and many other realists have in common', Robert Gilpin has written,

> is a belief that ethical and political behaviour will fail unless it takes into account the actual practice of states and teachings of sound theory. It is this dual commitment, to practice and theory, that sets realism apart from both idealism and the abstract theorizing that characterizes so much of the contemporary study of international relations.
>
> (Gilpin, 1986: 320)

In terms of the CSDP, therefore, the classical realist tradition has much to offer. Classical realism embodies a distinctive philosophical disposition coupled with some key assumptions about the nature of international politics. Classical realists are aware of the element of *tragedy* inherent in an anarchic self-help system, and emphasize the need to distinguish between what is *desirable* and what is *achievable*, given the structural constraints and opportunities of the international system. Classical realism also emphasizes the need to avoid 'moralism' in security policy, and to distinguish between core security objectives and second-order normative concerns (such as human rights and democracy promotion). The implication of this for the CSDP is that EU member states – which determine the goals and means of EU security policy – must match their aspirations to their capabilities, and base their security policy on a hard-headed calculation of the balance of power and competing conceptions of the *summum bonum*.

Whilst this realist perspective might be anathema to liberal-idealists in academia, it does resonate in some parts of the policy community. 'We are moving towards a multipolar world', Finnish Foreign Minister Alex Stubb has argued, 'where you have a set of eight to ten nation states which are taking a bigger role in world affairs, the likes of Turkey and Brazil and the likes of China and Russia and India and a few others.' In this context, 'We need to pick our fights better', he argues, adding that 'for too long we have been preaching, paternalising the rest of the world. Now it's time to take a new approach' (Castle, 2010). For the EU member states, this means recognizing and respecting rival views of the *summum bonum* outside of the Union, and acting as a 'calculator not a crusader'. It also means distinguishing between vital strategic interests and pursuing second-order normative concerns when structural opportunities present themselves. 'Politics', Niebuhr observed, 'will, to the end of history, be an area where conscience and power meet, where ethical and coercive factors of human life will interpenetrate and work out their tentative and uneasy compromises' (Niebuhr, 2005: 4).

Waltz's Copernican revolution

As a tradition of thought, realism is at one and the same time a *philosophical mood or disposition*; a form of practical knowledge concerned with the principles of statecraft; and a social scientific research paradigm. Whereas classical realism is primarily a philosophical mood and a form of practical knowledge, structural realism is essentially a form of what Michael Oakeshott termed 'scientific knowledge' or *scientia*. Practical knowledge is concerned with how we can affect and change the world in order to meet our needs and desires. Scientific knowledge, on the other hand, seeks to understand the world 'in respect of its independence of our hopes and desires, preferences and ambitions'. It involves 'constructing and exploring a rational world of related concepts to which every image recognised as a relevant "fact" … is given a place and an interpretation'. *Scientia*, or this 'impulse for rational understanding', 'exists only where this impulse is cultivated for its own sake unhindered by the intrusion of desire for power or prosperity' (Oakeshott, 1991: 505–6).

Although a number of classical realists were concerned to go beyond philosophic mood and policy advice in order to develop 'scientific knowledge', it is only really with the publication of Kenneth Waltz's *Theory of International Politics* (1979) that realism acquired the theoretical sophistication and analytical tools for explaining – rather than simply describing – international politics. Waltz's great achievement was in developing a parsimonious and deductive theory that established neorealism as a distinctive research paradigm able to generate cumulative knowledge (Vasquez, 1998: 39). In doing so, he produced a 'Copernican revolution' in international political theory by 'showing how much of states' actions and interactions, and how much of the outcomes their actions and interactions produce, can be explained by forces that operate at the level of the system, rather than at the level of the units' (Waltz, 1979: 69).

Neorealism has two defining characteristics. First, it is explicitly parsimonious and elegant, in the sense that it simplifies and abstracts reality in order to focus on a limited number of key variables. 'Explanatory power', Waltz argued, 'is gained by moving away from "reality", not staying close to it. A full description would be of least explanatory power, an elegant theory, of most' (Waltz, 1979: 9). Second, it is 'systemic' in that it seeks explanations for international outcomes at the level of the international system, rather than at that of individual actors. Waltz recognized that state behaviour (and therefore the behaviour of collective international actors like the EU) was self-evidently a consequence of both systemic pressures and domestic political preferences, but argued that his theory of international politics was a parsimonious one which focused on the systemic level because this was the least understood, and the one about which there were most misconceptions (Waltz, 1979: 174).

Neorealism therefore focuses on one key variable: the distribution of relative power capabilities. It does not aspire to explain specific security policy decision-making processes of individual states or of the CSDP, but rather seeks to explain recurrent patterns of behaviour over time. It does so by addressing two separate but related questions: (a) how the structural distribution of relative power capabilities 'shapes and shoves' the behaviour of the units in the system; and (b) how structural, or system-level, factors influence the nature and composition of units, i.e., how their domestic structures are shaped by systemic ('third image') factors – or what is sometimes called 'second image reversed' (Gourevitch, 1978).

Neorealism and the CSDP

A neorealist perspective on the CSDP is clearly one that abstracts and simplifies a complex reality, as one would expect of a parsimonious theory. Nonetheless, it does help focus attention on some of the key features of the EU as a strategic actor.

To begin with, neorealist analyses of the origins and emergence of the CSDP focus on the structural opportunities and constraints generated by global and regional distribution of relative power capabilities. Here, two developments have been crucial to the ESDP/CSDP initiative: the preponderance of US power globally ('unipolarity'), which meant that the USA could afford to pay less attention to the concerns of its European allies and devote less time to alliance management, leading to European perceptions that it was a capricious and unreliable partner (Mearsheimer, 2001: 391; Kagan, 2003; Mowle, 2004); and balanced multipolarity in Europe, which created the permissive conditions for regional cooperation to address shared concerns (Hyde-Price, 2007: 69–71). The CSDP is thus the product of the conflux of two systemic pressures: global unipolarity and regional multipolarity (Posen, 2004(a): 5–17; Posen, 2004(b): 33–8; Treacher, 2004: 49–66).

The CSDP can therefore be seen as the response of EU member states to the uncertainties of US security policy in the context of global unipolarity. As realism would predict, the process has been driven by the 'Big Three', and remains firmly inter-governmental (Grieco, 1993; Missiroli, 2001: 177–96). It is a collective instrument for developing a common security policy and a crisis management capability, as defined by the Petersberg tasks and the European Security Strategy. The CSDP provides an institutional and procedural framework for common security cooperation, primarily in order to collectively shape the Union's external milieu, using limited military coercion to back up its diplomacy where necessary. As a result of the structural pressures emanating from global unipolarity and balanced multipolarity in Europe, the EU is clearly beginning to develop the institutions and procedures to act as a 'centaur', and is ineluctably moving beyond the one-dimensional reflexes of a 'civilian' or 'normative' power.

Looking to the future, structural realism would suggest that Europe's major powers will continue jealously to guard their sovereign rights to pursue their own foreign and security policy priorities (Menon, 2004: 632). Consequently, the CSDP is likely to remain firmly intergovernmental, with cooperation in the second pillar limited to a set of 'second order' concerns agreed on the basis of the lowest common denominator (Waltz, 1979: 170). At the same time, the CSDP is likely to be driven by the EU's largest powers and those with significant crisis management capabilities (Smith, 2005: 757–73; Aliboni, 2005: 1–16; Lindley-French, 2002: 810–11). This was the case with the Contact Group and the Western Balkans in the 1990s, and was evident in terms of the role of the 'EU3' (France, Germany and Britain) in negotiating with Iran on its uranium enrichment programme (Allen and Smith, 2004: 97; Everts, 2004; Bowen and Kidd, 2004: 257–76; Gow, 1997; and Denza, 2005: 289–312).

Finally, a neorealist analysis would suggest that given the changed structural distribution of relative power capabilities following the demise of Cold War bipolarity, there are strong systemic incentives for the further development of the EU as a 'centaur'. Facing more pressing problems in Asia and the Middle East, the USA is focusing less on, and reducing its military commitment to, Europe, thereby generating further 'continental drift' in transatlantic relations. Consequently, there are strong structural pressures for EU member states to provide themselves with options for autonomous military and civilian crisis management. At the same time, EU member states are likely to pursue a variety of strategies towards America, from balancing to bandwaggoning. The divisions between 'old' and 'new' Europe that emerged during the Iraq crisis of 2002–3 are suggestive of the patterns of relations that could emerge, with some states allying with the USA and others pursuing a *Kleineuropa* ('small Europe') option of integration between a select group of 'core' states (Stahl *et al.*, 2004: 417–42). This is likely to perpetuate a continuing ambiguity in relations between the CSDP and NATO.

Beyond parsimony: the promise of neoclassical realism

As an explicitly parsimonious theory, neorealism can shed light on the systemic pressures affecting states and on the structural opportunities and constraints shaping the development of the CSDP. However, as Waltz notes, 'it cannot tell us just how, and how effectively, the units of a system will respond to those pressures and possibilities' (Waltz, 1979: 71). This is clearly a major limitation when it comes to understanding the CSDP. In order to gain greater theoretical traction on the development of the EU as a strategic actor, it is necessary to consider both systemic pressures and a range of variables at national and EU level (Finel, 2001).

For this reason, recent moves to develop a new research programme within the framework of 'neoclassical realism' hold considerable promise for a more fine-grained and nuanced realist analysis of the CSDP. Neoclassical realism combines the central insight of structural realism – namely the primacy of systemic factors in determining international outcomes – with an explicit recognition that a distinctive theory of foreign policy analysis requires an appreciation of the significance of domestic level factors (Rose, 1998). It builds on the complex relationship between state and society found in classical realism without sacrificing the central insight of neorealism about the constraints of international politics and the casual primacy of the international system. Seeking to address the limitations of parsimony identified by Waltz above, neoclassical realism uses the internal characteristics of states as a guide to unit responses to international constraints, and posits an intervening variable for elite perceptions of systemic variables (Lobell, Ripsman and Taliaferro, 2009: 12–13). Although this involves a move away from elegance and parsimony, when seeking to address complex empirical puzzles such as the CSDP, parsimony must be balanced against explanatory power. Consequently, neoclassical realism is explicitly not mono-casual in approach, but includes domestic-level variables such as regime type, decision-making processes, state–society relations and strategic culture (Lobell, Ripsman and Taliaferro, 2009: 23).

As a tool of analysis for thinking theoretically about the evolution of the CSDP, therefore, neoclassical realism offers a way of combining the richness of the classical realist tradition with the theoretical rigour of Waltzian neorealism. Although no major studies have yet emerged that utilize this approach, it offers one of the promising avenues of investigation for more fine-grained realist analyses of the fledgling European 'centaur'.

3

LIBERAL, CONSTRUCTIVIST AND CRITICAL STUDIES OF EUROPEAN SECURITY

Knud E. Jørgensen and Åsne K. Aarstad

The aim of this chapter is to review studies of European security that are informed by liberal, constructivist or critical theoretical orientations. The selected studies belong to the part of the literature that has proved to be of some consequence by setting research agendas, contributing innovative theoretical perspectives, providing comprehensive and significant new insights or reaching important or perhaps counter-intuitive conclusions. While briefly outlining the main characteristics of each of these theoretical perspectives, the main part of the chapter is devoted to critically reviewing the research that each of the three perspectives has produced, including their strengths and weaknesses. While allowing for a few historically significant excursions, the chapter focuses on research produced in the period 1990–2010, i.e., since the fall of the Berlin Wall and the end of the East–West division of Europe.

All three perspectives have delivered path-breaking research on European security. Within the liberal perspective, one of the most precious topics is the construction of Europe itself, significantly contributing, according to liberal arguments, to European security. The construction of Europe is seen as being based on three key liberal features: interdependence, peace-loving democracies and extensive institutionalization of (European) international politics. Moreover, liberal perspectives have been applied in studies of the EU's high-profile promotion of democracy and human rights. This inherently liberal internationalist political agenda has a strong security dimension, not least because the agenda promises to extend the global zones of peace, strengthen the institutionalization of international politics and deepen the dynamics of interdependence. Within constructivist perspectives, the identity–interests–policy axis has functioned as the backbone of scholarship. Put differently, policy-making has been explained by reference to the dynamics of European identity formation and derived processes of interest formation. The transformation of Europe has highlighted change to such an extent that constructivism has widely been seen, to some degree wrongly, as a predominantly change-oriented perspective. Moreover, novel or reinvented approaches such as security communities (with a constructivist twist) and cultures of national security have emerged, documenting the highly innovative features of the perspective. Within critical perspectives, much attention has been directed towards the politics of securitizing various fields of European policy areas and as such questioning who determines the European security agenda. A further significant theme has been the focus on individual security and emancipation, which underscores the conception of human security.

Three theoretical perspectives and four junctions

Most people agree that red, green and blue are different colours. However, when it comes to liberal, constructivist and critical perspectives, such common understandings tend to entirely evaporate. Some do not see any significant difference between the three approaches, for which reason they are lumped together under some common label (Mearsheimer, 1995a). Others believe that all three perspectives are substantive perspectives, for which reason it makes sense to compare and perhaps determine, in the manner of a beauty contest or gladiatorial combat, which one is the best, the winner or just the most beautiful (Jervis, 1999). Still others do not see crucially important differences *within* liberalism, *within* constructivism or *within* critical security studies, for which reason they mix and stir incommensurable assumptions, propositions and meta-theoretical positions, after which they pour a drink that is more muddy than clear and less than applicable in empirical research. In order to avoid such misleading understandings, Figure 3.1 shows that liberal, constructivist and critical perspectives both exist independent of each other, yet also overlap or intertwine. Moreover, had the figure been in 3D, it would have depicted the three perspectives at different levels of analysis.

In addition to visualizing our understanding of how liberal, constructivist and critical perspectives operate – alone or in combination – Figure 3.1 represents a stark contrast to those visualizations of the IR field that present various perspectives as exclusively categorically distinct and, often, as mutually exclusive (Barkin, 2010). These categorizations, however systematically beneficial, do not capture the multitude of combined theoretical perspectives that guide scholarly research. In order to present a comprehensive review of liberal, constructivist and critical studies of European security, it is thus important to acknowledge that the field is marked *both* by theoretically distinct perspectives, as well as combined perspectives.

To start with the former, clusters 1, 2 and 3 in Figure 3.1 are not characterized by any junction with competing or complementary perspectives. First, a major part of research informed by one or more of the main currents within the liberal tradition has little or nothing to do with constructivist and critical theoretical perspectives. Such research is based on different assumptions and subscribes to other epistemological commitments, including positivism and rationalism. Second, research informed by constructivism focuses on the dynamics of social

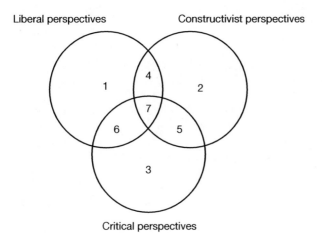

Figure 3.1 Liberal, constructivist and critical perspectives.

reality, hence the importance of exploring the boundary between social and material reality (Searle, 1995; Sørensen, 2008). Importantly, constructivist epistemological commitments do not necessarily necessitate subscription either to liberal assumptions or critical aspirations. Thus, alternative options include shaping or complementing realism (Barkin, 2010; Nau, 2002). Third, research informed by critical perspectives constitutes a further theoretical perspective, characterized by its own distinct assumptions and commitments. In contrast to the two aforementioned perspectives, critical perspectives can be seen as distinctively and deliberately *political* by acknowledging the political nature of political enquiry (Manners, 2006a; van Munster, 2007; Huysmans, 2002).

With reference to the latter overlapping perspectives, four clusters of research (4–7 in Figure 3.1) have been identified. Some liberalism-informed research is based on constructivist commitments and other clusters of liberal research have critical aspirations. We have termed these perspectives 'constructivist liberal studies' and 'critical liberal studies' respectively. In a similar way, some critical studies are based on a constructivist edifice, and thus constitute what we have termed 'constructivist critical studies'. Finally, cluster 7 refers to 'most mixed-perspectives', studies characterized by several theoretical overlaps.

If the theoretical perspectives seemingly constitute a maze, the notion of European security fares no better. Although there are very strong competitors, the notion of 'security' is among the most vague or underspecified notions one can imagine. While during much of the Cold War 'security' was understood as denoting military defence, the 1970s oil crisis extended the meaning to also cover a state's *economic* security, including its access to raw materials. During the late 1980s and up until today, broad notions of security have been introduced and cultivated to such an extent that linkages to defence are almost forgotten. The result is that contemporary notions of security have moved far beyond the security of the survival of the state, to also include security of the individual and the (local/global) society. Examples of the latter are the terms 'human security' and 'environmental security' respectively. As argued by Frédéric Mérand, Martial Foucault and Bastien Irondelle, 'European Security is no longer what it used to be' (2011: 3). The notion of European security has been a moving target and scholarship reflects this dynamic feature.

The following sections of the chapter have been structured by the above understandings, yet they focus foremost on how theoretical understandings have informed research on European security.

Liberal perspectives on European security

Liberal theories can best be collectively described as drawing on a set of assumptions about how the world works, ranging from an optimistic belief in human reason to the perceived positive effects of institutions in moulding anarchy or mitigating conflicts. It follows from this that liberal perspectives on European security are diverse, and come in many forms and shapes. Various liberal perspectives on European security proliferated in the first decade after the end of the Cold War, as orthodox approaches to security were found increasingly unsuitable to grasp the new reality on the Continent. Commercial, ideational and republican liberal theories seek to explain the nature of national preferences (Ikenberry and Moravcsik, 2001). From these perspectives, peace (security) is largely seen as a quality stemming from the liberal state in itself, through its commercial and political organization, and the interdependence between similarly organized states.

John Ikenberry and Andrew Moravcsik (2001) argue for a qualitative distinction between liberal theories of institutional delegation, design and compliance, and liberal theories of underlying preferences of states that motivate policy. The former – liberal institutionalist theories – focus on the ways in which variation in the distribution of information can stimulate incentives to cooperate, and as such reduce the likelihood of conflict. This branch of liberal theories can be seen as sharing many assumptions with the traditional branch of realism, as it assumes that state preferences are a given. In contrast, the latter seek to explain variation in underlying preferences themselves and direct focus towards norms and ideas. We therefore deal with these contributions in the 'constructivist liberal' section.

One of the first major liberal studies to appear immediately after the Cold War was Robert Keohane, Joseph Nye and Stanley Hoffmann's influential *After the Cold War: International Institutions and State Strategies in Europe, 1989–1991* (1994). The application of core components of neoliberal institutional perspectives to the domain of security is a novel feature of this volume, as such applications had previously been restricted to issue areas where the dangers of defection were seen as low, such as economic or environmental cooperation (Martin and Simmons, 2001: 6). During the 1990s, a range of liberal scholars such as John Duffield (1996), Robert McCalla (1996) and Celeste Wallander (2000) applied the neoliberal institutionalist framework to explain the endurance of NATO cooperation after the end of the Cold War. In *Imperfect Unions: Security Institutions through Time and Space* (1999) Helga Haftendorn, Keohane and Wallander make the claim that NATO successfully transformed from a threat-based military alliance to a risk-based security management institution, largely due to its permanent institutional assets aimed at dealing with instability and mistrust.

While Moravcsik's *The Choice for Europe: Social Purpose and State Power from Messina to Maastricht* (1998) does not focus directly on European security, its theoretical framework is nonetheless relevant for such studies. According to Moravcsik's liberal intergovernmentalist framework, the dynamics of European cooperation, in the realm of security as well, can be explained by processes of domestic preference formation within EU member states and by strategic bargaining among the governments of EU member states. The states are seen as the 'masters of the treaty', and integration is the outcome of processes of domestic preference-formation', bargaining and the pooling and delegation of sovereignty. Wolfgang Wagner (2003) draws on Moravcsik's approach when explaining why the CFSP is likely to remain intergovernmental, rather than 'communitarized/Europeanized'. Even though cooperation can be *enhanced* through the establishing of decision-making procedures that pool sovereignty, such as through the introduction of QMV, the overall structure will remain firmly intergovernmental (Wagner, 2003). Assessing the EU's foreign policy towards the Middle East, Costanza Musu applies a historical institutionalist perspective when she argues that the driving factor behind the EU's policy is more congruence rather than real convergence 'capable of producing a truly collective policy, an expression of a unitary European political strategy' (2011: 293).

Regardless of their scholarly popularity, the liberal perspectives have not been received uncritically. The enhanced prospects for institutional cooperation and the focus on absolute, rather than relative gains have been criticized by realist scholars such as John Mearsheimer (1995a) and Joseph Grieco (1995). Ronald Krebs (1999) similarly applies realist arguments when he criticizes liberal institutionalist contributions on NATO for neglecting intra-alliance conflicts, pointing to the difficult relationship between NATO members Greece and Turkey. From a different point of view, constructivist scholars such as Michael Barnett and Martha Finnemore (2001) and Alexandra Gheciu (2005) criticize the liberal institutionalist framework for not acknowledging that institutions can have functions *beyond* the goals that states give them.

Constructivist perspectives on European security

Constructivism, being not a substantive international relations theory but a set of ontological and epistemological commitments, can in principle be blended with a range of substantive theoretical traditions, including realism (Barkin, 2010), the English school (Dunne, 1995; Suganami, 2003), liberalism (Wendt, 1992; Finnemore, 1996) and the Critical Theory tradition (Price and Reus-Smith, 1998). The constructivist turn within IR has produced an avalanche of studies concerned with the role of ideas, norms and culture in politics, underlining intersubjective – shared social – understandings (Finnemore and Sikkink, 2001). While some studies address the key characteristics of constructivism at philosophical, meta-theoretical and theoretical levels, other studies are 'applied' and some of these applied studies focus on European security.

Ian Manners was the first to make use of the concept of 'normative power Europe' in his article of the same name from 2002, and in a revisited version stemming from 2006. Manners argues that the EU is vested with powers to promote norms and values beyond its own borders, which is a distinct capacity from other forms of state power, e.g. the traditional material notions of military or economic power. In other words, the EU's internal identity is said to constitute powers that the EU can use to influence international relations by the promotion of these norms abroad. Examples include the EU's abolition of the death penalty, as well as the promotion of human rights and democracy. While undoubtedly serving as an influential and important work on the impacts of norms on power, Manners has been criticized from various theoretical approaches, including Samir Amin and Ali El Kenz's Marxist critique, arguing that Manners' 'glorification' of the EU's foreign policy ambitions serves as a justification for neoliberal economic imperialism (2005). Adrian Hyde-Price frames his critique in neorealist terms, emphasizing the EU's intergovernmental dynamics and the aspirations of the great powers to 'continue to jealously guard their sovereign rights to pursue their own foreign and security policy priorities' (Hyde-Price, 2006: 231). Far from being a normative power, the EU is seen to be constituted by the powers of its member states, who continually value common security and defence cooperation as only a secondary priority.

Other important constructivist research on European security includes studies of European strategic culture, coercive diplomacy and immigration (Meyer, 2005; Wheeler, 2007; van Munster, 2009). Some of these (and a range of other) constructivist contributions are presented in the 'constructivist liberal' and 'constructivist critical' sections.

Critical perspectives on European security

Roughly speaking, two ways of understanding what constitutes critical security studies can be identified. One group see critical security studies (CCS) as 'a distinct project in its own right', pointing to the normatively guided research agenda of the Welsh school (often referred to as the Aberystwyth school). For others, however, critical security studies is seen as a label for a wide range of approaches critical to the dominance of realist contributions to security studies, including a range of various critical 'schools' (Williams, 2004).

For the purposes of this chapter, we contend that a broad take on critical perspectives applied to the study of European security is not compatible with narrow definitions or strictly defined research agendas. As the name suggests, critical perspectives are brought together more by their contentious relationship with conventional theories of international relations, than by shared theoretical underpinnings. Certain common characteristics, however, are being convincingly brought forward by Colin Hay, arguing that critical perspectives raise three distinct questions when making political enquiries: what is being studied?; what can we know?; and how are we going to know? (Hay, 2002). Thus, as a point of departure, critical perspectives move beyond rationalist theoretical approaches by refusing to accept that the knowledge of the world we inhabit is objective. Following this, theories are not seen as neutral tools to understand the driving forces in our society, stripped of values and partiality. On the contrary, critical perspectives see theories as distinctly political, by arguing that the conduct of political enquiry is by its very nature a political behaviour in itself. The *critique* is directed towards the static rationalist assumptions about human nature and action, the rationalist belief in empirically verifiable truths and the positivist research method (Price and Reus-Smith, 1998: 261). These broad common features taken into consideration, it should come as little surprise that the research contributions that could potentially fit under the heading 'critical security studies' are overwhelmingly many in number. Responding to questions such as '*who* determines the European security agenda?', '*what* is considered a security challenge?', 'for *whom* is it a security challenge?' and '*why* is/should this be a security challenge?', critical approaches to European security have proliferated over the last two decades (van Munster, 2007; CASE, 2006).

Given that critical approaches to the study of security have their intellectual roots in the positivism–post-positivism debate in the 1980s, critical approaches to European security owe much to the post-structural philosophies of Foucault and Derrida, the Marxist tradition of the Frankfurt school, peace-research institutes and their proponents as well as the constructivist research agenda more generally (Jørgensen, 2010: 156–69, CASE, 2006: 447–8). While this insight offers little help in conceptualizing the shape and content of critical security studies, it informs us that the critical approach to security has largely been cultivated in an environment marked by opposition towards the mainstream. Keith Krause and Michael C. Williams' edited volume *Critical Security Studies: Concepts and Cases* (1997) was an early, agenda-setting contribution that addressed the new security challenges of the 1990s. Among the many contributions, Beverly Crawford and Ronnie Lipschutz drew attention to how the politics of (in-)security was exploited to the full extent during the war in former Yugoslavia. The critique was directed towards attempts to structure the causes of the war in a deterministic manner (e.g. 'the conflict was bound to happen') in order to justify the late and incomplete reaction by the international community. By drawing attention to the construction of security, this contribution was an early application of what has become known as the securitization framework developed by Barry Buzan, Ole Wæver and Jaap de Wilde, also referred to as the Copenhagen school (1997). The social construction of security issues through various forms of communicative tools (speeches, images) has been picked up and developed further by critical scholars (Bigo, 1996, 2002; Hansen, 2006).

The Welsh school of critical security studies is characterized by stronger normative aspirations than those works already cited (van Munster, 2007: 235; Peoples and Vaughan-Williams, 2009: 18). The Welsh school cultivates a particular research agenda with a strong normative component, 'conceptualizing security in terms of human emancipation' (Williams, 2004: 144; see also Booth, 1991, 2005; Price and Reus-Smith, 1998; Wyn Jones, 2005). The normative component can be seen as a natural prolongation of the assumption that theoretical knowledge is socially constructed. If there can be no 'research without politics', the conceptual leap is short to advocating how 'good politics' can be better practised and 'bad politics' avoided. In a similar manner, the neo-Gramscian approach, advocated by Andrew Linklater, sees human equality as the goal for which research must pave the way (2000).

Constructivist liberal studies

While Alexander Wendt (1992) has pointed to a mixed zone of strong liberalism and constructivism, other constructivists have been reluctant or downright opposed to be identified with liberal positions. This somehow mirrors realist critics who, when addressing the constructivist turn, have been keen to employ standard realist critiques of liberalism (Mearsheimer, 1995a; Copeland, 2000). In contrast, Brent Steele (2007) argues vigorously that social constructivism is not liberalism, pointing to epistemological, ontological and normative distinctions between the two (see also Barkin, 2010). In short, the constructivist liberal position is deeply contested, yet also most capable of delivering significant studies. Four thematic areas have proved particularly attractive.

First, Emmanuel Adler and Michael Barnett's *Security Communities* (1998) draws upon Karl Deutsch's classic liberal work on security communities and 'role-identity'. Throughout this volume the prospect of security through community-based initiatives, rather than material factors, is a key theme. Others combine the security community perspective with alliance politics (Williams and Neumann, 2000). Generally, the security community perspective has informed a spate of studies.

Second, the distinctly liberal factor is often considered to be domestic politics. While Peter Katzenstein's *The Culture of National Security: Norms and Identity in World Politics* (1996) mixes several analytical components, its emphasis on identity and domestic cultures of security does suggest some affinities with liberal theoretical thinking. The volume's three case studies on German, French and British security policy support this interpretation. Otherwise, the theoretical framework is as systemically structural as neoliberal institutionalism, albeit focusing on global norms rather than international institutions (Kowert and Legro, 1996). Moreover, the focus in other studies on domestic preferences makes it possible to speak about a constructivist liberal research agenda, merging constructivist and liberal perspectives as demonstrated by Wendt (1999) and Risse-Kappen (1995).

Third, liberal and constructivist scholars tend to agree that institutions matter, indeed Keohane (1989) was among the first to point to this shared feature. Several constructivist studies follow up on this proposition in general terms (Finnemore, 1996; Barnett and Finnemore, 2001), while other constructivist studies focus on how European institutions matter in relation to European security (Smith, 1998; Glarbo, 1999; Jørgensen, 1997a). Similarly, Risse-Kappen (1996), Fierke and Wiener (1999) and Gheciu (2005) have drawn upon processes of socialization and identity to explain NATO's continued relevance in the post-Cold War era.

Fourth, liberal and constructivist characteristics intertwine in their key assumption that progress is possible, although not inevitable. While constructivists point to processes of the making of social reality and thus, in principle, are open to options of change, nothing in its key characteristics suggests that constructivists suffer from an inbuilt bias towards change. The issues of the importance of change and continuity, respectively, have frequently been addressed (see e.g. McSweeney, 1996; Buzan, Wæver and de Wilde, 1997).

Constructivist critical studies

Separating constructivist and critical approaches to European security studies can be seen as a somewhat artificial exercise, since substantial parts of the critical security scholarship adhere to the constructivist insistence on security as being socially constructed. In a similar manner, scholars such as Richard Price and Christian Reus-Smith (1998) and Hasan Ulusoy argue that constructivism as a whole is a *critical* exercise of research, in particular since 'it aims to recover the individual and shared meaning that motivates actors to do what they do' (Ulusoy, 2003). From this follows the realization that it is a far from clear-cut task to single out distinct constructivist critical security approaches, but as will be argued, there is nevertheless leverage in the literature for such a distinction.

According to Ted Hopf, constructivist approaches to security can be roughly separated into two camps, specifically the 'conventional' and the 'critical' (Hopf, 1998), an argument also presented by Theo Farrell (2002). Whereas the former camp refers to the large body of constructivist scholarship occupied with the roles and influences of norms and identity in international affairs (as described in previous sections), the latter is more concerned with the role played by discourse and linguistic methods in the construction of security challenges (Karacasulu and Uzgören, 2007: 30–1). According to this dividing line, critical constructivist approaches to the study of security are to be found in-between conventional constructivism and critical approaches with strong normative commitments (Karacasulu and Uzgören, 2007: 30–1).

The Copenhagen school's original outline of the securitization thesis, advanced in *Security: A New Framework for Analysis* by Buzan, Wæver and de Wilde (1997), can be placed within the critical constructivist camp. The social construction of security issues through various forms of communicative tools (speeches, images) over shorter or longer periods of time has been picked up and developed further by critical scholars. Among these, many adhere to the Paris school's sociological approach, emphasizing how security practices move across a wide spectrum of issue areas (Peoples and Vaughan-Williams, 2009: 10; see also Bigo, 2002; Huysmans, 2000, 2006; Aradau, 2004; Williams, 2004; CASE, 2006; and Hansen, 2006). In particular the securitization of immigration in Europe is a field that has received much attention (see Huysmans, 2000, 2006; Aradau and van Munster, 2009). Huysman (2006), to highlight one of the examples, shows in his contribution how specific securitizing moves within the EU have been initiated in order to govern the access of perceived 'dangerous' elements – that is immigrants, asylum-seekers, organized crime (van Munster, 2007: 239). The process of securitization has been facilitated, he argues, through the institutionalization of fear and hostility as an ordering principle (van Munster, 2007: 239; Huysman, 2006). Gross similarly sees strong securitization tendencies in the EU's treatments of the Balkans in her analysis of the EU's crisis management in the region (Gross, 2011). Finally, it should be mentioned that critical works focusing on security as practice have successfully combined different scholarly disciplines, exemplified by the work of Rens van Munster (critical constructivism) and Claudia Aradau (criminology) on the politics of exceptionalism in the face of terrorism (both in the USA and in Europe). As such, these critical constructivist studies can be said to look beyond the perceived disciplinary boundaries of IR theory.

Mikkel Vedby Rasmussen's 2006 *The Risk Society at War: Terror, Technology and Strategy in the Twenty-First Century* can also be placed within the critical constructivist camp. The risk society literature draws upon works by the sociologists Ulrich Beck (1992, 1999) and Anthony Giddens (1999), arguing that in the era of 'reflexive modernity' the risk society is preoccupied with self-manufactured risks. As risks, unlike threats, can never be eliminated, according to Rasmussen 'there is no such thing as perfect security' (2006: 3). Decision-making takes place under conditions of uncertainty, and can be conceptualized as 'a controlled extension of rational action' (Luhmann, 1993). Rasmussen (2001, 2006), Christopher Coker (2002) and Michael J. Williams (2008) have all drawn upon the risk society thesis to explain Western/European security policy over the last two decades, with particular focus on NATO's endurance and the manifestation of the precautionary principle as the new strategic doctrine. Anna Leander (2005) and Elke Krahmann (2011) have directed attention to how private security companies can contribute to shape security policies and preferences in the risk society drawing upon mixed constructivist critical perspectives.

Critical liberal studies

In Ken Booth's *Critical Security Studies* (2005) some of the contributors suggest that individuals – not states – should be the referent objects of security studies. This view does not necessarily make them liberals but does suggest that they share key concerns with both liberals and English school solidarists. Moreover, the position enables a research agenda on human security, i.e. an issue cultivated within both the UN and the European Union. Closely related to the emancipation of individuals as advocated by Ken Booth and Andrew Linklater, the human security framework stands out as a field worth noticing. Located within the security–development nexus, human security is a contested, yet widely popularized term, addressing security from the twin aspects of 'freedom from want – freedom from fear', targeting individuals, not states (Werthes and Debiel, 2006: 10). Mary Kaldor stands out as a scholar who has not only published influential studies in the field (Kaldor and Martin, 2009), but furthermore exercises some influence on the EU through the Human Security Study Group's publications (the Barcelona Report 2004; the Madrid Report 2007), initiated by former EU High Representative Javier Solana.

Most-mixed perspectives

Some would probably argue that this field of study is simply too complex or 'über-patch-work-like' to be helpful for analytical purposes. Yet in the real world, 'appliers' are often considerably more pragmatic than 'purist' theorists. In other words, this 'several-overlaps' position might not constitute a distinct theoretical position, yet nonetheless prove capable of producing numerous studies of European security. Moreover, while the 1980s and 1990s were predominantly characterized by competitive theory-testing and analytical MAD strategies, the times they are a-changing. Now it is notions of 'dialogue', 'bridge-building', 'complementary potentials' and even praise of theoretical eclecticism that characterize recommended research design (Sil and Katzenstein, 2010). We should therefore focus on scholars tracing the boundaries between analytical perspectives, for instance examining the boundary between critical security studies and the Copenhagen school (Buzan, 2004; see also Campbell, 1998) or discussing the mixed zone of strong liberalism and constructivism (Wendt, 1992).

In order to better understand junctions in this analytical 'Dreieck' of theoretical perspectives, we can ask if processes of securitization do not at least to some degree overlap with processes of domestic preference formation; if strategic bargaining does not constitute a distinct kind of social interaction defining the identity of actors involved; and if institutional design cannot be seen as part of the environmental structure in which processes of identity and interest formation are embedded, in turn defining the key parameters of policy-making. If yes, we have pointed to possible translations of the theoretical vocabulary that theorists employ.

When drawing out the consequences of the above ideas, two alternative pathways emerge as particularly intriguing. The first option is that we keep theoretical characteristics fairly fixed and look for a theoretical position that is the outcome of a conscious theoretical synthesis, in turn applied in studies of European security. In this case, Figure 3.1 turns out to be a badly shaped donut, yet with the empty centre intact. The second option is to acknowledge that empirical studies of European security often are nothing but a more or less messy set of variables, characterized by some varying leanings towards liberal, constructivist or critical analytical concerns.

Conclusion

As argued at the beginning of this chapter, studies of European security are characterized by a multitude of theoretical perspectives in combination with a multitude of understandings of what constitutes 'security' in the European context. Liberal, constructivist and critical theory perspectives are applied alone or in combination, contributing a constant chain of new insight and novel analyses. Within this broad and widely pluralistic field, it is nevertheless possible to single out some key areas of research that have proved particularly attractive to analysts working within the theoretical perspectives covered in this chapter:

- First, conflicts and interventions in the Western Balkans and the conduct of peace-support operations more generally have been among the most enduring challenges during the last twenty years. It is hardly surprising that these political challenges have been turned into analytical challenges and that liberal, constructivist and critical perspectives have been thoroughly employed.
- Second, NATO's endurance has constituted a genuine puzzle for analysts drawing on very different theoretical perspectives. In a wider perspective, analysts have explored international organizations and regimes that enjoy mandates to deal with security issues.
- Third, EU advances in the field of security have been analysed within identity perspectives, institutional dynamics (CFSP, CSDP), processes of socialization and interplays between European and national levels of policy- and decision-making. EU engagements in Asia, Africa, the Caucasus and the Middle East have been thoroughly analysed. The issue of strategic culture might mainly have been analysed by policy analysts but some theory-informed studies have also appeared. In this context, we also find various studies of European security strategies at both national and European levels.
- Fourth, the EU's neighbourhood and enlargements policies have got a fair deal of attention, although theory-informed studies have been relatively difficult to find.
- Finally, Russia constitutes kind of a constant in studies of European security. This analytical area includes issues such as nuclear security in the wake of the dissolution of the Soviet Union, Russia–CIS relations and energy security.

Merand, Foucault, and Irondelle argue that the contemporary European security architecture, as it has developed since the fall of the Berlin Wall, 'lacks a clear structure of political authority' (2011: 302). The shift from government to governance in the security domain is a related observation, pointing to increased fragmentation of political authority and the parallel growth of multiple centres of power and the multiplication of security actors in Europe (Webber *et al.*, 2004; Krahmann 2003). These two observations are well reflected in a theoretically rich, thematically broad, and ever-expanding scholarly literature on European security, as outlined in this review.

4

THE EUROPEAN SECURITY STRATEGY

Towards a grand strategy?

Sven Biscop

On 12 December 2003 the European Council adopted the *European Security Strategy* (ESS), sub-titled *A Secure Europe in a Better World*, the first-ever strategic document addressing EU external action in the broadest sense and therefore key to understanding the Union's role in security.[1] Starting from an analysis of what constitutes the core of the ESS, this chapter will argue that although it represents a milestone, it is not the alpha and omega of European strategic thinking. For it to function as a fully-fledged grand strategy, it needs to be completed and EU strategic thinking needs to be deepened, particularly in the area of security and defence.

Strategy can be defined as a policy-making tool which, on the basis of the values and interests of the actor in question, outlines the long-term policy objectives to be achieved and the instruments to be applied to that end, which serves as a reference framework for day-to-day policy-making in a rapidly evolving and complex environment and which guides the definition of the means that need to be developed. A grand strategy, defined by Gaddis (2009) as 'the calculated relationship between means and large ends', defines an actor's fundamental objective and the basic categories of instruments it chooses to apply to achieve that. Grand strategy thus equals the choice to be a certain type of actor or power. Grand strategy moreover has implications for internal policies as well. The ESS operates at this level. To be a strategic actor, the EU requires not just a clear strategy, but in addition both the means and the political will to actively pursue it.

An incomplete grand strategy

The core of the ESS can be summarized in three principles, which together constitute an approach, a method, to deal with the international environment.

The core of the ESS

The first core principle of the ESS is *prevention*: 'we should be ready to act before a crisis occurs. Conflict prevention and threat prevention cannot start too early', as the ESS states. A permanent strategy of prevention and stabilization, addressing the root causes of threats and challenges, aims to prevent conflict so that, ideally, coercion and the use of force will not be necessary. Addressing the root causes means closing the gap, both within and between countries, between the haves and the have-nots in terms of access to the core public goods to which all individuals aspire and are indeed entitled: security, prosperity, freedom and social equality. For this gap between haves and have-nots generates feelings of frustration and marginalization on the part of those that are excluded, as well as radicalization and extremism of various kinds, social and economic instability, massive migration flows and tension and conflicts within and between states. Effective prevention is an enormous challenge, for it means addressing a much wider range of issues, at a much earlier stage, across the globe, because as the ESS says 'the first line of defence will often be abroad'.

Closing the gap between the haves and the have-nots of necessity demands a *holistic* approach, the second principle, for the security, economic, political and social dimensions are inextricably related – an individual cannot enjoy any one core public good without having access to them all – and all are present, in differing degrees, in all threats and challenges. In the ESS: 'none of the new threats is purely military, nor can any be tackled by purely military means. Each requires a mixture of instruments.' Therefore every foreign policy must simultaneously address all dimensions, making use in an integrated way of all available instruments: 'Diplomatic efforts, development, trade and environmental policies, should follow the same agenda.' The core phrase in the ESS is perhaps the following:

> The best protection for our security is a world of well-governed democratic states. Spreading good governance, supporting social and political reform, dealing with corruption and abuse of power, establishing the rule of law and protecting human rights are the best means of strengthening the international order.

Such a holistic approach is best implemented via *multilateralism*, the third principle. 'We need to pursue our objectives both through multilateral cooperation in international organizations and through partnerships with key actors', according to the ESS. Only in cooperation with others can our objectives be achieved peacefully, and can global challenges be successfully addressed. 'The development of a stronger international society, well functioning international institutions and a rule-based international order is our objective', declares the ESS under the heading of 'effective multilateralism'. Multilateralism can be considered 'effective' to the extent that the ensemble of regimes, mechanisms and institutions manages to provide access to the core public goods to citizens worldwide.

From these three principles it follows that the EU must be a *global* actor. As the ESS states: 'As a Union of 25 [now 27] states with over 450 million people producing a quarter of the world's Gross National Product (GNP), and with a wide range of instruments at its disposal, the European Union is inevitably a global player.' In a globalized world, interdependence is such that none of these principles can be successfully applied at the regional level only, for the most pressing challenges are global challenges. The EU cannot insulate itself or its neighbourhood from the world.

These are indeed *principles* of foreign policy, i.e. the EU pursues them as a matter of principle, because they reflect the values on which the EU itself is based; therefore they determine the EU's soft power, i.e. the credibility and legitimacy of its foreign policy. From these principles, the ESS also draws certain implications for the means, notably the need to be more active, more capable and more coherent, and to work with partners.

These three principles constitute only a partial grand strategy, however. They represent an important strategic choice, but they mostly tell us *how* to do things – the ESS is much vaguer on *what* to do. The issue is not that the ESS is not valid or has been outdated – in fact, it already mentions all of the so-called new threats and challenges, e.g. climate change, energy shortages and large-scale migration, proof of the authors' foresight. The issue is that the ESS is incomplete in terms of the fundamental objectives which the EU aims to achieve. It is so because to start with it is not clear about the values and interests to be defended. Even with an incomplete grand strategy, the EU could have been more of a global power, beyond the area of trade, if it had not been for the half-hearted implementation of the ESS and Member States' reluctance to act proactively and collectively. A grand strategy must necessarily be translated into strategies, sub-strategies and policies for it to be put into action, but the objectives of 'building security in our neighbourhood' and 'effective multilateralism'[2] have proved too broad, and Member States far too hesitant to act upon the strategy that they have adopted, to generate clear priorities. As a result, the EU has not become markedly more proactive, capable or coherent since the adoption of the ESS. In other words, the EU has yet to become a real strategic actor.

The 2008 Report on the Implementation of the ESS

A chance to revisit the ESS presented itself when the December 2007 European Council mandated High Representative Javier Solana 'to examine the implementation of the Strategy with a view to proposing elements on how to improve the implementation and, as appropriate, elements to complement it'. The December 2008 European Council duly adopted a *Report on the Implementation of the European Security Strategy – Providing Security in a Changing World*, while deciding to leave the ESS itself untouched. Unfortunately, the Report did not offer concrete recommendations to improve implementation, although it recognized that 'despite all that has been achieved, implementation of the ESS remains work in progress'.

In view of the difficult circumstances, notably the delay in the ratification of the Lisbon Treaty, it was probably for the best not to have a fundamental strategic debate in 2008, so as not to run the risk of ending up with a weaker grand strategy than before. Nevertheless, because the ESS *is* incomplete, a true strategic review is necessary. That would bring enhanced clarity, for although the Report – which is longer than the ESS itself – 'does not replace the ESS, but reinforces it', the existence of the two documents alongside each other tends to lead to confusion. A new exercise in grand strategy need not start from scratch, as the ESS makes valid choices, but a fully-fledged revision is required in order to complete it (Biscop, 2009b).

Completing EU grand strategy

The first rule of strategy-making could simply be: know thyself. It is actually not that clear which values and interests the EU seeks to safeguard and which kind of international actor it wants to be.

Universal values

The Treaty defines the values on which the EU is based and which it states should also guide its foreign policy. The Lisbon Treaty has extended this definition, putting additional emphasis on the values of equality, solidarity and human dignity:

> The Union is founded on the values of respect for human dignity, freedom, democracy, equality, the rule of law and respect for human rights, including the rights of persons belonging to minorities. These values are common to the Member States in a society in which pluralism, non-discrimination, tolerance, justice, solidarity and equality between women and men prevail.
>
> (Art. 2 TEU)

> The Union's action on the international scene shall be guided by the principles which have inspired its own creation, development and enlargement, and which it seeks to advance in the wider world: democracy, the rule of law, the universality and indivisibility of human rights and fundamental freedoms, respect for human dignity, the principles of equality and solidarity, and respect for the principles of the United Nations Charter and international law.
>
> (Art. 21.1 TEU)

These values highlight what is most distinctive about the EU model of society: the combination of democracy, the market economy and strong state intervention, at Member State and EU levels, to ensure fair competition and social security. This European social model can be conceptualized as a social contract between EU citizens on the one hand, who are all entitled to an integral whole of public goods, and the EU and the governments of the Member States on the other hand, whose responsibility it is to provide these goods, which are the concrete expressions of the values on which the model is based:

- security or freedom from fear
- economic prosperity or freedom from want
- political freedom: democracy, respect for human rights and the rule of law
- social equality: health, education and a clean environment.

This social model as such is specific to the EU and thus not universal. Even within the EU there are obviously differences between individual Member States in how they have organized their democracy or social security. But the values *are* universal. Clearly, the more the values are respected within the EU and the stronger the cohesion of the European model that is based on them, the stronger the foundations on which to base EU foreign policy. Arguably, next to guaranteeing peace among its members, the European social model is Europe's most successful achievement, in material as well as in moral terms. The fundamental objective of EU grand strategy, both internally and externally, can thus be defined as the preservation and strengthening for its citizens of the security, economic, political and social dimensions of the European social model and the universal values on which it is based.

European interests

An assessment of the conditions that have to be fulfilled for this fundamental objective to be achieved allows us to identify the EU's vital interests, i.e. those that determine the very survival of its social model:

- defence against any military threat to the territory of the Union
- open lines of communication and trade (in physical as well as in cyber space)
- a secure supply of energy and other vital natural resources

- a sustainable environment
- manageable migration flows
- the maintenance of international law (including the UN Charter and the treaties and regulations of the key international organizations) and of universally agreed rights
- preserving the autonomy of the decision-making of the EU and its Member States.

These *vital* interests are common to all Member States, who no longer have national vital interests, i.e. vital interests different from those of other Member States. Moreover, not only do Member States share the same vital interests, they are also inextricably related, as a consequence of the ever-deepening political and economic integration within the EU. The vital interests of one Member State can no longer be separated from those of another; a threat to the vital interests of one inevitably threatens all. Even the two military powers in Europe, France and the UK, recognize this. In the Declaration on Defence and Security Cooperation adopted at the 2010 Franco-British Summit in London, they state that '[w]e do not see situations arising in which the vital interests of either nation could be threatened without the vital interests of the other also being threatened' (France and UK, 2010: 2). Finally, no single Member State any longer has the resources to safeguard all of its vital interests on its own – at the global level, all Member States are small states.

Although it is an issue about which the ESS largely remains silent, interests cannot be ignored. The negative connotation that the notion of interests has acquired in the eyes of many is neither justified nor rational, for interests are at the heart of policy-making. The EU evidently pursues its interests. In itself, that is neither positive nor negative – the question is *how* they are pursued, through which basic categories of instruments or, in other words, which kind of actor the EU decides to be.

Opportunities and threats in the global environment

The answer to the question which approach the EU can adopt to safeguard its interests is determined by the EU's adherence to what it judges to be universal values, which guide its foreign policy, but it is also conditioned by the international environment, i.e. the threats, challenges and actors which are analysed in the ESS and the Implementation Report.

In terms of threats, i.e. issues that imply a risk of violence and therefore may ultimately demand a military response, today's environment is relatively benign. As the ESS states: 'Large-scale aggression against any Member State is now improbable.' Other threats are 'more diverse, less visible and less predictable' – terrorism, proliferation of WMD, regional conflicts, state failure – but today none of these constitutes an immediate vital threat. That does not mean that these threats can be ignored, for they do produce negative effects for the Union, and if left unattended they may again develop into more serious direct threats. There does today remain a direct terrorist threat against EU territory, but '[c]ompared to interstate conflict, terrorism … is a minor menace'; it 'does not threaten our civilization, but our over-reaction to it could do so' (Gray, 2009: 24). In the long term, inter-state war between major actors cannot be excluded, unlikely though it appears today; even if the EU were not directly involved, the implications of war between the other great powers would be enormous. The risk of inter-state war in the near future either between the great powers or involving an EU Member State does seem limited, however. Consequently, the EU and its Member Stats, while obviously required to maintain a credible territorial defence as an insurance policy, fortunately can now afford not to focus on military power alone.

At the same time, today's environment contains a number of major challenges, which are all complex, global and interrelated, and which potentially have a multiplier effect on the threats: poverty, climate change, scarcity of energy, water and other natural resources, pandemics and large-scale migration. Because of globalization, the dependence of the EU and hence its vulnerability to these threats and challenges have greatly increased. Finally, in terms of actors, the environment is marked by growing multipolarity and a relative shift in the distribution of power: as the military, economic and soft power of other global actors increase (though not at the same pace in all dimensions of power or in all of these states), the relative importance of the EU declines, notably vis-à-vis the BRIC countries. Although in absolute terms the EU still is the major economic power, on par only with the USA, it is confronted with increasingly active other players, and thus sees its leverage decreasing, both in bilateral relations and in multilateral forums (Renard, 2009).

How to interpret this environment? Although it is undoubtedly very challenging, it also contains elements on which the EU can build constructive engagement with the world. For one, the EU has no enemies: today not a single state has the capacity or even the intention to directly confront it militarily. Second, the world is marked not just by increasing multipolarity, but also by increasing interdependence between the poles. All are increasingly interlinked economically, and all are confronted with the same complex global challenges that can be successfully addressed only in cooperation between them. This is what Grevi (2009) has dubbed 'interpolarity'. This context does not guarantee the absence of tension or strife between the powers, but it constitutes a great opportunity. For among the global actors 'controversy mainly revolves around the means and not the ends' (Grevi, 2010a: 5). There is a chance, in other words, to involve them in a comprehensive and multilateral strategy, as per the ESS.

Reaffirming the distinctive EU grand strategy

In the absence of enemies and in view of the need for cooperation to tackle common challenges, EU grand strategy need not be threat-based nor need it focus on the 'traditional', coercive use of power. Instead, it can continue to focus on values. The best way of defending our interests, in order to defend the EU model and the universal values on which it is based, is precisely to spread those universal values. For increasing the access of citizens worldwide to the same core public goods that are the concrete expression of these values (security, prosperity, freedom, equality) directly addresses the underlying causes of threats and challenges. The current global environment thus validates the preventive, holistic and multilateral approach of the ESS, the fundamental principles of which therefore do not have to be amended. If the fundamental objective of the EU is the preservation and strengthening of the European social model and the universal values on which it is based (its internal social contract), the best way of achieving that is to promote those universal values in the rest of the world (an external social contract). The idea is not to export the European model, for that is specific to the EU and the same universal values can inspire different models, as the variations within the EU itself demonstrate. Promoting the *values*, however, constitutes a positive agenda in its own right. EU grand strategy can thus be constructive, aimed at achieving objectives that are in the enlightened self-interest of the EU – that is what policy is about – but which also directly benefit others and thus express a feeling of responsibility for and solidarity with the have-nots.

Promoting democracy, human rights, etc. is extremely difficult, but the answer to these difficulties is not to abdicate when it comes to the promotion of values. The EU could not do so, for those values are at the heart of what the EU itself is – no foreign policy that runs counter to them would be tenable for long. Second, promoting those values is essential to the EU's strategic objectives, for without security, prosperity, democracy and equality there can be no real stability – that has been proved by the Tunisian and Egyptian people. What has to change, though, is the method of promoting these values. '[The EU's] achievements are the results of a distinctive European approach to foreign and security policy', states the Implementation Report. Distinctiveness is not an objective per se, but this is a distinctive grand strategy, different from that of all other global actors. The EU refrains from the aggressive use of force and uses coercion (by diplomatic, economic and, as a last resort, military means) only when vital interests are threatened, and does not seek to establish spheres of influence, but pursues its interests through a preventive, holistic and multilateral approach based on the promotion of universal values. It does not seek to coerce other states into adopting those, not even merely to entice them through conditionality. The EU seeks instead to *convince* others of the benefits of respecting those values through concrete cooperation and support, on the basis of shared interests and common challenges, but in a manner that also respects the universal values that it aims to promote. Thus by marrying multilateralism and partnership to multipolarity, the recognition of the universality of these values can be gradually and consensually increased.

Priorities of grand strategy

Having established what the universal values are on which the EU is based and which vital interests it needs to protect, and having reaffirmed the preventive, holistic and multilateral approach, the next step would be to translate grand strategy into clearer objectives and priorities. Of course, even a more complete grand strategy is not an operational document – it will always be a guide for day-to-day policy-making. But the clearer the strategic objectives, the more they will generate purposive action. Therefore, on the basis of its vital interests the EU should identify its specific interests in all of the key areas of foreign policy and set more concrete objectives, in order to direct its sub-strategies, policies and actions.

Implementing the Lisbon Treaty

To start with, the entry into force of the Lisbon Treaty on 1 December 2009 is an argument in itself in favour of continuing the strategic reflection process, in order to incorporate its innovations in the field of foreign and security policy. The Lisbon Treaty provides the EU with more and better tools for foreign and security policy – a grand strategy should tell us when and why to use them. It should also be clear where the institutional ownership of the ESS lies and who is responsible for its implementation. Experience with the ESS shows that an institutional follow-up structure is required, ensuring that a specific body is responsible for monitoring implementation, and setting deadlines for reporting back to the European Council. For lack of it, the ESS, although omnipresent in the public debate, failed to have sufficient impact on actual policy-making: officials habitually referred to the ESS when having to explain to various publics the EU's role in the world, but did not seem to refer to it very often in their own work. Most importantly, the remit of grand strategy must be perfectly clear. As it is, the ESS is too often seen as 'the Solana paper', pertaining only to the CFSP. Now that the Lisbon Treaty has entered into force, the High Representative/ Vice-President of the Commission, Catherine Ashton, supported by the External Action Service, should be formally entrusted with the development and implementation of strategy and take the lead in the Council and in the Political and Security Committee. As the High Representative will chair the Council when it deals with foreign policy, she will have a much greater impact on agenda-setting, which should allow her to schedule strategic-level debates as required, supported by a strong policy-planning branch with which the External Action Service should be endowed.

Eventually, a systematic ESS review process could be instituted, e.g. every five years, with clear follow-up and reporting mechanisms, in order to ensure that the EU, at the level of Heads of State and Government, regularly assesses and if necessary amends its grand strategy, which must be a dynamic document. A true strategic review would allow us to identify in which areas the grand strategy has yet to be translated into sub-strategies, policies and actions, to assess their effectiveness in areas where this has taken place and to establish where they overlap and contradict each other.

Lessons learned from implementing the ESS

Strategy development should take into account the lessons learned from implementing the ESS until now.[3] Although the principles on which the ESS is based are by now well established and the EU has sincerely sought to implement them in its foreign policy, their translation into practice has raised questions which the Implementation Report did not address. At least three core issues demand a thorough debate.

The EU has pursued its agenda mainly via 'positive conditionality', establishing comprehensive partnerships that promise benefits in function of reforms undertaken by the partner country in a variety of fields. In practice, except in the case of enlargement, that approach has seldom yielded the hoped-for results. On the one hand, the proverbial carrot on offer is not always what interests the partner the most, e.g. access to the EU's labour or agricultural market, while on the other hand it is often accorded quite regardless of the partner's performance. The EU too often applies double standards, condemning in one country what it discreetly overlooks in another, and too rarely manages a coherent approach, without one EU policy undercutting another. In combination with the fact that as a result of the rise of other global powers, the envisaged partner countries can now shop around and seek partnership with actors that are less demanding when it comes to human rights, for instance, EU leverage appears limited, especially vis-à-vis authoritarian regimes.

The fundamental dilemma that the EU has yet to solve is what to do when its interests (e.g. energy supply, managing migration, the fight against terrorism) generate short-term demands (e.g. cooperation with authoritarian regimes) that clash with its inherently long-term preventive, holistic and multilateral method of promoting the core public goods outside the EU. The EU cannot afford to continue to ignore this dilemma, for already the contrast between high-flown rhetoric about human rights and democracy and mostly rather hesitant policies in practice has greatly damaged its credibility and legitimacy. Too many perceive the EU as a status quo actor, prioritizing economic and security interests and not sincerely committed to promoting reform.

To begin with, serious debate is in order, about the objectives which the EU should set at the grand strategic level, and about how to translate those into strategies, sub-strategies, policies and actions, in order to ensure that the emphasis on the promotion of public goods does not lead to weakness. How can the EU dialogue with a regime and foster cooperation and reform while simultaneously remaining sufficiently critical of all violations of the values which cooperation and reform are to promote? Which 'carrots' can be offered to increase the effectiveness of conditionality? How can conditionality be more strictly applied? What is the minimum threshold below which the EU cannot agree to deal with any regime, even to the detriment of short-term interests? How can democratization movements be fostered and supported? That the EU, while it cannot hope to engineer democratization from the outside, must support any internal democratization movements is in any case beyond doubt. In doing so, it will not only stay true to its values, but it will then also have positioned itself as a partner of choice for any democratic regime that manages to establish itself, whereas otherwise it can only be put to shame by its previous all too uncritical support for the preceding authoritarian regime.

Second, the EU must in any case be conscious of the limits of conditionality: vis-à-vis other global powers it is not an option, for interdependence is too great and the scale of things too vast for the EU to have any serious direct leverage. Trade relations with China were not cut when Beijing refused to release the winner of the 2010 Nobel Peace Prize, Liu Xiaobo, from prison. Such actors can only be *convinced* of the value of the public goods which the EU promotes on the basis of shared interests and common challenges. The incomplete state of current EU strategic thinking and its lack of strategic actorness is made all the more evident by contrasting it with the much more purposive action of other global powers that do act strategically in terms of explicit interests, notably the BRIC countries, and of course the USA. Most of them do not regard the EU as a strategic actor, and are adept at playing off one Member State against the other, as the EU is all too good at 'divide and rule': by dividing itself, others rule. Naturally, the EU is hampered by its collective decision-making when compared with presidential or even authoritarian regimes: all the more reason to deepen its collective strategic thinking and give more direction to decision-making. Every analysis points in the same direction: the future will be dominated by large, strategic players (Howorth, 2009). If they want to safeguard their interests and not be pulled apart, Europeans have no choice but to act as a 'large, strategic player' themselves, i.e. to act collectively and with a clear sense of purpose. The second debate therefore concerns EU objectives as regards its strategic partnerships with these other global actors, as well as with regional organizations. That in turn implies a debate about the EU's view on the future of the multilateral institutions.

The third debate is more directly linked to CSDP: what to do if, in spite of all positive intentions, prevention fails and conflict does erupt? What is the EU view on the threat and use of force? The ESS remains vague. It calls for 'a strategic culture that fosters early, rapid, and when necessary, robust intervention'. Such intervention is put in a multilateral context, as regards who is to act – 'The United Nations Security Council has the primary responsibility for the maintenance of international peace and security' – and why to act – 'We want international organizations, regimes and treaties to be effective in confronting threats to international peace and security, and must therefore be ready to act when their rules are broken.' The EU and its Member States evidently see the use of force as an instrument of last resort, which in principle is used only with a Security Council mandate. Yet although a shared strategic culture seems to be emerging, this has never been translated into clear priorities for CSDP.

Towards a strategy for CSDP?

Why does Europe develop the military and civilian capabilities that it does? Why does it undertake the military and civilian operations that it does? And why in other cases does it refrain from action? The answers to these questions would amount to a specific civilian–military CSDP or crisis management strategy (Biscop, 2011). Starting from the EU's vital interests, an analysis of the threats and challenges to these interests, and the EU's foreign policy priorities, a CSDP strategy would outline the priority regions and issues for CSDP and, in function of the long-term political objectives and the appropriate political roadmap for those regions and issues, scenarios in which launching an operation could be appropriate.

The absence of a CSDP strategy has not stopped the EU from being active, witness the more than twenty civilian missions and military operations undertaken. But too often, action has been reactive, ad hoc, ill-thought-through – the result of the Boy Scout mentality: we should do something. And indeed, the EU should – but not in each and every case. Because the means are limited, choices must be made and priorities set. Without strategy, the EU can never be sure that the operations that it carries out are actually the most relevant and important that it could undertake. It cannot direct the operations that it does undertake to achieve the desired strategic effect. And it cannot focus capability development if it does not know its strategic priorities.

Priority regions and issues

The regions and issues on which CSDP ought to focus are those where the EU's vital interests are most directly at stake (Biscop, 2011). That does not mean that the EU will disregard other regions and issues, but it does provide the focus for early warning and prevention, and for permanent contingency planning.

In defining priority regions and issues, geopolitics is crucial. Because of its proximity, the most important priority area undoubtedly is the Neighbourhood: any crisis in the area from the Baltic to Gibraltar will have immediate spill-over effects on the EU, in terms of political and economic disruption, refugees and possibly even violence. Lines of communication and energy supply are obviously at stake; migration is also an issue, especially but not exclusively in the Southern Neighbourhood. In this region, the EU itself is the most powerful actor, hence it should take the lead in safeguarding peace and security, which is, not coincidentally, what our most important ally, the USA, expects from us.

1   The Eastern Neighbourhood (the Baltic to the Black Sea). With the persistence of the 'frozen conflicts', which, as the Russian–Georgian War of 2008 showed, can easily be sparked into open war, the region remains fundamentally unstable. The priority is to step up conflict prevention and stabilization efforts, but crisis management may be required, as in 2008. In view of Russian aspirations to maintain a sphere of influence, any operation or mission will be highly sensitive. Nevertheless, crisis management, including extricating EU citizens or civilians deployed on a CSDP mission, must be planned for in addition to preventive measures and peacekeeping.

2   The Southern Neighbourhood (the Dardanelles to Gibraltar). The everlasting Israeli–Palestinian conflict, but also disputes between Southern states and the inherent instability of authoritarian regimes and their unpredictable succession all contain serious potential for conflict. While we rejoice at the Arab spring, it does not automatically solve any of these issues and might complicate some of them even more. Here too, any intervention would be highly sensitive and ideally would take place with political, and preferably military, support from the region. Besides stepping up prevention, crisis management, evacuation and humanitarian operations must be planned for, as well as peacekeeping, notably in the event of a solution to the Israeli–Palestinian conflict.

Three regions immediately adjacent to the Neighbourhood also merit our particular attention. The Gulf and Central Asia are of obvious importance for energy supply, and the former also for trade routes; furthermore, crisis in either region risks generating important spill-over effects. In security terms, both regions probably form part of the EU's 'broader Neighbourhood'. In sub-Saharan Africa vital interests are less directly at stake, but Europe does have essential interests there as well as a continued responsibility, in view of its historical legacy, to assist the African Union in maintaining peace and security.

3   The Gulf. The emphasis has rightly been on preventive diplomacy, notably in the Iranian nuclear dossier, but the fact that some actors might see a *casus belli* here, even if the EU does not, should inform prudent planning. As in the Southern Neighbourhood, inherently unstable authoritarian regimes are a potential source of conflict. While our leverage is more limited, notably as compared to that of the USA, and operations at the higher end of the scale less likely, various scenarios may demand some contribution to crisis management. The EU could build on coordination between British and French pre-deployed assets.

4   Central Asia. The region is somewhat off the radar screen, but the same instability that comes with authoritarianism applies. While high-end operations are unlikely, other operations and missions might be called for.

5   Sub-Saharan Africa. There is as yet no end to the security problems from which Africa itself suffers, first and foremost. The EU can support the African Union and local actors with operations and missions across the spectrum, but would probably have more impact if it concentrated its efforts on a limited set of priorities rather than contributing piecemeal. In the long term the key is of course development.

Finally, two less region-specific issues also demand to be prioritized. The security of shipping lanes worldwide is vital to Europe as a trade power; migration and trafficking are issues, too. Because maintaining international law is a vital interest, the EU must contribute to its enforcement by the UN when it is violated.

6   Maritime Security. Except to the east, the EU has maritime borders, but planning ought to have a global focus, notably on the crucial zone from 'Suez to Shanghai' (Rogers, 2009), and increasingly on the Arctic. The EU should build a presence and contribute actively to the patrolling of key maritime routes in order to prevent other powers, or conflict between them, from dominating or disrupting them. Supporting operations and missions on land is another key task.

7   Collective Security. The collective security system of the UN can only work if it addresses everyone's security. In view of its vital interests as well as its values, the EU must shoulder its share of the burden, but cannot of course contribute to each and every operation. The 'Responsibility to Protect' can guide setting priorities.

If the main focus of CSDP is on the external security of the Union, it does have a complementary role to play in our internal security as well, notably in the implementation of the Solidarity Clause and in the future, perhaps, in our collective defence.

Conclusion: from strategy to action

Adopting a strategy for CSDP will not in itself guarantee resolute action in each and every crisis. But forging a consensus on priority regions and issues and drawing the conclusions from that for capabilities, including planning and conduct, will focus the Union's preventive, long-term efforts, and will certainly make it better prepared for action in any contingency. Being more prepared and knowing in advance what its priority regions and issues are, and why, will then hopefully also strengthen the political will to generate action under the EU flag by the able and willing Member States, and will thus make for an EU that carries its weight on the global stage. CSDP is only an instrument, however, a tool, hence a CSDP strategy only makes sense if it serves an overall EU grand strategy.

Notes

1 For an analysis of the origins of the ESS, see Bailes (2005) and Biscop (2005).
2 Under the heading of 'strategic objectives' the ESS also mentions 'addressing the threats', but rather than setting future-oriented targets, this section is limited to listing past actions and outlining the need for a preventive and holistic approach.
3 For an analysis of implementation during the first years of the ESS, see Biscop and Andersson (2008).

5

EUROPEAN STRATEGIC CULTURE

Taking stock and looking ahead

Christoph O. Meyer

The rapid evolution of the European Union's security and defence policy since 1999 visible in Treaty amendments, strategy papers, institutional differentiation and carefully delimited missions has always been accompanied by scepticism about its political foundations. To what extent have all these developments been driven by a relatively detached Brussels elite supported by the short-term tactical interests of national leaders, rather than a sustained and deep-rooted convergence of political ideas and norms about the use of force? Will the EU be able and willing to act in times of crisis (Biscop, 2004)? Even at the beginning of the ESDP process, Paul Cornish and Geoffrey Edwards (Cornish and Edwards, 2001) argued that European defence and security policy needed a common strategic culture to function. They defined it as the 'institutional confidence and processes to manage and deploy military force as part of the accepted range of legitimate and effective policy instruments, together with general recognition of the EU's legitimacy as an international actor with military capabilities' (Cornish and Edwards, 2001: 587). Two years later, the European Security Strategy echoed this call for 'a strategic culture that fosters early, rapid and when necessary robust intervention' (European Council, 2003).

Optimists argue that a European strategic culture is emerging through transnational advocacy coalitions for 'Global Power Europe' (Rogers, 2009a) or find evidence of convergence in policy documents as well as the operation of EU committees (Biava, 2011). Sceptics point out that these conceptions already propose *a specific kind* of strategic culture for the EU, closer to the British and French approach to the use of force, and question whether this particular conception is sufficiently shared among other European nations to be supported when difficult decisions need to be taken about how scarce resources are to be spend, how much risk countries are willing to take with their soldiers' and foreign citizens' lives, in alliances with whom and, above all, for what kind of purpose (Meyer, 2006). They highlight the ideational differences and outright incompatibilities between the non-aligned and neutral countries in Europe, those with historically ingrained pacifism and the new members of the EU who are more concerned about their territorial integrity and political independence than the defence and promotion of human rights and international law across the globe (Lindley-French, 2002; Rynning, 2003; Hyde-Price, 2004).

This chapter aims to examine the empirical evidence in support of and against the emergence of a European strategic culture, looking at the emergence of a Brussels-centred culture and its relationship to partially converging national cultures. It then proceeds to examine the implications of the findings for the future evolution of ESDP, its missions, capabilities and doctrines. It highlights the dynamic and at times discontinuous interplay of ideational and material factors as key determinants of ESDP, but also readily admits the scope for political leadership to shape ideas about the use of force and the role of the EU. However, before proceeding to the empirical part, the chapter will introduce the reader in brief to the argument about what a strategic culture is, how it can be measured, why it matters and how the concept can be used by those interested in understanding and shaping the evolution of security and defence in Europe.

Strategic culture: the concept and its uses

While there have been numerous scholarly attempts to consider cultural factors in warfare and consider 'national ways of war' (Uz Zaman, 2009), the first generation of academic writing using the explicit concept of strategic culture dates back to a report by Jack Snyder on the Soviet Union's nuclear strategy in 1977 for the RAND think tank in the USA (Snyder, 1977) and advanced by Colin Gray subsequently (Gray, 1981). After falling somewhat out of fashion, the concept has experienced a major resurgence in academic writing since the mid- and late 1990s, first with the pioneering work of Alistair Johnston on Chinese strategic culture (Johnston, 1995b) and then substantially advanced by other mainly US-based scholars such as Jeffrey Lantis or Peter Berger. There are close links with the work by Peter Katzenstein and others on security cultures (Katzenstein, 1996; Kirchner and Sperling, 2010) and the wave of writing in international relations employing a modernist constructivist framework (Adler, 1997), focusing on norms in relation to humanitarian intervention (Finnemore, 2003) and a 'Western way of war' (Shaw, 2005). While this is not the place for a full review of the debates about different definitions and uses of strategic culture (Greathouse, 2010), it is relevant to acknowledge one major disagreement among key authors: One strand of thinking sees culture as context, not a variable, and tends to include patterns of behaviour within its definition, while the other sees culture as a cause, either major or minor, of strategic behaviour and excludes actual behaviour from its definition.

My own perspective tends to side with the second strand. Here, strategic culture is seen as a causal factor of relatively high permanence, which has practical implications for explaining decisions about future military capabilities, the initiation and sustainability of military operations and the conditions under which dominant elites will perceive threats and opportunities. It is of particular value as a compass in situations of high uncertainty and crises when political actors tend most strongly to rely on their conventional analytical prisms and the instruments they trust, rather than question the adequacy of their pre-existing worldviews and beliefs about what works. The second function casts strategic culture as an annotated roadmap for accumulative and medium-term choices about the trajectory of a given political community, providing it not only with a sense of orientation and direction, but also with an understanding of which roads may be the least risky and quickest for getting from A to B. However, strategic cultures should not be confused with official strategy and planning papers, but operate at several higher levels of generality and may easily contradict some of the official analysis and make it redundant once real decisions have to be taken to put it in practice. Culture is much more powerful than paper, even though the paper itself is part of the discourse, which constitutes, reaffirms and occasionally also challenges the pre-existing culture.

What is strategic culture? First, I define it as the *socially transmitted, identity-derived norms, ideas, and habits of mind that are shared among the most influential actors and social groups within a given political community, which help to shape a ranked set of options for a community's pursuit of security and defence goals.* This definition makes explicit reference to norms in order to allow for a more nuanced description of different components of culture, which may at times contradict each other. Norms refer not just to notions of morality, about 'what is right', but also to beliefs about what 'works' in security and defence affairs (Farrell, 2005). In this sense, norms are closely related to ideas, defined as deeply ingrained views and perceptions of a political entity's proper role in the world, its perception of how states interact in international affairs and how security is achieved. Second, the definition reflects an understanding that norms, ideas and practices are not isolated variables, but should be rather seen as elements of and derived from an overarching identity narrative of a given community as it relates to the outside world. Third, this definition highlights how strategic culture can be quite heterogeneous and contested within societies in just the same way that national identity narratives are. Norms within the context of strategic culture can be conceptualized as beliefs about what is appropriate or legitimate or just in relation to the goals, ends and modalities concerning the use of force. And finally, habits of the mind can be broadly understood as cognitively internalized ways of discussing (societies), deciding (political actors) and doing things (armed forces) in matters of security and defence. These are mental constructs, which are acquired through experiences of success and reinforced through constant repetition as regularly occurs in any given policy field, but particularly in the realm of defence with its emphasis on doctrines, training and manoeuvres.

The value of strategic culture lies in its relative permanence over time, although this does not suggest that strategic culture is either monolithic or immutable. In fact, the very idea of the emergence of a European strategic culture is premised on processes of learning, socialization, peer pressure and advocacy at the level of elites and even whole societies, which would allow for the destabilization of existing norms, the introduction of new norms and ideas and their subsequent affirmation and internalization through practice and experience. Cultural change at the highest level of community identity narratives usually requires major crises such as military defeat to take place, whereas other forms of more gradual change in some normative domains may occur more gradually through the force of learning from minor failures or institutional socialization, as well as advocacy coalition and norm entrepreneurs. Studying changes in cultures is crucial to the debate about whether a European strategic culture is emerging among EU officials, key national representatives and senior offices on the one hand and those at the level of broader national elites, rank-and-file military personnel and public attitudes on the other.

In contrast to tanks, satellites and military personnel, strategic culture and its ideational component are more difficult to count and measure, which makes agreeing on how 'European' or 'common' the strategic culture is and how much convergence has occurred among European nations extraordinary difficult. There is no single agreed method of how to empirically analyse culture, but one can distinguish between those who draw on their understanding of historical experiences and actual behaviour to describe a given culture and those who use a range of empirical methods to inductively arrive at what it looks like and how it is changing by, for instance, analysing different official and non-official texts and discourses, conducting interviews and surveys among elite actors and taking major trends in public opinion into account. However, a first step to measure strategic culture is to unpack it a little more: it has been suggested that we should look at four types of norms regarding defence policy: (i) goals for which the use of force is considered legitimate, e.g. territorial defence, defence of human rights, pre-emptive action or cultural and territorial expansion; (ii) the degree to which force has to be domestically and internationally authorized in order to be considered legitimate, e.g. with or without UN mandate, peer support, parliamentary approval or consent of constitutional courts; (iii) the way in which force can be used, in particular, the tolerance to risks arising for a country's own and foreign troops and civilians; and finally, (iv) norms relating to the way in which a state should cooperate with other states and/or alliances, covering the spectrum from neutrality, acting within and through the European Union or together with the United States.

European strategic culture(s): compatibility and convergence

A coherent and deep European strategic culture would need to capture and draw upon similar norms, ideas and practices regarding security and defence policy and the legitimate use of force. If we go back to our generic definition of strategic culture, the key question for whether one can speak of a *European* strategic culture is, first, *whether there is an identifiable set of norms, beliefs and habits of mind regarding the use of force shared by the relevant political actors and societies,* and second, *whether the hierarchy and interpretation of these norms is derived from a sufficiently shared identity narrative of a European security community.*

The first problem here is how you define the circle of relevant political actors and societies. Strictly speaking, decision-making on ESDP matters relies on the unanimity rule so that all 27 national governments wield a formal veto on all operations and they all have varying degrees of say. De facto, however, the number of member states with the relevant interests, capabilities and experience which have shaped the course of ESDP together with the political actors in the EU central institutions is limited, while the rest tended to acquiesce, even if not all necessarily agreed with each and every mission or some of the wording in strategy documents. So only a limited number of member states are de facto shaping and participating in European security and defence policies, although this observation does not preclude the possibility that individual countries may raise concern in particular cases when vital national interests are affected such as Greece and Cyprus over relations to Turkey, the Baltic States over security issues relating to Russia and so forth. With this caveat in mind, it may make sense to look at degree of ideational convergence and commonality among the Big Three, plus Sweden, the Netherlands, Italy and Poland.

If one focuses on central institutions it is probably easiest to identify elements of an emerging European strategic culture in the discourses, both written and oral, which have emanated from the Council Secretariat under the previous High Representative Javier Solana (Howorth, 2007). The EU has experienced a rapid growth of personnel active in the broad area of security and defence policy, most importantly within the Council Secretariat through the strengthening of the HR Policy Unit and the EU Joint Situation Centre (SITCEN). In addition, we have seen the creation of regularly meeting committees composed of national ambassadors permanently based in Brussels, who have developed a common *esprit de corps* and a commitment to making ESDP a success. The socialization and cultivation effects arising from these structures, especially the PSC, the EUMC and the EUMS, have already been well studied and are likely to continue (Howorth, 2004; Duke, 2005; Juncos and Pomorska, 2006; Howorth, 2010; Biava, 2011). Hopes have been expressed that the new provisions for the double-hatted High Representative and the building of the new External Action Service would give an impetus to convergence in perceptions, strategies and actions (Whitman and Juncos, 2009). Yes, these have not materialized yet, as member states gave the important HR position to the political lightweight Catherine Ashton, who visibly struggled to make good and timely judgements and to express a strategic vision for the EU in foreign affairs during the first two years of her tenure (Howorth, 2010).

As James Rogers shows, key staff in the secretariat together with a limited number of actors in some national ministries, think tanks and academia formed a transnational discourse coalition in favour of making Europe 'more capable, more active, more coherent' as well as more 'global' (Biscop, 2009b; Rogers, 2009a). A European Union which does not shy away from using force abroad in pursuit of both altruistic goals relating to the mitigation of humanitarian disasters under UN auspices as well as for conventional self-interested purposes such as eliminating training-grounds for terrorist groups, securing trade and energy supplies, deterring potentially belligerent authoritarian regimes and soft-balancing of rapidly arming global powers such as China. Optimists can point to relatively consistent if not always very specific themes in the official discourse such as the emphasis on civilian as well as military means, its preference for broader international legitimacy through 'effective multilateralism' and support for international law and the downplaying of 'power' for its own sake.

This discourse has significant appeal across the EU's institutions, partly because it remains vague in key respects such as its relationship to the USA and NATO and questions of prioritization of goals and means. We also need to be careful not to mistake the rhetoric in official documents, even if they are labelled strategies, for those actual shared ideas, beliefs and deeply rooted habits of mind among the relevant actors and emerging habits of practice. An analysis of the 23 CSDP operations carried out since 2003 shows a clear preference for civilian over military means, a preference for close cooperation with UN and NATO, aversion to military risk through limited mandates in terms of scope and time as well as a divergence between the doctrinal commitment to prevention and the actual preoccupation with post-conflict stabilization missions (Biava, 2011). It is arguable that the antipathy to coercion varies somewhat between the EU Commission and the Council Secretariat, but on the whole the EU is more reluctant than for example either France or Britain to back up demands and policies with coercive means and prefers to work with positive incentives. What is generally true of the EU's behaviour in external affairs, is particularly true for the domain of using force, as Matlary argues when stating that the EU's strategic culture is incapable of 'coercive diplomacy' (Matlary, 2006).

Switching to the national level we must distinguish between strategic cultures of a country as a whole and military cultures. They are related but distinct. In fact, convergence pressures are most visible when looking at the transformation processes that have affected Europe's militaries and their relationships to the societies in which they are embedded (Forster, 2006; Mérand, 2008). One argument is that national strategic cultures are changing through intensified transnational links and interactions among national militaries, affecting particularly but not only the higher echelons (King, 2006; Mérand, 2008; Koivula, 2009). This is due to both intensified training exercises as well as interactions on military missions. The total number of European troops deployed on operations abroad rose from 39,000 in 1995 to just over 71,000 in 2007 (Giegerich and Nicoll, 2008). Mérand argues that gradual and accumulative effect of both training and operations is the deprioritization of the central military norm of patriotism – dying for one's country (Mérand, 2003, 2008). The emergence of transnational military links is reinforced by a strong pan-European trend towards a professionalization of the armed services (Giegerich and Nicoll, 2008), including a dramatic shift away from conscription and towards all-volunteer forces. After Belgium and the Netherlands made the start in the mid-1990s, they were followed, *inter alia*, by France (2001), Spain (2002), Italy (2006), Poland (2008) and Sweden (2009). Even Germany, one of the last notable EU countries to still hold on to conscription at least legally, decided to suspend it from March 2011 onwards – a momentous step towards a professionalization of the armed forces. These trends support Anthony King's argument that 'a more common, though not unified European military culture may become more discernible' (King, 2006: 273). This shift towards the expeditionary model and more professionalization does not necessarily equate to 'better warfighting' given stagnant or falling levels of defence spending. Tommi Koivula argues that the emergent EU military ethos is *not* geared towards high-intensity combat situations and emphasizes instead the mastery of a broader range of civilian skills (Koivula, 2009). This would tally with the argument made by Martin Shaw (2005) that Western societies are becoming increasingly risk-averse regarding the use of force and the 'culture of constraint' pervading EU institutions.

If we want to look at the strategic rather than military cultures of some of the most relevant countries, we can draw on two comparative studies of strategic cultures in the EU by single authors (Giegerich, 2006; Meyer, 2006) and one multi-authored project which investigated security rather than strategic cultures of key countries, including European ones (Kirchner and Sperling, 2010). Both Meyer and Giegerich found that the Big Three had become more similar to each other or more compatible in some respects, even though Giegerich hesitates to see this growing similarity as an indicator of a more deep-rooted, long-term convergence of cultures. In the following, I will attempt to elaborate on areas both of compatibility and incompatibility across the four dimensions concerning the use of force between Germany, France, Britain and Poland.

Probably the most publicized area of normative incompatibility concerns the Franco-British problem of how to relate to the United States in security and defence matters. It is this single issue, 'our Mount Everest' as a British diplomat called it, which has overshadowed the high degree of Anglo-French compatibility across many of the key dimensions concerning the use of force. Both countries have a relatively high degree of risk tolerance, both agree essentially on the importance of the UN and the legitimate goals for the use of force. However, the question of political and military autonomy from the USA remains divisive, especially at the level of experts and decision-makers. British officials find the French deep-rooted concern with independence from the USA 'bizarre' (interview, September 2004), especially when they see it as getting in the way of what British decision-makers frame as pragmatic and best solutions. 'Why should we not follow the leadership of a country on whose capabilities we depend and whose values we share?' (interview, September 2005). Conversely, many of the French interviewees characterize the relationship of the UK to the USA as one of 'servant and master' (interviews, September 2004). There is little equivalence in the UK to the anti-hegemonic instinct among the French policy community and public opinion.

Yet the salience of the issue is declining in the eyes of British public opinion as attachment to the USA has weakened. In the case of France, a generational change is under way as younger members of the security and defence policy community are gradually moving into positions of power, less influenced by Gaullist attitudes to the USA and in favour of finding a common ground for cooperation. The coming to power of President Sarkozy and his decision to take France back into the military command structure of NATO epitomizes this shift, even though the election of a Democratic US president will have also helped in selling this highly symbolic step to the wider French political elites and public opinion. In sum, incompatibility on this issue between Britain and France is still high, but the gap is closing, especially at the level of British public opinion and to a somewhat lesser degree among elites.

The second most important area of normative incompatibility is between France and Britain on the one hand and Germany, and, with some minor qualifications, Poland, on the other, regarding modes of war fighting. The deployment of ground troops in the case

Table 5.1 Convergence progress across norms

Horizontal perspective	
Broadly compatible	• De-prioritization of territorial defence and agreement on humanitarian intervention, including peace-making.
	• Agreement on stronger role for EU but without ceding sovereignty.
	• Agreement on desirability of UN authorization.
	• General preference for civilian over military instruments.
Incompatible, but possible medium-term convergence	• Use of force for tackling short-term security threats.
	• Relationship to NATO and the USA (among publics).
	• Parliamentary approval for use of force/domestic authorization thresholds.
	• European defence as step towards deeper political integration.
Broadly incompatible	• Use of force for democracy promotion and economic interests.
	• Relationship to the USA (especially among elites).
	• Use of force with high risk of casualties against enemy forces.

Source: Meyer 2006.

of Kosovo was assessed in Germany quite differently from how it was assessed in the other three countries, as German commentators advocated a return to diplomacy in reaction to pictures of civilian casualties from NATO bombing. More so than decision-makers and experts, German public opinion is very concerned not to cause foreign casualties, be they military or civilian, and thus shies away from all kinds of military missions which would involve the high end of using force. Interestingly, in German strategic culture, foreign casualties can be as difficult to digest as their own casualties since they raise the trauma of guilt and self-induced downfall. We can see this sensitivity played out in the public inquiry and resignations of the German defence minister over the involvement of German officers in ordering a US airstrike on a Taliban-hijacked petrol vehicle in September 2009 in Kunduz, Afghanistan, which killed 91, most of them civilians from nearby villages.

In contrast, Polish citizens voice a high readiness to die for their country, defending national independence and pride, but also, somewhat contradictorily, a very low degree of tolerance for their own casualties, as witnessed in the case of the Iraq occupation, because they raise the trauma of all-out war and defeat in World War II. The difference between Germany and Poland regarding risk tolerance is not only the much greater pacifist impulse and ideational underpinning, but also the high level of German domestic and international authorization required. The combination of both factors makes Germany an awkward partner to work with in security and defence matters from the British and French perspective, even though domestic authorization has also become more difficult in these countries.

The third major area of normative incompatibility concerns the question of whether security and defence should no longer be primarily concerned with defending the home country, but directed to other purposes. Both Germany and Poland are more attached to this goal than the permanent members of the UN Security Council, Britain and France, but have also taken steps towards developing a more flexible and capable professional army by suspending conscription, although strained resources will severely limit this transformation in the German case. Apart from the cleavage on the issue of territorial defence, substantial differences emerge between Germany and the other three countries regarding the pre-emptive use of force to tackle threats. German elites as well as decision-makers are highly sceptical of using force for any purpose other than for humanitarian reasons and against an immediate attack by a clearly identifiable enemy. The German centre-right government's abstention from the UN-authorized operation to protect civilians rising up against the Gaddafi regime in spring 2011 illustrates the widespread concern about the use of force to promote de facto regime change and the risks such operations entail (König, 2011). Another illustrative example is the resignation of German President Horst Köhler on 31 May 2010 after facing strong criticism from across the political spectrum for suggesting in an interview that German troops in Afghanistan were defending German economic interests as well, rather than using the standard argument of foregrounding a humanitarian justification of rebuilding a war-torn society mandated by the UN.

The fourth area of normative/ideational incompatibility is the question of building European defence as part of the political unification process, which may involve the ceding of some political autonomy in military and defence matters. This last area is important because it relates to whether conflicts between norms can be resolved by reference to an overarching identity narrative shared among members of a single community. There is broad support among both decision-makers and publics in most countries for a European Union that has an important role in also protecting its citizens militarily. While military means are not ruled out, the main preference is for the EU as a 'soft power', which promotes peace primarily through non-coercive means. Only a very small minority of decision-makers as well as members of the public say that defence should be solely a matter for national governments.

Beyond the conception of the EU as being active in providing security and promoting peace, the contention begins. While there is considerable support among citizens for using a kind of European army to 'defend European rights and undertake humanitarian missions', support among decision-makers and the public in Britain is considerably lower than in the other three countries. At the same time, support among British experts and decision-makers for the EU to advance its 'economic, political and security interest' with all available instruments, including the military, is considerably higher than average. I would argue that these cross-national differences, especially the stance of the UK and Poland, can at least in part be attributed to incompatibilities between the two countries' national identity conceptions and their perception of the EU.

In the case of Germany, support for ESDP is to a large extent driven by the positive vision of the EU as a political entity that can supplement Germany's fragile national identity and through which power can be exercised without risking the pitfalls of the country's past. For the French elites, the European project also has considerable ideational resonance, not least in the area of defence affairs, where French armed forces had for decades been somewhat isolated by virtue of staying outside of the NATO military structure. For Britain, however, discussing the finality of European defence, as with European integration more broadly, remains a highly controversial issue.

On the one hand, we can find considerable support for the vision of the EU as a global superpower pursuing its political and economic interests in a toned-down kind of neo-colonialism. However, British respondents were considerably more sceptical about the statement that the EU is a community of values that should use its means for the promotion of human rights and democracy across the world. British decision-makers predominantly have a vision of the EU as a kind of toolbox, which offers persuasive instruments to make other countries improve their capabilities as well as material instruments to advance the island's hard interests, but not as an entity that has its own values and takes decisions that may contradict British preferences. While the British public is generally, if only moderately, in support of building ESDP, it is less convinced about its purposes, especially if the enterprise is framed as diminishing the independence of British defence policy, the primacy of NATO and the standing of the British armed forces. The instinctive scepticism towards building European defence is most salient within the Conservative party.

For Poland, European political union and integrated defence are intrinsically problematic because of a historically rooted lack of trust in key neighbours that hinders the country from considering itself as a full part of a European security and political community. The election of Donald Tusk as Poland's prime minister in November 2007 has shifted policy towards a greater engagement with the EU, but one must doubt how quickly this will impact on the level of trust among Polish elites and publics in their neighbours. The decision by the new US administration to shelve missile defence in Eastern Europe may only reawaken fears of abandonment, even if it may benefit the EU, rather than NATO.

Conclusion

We are left with the picture of a European strategic culture like a thinly stretched hourglass. We find at the top institutional level relatively high and growing coherence and convergence of shared ideas about nature and hierarchy of threats that need to be addressed and the utility of the EU. At the bottom operational level of using force, we can witness national militaries deployed on a range of carefully delimited and legitimized multi-national missions and regularly training together within both EU and NATO contexts. These missions generally reflect and solidify the emerging strategic consensus, although they are often more limited in scope and less focused on prevention than one would have expected when reading the strategy documents. On the other hand, we must note a considerable degree of diversity and incompatibility among national political elites as well as the publics. Only a small set of norms is fully shared among key countries, without even considering some of the more fundamental concerns of non-aligned countries such as Austria and Ireland. In so far as role conceptions and identities are concerned, broad support for the EU as a global actor with a commitment to promoting humanitarian causes and peace exists, but there is currently no consensus on the promotion of democracy and *realpolitik* interests through coercive means.

These findings would best match the role model of a rather risk-averse Humanitarian Power Europe, rather than the vision of Global Power Europe. If different norms clash in a challenging case such as Iraq in 2003 or more recently in Libya in 2011, it remains extraordinarily difficult to reach a common European decision on priorities of response given that the underlying identity narratives remain quite stable and continue to raise compatibility problems. At the same time, many of the convergence pressures are likely to endure, such as increasingly common threat perceptions among Brussels-based elites and beyond; transnational advocacy coalitions and media pressure in favour of humanitarian interventions; further increasing cost pressures on national armed forces to transform and Europeanize; training for and deployment on common missions; institutional socialization through the External Action Service. Divergence forces are on balance weaker, but could arise, *inter alia*, from an unexpected crisis that overtaxes the EU's ability to agree and act, drastic changes in US leadership and foreign policy towards unilaterism, changing behaviour of Russia towards its 'near abroad', a confrontation between the British government and the EU over the repatriation of powers or deeper integration and the wider repercussions from a Eurozone crisis spilling over to the EU system as a whole. On balance, time is on the side of those who want to turn the EU into a fully-fledged security actor, but they are well advised not to overestimate progress and the permissive public consensus on European defence, to exercise great caution in selecting the missions undertaken and, finally, to develop the EU's ability to implement and take credit for preventive action. In this sense, research on a European strategic culture is neither inherently optimistic nor pessimistic about the EU as a security actor, but can act as socio-political reality check on Europeans' ability to think alike about the uses of force.

Acknowledgements

The author acknowledges past support from a Postdoctoral Marie Curie Research Fellowship (HPMF-CT-2002-01791) as well as a Starting Investigator Grant of the European Research Council for the Foresight project (no. 202022). The chapter draws on material contained in the author's following publications: Meyer (2006), Meyer (2011) and Meyer and Strickmann (2011).

PART II

Institutions, instruments and means

6

DIPLOMACY AND THE CFSP

With new hands on the wheel, have we something that's real?[1]

Geoffrey Edwards

Diplomacy and its role in the international system have been under continuous challenge from changes in the structure of the system, particularly from the advent of new technologies as well as new actors. Traditionally, diplomacy has been defined as the organized dialogue between states, its practices embedded in a Westphalian inter-state system. New challenges have meant that international relations, in the words of Der Derian, have been shifting 'from a realm defined by sovereign places, impermeable borders and rigid geopolitics, to a site of accelerating flows, contested borders and fluid chronopolitics. In short, pace displacing space' (Der Derian, 1992: 129). Within that reconstructed space, Europe, far from being any longer the 'centre of international gravity' that characterized Harold Nicolson's 'old diplomacy' (Nicolson, 1953: 77), has, nonetheless, assumed a new actorness.

With the Lisbon Treaty, the EU rather than simply the European Community (EC) gained legal personality. Under the Treaty of Rome, the EC had competence in the field of trade and aid and steadily accumulated responsibilities, whether wholly or partially in a growing range of other issues. This means that the EU can negotiate, sign agreements and treaties in line with the competences granted to the Union (Article 216 TFEU). Even if the EU's competences fall short of those of the traditional state, they reflect the widening concerns of the Member States and their perceived need to act on a more common or cooperative basis. That is inevitably reflected in the EU's external relations, many of which concern domestic as well as cross-boundary issues ranging from agriculture through education and public health to visas and the management of the EU's borders. At the same time, the EU, especially through its High Representative for Foreign Affairs, has sought – for both European as well as global consumption – to promote an identity distinguishable from that of its Member States, often described in terms of its normative or transformative power, a power to be exercised through, in particular, 'effective multilateralism' according to the European Security Strategy of 2003. If, in 1838, the Vicomte de Chateaubriand could lament that: 'Transactions are nowadays delayed by hindrances of which previously we were free. Yesterday it was only a question of material interests, of an increase in territory or commerce; now one deals with moral interests; the principles of social order figure in dispatches' (cited by Hamilton and Langhorne, 1995: 89), the subjects covered by today's European diplomats extend probably well beyond what might have been considered appropriate subjects for detailed discussion among the diplomatic elite.

But questions remain about the nature and mechanics of the political entity that the new legal persona reflects and what sort of dynamic it has created in the international system. On the one hand, foreign policy within the framework of the Common Foreign and Security Policy (CFSP) remains intergovernmental. On the other hand, CFSP has become increasingly institutionalized in Brussels with its High Representative and, since 2010, a European External Action Service (EEAS), a European diplomatic service.

The EU's High Representative, under the Amsterdam Treaty of 1997, was charged with representing the Union, to become at least the voice of a more united European foreign policy. While often working alongside the President of the Council and the President of the Commission in the so-called *troika*, the first High Representative, Javier Solana, far surpassed the expectations of many member governments in establishing a distinctive EU presence. The Lisbon Treaty seemingly endorsed this strengthened role of the High Representative – not least through the creation of the EEAS to fulfil the traditional functions of the diplomat, of representing the Union, promoting it, negotiating on its behalf and reporting back through the High Representative to the European institutions and the Member States. However, Lisbon also added certain potential constraints as well as leaving unresolved issues of representation. The Union, for example, is now also represented, at the level of heads of government, by a new President of the European Council. That the EU may still in certain circumstances be represented by the President of the European Commission and/or the country holding the six-monthly Presidency may add a degree of confusion to the EU's presence and certainly raises questions about its coherence and even legitimacy. This is compounded further by the fact that individual Member States continue to retain their own diplomatic services and, in many cases, remain determined to use them to protect and promote what they regard as their national interests. And, to make matters even more complicated, there have been frequent instances of the bigger Member States acting in concert, as a *directoire*, acting in or as if in the name of the EU.

Faces and reflections

This variable representation of the Union and its Member States may in some respects be peculiar to a highly complex regional entity. In other ways, though, this multiplicity of faces and voices simply reflects some of the complexities of the contemporary international system. States are no longer the only actors in the international system but have been joined by a proliferation of actors seeking to influence events, whether international organizations, subnational governments, multinational corporations, NGOs, transnational movements, both legal and criminal, and so on. What these disparate elements create is a challenge to the traditional hierarchical intergovernmental diplomatic process, creating a much more networked model of diplomacy in which states have perforce to seek different, sometimes transient allies (Hocking, 2008). As Hocking has also suggested, this 'multi-stakeholder model of diplomacy' raises further questions about the rules and norms of behaviour that lie behind it: 'The diplomatic system remains one founded ultimately on principles of sovereignty and non-intervention, however much these have become modified in practice. Non-state actors, such as NGOs, work to different norms, often rooted in the rejection of these principles' (Hocking, 2008: 72).

The resulting tensions create a much more complex and difficult environment with diverse actors pursuing their own diverse interests interacting at different levels and with each seeking to legitimate their position with both their own and other audiences in public. There is a resulting paradox, as Constantinou and Der Derian have suggested, in that:

> [C]onventional inter-state diplomacy is sustained by the very thing it defines itself against, or distinguishes itself from, namely sub-state or non-state diplomacy and this is because it needs to find a way of dealing with the plurality of voices around the world and to mediate more effectively the multiple forms of estrangement, which are never just interstate.
>
> (Constantinou and Der Derian, 2010: 12)

At the same time, the growing number of states in the international system – and the costs of maintaining diplomatic posts in them – has deepened the paradox, for, as Paul Sharp put it:

> [I]n international politics, as in domestic politics, there is a high expectation that governments can and should solve problems and a widespread reluctance to pay the price. The result is a dangerous cycle in which governments embark on difficult international projects with inadequate resources because a major mobilization of them cannot be justified.
>
> (Sharp, 1998: 100)

The resulting 'disjuncture between champagne tastes and beer budgets' (Sharp, 1998) has led governments towards greater collaboration with others – as in the EU – and/or to shrinking diplomatic services. After all, the speed of contemporary transport and communications allows a prime minister, a variety of ministers and officials to conduct negotiations personally, perhaps providing Harold Nicolson with a rather different answer to his question of 'Does this mean that a diplomatist today [i.e. 1953] is no more than a clerk at the end of a line?' (Nicolson, 1953: 82). And yet, some individual states, most explicitly perhaps the UK, have sought to buck this trend, confirming Nicolson in his view that ambassadors remain a critical source of information and interpretation and the chief channel of communication. A fundamental element in the UK argument is the belief that national interests can only be protected and advanced by national diplomatic services rather than a European service – with Hague adding somewhat typically that even if such a diplomatic service could be 'an extension of our influence in the world ... it is not a substitute for it' (Hague, 2011). That scepticism has created a wariness of 'competence creep' on the part of the EU.[2] Yet this has been the case despite continued recognition – even if in the UK sporadically challenged – of the value of the EU's diplomatic effort in support of its 'structural power', to use Keukeleire's term (Keukeleire, 2003), the objective being to shape structures, rules and processes not simply in the EU's neighbourhood but globally, too, in the interests of 'maintaining competitiveness, dealing with climate change, combating global poverty and even dealing collectively with foreign policy issues' (Hague, 2010).

Circumstances, it has been argued, have not been shifting in Europe's favour. As the French foreign minister put it:

> We are acutely aware of the rapidly changing balance of powers in the world; emerging powers want a place at the table and if we in turn really want to continue to have a say in world affairs we must join forces with one another, acquiring with that the ability to act at the European level. The European Union, which is the foremost economic power in the world and is home to half a billion people, should

be in a position to play a consequential role on the international stage. Because it is only at European level that we will have the same diplomatic weight as China, India or Brazil.

(Juppé, 2011)

But, as one former British ambassador described it, the EU is 'the world's principal under-performing asset' (Marshall, 2008). So, as Juppé's predecessor, Bernard Kouchner, declared:

The European Union must do a better job of asserting its influence and its interests in the world. Catherine Ashton must have the tools to fully carry out her tasks and thereby wholly live up to the expectations placed in her. This is of vital importance to Europe's future position and the success of our common values and interests on the international political stage.

(Kouchner, 2010)

Response and delivery

Such diverse statements in some respects reinforce Constantinou and Der Derian's paradox. Intra-EU diplomacy has been qualitatively changed rather than merely becoming perhaps an exaggerated form of institutionalized dialogue, for whether as a result of the range of issues covered or the continuousness of the interaction, diplomacy within the Union has evolved its own set of norms and procedures (Bátora, 2005). While allowing for a degree of down-grading of representation in other Member States, it has, of course, led to a strong focus on resources in Brussels as well as among the private offices of prime ministers, but not on the part of foreign ministries; other ministries have become so familiar with the Brussels policy-making process that they see little need for professional diplomats as intermediaries. But if MFAs have 'lost' the game in Brussels, they now face the dilemma brought about by both participating in and resisting the establishment of a strengthened CFSP.

In the pursuit of Juppé's 'consequential role' and to achieve the success of 'common values and interests', the EU inevitably reinforces change in diplomatic practice or at least its further development. Given the nature of those common values, it necessarily tends to move well beyond relations with governments to engage with economic interests ('a consumer-oriented diplomacy' to use Bruter's phrase (1999: 183)), and with civil society etc. a process subsumed within the term 'public diplomacy'. The process is hardly new, with much having been written about it, especially in the United States during the Cold War. Since then, as Hocking has suggested (2008: 63), in addition to globalization and regionalization and the revolution in communication and information technologies, 'Events following the wave of terrorist attacks that began in September 2001 have focused attention on the centrality of identities and values in world politics and, consequently, on the significance of images and ideas.' Together they not only emphasized the added complexities of diplomacy but pointed up the critical need for further attention to be given to public diplomacy. As Jim Murphy, when one of the UK Labour government's many European ministers, declared, 'public diplomacy must become an integral part of policy-making and delivery. Governments must go beyond simple messaging, towards dialogue and cooperation, in collective effort to find solutions to the global challenges exemplified by climate change, violent extremism or poverty' (Murphy, 2008: 5).

The 'delivery' of public diplomacy now involves not just communicating to govern-ment or civil society through speeches, visits or appearances on or in the media, but also through an increasing use of 'social media', blogging even tweeting, from foreign ministers to, presumably with departmental approval, first secretaries. For those in post, it creates, perhaps, a new dimension to Neumann's second or 'heroic' script for individual diplomats: they can indulge an element of individual braggadocio and report as close to the action as possible, even while continuing the more monotonous everyday routine or, with even more difficulty in many circumstances, being the self-effacing mediator (Neumann, 2005: 73).

But public diplomacy is undertaken in varying political environments where access to any public audience can be constrained. Indeed, access by the public to such information and diplomacy can often be highly restricted. One of lessons of the 'Arab spring' was just how important social media can be among demonstrators. The use of smart-phone cameras and videos has allowed the world to see a good deal more than governments may have wanted (as in Syria's case during the spring and summer of 2011), particularly when they have been disseminated globally by the electronic media. The immediacy of broadcasting these images within hours of events taking place re-emphasizes the challenge to diplomacy of speed. It raises once again what in the 1990s was often discussed under the label of the 'CNN effect'[3] (see, for example, Strobel, 1997 or Jakobsen, 2000), the impact of 24-hour news reportage on foreign policy. Whether such 'telediplomacy' (Ammon, 2001) changes policy is disputed, but it certainly creates additional pressures on governments to be seen to be doing something. It also, particularly in its coverage of disasters and crises, raises expectations that diplomats on the spot will be reporting back on radio if not television to assure home audiences that something is being done to protect nationals etc. The absence of such reportage by either diplomats or even more by governments can undermine reputations – events in Libya in 2011 being only the latest in a long line of crises reaching particular intensity during a summer vacation to cause problems for governments. Hocking, in fact, has gone further to suggest that the speed of an institution's reactivity and the intensity of its interaction has a more significant meaning in so far as 'the ability to respond speedily to the ever-quickening flow of events is deemed a key measure of actor capacity' (Hocking, 2004: 97)

Such speed and the possible adverse publicity surrounding such crises has often brought heads of government (HOGs) rushing back from their holidays to negotiate possible solutions or at least stop-gap measures with their counterparts in the Union (and beyond), whether bilaterally or multilaterally, by telephone or video-conferences. Such discussions, of course, take place in secret even if much is made of the fact that they have taken place and their outcomes are often widely disseminated. They take place in addition to increasingly frequent summit meetings. These, however regular they become, are still accompanied by a build-up of expectations beforehand and press conferences or reports to parliament afterwards with national victories perennially won or at least national interests protected. Such involvement of HOGs in summer summits would have been anathema to, say, Harold Nicolson, who, in his Chichele lectures in 1953 on the evolution of diplomatic method, had bemoaned what he labelled 'new diplomacy', especially conference diplomacy. These appeared then as sporadic and intermittent episodes, occasioned by crisis or war but which undermined the consistency and continuity of a long-term process carried out by professionals in confidence (1953: 76). In his view open diplomacy raised the prospect of continuous public controversy and immovable positions, whereas private negotiation allowed for concession and negotiation.[4]

Breadth ... and depth?

It is not simply a question of either traditional diplomacy or open diplomacy. Whereas the pressures for greater accountability as well as technological facilitation are likely to ensure that HOG diplomacy continues to intensify, their continued interaction is reinforced by the complexity of the range of different issues that have become so inter-linked within the national and international systems that only HOGs have the political weight to coordinate them. Within the EU framework, the Lisbon Treaty acknowledged these inter-depend-ences and the problems of continuity by establishing a more permanent President of the European Council (TFEU 15 (6)). Herman van Rompuy, a former Belgian prime minister, was appointed President in December 2009, not only to chair meetings of HOGs but to 'drive forward its work', facilitate cohesion and consensus in the European Council and to represent the EU at HOG level abroad.

Such discussions at summit level may engender their own familiarity and so on and clearly have an impact on diplomatic representation and the traditional role of mediation, particu-larly within the EU – though they are at the same time usually only too conscious of their political standing at home. But there are few, least of all in ministries of foreign affairs, who do not argue that for success at European Council and other summit meetings, they need more than a degree of authoritative knowledge and assessment of the context within which they and other HOGs are working. The classic role of the diplomat – and therefore of foreign ministries – of acquiring information and human intelligence therefore remains key. To cite William Hague again:

> It is necessary to know countries in detail – to know them geographically, to know personally their leaders and potential leaders, to know their languages and to under-stand their history – in order to be able to influence events. Those skills now need accentuating again. That is the clear and constant signal that I am sending out from the Foreign Office.
>
> (Hague, 2011)

Often, of course, diplomats may exist in a metropolitan bubble, talking mostly to those within the governing elite or to whom they have been directed by those in power. Certainly some of the diplomatic reports from posts suggest that they had been taken unawares by the Arab spring of 2011. But their reports remain of critical importance in constructing the framework within which political leaders interact.

The threat to domestic populations from terrorist attacks has inevitably meant not simply interaction at the level of HOGs but among interior ministers and intelligence agencies – the last from a multitude of different ministries as well as more autonomous agencies such as those who meet in the semi-formalized framework of the Berne Group of Interior Intelligence agencies. The impact of terrorism on diplomacy was one of the issues taken up by Der Derian, who pointed to two interrelated challenges: first, terrorism and counter-terrorism together raise problems of legitimate orders (Der Derian, 1992: 81); second, an increased dependence on intelligence, particularly the use of surveillance via satellite and cyber space, can be seen as a structural challenge to traditional diplomacy (Der Derian, 1992: 73). As Hocking, too, pointed out above, terrorism has raised concerns about portraying European values more effectively through more public diplomacy. It has also focused greater attention on gathering intelligence and, with the invasion of Iraq, the quality of that intelligence. If public diplo-macy almost by definition has involved a highly sensitive balance between promoting a state's interests and interfering publicly in the domestic affairs of another, there has always been an uneasy *modus vivendi* between the overt and covert means of gathering of information. But Der Derian's point that technology has made a structural difference in terms of diplomacy by creating hyper vigilance and intense distrust, a veritable 'cyber paranoia' (1992: 32), has been strongly reinforced by the cyber attacks on, for example, Estonia in 2007. The immediate

Estonian response was to blame Russia, both reinforcing and deepening Estonian suspicions and undermining any moves to improve wider EU–Russia relations. By 2009, 'intelligence chiefs' were warning 'that China may have gained the capability to shut down Britain by crippling its telecoms and utilities (*Sunday Times*, 29 March 2009), making relations with China as well as Russia even more sensitive.

And CFSP?

Covert intelligence-gathering and its assessment may not be a foremost characteristic attributed to the EU – whether accurately or not its institutions have always been held to be particularly leaky – yet its capacity for assessment was significantly enhanced with Solana as High Representative. The EU's Joint Situation Centre (SitCen), for example, offers strategic advice based on intelligence shared by the Member States on issues such as terrorism. Such intelligence may already have been assessed by Member governments; it may nonetheless provide a potentially useful, even vital basis on which to take or approve decisions for those with limited intelligence services of their own or who are not in a privileged position vis-à-vis the United States, from whom several of the bigger Member States receive restricted intelligence. It also provides the analysis on which the High Representative can recommend policy (Duke, 2006: 617). That intelligence may be reinforced by the information gathered more overtly by the EU's Special Representatives, who have been appointed usually in areas of especial interest to the EU as well as of high tension (Grevi, 2007).That information in the past was further augmented by information from Commission delegations, which now form a part of the EU's delegations/embassies.

The grounds on which William Hague justified the revitalization of British diplomacy in his diplomatic excellence initiative (the necessity 'to know countries in detail' etc.; see above) are presumably equally applicable to other diplomatic services, including that of the EU. Gathering comprehensive knowledge of local circumstances can lead to gaining an advantage over competitors. Better information, it is assumed, leads to better decisions. Much, of course, depends on the quality of the diplomatic service – even a Rolls Royce of a service if driven by madmen can still come off the road – but for some Member governments, the creation of the EEAS is something of a challenge. The concerns of the UK's minister for Europe about 'competence creep' is a case in point. But the UK is not alone; for France, too,

> there's no question of the EEAS becoming a 28th diplomatic service. The diplomatic service will give greater weight to Europe's action, in cooperation with the States. Baroness Ashton receives mandates from the States. The European Parliament, will, admittedly, try to put its stamp on this EU foreign policy, but – I stress this – there won't be a 28th EU foreign policy.
>
> (Lellouche, 2010)

Such statements reflect the continuous dilemma of Member States about how to influence international events that can be traced back to the establishment of European political cooperation in 1970 (Nuttall, 1992). For the UK and France in particular, EPC/CFSP has always been regarded as complementary to their national policies. And yet, at the same time, and somewhat paradoxically, they have constantly led or allowed the greater institutionalization of CFSP. The result has been that the creation of a common policy expressed by a single representative has been pursued in a somewhat crab-like manner and always under the shadow of complete immobilism when Member States cannot agree on an appropriate policy. Indeed, it has been suggested by Bickerton that, in part at least, 'what lies at the heart of EU foreign policy are a series of internal concerns, namely the need to broker agreement among the member states (damage limitation) and legitimize the inactivity of member states in foreign affairs' (Bickerton, 2011: 32). Certainly Juncos and Reynolds in their detailed examination of the Political and Security Committee concluded that 'the journey is as important as the destination: the process of Brussels-level information gathering, consultation, cooperation and consensual decision-making is essentially what the CSFP/ESDP is all about' (Juncos and Reynolds, 2007: 147). 'Procedure as substitute for policy' (Allen and Wallace, 1977) has a long conceptual and practical history, continually setting the European and national discourses at odds with one other.

The Solana phenomenon

Nonetheless, it can be argued that Solana both raised the costs of inactivity and created a wider base on which consensual decision-making could take place. He had begun, as he readily admitted, relying on the Member States, 'their diplomatic networks, their logistic capabilities, and their expertise in specific areas' (Solana, 1999). However, within only a few years, largely informally and on a personal basis, he had begun to institutionalize a significantly more effective foreign policy-making infrastructure in Brussels. Even allowing for a certain exaggeration, he could thereby claim that:

> As time goes by I do whatever I want. I know what people think. I pursue my own agenda. I don't have to check everything with everyone. I would rather have forgiveness than permission. If you ask permission, you never do anything.
>
> (Crowe, 2005: 15)

Such an approach might have been expected of a former Spanish foreign minister and NATO secretary general. It was complemented by a determined effort to make the EU a more visible world actor, especially by means of personal diplomacy. As he put it after a year in office:

> At the risk of sounding simplistic, I can quantify my own contribution in figures. Over the last 12 months I have travelled to 40 countries – not including the Balkans, which I have visited practically every month – clocking up more than 450,000 kms in the air. I have taken part in 17 Summit and political dialogue meetings, as well as over 20 other meetings at Head of Government and Ministerial level. One of my priorities is to maintain a substantive dialogue with a wide range of third countries. Equally, I put a considerable amount of effort into ensuring that the European Union is sufficiently present and active in international organisations, particularly the United Nations and the OSCE.
>
> (Solana, 2000)

But, as he went on:

> Travelling is of course not an end in itself. But I will continue to accumulate air miles for as long as I believe I can make a contribution to prompting the interests of the European Union in the world. We should be present and actively involved whenever and wherever issues of international order and security are on the agenda.
>
> (Solana, 2000)

Solana's highly personal diplomacy, his frequent visits to the United States, to the Balkans and to the Middle East were seemingly acceptable to Member States only in so far as his agenda did not appear in contradiction to their own. But while it raised the visibility and the sense of presence of the EU, it did not always result in Member State consensus. That tended to come under severe strain during moments of crisis when EU agreement was found lacking. Despite his close personal relations with Israeli, Palestinian and Egyptian leaders, for example, Solana was effectively silenced during the Israeli invasion of Gaza in 2008 when the EU Member States failed to agree to a response.

And the Ashton ... impact?

Even if sometimes silenced, much that Solana had established was codified and extended under the Lisbon Treaty. Indeed the role of the High Representative was now double-hatted to take on that of a Vice-President of the Commission responsible for much of the Community's external relations. But Solana's achievement meant that his successor was left with a particularly difficult legacy, even if one seemingly strengthened under the Treaty. What Member States appeared to give with one hand, they seemed determined to take back with the other – rather as few Member States wanted another Jacques Delors in 1995, for example, so even fewer of them were prepared for Solana to be succeeded by another former foreign minister from one of the larger Member States.

Prompted perhaps by some poor decisions, or at least some poor PR, as well as some difficult international events to which the EU as such had only limited responses, Lady Ashton appeared initially to be reluctant to engage in personal diplomacy to quite the same extent as her predecessor. The French appeared to be particularly critical from the outset. In the aftermath of the devastating Haitian earthquake of January 2010, *The Times*, for example, quoted Pierre Lellouche: "'There is no doubt that Mrs Ashton should have taken herself to Haiti immediately to wave the flag for Europe,' he said. "I guess that not everyone is a Nicolas Sarkozy"' (*The Times Online*, 30 January 2010). Whether her presence, following that of the US Secretary of State and many other prominent visitors, would have helped the victims of the earthquake is a moot point, but the issue was clear: whether or not it was practical, raising Europe's visibility in the eyes of Europe's public if not of others was regarded as of critical importance.

Except that visibility was not everything at all times. Despite the fact that she was visiting Moscow and later attended the inauguration of the Ukrainian president, Viktor Yanukovych, she earned the opprobrium of the French defence minister (among others) for missing an informal meeting of defence ministers.[5] Hervé Morin appeared incensed that, unlike Solana, Ashton had missed the meeting, declaring: 'Isn't it rich that this morning, to display the ties between NATO and the EU, we have the NATO secretary general (Anders Fogh Rasmussen) here but not the high representative for the first meeting since the Lisbon treaty came into effect' (*EUBusiness*, 25 February 2010). And even the British, initially (under Labour) defenders of her appointment, became critical during the Conservative government, citing her budgetary request – which resulted largely from the decision to move into a single building (rather than eight) and the costs of the EEAS – as indicative of over-ambition (David Lidington, quoted in the *International Herald Tribune*, 24 May 2011).

There was also considerable criticism of Ashton's lack of leadership during the 'Arab spring' of 2011, especially from many within the European Parliament. The Polish MEP Jacek Saryusz-Wolski, for one, criticized both the EU's inaction and the fruitlessness of holding innumerable meetings and simply issuing statement after statement, adding:

> Following Member States and waiting for permission from Foreign Ministers to go
> ahead has become Lady Ashton's doctrine and she treats it as virtue. It is the wrong
> approach. It condemns our foreign policy to the lowest common denominator and
> to always being late. We want a High Representative to lead, not to follow.
>
> (Saryusz-Wolski, 2011)

Interestingly, even if the reasons might be obvious, since the French had particular reasons
to lead in North Africa, and especially Libya, Ashton was encouraged by President Sarkozy
not to wait, not to 'try to systematically get the agreement of everyone before acting', adding:

> It's necessary to act according to what one believes is right for Europe, while getting
> the support of some, but while avoiding always having to get the agreement of the
> entire 27 before acting ... When you believe that something is important, do it. We
> will always be at your side if you act, if you show your ambition, if you have ideas.
>
> (*Daily Mail*, 16 April 2010)

Whether the High Representative has been ambitious enough or prefers to wait until all
27 Member States are on board, she has, nonetheless, begun to follow Solana's example of
entering into personal diplomacy – though often along with foreign ministers still intent
on maintaining their own national role and prime ministers and presidents visiting and
talking to the same governments and other actors.[6] She may well prefer 'quiet diplomacy',
as she declared on her appointment (Ashton, 2009), but she is also reported to set 'great
store by personal diplomacy ... But Cathy's not a diplomat by behaviour or background.
She doesn't like the classical diplomat' (Traynor, 2011). She has, however, been strategic in
that diplomacy, maintaining frequent contact with the United States and Hillary Clinton –
successfully in so far as Clinton declared that 'she now knows who to call when she wants
to speak to Europe about "life and death issues" and "children and shopping"' (BBC, 14
October 2010).

A real diplomatic service in the making?

Even if Ashton does not like classical diplomats she has the responsibility to create the
EEAS, described by Alain Juppé as 'this unprecedented adventure' that 'will modify the
way our diplomatic corps works and it already poses challenges we need to meet head on
(Juppé, 2011). Such was the challenge that France sent one of its most senior diplomats,
Pierre Vimont, a former French Ambassador to the United States, to become the Executive
Secretary General of the new service. It was a sentiment echoed by William Hague, who was
intent on 'ensuring that talented British candidates enter it' (Hague, 2011). Other Member
States have followed the appointment of staff to the new service, part seconded national
officials, part officials from the Council Secretariat and the third part from the Commission
with close interest, sometimes, as in the case of the Poles, convinced that the older Members
appeared to be winning the better posts (*Rzeczpospolita*, 28 August 2010). Who makes up
the new service, its purposes and its potential impact raise testing questions for Member
States and the European institutions as well as for traditional inter-state diplomacy. Pierre
Lellouche's remark above, for example, refers to the European Parliament's effort to gain
some control over the service via its powers over the budget and staff regulations.

The declared aim to create an efficient and effective diplomatic service was justified by
Ashton on the grounds that, as she told the *Washington Post*, 'The EU can be too slow, too

cumbersome and too bureaucratic. I want to help to put that right in the way the EU works with the rest of the world' (27 July 2010). Europe, as she declared to the European Parliament,

> cannot afford to act in a disparate manner in a world that is seeing fundamental power shifts and where problems are increasingly complex and inter-linked. We need to defend Europe's interests and project Europe's values in a more coherent and effective way. And we should be ambitious in how we do it. The European Union and the Member-States have an impressive array of instruments, resources, relationships and expertise to help build a better, more stable world. Now we need to bring all this together, to forge joined-up strategies and maximise our impact on the ground. Particularly in the troubled parts of the world, where our action matters the most.
>
> (Ashton, 2010)

The need was 'to build an integrated platform that projects our values and interests effectively around the world'. This would:

> Protect our security and prosperity: if we are going to do that, we need to think big and we need to be creative, to build integrated systems, breaking down the old silos that exist and be willing to do things differently to improve our effectiveness. I say more than anything: what matters is what works. We should be pragmatic and make sure that this is the approach we take.
>
> (Ashton, 2010)

Clearly 'breaking down the old silos' to build an integrated system with its own identity and sense of purpose was inevitably a challenge both to the European institutions and especially to the Member States. Ashton did not necessarily allay suspicion by declaring that 'This is not, as some critics say, a grab for power; but it is, unashamedly, a grab for effectiveness. The EAS can make a positive difference – and I am determined that it will' (*Washington Post*, 27 July 2010). To quote Juppé again:

> To the extent that each country retains its own diplomatic sovereignty and ability to defend itself (decisions are made unanimously) it is important first to try and distil a common vision of our collective interests. Then we can take action by making our national diplomacies and the EU instruments work together. The role of the European External Action Service (EEAS) and of the High Representative for Foreign Affairs and Security Policy is to help us achieve this ... We ... need to create a genuine, joint diplomatic culture within this institution; and of course we must rise to the occasion and provide the diplomatic service with the proper tools for reflection and decision-making so that for each major issue, a shared European interest emerges even while we ensure our national interests have also been taken into account.
>
> (Juppé, 2010)

But French support has not been without its ambiguities. As Pierre Lellouche put it:

> Member States' rights will be respected; in particular the EEAS will include staff from national diplomatic services, with these making up at least a third both of

the total EEAS staff in Brussels and the EU delegations. This is very important if we want to instil a common diplomatic culture in countries with great diplomatic traditions, countries with more modest ones and staff who have come from the Commission. The Common Security and Defence Policy structures, whilst being integrated into the European External Action Service, are seeing their autonomy maintained. In fine, the organizational set-up should ensure the new structure operates efficiently.

(Lellouche, 2010)

Tensions between the EEAS and the Member States were exacerbated by 'turf battles' between the European institutions. Barroso's detachment of enlargement, one of the EU's key foreign policy issues, from the Commissioner for External Policy portfolio (as under Ferrero-Waldner) suggested a policy of at least damage limitation. His appointment of João Vale de Almeida to the 'embassy' in Washington in February 2010 after less than a year as Director-General for External Relations (but rather longer as head of Barroso's *cabinet*) and well before the formal establishment of the EEAS was also generally regarded as an attempt to seize a particularly important post for the Commission.

The extent to which the disparate elements from the Commission, Council Secretariat and the Member States can be welded together to form a professional European diplomatic service with its own *esprit de corps* remains to be seen. If the Commission's external delegations have often been dismissed as technocrats lacking political nous given their preoccupation with trade and aid issues, they had nonetheless, and despite institutional confusion, become increasingly recognized as 'real embassies' (Bruter, 1999: 197). If officials from the Council Secretariat are more an unknown quantity, those seconded to the EEAS from the Member States are under double suspicion. On the one hand, they are suspect to representatives of the European institutions on the grounds that they may retain primary loyalty to, perhaps even continue to report to, their home government. On the other hand, they are under suspicion from home governments lest they 'go native'. Harold Nicolson suggested that there was always a danger that the diplomat posted abroad 'becomes denationalized, internationalized, and therefore dehydrated, an elegant, empty husk' (Nicolson, 1953, cited in Sharp, 1998: 107). Rather than a husk, elegant or otherwise, Sharp and others (for example Checkel, 2001) have made much of diplomats not just representing their capital's views to their host, but explaining, even pressing on their home government the views of their host government, their circumstances, environment, etc. There is perhaps always a fine line between reportage, explanation and advocacy. But what might be termed socialization may simply reflect a temporary professional commitment to a new service. It could, though, mean a growing identification with European norms (i.e. as distinct from national norms). Whichever might be the case, those seconded may have to reflect on the danger that they may come under suspicion, which might have an impact on their career once they return to their capitals (see Geuijen, Hart and Princen, 2008, for a study on other Commission officials).

The spinning wheel of EU representation

EEAS officials may well be reminded of their provenance not just by their former employers but by two further factors: the multiplicity of bodies that may still represent the Union and the reactions of the host government. A new unified voice and channel of communication is made difficult by the fact that at different times on different missions the EU can be represented by the President of the Council, the President of the Commission and by the foreign minister or even another minister of the rotating Presidency. Foreign ministers and national HOGs still expect to make their mark on the international scene, whether in traditional areas of national concern or in times of crisis – whether international or occasionally domestic. Although it took place before Lisbon came into effect, the example of the French and Czech EU Presidencies is indicative of the difficulties that remain. President Sarkozy appeared seemingly unbothered by the rotation of the EU Presidency from France to the Czech Republic at the end of December 2008 and continued to seek to negotiate with Israel, Egypt and the Palestinians over Gaza. Both the French President and Czech EU Presidency delegation visited the region, talking to many of the same people but in rather different accents.

It is therefore not surprising (*pace* Bruter, above) that occasionally third countries find it difficult to distinguish between the Commission and the EU and, even with the EEAS and the High Representative, they may well remain 'baffled by the many faces, names, and telephone numbers that the EU can have'. As was the case in the Sarkozy example, so, too, clarity was not necessarily served by the example of Moratinos during the Spanish EU Presidency, who was reported to have visited the Southern Caucasus '"on behalf of" Ashton … to convey the message that the three countries are "priorities for the EU"' (*EUBusiness*, 28 February 2010). An active Presidency or an issue covering more than just foreign and/or foreign economic issues allow for confusion of intermediaries – this in addition to the presence of other EU Member State embassies with or without ambassadors with ambition or a strong if somewhat outmoded sense of propriety. The EU is thus likely to remain subject to a degree of exploitation for those 'who have mastered the intricacies of the European machinery, [who will continue to] be able to work the system to their advantage, making use of disputes over competence or bureaucratic rivalries to further their interests' (Edwards and Rijks, 2008: 25).

And so?

Even against these odds and however 'unhusk-like' an individual EEAS representative might be, he or she is likely to be effective only to the extent that the EU has a common policy. As suggested above, there is an assumption that an EU interest will be reported back to Brussels and so form the basis for proposals from the High Representative to which the Member States react, to 'provide the foundation for implementing European interests through focused diplomacy', as the German foreign minister put it (Westerwelle, 2011). Given the frequent criticism that the EU too often cannot act, or cannot react quickly, the assumption that a High Representative even with an EEAS will make a qualitative difference is an optimistic one; there remain too many hands on the wheel. And yet, as is so often recognized by Member States, if the EU can agree and the consensus is firm, despite the efforts of those to whom the policy is directed to unpick the agreement, the EU's influence can be significant.[7] This is especially the case if it is known that it had been difficult to arrive at the consensus and would be even more difficult to change it, circumstances remaining largely the same. It is also the case if, in their bilateral relationships, the Member States hold to the common policy. The downside is that if circumstances do change, the policy may stick and the EU becomes marginalized or another decision is made to meet the new circumstances even while the former decision remains, making for inconsistency, which can then be exploited by a third party. And of course, Member States may flake off, leaving the EU and its representatives floundering.

Winning support among 27 states is rarely easy, and this can remain the case in actual negotiations even when the broad lines of policy have been laid down. Karen Smith, among others, was struck by the 'sheer amount of time member-state diplomats spend in EU coordination meetings', even if she was also impressed by their dedication to the process (K. E. Smith, 2006: 156). In so far as little time might actually remain for negotiating an agreement, the emphasis does, indeed, seem to be on the process and journey towards the common position rather than effecting its purported purpose. And long hours of coordination can still leave disagreement and inaction.

All of which leaves the EU representatives facing particular difficulties in terms of being the voice of the EU, whether in public or in private. The issues of speedy decision-making and timely decisions, of coherence and consistency remain. There may be no lack of ambition on the part of members of the EEAS – witness the optimism of Ambassador Almeida in Washington declaring:

> The new service will ensure consistency and coordination of the EU's external action. It will represent European interests via 136 EU Delegations that work in full cooperation with the diplomatic services of the Member States, as we do here in Washington, DC. The EEAS will consolidate the EU's Security and Defence Policy, crisis management and planning, civilian planning and military cooperation. And with other relevant European institutions and departments, it will work to integrate EU policy on, among others, the European Neighbourhood Policy, energy, climate change, development, democracy and human rights, nuclear safety and non-proliferation.
>
> (Almeida, 2010)

Doubtless many of those appointed will find that public role of critical importance in attempting to establish an autonomous identity for the new service, in addition to explaining the nature of the EU. Much of their time is likely to remain bound up with managing the differences among the Member States, as well as managing those with third countries.

While clearly the novelty of the EEAS makes predictions as to its impact on the Common Foreign and Security Policy of the EU somewhat meaningless, its establishment has revealed the continuing tensions caused by the pressures for cooperation, if not integration, within the EU to meet contemporary challenges and the determination of Member States to retain as much control as possible. While potentially Europeanized, the EEAS may not be wholly denationalized, stateless and neutered; it could well provide the basis for a new dynamic to come into play in European foreign policy-making as well as in its execution. While not new, the office of High Representative supported now by the EEAS has been strengthened to become yet another actor with at least some sort of voice to add to the cacophony of voices that characterize the EU. The efforts of both Solana and Ashton to further the EU as an international actor continue, with personal diplomacy a critical factor. However powerless, there is a dimension, pinpointed by Nicolaidis following Havel, of the power of the powerless in building networks and setting examples for managing relations, however flawed (Nicolaidis, 2004: 95).

That, of course, has to be set against the frequent incoherence and inconsistency of the EU and its Member States, and, indeed, the incoherence or (deliberate) misunderstanding of others – sometimes disregarding the EU in favour of the continuation of more historical relationships with particular Member States, at other times wanting closer relations yet seeing little value added if the EU is promoting norms that counter governments' vested interests – not least if this means treating with and perhaps even funding civil society groups that are regarded as essentially subversive. Any distinctiveness of the High Representative's voice may easily therefore be muffled. And yet, however flaky Member States may be in terms of their support, they seem nonetheless to acknowledge that a more coordinated effort is needed to meet some at least of the challenges of the contemporary international system. There is, too, an awareness that the establishment of a High Representative with their own diplomatic service may lead to a modification of national practices and even modify national behaviour, creating a new dimension to contemporary diplomacy.

Notes

1 With apologies to Willie Nelson.
2 David Lidington, UK minister for Europe, reported in *International Herald Tribune*, 24 May 2011.
3 As the German foreign minister told the *Guardian* on the eve of the UN Security Council vote on a no-fly zone: 'Your own instinct is to say "We have to do something". But military intervention is to take part in a civil war that could go on for a long time. Germany has a strong friendship with our European partners, but we won't take part in any military operation and I will not send German troops to Libya' (*Guardian*, 18 March 2011).
4 These themes of concession and counter-concession, mediation and negotiation have re-emerged in some of the diplomacy literature as in, for example, Sharp (1998) or Constantinou and Der Derian (2010).
5 Under the Lisbon Treaty the High Representative also chairs foreign ministers' meetings – including, when present, meetings of defence ministers. There have been some precedents for Ashton to ask the rotating Presidency to chair particular meetings at foreign or defence minister levels, as was the case with the Spanish foreign minister, Miguel Angel Moratinos, who chaired the EU Algeria Association Council in June 2010.
6 Ashton was questioned about whether it helped her when in Cairo that her visit coincided with the British prime minister's visit to the Middle East with 'a cohort of arms sellers' (*Newsnight*, BBC, 22 February 2011).
7 As *EUObserver* reported (20 May 2011), a paper by the Austrian government on the development of the EEAS began: 'Close co-operation between the diplomatic services of member states and the EEAS in Brussels and in third countries is the prerequisite for the Union's success in joint external action.'

7

MILITARY CSDP

The quest for capability

Sven Biscop and Jo Coelmont

In absolute terms and when taken as a bloc, the EU is the world's second largest military actor, preceded only by the USA. In 2009 the 26 EU Member States that collectively participate in the European Defence Agency (EDA) spent €194 billion on defence, having some 1.67 million men and women in uniform (EDA, 2010). However, of that impressive overall number, only a small share is employable for expeditionary operations: a meagre 10 per cent or some 170,000 troops (Horvath, 2011: 57). Because of the need for rotation, the EU can sustain about one third of those in the field, so a rate of deployment of 60,000 to 70,000 troops is the maximum effort which in the current state of its capabilities and under normal circumstances the EU can sustain. This more or less equals the level of ambition of the Headline Goal (HG) adopted by the European Council in Helsinki in 1999. The aim is to be able to deploy up to an army corps (50,000 to 60,000 troops), together with air and maritime forces, plus the required command and control, strategic transport and other support services, within 60 days, and to sustain that effort for at least one year.

In 1999, the number of 50,000 to 60,000 was arrived at by referring back to the launch of KFOR earlier that year: it was about the number of troops needed to stabilize Kosovo or, earlier, Bosnia and Herzegovina. Today, the EU and its Member States are actively engaged in many more theatres, a trend which is likely to continue as Europe strengthens its foreign policy, and as the USA is looking for burden-sharing with its European allies. As a result, EU Member States now usually deploy troop numbers equivalent to the HG or even higher, if all ongoing CSDP, NATO, UN and national operations in which they participate are counted, up to 83,000 in 2006 (EDA, 2010a). This much-increased rate of deployment has two major implications. On the one hand, operations last ever longer – usually much more than one year. On the other hand, in the event of a crisis occurring in addition to ongoing operations, EU Member States could not, or could only with great difficulty, deploy significant additional troops, except by improvising (as in the event of an emergency threat to vital interests they would, accepting the increased risks for the forces deployed which this would entail) or by withdrawing forces from ongoing operations.

In order to stay in tune with this higher level of activity, the HG should be interpreted broadly. First, the ambition in terms of sustainability ought to be increased. Second, the HG should be understood as a deployment which EU Member States must be able to undertake at any one time *over and above* ongoing operations. Having a second corps available, the

EU would be able to deal with every eventuality. Clearly, therefore, the transformation of Europe's armed forces must be stepped up.

The need for transformation

Transformation means reorienting the armed forces from territorial defence to expeditionary operations. The majority of Europe's armed forces used to consist of heavy formations with limited mobility geared to the defence of the national territory. This made perfect sense during the Cold War, as armies were stationed at striking distance on both sides of the Iron Curtain in preparation for a massive conventional onslaught. This legacy meant that once the Cold War ended, most of Europe had to start transformation with a severe handicap as compared to the USA.

Today's worldwide crisis management operations demand much more agile forces, able to deploy rapidly over long distances. This requires a different mix of capabilities: strategic air and maritime transport, the key 'strategic enablers' along with deployable force head-quarters (FHQs) and strategic intelligence and communications, but also equipment suitable for operations in various theatres. Doctrine and training, an integral part of any capability, must be adapted accordingly. Member States are aware of this challenge; all have initiated reform. Budgets are limited, however, and have considerably decreased since the end of the Cold War. At the same time, capabilities and operations have become increasingly expensive, hence transformation cannot be achieved in one big bang but proceeds mostly at a very slow pace. Often, the situation is aggravated by governments regarding the defence budget as easy pickings when additional savings are needed to balance the national budget. As a result, plans for transformation and restructuring of the armed forces often have to be abandoned midway through, when it turns out that the promised budgets are not accorded after all. A succession of unfinished reform plans has left many armed forces in disarray. The problems faced by the Member States of Central and Eastern Europe are particularly difficult, as they are burdened by even larger quantities of usually older legacy equipment, and have much more limited budgetary means.

The fundamental issue at the heart of both the problem, i.e. low deployability, and the slow pace of the solution, i.e. transformation, remains the fragmentation of Europe's defence effort. If the collective defence budget of the EU27 represents a very considerable sum of money, in reality it is of course not spent in a collective way. Rather it is fragmented across 27 separate armed forces. Most Member States remain reluctant to align national defence planning with that of other Member States and take into account the shortfall areas, as well as the areas in which there is overcapacity, that have been identified at the European level. Instead, they insist on remaining active in a relatively wide range of capability areas chosen in terms of national considerations, in spite of the decreasing defence budgets and size of their armed forces. Consequently, a plethora of ever smaller-scale capabilities are scattered across the EU's smaller Member States especially, which are neither cost-effective nor, usually, very deployable. At the same time, many Member States maintain large capabilities in spite of their having become redundant.

As many Member States through successive rounds of savings have had to cut the size of many capabilities, cost-effectiveness has decreased, because certain costs to a large extent remain fixed, regardless of the size of the capability. The cost of running an airbase, for example, does not decrease proportionately as the number of aircraft stationed there decreases. As a result, the unit cost increases, an ever larger share of the budget is spent on overhead and support structures and less money is available for investment in the needs of the manoeuvre units and for actually deploying them on operations. Moreover, many Member States sought to maintain the extensive superstructures of the former large-scale Cold War armed forces, such as division structures, even though mostly the actual size of the forces no longer warrants it. With the abolishment of conscription in most Member States, the reserve forces are gradually disappearing, so mobilization cannot serve to fill up these large structures either. In the area of overhead and support structures, great redundancy thus exists, so the potential for increasing cost-effectiveness is very large.

The answer to fragmentation is integration. But fragmentation has proved difficult to overcome. Even States that are members of the EU or NATO or both often decide on national defence planning with little or no reference to either. Their guidelines are usually trumped by considerations of prestige, by historical legacies, by national industrial interests, by very local politics and simply by budgetary pressure. As a result, even when Member States invest in defence, they do not necessarily invest in the right capabilities, nor do they always procure capabilities in the most cost-effective manner. Meanwhile, the strategic enablers required for the transformation to expeditionary operations are being developed only very slowly, if at all. In 2001, and at repeated instances ever since, the strategic shortfalls have been identified and prioritized by the EU and yet progress in addressing them has remained very limited indeed. At the same time, in other areas massive redundancies are maintained in spite of their limited usefulness.

Every successive round of budget cuts threatens to aggravate this already bad situation. Most recently, in the wake of the financial crisis, most nations as of 2010 have started to announce additional cuts. The worst that could happen under such circumstances is business as usual: each government deciding unilaterally, without any coordination with fellow members of NATO and the EU, where the cuts will be made. The great risk is always that States will scale down or axe altogether ongoing and future programmes and projects meant to generate the indispensable strategic enablers (Maulny, 2010), while hanging on to existing capabilities that are cheaper to maintain but that are already redundant. In the end the sum total of European capabilities will be even less coherent, and even less employable.

Creating a CSDP mechanism

The awareness of this European capability conundrum lies at the origin of the creation of ESDP, now CSDP, in 1999, following an initiative by Prime Minister Tony Blair and President Jacques Chirac at the Franco-British summit in St-Malo the year before. An intricate Capabilities Development Mechanism (CDM) was created in order to try and accelerate transformation and render Europe's forces more deployable by coordinating and cooperating at the EU level.

As defined in the CDM, follow-up of the 1999 HG is ensured by a working group of experts, the Headline Goal Task Force (HTF), with the support of the EU Military Staff (EUMS). First the Helsinki Headline Goal Catalogue (HHC) was drawn up, listing the capabilities required to achieve the HG. A call for voluntary contributions was then made. Following the first Capabilities Commitment Conference (CCC; November 2000), the results of this call were listed in the Force Catalogue. These amounted to about 100,000 troops, 400 combat aircraft and 100 naval vessels. Both the HHC and the Force Catalogue are regularly updated, taking into account additional requirements and adding new contributions. At the May 2003 CCC, notably contributions from the ten new Member States and the then six non-EU European members of NATO were added (although the latter does not count towards the assessment of capability shortfalls); the contribution from Romania and Bulgaria was included in 2007.

The comparison of the requirements of the HHC with the available capabilities according to the Force Catalogue led to the identification of a number of substantial qualitative shortfalls, listed in the Capability Improvement Chart. Following the second CCC (styled Capabilities Improvement Conference), a European Capability Action Plan (ECAP) was therefore adopted, in order to introduce a degree of top-down coordination to guide the bottom-up contributions by the Member States. Under the ECAP, 19 panels of national experts were launched, with at least 1 lead nation each, to propose solutions to remedy the original list of 42 shortfalls. In December 2001 the Laeken European Council stated that 'the Union is now capable of conducting some crisis management operations' – a careful but truthful declaration of operationality taking into account the remaining shortfalls. In May 2003 the Council confirmed and reinforced this statement, declaring that 'the EU now has operational capability across the full range of Petersberg Tasks'.

Progress towards solving the shortfalls was not as rapid as expected, however: out of a total of 62 identified shortfalls at that point, the next Capability Improvement Chart (May 2004) showed only 7 to have been solved and 4 where the situation had improved; 23 of the remaining unresolved shortfalls were considered 'significant in the assessment of capability'. The process seemed to suffer from a lack of leadership and coordination. Already at the 2003 CCC, a second phase of ECAP was therefore launched. On the basis of the Progress Catalogue, an analysis of the updated 2003 HHC and Force Catalogue, the ECAP panels were transformed into 15 project groups,[1] each with a lead nation, which were to focus on the implementation of concrete projects, giving due attention to options such as leasing, multinational cooperation and specialization.

The June 2004 European Council endorsed a new Headline Goal 2010. This involved the continued updating of the HHC and Force Catalogue, on the basis of the five illustrative scenarios elaborated by the EUMS: separation of parties by force; stabilization, reconstruction and military advice to third countries; conflict prevention; evacuation operations; assistance to humanitarian operations. On this basis a more detailed Requirements Catalogue was produced in lieu of the HHC. No additional quantitative objectives were set: the HG 2010 focuses instead on qualitative issues, i.e. interoperability, deployability and sustainability. Another specific aspect of the HG 2010 was the creation of the Battlegroups (BGs): the EU permanently has two BGs of about 1,500 troops on standby for rapid-response operations. The core of a BG is a battalion, plus all support services; all capabilities, including command and control arrangements, are pre-identified. After a training period and certification process, each BG is on standby for six months and can be deployed within ten days of a Council decision to launch an operation; sustainability is four months. Often wrongly perceived as representative of CSDP as a whole, the BGs obviously do not replace the HG but constitute one specific additional capacity to that overall capability objective, created because of a shortage of rapid-response elements.

In delivering the HG 2010, an important part was to be played by the European Defence Agency (EDA), established by Council Joint Action of 12 July 2004. The EDA uniquely combines four functions in as many directorates: capability development, armaments cooperation, industry and market, and research and technology. The Agency is a European – as opposed to national – actor that was intended to strengthen top-down coordination by involving the ministers of defence of the 26 participating Member States (Denmark does not take part), who constitute the board of the EDA, which is chaired by the High Representative. The EDA is not a large administration, but a small body. Yet it was hoped that high-level political involvement would enable the EDA to play a strong role of stimulation and coordination: coordinating existing initiatives and mechanisms for cooperation and stimulating Member States into action and new common initiatives by means of peer pressure. Decision-making power remains with the Member States, therefore it is up to the EDA to present as attractive a proposal as possible to convince Member States to harmonize requirements, to agree on specific solutions for specific commonly identified shortfalls and ideally to sign up to multinational programmes, which the Agency can then manage on their behalf. Alternatively, if the project phase is reached, management can also be taken care of by OCCAR, the Organisation Conjointe de Coopération en Matière d'Armement, a dedicated structure for running multinational projects created in 1996, which now has six Member States. Its combination of four functions allows the EDA to take a long-term perspective and initiate things far upstream, in the R&T phase, potentially generating maximal effectiveness.

Initially the EDA took over eight of the ECAP project groups. Following the informal European Council meeting at Hampton Court in October 2005, the EDA identified a much reduced set of priorities for the Capabilities Directorate (command, control and communication, strategic airlift and air-to-air refuelling) and for the Armaments Directorate (armoured fighting vehicles (AFVs)). The Agency's experience shows that generally it remains difficult to persuade Member States to commit to necessary but expensive measures. While the EDA has finished a number of studies, it has not yet been able to contract actual projects in many areas. In spite of the high expectations and the envisaged top-down steering, the EDA was not able to fundamentally alter Member States' behaviour. While it is true that in those cases where multinational programmes have been launched, experience has not been universally positive, the main reason being that they have not been multinational enough, as too many participating nations come up with too many specific national requirements. Such a 'gold-plating' strategy leads to the production of too many national versions of equipment and inevitably pushes up the price (Giegerich, 2010: 95). When money is short, 'the principle of nice to have should be replaced by need to have' (Zandee, 2011: 66). The basic fact remains that well-managed multinational programmes are more cost-effective than a plethora of national programmes duplicating one another. Furthermore, as national markets become smaller as a result of the diminishing size of defence budgets and armed forces, in many areas industry will require a multinational harmonization of the demand side in order to achieve the critical mass needed to launch a programme. Multinational programmes thus remain essential to a cost-effective European defence effort.

In 2006 the EDA in cooperation with the EUMC produced the *Long-Term Vision*, a broad prospective report assessing the nature of the capabilities which the EU will need in the future. The *Long-Term Vision* emphasized four characteristics: synergy, i.e. operating in coordination with civilian actors; agility and speed of deployment; selectivity, on the basis of the availability of a wide range of capabilities; and sustainability. These inform the major capability areas: command, inform, engage, protect, deploy and sustain. The Member States endorsed the *Long-Term Vision* in October 2006; at the end of the year, they tasked the EDA to elaborate a Capability Development Plan (CDP), in order to provide more specific and thus more operational guidance. The CDP, endorsed by the Member States on 8 July 2008, comprises four strands: the HG 2010, i.e. existing capability objectives in the short to medium term; the development of the global strategic context, of the threats and of technology informing Member States which capabilities might be required and which might be possible in the longer term (2025); lessons learned from operations in various frameworks (CSDP, NATO, etc.); and a database of Member States' current longer-term plans and programmes, which notably allows the EDA to identify opportunities for cooperation. The CDP is not one supranational defence plan that seeks to replace national defence planning; rather it is to provide the framework for defence planning at the national level, to function as a 'plan for planning'. The aim is to facilitate and, based on information on other Member States' intentions, inspire national choices on defence planning while stimulating cooperation and, in the longer term, convergence of Member States' plans.

At the same time as endorsing the overall approach of the CDP, Member States also selected 12 topics for specific action: counter–man portable air defence systems (MANPADs); computer network operations; mine counter-measures in littoral sea areas; military implications of the comprehensive approach; human intelligence; intelligence, surveillance, target acquisition and reconnaissance (ISTAR); medical support; CBRN defence; third-party logistic support; counter-improvised explosive device (IED); helicopters; network-enabled capability (NEC). These are to inform options for specific capability projects to be proposed by the EDA.

In a few years' time an intricate mechanism for capability development was thus developed. At the strategic level, starting from the European Security Strategy and how the EU sees its role in the world, Member States in the Council and in the Political and Security Committee (PSC) decide what the EU wants to be able to do militarily and which military capabilities it requires overall. At the planning level, on the basis of the advice of Member States' military representatives in the EUMC and of the work of the EUMS, it will then be established in a dynamic process which capabilities the EU already has (the Force Catalogue), what the detailed capability requirements are (the Requirements Catalogue) and what are the capability shortfalls to be addressed (the Progress Catalogue). At the level of implementation, the EDA, informed by the CDP, will assess the range of possible solutions for the shortfalls, and identify the most promising ones and the resources they require. Finally, it is up to each Member State to define its national defence planning and make specific capability choices, to be implemented through national or multinational projects.

Multinational cooperation alongside CSDP

Most contributions listed in the Force Catalogue are national capabilities, but nearly all Member States participate in multinational units. The depth of integration varies greatly from one multinational unit to the other. Whereas some can truly be considered a single multinational capability, others are more an expression of political intent than an operational reality. Three examples, from navy, army and air force, can serve to illustrate this.

An example of far-reaching multinational integration is Admiral Benelux (ABNL), the cooperation arrangement between the Belgian and Dutch navies, which became operational on 1 January 1996 (Parrein, 2010). Together the two navies operate 8 frigates, 16 mine hunters, 4 submarines, plus various support ships and a helicopter capacity. The operational staffs of both navies have been merged into a single Maritime Situation Centre in Den Helder (the Netherlands), which conducts national as well as combined operations, under the command of Admiral Benelux (always the commander of the Royal Dutch Navy) and Deputy-Admiral Benelux (always the commander of the Belgian Navy). A major degree of specialization has been achieved in terms of education, support and training: e.g. all mine hunters are maintained in Belgium and all frigates in the Netherlands; mine-warfare training is organized in Belgium as well as – true to type – training for catering, while training for deployment on frigates is organized in the Netherlands. At the beginning of 2011 the final step in education was taken by the creation of a bi-national technical school.

ABNL demonstrates how a combination of pooling and specialization can result in important savings and synergies, while at the same time maintaining great flexibility. Belgium and the Netherlands maintain the full sovereignty to engage in operations; the deployment of

Belgian ships does not entail the deployment of Dutch ships or vice versa; and for national operations a national operations commander is in charge. But both countries are committed to assist each other's operations through the combined command and control structure, which will serve the national operations commander, and through the specialized support and training capabilities. An important facilitating factor for integration is the use of the same or similar equipment, such as the commonly acquired and modernized Tripartite mine hunters (Belgium, the Netherlands, France). This factor was substantially strengthened when Belgium acquired the same type of multi-purpose frigates and lately also the same NH90 helicopter as the Netherlands. The obvious implication is that if both countries want to maintain the same degree of integration in the future, procurement decisions would ideally be harmonized.

One of the better-known multinational formations is the Eurocorps. Created in 1992 as a bilateral French–German arrangement, the initiative was subsequently opened to all EU and later to all NATO Member States, and now counts five so-called framework nations, following the accession of Belgium (1993), Spain (1994) and Luxemburg (1996). Next to the five full members, seven other nations send representatives to the Eurocorps staff: Austria, Greece, Italy, Poland, Romania, Turkey and the USA. Initially, Eurocorps was envisaged as a heavy army corps, to which France, Germany and Spain each contributed an armoured division and Belgium a mechanized brigade, in which a Luxemburg element was integrated. In view of the requirements of current crisis management operations, however, from 1999 onwards it was reoriented towards a rapid reaction corps. The main focus became the creation of a deployable headquarters available to the EU, NATO, and the UN (Eurocorps, 2009). The 390-strong HQ is based in Strasbourg, along with its some 400-strong Headquarters Support Battalion, and has seen deployment for SFOR in Bosnia (1998), KFOR in Kosovo (2000) and ISAF in Afghanistan (2004–5), and has been certified in the context of the NATO Response Force (2006 and 2010).

The Eurocorps HQ thus constitutes a real and useful capability. Interestingly however, there appears to be almost no discussion about the deployment of manoeuvre battalions in a Eurocorps context. For crisis management operations (which are more likely to require deployment below the corps level), the framework nations mostly do not seem to consider Eurocorps a likely framework for the combined deployment of manoeuvre battalions. As no units are permanently assigned to Eurocorps, participation has not promoted any significant degree of pooling or specialization among the armies of the framework nations. Important progress has been achieved in terms of harmonizing military procedures within Eurocorps, as well as, over the years, in terms of procurement of identical or compatible equipment. If ever manoeuvre units were to deploy in the Eurocorps framework, that would be vital. Arguably, opportunities have been missed, though, as there certainly is potential for pooling and specialization between the divisions and brigades concerned, notably in the organization of the various support and combat support capabilities.

A newly established multinational formation that has great potential is European Air Transport Command (EATC). EATC is a command and control structure that will assume operational control over most of the air transport fleet of Belgium, France, Germany and the Netherlands, in all about 170 strategic and tactical aircraft. EATC was formally stood up at a base in Eindhoven in the Netherlands in September 2010, with a staff of some 160. Currently, the participating nations operate C130 or C160 transport aircraft, but except for the Netherlands, which still has to decide on replacement, all will acquire the future Airbus A400M transport aircraft (including one funded by Luxemburg integrated in the Belgian capacity).[2] The integrated command structure allows for the maximally effective use of all available aircraft. Important savings are realized as only one 24/7 operations centre has to be maintained with far fewer staff required than in the four nations separately. Germany has for the moment gone the furthest by abolishing its national air transport command, which incidentally had more staff than EATC. Just as is the case in ABNL, operational flexibility can be safeguarded: the multinational command structure can conduct national and combined operations, without the deployment of aircraft of one nation automatically involving that of those of another nation, as long as all nations contribute to all operations through their contribution to the command structure. Aircraft will continue to be stationed on a number of national bases: a good spread of hubs helps to achieve maximum efficiency in flight operations. At the same time, though, the use of the same equipment will allow the participating Member States to create synergies in terms of logistics and maintenance; a degree of specialization in these tasks could also be possible. Meanwhile, in these functional areas EATC operates in a modular way, allowing each participating nation to tailor its degree of cooperation and integration according to its current needs and capabilities.

Capability development: an assessment

As the year 2010 passed without the HG 2010 being achieved, the question imposes itself: is the existing mechanism sufficient to generate the capabilities that the EU requires to live up to the ambitions of the ESS? The last Progress Catalogue still identifies more than 50 qualitative and quantitative shortfalls, mainly in the areas of survivability and force protection, deployability and transport and information superiority. The operational consequence is a high to very high risk of the objectives of an operation not being met, of delay in launching an operation and of incurring casualties and loss of equipment. True, capability development is a long-term process. But have the mechanisms that have been put in place the potential at least to generate the necessary quantum leap? The reasons why this appears doubtful can be found in the characteristics of the CSDP capability-development process.

To start with, the Force Catalogue is indeed no more than that: a catalogue. For each Member State it lists types and quantities of capabilities that can be made available to the EU, but it does not identify specific units. Hence there is no permanent link between the different national capabilities listed, such as combined training and manoeuvres. Obviously, this approach, while not hindering it, does not promote cooperation between Member States either. Only for actual operations, if a Member State decides to take part, are specific units identified. The availability of the capabilities listed in the Catalogue is thus not automatic but has to be decided on a case-by-case basis. The implications for preventive action and rapid deployment are obvious. Far from the 'Euro-army' that some fear, there exists only the assumption of the availability of national capabilities. The actual readiness of those national capabilities is judged only by each nation itself. As the process is based on self-certification, no EU body assesses just how ready the capabilities listed in the Catalogue really are.

Most if not all Member States have assigned part of their national capabilities to multinational units, but most of these formations display a rather low degree of integration. Except for the area of command and control, pooling and specialization mostly remain very limited. Hence many multinational formations do not amount to more than a catalogue themselves. Being assigned to a multinational unit should mean more than getting a new shoulder patch … This is linked to the fact that multinational units, especially for land forces, are not usually seen as a primary framework for deployment for actual operations. Unless they are, the drive to deepen integration in existing multinational units will probably remain limited. The 'enormous kaleidoscope of European multinational commands and units' was mapped by the

EUMS (Horvath, 2011: 59). The exercise revealed that 'while none of them is disinterested in CSDP ... what they may need is orientation – or indeed, some incentives – to fulfil a more challenging mission, such as to become part of the pooling and sharing of military capabilities for the EU' (Horvath, 2011: 59).

The only exception to the catalogue model are the Battlegroups. Each BG is composed of pre-identified units that train and exercise together during the stand-up phase, before starting their six-month standby period. Because of the small scale of a BG, this can be considered a useful and indeed successful experiment in military integration. The BGs have served to increase interoperability and in some Member States have helped to drive transformation. But unless the lessons learned from the BGs are brought into practice at a larger scale, they will remain an experiment. Furthermore, the effectiveness and credibility of the BGs will only be convincingly proved after their first deployment, which has yet to happen. Lindstrom (2011) outlines some of the possibilities to improve the usability of the BGs. One could have but a single BG on standby, but of larger, brigade-size (up to 5,000). The links between the BGs and the EU's civilian capabilities, e.g. the Civilian Response teams, could be strengthened so as to benefit from the added value of the BGs in humanitarian crises as well. Finally, the introduction of common funding to cover the cost of a BG deployment would remove one of the most important impediments to their use.

The fundamental obstacle to more substantial cooperation and integration is the almost exclusively bottom-up nature of the process, contrary to intentions at the launch of the ECAP and the creation of the EDA. Naturally, the mechanism relies on voluntary contributions by the Member States. Although in the EDA there is a key actor at the EU level, the capitals are the drivers. The intention was there, however, including in Paris and London, to complement this indispensable bottom-up dynamic with top-down guidance and coordination. During the European Convention and afterwards when the EDA was created, the ministers of defence especially had subscribed to this. That is why the EDA, which was included in the draft Constitutional Treaty, was set up in 2004, without waiting for the Treaty's ratification and entry into force. When the Constitutional Treaty and afterwards the Lisbon Treaty ran into difficulties, however, a number of Member States and political leaders that had until then been committed became more cautious and swallowed their ambitions, including in the field of CSDP. The EDA was among the main casualties, as Member States refused to provide it with more than the minimal budgetary and personnel means, rendering it very difficult for the tool that they had only just created to perform its ambitious tasks. Capability development thus suffered great collateral damage from the Union's institutional crisis.

As a result, an almost completely bottom-up capability-development mechanism emerged, which offers tactical-, but not strategic-level coordination of national capability development. Within the predominant focus on national contributions and with the limited means at its disposal, the EDA has made a valiant effort. It has analysed the needs and elaborated multinational options to address the priority shortfalls and, in specific capability areas, has attempted to convince Member States to abandon or to merge national projects in favour of multinational projects that focus on those shortfalls. When Member States are willing to join their efforts, in varying clusters according to the project, this approach does yield important results. But by and large Member States have not been willing to answer the call. Basically, Member States are still not motivated to invest in a capability area simply because at the EU level it has been identified as a priority shortfall. Rather they each look to the other capitals to make the first move, fearing as they do to contribute too much of their limited defence budgets to a common programme as compared to the extent that they expect to have to draw on it. Meanwhile their focus remains national, and defence-planning decisions continue to be taken in isolation, in terms of strictly national requirements, without much coordination, let alone alignment, with fellow Member States. Redundant capabilities are still being maintained while the strategic enablers are lacking, therefore.

The conclusion is that tactical-level coordination, i.e. on a project-by-project basis, is insufficient to alter the intrinsically national focus and bottom-up nature of CSDP. That requires top-down coordination at the strategic level, not just of specific projects or even individual capability areas, but of Member States' defence planning as such.

The future: Permanent Structured Cooperation or pooling and sharing?

CSDP needs a new stimulus therefore. The Lisbon Treaty (Art. 42.6) introduces a new mechanism that has great potential to re-dynamize capability development:

> Those Member States whose military capabilities fulfil higher criteria and which have made more binding commitments to one another in this area with a view to the most demanding missions shall establish permanent structured cooperation within the Union framework.

Permanent Structured Cooperation (PESCO) allows a group of Member States, on a voluntary basis, to work together more closely in the field of defence. By setting criteria for participation, for the first time participating Member States (pMS) would enter into binding commitments in the field of defence; furthermore they would allow the EDA to assess their performance. The Protocol on PESCO annexed to the Lisbon Treaty sets out two objectives (Art. 1), one of which, i.e. to supply or contribute to a Battlegroup, has already been achieved by most Member States. This leaves a single major objective: to proceed more intensively to develop defence capacities, which must of course be available and deployable, as Art. 2 (c) says. Thus by closer cooperation among themselves, PESCO should enable the pMS to achieve at a quicker pace than at present, as well as to increase, their national level of ambition in terms of deployability and sustainability. In other words pMS will be able to field more capabilities for the full range of operations in all frameworks in which they engage: CSDP, NATO, the UN and others. In doing so, they will contribute to the achievement of the overall objectives for the CFSP and CSDP to which they have agreed in the Lisbon Treaty.

Article 2 of the Protocol mentions five areas which have to be operationalized and translated into criteria for participation:

- to agree on objectives for the level of investment in defence equipment;
- to 'bring their defence apparatus into line with each other as far as possible', by harmonizing military needs, pooling and, 'where appropriate', specialization;
- to enhance their forces' availability, interoperability, flexibility and deployability, notably by setting 'common objectives regarding the commitment of forces';
- to address the shortfalls identified by the Capability Development Mechanism (CDM), including through multinational approaches;
- to take part, 'where appropriate', in equipment programmes in the context of the EDA.

There was an arduous debate in 2010 about whether, and if so how, to implement PESCO. In spite of the lack of common understanding of PESCO and the reluctance therefore to launch it, the ministers of defence of the EU Member States, urged on by the financial crisis, on 9 December 2010 agreed on potentially far-reaching conclusions: the so-called

Ghent Framework. Avoiding any explicit reference to PESCO, ministers focused on the immediate need for coordination in view of the budgetary cuts and proposed a concrete method. Member States were encouraged to 'systematically analyze their national military capabilities', aiming at 'measures to increase interoperability for capabilities to be maintained on a national level; exploring which capabilities offer potential for pooling; intensifying cooperation regarding capabilities, support structures and tasks which could be addressed on the basis of role- and task-sharing'. This pragmatic approach created a positive atmosphere. Subsequently, 'pooling and sharing' became the new buzzword in CSDP-town.

Pooling and sharing is of course not new. Many Member States have already pooled important capabilities with others for decades, through various bilateral and multilateral arrangements, and some have even engaged in role- and task-sharing or specialization. But they have never surpassed the tactical level of project-by-project cooperation, and have not solved the strategic shortfalls. There certainly is scope therefore to create many more synergies and effects of scale, as well as an increasing necessity, in view of the budgetary pressure and the ever-reduced size of most Member States' defence budgets and armed forces. Pooling and sharing also has limits, though. A critical mass of Member States must take ambitious initiatives, including in some significant capability areas, to set things in motion. More importantly, pooling and sharing what you have does not get you more. Pooling and sharing can allow existing capabilities to be made more cost-effective, and hopefully also more operationally effective. But it does not automatically lead to solutions for the capability shortfalls. The Ghent Framework not only has to be long term, it also has to create a platform to launch new capability initiatives.

For the Ghent Framework to yield results, it must be top-down. Not in the sense that Brussels dictates to the Member States, but in the sense that the ministers of defence, who are the capability providers, personally take the lead and steer their armed forces towards greater convergence in order to meet the common capability objectives. Useful inspiration can be found in the method used to launch CSDP operations: a Force Generation Conference. Once the capabilities required for a specific upcoming CSDP operation are identified and listed in the Statement of Requirements, a Force Generation Conference is organized among the potential Troop Contributing Nations. This process goes on until the entire list of requirements has been met by voluntary contributions by the Member States. Although such conferences can be difficult, in the end they have always yielded results.

In a similar vein, the Ghent Framework could be the first step towards a 'capability generation conference' of the ministers of defence of the willing Member States. The aim of such a conference would be to create a durable strategic-level framework for systematic exchange of information on national defence planning, as a basis for consultation and top-down coordination, on a voluntary basis. Today, Member States do their national defence planning in splendid isolation, without really taking into account either EU or NATO guidelines. In the future, a national defence White Book ought no longer to be the end of the process, but the starting point for an open dialogue among partners. As defence planning concerns the long term, such a dialogue will be permanent, hence a *Permanent Capability Conference*. Such a forum will create the certainty and confidence that capitals need in order to really align their national defence planning with fellow Member States and to focus it on the commonly identified shortfalls.

Only in the framework of a Permanent Capability Conference that provides them with a bird's-eye view of all participants' plans and intentions can Member State reliably assess the relevance of their national capabilities. It functions in effect as a peer-review mechanism of national defence planning. The advantages for national capability decisions are fourfold:

1   Member States can confidently choose to strengthen their relevance by *focusing* their defence effort on those capabilities required for crisis management operations that are in short supply and therefore critical at the EU level.

2   Member States can safely decide not to expand or even to disinvest in national capabilities of which at the EU level there is already overcapacity. Actually, Member States spent far more money on maintaining redundant capabilities than would be needed to solve the priority shortfalls. Doing away with those redundancies in a concerted way is the most effective cost-saver imaginable. Furthermore Member States can without risk decide to disinvest in a capability area either because existing national capabilities are obsolete and non-deployable or because, always on a voluntary basis, participating Member States have agreed on specialization among them.

3   In those capability areas in which they do remain active, Member States will be easily able to identify opportunities for increased pooling and sharing of capabilities, allowing them to organize them in a more cost-effective manner and increase operational effectiveness.

4   Pooling and sharing, specialization and doing away with redundancies will create budgetary margin, allowing Member States to find partners to launch multinational programmes to address the strategic shortfalls and generate *new* capabilities, including in those areas which go beyond the means of any individual nation and thus demand a combined initiative at the EU level.

The question can be asked: does this constitute PESCO? What is relevant here is not the label, but whether, for the Ghent Framework to be successful, a mechanism similar to PESCO is necessary. In all likelihood, not all Member States will be willing from the start to subscribe to a permanent and structured process along the lines of the Ghent Framework. It is crucial that those who are willing can do so *within* the EU and can make use of the EU institutions, notably the EDA. That will ensure that something like a Permanent Capability Conference remains fully in line with the overall development of CSDP, and will easily allow other Member States to join at a later stage, whenever they are able and willing. To allow that, the Protocol on PESCO annexed to the Lisbon Treaty could be activated, or Member States could agree to consider this as one of the subgroups established in the EDA, as long as the experience and expertise of the EDA can be put to use.

Conclusion

Europe's armed forces are simultaneously facing budgetary austerity and increasing deployment for crisis management operations. In spite of this, the political circumstances at first sight are not propitious to a new step in European defence cooperation. With Member States divided over the military dimension of Libyan crisis management in 2010, the enthusiasm for pooling and sharing of capabilities may have slackened. Yet operations in Libya have also highlighted once again the already well-known capability shortfalls. Precision-guided munitions (missiles), satellite observation, aircraft carriers, air-to-air refuelling: for lack of sufficient European capacity, 90 per cent of the strategic enablers that allow for a 'clean' air campaign were contributed by the USA.

Unfortunately, the political fallout of the Libyan crisis may negatively affect the Ghent Framework. There is a great risk that Member States will not be willing to engage in pooling and sharing with those seen as unlikely to join in when it comes to real operations. That impression can only be undone by those so accused, including by signalling their willingness to pool capabilities in substantive capability areas, to a substantive degree. That in turn will create the political energy necessary to ensure that 'Ghent' becomes a long-term process, in order to arrive eventually at a forum for effective strategic-level dialogue between national defence planning. Only through CSDP can such military convergence be achieved as the only way to produce more deployable capabilities by *all* Member States, which will thus also benefit the two militarily most powerful Member States, France and the UK.

While the degree to which Member States will engage in substantive pooling of capabilities remains to be seen, nevertheless at the 1 December 2011 Foreign Affairs Council, Member States did indeed make important decisions concerning the strategic shortfalls. In the fields of air-to-air refuelling and satellite communications especially, the projects announced, if follow-up is assured, will be key in providing Europeans with some of the strategic enablers required for autonomous operations. The solution requires thinking outside the box, for which 'Ghent' was the starting point. Only by aligning their defence efforts and *collectively* focusing it on those shortfalls can Europeans remain militarily relevant.

Notes

1   Air-to-air refuelling; combat search and rescue; headquarters; nuclear, biological and chemical protection; special operations forces; theatre ballistic missile defence; unmanned aerial vehicles; strategic airlift; space-based assets; interoperability issues and working procedures for evacuation and humanitarian operations; intelligence, surveillance, target acquisition and reconnaissance; strategic sealift; collective medical protection; attack helicopters; support helicopters.
2   The development of the A400M, which predates the creation of the EDA, can serve as an example of a potentially successful project: 6 Member States (Belgium, France, Germany, Luxemburg, Spain and the UK), plus 3 non-EU States (Malaysia, Turkey and South Africa) originally agreed to acquire a total of 192 aircraft. Cooperation thus allowed assembling the critical mass which industry required to launch such an expensive project. Unfortunately, the project was later derailed and suffered great delays; participants were forced to provide additional funding, but the budgetary crisis might at the same time lead to part of the order being cancelled.

8

CIVILIAN CSDP

A tool for state-building?

Catriona Gourlay

Despite initial misgivings about the value of creating civilian crisis management capacities from the EU's largest member states, history has been on the side of the Nordic states that pushed for an EU capacity to deploy civilians on missions in the framework of the European Security and Defence Policy (ESDP, now CSDP). The development of civilian CSDP since 1999 has coincided with a rise in demand for assistance for the development of the rule of law sectors, especially in states recovering from war. The EU's civilian monitoring missions in Aceh and Georgia have also demonstrated the utility of relatively small, unarmed missions in providing effective support to the implementation of a peace agreement. At the same time, it has been relatively easier to secure support from EU member states for civilian missions, which tend to be less expensive, less dangerous and less controversial than military ones. Indeed, while the West's military interventions in Iraq and Afghanistan have cast a shadow of doubt in many EU states over the compatibility of military deployments with peace-building objectives, there is rising appreciation of the importance of state-building for consolidating peace and fostering development.

In short, the initial reservations of some EU member states about the utility of creating a distinctly civilian dimension of CSDP have proved unfounded. On the contrary, the early history of CSDP has shown how civilian missions have been a useful and relatively flexible instrument that has enabled the EU to provide support for peace processes in ways that would not otherwise have been possible using military or other EU aid instruments. Civilian missions have arguably now become member states' principal instrument of choice when faced with internal or external demand to visibly respond to a crisis, to support states struggling to recover from conflict or to address violent challenges. In the sense that civilian CSDP is a tool that has been adapted for an ever-expanding variety of tasks, one might therefore conclude that it is indeed a tool for all trades engaged in peace consolidation.

It does not, however, follow from the relative popularity of the civilian CSDP tool that it is necessarily well adapted to the various roles it has been tasked with. Assessing whether civilian CSDP missions have, in practice, been well suited to the mandates ascribed to them evidently requires detailed empirical analysis of their functioning and impact on a case-by-case basis. This is beyond the scope of this chapter. Rather than address whether the tool of civilian CSDP actually works, this chapter aims to identify the operational limits of civilian CSDP from an EU institutional perspective. It concludes with a brief assessment of how the instrument may be further adapted in light of changing conditions. These include the post-Lisbon reforms, including the EU's ambition to boost its external political influence through the European External Action Service.

What is the policy framework for civilian CSDP and state-building?

Conceptually, civilian CSDP has been tied to the objective of state-building. For example, the EU 2003 Security Strategy stated that 'civilian crisis management helps restore civil government' (European Council, 2003) and the majority of civilian missions have institutional capacity-building mandates in the rule of law sectors. In addition to building government capacity through 'supportive' tasks, however, civilian CSDP has also been designed to 'substitute' for local government capacity through missions with executive mandates. Hence civilian CSDP is also conceptually associated with the objective of promoting stability by directly providing international police and justice services on an interim basis. For a number of states this was the initial purpose for creating civilian CSDP and the link with directly providing public order is maintained. For instance, the EU 2008 *Report on the Implementation of the European Security Strategy* (European Council, 2008a) identifies 'building stability in Europe and beyond' as a core EU security objective that can be pursued by combination of CSDP and development actions attuned to fragile or post-conflict situations (European Council, 2008a: 8).

While the EU ambition to promote stability and help (re)build states, including through civilian CSDP, is clearly stated in its security strategy and the Lisbon Treaty, EU policy is far less clear on how to tailor specific state-building interventions to different contexts and which tools are best adapted to specific cases and tasks. In other words, there is no clear policy guidance regarding how to combine different EU tools in fragile or post-conflict contexts. This is not surprising given that that the evidence base for state-building practice remains weak and that international policy discourse has only recently focused on how to calibrate international interventions towards promoting more resilient states in challenging contexts. For instance, it was only in 2007 that the Organisation for Economic Co-operation and Development (OECD) Development Assistance Committee (DAC) – one of the principal forums for developing and consolidating guidance for donor policies – first explicitly prioritized state-building as the central objective of international partnerships in fragile situations and in countries emerging from conflict in its *Principles for Good International Engagement in Fragile States and Situations* (OECD, 2007). Since then, donors working together in the framework of OECD DAC have explored the potential of international assistance to inadvertently do harm to state-building processes and have focused on how to better adapt aid disbursement modalities, programming and technical assistance in these contexts. Similarly, international financial institutions have recently turned their attention to the challenges of supporting state-building. For example, the central thesis of the World Bank 2011 World Development Report is that legitimacy of government actions is essential for sustained development success. It critically reflects on international efforts to support state-building, stressing the importance of function over institutional form, and calls for greater investment in preventive programming and the rule of law sectors (World Bank, 2011).

Recent policy reflection in the donor and development communities has confirmed the centrality of the state-building objective but called for greater modesty and sensitivity in relation to how international engagement can support it. This is, for example, reflected in recent OECD DAC policy guidance for *Supporting State-Building in Situations of Conflict and Fragility* (OECD, 2011). This policy guidance emphasizes the importance of understanding state-building processes and the context in which they take place as the starting point for any international engagement and support. State-building is also seen as a largely endogenous process, and the challenge for international engagement is in judging how to strengthen constructive state–society engagement through country programmes, aid modalities and technical assistance. The OECD DAC guidance recommends that international assistance should prioritize support for: local conflict management and resolution mechanisms; inclusive political settlements or processes that strengthen state–society interaction and accountability; and functions that are strategically important for state-building. These include the functions of security and justice, revenue and expenditure management, economic development – especially job creation – and service delivery.

Although there is a broad consensus within the EU that assistance for state-building is most effective when different tools are employed in a comprehensive fashion, towards common strategic objectives in a way that is tailored to local context, this remains an aspiration rather than reality. The fragmented nature of decision-making within the EU means that there is no single venue in which discussions over strategic priorities and how best to achieve them take place. Rather, decision-making is sector-specific, and takes place in different institutional contexts and with different actors. Decisions over the deployment of aid instruments have, to date, been made by *functionnaires* within a number of Commission directorate generals (with mandates for development, humanitarian aid and external relations), while decisions over CSDP deployments are taken by EU member state ambassadors in the Political and Security Committee. In practice, therefore, there is no tradition within the EU context of a common deliberation over which is the appropriate strategy or mix of instruments to deploy in response to a crisis or for state-building purposes. Rather, the mix 'emerges' from a number of separate analysis and decision-making processes across EU institutions, few if any of which use a state-building lens in their analysis and decision-making.

What are the EU's development tools for state-building?

CSDP is but one of a range of tools that the EU deploys for institution-building in the area of justice and security. EU 'development' tools of state-building also include a range of options for disbursing aid and providing technical assistance. There are three main options for disbursing aid. The first is direct budget support to national governments. However, concerns over government capacity and/or legitimacy mean that it is rarely used in early recovery or fragile contexts. Although the EU, together with other donors, is exploring how this instrument might be extended to more challenging contexts through greater use of joint management provisions, its use in fragile contexts remains marginal. The second option for disbursing EU funds that is much more common in post-conflict contexts is the pooled-funding mechanism of Multi-Donor Trust Funds (MDTFs). These are typically administered by the UN Development Programme or World Bank. They may be sector-specific, for instance, supporting a range of government capacity-building activities to strengthen the rule of law.[1] Alternatively, they may provide a pool of funding for reconstruction that can be used to fund activities across police, justice, governance and socio-economic development sectors.[2] Although the MDTF mechanism has been criticized for being relatively slow in disbursing funds or for indirectly undermining state structures by creating parallel management structures, there is broad consensus amongst donors that it is a useful mechanism for channelling aid in fragile situations in a way that also has the potential to strengthen state capacities and harmonize international support. The EU, however, tends to channel its funding for state-building through MDTFs or pooled-funding mechanisms only in high-profile cases which receive large volumes of aid from the EU budget, for instance in Iraq and Afghanistan.[3]

The third modality for disbursing EU aid in post-conflict or fragile situations is through programmes administered through EU 'implementing partners'. The majority of this programming aid originates from geographic budget lines that are administered in line with long-term Country Strategy Papers and programming objectives. A relatively small proportion (2 per cent) originates from the Instrument for Stability – a funding mechanism that allows greater flexibility in the administration of aid and is explicitly intended to support efforts to promote stability and prevent conflict. It is also often the source of funding for so-called 'flanking' measures designed to complement CSDP operations.

While in principle all three aid modalities can support institutional reform and capacity-building, the EU's direct support for and control over the deployment of technical assistance is limited to programmable aid. In the context of EU-funded development programmes designed to build state capacity, technical assistance (TA) is commonly provided through private consultancies. Consultants are often embedded in government ministries across the public administration and rule of law sectors and engaged in discrete tasks aimed at filling capacity gaps or providing specialist advice related to broader programme objectives.

The model is somewhat different in Europe's near abroad, however, where EU programmes that draw on member state civil servants have been privileged over traditional TA based on outsourcing to private consultancies. The 'Twinning' programme, for example, involved the secondment of EU member state civil servants for one to three years to work with their country counterparts. And the TAIEX programme was developed for short-term secondments of national experts, including in the security and justice sectors, in response to requests from eligible counties.[4]

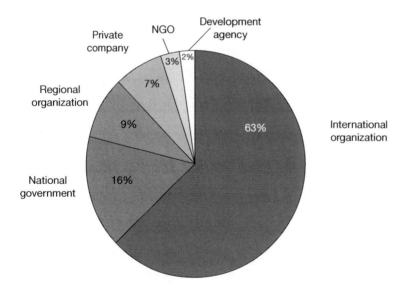

Source: European Commission, 2009b.

Note: Figures for the main 48 contractors, representing 83% of total amount contracted

Figure 8.1 European Commission implementing partners for conflict prevention and peace-building 2001–8 (not including the Balkans).

Although the Commission's practices of outsourcing the implementation of institutional capacity-building expertise has not been fundamentally challenged,[5] independent evaluations have highlighted the fact that EU TA (whether outsourced or directly administered) is most effective in contexts where there is political commitment to and a strategy for public administration reform (notably in EU accession countries) as well as basic administrative capacity (Cooper and Johansen, 2003). This is consistent with the experience of other donors. OECD DAC guidance, for instance, recognizes that:

> There are many challenges associated with providing technical assistance (TA) in fragile situations, where the conditions needed to make TA work tend to be weak or absent. This requires a long-term vision of where TA personnel fit into the change agenda, embedding TA in national structures as quickly as possible, and developing state capacity to manage and co-ordinate TA.
>
> (OECD, 2010)

Yet, despite the challenges Collier (2008) has shown that aid as technical assistance can help turn around failing states. There is, for example, statistical evidence that technical assistance in the first years of an incipient reform has a big favourable effect on the chances that the momentum of the reforms will be maintained (Collier, 2008: 114).

What is the civilian CSDP approach to state-building?

Although it shares the objective of building institutional capacity in the sectors of justice, security and public administration, civilian CSDP is not associated with the established aid 'trade' or approach to capacity-building. Rather it is seen as an instrument of crisis management and is deployed in accordance with military planning methodology. Also, although civilian CSDP missions are deployed in line with the EU the Common Foreign and Security Policy (CFSP), CSDP is not associated with the diplomatic 'trade' or with the formal 'offices' of CFSP, notably EU Special Representatives. Rather, while civilian missions have political objectives in line with CFSP they are often viewed as essentially technical instruments, especially in relation to missions with supportive capacity-building mandates. They are also most commonly associated with the domestic trades of police and justice since the majority of missions are Police or Rule of Law Missions and the majority of those deployed are recruited from these sectors within EU member states. In other words civilian CSDP is an experiment in how crisis management 'missions' can be adapted for tasks related to the (re)building of state structures through the deployment of teams of national civil servants with relevant expertise in the rule of law sectors. The *assumptions* underlying their deployment is that these instruments are better adapted to fragile contexts where state capacity is weak. This is because they are often considered to be more robust forms of technical assistance, able to effectively substitute for elements of state capacity while also building them.

Although CSDP missions can be deployed globally and in a wide range of contexts, missions deploy a similar model for institutional capacity-building by 'monitoring mentoring and advising actions'. This is also similar to the European Commission's approach in which the emphasis is typically on improving formal legal, administrative and financial frameworks through placing EU mission personnel with counterparts at 'strategic' levels. This was, for example, the model first developed for the EU Police Mission in Bosnia and Herzegovina. But it has also been deployed in the Democratic Republic of Congo and Afghanistan.[6]

Similarly the EU's largest Rule of Law mission, EULEX in Kosovo, also employs a similar approach to 'monitoring, mentoring and advising', although it is managed differently.[7]

While EU officials regularly emphasize the technical nature of civilian CSDP missions, it is also clear that the deployment of experts within this framework is politically and symbolically significant. CSDP missions not only visibly convey high-level EU political commitment to a particular country, often together with a particular vision for its development. By framing an EU intervention in terms of crisis management, they also signify the contested or fragile context in which the mission operates. Both of these symbolic aspects of CSDP interventions have been operationally significant. For example, the demand for a first EU Rule of Law mission to take place in Georgia was linked to the Georgian policy of promoting closer political relationship with EU.[8] Conversely, the CSDP Police Mission in Macedonia (EU Proxima) was effectively transformed into a series of Commission-funded projects because the Macedonian authorities believed that this represented a normalization of relations with the EU which would, in turn, enhance their accession prospects (Gourlay, 2011). In short, regardless of the operational approach that the mission takes, a civilian CSDP intervention is widely viewed by officials both within and outside the EU as qualitatively distinct from technical assistance delivered through aid instruments. Since they derive their authority from an overtly political decision-making body, the Political and Security Committee, it is also widely assumed that civilian CSDP missions have greater political clout or leverage with national elites and are therefore better equipped to influence capacity-building in politically contested contexts.

Whether civilian CSDP capacity-building missions are better suited to contexts in which capacity and commitment to reform processes are weak is far from certain, however. In some cases it is clear that an EU mission had limited or no leverage over national authorities. For instance, the limited results of both the EU's first Security Sector Reform mission in the DRC and its small SSR mission in Guinea Bissau have been explained by the mission's relative impotence in influencing domestic political conflicts (Gourlay, 2010; Clément, 2009). Others have argued that the CSDP model is not best suited to capacity-building in situations where institutional structures are extremely weak. Both the EUPOL mission in Afghanistan and the EUPOL mission in Eastern DRC have been criticized for prioritizing reforms at the strategic level. For example, in relation to EUPOL Afghanistan's intention to provide advice at senior, strategic levels, Korski argues that 'this approach shows few results in places like Afghanistan, where legal and administrative traditions are limited, corruption pervasive, the skill base low and illiteracy high, even at senior levels' (Korski, 2009: 9).

Just as technical approaches to capacity-building and reform delivered through Commission programmes were less effective outside the accession context, it is not clear whether CSDP missions manage to translate their assumed political authority into local influence in support of EU visions for reform and capacity-building. It is, however, extremely difficult to assess the relative effectiveness of the CSDP model in the absence of robust monitoring and evaluation systems. At present, the internal CSDP processes of lesson-learning are not designed to measure impact, sustainability or cost-effectiveness. Commission competence for evaluating CSDP missions is also limited to the evaluation of financial management, an area for which it remains directly responsible. Given the potential for Monitoring and Evaluation to promote institutional learning and feed into mission design, however, some within the Crisis Management and Planning Directorate and Civilian Conduct and Planning Capacity within the Council Secretariat are working on building feedback and impact-assessment mechanisms into operational evaluation and planning processes. This draws on best practice within domestic EU contexts in which resources are targeted at high-risk areas or 'hot spots'.

However, this work remains at an early stage and is, in practice, often difficult to reconcile with established military approaches to planning.

Although the EU has responded to demand for state-building assistance with aid, capacity-building programmes and civilian CSDP missions designed to harness EU technical expertise, the EU still knows relatively little about how best to engineer institutional change in dynamic and politically contested contexts. Nor is there sufficient evidence to suggest which tools work best in which circumstances. Consequently, in the absence of strong evidence-based feedback, the deployment and evolution of specific tools for crisis management are often based on assumptions about what works as well as political and financial considerations internal to the EU. The following account of the evolution of civilian CSDP traces how operational demands and the internal politics of civilian CSDP have shaped their capacities, structures and approach.

How has the civilian CSDP evolved to address its main tasks?

The roles and capacities of civilian crisis management have evolved incrementally, principally in response to operational demands. This section traces the evolution of internal CSDP capacities, showing how its approach to institutional capacity-building has been shaped in line with the military approach to capacity development.

The creation of civilian CSDP followed in the wake of the 1998 decision taken by France and the UK at St-Malo to create EU military capabilities. But the motivation for and principal drivers behind civilian CSDP were always distinct from those driving military CSDP. The British and the French were not initially in favour of the idea, but did agree that additional civilian police capacities were needed to fill a gap in international civilian *executive* policing capabilities.[9] For others, including the Swedish, Finns and Germans, civilian CSDP was in part a normative reaction to the development of military CSDP, and represented an attempt to 'round out' EU military capabilities, building on the EU heritage as a civilian power. Initially, therefore, there was no common vision about what civilian CSDP should do or be.

This is apparent from the loosely worded decision of the 1999 Helsinki European Council to establish 'a non-military crisis management mechanism to coordinate and make more effective the various civilian means and resources, in parallel with the military ones, at the disposal of the Union and the member states' (European Council, 1999). More specifically, the Helsinki European Council agreed an 'Action Plan on Non-Military Crisis Management of the EU' (European Council, 1999) that tasked the EU with developing a rapid-reaction capability for the deployment of civilian personnel in response to crisis. It requested further preparatory work to clarify the scope and purpose of this capability and to define concrete targets with respect to civilian deployments.

The EU role in civilian crisis management was therefore originally conceived as merely one of improved coordination. Consequently, the methodology for the build-up of civilian capabilities was supply-driven. The identification of concrete targets during the Portuguese Presidency drew on a 1999 stock-taking exercise which identified potentially relevant areas of member state civilian expertise. The approach also followed the military model of capacity generation involving the establishment of quantitative targets followed by pledging conferences. Specifically, the European Council in Santa Maria da Feira in June 2000 established four priority areas for capability development. These were police, rule of law, civilian administration and civil protection. In each priority area the EU then established 'concepts' clarifying operational procedures for missions designed either to substitute for local capacity or to support capacity-building in these distinct areas.

Reservations about the original approach to capability development were raised as early as 2001. For example, during its Presidency in 2001, Sweden had argued that the range of civilian expertise be expanded and that a more comprehensive approach to deploying police and rule of law expertise be considered in line with developments in the UN system, notably the recommendations of the Brahimi report. In practice, however, it was only in response to operational experience and requests for assistance that the EU adopted a broader and more flexible approach to the deployment of civilians in the framework of CSDP. This followed criticism of the limited utility of EU 'concepts'[10] and feedback from the field that stressed the need for a more integrated approach to police and rule of law deployments. For instance, although the UN had recommended an integrated Rule of Law Mission take over from the IPTF in Bosnia in 2003, this was not perceived as possible given the EU early focus on police-only missions. Practitioners also criticized the military-style approach to pre-planning for privileging structures over programming. This has since been partially addressed through the practice of more robust and inclusive pre-planning missions and, in the case of EULEX in Kosovo, the adoption of an explicit 'programming approach' to mission planning. Weaknesses in planning were, in any case, arguably inevitable given the limited resources that were dedicated to civilian mission planning. By 2005, there were only some 30 staff working on civilian aspects of crisis management in the Council General Secretariat, including capacity-building, strategic and operational planning and mission support. The EU Military Staff, on the other hand, responsible for strategic planning for military missions (alone), numbered over 140.

Paradoxically, despite the early emphasis on the development of military infrastructures and capabilities, the first years of CSDP saw a rapid rise in the number and scope of civilian operations. The first CSDP operation (EU Police Mission in Bosnia) was a police mission launched in 2003, and by 2005 the EU had launched no fewer than 10 civilian missions. These included missions to strengthen police capacity (in Bosnia, Macedonia, Palestine and the Democratic Republic of Congo), to strengthen local justice systems (in Georgia and Iraq) and to monitor disarmament and demobilization processes (in Aceh) and borders (in Moldova/Ukraine and Gaza). In response to operational demands, the EU expanded the scope of its ambitions for crisis management missions. The 2004 Action Plan for Civilian Aspects of CSDP expanded the number of 'priority areas' for civilian CSDP up to six (police, rule of law, civilian administration, civil protection, monitoring and support to EU Special Representatives) and introduced a more agile format for deployment of civilian experts. In 2005 the scope of CSDP tasks was effectively extended again, when the Council agreed a concept guiding how CSDP missions could be deployed in support of Security Sector Reform (European Council, 2005c). This was, in turn, followed by the agreement in 2006 of a Joint Council/Commission Concept guiding the provision of EU financial and technical support to Disarmament, Demobilisation and Reintegration (DDR) programmes (European Council, 2006b), which paved the way for CSDP DDR missions. Moreover, to enable the EU to undertake such a potentially broad range of monitoring and assistance tasks, the 2004 Action Plan (European Council, 2004b) called for the expansion in the range of expertise that the EU might draw on for CSDP mission design and implementation. Specifically, it called for experts in human rights, political affairs, security sector reform (SSR), mediation, border control, disarmament demobilization and reintegration (DDR) and media policy. The Action Plan also introduced the possibility that civilian experts could be deployed in support of Special Representatives, thereby providing a means to boost their role in supporting peace processes. As a means for the rapid recruitment of such diverse expertise the Action Plan incorporated a proposal introduced by the Swedish for the EU to be able to deploy tailored 'packages' of experts with a mix of expertise. These Crisis Response Teams (CRTs) can, in principle, be deployed in support of CSDP missions or in support of EU Special Representatives. Although the CRTs were declared operational in 2006, this instrument for rapid recruitment has in practice only functioned as a roster from which a few individuals have been selected to serve on fact-finding or pre-planning missions.

To summarize, EU civilian crisis management capabilities have developed so that EU missions can now deploy a wider range of experts in a range of formats. While the majority of deployed missions have been relatively small in size and have focused on providing technical assistance for a specific institution or sector (most commonly police and justice), the EU ability to deploy a large mission, including executive and supportive components has also been tested in Kosovo. The relatively large scale of the Kosovo EULEX deployment, which accounts for the steep increase in the number of civilians deployed in CSDP missions since 2008, is reflected in Figure 8.2.

EU capacity ambitions for future deployments have been made explicit in the Civilian Headline Goal 2008. This confirmed the EU ambitions to field both executive and supportive missions:

> The EU aims to have sufficient capability to deploy a small number of executive missions that substitute for local capacity, while concurrently deploying a larger number of smaller civilian missions which aim to provide technical assistance and political support to state-building and reform processes in fragile or post-conflict contexts.
>
> (European Council, 2008b)

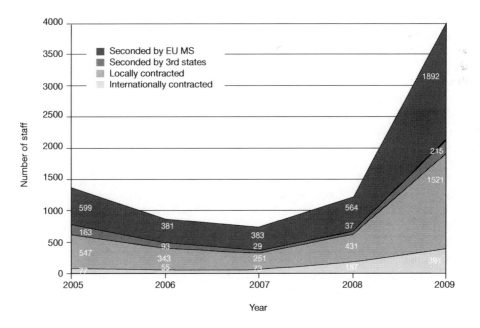

Source: Crisis Management and Planning Directorate, Council General Secretariat, 2010.

Figure 8.2 Numbers of personnel deployed in civilian CSDP missions.

Current EU capacity-development efforts focus on the greatest perceived challenge to civilian deployments, namely, attracting and recruiting sufficient numbers of suitably qualified and trained staff for missions, especially those in hostile or fragile environments. These challenges have been extensively documented (Gowan and Korski, 2009) and de Coning's comparative analysis of civilian capacity challenges clearly shows that it is only organizations that rely on secondments from national civil services that report a shortage of civilian candidates. The reasons for this are well known. As de Coning explains, most civil services do not have sufficient surplus staff to enable them to contribute civilian personnel to international missions. National departments are reluctant to release their staff, especially their best. Highly specialized categories of staff are in short supply (de Coning, 2010). Working together with EU member states, efforts are now underway to create better incentives for international deployments within national civil services and to address shortfalls in specialist capacity (for example, in security sector reform) through establishing rosters. Yet many doubt that these efforts will be sufficient and some argue that the secondment model should be complemented with increased use of personnel from 'third states,' employed using short-term contractual arrangements (Gowan and Korski, 2009).

Nevertheless the principal 'secondment' approach of the CSDP model is not in question. The EU is committed to using CSDP as a way to harness member state expertise to assist with state-building in post-war or fragile contexts. Moreover, officials within the Crisis Management and Planning Directorate attest that the model of small strategic-level 'supportive' capacity-building missions is likely to remain the most popular one. However, missions with a mandate to support peace processes through monitoring implementation of peace agreements and playing an active role in dispute resolution, notably in the EU monitoring mission in Georgia, indicate a potential growth area for civilian CSDP. Monitoring missions raise the possibility that, in future, EU civilian missions could look more like the 'political' missions deployed by the UN or other regional organizations, which have 'political process management' at their core.[11]

What are the political constraints on the use of the civilian CSDP tool?

As mentioned above, all CSDP missions are subject to an overtly political decision-making process in the Political and Security Committee. In previous research on the internal decision-making process that that resulted in the launch of civilian CSDP missions, the author has shown the importance of the role of the Presidency and of member state 'interests' in specific countries and missions in PSC decision-making (Gourlay 2011). A summary of these findings is presented in Table 8.1.

More specifically, Table 8.1 provides an overview of the source of the initial proposal to consider each civilian CSDP mission. It suggests that CSDP missions are reactive in so far as the majority of CSDP missions have been triggered by requests for assistance from the governments of affected states or international organizations engaged in crisis management. Although an invitation of the host nation or authorization by the UN Security Council are formal conditions for civilian CSDP missions and form a critical source of their legitimacy, this table is not intended simply to indicate the legal basis of the mission. In some cases, for example EUSEC in DRC, in which a letter of invitation constitutes the legal basis of the mission, the mission was clearly not triggered by a host-nation request. Indeed in this and a number of other cases, the formal invitation was received 'at the last minute'.[12]

Table 8.1 also makes clear that internal leadership or 'champions' are required for external requests to be translated into a proposal for member states to consider. In other

Table 8.1 Source of initial request and proposal for civilian CSDP missions

Mission code name and country	Host state	International organization	Non-state actor	EU member state(s)	The HR/SG
EUPM Bosnia Herzegovina		x		x (France)	
EUPOL Proxima FYROM	x	x			x
EUJUST Themis Georgia	x			x (Baltic states)	
EUPOL Kinshasa DRC	x	x		x (France/Belgium)	
EUSEC DR Congo				x (France/Belgium)	
EUJUST LEX Iraq				x (UK, NL)	
AMIS EU Supporting Action		x		x (UK Presidency)	
AMM Aceh			x	x (UK Presidency)	x
EU BAM Rafah	x			x (UK Presidency)	x
EU BAM Ukraine-Moldova					
EUPOL COPPS Palestine	x (PA)			x (UK Presidency)	x
EUPT/EULEX Kosovo		x		x	x
EUPOL RD Congo				x (Belgium/France)	
EUPOL Afghanistan	x			x (Finnish and German Presidencies)	
EU SSR Guinea Bissau	[x]			x (Portuguese Presidency and UK)	
EUMM Georgia	[x]			x (French Presidency)	

Source: Gourlay, 2011.

Note: A cross in brackets [x] indicates a relatively less critical role in initiating inter-governmental discussions on the proposal.

words, CSDP decision-making is proactively reactive, requiring in most cases high-level leadership from one or more member states. In the 16 civilian missions reviewed, the Presidency (German, Finnish, French, Portuguese and UK) played a critical leadership role in securing the decision to launch the mission half of the cases (8 missions). This highlights the importance of the rotating Presidency as a source of political will. Indeed, some officials argue that the political activism of the Presidency in the era of CSDP has been linked to the desire of member states holding the Presidency to demonstrate tangible political accomplishments during their term. They argue that the steady stream of new missions (one or two missions during each Presidency[13]) can be partly explained by the 'traditionally' proactive role of the Presidency. Officials also attest to the impact of the Presidency dynamic on CSDP decision-making. Countries that are soon to hold the Presidency are said to be more compliant and less obstructive within the PSC on the basis that this will help them secure support during their Presidency. In the words of one official, 'objections tend not to come from countries sitting on the right of the chair' (i.e. countries that are next in line to hold the Presidency).

This, in turn, raises the question of whether the implementation of Lisbon Treaty reforms which replace the rotating Presidency with a permanent President will result in a less active CSDP, with member states not driven by the occasional significant combination of pressure and opportunity to 'make their mark' during their short turn at the helm. Conversely, and unlike military CSDP, the overview suggests that while the UK and France have been important drivers of civilian missions, a number of smaller member states have played a critical role in initiating civilian missions, notably the Baltic states in the case of EUJUST Themis and Portugal in Guinea Bissau. These missions therefore reflect national geographical interests and point to the critical 'opportunity' that the Presidency system presented to member states to shape CSDP priorities.

The above overview also points to the role of the High Representative/Secretary General in transmitting requests for assistance from other international organizations. Approximately one third of EU civilian missions were triggered by a request from another international organization, and in one case (AMM) a non-governmental actor.

It is also striking that proposals for CSDP missions have never originated from assessments undertaken at the working level in the Commission or Council Secretariat, possibly with the exception of the Commission-led EU BAM Moldova mission, which is technically not a CSDP operation. Similarly, in only one case, EUJUST Themis, was the proposal for a mission first introduced by member states in CIVCOM rather than at ambassadorial level in the PSC. This informs the widespread impression amongst officials that CSDP decision-making is essentially top-down and that proposals for new missions 'cascade down' to the Council working committees and General Secretariat.

CSDP is essentially reactive in so far as CSDP decisions do not build on internal procedures which are meant to translate early warning into early (proposals for) action. Nor are they typically linked in to ongoing conflict analysis, needs assessments and planning processes of other actors, including those within the EU, which aim to identify gaps and opportunities for action. The exception of the Aceh Monitoring Mission appears to prove this rule in so far as the suggestion for a CSDP mission was introduced through high-level contacts between former President Ahtisaari (the mediator in the peace talks) and the HR/SG and UK Presidency, rather than through the Commission which had financed the peace talks or the Council situation assessment and working-group mechanisms. Similarly, there is relatively little evidence of early consultations with external actors – notably the UN – in the political, pre-planning phase of civilian operations. Only in the cases where the EU was taking over from UN missions (EUPM and EUPT/EULEX) were there extensive consultations at an early stage. Where EU civilian missions were deployed in countries where the UN had active missions (the DRC, Afghanistan and Georgia), the only mission that was significantly shaped by early consultations with the UN (in-country) was the first EU police mission in the Democratic Republic of Congo. This suggests that CSDP decision-making has often privileged the principle of 'decision-making autonomy' over the principle of 'added value' and the EU's strategic preference for 'effective multilateralism'. It also highlights the dominance of internal political drivers over considerations of external coherence of action.

By the same token, analysis reveals that PSC decision-making is not strategic vis-à-vis intended impact on the ground. There is little evidence to suggest that the pre-planning phase, including the work of fact-finding missions, provided strategic guidance based on broad-based analysis of conflict dynamics or of specific state-building processes. Rather, the pre-planning methodology was technical in its approach – seeking to take stock of institutional weaknesses in affected states and EU civilian capabilities, and proposing CSDP action where supply appeared to meet technical rather than political demand. Subsequent discussions tended to refine what was politically feasible in terms of member state contributions and to adapt mission size and mandates accordingly. Thus, arguably CSDP decision-making was insufficiently politically strategic with regard to local political dynamics in the host country. A focus on internal EU political motivations and capacities often resulted in clear indications of mission size and type but relatively vague mandates with regard to programming priorities and approach. This further suggests that intra-EU politics have privileged considerations of the mission's potential impact on CSDP over its impact in theatre – which tends to be assumed rather than explored in the political CSDP decision-making phase.

The essentially top-down and EU-centric nature of CSDP decision-making does not, however, mean that it is insufficiently strategic with respect to CSDP and EU interests. On the contrary, CSDP decision-making bodies privileged consideration of the extent to which a potential mission would benefit CSDP and EU interests. In politically contested missions such as Aceh, Iraq and Afghanistan, the controversy reflected in large part different interpretations of the strategic interest of the country for the EU and the potential benefits and risks – material and reputational – of launching an EU mission there. Indeed, the importance of perceived relevance to EU interests suggests that the CSDP tool is most likely to be deployed in the EU's near abroad or in countries of strategic/former colonial interest to a number of powerful EU states. By the same token, however, this analysis suggests that it is unlikely that the civilian CSDP tool will be deployed in the majority of fragile states or states recovering from war.

Conclusion

The capacity constraints on mobilizing civilian CSDP personnel from national civil services combined with the dynamics of decision-making within the PSC suggest that the civilian CSDP tool is likely to be deployed in relatively few cases: notably in Europe's near abroad, and beyond this only where some EU states have strong interests or where there is strong international pressure for additional EU assistance. This suggests that civilian CSDP is certainly not a tool for all places. Nor should it be, since the EU's current CSDP model of capacity-building is arguably best suited to providing 'technical' assistance at the strategic level where state capacity is relatively robust and where buy-in to the reform agenda is sincere and relatively uncontested.

Were it not for the new opportunities provided by the Lisbon Treaty reforms, this chapter would end here with a call for combining more robust consultation and analysis of specific state-building dynamics in mission decision-making and planning with greater modesty in the ambition and scope of civilian CSDP as a tool for state-building. However, the post-Lisbon reform agenda has great potential to increase the flexibility with which the EU conceives and manages its civilian interventions. Crucially, it also has the potential to empower EU Delegations so that they are better able to understand complex state-building processes and play a more nuanced role in supporting or mediating public sector reforms and tailoring EU's capacity-building assistance to local context. Opportunities provided by Lisbon could also be exploited by strengthening the political and *operational* dimensions of the offices of EU Special Representatives and EU Delegations in fragile contexts so that they can assume some of the functions of missions with mandates to provide political and capacity-building support. Empowering the function of EU political representatives and combining them with operational functions should serve to increase the geographical reach of EU support for peace processes and state-building. It would also help ensure greater continuity of EU support in fragile contexts and where CSDP missions are winding down. Conversely, strengthened EU Delegations should have greater authority and capacity to influence CSDP planning and decision-making and to support the External Action Service in developing a more strategic approach to deciding the appropriate mix of EU state-building instruments to be deployed in a specific context.

Notes

1   In Afghanistan, for instance, the EU uses a variety of aid and CSDP instruments. The Commission funds the Afghan National Police through the Law and Order Trust Fund for Afghanistan (LOFTA), which is managed by UNDP. It also manages a Rule of Law programme directly. In addition, an EU Police Mission is deployed in the framework of CSDP.

2   In Iraq, for instance, a large proportion of EC funding was channelled to the International Reconstruction Fund Facility for Iraq (IRFFI). This consists of the UN Development Group Iraq Trust Fund and the World Bank Iraq Trust Fund. Approximately half of these funds were dedicated to the development of basic services, a quarter to human development (poverty reduction, agriculture, refugees, landmine action) and a quarter to capacity-building in rule of law, elections, human rights and civil society.

3   The use of MDTFs in post-conflict contexts and the fact that a high proportion of aid is channelled to a few high-profile cases also helps explain why such a large proportion (63 per cent) of EU funding for peacebuilding is channelled through international organizations. See Figure 8.1.

4   More specifically, in 2005 TAIEX Programme operations totaled €24 million and covered a range of activities including expert missions and study visits, peer reviews and assessment missions, train-the-trainers programmes, multi-country workshops as well as legislation screening and translation activities. In 2005 alone, TAIEX mobilized more than 5,000 member state experts to participate in 1,300 missions reaching 40,000 officials from beneficiary countries (European Commission, 2005b).

5   To the extent that it has been challenged – by the European Court of Auditors in 1997 – criticism focused on the Commission's reliance on consultants for monitoring and evaluation (M&E) tasks, which the Court believed should be conducted in-house or more strictly supervised by the Commission (cited in OECD, 1998: 98). Moreover, an independent evaluation of EU funding channelled through the UN found that in many cases the UN was the only implementing partner with sufficient capacity and legitimacy to implement projects, and an evaluation of programme results found that these were equivalent to results delivered by other organizations (European Commission, 2009b).

6   However, the EU's first police mission in DRC in 2005/2006 was arguably an exception to this model since it helped establish and train an Integrated Police Unit in Kinshasa.

7   EULEX is geographically more decentralized and also operates at a regional level. It also combines a development-style 'programming approach' to designing monitoring, mentoring and advising 'actions' in the justice, police and customs sectors with an executive mandate in the justice sector.

8   Although the Commission was also funding work in this area, the Georgians pushed for a CSDP mission precisely because it was a more visible symbol of EU commitment to Georgia.

9   This was linked to events in the Balkans, notably the EU's inability to assist in establishing public order and preventing violent clashes between Kosovar Albanian and Serbian civilians in the divided city of Mitrovica (Dwan, 2002, 2004). This was highlighted by the failure of the UN to raise sufficient civilian police authorized for the UN mission in Kosovo (UNMIK). Despite appeals from the head of the UN in Kosovo, Bernard Kouchner, and the newly established HR/SG Javier Solana, less than 2,000 of the 4,178 police authorized for UNMIK were in place in early 2000. And of these only 22 per cent came from EU member states (Fitchet, 2000).

10 For instance, the planning for the first two EU police missions launched in 2003, EUPM in Bosnia Herzegovina and Operation Proxima in the Former Yugoslav Republic of Macedonia (FYROM), relied principally on the generic EU Crisis Management Concept rather than the police concepts. Moreover, the internal lessons-learned review of planning for EUPM found that the CSDP 'Concepts' served as constraints to planning, and argued that they should serve as guidance only. Rather, more emphasis should be placed on needs assessments in the form of fact-finding missions, and where these were restricted in time, consideration should be given to more flexible planning processes which would allow the EU to revisit planning estimates. The internal review also called for a greater breadth of expertise to be included in planning teams.

11 This term is used by Ian Johnstone to describe the core function of political missions (Johnstone, 2010). It was also used to describe the political functions of the head of UN peace-keeping operations by Lakhdar Brahimi and Salman Ahmed (Ahmed and Brahimi, 2008).

12 Moreover, in some cases, such as EUPOL Afghanistan, a mission goes ahead without a status of mission agreement with the host nation. The absence of a formal request by the Afghan authorities delayed the launch of the mission and, in the absence of a formal agreement, an exchange of letters constitutes its legal base.

13 For a clear illustration of the timelines of all CSDP missions to date, see <http://www.csdpmap.eu/images/chart.gif>.

9

DEFENCE INDUSTRY AND TECHNOLOGY

The base for a more capable Europe

Jan Joel Andersson

The European defence industry and technological base makes a major contribution to the security and defence of Europe. Some of the world's most advanced weaponry and defence technologies are of European origin and give Europe a cutting edge in conflict and war. Areas of European specialty are, for example, radar systems, missiles, conventional submarines, helicopters and armoured vehicles as well as a strong emerging 'homeland security' industry. The ability to develop and produce advanced weaponry and associated technologies not only ensures a degree of political independence but also provides Europe with an important tool for politico-military influence around the world. With some 700,000 people employed and a contribution of around 2 per cent of EU GDP, the economic importance of the security and defence industry to European employment and exports should not be underestimated, either.

The European defence industry and technological base is today highly capable, and in many areas world-leading, but is largely the result of past investments. Since the end of the Cold War, Europe's overall levels of defence expenditure have sharply fallen and with it investment in its defence industrial and technological base. At the same time, the costs and complexity of defence systems have continued to grow and competition in overseas markets has become ever more intense from not only the United States but also from Russia, and countries in Asia and Latin America. Given declining defence budgets in Europe and increasing competition in overseas markets from the USA and other countries' industries, the question is whether the European defence industry can continue to be the base for a more capable Europe in the future.

In this chapter, the European defence industrial and technological base (DITB) will be examined with a focus on the major actors and market trends. The efforts of the European Defence Agency (EDA) and other European institutions to establish a competitive European defence technological and industrial base and an open and transparent European defence equipment market, which are fundamental for underpinning European military capabilities, will be analysed.

The European defence industrial and technological base

Almost all countries in Europe produce arms. For reasons of national security and industrial policy many countries have chosen to support domestic defence industries. Thanks to national requirements, subsidies and protection from common market regulations, national defence industries have been able to survive across Europe. For example, Austria, Belgium and Finland all have long traditions of high-quality arms production and continue to produce arms today. The European ability to develop and produce advanced weaponry is, however, increasingly concentrated in a handful of countries. The most important of these are Britain, France, Germany, Italy, Spain and Sweden. Despite this concentration, the European defence industry and market remains fragmented along national lines, leading to inefficient duplication of programmes. It is therefore increasingly recognized in Europe that a fully adequate defence industry and technological base is no longer sustainable on a strictly national basis. Both within EU institutions and in national defence ministries there is a realization that Europe needs a European DITB that is more than the sum of its national parts.

The 26 EU Member States of the European Defence Agency collectively spent 1.67 per cent of GDP, or €194 billion, on defence in 2009.[1] Of this sum, 21 per cent, or close to €41 billion, went to investment in equipment procurement and research and development (R&D). While this sum may seem large, it is small in comparison to what the United States is spending. In 2009, the United States spent 4.90 per cent of GDP, or the equivalent of €498 billion, on defence. Of this sum, €154.5 billion went to investment on equipment procurement and R&D. The difference between Europe and the USA is even more pronounced if one considers R&D spending separately. In 2009, the EU spent €8.4 billion on R&D while the US spent €57.4 billion. In this central category, the USA outspends the EU by nearly seven to one (EDA, 2010a, 2010b).

To maintain and strengthen the European DITB, more money needs to be spent on procurement and R&D. In the European Security Strategy from 2003, the EU called for more resources for defence (European Council, 2003: 13). The call for more resources was repeated in the follow-up implementation report of the European Security Strategy in 2008. This time the EU specifically underlined that the efforts to increase European key capabilities 'must be supported by a competitive and robust defence industry across Europe, with greater investment in research and development' (European Council, 2008: 10). However, given current national budget difficulties across Europe and existing operational military commitments in Afghanistan and other places, more money for defence procurement and R&D from cash-strapped governments is highly unlikely to appear. The only solution is therefore more European collaboration and integration.

To achieve a stronger European DITB, both sides of the market in Europe need to be more integrated. European governments must align and combine their various needs in shared equipment requirements and the European defence industry must work to consolidate even further to eliminate duplication and achieve economies of scale. It is no longer economically sustainable for any country in Europe to individually set equipment and research requirements, develop them through separate national efforts and procure them through individual national programmes. This approach is also increasingly unacceptable at a time when European forces primarily serve together in multinational operations.

The European defence industry companies

Rapidly increasing costs of research and development in combination with diminished defence spending after the end of the Cold War and stiff competition in overseas export markets have led to a consolidation of the European defence industry. After a series of national mergers, the European defence industry began in the late 1990s and early 2000s an industry-led series of groundbreaking European cross-border mergers and acquisitions restructuring the aerospace and defence sector from the bottom up (Schmitt, 2000; Andersson, 2003).

Today, the European defence industry is increasingly concentrated in a handful of companies. At the highest level, global market leaders such as BAE Systems, EADS, Thales and Finmeccanica are all among the top ten arms producers in the world (SIPRI, 2010). Rapid advances in technological development have also made distinctions between aerospace, land armaments and naval systems less relevant. Defence giant BAE Systems produces the full range of armaments from artillery and fighter jets to nuclear attack submarines. Similarly, EADS produces military aircraft, electronic systems and missiles in several European countries. The exception to this trend of European and international concentration is the armoured vehicle and small arms industry which largely remains fragmented across many programmes and countries (Andersson, 2001).

BAE Systems, formerly known as British Aerospace, became the world's largest arms producer in the Stockholm International Peace Research Institute's (SIPRI) annual ranking in 2008 with arms sales reaching $32.4 billion and some 107,000 employees. BAE Systems is the result of a long series of domestic mergers and international acquisitions. Legendary names in the defence industry such as Vickers in Britain, United Defense in the USA and Bofors in Sweden have all been acquired by BAE Systems, turning the British defence giant into a global company with equal businesses in Europe and the United States. BAE Systems is currently the fourth largest provider of arms and services to the US Department of Defense and with substantial presence in Australia and South Africa (SIPRI, 2010; BAE Systems, 2010).

The second European defence industry giant is EADS (European Aeronautic Defence and Space Company NV). EADS was formed on 10 July 2000 by the cross-border merger of DaimlerChrysler Aerospace AG (DASA) in Germany, Aérospatiale-Matra in France and Construcciones Aeronáuticas SA (CASA) in Spain. The company's headquarters is in Leiden in the Netherlands and operates under Dutch law. EADS employs some 120,000 people and produces civil and military aircraft, communications systems, and missiles and satellites. Today, EADS is the seventh largest defence industry company in the world with $17.9 billion in arms sales in 2008. While still a company with a primarily European identity, EADS aims to better balance its European roots and global markets. To gain access to new markets and technology resources, EADS aims to have 20 per cent of employees and 40 per cent of sourcing outside Europe in 2020 (SIPRI, 2010; EADS, 2010).

Finmeccanica of Italy is the third largest European defence company and the eighth largest in the world. With activities in the fields of defence, aerospace, security, automation, transport and energy and with some 77,000 employees, Finmeccanica's arms sales reached $13 billion in 2008. Beginning in the late 1980s and early 1990s, the Italian defence industry underwent a series of mergers. Companies such as Agusta, Oto Melara, Officine Galileo and Breda passed into the hands of Finmeccanica, which became one of the most important industrial groups in Italy. Today, Finmeccanica has a substantial presence in Italy, the UK, and the USA, with a significant presence in France, Germany and Poland. Previously fully state owned by IRI, Finmeccanica became partly privatized in

1993 but with the Italian government still holding about 30 per cent of the shares (SIPRI, 2010; Finmeccanica, 2010).

Thales of France is Europe's fourth largest and the world's tenth largest defence industry company, with some $10.76 billion in arms sales in 2008. A result of mergers and acquisitions beginning in the late 1960s in the French defence and electronics industry, Thales is today a world leader in mission-critical information systems for defence and security, aerospace, naval and transportation systems. With operations in 50 countries and 68,000 employees, Thales is a global defence industry actor with home markets in several countries. Thales UK, for example, is Britain's second largest defence contractor, and has been selected by the UK Ministry of Defence for a number of major programmes, including the Royal Navy's future aircraft carriers. Thales was privatized in 1998, but with the French government still holding 27 per cent of the shares (SIPRI, 2010; Thales, 2010).

Behind this group of major arms producers, there are smaller but still important European defence industry companies such as the world-leading British engine maker Rolls Royce, major French naval producer DCNS, Swedish aerospace company SAAB, French fighter producer Dassault and German armoured-vehicle specialists Rheinmetall and Krauss-Maffei Wegmann. Moreover, there are several defence industry companies in Europe owned by US interests. Classic European arms producers such as Steyr-Daimler-Puch Spezialfahrzeug GmbH (STEYR-SSF) in Austria, MOWAG GmbH in Switzerland and Santa Bárbara Sistemas in Spain are all part of General Dynamics European Land Systems (GDELS), a business unit of US defence giant General Dynamics (SIPRI, 2010; General Dynamics, 2010).

In addition to traditional defence industry companies in Europe, there is a burgeoning civil security sector industry focusing on 'homeland security'. These companies typically draw on civil and dual-use technology and employ human capital and sources of innovation in universities, SMEs and companies across Europe not traditionally regarded as part of the 'defence industries'.

Organization on the European level

The European defence industry is organized in national defence industry associations. These organizations are in turn organized in the Aerospace and Defence Industries Association of Europe (ASD). ASD's members are 28 national trade associations in 20 countries across Europe, representing over 2,000 aeronautics, space and defence companies. These companies employ in total around 676,000 employees with a turnover of over €137 billion in 2008. The ASD is the result of a merger in 2004 of AECMA, EDIG and EUROSPACE to reflect the integrated nature of civilian and military technologies and the integration of aerospace and defence. In the defence areas, ASD also took over the role played by the European Defence Industries Group (EDIG) as the industry counterpart to the European national armaments directors (ASD, 2010).

In 1976, EDIG was founded as a body responsive to the National Armaments Directors (NADs) of the Independent European Programme Group (IEPG) nations (see below). The role of EDIG was to bring together and represent the European defence industry's positions vis-à-vis the policy-making bodies at the European level. In 1984, EDIG was formally recognized by the IEPG as 'the designated forum to advise the IEPG on industrial matters' (ASD, 2010). The simultaneous creation by the EU of the European Defence Agency (EDA) in 2004 meant that both the European defence industry and the EU for the first time had a unified contact point for the discussion and exchange of views on defence industrial issues.

European efforts to strengthen the base

The European Security Strategy (ESS) of 2003 made it clear that if the EU was to make a contribution to global security that matches its potential, Europe needed to be more capable. The Implementation Report on the ESS in 2008 underlined the need for key capabilities such as strategic airlift, helicopters, space assets and maritime surveillance and that these efforts had to be supported by 'a competitive and robust defence industry across Europe, with greater investment in research and development' (European Council, 2008a: 10).

There is a long history of government initiatives in Europe to promote a stronger European defence industrial and technological base, but with mixed results. In 1976, the European NATO nations established the Independent European Programme Group (IEPG) as a forum for armaments cooperation. IEPG, however, did not achieve much progress. In 1992, IEPG's functions were transferred to the Western European Union (WEU) and became known as the Western European Armaments Group (WEAG, 2005a).[2] Despite the transfer to the WEU, an ambitious proposal in 1993 to create a European Armaments Agency 'conducting the full range of procurement activities on behalf of the WEAG nations' went nowhere. In its place, but considerably less ambitious, the WEAG nations established in 1996 the Western European Armaments Organisation (WEAO) as a WEU subsidiary body to manage any cooperative armaments activities that WEAG nations would assign to it. In the end, WEAO ended up being only a small research cell managing certain cooperative defence research and technology projects between the Member States (WEAO, 2006).

With little progress in WEAG and increasingly concerned by the state of the European defence industry, the major arms-producing countries in Europe pressed ahead in various smaller ad hoc groupings outside of existing institutional frameworks. In November 1996, the defence ministers of France, Germany, Italy and the UK established the Organisation Conjointe de Coopération en matière d'Armement (OCCAR). Its aim was to provide more effective and efficient arrangements for the management of some existing and future collaborative armament programmes. The four founding governments went on to sign the 'OCCAR Convention', a treaty which came into force in January 2001. Belgium joined OCCAR in 2003 and Spain in 2005. Finland, Luxemburg, the Netherlands, Poland, Sweden and Turkey are today participating in OCCAR-managed programmes but without being members of the organization (OCCAR, 2010).

Another ad hoc intergovernmental initiative to promote European armaments collaboration was the signing of a Letter of Intent (LoI) to facilitate cross-border defence-industry restructuring by the six major European arms-producing nations, Britain, France, Germany, Italy, Spain and Sweden, in July 1998. The aim of the LoI group of countries was to remove some of the barriers to European industrial restructuring and improve equipment cooperation in the areas of security of supply, export procedures, security of information, R&T, treatment of technical information and harmonization of military requirements. A final agreement amongst the six was signed in 2000 as the 'Framework Agreement' which is a legally binding international treaty outside of the EU (Framework Agreement, 2001).

The EU was for a long time not active in discussions on the defence industry. With the defence-equipment market exempt from internal market rules for national security reasons by Article 296 of the TEC (now Article 346 of the TFEU) there was little for the Commission to do.[3] However, increasingly concerned by the deteriorating competitiveness and rapid loss of jobs in the European defence industry in the mid-1990s, the European Commission launched a series of initiatives to bring the defence industry under the internal market. In January 1996, a Commission Communication outlined the challenges facing European defence-related industries and how the sector could maintain its short-term competitiveness by subjecting it as far as possible to EU law on public procurement, intra-EU trade and the monitoring of competition with particular regard to aid. With little response from the Member States, the Commission issued another Communication in December 1997 calling for urgent restructuring in the EU defence industry and for a single market for defence products to meet increasing competition from US firms (Commission of the European Communities, 1997). These initiatives contributed to the decision by the European Council in Cologne in June 1999 to adopt a common position on the framing of a European armaments policy and strengthening the European defence industrial and technological base.

Initiatives such as OCCAR, the LoI and the communications from the EU increased pressure for more European armaments cooperation in WEAG. In November 1998, WEAG ministers agreed to a 'Masterplan' for a European Armaments Agency and to study and develop the necessary rules and regulations as well as structure and working procedures for such an Agency. By May 2002, WEAG ministers had endorsed the concept of an evolutionary process, envisaging the establishment of a European Armaments Agency as soon as all appropriate conditions were met and political consensus reached (WEAG, 2005b). However, with the increasing transfer of functions from the WEU to the EU and the establishment of the European Defence Agency in 2004, it was recognized that any future European armaments cooperation would take place within the European Union. As a consequence, WEAG ceased its activities on 30 June 2005.

The European Defence Agency (EDA)

The EDA is the central actor for EU discussions on the defence industry. The head of the agency and chairman of the steering board is the High Representative of the Union for Foreign Affairs and Security Policy, Catherine Ashton. The Steering Board acts under the authority and guidelines of the Council and is composed of the defence ministers of the 26 participating Member States and the European Commission. In addition, the Steering Board meets regularly at sub-ministerial levels, such as National Armaments Directors, Capability Directors or R&T Directors. The central role played by the EDA in discussions on the European DITB is underlined by the fact that the Agency's stakeholders are not only the Member States participating in the Agency but also the Council and the Commission as well as third parties such as OCCAR, the LoI group and NATO (EDA, 2010c).

The European Defence Agency's mission is to support the EU Member States and the European Council in their effort to improve European defence capabilities. The central role played by the EDA is pointed out in both the European Security Strategy of 2003 and the Implementation Report on the ESS from 2008. The EDA's functions and tasks are to develop defence capabilities, promote defence research and technology (R&T), promote armaments cooperation and create a competitive European defence equipment market and strengthen the European defence industrial and technological base. These functions aim to improve Europe's defence performance by promoting coherence. The argument is that a more integrated approach to capability development will contribute to future common requirements on which armaments collaboration and R&T can be built. The hope is that more collaboration will not only provide opportunities for industrial restructuring but also promote larger demand and an expanding market (EDA, 2010c).

While EDA is still a rather new agency, there have been some early results. The first major achievement was the approval in November 2005 by the Member States of a voluntary Code of Conduct on defence procurement to cover defence equipment purchases of more than €1 million where provisions of Article 346 of the TFEU (ex-Article 296 of the TEC) are applicable.[4] This decision changed the long-established practice of exempting defence procurement from cross-border competition. On 1 July 2006, the Code of Conduct became operational with the participation at that time of 22 of the 24 participating Member States of the EDA. Today, all Member States except Romania participate in the Code of Conduct, as does non-EDA member Norway. The participating Member States now publish their contract opportunities on the so-called Electronic Bulletin Board on EDA's website for suppliers across Europe to bid on. The Code of Conduct is underpinned by a reporting and monitoring system to help ensure that transparency and accountability are maintained among subscribing Member States. Complementing the Code of Conduct regime is a Code of Best Practice in the Supply Chain (CoBPSC) which extends the principle of greater competition through the supply chain to lower-tier companies and small and medium-sized companies who may not be able to bid for contracts directly but could act as subcontractors (EDA, 2008).[5]

On 20 September 2006, the EDA Steering Board also agreed on important new elements to support the development of a truly Europen Defence Equipment Market, by enhancing Security of Supply and Security of Information across national borders. Member States subscribing to the regime have committed themselves to endeavour to meet requests from fellow Member State for goods and services during an emergency, crisis or armed conflict, including from their own stocks if necessary. Agreed also were rules governing the security of classified and commercially sensitive information relating to defence procurement. Another early result was the approval of a joint R&T investment programme with the aim of developing new technologies helping to provide better protection for European armed forces. Under this programme, 20 European governments pledged a budget of more than €55 million in an effort to follow the European defence ministers' call to 'spend more' and spend 'more together' on defence research and technology. Moreover, in October 2006 the EU defence ministers endorsed EDA's long-term vision (LTV), in which joint European capability and capacity needs are defined in the timeframe 2020–30 to assist in steering European defence R&T and armament collaborations in the long term (EDA, 2006).

In a further effort to strengthen the European defence industrial and technological base, the Ministerial Steering Board of the EDA approved in November 2007 four collective benchmarks for equipment procurement and R&D (including R&T):

- equipment procurement (including R&D/R&T): 20% of total defence spending
- European collaborative equipment procurement: 35% of total equipment spending
- defence research and technology: 2% of total defence spending
- European collaborative defence R&T: 20% of total defence R&T spending.

While sound benchmarks, their practical impact is limited due to the fact that they are collective in that they apply to the total sum spent by all participating EU Member States together, and that they are voluntary since turning them into national targets is optional. Moreover, there are no timelines for realizing these benchmarks.

Collective European spending on defence equipment (including R&D) as a percentage of total defence expenditure in 2009 was 21.1 per cent and, in fact, currently exceeds EDA's benchmark of 20 per cent. However, the greatest part of defence procurement takes place on a national basis, causing inefficient duplication and overhead. Of a total sum of €32.5 billion spent on defence equipment procurement in 2009, nearly 75 per cent, worth some €24.3 billion, was allocated to national programmes.[6] Only 22 per cent, valued at €7.14 billion, and far short of the EDA benchmark of 35 per cent was allocated to European collaborative projects. Another 3.3 per cent, worth €1.09 billion, was spent on other collaborative projects.[7] European spending on defence R&T was even more nationally focused.[8] Nearly 86 per cent of the European R&T spending in 2009 went to national programmes. Only 12.8 per cent, also far from the EDA benchmark of 20 per cent, was allocated to European collaborative R&T programmes (EDA, 2010b).

The future base

Given the low levels of European investment in defence over the past decades in combination with growing costs and complexity of new systems and competition in overseas export markets, Europe needs to fundamentally reconsider how it manages its defence industrial and technological base in the future. Europe's defence sector remains fragmented at national level with some 25 different customers and regulatory frameworks. This fragmentation is a major obstacle to both intra-European defence industry collaboration and competition. It creates extra costs and inefficiencies, negatively affecting industrial competitiveness as well as the ability of Member States to equip their armed forces. With little prospect for more money for defence, consolidation and integration will be required on both sides of the market.

National governments must begin to align and combine their various needs in shared equipment requirements. These shared equipment requirements must be met by an increasingly integrated European defence industrial and technological base. This base must be able to meet the real operational requirements of future European armed forces while ensuring necessary levels of European and national operational sovereignty. At the same time, industry must be at the forefront of technology and be competitive in both European and overseas export markets. To succeed, such an industrial and technological base needs to integrate, specialize and eliminate duplication at all levels. To succeed, the 'traditional' defence industry must also be more integrated with the broader, European non-defence industrial and technological base. A major challenge for industry is to balance cooperation with, and imports from, overseas defence industries while at the same time ensuring access to foreign markets. The continuing challenge for European companies to gain access to the US defence market and managing a balanced technology exchange across the Atlantic is a reminder that it may be necessary for European countries and companies to cooperate more closely to limit dependence on non-European sources for key defence technologies and to ensure the future of the European base. Another difficult challenge for industry is how to identify centres of excellence while taking into account political requirements for a politically acceptable regional distribution of production and R&D.

The defence industry is a political industry since it depends on governments in their role as regulators, customers and investors. While more certainly can and must be done on the industrial side to further consolidate and integrate the sector, there is a key role for European governments in moving forward towards a truly European defence industrial and technological base. First, European governments need to clarify and communicate their priorities and capability needs to industry in a timely fashion. This includes identifying and agreeing on key technologies and industrial capacities that need to be developed or preserved in Europe. Second, European governments must also consolidate demand by aligning and combining future materiel requirements of their armed forces. This will require a willingness to always consider European collaboration as an option in all procurement and equipment decisions. Third, a truly European defence industrial and technological base will never emerge if EU

Member States cannot be guaranteed that increased mutual dependence for supply of defence goods and services is met by increased mutual assurance of that supply.

Most important for a strong future European DITB, however, is to increase competition in European defence procurement. Traditionally, EU Member States have heavily relied on the 'national security' exception in Article 296 of the TEC to procure the majority of their defence needs on a national basis. The decision in November 2005 to introduce a code of conduct on defence procurement that commits the EU Member States to open national defence markets, on a voluntary and reciprocal basis, to suppliers based in other Member States was an important step towards a proper European defence equipment market (EDA, 2005). However, transparency and mutual confidence must be improved if the industry is to be convinced that a level playing field really exists. Much work clearly remains in this area, but several initiatives by the Commission to clarify the conditions for the application of Article 296 (now Article 346 of the TFEU) and the EU's existing legal framework have been important to promote the process (Commission of the European Communities, 2003, 2004, 2005). These contributions also demonstrate the active and increasing role of the Commission in the area of defence industrial policy.

Nevertheless, as late as an EU defence ministers' meeting in December 2010, it was reaffirmed that achieving a European defence equipment market and level playing field is 'a strategic and long-term exercise' that must overcome strong vested interests in many countries. Sensitive issues such as Member States requiring their defence imports to be 'offset' by purchases or investments and/or hidden government subsidies to domestic companies all work against fair competition and a level playing field.

While increased competition is crucial, collaboration may at times be more appropriate. The history of armaments collaboration in Europe is mixed. Some European projects have been very successful while others have been clear failures with too much focus on national defence industrial concerns. National governments should therefore refrain from invoking any principle of *juste retour* (or 'fair shares') and let industry find the most efficient collaborative solution. Governments, however, can do more to initiate collaborative efforts by issuing shared requirements early in the process where possible applications of new technologies are explored. R&T collaborations are also easier to achieve than major equipment collaborations and the sums of money involved smaller and therefore may more easily and quickly be made available.

Conclusion

Europe has today a highly capable and, in many cases, world-leading defence industrial and technological base (DITB). The future status of this base is, however, less certain. The USA is outspending Europe nearly seven to one in defence R&D and devotes a far greater share of its much larger defence expenditures to investment in equipment procurement. If the trend continues, Europe will be unable to sustain a DITB which matches the best in the world and the European defence industry may very well be reduced to niche specialists and subcontractors to the US defence industry. While higher investments are necessary to ensure a world-leading DITB, there is little prospect for more money for defence given the state of the European economy. Europe therefore needs to spend its limited defence money more wisely by investing in joint future capability needs rather than maintaining national Cold War programmes and production lines. Europe also needs to eliminate wasteful duplication and reach an economically viable scale of production by integrating its fragmented defence market.

To achieve 'smarter' spending, European governments and industry must work together to further consolidate both the demand and supply side of the defence market. The European defence industry has shown itself ready to do so and is in many cases ahead of national governments in their thinking on the need for reform as well as on how to draw on civil and dual-use technology in their production. National governments and EU institutions must in turn show the political will and courage to make decisions at a European level about joint requirements and determine what technologies and capabilities should be preserved and developed in Europe, and what can be safely procured on the global market. With 'smarter' spending and a political willingness from national governments to follow through on the code of conduct agreement on defence procurement and a level playing field, there is a good possibility the European defence industrial and technological base will continue to serve as the base for a more capable Europe, not only now, but also in the future.

Notes

1. Denmark is not a member of the European Defence Agency.
2. In November 2000, WEAG defence ministers agreed to the accession of six new nations: Austria, the Czech Republic, Finland, Hungary, Poland and Sweden to full membership in WEAG.
3. Article 296 paragraph 1 of the TEC stated that 'any Member State may take such measures as it considers necessary for the protection of the essential interests of its security which are connected with the production of or trade in arms, munitions and war material'.
4. Article 296 of the TEC is relabelled Article 346 in the Treaty on the Functioning of the European Union (Lisbon Treaty).
5. The Electronic Bulletin Board Industry Contracts (IC) was launched on 29 March 2007 in the same interface for the Defence Contract Opportunities on EDA's website to enable Prime Contractors and other commercial actors to advertise subcontract opportunities.
6. Defence equipment procurement expenditure includes expenditure for all major equipment categories.
7. European Collaboration is defined as a subset of Collaboration: agreement by at least two EU Member States' ministries of defence for project or programme contracts. Possible non-EU partners' share in such contracts is lower than 50 per cent. Other Collaborations are all collaboration that does not fall under the European Collaboration definition.
8. Research and Technology (R&T) is a subset of R&D: expenditure for basic research, applied research and technology demonstration for defence purposes.

10

SECURITY THROUGH DEMOCRACY

Between aspiration and pretence

Richard Youngs

The EU has constructed an impressively comprehensive edifice predicated on a singular line of reasoning: politics matter to security. At a myriad of levels and within a plethora of different component parts of security policy, the EU asserts that political trends and structures within third countries have an impact on Europe's own security. And the formal line runs that it is democratic politics that are best sought in pursuit of security.

In theory, democracy is diplomacy's multi-purpose tool, with a logic for each predicament: democracy is the means of smoothing relations with antagonist governments; it is the route to deradicalizing terrorists and insurgents within states; it is the way to cement peace deals in civil conflict; it is the remedy to a host of soft security challenges, including migration, economic security and the need for greater transparency in energy supplies.

Democracy provides the political foundation necessary to sustaining all other dimensions of security. It is the bedrock judged necessary to the success of 'mainstream' security strategies. Without democracy advancing and stabilizing beyond Europe, Common Security and Defence Policy (CSDP) missions, defence capabilities initiatives, counter-surveillance and external military cooperation are all likely to stumble on the stony ground of political obstacles. EU High Representative Catherine Ashton has described the concern with human rights and democracy as the 'silver thread' running through the whole gamut of EU external strategic policy.

Or at least, that is the contention. The reality is less straightforward. Few will be taken aback by the observation that the EU has not fully lived up to its commitments to support worldwide democracy. But also pertinent is the way in which the conceptual relationship between democracy and security is understood. Of course, it is well known that there are two extremes in this debate: traditional *realpolitik* sees security and liberal values as being mutually exclusive foreign policy choices; in diametric contrast, the liberal internationalist position is that democratic ideals and self-interest go hand in hand. Perhaps unsurprisingly, most EU policy is positioned somewhere between these two extremes.

The conviction is well rooted amongst policy-makers that a more democratic world would in very broad terms be a more peaceable and prosperous one. Undoubtedly, democracy has extended roots into the European security psyche. But the logic is not quite one of 'security through democracy'. Rather, it might best be captured as: 'security alongside democracy, when other conditions are fulfilled'. Many accounts point to the way that immediate security interests discourage democracy promotion. This should hardly surprise us; nor is it especially noteworthy. The issue of greater significance is that even where one detects good logic for the EU to be interested in fostering a wider sphere of democracy over the longer term, its policies do not appear to be driven in any priority sense by a conviction that changes in political process contribute to good geostrategy.

This chapter is not about whether supporting democracy is a good thing or not. Suffice it to say that lively academic debate persists over democracy's security-enhancing worth. In each area of security concern – inter-state relations, soft security, counter-terrorism, conflict resolution – democracy's value is asserted robustly by many, but also increasingly questioned by other analysts. This chapter provides a broad-brush overview of how we might classify the EU's approach towards the security–democracy link and reflects on how this impacts on the broad panoply of traditional security initiatives.

Inter-state relations: integrative versus democratic dynamics

The security–democracy nexus can be broken down into four different strategic logics. The first proposition is that the EU is likely to be able to establish more peaceable relations with democratic than with autocratic regimes. Security aims are more likely to be achieved with states whose governments are open, accountable, predicable and transparent. This is, of course, the essence of the democratic peace theory; this is much debated but of abiding influence over security thinking.

The EU may indeed prefer that democracy prevail in those states presenting Europe with its thorniest strategic challenges. But policy focuses on other means of addressing those challenges, with democracy an apparently marginally contributing long-term goal. Democracy is not prioritized as the means of improving relations with other powers. It is supported as and when security aims in inter-state relations allow it. It is not completely absent from the EU security equation; but it is a residual, not geostrategy's core driver.

With 'states of concern', the policy is to integrate non-democratic regimes into interdependent processes and structures that constrain their behaviour. It is about 'locking them in' rather than pressing democratic reform. Interdependence is seen as a more potent security driver than democratization. This can be seen in the cases of China and Russia. In the case of the former, the strategic logic appears, if almost by default, to be one of commercial lock-in; in the case of the latter, a more political lock-in.

Recent deliberation over policy towards Russia has centred on President Medvedev's proposal for a new European security pact. European governments have responded cautiously to these proposals, grappling with the question of how best to improve relations with Moscow. Most governments are not convinced that new institutional structures would be appropriate, but have declared themselves favourable towards the idea of reconstituting a security partnership with Russia on modified terms. There seems broad agreement that the question of Russian democracy today merits little priority policy focus. The Medvedev pact would row back from the Helsinki Accords' inclusion of human rights commitments. It is essentially about state-to-state hard security cooperation. European governments may be reluctant to agree a thorough-going change to formal institutional structures, but they appear to concur with the Russian vision of a return to more traditional inter-state diplomacy.

Many EU diplomats are positively disposed towards the notion of integrating Russia into a genuinely pan-European security architecture as a means of counter-balancing Asia's rising powers. While the EU insists that it does not buy into Russia's spheres of influence argument, the actions of several member states suggest that they do have increasing sympathy with just such thinking. They have ceded a dilution of OSCE pro-democracy actions and withdrawn their support for using NATO enlargement as an incentive to democratic reform. The EU and Russia are now exploring the possibility of undertaking joint peacekeeping missions together. At the end of June 2010 Angela Merkel teamed up with President Medvedev to propose a new EU–Russia security council. Putting flesh on the bones of this idea, in October 2010 the French and German governments proposed a new EU–Russian Political and Security Committee.

After the Russia–Georgia conflict of 2008, the focus on democracy was reduced in both these countries. For one group of EU member states, the concern after the Russian invasion of South Ossetia was not to risk undermining Georgian national unity by pressing President Mikhail Saakashvili hard to rein in his semi-authoritarian peccadilloes. Georgia received a huge injection of donor funding after 2008, just as Saakashvili's administration changed its rallying call from democratization to 'modernization' and the president introduced reforms many saw as paving his way into a powerful prime-ministerial office after the end of his term in 2012. For another group of states, the lesson drawn from the conflict was the need to engage Russia on early-warning mechanisms and regional cooperation, entailing an even further sidelining of criticism over Russia's internal political trends. The European Union Monitoring Mission almost seems to be policing the post-invasion borders on Russia's behalf, stopping Georgian incursions into South Ossetia while Russia denies it access to the enclave. EU officials say that their stress is on the humanitarian dimension and maintaining strict operational neutrality, rather than the mission getting 'dragged into' things like civil society support.

There are important and valid reasons for resurrecting such cooperation with Russia, after a period of prickly tension between Moscow and several European governments. But what is of relevance here is that there is little evidence that current security policy debates are driven by a concern to see Russia return to the path of democratization. The focus is on discussing a whole range of potential new means of practical cooperation with Russia. The EU perceives Russia as a necessary partner for key immediate global and regional security aims. An EU–Russia Modernization Partnership has been agreed that does formally include a focus on the rule of law. But the centre of gravity in EU policy has shifted towards assuaging Russia's feeling of victimization, and away from the desirability of its democratization.[1] Most think-tank advocacy now pushes in the same direction, recommending collective EU–Russian problem-solving and greater 'accommodation' with Russia's de-democratization.[2]

In the case of China, European security has been clearly led by a commercial logic – and indeed, some might feel, emasculated by economics. China might be conceived of as today's most vital laboratory for a test of the democratic peace hypothesis. Its results are less than conclusive. European diplomats may be genuine in their assertions that over the longer term a more democratic China would be preferable. But this is not a desire that informs today's policy decisions in any tangible manner.

The predominant view is that China's power means that it is hardly worth trying to support democracy in this case; that the chance of making any impact is so slim that there is far more to lose than to gain from attempting to prompt a loosening of the Chinese Communist Party's political control. European efforts to support reform in China are weakening. Support for village elections has been discontinued. The EU–China Legal and Judicial Cooperation Programme limits itself to the issues of commercial law that are of direct interest to European investors. A number of European NGOs have even been excluded from the EU–China human rights dialogue. European governments have been reluctant to criticize repression against the Uighur Muslim minority; they stay clear of the Charter 08 pro-democracy movement; and all now formally recognize Chinese sovereignty over Tibet. The EU arms embargo has not prevented increased weapons sales to China. The Chinese leadership has cancelled summits and meetings with European governments without sanction (House of Lords, 2010).

China appears to disprove one of the central pillars of the democratic peace, namely that democracy works well in security terms because it generally spurs economic interdependence. In China's case, of course, political reform has not been necessary to tie the People's Republic into mutual dependency with Western economies – seen in heightened form in the context of the current economic crisis. What is striking is that EU policy is led very much by trade and commercial concerns, with a rather easily-made assumption that the more economic lock-in that can be achieved, the better for security. The erstwhile support for China's accession to the World Trade Organization – and this body's plethora of limiting rules – can be seen as the epitome of such reasoning. One expert detects here 'an overly-expansive Commission-led agenda', largely bereft of political focus (Small, 2010). What is lacking is any far-reaching strategizing on how China's internal politics relates to such policy trends.

Additionally, beyond its great power diplomacy, the EU pursues many policies of counter-balancing. While these entail deepening partnerships with some notable middle-ranking democracies, such as Indonesia, Mexico, South Africa and South Korea, they also propel strategic alliance-building with a range of dictatorships. In broad terms, the EU has rejected the notion of geostrategy being based on an alliance of democracies. It might be felt that this is a wise judgement. But it has also gone hand in hand with a dilution of European contributions to consolidating new democracies that might be expected to be more strategically significant in the future. Not only is the EU sceptical about getting emerging democracies signed up to multilateral democracy promotion, but it is pulling back in its own democracy-support efforts as part of a strategic logic that accords such powers a more leading role in their own respective regions.

Of course, in all this there may be an undeclared, hyper-Machiavellian, well-worked strategy of keeping 'rival powers' weak by actively seeking to deprive them of high-quality consolidated democracy. More probably, the concern must be that the EU is simply failing to look to the long term. Many would predict that over the longer-term dangers may lie in the possible fragmentation of states such as Russia and China and the prospect of nationalistic expansionism in a second-tier group of emerging powers that may prove to be the states of most serious concern by mid-century. It is unlikely that pure alliance-building will suffice to temper such concerns.

The 'single issue' syndrome

Such are the policy balances at play in the EU's general strategizing towards important powers. But what about the approach towards more specific policy issues? This represents the second strategic logic, which holds that democracy should help sustain diplomatic gains made in relation to particular short-term security objectives. The evidence suggests that, in practice, in dealing with individual issues of concern the EU's policy is to negotiate trade-offs and deals on the particular matter in question in a way that deliberately keeps the democracy agenda separate. The EU suffers from what might be called 'single issue syndrome'.

Several illustrative examples of this malady can be mentioned. One is policy towards the Iranian nuclear programme. The EU's position has been that the nuclear and democracy issues should be kept separate. Iran's democratization is certainly a genuinely held European aspiration. But while talks over the nuclear issue proceed, the main concern has been that pressure on the regime for human rights improvements will make it feel more threatened and thus more determined to proceed with its nuclear programme. The EU–Iran human rights dialogue was effectively wound up in 2004. Many new carrots have been put on the table, including promises of aid, trade preferences and all kinds of social exchanges, as an incentive for Iran to relent on its nuclear programme. But these have not been linked to resumed cooperation on human rights.

Diplomats are invariably minded to point out that Iran's opposition forces also defend the Islamic Republic's right to develop nuclear capabilities. This appears to be a more potent influence over policy than the fact that the opposition has called for more harmony and flexibility in the way that Iran manages its relations with the West. The trade-off between the democracy and nuclear agendas has become more apparent since Iran's 2009 elections. As protests have raged in Iran since these elections the EU has offered an implicit trade-off: no pressure on a reeling Iranian regime in return for the latter compromising on its nuclear programme. The EU did not even extend its list of visa bans on Iranian officials after the violence of 2009. Policy-makers admit to a lack of deep reflection on how complex the relationship is between Iran's internal political trends and the prospects of a satisfactory nuclear deal.

Another case of 'single issue syndrome' relates to the security impact of climate change. Many European diplomats are entirely candid in arguing that pressure on human rights and peace-building is and will be forgone in order to get the maximum number of countries signed up to internationally agreed climate change commitments. Indeed, some even argue that democratization in many developing states would make it harder for regimes to make the concessions necessary to cut carbon emissions (Shearman and Smith, 2007). The growing feeling that liberal democracy is irrelevant to these kind of existential problems may herald a return to elitist visions of technocratic experts running the international system.

A further example is the parcelled-up approach to energy security. The EU espouses an approach to energy security based on rules-based governance norms. Not only in its immediate periphery but further afield too, the EU seeks to export its own internal energy market rules that touch upon a whole host of good governance standards. In practice, energy questions and deliberation on democracy support are simply not linked up within EU policy-making. This is not simply a matter of pointing to the obvious fact that energy deals are done with autocrats. It relates also to the way in which the EU conceives the relationship between economic and political power. In several countries, such as Russia and Iran, it is clear that the conjoining of economic and political power causes profound problems for energy security. Yet the main thrust of EU policy limits itself to improving governance standards in other countries' energy sectors in a way that is ring-fenced from systemic-level political problems and considerations (Youngs, 2009).

Finally, the management of migration. Most European politicians would rank migration, especially illegal or irregular flows of people into Europe, as representing a more immediate 'security threat' than traditional 'hard' strategic questions. European policy documents insist that support for more open politics in developing states is a central pillar of immigration-reducing strategy. In practice, it is not. Offered a choice between spending €100 million on a democracy initiative or on measures to boost physical controls on migration flows, few European politicians would have the long-term foresight to plump for the former. Democratization is, if anything, feared as a possible trigger of greater, not reduced, illegal migration. Southern European states frequently make the argument that they have to be more cautious about political reform in North Africa because they receive more migrants from this region than do northern EU member states. If they were true to EU rhetoric, their geographical proximity to North Africa should give them greater, not lesser, reason to see democracy prevail in Morocco, Algeria, Tunisia and Egypt. In October 2010 the EU granted the Libyan government an extra €50 million to beef up the country's border controls and surveillance technology, and stem migration into Europe. Colonel Gaddafi requested such payment as a means, in his delicate and delightful phraseology, to ward off the instability of a 'black Europe'. European leaders seem more mindful of this 'security' threat than they are of anything emanating from Gaddafi's brutal repression of his own population.

Counter-terrorism and deradicalization

The third logic: since the mid-1990s, the EU has espoused the notion that democratic reform is the best means of tempering the radicalization that underpins international terrorism. While this strategic logic was invested with greater commitment and urgency in light of the terrorist attacks in Washington, Madrid and London, it is now losing force as a driver of EU security policy. It was always unduly simplistic to paint democracy as a panacea for radicalization; but now the pendulum appears to have swung back to the other extreme, where democracy support in the Middle East and South Asia is seen as either irrelevant or in some instances prejudicial to effective counter-terrorism.

Several European governments do fund a smattering of initiatives that link human rights to counter-terrorism (CT). The UK has funded local human rights organizations to monitor security services' treatment of terrorist suspects in Jordan. Several European governments fund rule of law programmes in the tribally administered areas of Pakistan. But such initiatives are relatively few in number and of limited scale. Their aim is not so much to support those seeking fundamentally different types of political system in the Middle East and Asia, but more modestly to include some degree of focus on human rights within beefed-up state-to-state counter-terrorist cooperation.

The 'reformist' strand in European policy is generally equated with exporting and fostering 'moderation'. This is entirely laudable but is not synonymous with – nor does it necessarily involve – supporting democratization. European governments run programmes on training moderate imams; but they do little to break the links through which authoritarian regimes promote more radical imams to senior positions. Dialogue forums and initiatives such as the Ana Lindh Foundation and the Alliance of Civilizations carry out much admirable work but have declined to build a focus on democracy into their funding initiatives. Muslims complain that such initiatives are not designed to talk about human rights on the basis of a common Europeanness, but rather entail Christian or secular majorities using human rights discourse as a means of restraining Muslim identity. Such approaches conflate and confuse CT and the challenges of integration.

EU positions towards political Islam have evolved. But the increasing vibrancy and professionalism of Islamist opposition forces across the Middle East are judged to be a reason for putting the brakes on support for democracy, more than it is seen as an opportunity for fostering effective alternatives to autocratic regimes. European rhetoric now routinely insists that Islamists must play a full political role. Yet, Islamists are still excluded from European support programmes and the EU declines to defend Islamists rounded up by the security forces of authoritarian regimes. Despite plentiful rhetoric to the contrary, European governments still adhere to a nervous and static view of political Islam: they focus on what short-run negative effects might occur if democracy allowed Islamist parties to assume power far more than on how the democratic process might over time contribute to encouraging moderation.

European governments have extended support and cooperation to countries such as Pakistan, Algeria and Egypt to boost border controls and surveillance measures. Vastly increased amounts of weapons are now channelled from Europe to the security forces of these countries in the name of cooperation on CT. One commentator argues that the internal–external link in CT policy is seen most clearly in member states such as the UK exporting their own new surveillance technology to dictatorial regimes in the Middle East and Asia (Kampfner, 2009: 200, 209). The British Parliament's Human Rights Committee has expressed concerns over the depth of UK security cooperation, in particular with Pakistani and Saudi Arabian security services, sitting uneasily with rights commitments in these countries (House of Commons, 2009). The European Parliament regularly criticizes the use of EU development aid for equipping non-European security forces. A CT clause now competes with the democracy clause within EU external agreements. With 'ally' regimes the policy is to equip and train rather than chivvy elites into allowing democratic reform.

EU governments have to date agreed three major packages of counter-terrorist measures that all focus primarily on strengthening law enforcement and monitoring measures. These formal counter-terrorist strategies mention the importance of supporting reform outside the Union, but are bereft of concrete initiatives designed to contribute to this end. Budgets for beefing up 'homeland' defences vastly exceed those projecting European reform and counter-radicalization efforts outwards. Only a small proportion of the resources made available under Contest 2, the UK's CT strategy introduced in March 2009, are allocated for counter-radicalization activities outside Europe (Her Majesty's Government, 2009: 4). Deradicalization initiatives have proliferated mainly *within* the EU's own borders, particularly in the UK, Spain and France. Counter-terrorist policy within Europe is gradually assuming a more forward-looking focus on the roots of radicalization, and some of the more draconian civil rights restrictions introduced in the early 2000s are being repealed. Paradoxically, if there is a shift in *external* policy it is if anything in the opposite direction.

The foreign policy input to the CT dossier remains limited. In mid-2010 a new EU committee was created comprising member state representatives working specifically on internal security. European Union CT coordinator Gilles de Kerchove has endeavoured to keep the focus on the importance of external democracy support, but has struggled to influence other departments to move policy in this direction. Experts agree that the external dimension of CT strategy has remained hardly visible, that the Commission has stepped back from pushing a common strategy in this area and that the focus is on the still-lagging technical implementation of internal CT agreements. This author is struck by the fact that when asked about the link between CT and human rights, European diplomats answer with reference to US abuses at Guantánamo Bay and Abu Ghraib far, far more than to repression in the Middle East.

A major security concern in recent years derives from a spate of kidnappings of European citizens by radical Islamist groups. On such occasions, several member states – in particular Spain, Italy and France – have had no qualms about cutting deals with radicals. Some basic principles have gone out of the window when European governments have been faced with their citizens being taken hostage by Islamic groups. Several member states have increasingly resorted to paying ransom money as the frequency of kidnappings of European citizens has increased. On several occasions they have even pressed authoritarian regimes to release terror suspects as the price for the kidnappers to free their hostages. Such responses to the horrible moral dilemma of hostage negotiations might be perfectly understandable; but these episodes have provoked complaints from Middle Eastern governments that European double standards are giving further incentive to radicals on their soil.

The EU's downplaying of political structures contrasts with debates over trends in the Middle East. Analytically there is increasing breadth of agreement that it is political repression that lies at the heart of what appear to be religious tensions in this region. The notorious protests across the Muslim world against the Mohammed cartoons published in Denmark were orchestrated by regimes, not Islamist parties. Arab regimes have done a much better job of wiping out secular opposition parties than the Islamists. Islamist parties have organized themselves a lot better to navigate the limited political space available; that is why they have attracted support, rather than because of a wave of pious purity. Middle Eastern regimes are still playing divide-and-rule over the Islamist and secularist constituencies, with the international community playing along. One of the main complaints of radicals in Saudi Arabia is the amount spent by the regime on foreign military equipment. All these features speak to profoundly political machinations. Many other trends portend the same: European security policy risks underplaying all such political considerations and overplaying religious tolerance as the supposed panacea in Western–Muslim world relations.

Conflict

A fourth and final strand of policy is the commitment to support democracy as part of peace-building strategies in conflict scenarios. Democracy-building funding initiatives are now undertaken in all situations where the EU jointly or member states individually intervene in peace support missions. Democracy is presented as needed for installing and maintaining peaceable politics between warring factions. It is seen as the means of combating insurgencies, bringing fighters into mainstream political processes. Once again, however, many aspects of EU policy belie such reasoning. Advancing democracy is rarely the motive per se of peace-support interventions, but has been described as more of a 'retrofitted rationale' introduced quite separately from the factors seen as causally related to conflict (Mitchell, 2007: 36).

Space precludes a detailed overview of European democracy-building programmes in situations of fragility. It suffices to register that such initiatives have grown in scale and comprehensiveness in recent years. Most member states now have dedicated stabilization (or similar) units charged with engaging on the underlying politics of civil conflict. Growing shares of global democracy assistance are spent in conflict scenarios and invested with clear peace-building relevance. For several years now, exhaustive attention has been paid to ensuring that the large amounts of standard development assistance spent in fragile states incorporate elements designed to assuage grievances through increased political participation. The Extractives Industry Transparency Initiative (EITI) is the best known of such efforts to link security, development and governance reform in a more seamless fashion.

However, several reports have charted the political dimensions of EU conflict interventions and all conclude similarly that support for democratic institution-building is of limited effect. In all cases where the EU has intervened in situations of fragility, the autocracy-derived drivers of conflict persist and have scarcely abated in their intensity. A long-awaited Action Plan ostensibly oriented to participative approaches to peace-building remains stalled.

A number of features prevail in EU interventions that often rub uneasily against the ostensible commitment to democracy.[3] The main priority of such engagements is crisis management. The EU has made most progress in improving its contribution to short-term crisis management, investing particular attention to civilian–military linkages. Democracy-building efforts have increasingly been left behind relative to this priority focus. Closely linked to this is the fact that in many conflicts counter-insurgency now represents the overwhelming bulk of policy effort. The objectives are phrased in terms of defeating insurgents far more than building democratic states.

Another feature is the focus on mediation aimed at peace deals rather than reform of political processes as such. The EU's engagement follows a similar pattern across different conflicts, and tends to limit itself to mediating a ceasefire; sponsoring a reconciliation process; and then funding preparations for elections, but without following through to ensure that such polls are carried out in a free and fair manner. Each stage entails seeing the autocratic regime as part of the solution, rather than part of the problem (Haine, 2009: 467). The experience of Iraq, where the absence of a basic political accord has militated against institution-building and stability, has encouraged agencies such as the UK Department for International Development (DfID) to shift their focus to helping craft 'political settlements' – not an approach that is necessarily anti-democracy, but one which turns the primary policy attention away from competitive politics.

Under the Lisbon Treaty attention has centred on the setting up of a mediation unit. In terms of local, third-country political structures, this approach entails 'working with what there is'. Donors now rely increasingly on 'traditional' structures, such as village councils. Talk abounds of increased support for and recognition of 'indigenous concepts of reconciliation' informed by anthropological accounts of difference. In conflict situations, donors like DfID talk of the need for 'responsive government' without stipulating whether they see democracy as most likely to provide such responsiveness.

And the main thrust of funding initiatives is towards building state capabilities. What the EU really judges to be most necessary to stabilizing fragile polities is a strong, rather than a democratically accountable state. One lesson firmly learned is that elections should not be held before institutional structures are strengthened. The logic is to press political elites and/or insurgents to conclude a power-sharing peace deal and then broaden participation and accountability over the longer term. The reality is that this longer-term aspiration is invariably and indefinitely deferred. Most funding in conflict states still goes on high-impact, state-focused development projects rather than on less noticeable, less tangible programmes aimed at long-term efforts to modify the patterns of decision-making. It is recognized that many such state-enhancing programmes have shored up repressive leaders in the search for quick, quantitative measures of stabilization (ODI and Netherlands Ministry of Foreign Affairs, 2010: vii).

Conflict resolution and fragile state policy is an area of security strategy where the formal design of and thinking behind European policy have certainly evolved into impressively sophisticated approaches. Agencies such as DfID have elaborated a range of strategies that assess carefully the complex nature of political processes effecting conflict. But they equally acknowledge that implementing such holistic reform-oriented thinking remains difficult and that donors' state-building efforts have 'tended to strengthen or ignore predatory elites', undermining long-term state capacity (DfID, 2009: 9 and 15). The concern with 'joining up' different departmental processes, within the bafflingly complex multi-actored bureaucratic processes that have now emerged in the field of conflict stabilization, risks diverting attention from some of the straightforward political issues that emanate from the nature of unstable regimes (Teuten and Korski, 2010).

The risk is that the pre-eminence of these guiding principles means that reform-oriented initiatives can often contradict their own premises. Much formal state-building has ended up serving an intimate cabal of the international aid complex and local elites, to the detriment of democratic vibrancy at the community level (Ghani and Lockhart, 2008). Support for power-sharing solutions invariably ends up being used 'as an informal strategy to circumvent democratic obligations' (Mezzera, Pavici and Specker, 2009: 36). The security sector reform (SSR) brief has so far hardly taken concrete form in trying to check militaries' political power. Many initiatives carried out under the SSR banner look like fairly standard defence cooperation programmes, with few tangible reform aspects. Growing support for traditional forms of justice and local militias can sit uneasily with international human rights standards (Scheye, 2009: 36). One of the leading experts on state-building has recently gone as far as suggesting that the EU's democracy discourse is entirely misleading: the fact that European policies support the strong state and rule of law rather than bottom-up liberal pluralism reveals that the concern is really with 'managerial control' and restricting conflict states' de facto sovereignty (Chandler, 2010).

Conclusion

These four security logics overlap in practice. Separating them out here helps simply to demonstrate analytically the multi-faceted reasoning behind the democracy–security linkage. And it assists in identifying the limitations to democracy-enhancing policy efforts in different areas of security. These limitations remain significant. The senior kernel of hard security diplomats, defence specialists and armed forces personnel remains largely unconvinced by the democracy agenda. This agenda is promoted mainly by other centres of EU policy-making with a more indirect purchase on security policy. Democracy has found its place within conflict policies, at the levels of conflict prevention, peace support missions and post-conflict strategy; but it is not the all-encompassing, primary or guiding logic of CSDP missions and other interventions. In their counter-terrorist and soft-security thinking, European diplomats still need to give substance to the ostensible recognition that stability and the status quo are not synonymous.

There has been a move away from the most directly instrumental security thinking on democracy: regime change as a means of installing more pro-Western leaders. Today the focus is ostensibly more on the process of democracy. At the same time, much of diplomacy in practice still hinges on perceptions of the nature of particular leaders rather than the adequacy of underlying political process in dealing with social grievances. This leader focus today generally militates against democracy support. Some experts fear that the fall-out from the Iraq debacle has undermined the whole general conviction that Western interests are served by strong commitment to helping spread democracy (Whitehead, 2009).

None of this is to suggest that democracy is not at all supported. EU diplomats paint these trends in a positive light: we have, they insist, stepped back from our 1990s missionary zeal for democracy and now have a correct balance in understanding the advantages and problems of democracy. Democracy is supported through technocratic, functional cooperation because this is compatible with short-term, collective problem-solving on security issues.

The EU may have moved away from overly effusive interventionism towards an opposing extreme of classic nineteenth-century 'masterly inactivity', content to let political pathologies weaken potential rivals – notwithstanding all its rhetoric about positive-sum security enhancement.

And the logic is increasingly muddied: when the EU does give substance to its democracy commitments, it is often despite, not because of security concerns. Encapsulating these overarching trends, David Cameron has made an early judgement in his government's incipient foreign policy: the UK is to preserve status through withdrawing from seeking to 'do good abroad', while striking new alliances with emerging powers and fighting to retain its formal top-seat representation in international bodies (Stephens, 2010). Arguably, this turns the declared EU security logic on its very head. Support for democracy provides not the central driving force of the EU's security efforts, but fills the spaces left by other strategic policies. Most would say it is an extremely heroic assumption which holds that the combination of technical cooperation with collective problem-solving really constitutes tangible democracy promotion to the extent that diplomats claim. In explanatory terms, this ought to turn our attention to the role of varied rationalist calculations that persist alongside the constructivist-identity logic often said to form the heart of common European security approaches.

In short, democracy is not the alpha and omega of European security, but a secondary desideratum. European allegiances to democratic norms today exhibit more pusillanimous contrition than geopolitical conviction. The EU's commitment to supporting democracy as part of its overarching security policies can best be described as passively aspirational rather than operationally constitutive of those strategies. In this sense, EU security policy often resembles the traveller set on a Western destination who sets off to the East – but is still convinced that eventually he will come round to his journey's end.

Notes

1   For an overview of current European debates on the Medvedev proposals, see Vaquer (2010).
2   For one recent example, see Krastev and Leonard (2010).
3   Key examples of such reports and assessments are: Grevi, Helley and Keohane (2009); Anten (2009); Commission of the European Communities and Soges SpA (2008); and Faria and Ferreira (2007).

11

SECURITY AND DEVELOPMENT IN EU EXTERNAL RELATIONS

Converging, but in which direction?

Karen Del Biondo, Stefan Oltsch and Jan Orbie

The nexus between security and development policies has received great attention in recent years from policy-makers and academics alike. However, the notion of a correlation between security aspirations and economic development is not new at all: the European integration process is based on the idea that common economic development increases the security of Europe. New, however, is the intensity and the form of cooperation, coordination, coherence or harmonization aspired to by the two policy fields that used to follow rather separate policy objectives – while indeed development aid all too often was granted following the geo-strategic or economic interests of the donor.

The main assumption of the so-called security–development nexus is that both policy areas are mutually enhancing. Situations of severe insecurity – like armed conflicts – hinder economic development and destroy development investments; and lack of development – like severe poverty (or rather unequal access to resources) – might create causes for insecurity or feed into conflicts. Yet, the actual causal connections between development and security are far from being satisfactorily investigated, and thus, the characteristics and practical consequences for policy actors like the European Union (EU) remain 'elusive and disputed' (Büger and Vennesson, 2009: 4). Many controversies result from the fact that, as Büger and Vennesson point out, 'the notions of development and security are broad and often ill-defined and the link between them can refer to many different, potentially contradictory, ends and means'. This is confirmed by research by Youngs, who found 'notable discrepancies over basic definitions of what constitutes "development" and what constitutes "security"' in interviews with EU policy-makers (Youngs, 2008: 426).

Thus, the next part of the chapter provides a brief conceptual clarification of the security–development nexus along two dimensions:[1] (1) in relation to policy *instruments*, development and security might tend either to diverge or to converge, when they are perceived as having either compatible or incompatible toolboxes; (2) in relation to policy *goals*, there might be a primacy of traditional development or of security policies. Taking these two dimensions into account, the subsequent parts of this chapter provide an overview of the security–development nexus in EU external relations by looking at the EU's policy declarations and institutional reforms and at recent EU initiatives and activities. We conclude that while the security and development spheres seem to be converging (dimension 1), there are also indications that security considerations are increasingly taking priority over the objectives of development aid (dimension 2).

Conceptualizing the security–development nexus: interconnected, but how?

Security approaches development: the two dimensions of human security

The question of what is seen as relevant to security policies has changed significantly during the last two decades. After the Second World War, the predominant concept for security policy was national security. Security policy had to secure the state from military threats by military (and diplomatic) means. Following the perception that, in addition to power-political threats, insecurity could also have economic, social, cultural or environmental causes, security policy concepts were extended and the spectrum of instruments for security policy to de-escalate crises had to be broadened – including civilian strategies. However, the state remained the reference object for security. This is problematic in so far as states themselves are among the biggest threats to human beings and a secure state does not necessarily guarantee or provide security for its residents.

The concept of human security meets these concerns. Human security is related to the security of people instead of states and defines security as the absence of severe threats to various areas of individual human survival. Individual human beings perceive various different threats to their security, such as losing their job, not having enough food, getting ill or being affected by violence or crimes. These threats now get into the focus of security-related policies. Hence, the necessary tools to achieve security must be enhanced as well, including mainly civilian and preventive measures.

It is worth mentioning that the concept was coined from a development perspective, namely by the UNDP Human Development Report (HDR), *New Dimensions in Human Security*, in 1994. The HDR defined human security in an all-embracing and quite unspecific manner as 'freedom from fear' (meaning freedom from direct threats to survival) and 'freedom from want' (encompassing economic threats, health issues, etc.) (UNDP, 1994). According to these two basic concepts, two main approaches to human security emerged in the course of the discussion during the 1990s: a narrow concept of human security, being limited to security from all kinds of violence, as in wars, violent conflicts, crimes or human right violations; and a broad concept, encompassing economic risks, health and social security, environmental risks, questions of education and even mental well-being and self-development.

In principle, the EU addresses both approaches to human security. In regard to the narrow concept – or the 'protection dimension' of human security (McFarlane and Khong, 2006) – the EU is an increasingly important actor in the protection of civilians in violent conflicts, which played a significant role in the development of the CFSP. Accordingly, the EU participates actively in the fight against land mines and small and light weapons, combats impunity from grave violations of human rights and played a large role in the creation of the International Criminal Court. The broader approach – the development dimension – of human security is pursued by the EU through adding it as an underlying principle of external assistance. For example, the EU Consensus on Development takes a 'multi-dimensional' approach to poverty, including issues of human security (European Union, 2006: 3).

Development approaches security: securitization and conflict sensitivity of development

Concepts of development policy have experienced a similar broadening in recent years. Actually, one background for effective development policy can be seen in the Marshall Plan, which was, in Marshall's own words, directed against 'hunger, poverty, desperation, and chaos', which as Büger and Vennesson (2009: 7) note, 'is as good a definition of fragility as any'. Nevertheless, development cooperation initially focused on economic growth of partner countries – trying to trigger a trickle-down effect to increase the wealth of the population. Yet, this effect often failed to appear. In addition, connecting development policies to geo-strategic interests of the donors in the Cold War context rather undermined the development efforts and increased insecurity.

Hence, development concepts were gradually broadened and deepened. On the one hand, the referent objects shifted from nations to sub-state actors, communities, grassroots organizations or even households. On the other hand, focus issues were gradually expanded from economic growth over basic needs concepts, gender issues, environmental sustainability, human rights, good governance and civil conflict transformation to its recent objectives: the Millennium Development Goals. Both evolutions can be equally observed in the EU's development policies. The Cotonou Partnership Agreement (2000) considers 'social and human development' as an area of support and mentions issues such as gender, sustainable development, human rights, democratization and good governance, security and the MDGs.

The concept of human development focuses on individual human beings in development cooperation and emphasizes the diversity of human needs and general improvement of human life in addition to pure economic growth.[2] This conceptual shift anticipated the theoretical and ethical shift that later was repeated by the human security discussion emerging out of traditional national security concepts. Like human security, the concept of human development focuses on people rather than on states and aims at the development of the potential of people and the enlargement of choices and well-being.[3]

Securitization of development issues might be in the interest of both security and development actors. From the development perspective, securitization would raise legitimate development objectives on the political agenda. Linking development issues with security concerns was often supposed to redirect security funds – such as the peace dividend after the Cold War – to development policy. This partly explains why the EU member states agreed to increase their spending of Official Development Assistance (ODA) following the 11 September terrorist attacks (Santiso, 2002). From the security perspective, securitization of development policy could be used to legitimize a shift of development objectives to areas of severe insecurity and to use development funds as well as the development toolbox to primarily reach security policy goals. Several commentators have warned against the development impact of such an evolution, also in EU external relations (e.g. Hadfield, 2007).

The existence of a general correlation between poverty, instability and violent conflicts is undisputed. Nevertheless, the real causality of the linkage is yet to be fully analysed (Tschirgi, 2006: 47; Tschirgi *et al.*, 2010: 2; Büger and Vennesson, 2009: 25). There is plenty of evidence that violent conflicts are more likely to occur in areas with low levels of economic development and a high level of inequality than in more prosperous regions. It can also be observed that most wars happen in the poorest regions of the world. However, poverty does not necessarily lead to conflict – it is only one of many factors (Tschirgi *et al.*, 2010: 3). It is equally clear that development policies can be undermined by insecure environments and that conflicts destroy development investments (Stewart, 2004: 5). On the other hand, a strict focus on development goals can also increase insecurity, since development 'is transitional by definition and therefore gives rise to instability' (Tadjbakhsh and Chenoy, 2006: 99). As overall growth may fail to improve life for the poorest groups, development might increase inequality. In the development community it is furthermore widely acknowledged that development cooperation and humanitarian aid cannot be entirely neutral in areas of conflict but will become a part of it. By just pursuing legitimate development or humanitarian goals, it might feed into social conflicts by unintentionally strengthening dividing factors within the societies (Anderson, 1999).

Since development cooperation thus cannot work around conflicts and insecurity, security issues at least have to be taken into account: development policies need to be sensitive to their security outcome. In addition to conflict-sensitive development policy, development actors are well equipped to use their approaches and methods to directly support civil conflict transformation.

How to merge EU policies?

Given this empirical uncertainty over the relation between security and development, it may not come as a surprise that merging these two policy areas is highly disputed. On the one hand, the merger of security and development policies might open various options to improve European foreign policies. On the other, even given all the consonance and correlations, development and security still enjoy separate objectives, and concentrating on the nexus might bear the risk of neglecting or subordinating these objectives under the goals of another policy field. Apart from the ideas behind the enhancement of the security–development nexus, there are also bureaucratic interests involved. In the EU context, it can be seen as an opportunity to detach development funds for security purposes, which are typically located in the European Commission (Bagayoko and Gilbert, 2009), but also as an opportunity for policy-makers at the Commission's DG Development to increase their relevance and to broaden their scope (Büger and Vennesson, 2009: 11).

Büger and Vennesson's (2009: 4) matrix provides insight into the sensitive political questions that emerge because of the overlap between security and development. The first dimension refers to a potential *convergence or divergence* of the two policy fields. To what extent are the toolboxes of EU development and security policies compatible with each other? Convergence implies that organizations or practices in the policy fields could in principle be integrated into one single set of policies. Although divergence would mean that cooperation between the security and development realm is difficult, this does not necessary imply that both spheres are conflictive or incoherent. Rather, divergence refers to the independence of security and development policies. Apart from the question whether there is convergence or divergence, a second question refers to which policy field is prioritized. Does the EU give priority to security or development goals? What is integrated into what? The second dimension thus looks at whether there is a *primacy* of security or development objectives. Keeping these two dimensions in mind, the following sections will examine the EU's documents and activities in relation to the security–development nexus.

The security–development nexus in the EU's discourse and institutions

The merger of security and development policies can easily be found in the EU's policy declarations and it can be considered one of the guiding motives behind the institutional reforms over the past decade. The first concrete EU document reflecting this merger was the 2001 Commission Communication on Conflict Prevention, which emphasized that 'development policy and other co-operation programmes provide, without doubt, the most powerful instruments at the Community's disposal for treating the root causes of conflict' (European Commission, 2001: 9). The Communication was followed by the Gothenburg Programme for the Prevention of Violent Conflict, adopted by the European Council in June 2001, which made conflict prevention a central objective of the EU's external relations and invited the European Commission to strengthen the conflict prevention elements in the Country Strategy Papers setting out the development strategies. Many more documents have followed, both from the development and the security realm, inspired by a change from mono-causal thinking whereby development determines security, to a more cyclical view on the complex relation between both concepts (Hadfield, 2007).

From a development perspective, two important documents clearly illustrate this evolution: the European Consensus on Development of 2005, which replaces the Development Policy Statement of 2000; and the revised Cotonou Partnership Agreement of 2005, which replaces the Cotonou Agreement signed in 2000. The European Consensus states that 'Without peace and security development and poverty eradication are not possible, and without development and poverty eradication no sustainable peace will occur.' Article 11 of the revised Cotonou Agreement with the African, Caribbean and Pacific (ACP) group of countries introduced new sections on the 'Fight against terrorism' and 'Cooperation in countering the proliferation of weapons of mass destruction'. Cooperation on countering the proliferation of weapons of mass destruction became an 'essential element' of the agreement, alongside human rights, democracy and the rule of law.[4] The second revision of Cotonou in 2010 further amended Article 11, emphasizing the parties' commitment to addressing situations of fragility. There is also a reference to human security and a commitment that 'the interdependence between security and development shall inform the activities in the field of peace building, conflict prevention and resolution, which shall combine short and long-term approaches'.

The Policy Coherence for Development (PCD) (2005) initiative, another key document on EU development policies, identifies security as one of the 12 priority areas and reiterates that 'there can be no development without peace and security; and no peace and security without development' (European Commission, 2005b).[5] The Joint Africa–Europe Strategy of 2007 also has a separate partnership on peace and security. It states that 'peace and security lie at the foundation of progress and sustainable development'. However, somewhat surprisingly, the reverse relationship is less pronounced. Equally, the partnership on the MDGs does not refer to peace and security (except for food security).

This brings us to the security perspective. Here the landmark document is the European Security Strategy (ESS) of 2003, which clearly states that 'security is a precondition of development'. In addition, the ESS considers 'development activities' as one of the tools at the Union's disposal to pursue its 'strategic objectives'. Within the development community and the academic world, the ESS has been castigated for putting too much emphasis on threats and defence rather than on the root causes of conflict and insecurity, hence turning away from human security and from the conflict prevention objectives of the Gothenburg Programme (Kaldor and Glasius, n.d.: 5; see also Manners, 2006a; European Peacebuilding Liaison Office, 2006). According to Youngs (2008), in Brussels the ESS is mainly seen as 'Solana's baby', from which the Commission distances itself. In this context, he also states that the then Development Commissioner, Nielson, 'was progressively excluded from policy deliberations after the September 11 attacks and that, despite cultivating a higher profile, his successor Louis Michel has failed to reverse this trend'.

This apparent lack of convergence between the security and development spheres has been addressed through various institutional reforms in the past decade (dimension 1 on policy instruments). However, here too, fears that security would be prioritized over development have emerged (dimension 2 on policy goals, see above). Already in the context of the Gothenburg Programme, a Crisis Management and Conflict Prevention Unit was established within DG Relex in order to coordinate and mainstream the Commission's conflict prevention and management activities *and* to provide the link with their Council counterparts. Yet discussions on the making of a 'European Civilian Peace Corps' and a 'Human Security Doctrine for Europe' were not productive (see Gänzle, 2009). Moreover, a number of reforms of the EU's development policy architecture fuelled fears that more convergence might equal less development; or more specifically, that development would be subordinated to foreign policy and security goals. First, the establishment of EuropeAid for the implementation of aid policies in 2001 strengthened the power of the Commissioner for External Relations, who chaired the new agency's board, while the Development Commissioner is Chief Executive. Second, the Development Council was abolished as a formal body and integrated in the broader General Affairs and External Relations Council in 2002. Still, the Development Council continued to meet informally (Orbie and Versluys, 2008: 82).

Institutional innovations from the Lisbon Treaty are undoubtedly more far-reaching. While the new treaty aims to improve coherence of the EU's external action, the concerns mentioned above that the Commission's aid budgets would be controlled by those in charge of foreign and security policy have only increased. To be sure, the treaty recognizes development aid as an independent policy area with the eradication of poverty as its principal aim.[6] Provisions on development cooperation also include a commitment to PCD, by stating that 'The Union shall take account of the objectives of development cooperation in the policies that it implements which are likely to affect developing countries' (Art. 208). However, the main responsibility for the coherence of the EU's international action lays with the newly established function of the High Representative of the Union for Foreign Affairs and Security Policy (HR), who is also the vice-president of the European Commission. In the context of the Common Security and Defence Policy, the Treaty (Art. 42(4)) states that the HR 'may propose the use of both national resources and Union instruments, together with the Commission where appropriate'. The question whether this 'EU Foreign Affairs Minister' would eclipse the development sphere was central in the discussions on the creation of a European External Action Service (EEAS), which according to the Lisbon Treaty should assist the HR and will comprise officials from the Council General Secretariat, the Commission and the member states' diplomatic services. The Council decision establishing the EEAS stipulates that the agency should respect the development objectives set out in the Lisbon Treaty. However, the whole debate revolved around the incorporation of development budget and staff in the EEAS. The EEAS decision states that the HR will 'ensure overall political coordination of the EU's external action', including through the EU's budgetary instruments. The programming and management of these instruments (e.g. Country Strategy Papers and National Indicative Programmes) will be prepared by the EEAS in cooperation with the Commission.

Decisions in relation to the European Development Fund (EDF) and the Development Cooperation Instrument (DCI) need to be approved by the EEAS, but will be prepared under the responsibility of the Development Commissioner (Council of the EU, 2010b). It is unclear how this 'dual key' between the HR and the Development Commissioner will work in practice (Furness, 2010). The latter's ability to leave a stamp on these decisions can be questioned, given the reduced number of staff at DG Development (DG DEV). Indeed, 93 employees at DG DEV, including staff from the geographical desks, have moved to the new agency, together with the entire staff from DG Relex, which has been abolished (European Union, 2010b). The remaining part of DG DEV has merged with former DG AIDCO or EuropeAid, responsible for the implementation of EU development assistance, forming the new DG Development and Cooperation (DG DEVCO). Hence, DG Development, formerly responsible for the entire aid programming and political relations with the ACP region, has now been transformed into an administration responsible in the first place for the implementation stages of EU development policies (such as establishing annual action programmes and implementation) in all regions. In addition, the new EU Delegations in the field, which provide much input into the programming and management of aid funds, will henceforth report to the HR (interview, 11 August 2010).[7] However, fears that the Commission's responsibilities in aid programming would be fully assumed by the EEAS were not wholly confirmed. Indeed, despite earlier plans to move the entire geographical desks to the EEAS, the new DG DEVCO will continue to have geographical desks, with which the EEAS will cooperate in the programming phases. Moreover, this cooperation will also take place in the EU Delegations, which will comprise diplomats from EU member states, EEAS staff and people from DG DEVCO (personal communication, 6 October 2011). Various development NGOs argue that the EEAS goes against the spirit and the letter of the Lisbon Treaty and that its role should be restricted to the CFSP, whereas decisions on the spending of development aid should remain within the Commission (CIDSE *et al.*, 2010). Some advocate a more formal and comprehensive coordination of aid programming between the EEAS and the Commission. They argue that the EEAS development structure should be reinforced by establishing a separate Development Directorate. Under these conditions, the EEAS could be an opportunity for a more effective development policy embedded in a more coherent external European policy (ECDPM and ODI, 2010; Furness, 2010).

Officials close to the HR stress that poverty reduction objectives will continue to guide the management of development budgets, but at the same time emphasize that development can no longer be separated from foreign policy considerations:

> We are unfortunately living in a world where development depends on political factors. You do not make development in the Sudan or Somalia and forget that there is a political context. That is what the EEAS is about. It is not a way of trying to divert development money to so-called political purposes. It's about how you best promote the interests of that particular country.

> (quoted in *EUObserver*, 27 April 2010)

Summarizing, over the past decade the EU's main documents and institutional structures have continually emphasized the need to address the challenges in the security–development nexus. Yet it is unclear to what extent security and development policies have converged in practice. Moreover, there has been a constant concern that development goals could become subordinated to foreign and security policy purposes. The next section takes a closer look at both perspectives by considering the EU's activities and initiatives in the security–development realm.

The security–development nexus in EU policy practice

Increasing convergence?

Is the EU's aim to increase convergence between security and development more than lip service? The EU's foreign policy system is notorious for its compartmentalization, facilitating stove-piping and hindering a coherent approach between the various sub-systems (see e.g. Pilegaard, 2009; Olsen, 2009b). In relation to security and development, there are indeed indications that, in practice, there are still high walls between both spheres. Echoing the results of several studies on this topic, Büger and Vennesson (2009: 32–3) criticize the fact that the EU's rhetorical commitment to 'coordinating more' has barely impacted on concrete situations on the ground. They stress that 'there is no clear indication that current coordination initiatives have led to either a subordination or prioritization of security or development policies, *because coordination has not been functioning well*' (emphasis added). The 'coordination bubble' in Brussels even has the adverse effect that it diffuses policy responsibility over European decisions on difficult conflict situations. Similarly, in an empirically rich account of the EU's conflict and development policies, Faria and Youngs (2010: 4) emphasize that the security and development spheres have hardly been integrated in the field: 'ESDP missions are still not actually "integrated", but simply have military and civilian strands running in parallel – "in awkward juxtaposition and rarely dovetailing well"'. The priority is still on short-term and crisis management operations, which overshadow long-term and development issues and neglect the reform of state structures and the fundamental causes of conflict. There is first a military decision, and only in a second stadium are development, governance or security experts consulted. For example, Security Sector Reform (SSR) initiatives promoted by the EU still look like 'fairly standard counter-terrorist programmes, with few tangible reform aspects' (Faria and Youngs, 2010: 2). Although only projects to increase the democratic responsiveness of armed forces are accepted as development aid according to the OECD-DAC criteria for ODA (OECD, 2007b) and the EU considers good governance as a 'link in the chain' between security and development (Youngs, 2008: 16), SSR missions have focused much more on the efficiency than the accountability of armed forces in developing states (Youngs, 2008: 7). An OECD-DAC evaluation voiced similar concerns on the limited connection between ESDP missions and long-term development planning (OECD, 2007c: 66). One of the main reasons for this lack of convergence is the 'ramshackle institutional machinery' (Sheriff, 2007: 89) of the EU, with the Council focusing on short-term actions such as crisis management, and the Commission being concerned with long-term activities including conflict prevention and good governance. The difficulty of overcoming this institutional divide is shown by the drafting process of an EU Concept on SSR: both the Council and the Commission prepared their own documents. Thus, the problem seems not that EU development has become securitized, but rather that its security initiatives are not being 'developmentalized', and that both foreign policy subsystems are still going their own way.

Several authors suggest that the security foreign policy sub-system is not really interested in or well informed on development issues, while development actors remain highly sceptical of the security sphere (Youngs, 2008; see also Olsen, 2009b). When analysing the Country Strategy Papers (CSPs) of the EU (2007–13), Hout (2010) also comes to the conclusion that the complexity of security, development and related governance issues is recognized in the country analysis, but that it remains limited to technocratic reforms which do not tackle fundamental reforms in a country, including developmental issues. CSPs include a security dimension only in theory, but not really in practice. Thus, the two policy fields are still far from integrating – and increased coordination is necessary. The same divergence also seems to exist between humanitarian aid and ESDP policies such as civilian crisis management and conflict prevention (OECD, 2007c: 98).

Over the past five years, several EU initiatives have been launched to increase convergence. Two sets of Council Conclusions were prepared in the course of 2007 and adopted in November 2007. The first conclusions on Security and Development were prepared by DG Relex and focused on the need to coordinate between short- and long-term planning and actions, and between security, development and foreign policies (Council of the EU, 2007c). The second conclusions recognized the need to address the problem of fragile states, which are perceived as security threats by the EU (see, for example, the ESS) because these countries are the breeding ground for terrorism and organized crime. Both Council Conclusions emphasize the need to address institutional divergence by adopting a 'whole-of-government approach': getting different ministries to act as a coherent whole (Doelle and de Harven, 2008: 47). For example, in the case of SSR, this can be achieved by enhancing information flows on SSR activities, pursuing field coordination, carrying out joint assessments, pooled funding, etc. (Council of the EU, 2007d). As a follow-up to these conclusions, it was agreed that the EU would adopt an Action Plan in 2009 for implementing the Council Conclusions on both topics, jointly prepared by development and security officials. Four areas for increasing coherence were identified: strategic planning, SSR, partnerships with (sub)regional organizations and humanitarian aid and security. In this context, two studies were commissioned which provide an interesting overview of the EU's policies in the security–development nexus and which both recommend a more convergent and comprehensive EU approach (Commission of the European Communities and Soges SpA, 2008; HTSPE Ltd, 2008). Meanwhile, the OECD-DAC had also issued a critical evaluation of the limited convergence in the EU's approach to fragile states (OECD, 2007c: 66–7). In a recent document on Policy Coherence in Development (European Commission, 2010d: 33–40), the Commission suggests that there is still room for improvement in the coherence of development and security. The report makes several suggestions, such as the full involvement of development actors in the planning and implementation of crisis management missions, taking development objectives into account in security spending, making development plans more conflict sensitive and using the various instruments for conflict prevention more coherently. The long-expected action plan has still not been finalized; however, a concrete implementation of the conclusions is currently being tried with the EEAS's Strategy for Security and Development in the Sahel, which is intended as a joint strategy with different pillars (conflict resolution, governance, fight against terrorism, economic development, etc.) (personal communication, 6 October 2011).

Another attempt to cope with the apparent divergence between security and development policies is the introduction of the Instrument for Stability (IfS) in 2007 to finance projects that operate in the grey zone between security and development policy. The Commission and European Parliament wanted a more ambitious instrument which also includes peacekeeping and peace support, but the Council eliminated these concepts from the original proposal (Gänzle, 2009: 59–60). Its primary goal is to enable the EU to respond rapidly to emerging crises. However, short-term security aims seem to dominate in the use of the IfS. The crisis response component accounts for the majority of the IfS (at least 73 per cent of the budget), while the rest goes to a long-term component, meant to provide assistance in the context of stable conditions for cooperation. According to Faria and Youngs (2010: 2), 'The Commission itself stresses that the Stability Instrument … has not been designed to feed into development goals. Funding from this budget has gone to immediate crisis response priorities such as mediation, demobilisation, security cooperation, displaced persons and transitional justice.' The Commission has indeed acknowledged that synergies between the EDF and the DCI, which are mainly geared towards development objectives, and the IfS, which is mainly used for conflict prevention, peace-building and security purposes, could be enhanced (European Commission, 2010d: 39–40). There is also an institutional obstacle to more convergence between security and development in the implementation of the IfS: its management was the responsibility of DG Relex, while aid allocations to the ACP countries fell within the mandate of DG Development (Commission of the European Communities and Soges SpA, 2008: 90–1). Although the new EEAS could be an improvement in this regard, the fact that the EEAS will be responsible for the programming phases of the IfS, while EDF and DCI funds are jointly programmed by DG DEVCO and the EEAS, indicates that the IfS is still being regarded in the first place as a foreign policy instrument, in contrast to the development-oriented EDF and DCI. The IfS has increased the speed of Community responses, and has potential to improve convergence. However, its success will ultimately depend on the political will of member states in the Political and Security Committee and the geographical working groups to coordinate closely with the Commission on embedding IfS measures within the EU's broader foreign and security policy (Gänzle, 2009: 8).

Coherence for development, or primacy of security?

At the same time, there are indications that security considerations are more and more overshadowing the EU's development policy. As suggested by Woods (2005: 13), 'in the name of coherence, a greater diversion of aid flows for geostrategic purposes may take place, and increased coordination would magnify that effect'. Can such criticisms, mainly based on policy documents and institutional reforms (see above), also be confirmed in the EU's concrete initiatives and activities? Although it is too early to give a definitive verdict, we will attempt to offer some insights by 'following the money': to what extent is EU ODA, as defined by the Organisation for Economic Co-operation and Development's Development Assistance Committee (OECD-DAC), used for geopolitical and security-related goals?

The most obvious example of a diversion of EU development money is the financing of the African Peace Facility (APF) for peacekeeping and peace enforcement with money from the EDF. While the IfS is an example of additional development funds for security-related expenses, security-related EDF expenditures for the APF are not compensated with additional budgets for development. The EDF regulation suggests that, in the choice of projects financed by the APF, ODA-eligible projects are given priority. However, almost half of the entire APF budget until now has been contributed to the African Union Mission in Sudan (AMIS), which does not qualify as ODA. Faria and Youngs (2010: 2) conclude that development activities in the context of the APF 'still represent the lowest share of all APF priorities'.

More generally, it should be noticed that some EU countries, such as the Netherlands, Portugal and Italy, supported by the US, provoked a fierce debate within the OECD-DAC with their demand to broaden the definition of ODA to include peacekeeping operations. They were opposed by Sweden, the UK, Norway and Japan, and to a lesser extent Germany (interview, 25 August 2010). Eventually, a limited extension of 'conflict-, peace- and security-' related expenses was qualified as 'DAC'-able' from 2004/5 onwards.[8] This extension did not immediately lead to a great increase in the European Commission's and EU15's spending on conflict, peace and security, which remained about 1 per cent of their total ODA. However, in recent years, a considerable surge can be noted. The Commission now spends over 3.5 per cent of its ODA on this category, which is similar to the USA's share of security-related ODA and slightly higher than the EU15 (see Figure 11.1), which saw large increases by the Netherlands, Sweden, Germany and the UK.

In addition, recent reports by the NGO consortia CONCORD and AidWatch point out that some EU member states such as Germany and the Netherlands have been trying to include peacekeeping costs, for example in Afghanistan, as ODA. The new member states, which hardly have any OECD monitoring and public scrutiny of development, are known for spending much of their development aid on security-related expenses. For example, a large part of Lithuanian aid goes to the NATO mission in Afghanistan (CONCORD and AidWatch, 2009: 41) and about one third of Poland and Hungary's ODA goes to Afghanistan (CONCORD and Aidwatch, 2010: 12).[9] In 2009, the European Commission again raised the issue, suggesting that discussion in the OECD-DAC should continue to resolve the situation of many peace- and security-related activities that are not covered by the current ODA definition (European Commission, 2009b: 32).

Another indication comes from the main beneficiaries of EU development aid. While the top ten of EU beneficiaries were almost exclusively sub-Saharan African countries in the period 1989–95, European countries in the Western Balkans became increasingly important from 1999 onwards. Turkey, an upper-middle-income country, but strategically closely located to the EU and a candidate for EU membership, is the top recipient since 2004. In addition, Afghanistan appeared on the list after the terrorist attacks of 9/11 and the US military invasion. Even in sub-Saharan Africa, countries in conflict such as the Democratic Republic of Congo and Sudan or partner countries in the fight against terrorism such as Ethiopia are preferred aid recipients. On the other hand, there were also some least-developed countries (LDCs) not very important to the EU's security interests, such as Tanzania, Mozambique and Uganda, in the top ten in 2004/5 and 2007/8 (see Figure 11.2).

Linked to the discussion on poverty reduction versus EU strategic interests is the regional distribution of EU funds. Multilateral EU aid does not seem to go primarily to the poorest countries in the world – actually it never has and was always given to countries with special relationships with or of specific interest to donor countries. This is even more so for the EU, which is focused on other regions such as the European neighbourhood, than for EU member states. However, after the Cold War, geopolitical interests had become less important in aid distribution. This trend has changed again, and in recent years the EU has distributed its funds increasingly to countries that are important for the EU's own security interests. Aid to sub-Saharan Africa has fluctuated in the last decennium, reaching its lowest points in 1997 and 2002, but has remained mostly above 40 per cent. Aid to Europe has increased even further since 1999, and reached no less than one third of total aid in 2007 (Figure 11.2).[10] Although the EU claims poverty reduction to be the main objective of its development assistance (European Union, 2006; Lisbon Treaty Article 208), its ODA to LDCs has known a sharp decrease since the mid-1990s. While LDCs still received over 40 per cent of total EU aid in 1995, this was only 33.1 per cent in 2008. Similarly, aid to lower-middle-income countries declined by almost 20 percentage points between 1997 and 2008. In contrast, aid to upper-middle-income countries, such as Belarus, Croatia, Turkey or Serbia, grew steadily from about 7 per cent in 1995 to almost 25 per cent in 2008 (Figure 11.3).

Thus, it is clear that countries in the EU's neighbourhood, which undoubtedly constitutes a region of strategic priority, are the main beneficiaries of EU development aid. If we extend the list of strategically important countries and regions for the EU, adding those that are referred to as threats in the ESS (e.g. the Great Lakes region, India and Pakistan in relation to Kashmir, North Korea, the Middle East, fragile states), or that are either important partners in the fight against terrorism (Ethiopia, Djibouti, Nigeria) or provide a potential breeding ground or safe haven for terrorists (Yemen, Afghanistan, Somalia), countries that are crucial in the fight against drug trafficking (Colombia) or that are identified as strategic in Biscop's chapter in this volume (e.g. Sudan/Darfur and neighbouring countries; the Sahel as a whole, the Horn of Africa, the Gulf Region), we come to the conclusion that they constituted more than 60 per cent of all EC aid in 2008.[11] In addition, those states that can be defined as 'fragile' (according to the World Bank LICUS index) but that *cannot* be considered as strategic have received only a limited amount of EU development aid (on average about 7 per cent, only 3.2 per cent in 2008) over the past decade. Similarly, if we take the group of LDCs that are not strategic, these have only received 15 per cent of total EU aid on average since 1999.

Conclusion

While a consensus has emerged that security and development objectives are mutually enhancing, the interaction between both external policy spheres raises sensitive political issues. These are perhaps even more prominent in the EU which has considerable experience with development aid, but has only recently embarked on a foreign security policy. Therefore, these discussions also touch on the very nature of the EU's (putative) international identity as a civilian or normative power.

Since the security–development nexus is a relatively recent topic on the EU's agenda (e.g. Instrument for Stability in 2007, Council Conclusions on fragile states in the same year, current discussions on ODA definition, forthcoming action plan on security–development, etc.), it is too early to draw definitive conclusions on where the EU is heading to. Indeed, it seems that the EU is still in the process of defining its approach to the security–development nexus. However, based on recent discourses and initiatives, and referring to the matrix outlined in the first part of the chapter, we can tentatively say that the development and security toolboxes seem to be converging (dimension 1 on policy instruments), and that this goes with a prioritization of security over developmental objectives (dimension 2 on policy goals). A closer examination of ODA flows also revealed that a large part of EU aid budgets are directed towards countries that are strategically important for the EU, to the detriment of countries that are of less importance from a security perspective. This trend might be reinforced through the post-Lisbon foreign policy arrangements which enhance the muscle of Europe's foreign and security policy apparatus over development issues.

This resonates with the more general finding in the literature that the EU is increasingly aspiring to a 'great power' status on the international scene. A paradigmatic shift seems to be taking place whereby the EU is abandoning its civilian or normative power role which emphasizes non-traditional, 'human' security issues, in favour of a 'drive towards martial potency' (Manners, 2006a), a 'global power' (Rogers, 2009a) and a 'superpower temptation' (Diez, 2009). Other authors have suggested that the EU's new attention for security issues in Africa cannot only be explained by real concerns for the security situation, but also by their symbolic role in establishing the EU as a significant and legitimate player on the international scene (Olsen, 2004; Bagayoko and Gilbert, 2009).

Is the 'Europe as a peace project' idea clearing the ground for 'EU superpower' ambitions (Kaldor and Glasius, n.d.: 1)? As emphasized above, definitive conclusions are hard to draw. However, given the EU's increased aspirations on the foreign security front, it is questionable whether a sustainable balance in the security–development nexus can be maintained.

Annexe

Table 11.1 Top ten recipients of EC ODA, 1989–2008

	1989–90	*1994–5*	*1999–2000*	*2004–5*	*2007–8*
1	Côte d'Ivoire	Morocco	Former Republic of Yugoslavia	Turkey	Turkey
2	Cameroon	Ethiopia	Morocco	Serbia and Montenegro	Palestinian Adm. Areas
3	Mozambique	Egypt	Bosnia and Herzegovina	Morocco	Ethiopia
4	India	Ex-Yugoslavia	Sts. Ex-Yugoslavia unsp.	Afghanistan	Morocco
5	Ethiopia	Côte d'Ivoire	Egypt	Congo, Dem. Rep.	Serbia
6	Bangladesh	Mozambique	Tunisia	Egypt	Afghanistan
7	Sudan	Cameroon	South Africa	Palestinian Adm. Areas	Sudan
8	Egypt	Zimbabwe	Turkey	India	Egypt
9	Congo, Dem. Rep.	Uganda	Albania	Mozambique	Croatia
10	Kenya	Bangladesh	Macedonia/ FYROM	Tanzania	Uganda

Source: OECD (2002; 2007c).

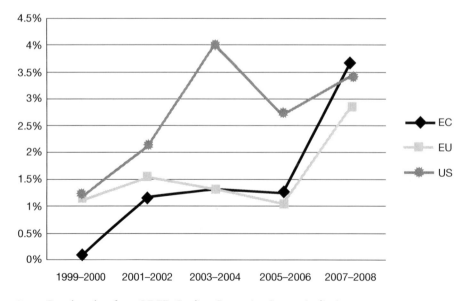

Source: Based on data from OECD Creditor Reporting System (online).

Figure 11.1 ODA commitments: conflict, peace and security, EC, EU and US (percentages).

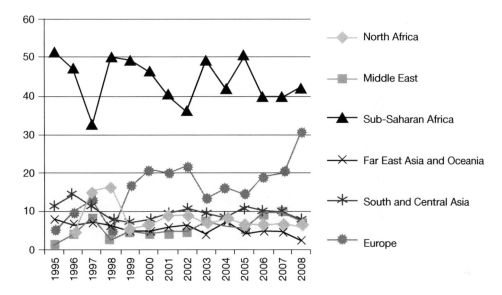

Source: Based on data from OECD Creditor Reporting System (online).

Figure 11.2 EC ODA commitments by region (percentages).

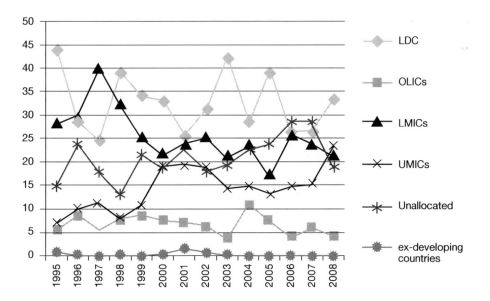

Source: Based on data from OECD Creditor Reporting System (online).

Figure 11.3 EC ODA commitments by income category (percentages).

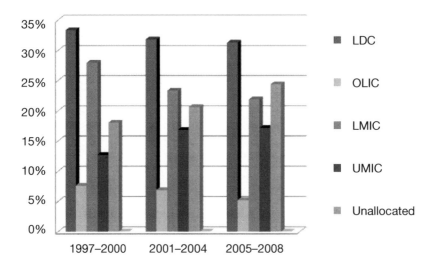

Source: Based on data from OECD Creditor Reporting System (online).

Figure 11.4 EC ODA commitments by income category.

Notes

1 These two dimensions are based on a matrix Büger and Vennesson proposed in their paper 'Security, development and the EU's development policy' (2009).
2 According to the definition of the United Nations Development Program (UNDP), '[h]uman development is about much more than the rise or fall of national incomes. It is about creating an environment in which people can develop their full potential and lead productive, creative lives in accord with their needs and interests. ... Fundamental to enlarging these choices is building human capabilities – the range of things that people can do or be in life. The most basic capabilities for human development are to lead long and healthy lives, to be knowledgeable, to have access to the resources needed for a decent standard of living and to be able to participate in the life of the community' (UNDP 2001: 9).
3 Although a lot of consonance can be found, the concepts must not just be equated with each other. Human security pledges for the capability to cope with insecurities to allow a life free from dangers. Development aims at the continuous improvement of the conditions in which humans live. Human development means an extension of human possibilities and human security means the potential to make use of those possibilities. The focus of development thus is growth; the focus of security is the prevention of crises or, as Amartya Sen puts it: 'Growth with equity', 'downturn with security' (Sen, 2000).
4 For a detailed analysis, see Hadfield, 2007; Gänzle, 2009: 39.
5 In addition, the new PCD approach proposed in 2009 identifies 'security and development' as one of the five priorities (European Commission, 2009b).
6 The eradication of poverty also appears among the general objectives of EU external action, see Art. 3(5) and Art. 21(2).
7 In addition, some interesting evolutions are taking place at the level of the Council of Ministers. Although it seems that the meetings of development ministers will henceforth be held separately from the meetings with the ministers of foreign affairs, and will be prepared by the CODEV and ACP committees, they will also be chaired by the HR. Ashton has already vowed to 'seriously

influence' the agenda, e.g. by putting Afghanistan and Somalia on the top of the development agenda in 2010 (interview, 11 August 2010).

8 Five categories were identified: (1) management of security expenditure; (2) enhancing civil society's role in the security system; (3) prevention of the recruitment of child soldiers; (4) security system reform; (5) civilian peace-building, conflict prevention and resolution; and (6) the prevention of the proliferation of small arms and light weapons (OECD, 2008).

9 Nevertheless, not all examples point towards a tendency to include more and more security-related expenses as ODA. Although it has a large military presence in Afghanistan, the UK reports only little security assistance as ODA (CONCORD and AidWatch, 2010).

10 Albania, Belarus, Bosnia-Herzegovina, Croatia, Cyprus (until 1996), Former Yugoslav Republic of Macedonia, Malta, Moldova, Montenegro, Serbia, Slovenia (until 2002), Turkey.

11 Somalia, Sudan, Djibouti, Ethiopia, Eritrea, Kenya, Nigeria, Central African Republic, Chad, Rwanda, Burundi, DR Congo, Uganda, Mauritania, Mali, Niger, Senegal, Burkina Faso, Iraq, Afghanistan, Iran, Syria, Lebanon, Yemen, Pakistan, India, Kosovo, Bosnia-Herzegovina, Albania, Macedonia, Serbia, Montenegro, Croatia, Russia, Belarus, Ukraine, Azerbaijan, Georgia, Armenia, Morocco, Algeria, Tunisia, Libya, Egypt, Moldova, Turkey, Colombia, Palestinian Territories, North Korea.

PART III

Policies

12

THE CSDP IN THE WESTERN BALKANS

From experimental pilot to security governance

Michael Merlingen

In 1990 realist international relations scholar John Mearsheimer (1990) wrote about the impending return to instability and interstate competition in Europe. His prediction was prompted by the end of the Cold War, which he regarded as one of the pacifiers and stabilizers of the continent. In the absence of the bipolar divide, Europe was destined to return to its own past, which was characterized by competitive security policies in a multipolar regional order. The Western Balkans had for centuries been an important European arena in the international struggle for power. If the realist scenario had been right, the region would once again have become a source of geopolitical competition among major European and non-European powers. Yet history unfolded according to a different scenario. To make sense of it, this chapter draws on the concept of governance. Mearsheimer's scenario is based on a view of states as sovereignty-bound actors which are primarily concerned about their military power. Governance scholars argue that the EU has partly transcended the sovereign state (Kirchner and Sperling, 2007; Sperling, 2009; Webber *et al.*, 2004). It is in some sense a post-Westphalian community of action. Its internal relations are those of a mature security community in which war has become unthinkable. Its foreign policy in its neighbourhood is structural in orientation (Keukeleire, 2004). It is a long-term policy embedded in contractual relations and aimed at transforming conflict-prone and underdeveloped countries into well-governed market democracies. Brussels' transformative diplomacy works by transferring EU rules and practices to target countries. This makes EU foreign policy a form of extra-territorial governance (Lavenex and Schimmelfennig, 2010; Schimmelfennig and Sedelmeier, 2004).

The chapter proceeds as follows. It first identifies the mixed motives driving EU policy towards the Western Balkans. It then conceptualizes CSDP missions as an instrument of EU external security governance before providing a brief overview of the activities and achievements of the five CSDP missions that the EU has deployed in the Western Balkans. Next the chapter discusses the other main EU governance policies in the region. In the two sections that follow the chapter first identifies the main successes and limitations of the EU's Balkan

policy and then explains its mixed record. The chapter ends by providing five recommendations on how to improve the EU record in the region. Throughout the chapter, the empirical
focus is on those three countries in which the EU deploys or deployed CSDP operations:
Bosnia, Kosovo and Macedonia.

Ethics and strategic interests: the normative, political and security objectives of EU policy in the Western Balkans

The EU is often described in normative terms as a cosmopolitan actor. Unlike sovereignty-
bound states, the post-Westphalian EU is committed to the diffusion of the universal norms
and values that it embodies, including peace, the rule of law and human rights. In Ian
Manners' (2002: 252) influential view, the EU is a normative power primarily because of
what it is or represents rather than because of what it does. In the Western Balkans, the
limits of this conceptualization of EU foreign policy are readily visible. There the EU's role
in changing the norms and functioning of domestic institutions, inter-ethnic relations and
civil societies has been heavily dependent on its civilian and military actions, including the
conditional offer of material incentives. Another normative approach is better suited to make
sense of EU foreign policy in the Western Balkans. The notion of ethical foreign policy
squarely places the emphasis on the actions of the EU rather than on its presence in international affairs (Aggestam, 2008). Yet this approach, too, is insufficient to explain the role and
impact of the EU in the Western Balkans. Irrespective of official discourse, the record shows
that EU policy has been driven both by other-regarding normative and egoistical material
motives. While the conceptualization of the EU as a post-Westphalian community of action
is useful to analyse EU policy in the region, the concept has to be broad enough to allow for
non-normative sources of policy.

An important impetus for EU actions in the Western Balkans has been related to self-centred
policy objectives. The EU has sought to protect itself against transnational threats emanating
from the former Yugoslavia and to strengthen its international identity. As a post-Westphalian
actor the EU no longer seeks to maintain a protective shell around its territory. It is committed
to keeping its borders open to transnational flows of tourists, goods, services and capital. Yet
as borders have become porous, new non-traditional security threats and new referent objects
in need of being secured have emerged. This is reflected in EU policy towards the Western
Balkans. The violent breakup of Yugoslavia in the 1990s and the associated prospect of failing
states were considered by European authorities to pose serious security problems for the EU.
They allowed organized crime to take root in the region and to penetrate the EU with its illicit
activities such as trafficking in drugs and small weapons. They caused large refugee inflows and
illegal migration that put strain on societal identities and social cohesion in EU states and taxed
their labour markets and welfare systems. They threatened to create safe havens for terrorists
from which they might launch attacks against the EU. The CSDP missions in the Western
Balkans and EU policy towards the region more generally have been partly a response to these
threat assessments. They have been motivated by the objective to promote the security and
well-being of EU citizens, even when this has come at the expense of the interests of Western
Balkan citizens. For instance, until recently most citizens of the region faced unwelcome visa
restrictions when they wanted to travel to the EU.

Another self-centred objective underpinning EU policy in the Western Balkans has been
about EU identity. A stronger international identity is a means for the EU to raise its status
or prestige, which is a currency of international influence. Also, the identity card plays well
with European publics who are otherwise disenchanted with many aspects of the EU. The

Western Balkans have played an important role in the EU's branding strategy. Its disastrous performance as conflict preventer and peacemaker in the former Yugoslavia severely damaged its reputation as an international actor. An important objective of the CSDP missions in the Western Balkans has been to show to EU publics and the world that the EU has finally got its act together and that, therefore, it has to be taken seriously as an international security provider.

Other-regarding policy goals, too, have been present in EU policy towards the region. Brussels has showed border-crossing solidarity with the victims of genocide and mass atrocity crimes both by welcoming refugees and by its actions in the region. It has advanced human security, including through conflict prevention and the promotion of human rights and economic development. More important still in the long run is that the EU has committed itself to giving all Western Balkan countries a European perspective. While the promise acts as a carrot that, when linked to policies of conditionality, gives the EU a powerful instrument to shape the institutional and policy trajectories of the countries concerned, there is more to the policy than self-interest. The enlargement promise is grounded in the conviction on the part of the EU that it has a moral obligation to make amends to the region for its foreign policy failures there in the 1990s. Brussels genuinely wishes to extend its peace project to the Western Balkans. There is thus a non-negligible element of cosmopolitanism in EU policy towards the region. To conclude, EU policy towards the Western Balkans has been driven by mixed motives. It has been both rational in that it has promoted the security and political interests of the EU and appropriate or reasonable in that it has been in accordance with certain standards of justice or fairness.

EU external governance in the Western Balkans

The EU has evolved a number of instruments to influence third countries. They include the EU enlargement policy; policies of conditionality without the carrot of membership such as the European Neighbourhood Policy (ENP); and the extension of EU-based policy networks to third countries. The CSDP is yet another EU external governance tool. One of its purposes is to deal in a cost-efficient manner with transnational security threats and the associated blurred boundary between internal and external security (Krahmann, 2005; Lutterbeck, 2005). On the one hand, civilian CSDP missions are an instance of the externalization of domestic law enforcement and judicial functions. EU police officers replace, train or support their local counterparts in post-conflict societies. EU judges and lawyers operating under the CSDP flag do the same for local judiciaries. On the other hand, military CSDP operations are an instance of the 'politicization' of soldiering. Troops are asked to carry out civilian tasks as peacebuilders and security sector reformers. The point is that CSDP missions (military and civilian) tackle transnational security threats by contributing to the stabilization and reconstruction of post-conflict societies. Just like other governance policies, they do so by extending to them EU rules, norms and practices.

The CSDP operations

The early CSDP deployments in the Western Balkans have been the main testing ground for the functionality and viability of the brand-new CSDP, including the EU's ability finally to transform itself from a mere civilian power into a military actor. If the EU showed itself incapable of getting the CSDP right in its own backyard, its aspiration to be a global security player would for the foreseeable future remain unfulfilled. Also, more so than elsewhere, the impact of EU policy in the Western Balkans has depended on the success of its CSDP missions. Especially important for the EU's policy objectives of extending peace and market democracies to the region have been the EU military operation in Bosnia and the civilian mission in Kosovo. In short, the stakes of the missions in the Western Balkans have been considerably higher than those of EU missions elsewhere.

The EUPM in Bosnia (January 2003–June 2012)

In Bosnia, the violent disintegration of Yugoslavia reached its apex. The three-year-long civil war involved massive human rights violations, including widespread ethnic cleansing. The police acted as an instrument of ethnic repression. The war was brought to an end by a US-led NATO air campaign. The 1995 Dayton peace accords established an internationally supervised power-sharing arrangement among the three major Bosnian ethnicities – the Bosniaks, Croats and Serbs. To oversee the transition to peace and democracy, the accords established the Office of the High Representative (OHR). A United Nations (UN) International Police Task Force was set up to build a professional and accountable Bosnian police. While the UN police officers had achieved much by the time their mandate expired at the end of 2002, the international community felt that the local police needed further international control and guidance. The EU volunteered to take over from the UN.

The EU police mission (EUPM), which was finalising its closure at the time of writing in the summer of 2012, was tasked to reform the local police in accordance with best European and international practices. Police experts and political advisers monitored the conduct of locals, mentored them on best practices and provided them with policy and strategic advice. At its peak, the mission had 540 internationals. In its first three years of operation, the EUPM pursued a wide range of reforms. It ran seven capacity-building programmes. They comprised about 120 reform projects (Merlingen, with Ostrauskaite', 2006; Mühlmann, 2008). Many EUPM projects were funded by the European Commission. After 2005, the mission mandate zeroed in on two main objectives. First, the EUPM was to support the consolidation of the highly fragmented Bosnian police system. This proved difficult as the territorial reorganization of policing has been politically controversial among Bosnians. Second, the mission was tasked to enhance the capacity of the local police to combat organized crime. To achieve this goal, it built an in-house capacity to improve police–prosecutor relations. They were a choke point in its previous efforts to upgrade local law enforcement. Also, the EUPM zeroed in on improving local police accountability. Among other things, it supervised the exercise of political authority over the police and the conduct of officers during crime-busting operations. Police corruption, misconduct and political interference in operational policing decisions have been among those factors hampering the fight against organized crime. After 2009, the refocused mission mandate emphasized the fight against corruption and organized crime.

The Bosnian police has come a long way since the days of the civil war, especially in police-technical terms. The EUPM played an important role in this development, notably regarding the development of policing competencies and standards of professionalism of the rank and file and mid-level police managers. Among other things, it succeeded in making the local police more accountable (e.g. by setting up, training and mentoring internal control units that investigate police misconduct); and more professional and effective (e.g. through developing new curricula for police training and through restructuring the country's criminal investigation departments) (Juncos, 2007; Merlingen, 2009). In terms of the broader political framework of policing, the EUPM had less impact. This is especially true of the de-politicization (and de-ethnicization) of the senior police management, a process which touches on issues such as police forces having their own independent operational budgets, the clear legal and practical separation of interior ministers and police commissioners and the enforcement of laws on merit-based recruitment and promotion of police officials.

EUFOR Althea (December 2004–)

In the wake of the Dayton peace deal, NATO was put in charge of keeping the peace in Bosnia. In December 2004, the 7,000-strong EUFOR Althea took over NATO's peace-keeping tasks. It has been the largest-ever military CSDP operation. It relies on NATO capabilities and assets under the Berlin Plus agreements. Its Operation Commander is NATO's Deputy Supreme Allied Commander Europe (D-SACEUR). The transition from NATO troops to EUFOR was smooth. EU military planners benefited from the alliance's extensive experience on the ground. Also, the capabilities and assets the EU wanted to borrow from NATO were already in place. Cooperation between the two sides has been good ever since. Denmark, Cyprus and Malta are the only EU states that have not participated in the force. Altogether 33 countries contributed to Althea when it was deployed.

Althea's main function has been to ensure a safe and secure environment in Bosnia. Initially, EUFOR focused on deterring possible spoilers of the Dayton peace accords, notably the ethnically and institutionally divided armed forces. Another key focus of EUFOR's earlier activities was compellence – the initiation of military action (peaceful or violent) in an attempt to stop adversaries from continuing to engage in undesirable action (Art, 2007). The first Force Commander used his troops proactively and at a high operational tempo. His aim was to disrupt the local networks that obstructed the efforts of the international community to bring to justice individuals indicted by the Yugoslav war crimes tribunal. For instance, early on in its deployment EUFOR conducted a large-scale operation to seize control of all underground military facilities in the country where war crimes fugitives were believed to hide (Bertin, 2008). Also, the Force Commander adopted a forceful approach in combating organized crime. The phenomenon was thought to be linked to the support networks of indicted war criminals. Interpreting his mandate liberally, the General drew on EUFOR's own armed police force and regular troops to carry out country-wide anti-organized-crime operations. Often he did not bother to inform either the local police or the EUPM. This resulted in confusion both in the EU family and among Bosnian authorities over who was in charge of improving local law enforcement. Also, it created some bad blood between Althea and the EUPM. The latter complained that the 'executive' approach of the military undermined its capacity-building approach based on local ownership. Finally, Brussels designated the EUPM as the lead actor on the issue of combating organized crime.

As peace took root in Bosnia and inter-ethnic relations were increasingly channelled through and moderated by democratic political institutions, Althea's deterrence and compellence functions became obsolete. On the military front, a milestone in this development was the national defence reform at the end of 2005, which established unified, democratically controlled armed forces. Responding to the evolving situation on the ground, the EU gradually reduced Althea to around 2,000 troops. They are backed up by over-the-horizon reserves. The slimmed-down EUFOR has strengthened its reassurance function. Liaison Observation Teams (LOTs) have been its main means. They consist of small groups of soldiers who live in local communities. LOTs are used throughout Bosnia to build close relationships with locals and to reassure them that the EU will not allow a return to conflict. In 2010, the EU reinforced Althea's contribution to the training of the Bosnian armed forces.

EUFOR set up a specialized training and capacity-building unit whose mobile teams focus on medical evacuation, information systems, leadership and weapons training. At the time of writing, Althea has about 1,200 troops in theatre, with preparations in 2012.

EUFOR Althea has been a success. It has kept the peace in Bosnia and carried out civilian tasks that have improved public security and enhanced the professionalization of the Bosnian armed forces. Moreover, the operation has demonstrated that the EU can successfully run a sizeable peacekeeping operation. Althea's success has prompted a number of contributing EU states to call for its termination.

EUFOR Concordia (March–December 2003)

The separation of Macedonia from Yugoslavia proceeded peacefully. Yet relations between the Slav-Macedonian majority and the ethnic Albanian minority subsequently deteriorated. Macedonian Albanians were discriminated against in the fields of culture, education and language (Brown, 2000). When neighbouring Kosovo plunged into full-blown violence, Macedonian Albanians were radicalized. Ethnic fighting ensued between the Macedonian Albanian National Liberation Army (NLA) and government forces. Full-scale civil war was prevented by a joint NATO and EU diplomatic intervention. Under international pressure, the Slav Macedonians agreed to a peace deal. It gave the Albanian minority more rights and autonomy.

The Ohrid Framework Agreement was signed in August 2001. It called for the disbandment of the NLA. NATO deployed a force to assist in the process. Its follow-up operations were tasked to monitor the former crisis area in the northwest of the country where ethnic clashes had occurred and to advise the government on defence-related security sector reform. On 31 March 2003, EUFOR Concordia took over the monitoring tasks from NATO. The 350-strong Concordia was the first-ever EU military operation. All member states bar Denmark and Ireland took part in it. In addition, 14 non-EU states participated. Concordia could easily have been launched without recourse to NATO assets. An autonomous CSDP mission is precisely what France called for. However, Atlanticist EU members and Germany insisted, for political rather than operational reasons, that the EU force be run in cooperation with NATO under the Berlin Plus agreements. They wanted to signal to Washington that the CSDP was a supplement to NATO and not an ersatz alliance. Their view prevailed. Minor hiccups notwithstanding, cooperation between Concordia and NATO was smooth, both during the transition from NATO to EUFOR troops and once Concordia was up and running (Gross, 2009).

EUFOR Concordia was tasked to contribute to a stable and secure environment. The initial mandate lasted six months. To implement it, Concordia deployed Field Liaison Teams to patrol the former crisis area (Mace, 2003). The operation was extended for three months. This allowed for an uninterrupted transition from Concordia to the CSDP follow-on mission EUPOL Proxima. Concordia was a success in that it kept the peace in the country. Yet given the stable situation on the ground, this was no big achievement. Concordia's significance lay elsewhere. The EU peacekeeping force mattered because it was a successful test of the military CSDP and the Berlin Plus procedures.

EUPOL Proxima (December 2003–December 2005)

Police reforms were a central plank of the 2001 Ohrid peace accord. The Slav-dominated police had a record of misconduct. Its violence often targeted the Albanian minority (Abrahams, 1998). Against this backdrop, the EU deployed its second CSDP police mission.

Proxima had a one-year mandate. It was to contribute to the consolidation of law and order; the reform of the ministry of the interior; the development of a civilian border police; and confidence-building measures between the police and the Albanian minority. In view of the short mandate, the mission leadership initially decided against project-based reforms. However, the resulting absence of strategic focus threatened the achievement of the mandate. Also, personal rivalry undermined the effectiveness of the mission. There was little coordination between, on the one hand, the head of Proxima and, on the other, the EU Special Representative (EUSR) and the head of the Commission Delegation. Under pressure from Brussels, the mission was re-engineered. It established 5 reform programmes, which together comprised 28 projects (Merlingen, with Ostrauskaite', 2006). They ranged from the organization of workshops on detecting forged travel documents to the production of policing manuals on the investigation of human trafficking. The programmatic approach reinvigorated the mission. But it came too late. Proxima only had six months to implement its reform projects. This was not long enough to have an impact on Macedonian law enforcement. To save the mission from failure, the EU Council decided to prolong it for one more year.

Proxima 1 was deployed in over 20 locations in the former crisis area. It had a staff of about 180 international police officers. Proxima 2 had its personnel strength cut to about 120. At the same time, it was rolled out throughout the country. To make ends meet, the mission's new leadership was asked by Brussels to reduce the reform programmes to three. The projects were for the most part a continuation of the uncompleted activities of Proxima 1. Proxima 2 was followed by an EU Police Advisory Team of about 30 experts. They were deployed from December 2005 to June 2006. EUPAT was a bridging measure until the European Commission follow-on police reform project kicked in.

Proxima (1 and 2) made a difference on the ground. Among their noteworthy achievements were the improvement of the accountability of police officers to citizens and the upgrade of the interface between law enforcement and the judiciary (Ioannides, 2007; Flessenkemper, 2008). This said, the mission was more about symbolic and intra-EU politics than about reforming the local police. It was deployed about two and a half years after the Ohrid peace deal had been signed. In the meantime numerous international actors had successfully engaged the local police in reforms (Merlingen and Ostrauskaite, 2005a). And yet the EU Council decided to maintain a CSDP presence in the country after EUFOR Concordia was terminated. On the one hand, it wanted to underline the EU's continuing political commitment to Macedonia. On the other hand, it wanted to signal to the European Commission that it intended to take a broad view of civilian crisis management. It staked out a large policy space for the CSDP in what the Commission has traditionally considered its turf.

EULEX Kosovo (December 2008–)

Kosovo is a poverty-stricken corner of Europe mainly populated by ethnic Albanians. In 1989, the Yugoslav government abolished the limited autonomy the province had previously enjoyed. Martial law was proclaimed. Instead of quelling ethnic unrest, this move fuelled it. Within a few years, Serb security forces and the Kosovo Liberation Army battled each other. At the beginning of 1999, an international conference was held in Rambouillet, France, to find a peaceful settlement. The West blamed its failure on Belgrade. NATO began bombing Serb targets in the province as well as in Montenegro and Serbia proper to stop the bloody repression of Kosovars. After an air campaign of about two and a half months, operation Allied Force achieved its objective. Serb President Milošević agreed to withdraw his military forces from the province. In June 1999, UN Security Council Resolution 1244 transformed Kosovo into an international protectorate run by the UN Special Representative of the Secretary-General (SRSG), who also heads the UN Interim Administration Mission in Kosovo (UNMIK). In 2006, the UN Secretary-General appointed a Special Envoy to find a solution for the future status of Kosovo. Within a year, Martti Ahtisaari tabled a proposal to grant Kosovo independence. It was rejected by Belgrade. After international mediation failed, Kosovo unilaterally declared its independence in February 2008. It was recognized by the USA and the majority of EU members as well as assorted other countries. Although EU governments failed to agree on a common position on this issue, they did agree on dispatching a CSDP mission to Kosovo. The mission operates 'under the overall authority and within the status-neutral framework of the United Nations' (United Nations Security Council, 2008: 11; Council of the European Union, 2008d). Failure to dispatch a CSDP mission would have resulted in a mission composed of a coalition of willing EU states led by America (Koeth, 2010). This would have been a severe blow to the newly established credibility of the CFSP. The SRSG and UNMIK have been sidelined since Kosovo's declaration of independence.

EULEX Kosovo is an integrated rule-of-law mission tasked to construct an independent and multi-ethnic criminal justice and customs system in Kosovo. It has three main components, which deal with the police, judiciary and customs. The police component is the largest. In addition to general police development work, EULEX police investigates war crimes, corruption and financial crime, especially money laundering. EULEX judges and prosecutors investigate war crimes, organized crime and corruption. Case management is handled jointly with local judges and prosecutors. The customs component is the one least involved in executive tasks. It focuses on monitoring, mentoring and advising activities. The ministerial-level Joint Rule of Law Co-ordination Board is the main venue for official cooperation between EULEX and the Kosovo authorities on all key rule-of-law issues.

EULEX has a number of unique features. First, it is the largest-ever civilian CSDP deployment. It has an authorized strength of about 1,900 internationals and 1,100 locals. Twenty-six EU states contributed to the mission when it was launched. Second, EULEX is the first civilian operation with executive competencies. It is authorized to run independent police investigations, to conduct trials and to annul decisions taken by local authorities. Last but not least, it is the first CSDP mission with US participation. An informal deal was struck between Washington and Brussels in early 2007. Washington agreed to have US personnel serve in EULEX. Brussels agreed to deploy a CSDP police mission to Afghanistan. About 80 US police officers, judges, and prosecutors joined EULEX when it was launched.

The mission faces daunting challenges. Kosovo remains awash in weapons. The government in Priština has limited authority over the rule-of-law sector in predominantly Serb-populated North Kosovo, though in 2011 it stepped up its efforts to reinforce its presence there (see further below). Crime throughout the country remains rampant, especially money laundering, corruption and human trafficking (European Commission, 2008b, 2009a, 2011a). As in other ex-Yugoslav territories, political interference in operational policing decisions is common. The judiciary is regarded by the international community as the weakest of all of Kosovo's institutions (Organisation for Security and Co-operation in Europe, 2008; International Crisis Group, 2010). For instance, in 2008 the overstretched court system had a backlog of nearly 40,000 criminal cases. The backlog of civil cases, many of which are related to property claims, was even larger.

Two key challenges the mission faces are how to handle the very different expectations addressed to EULEX by Serbs and Kosovars and the lack of a coherent EU position on

Kosovo. For the Serbs, EULEX is there to protect endangered ethnic Serbian communities in a Serbian province. For the Kosovars, the mission is about helping the Kosovo government to build a functioning sovereign state. Reflecting these different expectations, the mission juggles with contradictory objectives. On the one hand, its mandate is to help build a viable, effective and democratic justice and customs system. On the other hand, the mission remains neutral as to the future of the political organization of Kosovo.

EU external governance policies beyond the CSDP

Since 2000 the EU has had a comprehensive and well-resourced strategic framework in place to provide policy guidance and financial assistance to the Western Balkan countries with a view to promoting stability, market democracy and regional cooperation. The Stabilisation and Association Process (SAP) was upgraded by the Thessaloniki European Council in 2003, at which the EU committed itself to giving EU membership to all concerned countries when they meet the accession criteria. The Stabilisation and Association Agreements (SAAs) are the centrepiece of the SAP. They establish close and comprehensive contractual relations between the EU and the Western Balkan governments. The SAAs are designed to help the countries approximate the EU *acquis communautaire* and to prepare them for participation in the EU single market. Throughout the SAP process, the Commission monitors and assesses the reforms in annual progress reports. When it deems a country to have approximated EU standards, it recommends to the Council of Ministers that enlargement negotiations be opened. In addition to the SAP, the EU initiated and was a principal participant in the Stability Pact for South Eastern Europe. Launched in 1999 and operative until 2008, it promoted democratization, economic reconstruction and security in the region and encouraged regional cooperation. In 2008, it was replaced by the Regional Cooperation Council. The EU remains active in the new body, which focuses on regional policy coordination. Last but not least, individual EU states have provided considerable bilateral assistance to Western Balkan states.

The SAP has been the main pillar of EU policy towards the Western Balkans. Its most powerful carrot has been EU membership. Also, the SAP has made a difference because of the EU funding it involves. From 2000 to 2006, CARDS (Community Assistance for Reconstruction, Development and Stabilisation) was the main instrument for financial aid to the region. It allocated €298.2 million to Macedonia, €502.8 million to Bosnia and €583.8 million to Kosovo. In 2007, CARDS was replaced by the Instrument for Pre-accession Assistance (IPA). From 2007 to 2010, it has allocated €302.8 million to Macedonia, €332 million to Bosnia and €426.4 million to Kosovo. Most of the funding has been channelled into economic development and institution- and capacity-building projects, with a special focus on the rule of law, border management and democracy promotion. Beyond the SAP, EU policy conditionality, which links concessions by Brussels such as visa liberalization and financial aid to certain domestic reforms, has been a powerful influence instrument (Trauner, 2009).

Successes and limitations of EU policy in the Western Balkans

Any overall assessment of EU policy in the Western Balkans has to take account of the fact that accomplishments and shortcomings are finely balanced. The EU record in the region may either be described as a glass half-empty or half-full. The assessment that follows avoids such an 'either–or evaluation' in favour of a nuanced assessment, focusing on the CSDP.

Beginning with the successes, CSDP troops have successfully kept the peace in Bosnia and Macedonia. CSDP police officers have made law enforcement more effective and accountable in Macedonia and Bosnia and they have started to do the same in Kosovo. EULEX judges and prosecutors help to strengthen the rule of law. In carrying out their tasks, the CSDP missions have prevented a return to conflict, promoted public order and contributed to good governance. Second, the CSDP operations have undoubtedly strengthened EU internal security. Through their security sector reforms, they have combated organized crime and the threats to the EU associated with it such as drug trafficking, weapons smuggling and illegal migration. The EU has further enhanced the impact of its Western Balkan CSDP interventions on homeland security by coordinating them with the external dimension of EU Justice and Home Affairs (Mounier, 2009). Third, the CSDP operations have helped repair the tarnished reputation of the EU in the region. Moreover, they have strengthened the visibility and political influence of the EU and given it additional diplomatic leverage in relations with the concerned governments. Overall, the CSDP has evolved from experimental pilot to an important instrument of EU external governance in the Western Balkans. EU policy has been crucial in transforming the region from a bad neighbourhood into a relatively decent one in which peace and democracy are well entrenched.

On the downside, the missions and EU policy more generally have faced a series of operational and political challenges. Beginning with the former, first, the civilian missions in Bosnia and Macedonia were initially hampered by their narrow mandates, which focused on just one component of the justice system – policing. The mandates thus ignored the functional interdependence between the various components of the justice system, notably between policing and the judiciary. The narrow objectives of the first generation of civilian CSDP missions reflected the decision by the EU to build up the civilian CSDP around discrete priority areas such as law enforcement and the rule of law. The second-generation mission in Kosovo no longer suffers from this problem. It has benefited from the EU's turn to multi-functional mission designs. Second, among the most bothersome issues for the civilian CSDP missions have been the cumbersome procurement procedures and difficulties in recruiting and retaining qualified personnel. European Commission red tape has caused many delays in the procurement of basic mission equipment such as computers and telephones. Insufficient recruitment mechanisms at the level of EU states and a patchy multi-layered training regime account for the fact that the missions in Bosnia and Kosovo have struggled to attract sufficient high-quality secondees to carry out their mandates. Third, both civilian and military missions have been affected by bureaucratic infighting among different branches of EU foreign policy and by related difficulties in coordinating action on the ground among different members of the EU family. Institutional politicking and turfing have degraded mandate implementation. They have also prevented the EU from making the most of its comprehensive foreign-policy toolbox in its efforts to transform the Western Balkans. The Lisbon Treaty tackles some of the challenges raised by points two and three through new rapid-funding procedures and the European External Action Service (EEAS). For instance, with the creation of the EEAS, which incorporates both heads of EU delegations and EU Special Representatives (EUSRs), the post of the EUSR in Bosnia was decoupled from that of the High Representative in 2011. In turn, the head of the EU delegation to Bosnia was double-hatted as EUSR, which will doubtlessly make EU policy towards Bosnia more coherent.

As to the political challenges faced by the EU in the three countries concerned, first, nepotism and undue partisan influence in the policing and the rule-of-law sectors remain rampant. Second, inter-ethnic tensions and ethnic polarization penetrate deep into the criminal justice systems. Third, EU pressure notwithstanding, law enforcement and judiciaries have shown only a limited capacity and willingness to combat corruption and organized crime. Finally, given the political attention given to the concerned countries and the resources pumped into them, progress on the road to the EU has been slow. Although it signed an SAA with Brussels in 2007, Bosnia continues to be institutionally fragmented and politically divided. Not surprisingly, progress on the road towards the EU has been very slow and uneven (European Commission, 2011b). The constitutional changes advocated by the West to strengthen the central state and ensure the political and economic viability of the country remain elusive. Kosovo lags even further behind. More than ten years after the international community took charge of Kosovo, the country's political and economic survival remains dependent on its external benefactors. On key indicators of democratic development such as the rule of law, freedom of the media and corruption the country persistently receives low scores from the EU. Relations with Serbia and inter-ethnic relations in Kosovo remain prickly, as the (attempted) takeover by force of border checkpoints in North Kosovo in the summer of 2011 by Kosovar special police, and the tensions between Serbia and Kosovo and between the ethnic communities in North Kosovo that ensued, demonstrate. The EU, which had no advance warning of the Kosovar operation, succeeded in defusing the ethnic tensions, even brokering a deal on Kosovo customs stamp that has allowed the reopening of trade between Kosovo and Serbia. Yet the incident reinforces the impression that Brussels has, somewhat paradoxically, a greater moderating and Europeanizing influence on Serbia, whose government pursues a pronounced pro-EU course, than on Kosovo even though its footprint in the country is large. The country is destined to be a Western protectorate for the foreseeable future. Macedonia is most advanced on the road to the EU, though progress has occurred at a snail's pace. Already in 2001 it signed an SAA with the EU. In 2005, it was granted EU candidate status. However, it took the European Commission until the end of 2009 to recommend opening enlargement negotiations, which have not yet started. The country still faces ethnic tensions, with the nationalistic feelings of the Slav majority running high, fuelled by the dispute with Greece over the name 'Macedonia'. Moreover, the government has recently clamped down on the political opposition. In 2011, one prominent opposition leader was arrested and a number of opposition media outlets were forced to close as they faced tax-evasion charges, a fact which led the European Commission to conclude in its 2011 Progress Report on Macedonia that the 'diversity of the media landscape has been weakened' (European Commission, 2011c: 16).

Explaining the mixed EU record

What explains the successes and shortcomings of the CSDP in the Western Balkans? A principal reason for the relative success of the CSDP missions in the region is the fact that the consensus–expectations gap has been relatively narrow. The CSDP is often hampered by a 'lack of decision-making procedures capable of overcoming dissent [which opens] a gap between what the member-states are expected to agree on and what they are actually able to consent to' (Toje, 2008a: 122). This gap accounts for the fact that outside the Western Balkans the CSDP operational record lacks ambition (Witney, 2008: 41). EU policy towards the Western Balkans has been partly different because on this issue national interests have been more convergent than divergent. The lack of an actionable security strategy and a robust strategic culture have not prevented the EU from evolving a largely consensual assessment of the soft security threats emanating from the region, from giving the CSDP missions clear and robust mandates to counter them and from mobilizing considerable resources (personnel, financial and diplomatic) to empower them to implement their mandates. A further reason is that the CSDP missions have benefited from the pronounced structure of inequality that binds southeastern Europe to the EU. The depth of these dependency relations sets the region apart from the relations the EU has with Eastern Europe, Africa and Asia, where Brussels' geoeconomic and geopolitical influence is held in check by limited ties or by alternative power centres such as the USA, Russia or China. The economic and political future of the Western Balkans squarely depends on the EU, which makes the countries concerned both more vulnerable to its pressure and more willing to comply with its demands. This has been a general empowering condition for the CSDP missions. A related, albeit more specific factor is that the missions have been able to leverage their influence by linking their reforms to broader EU membership and policy conditionality. Despite the turfing problems mentioned earlier, the CSDP missions and the Commission have generally reinforced their respective impact on the security sectors of their host countries.

Turning to the reasons for the shortcomings of EU policy in the Western Balkans, there is, first, the fact that the CSDP deployments in Bosnia and Macedonia were among the very first missions. They thus encountered teething problems, ranging from their non-holistic mandates to logistical problems. Second, a more persistent challenge to EU effectiveness has been domestic politics in the target countries, especially the continuing importance of divisive ethnic identities and the associated politicization of public life along ethnic lines (Freyburg and Richter, 2010). Local identity politics has limited the ability of CSDP missions to promote the professionalization of the criminal justice system and of the incentives-based policies of the Commission. Third, the EU's impact on the ground has been degraded by local scepticism regarding the legitimacy of some of its demands and policies (Noutcheva, 2009). For instance, Republica Srpska policy-makers have charged the international community, including the EUPM, that their insistence on the centralization of Bosnian policing hides an illegitimate political agenda aimed at changing the country's constitution through the backdoor. These charges have been particularly vocal when it comes to the EU given that its demands are not backed up by any *acquis communautaire* on the appropriate territorial organization of policing. In a similar vein, the deal struck by the EU and Serbia to allow Serb police station commanders in the north of Kosovo to report to EULEX and not to the Kosovo-Albanian-dominated Kosovo Police Service has been regarded as illegitimate by Kosovar authorities.

Fourth, the widespread perception in the three countries that the EU is reluctant to accept them as members and seeks excuses to push accession into a distant future has negatively affected Brussels' ability to fully leverage the membership carrot for advancing domestic reforms, including CSDP-driven reforms. The effectiveness of incentives-based policies relies on, among other things, a clear time horizon for when the benefits can be expected. Last but not least, EU policy towards the region has been hampered by intra-EU disagreements. In the case of Macedonia, the start of enlargement negotiations has been delayed by Greece, which has been locked with Macedonia in an emotional dispute over the latter's name. Athens claims the name Macedonia for one of its own northern regions and calls on its neighbour to change its name. In the case of Kosovo, EU accession policy and EULEX have faced a more fundamental problem. Brussels has been unable to formulate a coherent strategy on Kosovo (Koeth, 2010). On the one hand, EU states have underlined their willingness to give Kosovo 'a clear European perspective, in line with the European perspective of the region' (European Council, 2008: 16). On the other hand, Kosovo's status remains controversial within the EU, notwithstanding the 2010 judgement of the International Court of Justice that Kosovo's self-declared independence is compatible with international law. EU states Cyprus, Greece, Romania, Slovakia and Spain do not recognize its sovereignty. The split has forced the EU to adopt a status-neutral position on the future of Kosovo. At the same time, the brief of the International Civilian Representative in Priština, who is backed by most EU states and double-hatted as EUSR, is to build up Kosovo as a functioning sovereign state. EU policy towards Kosovo, including EULEX, is thus characterized by a fundamental political contradiction. As long as it remains unresolved, Brussels' impact on the ground will suffer.

Conclusion

To conclude, the chapter provides five policy recommendations on how to improve the EU record in the Western Balkans. First, the EU prides itself in making the notion of local ownership and partnership a key pillar of its CSDP operations and its structural foreign policy. Yet action only partly reflects discourse. The gap engenders the risk that EU supervised nation-building ends up stunting the growth of local democracy rather than advancing it. Both in Bosnia and Kosovo, EU foreign policy, including the EULEX mission, has to do more to avert such a dysfunctional outcome. In Bosnia, the EU has been part of international nation-building policies that have marginalized local ownership to such an extent that some critics refer to the role of the international community in the country as faking democracy (Chandler, 2000). The EUPM did not live up, either, to its verbal commitment to the local ownership of Bosnian police reforms (Merlingen, 2007). The heavy expatriate footprint in Bosnia has fostered a culture of dependency. Domestic political elites act irresponsibly, failing to cooperate with each other in reforming the country and instead pursuing maximalist positions in the knowledge that if push comes to shove the internationals will preserve the peace and impose their solutions. Furthermore, policy-makers and citizens alike have become cynical about politics because they know that whatever the outcome of the local democratic process, in the end the final arbiters of what goes and does not go in Bosnia are the internationals. In Kosovo the heavy EU footprint, including that of the executive EULEX mission, engenders the same risks. It is up to the EU to avoid it and to act towards Bosnia and Kosovo and the other Western Balkan countries more as a partner than a suzerain. If it does insist, as it sometimes will have to, on policy conditionalities, it should not hide behind the technocratic rhetoric of best practice but assume political responsibility for its efforts to shape local polities, politics and policies.

Second, the EU should avoid piling up new or changing existing requirements that Western Balkan countries have to meet before they can join the EU. Unclear and proliferating conditions are perceived as a delaying tactic by the concerned countries, and they reduce EU leverage over them. Third, the EU should discontinue its CSDP operation in Bosnia, where there is no longer a need for crisis management. It should make the freed resources available for more urgent tasks, including in Afghanistan, where the EU police mission remains notoriously understaffed. Fourth and closely related, the EU should launch a new military operation in the Western Balkans to take over from the NATO-led Kosovo Force (KFOR). This would inject new momentum into the build-up of the military CSDP and show that the EU remains serious about becoming a military security provider by improving its record of military deployments that have recently been limited to mainly cosmetic interventions in Africa, which generate headlines but do not contribute to sustainable improvements on the ground. The EU should make Bosnia and Kosovo a test case for its post-Lisbon foreign policy. The European External Action Service should make the region a priority to demonstrate that it can deliver on its promise to streamline and sharpen EU foreign policy across the divide between the intergovernmental CSDP and the communitarian enlargement policy.

13

THE THREE PARADIGMS OF EUROPEAN SECURITY IN EASTERN EUROPE

Co-operation, competition and conflict

Hiski Haukkala

When it comes to Eastern Europe the term security should be understood in the broadest possible sense.[1] For the European Union the increasing exposure to Eastern Europe, or what is increasingly known simply as the 'Eastern neighbourhood', spells a myriad of security challenges, both soft and hard. The area is home to some of the most impoverished and unstable countries in the world. For example, of the 12 countries in the area, altogether 4 feature prominently in the top 60 on *Foreign Policy*'s failed state index: Kyrgyzstan (31), Uzbekistan and Tajikistan (tied at 39) and Georgia (47) (*Foreign Policy*, 2011). In addition, the relations between the countries in the region are often strained and the area is home to some of the most protracted and difficult inter- as well as intrastate conflicts in the world. What is more, the area also includes a less than fully stable regional hegemon, Russia, that jealously guards its perceived sphere of influence and has eyed the EU's increasing role with some suspicion.

Yet it is in the EU's own interests to engage with the region in a substantial and comprehensive manner (Bonvicini, 2006). It is also a region where the EU increasingly is expected to take the lead as well as shoulder the primary responsibility of peace, stability and security (Biscop, 2005: 37). This is something the EU itself has acknowledged as well. This was reflected in, for example, the EU's own European Security Strategy (ESS) from 2003, which stated quite unambiguously how 'building security in our neighbourhood' was a key strategic objective for the Union (European Council, 2003). This view was reiterated in the Implementation Report of December 2008 (European Council, 2008a) as well.

That the EU itself thinks that Eastern Europe – and by extension Central Asia – is of considerable importance and interest is not to be doubted. Since the 'Big Bang' enlargement of 2004, the EU has gained direct access and at times unwelcome exposure to the volatile dynamics in the region. What is more, in recent years Brussels has been on its way to increasingly becoming a recognized and even welcomed actor in the region (for more about the role of recognition in the EU's policies in the East, see Bengtsson, 2010). That said, this chapter nevertheless ventures on to analyse whether the EU's voiced ambitions have been matched by the events on the ground. To a large degree, the result is a qualified no: despite the fact that the EU clearly has vital interests and grand objectives, to date there have been not many actual deliverables, at least outright successes, for the Union to point to.

It is argued that the main reason for the relatively lacklustre performance by the Union stems from the conflicting logics at play in the region. The EU – which often is a one-size-fits-all actor internationally – is faced with three conflicting logics of interaction, or paradigms of security, in the East: co-operation, competition and conflict. This chapter will discuss all of them in turn and will end with some concluding thoughts pondering the relative weight the three paradigms can be expected to have in the future, as well as discussing the EU role in the region. Obviously a short chapter like this does not allow a full analysis of the issues both thematically and geographically. Instead, examples are selected from both categories with a view to arriving at as comprehensive a picture of the issues at hand as possible.

Co-operation

The dissolution of the Soviet Union catapulted the then EC into leadership in Europe (Pelkmans and Murphy, 1991). The challenge was perhaps the most acute in the East, where in January 1992 the Community was faced with the challenge of having 15 new countries altogether in the former Soviet Union (FSU). To be sure, in the first instance the challenge was mainly a negative one: to prevent the further disintegration of the former Soviet space and the significant rise in the EC's responsibilities in the region that would obviously ensue (Lippert, 1993: 130). Therefore the policy line chosen was based on the need to solidify a new and stable order in the post-Cold War Europe. Karen E. Smith has summed up the EC's line of reasoning by arguing that its approach was to be based on economic aid that was 'intended to facilitate economic reforms; reforms would help reintegrate each country into the world economy; and this would help create a new European regional security order' (K. E. Smith, 1999: 49; see also Webber, 2007: ch. 5). In addition to this, one more piece of the puzzle was also certain: full accession into the EC was not on the cards, especially for the countries of the FSU, with the notable exception of the three Baltic states that did indeed accede in 2004.

Regardless of the membership perspective, the EC's policy line towards the East was based on the uniform assumption that the eventual interaction and integration was to be based on common norms and values. This understanding followed logically from the developments at the end of the Cold War (the events have been discussed in detail in K. E. Smith, 1999). The spirit of the age was that of the triumphalism of Western liberal values. Therefore the destination ahead was certain – liberal democracy and market economy – and the road to be taken was that of transition (and not more open-ended transformation) to Western liberal norms and values (Ikenberry, 2001: 215–16).

It is against this background that the Union's enhanced attention to the role of political conditionality based on liberal principles in the Union's relations with third parties during the post-Cold War era should be understood. Despite the crucial differences in the nature of the Community's offer in the Partnership and Co-operation Agreements (PCAs) that were negotiated with the countries of the FSU and the Europe Agreements that resulted in eventual EU accession, the logic in the arrangements was largely the same, with the offer being made conditional upon meeting the key criteria put forth by the Community itself: in exchange for adherence to a set of 'European values' and the implementation of liberal economic reforms, the Community would allocate assistance and grant closer forms of association when necessary (Vahl, 2001: 9). In essence, in devising a dense network of bilateral relations with the countries in Eastern Europe, the Community not only responded to external demands, but also showed strategic actorness by consciously seeking to project its views about good governance on its new partners (K. E. Smith, 1999: 173). All in all, the policy choices during the 1990s amounted to what can be called the Union's claim of regional normative hegemony, as exemplified best by the accession and European Neighbourhood Policy (ENP) processes (Haukkala, 2008, 2010).

The 'Big Bang' Eastern enlargement of 2004 created a group of new issues for the EU. It now acquired a set of new neighbours that presented it with a host of new challenges. It is safe to say that for the first time the EU acquired a direct stake in the volatile dynamics of Eastern Europe, including the Southern Caucasus. The EU was also faced with the pressing question of how to deal with the fresh calls for accession that started to emerge from the forthcoming 'new neighbours'. To all intents and purposes, the enlargement process seemed to have become a perpetual motion engine, a fact not all the member states and wider public were equally comfortable with.

It is against this backdrop that the emergence of European Neighbourhood Policy in 2003 should be examined. The ENP can be seen as having a threefold function: First and foremost, it is a security and stability policy in its own right. Second, it is an attempt to devise an alternative to further enlargements of the Union. Instead of full integration and institutional immersion, the 'neighbours' are offered wide-ranging co-operation and association. Third, it is an attempt at (re)injecting the Union's normative agenda and the application of conditionality more strongly into relations with non-candidate countries (see Kelley, 2006; Dannreuther, 2006; Sasse, 2008). As such, it is a conscious attempt at squaring the circle of relinquishing enlargement while retaining the Union's normative power in Europe.

At the heart of the initiative is the EU's offer of enhanced relations and closer integration based on shared values between the Union and its neighbours. The mechanism is simple: in return for effective implementation of reforms (including aligning significant parts of national legislation with the EU *acquis*), the EU will grant closer economic integration and association with its partners (European Commission and High Representative of the European Union for Foreign Affairs and Security Policy, 2011). The approach is twofold, as the EU wanted first to tap the full potential of the already existing PCAs, namely the gradual harmonization of legal norms with the EU *acquis* and the creation of free trade and only then move towards a set of new 'neighbourhood agreements' that would include a deep and comprehensive free trade area (DCFTA) as well as the prospect of closer political association with the Union.

The ENP also envisaged a process based on clear differentiation between countries and regular monitoring of progress. It is, however, here that the Union's attempt at normative hegemony in its neighbourhood becomes clearly visible, as the process is built on a set of bilateral relationships between the individual neighbours and the EU. Scholars seem to be in agreement that this is a deliberate choice on the part of the Union to maximize its leverage over the neighbours (K. E. Smith, 2005: 762–3; Vahl, 2005; Haukkala, 2008). Therefore, to all intents and purposes the Union does not give much meaningful say to the neighbours in setting the normative agenda: the objectives and the means are non-negotiable and the only time the partners have been consulted is when the individual action plans with clear benchmarks and timetables are being agreed upon. As such, the Union has been offering (or withholding) economic benefits depending on the neighbours' ability and willingness to implement the Union's normative agenda, and the EU is willing to give its neighbours influence basically only over *when* they want to implement the Union's demands and not *how* that is to be done (see also Bicchi, 2006).

The ENP also includes an aid component. The main instrument is the European Neighbourhood and Partnership Instrument (ENPI) that was introduced in 2007 and has replaced the TACIS funding in Eastern Europe. The budget for the Financial Framework 2007–13 is altogether €12 billion, an increase of 32 per cent compared with the previous budgetary cycle (European Commission, 2010).

Although the EU itself has been convinced of the credentials of its initiative, the neighbours themselves have been less impressed (Bengtsson, 2010; Bechev and Nicolaïdis, 2010). Ukraine is a case in point that has repeatedly voiced its frustration over the lack of credible accession prospects as well as the nimble level of market access and economic aid coming from the Union (Haukkala, 2008; Sasse, 2008). At the same time the lack of any serious progress in reforms in many of the neighbours has made it fairly easy for the Union to defer any further serious concessions.

Nevertheless, to allay some of the criticism the EU launched the Eastern Partnership in 2009. Compared to the ENP, the main new innovation in the EaP is the new multilateral component that encourages the convergence of the partner countries' legislation, norms and practices to those of the Union. The practical implementation of the multilateral track takes place through four thematic platforms: (i) democracy, good governance and stability; (ii) economic integration and convergence with EU policies; (iii) energy security; and (iv) people-to-people contacts. The multilateral track also provides for civil society participation through a separate Forum whose results will feed into the thematic platforms. Visibility and concrete substance are brought to the EaP through a number of regional flagship projects ranging from border management to energy efficiency and environmental concerns. Once again, political association and deeper economic integration are on offer for those partner countries which advance in agreed reforms. A related plan is to encourage free trade within the region itself. Of concrete and most immediate interest to the citizens of the partner countries is the facilitation of mobility. The EaP expands on the already set goal of country-by-country advancement to visa facilitation and readmission agreements with prospects for a visa dialogue with the possibility of eventual visa freedom. Integral to the success of this path is the the partner countries' ability to deal with the challenges posed by illegal immigration and other border-security-related issues.

Despite an impressive catalogue of new instruments and initiatives, the actual results from this flurry of activism have remained fairly meagre. To a degree this is due to Russia's suspicions, discussed in detail in the next section, but the nature of the EU's own policy template is also part of the problem. As Christou (2010) has argued, both the ENP and the EaP are based on binary logics of co-operation and containment where the essential securitization of the Eastern neighbourhood in effect limits and prevents the EU from effecting meaningful change through its policies: Instead of being able to offer its neighbours full benefits of freedom and interaction, the EU ends up shielding and protecting itself behind various policies that undercut the transformative potential of the EU in the East.

That said, the nature of the Eastern neighbours and indeed the very neighbourhood plays a role also. Countries in the region are usually weak states with limited administrative capacity. Corruption is entrenched and they are often divided states, either physically, as is the case with Georgia or Moldova, or mentally and politically when it comes to their place in Europe, as is the case with, for example, Ukraine. As a consequence, the countries have faced severe limitations in their ability and even basic willingness to engage in the kinds of reforms propagated by the Union (Lynch, 2005: 36).

A case in point is Ukraine. Despite repeatedly professing its European calling and credentials, Ukraine has failed to fully embrace the kind of societal change and reforms that would take it genuinely closer to the European Union. The brief 'romance' with the EU that followed the Orange Revolution of 2004 has increasingly been replaced with mounting fatigue and disillusionment on both sides. To better understand the difficulties Ukraine has faced in effecting its European calling we should keep in mind that the country is essentially what North *et al.* (2009) have called a natural state. Natural states are essentially limited-access orders that are based on a close fusion of economics and politics, patron–client relationships and rent-seeking. By contrast, open-access orders separate economic and political interests to a large degree and are contractual and rule-governed while allowing mass access to rents (for a useful discussion in the IR context, see Buzan, 2010). In essence, the EU has been propagating open-access solutions to a still predominantly closed Ukrainian order (for a discussion that highlights these characteristics in the Ukrainian society, see Kuzio, 2011). Responsible Ukrainian elites, too, acknowledge this conundrum and would in fact prefer to move towards a more open order, as exemplified by the repeated Ukrainian calls for domestic reforms and integration with the EU.

But the transition from a closed to an open-access order is difficult, even dangerous, as developments that favour the move towards open access orders tend to destabilize natural states, threatening potential instability, even chaos. The fate of the Orange Revolution shows how even the best of liberal intentions can succumb to the pressure of the clannish and oligarchic political and economic structures of Ukraine. In the process EU-led initiatives for reform can be perverted to serve the needs of local elites in prolonging and even enhancing their grip on power (Börzel, 2010). As a consequence, the EU is in danger of ending up propping up regimes with authoritarian tendencies instead of reforming them.

It can be argued that these characteristics are not unique to Ukraine but that the same principles can be seen as being at work in other Eastern neighbours as well, including Russia. Therefore the crux of the issue is that to all intents and purposes the EU is asking too much and giving too little in return in the East. The EU is asking for a radical transformation of a set of countries without offering them the full European perspective. What is more, the EU is expecting them to part ways with domestic governance structures, such as rent-seeking and political patronage, even patrimonialism, in favour of an open-market economy, liberal democracy and rule of law, which, while they might in the long term be beneficial for the countries in question, could in the short term put their stability, or at least put the standing and prosperity of the current elites in jeopardy (cf. Holden, 2009: 93, 121). To be sure, here we are faced with a genuine chicken-and-egg dilemma, as by and large the Eastern neighbours simply are not ready for deeper forms of engagement with the EU until they have engaged in substantial domestic reforms, which, however, might prove unattainable without the golden carrot of full EU accession (Missiroli, 2004). Whether extending the Union's membership further to the East is a realistic proposition is an altogether different matter, however, and one that must remain outside the scope of this chapter (for a discussion, see Haukkala, 2008).

Competition

The EU's role in Eastern Europe is further complicated by the element of competition. In essence, the EU has become locked into integration competition with Russia. Although the EU has done its best to convince the Russians that it is not interested in exclusive spheres of influence but is seeking consensual win–win outcomes instead, Moscow has decided to treat the EU's presence in the region largely in a classical zero-sum manner. This is largely due to the fact that the Russian elites frame international relations in general in terms of fierce competition and consequent spheres of interests and influence (Zagorski, 2009; Trenin, 2009). This has been reflected in the fact that Russia decided to opt out of the value-laden

ENP and has insisted on and been granted a more interest-driven strategic partnership instead (Sergounin, 2006).

This is not to suggest that the relations between the EU and Russia are wholly competitive, as the two obviously do co-operate with each other (for a discussion, see Haukkala, 2010). But in the context of European security Russia has taken a series of steps to counter the EU's impact in Eastern Europe and has increasingly put forth its own policies that in effect have undermined the Union's influence in the region. As Leonard and Popescu (2007: 17) have noted, in certain respects Russia has in fact had a much more robust strategy and policy in place than has been appreciated either in the EU or the United States.

Russia's competitive approach to the region takes three main forms. First, oil-rich Russia can use a whole array of mechanisms, both positive and negative, that are not necessarily at the Union's disposal to foster bilateral relationships. Russia's biggest asset may be its ability to engage in business deals with countries that the EU finds hard to engage. In short, Russia can offer economic partnerships and benefits that the EU at times cannot match because Russia does not have any problems in supporting authoritarian regimes. A case in point is Central Asia, where Russia has for years been operating at full economic and political speed with the Union still contemplating the merits and possible limits of engaging countries with severe problems in their democratic and human rights credentials (Melvin, 2007). In Eastern Europe the same lesson also seems to apply: it has been largely thanks to political and economic support from Moscow that President Lukashenko has been able to hold on to power for so long in Belarus (Moshes, 2010). More recently, President Victor Yanukovych's Ukraine has to a degree been lured back to line with a set of preferential gas deals that have kept the country's crisis-ridden economy afloat while lessening the prospects of successful economic modernization and eventual integration with Europe.

As a consequence, Russia seems increasingly to position itself as a counter-force to the Union's approaches to their 'common neighbourhood' (Popescu and Wilson, 2009). This has been highlighted in the fact that increasingly Russia seems less interested in joining the EU in a pan-European free trade area (as envisaged by the current PCA) and is instead investing political energies into developing a competing Customs Union of its own with some countries of the CIS, notably Belarus and Kazakhstan.

Second, Russia plays a major role in the conflicts that also affect the Union's neighbourhood. Russia is a player (in one form or another) in all the still simmering conflicts in the region. For example, the independence-minded 'kleptocracy' of Igor Smirnov in Transdniestria relies on Moscow's political and economic support. Russia also holds considerable sway in the deadlocked settlement of Nagorno-Karabakh between Armenia and Azerbaijan. In most cases it seems as if Russia is playing the role of spoiler, frustrating the Union's and other international actors' attempts to resolve the conflicts; essentially preferring the status quo and the perceived spheres of influence to the risk of the EU and its normative and economic reach achieving stronger sway in the region, perhaps even supplanting Russia's role in the process (Akçakoca *et al.*, 2009: 23–5; Meister, 2011: 17). To a degree, the brief Russo-Georgian war in August 2008 is a case apart and will be discussed in the next section.

Third, Russia has sought to develop an alternative model of economic modernization and societal development to that promoted by the EU. In this respect, however, it seems that Russia's effectiveness has at least so far been hindered by the fact that Moscow has failed to come up with an idea or theme to provide its policies with sound intellectual underpinnings that would have a wider international resonance. As a consequence, compared with the magnetic pull of the Union already mentioned, Russia's 'soft power' has been lacking (Tsygankov, 2006). Although the concept of 'sovereign democracy' has proven useful internally in resisting (the perceived) external encroachments on Russia's domestic juris-diction, it seems clear that, externally, the concept has not had much export potential. As a consequence, it has remained a home-grown Russian variant of a semi-authoritarian and state-capitalist thinking with rather weak intellectual underpinnings. That said, it should be noted that although the slogan and the ideology may not travel very well, the actual practice of resisting the Union's normative power and political conditionality seems to be a commodity that is in higher demand: engaging the European Union through its ENP requires sustained efforts at good governance on the part of the partner countries. Russia has shown how the EU can be successfully resisted, pointing out that being the Union's neigh-bour does not necessarily entail accepting its normative agenda as the basis for relations (see Karaganov, 2007).

The element of competition between the EU and Russia has not gone unnoticed by the countries residing in-between. In fact, the present constellation has invited and enabled a recurring political pattern where the states in the 'common neighbourhood' alternate their allegiances between the EU and Russia, always looking for a better political and economic deal. Therefore instead of fully Europeanizing or falling loyally into Russia's orbit the coun-tries use the two protagonists as bargaining chips and sources of political leverage to buttress their own sovereignty and freedom of manoeuvre (Popescu and Wilson, 2009; Wilson, 2010). As a result there exists potential for an unhappy outcome where neither the EU nor Russia manages to achieve their aims but both end up being played by the countries in-between. What is more, this process feeds into the feeling of latent competition in the region, eroding trust and hindering the development of co-operation further while creating potential for conflicts in the future.

To be sure, the Union's immediate Eastern neighbourhood is not the only theatre where this game has been played. In Central Asia the same tendencies have been present, with the notable exception that there the EU is not the second important contender with Russia but comes perhaps distant fourth after the United States and China, which have both been vying for influence with more vigour and success than the EU. Despite the adoption of Strategy for Central Asia in 2007, the EU has remained hamstrung between its voiced objectives of promoting human rights, democracy and good governance and the harsh realities of authori-tarianism and carbon-hydrate-based geopolitical competition in the region (Melvin, 2007; Emerson *et al.*, 2010). The EU's challenges in the region have been exacerbated further by the fact that it is Central Asia where Russia has been most concerned with the erosion of its standing and has therefore adopted an even harsher zero-sum mentality than has perhaps been the case in Eastern Europe (Torbakov, 2010; Deyermond, 2009).

Conflict

Since 2003 the EU has launched altogether 24 ESDP/CSDP operations, both civilian and military (Council of the European Union, 2011; Pirozzi and Sandawi, 2009). Of these only three have been conducted in the EU's Eastern neighbourhood. By contrast, ten operations have been conducted in Africa, suggesting a conclusion that the dispersion of missions tells more about the colonial past of many EU countries than the strategic importance of the Eastern neighbourhood to the European Union. Indeed, as Biscop and Coelmont (2010: 7) have noted, the missions often reflect political convenience or the parochial interests of only some of the member states rather than purely strategic considerations on the part of the EU.

To be sure, for a consensual win–win actor like the EU conflicts are always a challenge. In this respect Eastern Europe and Central Asia are a particularly challenging environment for the EU, as they are home to some of the most protracted and difficult conflicts in the world. The EU's difficulties in dealing with them have been manifest in a certain basic reluctance to become fully engaged in conflict settlement and crisis management in the area. When the EU has acted, it has mainly reacted and has not portrayed strategic and proactive actorness in the region (Khasson *et al.*, 2008: 221).

The EU itself sees its very presence in the region as playing a useful role in conflict resolution (Tocci, 2008). For example, conflict settlement features prominently in the ENP Action Plans (Helly, 2008). That said, the limits of the EU's 'constructive engagement' have also become obvious. Often the EU's impact is lowered by the low objective value of the Union's offers in the region (Tocci, 2008). Therefore, at best the ENP can be seen as an indirect conflict-settlement and -prevention policy: by seeking to improve the economic conditions and fostering people-to-people contacts, the policy can play a role in creating conditions for settlements while perhaps mitigating the harmful effects of conflicts without actually directly helping to solve them (Khasson *et al.*, 2008: 222).

There are several reasons for the EU's performance in the region. The region has already been crowded by other actors, especially the OSCE, and the EU has been fairly content to give pride of place to the multilateral body (Lynch, 2009; Khasson *et al.*, 2008: 222). The main reason behind the reluctance to engage the region stems from the internal political divisions in the Union, with several key member states preferring to keep a low profile in the hope of avoiding antagonizing Russia. As a consequence, the EU has punched below its weight in promoting conflict resolution in the East (Tocci, 2008: 882).

Also the nature of the missions in the East testifies to the same effect. The first mission, EUJUST Themis, was the first ever civilian rule-of-law mission launched by the Union. Between July 2004 and July 2005 altogether ten legal experts were sent to Georgia with a view to helping to develop rule of law in the country (for more about the mission and its mandate, see Kurowska, 2008). As such, the mission and the decision to target Georgia reflected more the ambitions of the Council Secretariat to move the civilian ESDP 'out of the police box' and the interests of certain member states in engaging particularly Georgia rather than any serious strategic calculation concerning what were the most burning issues to be tackled in the area (Kurowska, 2008: 100).

As a consequence EUJUST Themis can hardly be called a resounding success for the Union. The mission was plagued by internal coordination problems within the Union as well as political problems on the ground in Georgia (Kurowska, 2008). More importantly, although based on good intentions, the mission did not try to address the biggest security issue in Georgia, namely the ostensibly 'frozen' conflicts with South Ossetia and Abkhazia, which were sparked into a intensive although brief armed conflict between Russia and Georgia in August 2008 (of which more below).

The second mission, the EU Border Assistance Mission to the Republic of Moldova and Ukraine (EUBAM Moldova-Ukraine), can be assessed in a more positive light. The decision to launch the mission in late 2005 was based on a joint request from Moldova and Ukraine for EU assistance to develop their joint border control/customs practices in order to rein in the widespread smuggling and other illegal activities in the breakaway Transdniestria (for more about the mission, see Dura, 2009). The underlying rationale for the mission, which at the time of writing is still ongoing, was that in addition to stopping criminal activities the EU could help to put economic pressure on Tiraspol and therefore contribute to conflict settlement between Transdniestria and Moldova proper. Although the mission has been success in the former task, the latter goal has proven elusive. This is largely due to the economic and political support of Russia, which has enabled Transdniestria to withstand the economic losses incurred by the mission's activities. As a consequence the overall track record of the mission has been mixed: it has clearly proven useful in upgrading border management and fostering co-operation between Moldova and Ukraine, but it has failed to make a difference when it comes to the most profound underlying problem, the conflict concerning the future of Moldova (Dura, 2009; Parmentier, 2008).

Furthermore, the biggest success the EU has claimed, brokering the cease-fire between Russia and Georgia in August 2008, has not become an entirely unqualified success. At first sight, the EU's – or the Council Presidency France's and its President Nicolas Sarkozy's – performance was impressive: the EU managed, together with the Finnish OSCE Chairmanship to broker a six-point agreement that ended hostilities between the parties and managed to contain the conflict so that it did not entail the destruction of the whole of Georgia or loss of its sovereignty (the EU performance in the crisis has been discussed at length in Whitman and Wolff, 2010; Forsberg and Seppo, 2011). The EU was also able to field a substantial ESDP civilian Monitoring Mission in Georgia (EUMM) to supervise the implementation of the agreement. The EU has also secured, together with the UN and the OSCE, a leading role as a co-chair in the so-called Geneva Process that has been mandated to look for a more lasting settlement between all parties.

Yet all these successes can also been seen as failures of sorts. First, the EU's ability to act was largely made possible by the fact that Russia allowed it in the first place. For example, the cease-fire was agreed by Russia only after it had essentially achieved all of its primary military aims (Whitman and Wolff, 2010: 97). Russia's preponderance in the process is further underlined by the fact that Moscow has not lived up to its commitments in the six-point plan. For example, despite Russia assuming an obligation to withdraw its troops behind the pre-conflict lines it has not done so, and the EU has been forced to accept this as a *fait accompli*. Moreover, the ability of the EUMM to fully stabilize the situation on the ground has been substantially limited by the fact that Russia has not allowed the monitors any access to the breakaway regions themselves (Fischer, 2009: 385–6; Pirozzi and Sandawi, 2009: 6). Finally, in the Geneva talks the EU's role has remained weak, and the process has not produced any significant results but has to all intents and purposes degenerated into a mere refreezing exercise of the conflict.

None of this should be taken to mean that the EU has been useless on the ground. Although it has not been able to enforce the six-point plan, it was able to play a role in limiting the conflict. The monitoring mission has undoubtedly played a role in pacifying the area, too, and preventing small-scale skirmishes escalating into another shoot-out between the parties. In this respect the EUMM has become a useful trip wire that has at least thus far deterred all parties from any further aggression.

Conclusion

By its nature the EU's engagement and the policies it seeks to promote in its Eastern neighbourhood deal with security. Yet the analysis in this chapter highlights the certain and very real incompleteness of the EU as a security actor. It also highlights the certain discomfort the EU feels when operating in a region of vast importance where it nevertheless is for historical, cultural, economic and social reasons hampered and at times even undercut.

The chapter has argued that in the region the EU is faced with three different paradigms of European security – co-operation, competition and conflict – and that they create a rather mixed playground for the Union. In fact, for different reasons the EU has been hamstrung in playing all of them. In the sphere of co-operation the EU has been asking too much while being able to give too little to the troubled countries in the East. As a consequence, the EU's partnership-oriented project of association and small-scale integration has progressed in fits and starts, if at all. The EU has also been unable, and perhaps even more importantly, basically unwilling, to compete for influence in the region. This has probably been a wise move on the part of the Union, as engaging Russia in a geopolitical competition over the 'common neighbourhood' would only have served to further aggravate tensions without solving any of the underlying problems in the region.

The sphere of conflict resolution has highlighted a certain incompleteness of the EU as an international actor. In addition, the EU has clearly been unwilling to assume a larger role, largely in hopes of avoiding antagonizing Russia in the process. The EU is also suffering from a certain strategic deficit as all the other players in the region – Russia, China and the United States – as well as the countries residing in-between portray characteristics of more robust strategic culture and actorness. For example, the EUJUST Themis shows how the decision to launch particular missions often reflects more the internal ambitions of the Union and not the actual needs on the ground. In addition, the mission showed how the inter-institutional competition in Brussels between the different bodies can hamper the attainment of goals. To be sure, inter-institutional rivalry was not invented by Brussels – every international actor worthy of the name surely suffers from the same syndrome – but it seems evident that the EU is suffering from it perhaps more than most other actors. It is possible that some of these problems will be alleviated under the Lisbon Treaty and in the new External Action Service. At the same time the very process of creating the EAS has also shown that these competing pressures are real and can even hamper the development of otherwise badly needed new initiatives in the EU.

Equally, the problems faced by the EUMM in Georgia show how the success of the EU is crucially dependent on the attitude of other players in the region, especially Russia. As already noted, the EU has been unable to sanction Russia to withdraw behind the pre-conflict lines as it was supposed to do in the six-point plan. The EU has also been denied access to South Ossetia and Abkhazia, which has meant that its ability to reach all of its goals has been severely hampered. As a consequence, the EU has been forced to limit its actual impact to monitoring the new 'border' between Georgia proper and the break-away entities, in effect becoming a structural factor cementing the new status quo in the area.

None of this should be taken as a full rebuttal of the EU's role in the East, far from it. It should be borne in mind that the EU has come a long way as an international actor during the 2000s. The Georgian war has showed that the EU, when united and led by a leader with both authority and resolve, can make a difference. The fact that other international actors have been removed from the scene only serves to underline the importance of EU presence on the ground. Moreover, the EU is, finally, a fully engaged and recognized player in the region. Clearly the current state of affairs is not fully satisfactory for the EU and its member states, but it is a beginning on which the EU can and should seek to build more.

What is more, recently some weak signals of potential change in Russia have begun to emerge that offer some prospects of change also in the Russian view of the role of European Union in the East. These changes have largely been due to the wider 'reset' of US–Russian relations that have also spilled over to NATO–Russia relations as well (Antonenko and Yurgens, 2010). Some Russians have even begun to argue that a wide-ranging economic and political union between Russia and the EU is called for (Karaganov, 2010). Yet it is too early to conclude that a decisive shift has taken place in Russia. The long history of false starts in EU–Russian and US–Russian relations cautions against excessive optimism. Therefore it seems likely that the EU will continue to be hamstrung between the imperatives of its own security, its voiced ambitions and the realities on the ground in the East. By and large these realities are based on the conflicting logics of interaction prevalent in the area, which in their turn are based on deep-seated structural factors that are unlikely to change very quickly. As a consequence, it seems safe to conclude that the EU's uneasy balancing act in the East is here to stay, well into the future.

Acknowledgements

I want to thank Kari Möttölä for helpful comments on an earlier draft of this chapter. The usual disclaimer applies.

Note

1   In this chapter the term Eastern Europe, or 'Eastern neighbourhood', is used as a shorthand for the whole area of the former Soviet Union (with the exception of the three Baltic states). The focus will be largely, but not solely, on the EU's immediate Eastern periphery, the area covered by the European Neighbourhood Policy (ENP).

14

EUROPE, THE SOUTHERN NEIGHBOURHOOD AND THE MIDDLE EAST

Struggling for coherence

Costanza Musu

Europe's relations with the broader Mediterranean area are complex and deeply affected by the legacy of intricate historical ties.[1] Several members of the European Union have a past as colonial and Mandate powers in the region; World War II and the Holocaust cast a long shadow on relations with Israel; and the Mediterranean Sea has long been both the meeting point of the 'North' and the 'South' and the fracture line dividing three continents: Europe, North Africa and Asia.

Since the end of the Cold War the European Union (EU) has attempted to systematically identify and conceptualize its ties and interests in the region, and to elaborate a comprehensive and coherent policy that would reinforce its relations with the 'Southern Neighbourhood' and promote at the same time the EU's values and interests. However, while in developing its relations with Eastern Europe and former communist bloc countries the EU has been able to utilize the prospect of accession as a powerful tool of negotiations, no such possibility is on the table for the Southern partners, and this has left the EU struggling in its attempts to build effective and comprehensive initiatives. Relations have been further complicated (at times to the point of paralysis) by the unresolved Arab–Israeli conflict, which has been and continues to be a constant source of tension.

It is important to underline that for Europe, Middle East policy overlaps with Mediterranean policy. The EU considers the Mediterranean as a coherent geo-strategic region, and in this perspective it sees political instability in the Middle East as a potential danger to the political stability of the whole region. As Volker Perthes put it:

> [T]he European discourse alternatively emphasises Europe's common destiny with the peoples of the region and its responsibility for furthering peace, democracy and development among its neighbours, or European security and economic interests which require both socio-economic development and political progress in the region including, prominently, the peaceful regulation of the Arab–Israeli conflict.
>
> (Perthes, 2000: 43)

170

There are several reasons that explain why and how the Mediterranean matters to Europe: its potential for political and social instability; the uncontrolled migration flows generated by the scarcity of jobs and North–South economic disparity; the dependence of Europe on the energy resources of the Southern Mediterranean region (particularly gas); the possibility that countries in the Southern Mediterranean region might prove to be a fertile breeding ground for terrorism; the importance of the Mediterranean's transit points (the Straits of Gibraltar, the Dardanelles/Bosporus Straits, the Sicilian Channel and the Suez Canal), all critical both in terms of the energy security of the West and the general stability of maritime trade routes; and, as mentioned, the unresolved Arab–Israeli conflict, which is a constant source of tension.

The European Union has tried to build regional initiatives that would create positive linkages around common interests, and has attempted to improve South Mediterranean economies and thus prevent uncontrolled migration flows towards Europe. It has also endeavoured to organize relations along the guidelines of basic shared European values, such as the spread of democratic values, the rule of law and respect for human rights. Parallel but connected to these efforts have been the EU's attempts at cutting for itself a significant role in the Arab–Israeli peace process, attempts that in fact date back to the early 1970s and have become more consistent and systematic since 1991.

The EU's record of success with these initiatives is at best mixed. As this chapter will show, a number of factors have weakened the incisiveness of Europe's policies, including the persistence of sometimes conflicting European national agendas, the inherent contradictions of some aspects of the EU's strategy towards the region, the reluctance of several Southern Mediterranean governments to carry out significant reforms and the constant interference of the Arab–Israeli conflict that has severely hampered progress towards regional integration.

This chapter first analyses the strategic documents and official declarations that have defined the guidelines of the EU's policy towards the Mediterranean region. It then critically assesses and evaluates the EU's concrete policy initiatives. The analysis then focuses on the EU's policy towards the Arab–Israeli peace process. Finally, the conclusion offers a discussion of the way forward, especially in light of the political evolution in the EU's Southern Neighbourhood after the sudden regime changes in Tunisia and Egypt at the beginning of 2011.

Defining a strategy: milestones of EU policy towards the Mediterranean region

From the Barcelona Declaration to the Union for the Mediterranean

After the end of the Cold War, and with the intensification of the EU's relations with Eastern Europe, the southern EU member states increasingly requested a rebalancing of the Union's commitments towards Central and Eastern European countries and the South, as well as a revaluation of the Mediterranean region as a foreign policy priority. The so-called Mediterranean lobby (mostly Italy, France and Spain) within the Union became a 'vociferous advocate of a new approach' (Gomez, 1998: 140), and their pressures eventually led to the organization of a conference in Barcelona in 1995 to discuss ways of promoting a regional dialogue and co-operation, with the aim of reducing economic, social and demographic imbalances existing between the two shores of the Mediterranean.

The EU's long-term strategic approach to the Mediterranean region was focused on four objectives:

- first, to promote democratization, since – in the European experience – democratic structures have proven to be efficient instruments of conflict resolution within states, and also effective in diminishing the risk of conflicts erupting between states;
- second, to promote economic development and integration, an objective based on the assumption that free-market economies and liberalized international trade relations improve overall standards of living;
- third, to contribute to the construction of a framework of effective regional institutions, which could provide mechanisms for the peaceful resolution of conflicts;
- fourth, to favour a broader cultural dialogue underpinning all levels of political, economic and social interactions, in order to promote a Mediterranean identity on which more stable cross-regional relations could be based (Behrendt and Hanelt, 2000: 13).

The 1995 Conference approved the Barcelona Declaration, which endorsed the creation of a Euro-Mediterranean Partnership (EMP) between the then 15 EU member states and 12 Mediterranean Partners: Algeria, Cyprus, Egypt, Israel, Jordan, Lebanon, Malta, Morocco, Syria, Tunisia, Turkey and the Palestinian Authority.

To use the words of former Commission Vice President Manuel Marin, 'The Euro-Mediterranean Partnership provided for the first time a clear geopolitical and economic scenario for a priority region in the Union's foreign policy, and it designed a far-reaching double structure at both the multilateral and bilateral level.'[2]

The EMP (also known as the Barcelona Process, BP) had three main declared objectives or pillars: to establish a common Euro-Mediterranean area of peace and stability, to create an area of shared prosperity through the establishment of a free-trade area and to promote understanding between cultures and rapprochement of the peoples in the Euro-Mediterranean region. It was designed to operate both at the bilateral and multilateral levels.

At the bilateral level, the BP's strategy consisted of concluding Euro-Mediterranean Association Agreements between the Union and its Mediterranean partners,[3] and establishing national indicative programmes for financial assistance under the Community's MEDA program.[4] In the multilateral or regional track, the EU and its Mediterranean Partners developed an architecture of regularly meeting co-ordination bodies including Euro-Mediterranean foreign ministers' conferences.

The Barcelona Process was meant from the beginning to be independent from but parallel to the Middle East peace process: the peace process would achieve the political breakthrough; the BP would set up the real conditions for long-term stability and economic development. It would also offer a forum for the parties involved in the peace process to meet in a different context from that of the difficult and controversial negotiations on political and security issues. However, it soon became apparent that the formal separation between the Partnership and the peace process could not serve to prevent the de facto linkages emerging between the processes, and that any progress in the field of Mediterranean regional co-operation was continuously hampered by the difficulties encountered by the peace process. In other words, the EU's aspiration to be able to keep the process of economic co-operation and development isolated from the spill-over of the political consequences of the stalemate in the peace process proved to be an illusion (Musu, 2010).

In June 2000 the EU adopted a 'Common Strategy for the Mediterranean Region'. The Strategy built on the EMP and restated the European Union's goal of helping to secure peace, stability and prosperity in the region. It also acknowledged the inevitable link between any possible progress in the field of regional co-operation and a successful outcome of the Middle

East peace process, stating that 'The EU is convinced that the successful conclusion of the Middle East Peace Process on all its tracks, and the resolution of other conflicts in the region, are important prerequisites for peace and stability in the Mediterranean.'[5]

The same concepts were picked up and repeated in the 2003 European Security Strategy[6] and later in the 2006 Regional Strategy Paper for the Euro-Mediterranean Partnership,[7] which again underlined the strategic importance of the Mediterranean region to the EU in both economic and political terms, and identified three priority objectives for the EU:

- a common Euro-Mediterranean area of justice, security and migration co-operation;
- a common sustainable economic area, with a focus on trade liberalization, regional trade integration, infrastructure networks and environmental protection;
- a common sphere for socio-cultural exchanges.

Despite the political and economic commitments on the part of the EU, the Barcelona Process failed to yield any significant progress in these areas. In 2008 the French EU Presidency launched a new initiative and announced the creation of a 'Union for the Mediterranean', with the objective of infusing new life into the faltering Euro-Mediterranean Partnership. The initiative met initially with some resistance from within the EU itself, especially because it was not clear how it would fit with the existing structures of the Barcelona Process and whether it would end up adding another layer to the already complex picture of the EU's policies vis-à-vis the region (Emerson, 2008). Internal EU negotiations transformed the 'new' project into the official policy of the EU towards the Mediterranean, so that all future EMP initiatives would be implemented through the Union for the Mediterranean, but per se the Union for the Mediterranean offered little if any new substance to the pre-existing frameworks.

The bilateral dimension: the European Neighbourhood Policy and the Action Plans

In 2004, in the context of enlargement to ten new countries, the EU developed the European Neighbourhood Policy (ENP) with the objective of 'avoiding the emergence of new dividing lines between the enlarged EU and its neighbours, and of strengthening the prosperity, stability and security of all concerned'.[8] The ENP applies to the EU's immediate neighbours and includes the Mediterranean partners of the Barcelona Process. The objective of the ENP is to deepen the EU's bilateral relations with neighbouring states, partly as a means of using the bilateral approach to overcome the blockages inherent in region-wide policies such as the Barcelona Process. In fact with the introduction of the ENP the Barcelona Process essentially became the multilateral forum of dialogue and co-operation between the EU and its Mediterranean partners, while complementary bilateral relations were managed mainly under the ENP and through Association Agreements signed with each partner country.

The central elements of the ENP are the bilateral Action Plans (APs) agreed between the EU and each partner, which set out an agenda of political and economic reforms. At the beginning of 2011 the EU had signed Action Plans with several Mediterranean partners: Egypt, Israel, Jordan, Morocco, Tunisia, the Palestinian Authority and Lebanon. While the Barcelona Process (in its revamped format of Union for the Mediterranean) remains the cornerstone of the partnership with the Mediterranean, the Neighbourhood Policy is supposed to give the EU the chance to work more flexibly to meet the interests of each Southern Mediterranean country, also through the new European Neighbourhood and Partnership Instrument, which in 2007 replaced the already mentioned MEDA programme, until then the principal financial instrument of the EU for the implementation of the Barcelona Process.

From the above analysis it appears clear that the EU has both recognized the importance of building good relations with its Southern Mediterranean neighbours and dedicated a large amount of resources, both political and economic, to the task. At the same time it is difficult to claim that the EU has been able to achieve its objectives, primarily those of bringing about significant economic development and introducing deep democratic change.

One major obstacle hampered European strategy for years: the persistence of authoritarian governments in the region. The EU has tried to build a strong civil society in the Southern Mediterranean countries, introduce the rule of law, promote transparency and accountability in the armed forces and improve economies. At the same time, however, its main partners in the introduction of these profound changes have been authoritarian governments and regimes that had a lot to lose from the introduction of these very reforms, since their survival was guaranteed by the absence of a strong and politically aware civil society and by an alliance with the armed forces that perpetuated their grip on power and the economy. Furthermore, the introduction of a Euro-Mediterranean free-trade area has been hampered by the almost complete absence of South–South commercial and economic relations. The introduction of ENP and the shift of the focus to bilateral relations underline the continued presence of insurmountable obstacles in the development of an effective regional framework.

The events of early 2011, which brought about the downfall of the authoritarian regimes in Tunisia and Egypt, were received with a mixture of hope and apprehension in Europe's capitals. While enthusiasm for these popular revolutions opened the door to the hope of a new democratic phase in the region, there was a marked preoccupation with the transitions' final outcome, compounded by the uncertainly with regard to the role that Islamic parties would play in the new governments. At the time of writing events are still unfolding at a very fast pace, and popular demonstrations are starting to shake Algeria and Jordan. While the final outcome in each country is still unclear, it appears evident that these protests signal a deep change in these countries' societies, where millions of educated but impoverished citizens have ceased to be scared of their regimes and taken to the streets in an attempt to take their destiny back in their hands.

EU policy towards the Middle East peace process

Shaping the guidelines of a common European policy

The Arab–Israeli conflict and the subsequent peace process have been among the most strongly debated issues by EU member states, not only since the creation of the Common Foreign and Security Policy (CFSP) in 1991, but since the establishment of European Political Co-operation (EPC) in 1970. The peace process has been the subject of innumerable joint declarations and joint actions on the part first of the European Community and later of the European Union, and as such it has always remained a high priority issue on Europe's foreign policy agenda.

Many of the key principles of the EU's strategy toward the conflict have been laid out already in the 1980 Venice Declaration, and are still valid today. They include the centrality of the Palestinian question, the need to achieve a two-state solution, the importance attached to UN resolutions and to the principles of international law and the insistence on the need for all the relevant issues to be taken on simultaneously through the convening of an international peace conference where regional actors could meet in a multilateral framework.

While the member states of the European Union have found a basic agreement around these fundamental principles, the EU has struggled to cut an important role for itself in the peace process. The reasons for this difficulty lie in the contradictions of different member states' positions and agendas, in the United States' desire to maintain control over the peace process and in Israel's reluctance to accept the EU as a mediator.

Since 2002 the EU has been an official member of the so-called Quartet for Peace in the Middle East, alongside the USA, the UN and Russia. An initiative heralded by the US State Department in the wake of the 9/11 attacks, the Quartet represents a – limited – attempt on the part of the United States to advance the stalled Middle East peace process pursuing a multilateral approach, with co-operation with European governments as a key factor. The Quartet elaborated a 'Roadmap to a Permanent Two-State Solution to the Israeli-Palestinian Conflict', partially based on European ideas, that laid out a phased plan for the resolution of the conflict. While the Quartet has clearly failed to bring about a resolution to the conflict, the EU's participation in this initiative has arguably marked an important qualitative shift in Europe's role in the peace process, tying it to that of the USA and reinforcing the EU's credibility as an official mediator.

The 2003 European Security Strategy mentioned the conflict in the Middle East among the key threats that impact on European interests directly and indirectly. It restated the EU's commitment to its resolution while also underlining that 'regional conflicts need political solutions but military assets and effective policing may be needed in the post conflict phase. Economic instruments serve reconstruction, and civilian crisis management helps restore civil government. The European Union is particularly well equipped to respond to such multi-faceted situations.'[9] The words of the ESS underline Europe's desire to cut for itself a prominent role in the peace process, a role that could require not only economic instruments, but also military instruments and the specific civilian crisis management expertise that the EU has accumulated since the creation of the Common Foreign and Security Policy.

The policy initiatives: economic aid

For a long time Europe's role in the peace process has been mostly economic, a fact that has led many to call the EU 'a payer but not a player'. In the past two decades the EU's direct economic support of the peace process has indeed been enormous: the EU is the largest donor of non-military aid to the MEPP, and it's also the first donor of financial and technical assistance to the Palestinian Authority (PA).[10] The PA is also a full partner within the European Neighbourhood Policy, and a joint EU–PA Action Plan concluded in 2005 sets the agenda for economic and political co-operation with the EU. In 2008 the EU created PEGASE (Mécanisme Palestino-Européen de Gestion de l'Aide Socio-Économique), which channels EU assistance to support a Palestinian Reform and Development Plan prepared by the Palestinian Authority.[11] EU support has been a lifeline for the Palestinian people, providing much-needed economic support meant to prevent a complete collapse and humanitarian catastrophe in the occupied territories; on the other hand, the PEGASE mechanism has focused EU efforts more on crisis management and less on institution building and development, two goals that remain crucial to ensure the viability of the future Palestinian state.

The policy initiatives: diplomacy

Arguably one of the most significant steps taken by the EU in its policy towards the peace process has been the creation in 1996 of the position of EU Special Envoy (now Special Representative, SR) to the Middle East Peace Process through the adoption of a CFSP joint action.[12] The main objective of this appointment was to pursue better co-ordination of individual member state policies; undeniably Mr Moratinos first and later Mr Otte have not only contributed significantly to the preparation of common positions and the development of European initiatives aimed at promoting progress in the peace negotiations, but have also participated directly in many stages of these negotiations, earning the trust and respect of all the main actors involved. The problem, however, is that their activities have been hampered by the very terms of their mandate, which is formally quite broad but still provides that their action must take place in a strictly intergovernmental framework.[13] The SR is guided by and reports to the Presidency and the Council of the European Union; as a result, his scope for autonomous initiative is very limited and tightly bound to the indications he receives from the Council. He cannot officially commit any member state to any step which has not been previously agreed upon, and it is therefore hard to envisage for him a role beyond that of 'facilitator' of the peace talks.

The policy initiatives: CSDP missions

In June 2004 EU leaders declared their readiness to support the Palestinian Authority in taking responsibility for law and order and, in particular, in improving its civil police and law enforcement capacity. In January 2005 the EU Co-ordination Office for Palestinian Police Support (EU COPPS)[14] was established within the office of the EU Special Representative Marc Otte. In November the Council established the so-called EUPOL COPPS mission, a civilian mission in the framework of the Common Security and Defence Policy (CSDP) which builds on the work of EU COPPS and aims at contributing to the establishment of effective policing arrangements under Palestinian ownership in accordance with international standards. The mission was set to start operating in January 2006, but was largely paralysed after Hamas' electoral victory and started operating – and only in the West Bank – after the Hamas–Fatah split of June 2007. EUPOL COPPS is rather small, with 32 unarmed members of staff, of whom 27 are seconded from EU member states and 5 are local. The Head of Mission receives guidance from the High Representative for CFSP, through the Special Representative Mr Otte. The mission also co-ordinates EU member states' and international assistance to the Palestinian Civil Police and advises on police-related criminal justice elements, activities in line with EU's efforts in building and reinforcing Palestinian institutions.

In November 2005 the Council of the EU agreed to establish another civilian mission under the CSDP. The mission, called EUBAM Rafah (EU Border Assistant Mission Rafah), was tasked with monitoring the operations of the Rafah border-crossing point between Gaza and Egypt, in accordance with the 'Agreement on Movement and Access' signed by Israel and the Palestinian Authority following the unilateral withdrawal of Israel from the Gaza Strip. The operational phase of the Mission began on 30 November 2005 and was meant to last 12 months. In 2007 the Council adopted another joint action extending the mandate of the mission by a year. The operations of EUBAM, however, were suspended in June 2007 due to the Hamas takeover of the Gaza Strip. Since the closure of the crossing point the mission has maintained its operational capability, and the European Union has announced that it is prepared to redeploy its personnel at the border as soon as conditions permit.

There are two ways to look at this operation. On the one hand it can be seen as a qualitative step forward in EU's involvement in the security dimension of the peace process. For the first time a small group of EU military personnel (90 police and custom officers) were called in to supervise a check point previously under Israeli control and to monitor the compliance of the Palestinian Authority with the principles of the 'Agreement on Movement and Access'. The initiative was limited, and Israel maintained the right to close the crossing point; nevertheless the EU had for the first time visible 'boots on the ground'. On the other hand EUBAM turned out to be largely a failure: while it did succeed in facilitating the crossing of almost half a million people, it was also constantly hostage to the developments on the ground. As Colonel Faugeras, the Head of EUBAM, put it in an interview in 2009, '[The] EU's job was limited when it came to security. It has monitors at Rafah … but it is not an enforcement body; its role is to report observations to Israel and the Palestinian Authority.'[15] The consequences of this limited mandate are that EUBAM was unable to really control the security situation or the building of tunnels between Gaza and Egypt (used to smuggle everything from arms and explosives to food and cigarettes) and, when Hamas took power in June 2007, it could do nothing but suspend operations and wait in hope that an agreement would be reached between Israel, the Palestinian Authority, Hamas and Egypt. All this resulted in no real improvement or consolidation of the EU's credibility as a security actor in the eyes of both the Palestinians and the Israelis.

Essentially, after years of efforts to gain political influence, and having poured huge sums of money into the peace process, the European Union still finds itself today in a secondary role. It is however worth underlining two crucial issues. First, the basic principles that have guided Europe's policy since 1980, i.e. the centrality of the Palestinian question and the pursuit of a two-state solution, have now become accepted by all the actors involved in the peace process, including the United States and, albeit reluctantly, Israel. Second, there are limits to how much any external actor, including the United States, can aspire to influence the outcome of the conflict between Israel and the Palestinians. As the European Security Strategy underlined, 'Implementing [the two-state solution] will require a united and cooperative effort by the European Union, the United States, the United Nations and Russia, and the countries of the region, but above all by the Israelis and the Palestinians themselves.'

Conclusion

In early 2011 the situation in the Southern Mediterranean countries is in turmoil. Winds of change are sweeping several partners of the Euro Mediterranean Partnership, including Tunisia, Egypt, Jordan and Algeria. The EU and its member states, like all other Western countries, have had mixed reactions to the unfolding events. Hope for a democratic future for the region is intertwined with fear for the uncertainty that these sudden regime changes are bringing about. Questions about the type and length of the democratic transition, the role of the armed forces, the space that political Islam will have in the new governments and the stability of the region are being raised. The EU's reaction to regime change in Tunisia and, even more, in Egypt has been extremely prudent, and support for the 'hopes of the people' has been mixed with calls for calmness, peaceful transitions and the maintenance of regional stability.

While the role of external actors in these fundamentally national transformation processes is, and should be, limited, the EU has a duty to indicate its support for democratic change, but also an opportunity to favour it, by offering for example support for the organization and monitoring of new elections, and by relaunching programmes for the consolidation of civil society, democracy and the rule of law.

Notes

1 This chapter will refer to the broader Mediterranean as an area that includes North Africa (Algeria, Libya, Mauritania, Morocco, Tunisia) and the Levant (Egypt, Israel, the Palestinian Territories, Jordan, Lebanon and Syria).
2 See 'The Role of the European Union in the Middle East Peace Process and its Future Assistance', Executive Summary of the Communication to the Council of Ministers and the European Parliament made by Manuel Marin, Vice President of the European Commission, European Commission, 26 January 1998.
3 The provisions of the Euro-Mediterranean Association Agreements governing bilateral relations vary from one Mediterranean Partner to the other but have certain aspects in common: (a) political dialogue; (b) respect for human rights and democracy; (c) establishment of WTO-compatible free trade over a transitional period of up to 12 years; (d) provisions relating to intellectual property, services, public procurement, competition rules, state aids and monopolies; (e) economic co-operation in a wide range of sectors; (f) co-operation relating to social affairs and migration (including readmission of illegal immigrants); (g) cultural co-operation.
4 Until 2007 the MEDA (mesures d'accompagnement financières et techniques) programme was the principal financial instrument of the European Union for the implementation of the Euro-Mediterranean Partnership. The Programme offers technical and financial support measures to accompany the reform of economic and social structures in the Mediterranean partner countries.
5 The Common Strategy for the Mediterranean, available at http://www.consilium.europa.eu/uedocs/cmsUpload/mediEN.pdf.
6 Available at http://www.consilium.europa.eu/uedocs/cmsUpload/78367.pdf.
7 Available at http://ec.europa.eu/world/enp/pdf/country/enpi_euromed_rsp_en.pdf.
8 http://ec.europa.eu/world/enp/policy_en.htm.
9 'A Secure Europe in a Better World'. European Security Strategy. 12 December 2003. Available at http://www.consilium.europa.eu/uedocs/cmsUpload/78367.pdf.
10 See http://europa.eu.int/comm/external_relations.
11 See http://www.delwbg.ec.europa.eu/en/funding/pegas_documents.htm.
12 The first Special Representative appointed was Mr Miguel Angel Moratinos, who was succeeded in 2003 by Mr Marc Otte.
13 The annual mandate, successively prolonged by the Council of Ministers until today, gives wide-ranging responsibilities (see http://consilium.europa.eu/cms3_fo/showPage.asp?id=452&lang=EN), which include among others:

- to establish and maintain close contact with all the parties to the peace process, and all other key regional and international countries and organizations;
- to observe negotiations and to be ready to offer the EU's advice and good offices should the parties request this;
- to contribute, where requested, to the implementation of agreements reached between the parties, and to engage with them diplomatically in the event of non-compliance with the terms of these agreements;
- to engage constructively with signatories to agreements within the framework of the peace process in order to promote compliance with the basic norms of democracy, including respect of human rights and the rule of law.

14 See http://www.consilium.europa.eu/ueDocs/cms_Data/docs/pressData/en/declarations/84603.pdf.
15 See 'EUBAM head: Keeping Rafah open is the trick', *Jerusalem Post*, 6 February 2009, at http://www.consilium.europa.eu/uedocs/cmsUpload/090206JerusalemPostEUBAMHEADKeepingGazabordeopenisthetrick.pdf.

15

THE EU AND IRAN

Walter Posch

Formal relations between the European Union (EU) and the Islamic Republic of Iran commenced with the Edinburgh Declaration in 1992. This declaration came more than a decade after the 1979 revolution, four years after the UN-brokered ceasefire that ended the Iran–Iraq war (1980–8) and barely three years after the Islamic Republic of Iran's founder, Grand Ayatollah Rouhollah Mousavi Khomeini (the 'imam'), passed away in 1989. Hence, after a decade of de facto no relations between Europe and Iran, European heads of state and government decided to examine how to conduct EU–Iranian relations in the future.[1]

The Europeans had both realistic and idealistic reasons for breaking the diplomatic ice in Edinburgh. First, on the realist side, the argument ran, Europe simply could not afford to ignore a country with Iran's economic and geo-political importance, not in regional policy and certainly not regarding energy. Second, a successful Iran policy would prove essential to demonstrating the value of emerging EU foreign policy leadership.

The first engagement

It was developments within Iran, however, that tipped the balance towards – cautious – engagement. After a decade of war and revolutionary turmoil President Ali Akbar Hashemi Rafsanjani was compelled to try to allow for his country to enjoy some post-revolutionary normality, both in the domestic and foreign policy arenas.

This said, there was no way of beginning 'business as usual' by concluding a Trade and Cooperation Agreement (TCA) or a Political Dialogue Agreement (PDA), the EU's conventional starting points for strengthening relations with other countries. After all, a decade of alienation would not vanish overnight. Thus, in order to establish the trust necessary for good relations, the EU had to embark on a policy which would address the long list of disagreements and problems rattling both the respective bilateral and the EU-level relationships with the Islamic Republic.

The response was the initiation of the so called Critical Dialogue (CD). 'Critical', because none of the issues the Europeans found worrisome – be it Iran's abysmal human rights record, terrorism or its opposition to the Middle East Peace process (and back then to a lesser degree non-proliferation) – was excluded. But it was still a dialogue in which Europeans and Iranians listened and were listened to. The dialogue format proved a test for both sides: for Iran its engagement with the EU was the first real test for its newly created post-revolutionary diplomatic elite, and for the Europeans Iran policy immediately became a test case for the EU's newly initiated Common Foreign and Security Policy (CFSP).[2]

Small tangible successes notwithstanding, the Critical Dialogue immediately came under fire from many in Europe, the USA and of course Israel. In a nutshell, the argument asserted that the Critical Dialogue was just cheap cover for booming European business relations with the Islamic Republic. Ignoring the bilateral basis for trade and finance, critics charged that the EU deliberately and strategically chose to overlook Iran's destructive policies and ongoing human rights violations. Such criticisms of EU policy ignored the extent to which the Critical Dialogue forced the Iranians to look at internal human rights and to even admit, as they have done, that there is an 'issue' at all. This was a significant step considering that Iran had generally dismissed human rights as just another weapon in the arsenal of the 'cultural onslaught by the West'. Years later, in 2010, Iran's quixotic attempt to run for the chairmanship of the UN Human Rights Council gave grimly humorous proof that the Islamic Republic cannot ignore the human rights debate any longer.

Nonetheless, EU–Iran relations deteriorated again within five years. A 1997 German court verdict condemning Iranian officials for involvement in terrorist activities in Berlin during the 1980s (the so-called Mykonos Affair) proved a defining turning point. Iran's unacceptable reaction to the verdict led to the now famous pull-out of EU ambassadors later that year (Ghaissari and Nasr, 2006: 127). By that time, relations seemed to be beyond repair, at least from the vantage point of the EU.

The reformist era

In the end it was Iranian domestic policy that again changed the dynamics and reversed the trend which was leading towards diplomatic stalemate. The 1997 surprise victory of the reformist platform of Mohammad Khatami and his democratization policy made re-engagement possible. Nevertheless, Khatami's election did not bring any decisive resolution to the divisive issues between the EU and Iran. Recognizing the positive potential within the changed environment, the EU decided to revamp the Critical Dialogue; a new CD – 'Comprehensive Dialogue' – was initiated. Within this format EU and Iranian officials met twice a year at the level of under-secretary of state. The range of issues was also enhanced and human rights and non-proliferation issues were put higher on the agenda. Working groups were established covering classic fields of cooperation such as energy, drugs, refugees and trade and investment.

After Khatami's 2001 re-election, the EU moved to further intensify the relationship. Based on a Communication[3] it decided on a formula to:

1   combine (pre-)negotiations on a TCA (conducted by the EU Commission) with success in the Political Dialogue (conducted on behalf of the Council, i.e. led by Council presidency); and
2   stipulated the need for 'significant' positive steps on behalf of the Islamic Republic in all divisive policy areas (e.g. human rights, nuclear non-proliferation, and the Middle East peace process, to mention just the most important ones).

Furthermore, in addition to the Political Dialogue the EU and Iran conducted a Human Rights Dialogue, the last round of which took place in 2004 and has been suspended ever since Iran cancelled the next round which was to take place in 2006 (but never materialized).

In the Khatami era EU–Iran relations flourished on all levels: social, academic, cultural/ arts, and, of course, economic. Without question, European enterprises moved quickly to seize opportunities opened when US businesses were forced to cut investments under the Iran and Libya Sanctions Act (ILSA). With an amiable president like Khatami heading the state apparatus, Iran began to acquire a relatively attractive image across the EU countries, where efforts to deepen relations were deemed to be well founded.

Impressed by reports of the emergence of a serious debate on democracy and human rights inside Iran, many Europeans hoped, and not without reason, that further engagement, i.e. conclusion of TC and PD agreements, coupled with a continuation of the human rights dialogue, would strengthen the reformists and pave the way for a measurable shift towards a more democratic – rather than hard-line Islamic – Republic.

However, such hopes appeared to be delusional when a hitherto undeclared Iranian nuclear site was discovered in 2002. Consequently, the nuclear issue took priority over all other policy issues. Even so, in 2002 and 2003 European diplomacy and policy were firmly focused on haggling with the USA over Iraq, which made Iran policy less of a priority despite the Council regularly addressing the nuclear issue.

The nuclear issue

A few months after the fall of Baghdad in 2003, Iran was again high on the agenda. This time Iran became a clear 'test case' for the EU in several respects.

First, if the EU failed to show unity this time, its role as an independent and important actor on the international stage would be irreparably damaged. Secondly, by mid-2003 European decision-makers could not rule out another unilateral US military attack, this time on Iran. Third, US unilateralism could turn the whole international system of verification and control as conducted by the Vienna-based International Atomic Energy Agency (IAEA) into a shambles, thus further weakening the NPT regime. Finally, every European country realized that it had to ameliorate its relationship with the USA bilaterally and on the EU level.

Needless to say combining these various and partially conflicting agendas was no easy task. Even more so, when one considers the cumbersome, consensus-driven EU decision-making processes.

It was with this insight that the foreign ministers of the 'EU's Big 3' (i.e. the UK, France and Germany) decided to take matters in their own hands and in autumn 2003 travelled to Tehran in order to persuade the Iranians to sign the Additional Protocol; to allow intrusive inspections on behalf of the IAEA; and to suspend uranium enrichment. This trip became known as the 'E3 initiative' (also 'Big Three' or 'EU-Three') and ever since then the three European lead powers have been directly involved in all aspects of the Iranian nuclear saga.

The initiative proved to be the 'jolt' necessary to jumpstart the EU's diplomatic machine, and towards the end of 2003 Javier Solana, the EU Council's secretary general and foreign policy czar, was added to the team. The involvement of the general secretariat alleviated grievances held by many EU member states, some of whom scorned what they feared was the installation of an 'E3-*directoire*' superseding the EU presidency,[4] others of whom refused to see the EU dimension of the E3 initiative and almost all of whom felt they were insufficiently informed.

These fears were quickly overcome: short briefings given by the E3 ambassadors and later by the Council's political director at meetings of the Political and Security Committee (PSC) satisfied the need for more information. On the political level, Solana's presence placed the full weight of the EU's 15 (and later 27) member states behind the E3. This is remarkable in so far as the Council endorsed the E3/EU approach for the first time at a GAERC meeting in October 2005! In exchange the E3 enabled the EU – via the high representative – to be present and later on to play a role in an important matter of international security. In other words the E3 and the EU mutually reinforced their weight in international relations. Javier Solana's role grew, therefore, as he managed to make the Council a clearing house and coordination cell between the EU-Three and the rest of the EU.

With Solana on board the 'E3/EU' initiative became a fixed format with clear procedures and close cooperation on all levels from E3 and EU desk officers up to political directors. And this constellation – i.e. the format – also became the main framework to coordinate and to backchannel with the USA. By 2004 the E3/EU format became the EU's *modus operandi* regarding relations with the Islamic Republic of Iran. As a consequence the nuclear issue put all other policies towards Iran on hold, be they Commission- or Council-driven.

E3/EU diplomatic efforts peaked with the Paris Agreement of 15 November 2004,[5] which extended to cover broader issues, such as terrorism, whilst retaining the NPT issues and Iran's voluntary cessation of enrichment activities as the Agreement's central objectives. Immediately after signing the Paris Agreement the Iranian government came under immense domestic pressure as the anti-reformist opposition forces regained the political initiative which they had lost to the reformist coalition during the two Khatami presidencies. The nuclear issue became the linchpin of the country's technological progress and international standing, hence Iranian sovereignty and dignity.

Missing an agreement

According to uncorroborated Iranian sources no one understood this point better than French president Jacques Chirac and he attempted to strike a deal in March 2005 stating that 'one could not prevent the technological progress of this [Iranian] nation' (Mohammadi, 2005). Hereby Chirac grasped the typical third-worldish nature of the regime, which at the end of the day trumps its Islamic identity. In fact, the EU and Iran could never have experienced more favourable conditions for reaching a solution than those which characterized that meeting.

However, circumstances at that time were not favourable for a deal, especially since domestically the reformists were being accused of betraying the Iranian national interest. Viewed from this perspective, Khatami and his team needed a deal more desperately than the Europeans – and they needed it before the June 2005 elections, if they were to stand a chance of having someone from their camp elected.

For the Europeans the Khatami presidency was a mixed blessing. They were aware of the fact that Khatami faced fierce domestic resistance from undefined 'radical forces'. On the other hand, it became increasingly clear that former president Ali Akbar Hashemi Rafsanjani would once again run for president. Rafsanjani, whose economic policy was warmly remembered in European business circles, evoked the image of being someone who would be both powerful and pragmatic enough to strike a deal on the sensitive nuclear issue. Khatami in comparison appeared to be a lame duck president. Thus, the European offer concerning a nuclear understanding between Iran and the West did not reach Tehran until after the elections. But it was Dr Mahmud Ahmadinejad, a back-bench politician with political roots in the intelligence apparatus, who would win the election.

The Iranian reaction to the offer can be characterized as a furious rejection spurred on by their perception of it as worthless in the context of the following important issues:

1   There were no incentives for Iran to give up its 'inalienable' nuclear rights.
2   They bemoaned the lack of any guarantees or firm commitment by the EU to honour its agreement.
3   The offer lacked any negative security guarantees granted by the nuclear powers including the USA.

Whether or not the offer was a good one is less important than Iran's interpretation, according to which the Europeans could not deliver the USA. In fact, Tehran was unsure whether the USA would back this offer at all. The Europeans pursued an incremental approach and the 2005 offer was intended to be an important step towards bringing the Iranians and the USA to the negotiating table at a later date. The Iranians, however, took the presence of the USA as a given. Hence, Tehran scorned the 'self-righteous behaviour' of the EU. Answering on behalf of the EU, the British presidency summed up the most significant differences between Iran and the Europeans by asking why Iran would insist on the nuclear fuel cycle when the country has no nuclear facility to feed it into?[6] Hence the European lack of faith in Iran's self-proclaimed peaceful intentions. In the end, Iran and Europe could only agree on the lack of mutual trust.

On the partisan level, the Iranian team was still reporting to Khatami because Ahmadinejad was not yet sworn in and he had not yet promoted his followers to key positions. What the Europeans did not know was that the new president's followers were to be found among the radical forces that played a major role in derailing the reform process and who had opposed a nuclear deal earlier in that same year, 2005. Interestingly enough this fact had never really had a significant impact on the substance of Iran's nuclear policy; however, its impact on the Islamic Republic's political style was tremendous.

Diplomatic escalation

A sharp reckoning came when the new president Ahmadinejad 'elaborated' in detail on the Holocaust and the need to make the State of Israel 'vanish from the page of history'. European governments could barely contain their shock over these remarks, but despite protests, they continued to work on a negotiated solution with the Iranians. In fact, the Europeans went the extra mile in September 2005: after an unfavourable resolution for Iran was handed down by the IAEA Board of Governors, the Europeans declined to refer Iran's nuclear file to the UNSC in order to allow for further negotiations. However, progress on key objectives remained difficult for three reasons:

1   There was principle disagreement over the question of enrichment, with the Iranians insisting on a different interpretation of the NPT.
2   Ahmadinejad's inexperienced team of diplomats and negotiators had no previous experience with Europeans or international politics, much less experience in negotiations, and therefore they lacked the competency to exploit diplomatic openings.
3   There was a deficit of trust on both sides; what little had been developed vanished rather quickly.

Contrary to the dexterous manoeuvring exhibited by Khatami's policies, which meticulously avoided referral of the nuclear issue to the UN Security Council, the new president proved to be a risk-taker. For instance, after the unfavourable result of the September 2005 Board of Governors decision Iranian diplomacy risked just another confrontation by putting forth an uncompromising stance at the Vienna meeting with the E3/EU on 21 December 2005. After the negotiations ended inconclusively Iran again upped the ante by restarting parts of the nuclear programme that they had previously agreed to stop voluntarily.

The Iranian calculation was twofold: restarting parts of its nuclear programme under IAEA supervision would emphasize its legality and reduce the importance of the E3/EU negotiations mechanism. In other words, the Iranians hoped they could ignore international politics as represented via the E3/EU and insist on their own – third-worldish – reading of the NPT treaty. The second aspect was equally ideological: relying on Iran's anti-imperialist credentials in foreign policy, Ahmadinejad's new team gravely overestimated both the influence of the countries of the Non-Aligned Movement (NAM) in the IAEA and Iran's standing amongst the NAM countries.

The litmus test came at an extraordinary meeting of IAEA governors a month later. True, Iran had supporters in the IAEA meeting, but important countries like India did not support Iran and even China and Russia sided with the E3 and the US (Posch, 2006: 107). Finally, in February 2006, Iran's nuclear file was referred to the UNSC. From that point onwards, Euro–Iranian relations would be debated in a new format and offers for Iran would be accompanied with sanctions.

The EU's Iranian nuclear policy: offers and sanctions

After the Iranian nuclear file was sent to the UNSC, the EU met in a new format labelled either 'P5+1' (the UNSC permanent five members plus Germany), 'EU3+3' or more commonly 'E3+3' and finally 'E3/EU+3', i.e. the EU's 'Big Three' and the EU's high representative plus the USA, China and Russia. This was highly innovative. Depending on one's viewpoint, one could see the new arrangement as the addition of Germany and the EU to the UNSC, or the joining of the non-European P5 members with the E3/EU. The role of the High Representative only increased, and he was now acting as the official representative not only of the EU, but also of the international community as represented by the UNSC. On two occasions (in 2006 and in 2008), Solana presented offers for a negotiated solution to the Iranians. Concurrently, Solana de facto became the sole negotiator with the Iranians, a development which became particularly observable during Ali Larijani's tenure as the head of the Iranian negotiations team in 2005–7. Thus, the continuation of negotiations and the avoidance of a diplomatic meltdown are fully attributable to these two men. These years were critical because during this time several UNSC resolutions were issued and the Europeans began to debate and impose sanctions against Iran.

In June 2006 Solana travelled to Iran with a new package deal[7] covering all fields of cooperation. And since the deal was backed by the P5, the question whether the USA would ultimately support a European offer, one of the Iranians' biggest concerns, was alleviated. When Iran refused this offer as well, UNSC Resolution 1696 was adopted on 31 July 2006 obliging Iran to suspend its enrichment activities, which Iran – as expected – refused to do.

With the passing of UNSCR 1696 a whole cycle of resolutions commenced reflecting the increasingly tense relationship between the E3+3 and Iran. In fact, resolutions were issued almost twice a year: 1737 and 1747 in 2007, 1803 and 1835 in 2008 and 1887 in 2009, steadily increasing the pressure on Iran's economy and hindering the ability of some regime luminaries to travel. All of these resolutions were preceded by complicated negotiations where the EU took the middle position between Russia and China on one hand, and the USA on the other. Pundits and politicians in the USA and elsewhere found this position unacceptable and accused the EU of 'being weak' on Iran and of 'condoning' the Islamic Republic. However, the European middle position made sense because it helped retain the support of Russia and China, who were less enthusiastic about upholding the sanctions regime.

The incremental approach and the combination of sanctions and offers helped to promote the Western position in the IAEA because NAM countries recognized that any pressure exerted on Iran was preceded by offers to negotiate. Although everybody knew that the USA was the driving force behind passing sanctions resolutions against Iran, America was not acting unilaterally and, more importantly, America was not perceived to be acting unilaterally. In other words, lighter sanctions carried a heavier weight on the international scene.

The sanctions path was always accompanied by offers of cooperation, and many formal and informal contacts with the Islamic Republic were maintained on bilateral and EU levels. This changed – in some cases dramatically – when Ahmadinejad condoned the Holocaust 'conference' (in fact a jamboree of European and American fascists and Holocaust deniers) in late 2006. This had long-term consequences because it completely destroyed political goodwill. Furthermore, academic cooperation with Iran – notably in the think-tank world, but also with universities – steadily decreased and the tight web of academic cooperation which had been built up under Khatami ultimately unravelled.

The president's personal politics also came into play. In 2007 he replaced the aristocratic Ali Larijani with Dr Saeed Jalili, an ideologue and a confidant of his with no previous experience on the international scene. Dr Jalili quickly exacerbated the Europeans' frustration, but the EU remained determined to try to find a negotiated solution, while at the same time continuing the sanctions regime, in order to get the Iranians back to the negotiating table. This dual approach was also aimed at supporting European credibility vis-à-vis the USA.

The final offer

Throughout 2007 and 2008 the necessity of direct US–Iranian engagement became increasingly pressing. Preliminary contacts, for instance in the wake of the Iraqi neighbours initiative and other similar venues, never allowed for a breakthrough. As seen from a European perspective Iran was now definitively reduced to nuclear policy, because attempts to try other approaches concentrating on issues such as energy security, economic cooperation or regional security, to name the most utilized ones, went nowhere. Hence, the focus became maintaining unity both within the EU as well as with the E3+3 format, in order to push for more resolutions, but also to make another credible offer to the Iranians.

On 12 June 2008 High Representative Javier Solana met Iranian Foreign Minister Manuchehr Mottakai and handed him a letter signed by the foreign ministers of the E3+3 and himself. Attached to the letter was a proposal (INFCIRC 730) covering all fields of cooperation between Iran and the international community such as nuclear energy, political issues, economy, a privileged energy partnership with Europe, civil aviation and other things of that nature.[8] The text was rather short as it was intended to provide a basic understanding of common interests. It was also an impressive opening on behalf of the USA towards the Iranians and, as seen from a European perspective, a final political confirmation of the EU's engagement policy with Iran. The Iranians did not react to this offer, which is still on the table and the sole basis of a possible re-engagement with the Islamic Republic.

Arguably, this could have been the point at which the EU's involvement as a serious actor in the Iran saga ended. After all, the EU's engagement policy with Iran centred on bringing the Iranians and the Americans to the negotiating table, directly or indirectly. This, the EU managed to do, but success or failure was always a bilateral Irano-American affair. Even so, the E3+3 format and, therefore, the EU's central role in it continued after the 'handover' from Javier Solana to Catherine Ashton at the helm of the European Foreign Affairs and Security Policy. As a matter of fact E3+3 remains the only forum to coordinate Iran policy (attempts to supersede it with the G8 or other formats led nowhere) and as such, whatever turn Iran policy will take, towards more sanctions or towards engagement, will be conducted via the E3+3.

Following the delivery of Solana's last offer to the Iranians, the EU joined everyone else in awaiting the election of a new American president (November 2008), and the then hoped-for change through Iran's presidential elections (June 2009). Regardless of the two outcomes, by 2009 EU policy towards Iran was already reduced to the NPT and ever narrower: to sanctioning policy, conducted mainly on behalf of the E3. The imposition of UNSCR 1929[9] in June 2010 and the Council Decision of 26 July 2010 'concerning restrictive measures against Iran' (Official Journal of the EU, L 195/39) are the final points in a long development. Now EU sanctions against Iran come very close to the scope of US sanctions, leaving few chances to pursue any economic activity with the Islamic Republic.

It is our view that one has to keep this background in mind when seeking to understand why Tehran would engage with Turkey and Brazil in May 2010. The Iranians quickly realized how much more painful sanctions could become and eagerly seized the opportunity when Turkey and Brazil took the initiative and tried to promote their own solution for Iran's nuclear file, which failed. This outcome was not surprising because the main crux for a negotiated solution was the lack of bilateral relations between Tehran and Washington. Even so, Tehran had won time, ensured Turkey's negative vote at the UNSC and effectively stressed common interests with two important and economically vibrant aspiring powers. It is hard to imagine why Tehran would choose a go-between when it could have direct negotiations with the E3+3, and thereby with the USA.

A few months before the Turkish–Brazilian interlude, in October 2009 the E3+3 met with an Iranian delegation in Geneva. Negotiations must have reached an advanced level, but a possible solution broke down in the stormy waters of factional politics in Tehran. Ahmadinejad's attempts to reach a solution have been shot down by his own radical followers and of course by opposition leaders, who exploit this topic in order to attack him. On the Iranian side, domestic turmoil after the June 2009 presidential elections led to a stalemate situation among the decision-makers. As a result of this situation a mechanism developed through which any positive step on behalf of the Iranian government (e.g. acceptance of mandates for enrichment outside of Iran) had to be accompanied by a show of force (e.g. firing missiles or ordering enrichment to be upped to 20 per cent). Needless to say, such behaviour on Iran's part leaves the international community confused, frustrated and without many viable options.

In order to strengthen his own domestic position Iran's contested president hoped to forge an agreement with the West whilst at the same time abiding by Iran's revolutionary identity (Posch, 2011). Hence, the ironic situation emerges in which a radical president like Ahmadinejad would want to strike a deal on the nuclear issue with the international community. Without the permanent engagement on behalf of the EU this policy option would not even exist.

The last meetings between the E3+3 and Iran took place in December 2010 in Geneva and in January 2011 in Istanbul. Obviously the results were hardly satisfying for either side. High Representative Ashton expressed her disappointment with the outcome when she explained the E3+3's rejection of Iranian preconditions,[10] namely the acceptance of the full fuel cycle and the lifting of sanctions. Interestingly enough the Iranian side came away with a slightly positive take on the negotiations. After months of virtually no communication other than EU complaints and demarches against Iran's steadily deteriorating human rights situation,

EU High Representative Catherine Ashton commented on behalf of the E3/EU+3 on the last IAEA report on Iran.[11] In her comment, she repeated the need for Iran to honour its international obligations, but she also underscored the international community's will to 'engage with Iran in a constructive dialogue on the basis of reciprocity' and reaffirmed the 'offer of June 2008 and the proposals … made to Iran in Istanbul in January'.[12] The explicit reference to the 2008 offer is an interesting change of EU language, which had dramatically hardened after the passing of UNSCR 1929 in June 2010. Hence the EU made it clear to Iran that the international community still hopes for a negotiated solution.

Conclusion

For years EU–Iranian relations have been focused on the nuclear issue. Here the EU has not been without success: it managed to provide assurances as to the efficacy of the role of the IAEA regarding Iran. It sensed a policy change towards engagement with Iran in the USA (clearly apparent during the second Bush presidency) and recognized the chance to win some key concessions from the Iranians, i.e. the temporary suspension of nuclear enrichment, the signing of the Additional Protocol and increased openness to IAEA scrutiny of Iranian nuclear activities. And, most importantly, the EU was the driving force behind the E3+3 format; a unique overlap between the EU (High Representative), select member states (E3) and the Security Council (P5). Viewed from this perspective the EU has ensured its place as a primary actor on the international scene. This should create a new sense of European *realpolitik* through which the E3 plays a central role in engaging the larger EU in matters of great political gravity, such as the Iranian nuclear case.

On the other hand, once relations with Iran came to be viewed only through the prism of Teheran's nuclear programme, alternatives were ignored and actively discouraged. For instance, by weighing one issue against the other, the EU was unable to develop a unified Iran strategy that would take into account human rights, regional issues, energy and the nuclear file. This type of comprehensive approach is necessary in order to be able to formulate alternative policies. This is not to suggest dropping the nuclear issue under current conditions; however, formulating alternative strategies is crucial if one wants to be able to react to unexpected changes in the geo-political setup of the region. At the very least, there should be a European vision encompassing both Iran and the larger region which would allow the EU to react properly and in a timely manner to any geo-political shift. The need for greater political dexterity could become more urgent in the near future, given the fact that the outcome of the 'Arab Spring' and its future implications and ramifications for Europe are far from clear.

Interestingly enough, both sides, the EU and the USA on one hand, and the Iranians, on the other, insist the Arab Spring would alter the strategic balance to their own advantage. This augurs badly for the nuclear standoff because each side assumes it is in the stronger position. For instance, after the Iranians passed up the opportunity to benefit from the June 2008 offer the E3+3's patient policy succeeded in isolating Iran within the IAEA. On the other side, Iran feels tempted to put its nuclear programme in a regional NPT context. Depending on the outcome of recent developments it may indeed find more Arab states sympathizing with its strategic posture, thus counterbalancing the hostile position of Saudi Arabia and the Gulf States.

But after several years of negotiations, political sympathies are not enough to alter the political parameters in which the Islamic Republic conducts its nuclear policy and that is the E3+3 format and the fact that the ball is in Iran's court, as it actually has been ever since June 2008.

Notes

1 There is a surprising lack of scholarly literature devoted to EU–Iranian relations. For an Iranian point of view see Mousavian, 2008; for a European perspective see Posch, 2006.
2 The first to fully grasp the importance of the Iran issue for CFSP was Everts, 2004.
3 *EU Relations with Iran* (Communication from the Commission to the European Parliament and the Council) COM(2001) 71, Brussels ,7 February 2001; until now this is the only document providing a strategic vision on EU Iranian relations. For further EU documents on Iran see the European External Action Services site 'Brief History of Relations between EU and Iran' available at <http://eeas.europa.eu/iran/relations_en.htm> (general issues) and <http://eeas.europa.eu/iran/nuclear_en.htm> (nuclear issue).
4 Quite tellingly many journalists and many more academics dealing with the EU–Iran saga referred to the 'E3' erroneously as the 'EU *troika*' (which is actually the current, past and future EU presidency). Admittedly there is some *realpolitik* truth in that misnomer.
5 See IAEA, 2004. All IAEA documents concerning Iran from the period 2003–9 have been translated and published in Iran. See Gharibabadi and Qasempur, 2009. Among the vast literature on Iran's nuclear saga Chubin, 2006, is outstanding.
6 'Statement of the United Kingdom on behalf of the European Union at the IAEA Board of Governors', Vienna, 9 August 2005, available at <http://www.iaea.org/NewsCenter/Focus/IaeaIran/bog092005_statement-eu.pdf>.
7 'Elements of a proposal to Iran as approved on 1 June at the meeting in Vienna of China, France, Germany, the Russian Federation, the United Kingdom, the United States of America and the European Union' (S202/66), available at <http://www.consilium.europa.eu/ueDocs/cms_Data/docs/pressdata/EN/reports/90569.pdf>.
8 <http://www.iaea.org/Publications/Documents/Infcircs/2008/infcirc730.pdf>.
9 <http://www.iaea.org/newscenter/focus/iaeairan/unsc_res1929-2010.pdf>.
10 See Ashton, 2011a.
11 'Implementation of the NPT Safeguards Agreement and relevant provisions of Security Council resolutions in the Islamic Republic of Iran' (GOV/2011/54), 2 September 2011, available at <http://iaea.org/Publications/Documents/Board/2011/gov2011-54.pdf>.
12 Ashton, 2011b.

16

THE EU AND SUB-SAHARAN AFRICA

Richard G. Whitman

There is now a need for a new phase in the Africa-EU relationship, a new strategic partnership and a Joint Africa-EU Strategy as a political vision and roadmap for the future cooperation between the two continents in existing and new areas and arenas.[1]

Conflict is often linked to state fragility. Countries like Somalia are caught in a vicious cycle of weak governance and recurring conflict. We have sought to break this, both through development assistance and measures to ensure better security. Security Sector Reform and Disarmament, Demobilisation and Reintegration are a key part of postconflict stabilisation and reconstruction, and have been a focus of our missions in Guinea-Bissau or DR Congo. This is most successful when done in partnership with the international community and local stakeholders.[2]

Introduction

The EU's Common Foreign and Security Policy (CFSP) and its attendant European Security and Defence Policy (CSDP) have had an engagement with sub-Saharan Africa as a central strand of activities since their foundation.[3]

Commentary upon this sub-Saharan African strand of the CFSP/CSDP has consequently been an important component of the wider literature describing the evolution of the CSDP.[4] To date this literature on the CFSP/CSDP and Africa has for the most part sought to explore CFSP towards third countries and issues and individual CSDP operations and activities as the EU has engaged in more activity which, in turn, has provided scholars with greater opportunities for empirical work.

Sub-Saharan Africa is of considerable interest as a 'test bed' of CSDP activity as almost the full panoply of both civilian and military types of CSDP activity have been used on the continent since the initiation of CSDP activities in 2003. The EU has deployed military operations in support of Petersberg tasks, peace support operations, policing and police support operations and security sector reform operations (only rule of law and border assistance missions have not been utilized). Furthermore sub-Saharan Africa has been the sole location for some distinctive military operations: the CSDP's first naval operation, EUNAVFOR, the Artemis non-Berlin Plus operation and the AMIS peace support operation. With 10 of the EU's total of 24 CSDP operations to date taking place in sub-Saharan Africa the continent has therefore been an important theatre of operations for the development of the operational practices of the CSDP. This has given rise to a particular characteristic to the EU's strategic behaviour which we will explore in the section on 'Strategic behaviour: operational activity' below.

Examining the decision-making processes that resulted in some of these operations has also been an important generator of theoretical insight. Case study analysis has been used to analyse EU decision-making processes as the basis for accounting for particular policy outcomes.[5] We will side-step these decision-making processes in the body of this chapter but return to this issue in the conclusion.

Where there is currently a gap in the literature is the extent to which the EU's CSDP activities in sub-Saharan Africa have contributed to the development of an EU 'strategic culture'. This chapter contends that there has been an analytical neglect of the importance of sub-Saharan Africa to the refinement of the EU's definition of what constitute security threats, how these threats are seen by the EU to be particularly acute on the African continent and how the EU has used its foreign, security and defence policy interventions on the continent to test and refine its policy instruments.

As an attempt to generate a debate on the relationship between the EU's CSDP activities in sub-Saharan Africa and its strategic culture this chapter is very much a preliminary exercise in theoretical and empirical agenda setting. The chapter is intended as something of a tentative exercise to facilitate further and future empirical work.

The chapter proceeds by introducing the notion of strategic culture as applied to the EU before then seeking to refine the concept. It then makes a preliminary examination of what is considered to be a symbiotic relationship between the EU's strategic culture and sub-Saharan Africa.

An EU strategic culture?

Debate around whether the EU possesses a strategic culture has been ongoing since the foundation of the CSDP in the late 1990s. The central issue of debate is whether the EU is developing a strategic culture and, furthermore, what its characteristics are. Why is the notion of the EU's possession, or not, of a strategic culture of such importance? To address this question it is necessary to briefly examine the wider literature on generic strategic cultures in addition to the literature that deals specifically owithn EU strategic culturee.

Strategic culture defined

The literature on strategic culture (SC) is concerned with the assertion that there is a relationship between the strategies pursued by individual international actors and that these actors 'have different predominant strategic preferences that are rooted in the early or formative experiences of the state, and are influenced to some degree by the philosophical, political, cultural, cognitive characteristics of the state and its elites'.[6]

Literature on SC developed during the Cold War with a predominant focus on the two superpowers and with generalizations about the superpowers' appetites for risk and the propensities in the use of force used to inform strategies for the conduct of nuclear war in the USA.[7] From this starting point has emerged a burgeoning literature that examines the SC of a variety of states, including those of individual EU member states.[8] Applying the concept to the EU represents a particular set of empirical and theoretical challenges as there are 27 distinctive security cultures in existence alongside a putative EU SC. The interrelationship between the individual member state security cultures and the EU's emergent SC raises the question as to whether the process at work is symbiotic. Furthermore, if the EU is developing an SC, how and where can this be identified?

As with all concepts in the social sciences there is considerable contestation on the deployment of the notion of SC. All of these arguments cannot be rehearsed here. For SC theorists a key area of debate concerns the relationship between SC and strategic behaviour (SB). This is a distinction which is of crucial relevance for study of the EU, as will be explored below. For Gray, SB 'means behaviour relevant to the threat or use of force for political purposes'.[9] The relationship between SC and SB can be further conceptually distinguished: '[S]trategic culture can be conceived as a context out there that surrounds, and gives meaning to, strategic behaviour, as the total warp and woof of matters strategic that are thoroughly woven together, or as both.'[10]

This distinction between SC and SB is important because, as will be seen below, these are often conflated in discussion on the EU and SC.

The EU and strategic culture

Since the inception of the CSDP in the late 1990s there has been debate on the existence of an EU SC as an important necessary component of the EU realizing its ambitions for its foreign, security and defence policy. For the most part this literature glosses over definitions of SC itself in a rush to judgement as to whether the EU has an embryonic SC. What the nature of an SC is has been much less contested than whether the EU is acquiring one.

A dividing line within the literature on the EU and SC that Rynning identified in 2003 still holds.[11] Rynning distinguished between optimistic and pessimistic assessments on the EU's possession of an SC. What divides these assessments is the conclusion as to whether the EU is gaining both the *ability* and the *confidence* to use military force to address perceived threats to EU security.

The most frequently cited and well-rehearsed discussions on the EU and SC are the two companion chapters by Cornish and Edwards.[12] Cornish and Edwards seek to evaluate whether the EU has acquired an SC by examining four areas: military *capabilities*; whether CSDP *experiences* are engendering a sense of reliability and legitimacy for autonomous EU action; whether policy-making processes of the EU now ensure a *political culture* with the appropriate level and depth of civil–military integration; and the evolving relationship between the *EU and NATO*. Cornish and Edwards entwine elements of SC and SB in their analysis and the conclusion drawn in 2005 was that the EU has an SC that is a work in progress.[13] Five years from this analysis – and ten years from the foundation of the CSDP – general stocktaking exercises on the CSDP conclude that the policy domain, and by implication the EU's SC, is something of a curate's egg.[14]

EU strategic culture and sub-Saharan Africa: making the case

Examining the EU's SC with reference to sub-Saharan Africa represents a twofold challenge. First, and as indicated above, the EU's SC is a work in progress. Second, the wider literature on SC has not been applied systematically to the EU itself and, consequently, does not provide a well-trodden path of established frameworks of analysis by which to analyse the EU's SC through examination of policy towards a region, continent or theatre of operations.

Furthermore, sub-Saharan Africa may not appear to be the most appropriate case study through which to explore the EU's SC. The Western Balkans would appear to be a more promising case as it has been the location of a sustained engagement of the EU's foreign and security policies since the foundation of the CFSP in 1993 and onwards through the development of the European Security and Defence Identity (ESDI) and the eventual creation of the CSDP.

However, there are two distinct disadvantages that accrue to such an examination of the Western Balkans. The first is that the EU has defined a particular endpoint to its engagement with this region, which is to draw these states closer to the EU through a route map to EU accession. The second is that there have actually been more CSDP operations that have taken place in sub-Saharan Africa in comparison to the Western Balkans.[15]

The EU's sub-Saharan Africa CSDP operations therefore provide an extremely important case through which it is possible to examine manifestations of the EU's SB.[16] As noted above, SB and SC are in a symbiotic relationship. By examining the EU's SB, as manifested through the EU's CSDP operations in sub-Saharan Africa, it is anticipated that the chapter will be able to draw preliminary conclusions on the wider EU SC. This will be attempted by examining two elements of the EU's engagement with the continent. First, in clarifying in what terms the EU has defined sub-Saharan Africa as a theatre of operations for its foreign, security and defence policies there will be the examination of key strategic declaratory instruments used by the EU.[17] Second, examining SB through the CSDP operations where the EU has used either force or the threat of force as a policy instrument.

Sub-Saharan Africa and strategic culture: strategy defined

There is a longstanding literature which has examined the interrelationship between the European integration process, EU member states and sub-Saharan Africa. The ECSC/EEC/EU's engagement with sub-Saharan Africa dates to the commencement of the European integration process itself. Consequently, the continent is one of the oldest subjects and objects of EU member state collective foreign policy formation. During the period of the Cold War the member states' foreign policy was largely pursued through development policy instruments and through the Yaoundé and Lomé Conventions.[18]

The purpose of this chapter is not to seek to account for the EU's wider foreign policy objectives within sub-Saharan Africa or even the full gamut of the EU's CFSP towards the continent. Rather the intention is to examine the EU's CSDP activities within the region to more clearly discern its SB. The wider literature on the EU and Africa suggests that the EU's policy towards sub-Saharan Africa developed a new dimension in the 1990s with an increasing interest in conflict prevention and conflict management.[19] This assertion will be probed as an important step to discerning the evolution of the EU's SB.

Since this period, and alongside the EU's CSDP operations, the EU used a set of strategic declaratory pronouncements which provide the framework within which EU policy is being defined and organized. There is a hierarchy to this *informational diffusion* and in this chapter the pronouncements will be used as markers of the component of the EU's SB which have informed the EU's policy towards sub-Saharan Africa.[20] These documents are used to illustrate that the EU has established two key strands through its strategic declarations: the *security–development nexus* and the *human security imperative*.

European Security Strategy: sub-Saharan Africa within the EU's Grand Strategy

A key starting point for analysis of the EU's strategic declarations is the EU's first security strategy in December 2003.[21] In the words of the Heads of State and Government:

The European security strategy reaffirms our common determination to face our responsibility for guaranteeing a secure Europe in a better world. It will enable the European Union to deal better with the threats and global challenges and realise the opportunities facing us. An active, capable and more coherent European Union would make an impact on a global scale. In doing so, it would contribute to an effective multilateral system leading to a fairer, safer and more united world.[22]

Furthermore, as the European Council conclusions also noted, the appropriate consequence of the 'strategic orientation[s]' contained in the document was that they had to 'mainstream them into all relevant European policies'. Consequently the European Security Strategy (ESS) is supposed to provide the EU and its member states with the road map for a route march to greater global impact.[23]

The ESS defines Europe's security interests and priorities across three parts of the document: *global challenges and key threats* – this identifies what the document calls 'the security environment'; *strategic objectives* – how to address these threats; and *policy implications for Europe*. Sub-Saharan Africa features in each of these three sections of the document.

In the identification of global challenges and key threats the document is very much touched by its historical moment in international relations – terrorism, proliferation of WMD, regional conflicts, state failure and organized crime all appear. In this section of the document sub-Saharan Africa is used to illustrate a linkage between lack of development and political instability and conflict and the assertion that security is a precondition for development.[24] This is an embryonic expression of the security–development nexus that has subsequently become a key strand in the EU's strategy, as will become apparent below.

The second section of the document – on strategic objectives – identifies three strategic objectives: 'addressing the threats', 'building security in our neighbourhood' and an 'international order based on effective multilateralism'. 'Effective multilateralism' has become an overwhelming objective of the ESS. It is the EU's equivalent of the US Cold War notion of *containment* as the key objective of the EU internationally. In this section of the Strategy sub-Saharan Africa appears as illustrative of the manner in which the EU has already addressed threats (with reference to the DRC – 'to help deal with regional conflicts and to put failed states back on their feet') and as illustrative that 'State failure and organised crime spread if they are neglected – as we have seen in West Africa.' Sub-Saharan Africa is not defined as part of the neighbourhood but appears later in the document as 'partner' alongside Latin America and Asia. The African Union features as a component of the argument for effective multilateralism and the assertion that regional organizations strengthen global governance.

The third section of the document is almost all about capabilities development, which has been a collective concern since the early 1990s, and West Africa is used as illustrative of the assertion that 'Problems are rarely solved on a single country basis.' Strikingly, and unlike its references to other continents, the EU did not identify an African candidate for the 'strategic partnerships' that it was seeking to develop.

In its December 2008 five-year review of the implementation of the Security Strategy the EU has summarized the foreign and security policy evolution generally, and, for the purposes of this chapter, how sub-Saharan Africa fits within the EU's wider grand strategy.[25] Human security is enshrined in the review document as a central concept for the EU. The refinement of this concept as a guiding principle for the EU was an important element of the work undertaken to implement the ESS after its publication.[26] There is also a section of the document devoted to the security–development nexus and with Somalia cited as illustrative of the inter-linkage. Guinea–Bissau and the DRC are both cited as instances where the EU's intervention has been driven by the drive for post-conflict stabilization and reconstruction. This documentation represents a good snap-shot of the various strands of the EU's policy towards the region as they have consolidated over the last half decade. Stress is also placed on how the EU is working with the AU and also how the Joint Africa–EU Strategy is being used as a vehicle through which to enhance African capabilities in crisis management. There is also reference to the development of a more significant relationship with South Africa since 2003.

The EU's Security Strategy and its implementation across the last five years provide key indicators to the EU's SB which are echoed in key documents that deal specifically with sub-Saharan Africa. The key CFSP document that encapsulates the EU's strategic objectives for sub-Saharan Africa is the Common Position adopted in January 2004 concerning conflict prevention, management and resolution in Africa.[27] It establishes a number of principles that have guided EU policy. First, that the EU seeks to 'contribute to the prevention, management and resolution of violent conflicts in Africa by strengthening African capacity and means of action in this field'. Second, that to implement the policy there is close cooperation with the UN, regional and sub-regional organizations. Third, that conflict prevention, management and resolution need to be tackled through capacity-building at the international, regional and country level. The Common Position has been the platform on which the EU has developed a number of strands to its policy that have focused on capacity-building, and the disarmament, demobilization and reintegration of combatants and on combating the destabilizing accumulation and spread of small arms and light weapons.[28]

Sub-Saharan African strategic declarations

From 2003 onwards strategic declaratory statements of the EU on sub-Saharan Africa have contained significant reference to both the security–development nexus and the human security imperative. The EU has 'uploaded' these two key strands of its strategic behaviour into its strategic objectives for the continent.

The security–development nexus was central to the European Africa Strategy adopted by the EU in October 2005, the central objective of which is to guide the EU's response in assisting with the realization of the Millennium Development Goals (MDGs) with an aim to 'strengthen its support in the areas considered prerequisites for attaining the MDGs (peace, security, good governance), areas that create a favourable economic environment for growth, trade and interconnection and areas targeting social cohesion and environment'.

Furthermore the EU outlined its response strategy to these objectives:

> The EU will step up its efforts to foster peace and security by means of a wide range of actions, ranging from the support for African peace operations to a comprehensive approach to conflict prevention addressing the root causes of violent conflict. These actions also target cooperation in the fight against terrorism and the non-proliferation of weapons of mass destruction, as well as support for regional and national strategies for disarmament, demobilisation, reintegration and reinsertion in order to contribute to the reintegration of ex-combatants – including child soldiers – and stabilisation of post-conflict situations.[29]

This theme was reinforced at the second Africa–EU summit, 8–9 December 2007, in Lisbon under the Portuguese EU Presidency and at the level of heads of state and government from Africa and the EU. Running through the key declarations and documents of the summit

– the Lisbon Declaration and the Joint EU–Africa Strategy – is the characterization of the relationship as 'Strategic Partnership'. This Partnership is to be structured through eight strands and with the objectives set out in a two-year Action Plan.

The Joint EU–Africa Strategy is replete with references to human security. The Strategy also makes peace and security one of the fourfold objectives of the partnership.[30] The security–development nexus is also presented as shared understanding that underpins the objectives for the partnership: 'Africa and Europe understand the importance of peace and security as preconditions for political, economic and social development.' The 'Peace and Security' section of the Joint Strategy and its attendant action plan are primarily concerned with the EU facilitating African ownership of conflict prevention and conflict management and with the EU playing a facilitating, mentoring and assisting role.[31] Two key priorities are given to achieving full operationalization of the African Peace and Security Architecture (APSA) and Predictable Funding for Africa-led Peace Support Operations.

These two elements of the Action Plan highlight a sub-Saharan Africa region-specific aspect of the EU's SB. This is to sub-contract operational activity to African third parties – a *preference for local enforcement*. This aspect of the EU's SB was systematically codified in the peace and security cluster part of the *EU Strategy for Africa*, adopted by the European Council in December 2005. This, in turn, was developed at greater length in the *EU Concept for Strengthening African Capabilities for the Prevention, Management and Resolution of Conflicts* in November 2006.[32] Measures and initiatives proposed in the concept would directly support the AU's ongoing establishment of an APSA, including the creation of the African Stand-by Force (ASF).

These activities are being financed via the African Peace Facility (APF) intended to facilitate the African Union taking responsibility for African security. The APF provides EU financial support to facilitate capacity-building by African states and the AU particularly for the training of African troops to perform peace and security operations. Building African capabilities also diminishes the requirement for direct European military involvement on the continent. The APF funding is drawn from the European Development Fund (EDF) and for 2008–10 stood at €300 million. The initial €250 million funding of the Facility at its foundation in 2004 proved to be insufficient, particularly because of the costs involved with the AMIS operation, and funding was raised to €440 million by 2007.[33]

In examining a set of the EU's strategic declaratory instruments as indicators of the EU's SB it has been suggested that there are three strands which are apparent. Two of these strands are considered to be general and generic strands of the SB – the security–development nexus and the human security imperative – and there is a distinctive sub-Saharan Africa specific strand which is the preference for local enforcement.

Strategic behaviour: operational activity

Sub-Saharan Africa has seen the most significant cluster of CSDP activity since the initiation of such operations in 2003. These CSDP operations provide an important basis from which to assess the operational activity aspects of the EU's behavioural culture. As indicated above the EU has established two key strands of its SB which can be identified through strategic declarations: the security–development nexus and the human security imperative. Through an examination of the sub-Saharan CSDP operations we can also see the third of strand of SB, which is the preference for local enforcement.

Each of the individual CSDP operations has been the subject of academic and policy analysis.[34] This analysis has been primarily to assess the motivations behind the deployment of each of the operations, the difficulties with converting the mandate of the GAERC into a CSDP operation and whether the operation constituted a successful realization of its objectives. The interest for the purposes of this chapter is to examine these CSDP operations in totality to see what patterns can be discerned that are relevant for the characterizations of the EU's SB.

To analyse the ten sub-Saharan African CSDP operations they will first be considered against a typology of *operational types* and then against a set of *rationales* providing an indication as to where each fits with the three strands of SB outlined above.

Operational types

The fivefold operational types are presented in Figure 16.1. The sub-Saharan CSDP operations have been categorized on the basis of the mandate criteria outlined in the Joint Action authoring the operation. All the EU's CSDP operations can also be placed on both a civilian–military spectrum and defined in terms of their operation type. The sub-Saharan operations to date account for four of these five types, with only a border assistance and monitoring mission not being deployed. Through the use of these four types of operations the EU has generated a particular set of characteristics for the operational aspects of its SB in sub-Saharan Africa. Of the CSDP deployments to date Artemis, EUFOR DRC, EUFOR Chad–Central African Republic, EUNAVFOR Somalia/Operation Atalanta and the EU's support to the African Union's AMIS II operation in Sudan can be viewed as being at the military end of the civil–military spectrum. As we shall see below the circumscribed nature of these operations also fits within the human security imperatives identified above.

Policing and police support operations: two out of the nine CSDP operations to date can be characterized as this operational type – EUPOL Kinshasa and EUPOL, DR Congo. The second of these two operations was a successor operation to the first.

Reform-focused operations: rule of law and security sector reform. Three operations have been conducted under this category to date, the first the ongoing EU security sector reform mission EUSEC, DR Congo. The second operation is the completed EU SSR security sector reform mission in Guinea-Bissau. The third operation is the EU training mission to Somalia that was initiated last April. This is a military training mission for the development of the Somali security sector through the provision of specific military training, and support to the training provided by Uganda of 2,000 Somali recruits.

Logistical assistance. Only one CSDP operation to date has fallen into this category, which is the EU support to AMIS (Darfur) and which was EU technical support to the African Union, to assist it in the mounting of the AU's first ever large-scale peace support operation (AMIS II) in the Darfur region of Sudan. This was concluded on 31 December 2007, when AMIS was succeeded by UNAMID.

Military deployments in support of Petersberg tasks. Four military deployments have taken place in support of Petersberg tasks. First, the Artemis operation in the Congo (June–September 2003). Second, the EUFOR DRC (April–November 2006) operation to provide security for the general election process in the DRC. The third operation has also been concluded and was the EUFOR Chad–Central African Republic operation to protect the camps of refugees and displaced persons in the east of Chad and the north of the Central African Republic. The fourth and final operation of this type to date is the ongoing EUNAVFOR Somalia/Operation Atalanta, which is devoted to anti-piracy and anti-robbery operations off the coast of Somalia.

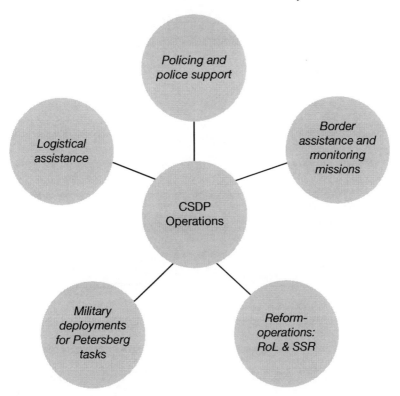

Figure 16.1 A typology of CSDP operations.

CSDP operations rationale-types

Each of the CSDP operations can also be categorized on the basis of their correspondence to the security–development nexus, the human security imperative and the preference for local enforcement (see Figure 16.2).

The assessment of each CSDP operation has been through a combination of examination of the mission mandate, the activities undertaken during the mission's duration and the actors involved in the implementation. The material used as the basis for the assessment is the IISS's *Strategic Survey*, development indices, EU documentation and secondary source analysis.[35]

The CSDP operations can be categorized according to their correspondence to different aspects of the EU's SB.

Security–development nexus. The majority of the EU's sub-Saharan African CSDP operations demonstrate evidence of a the security–development nexus as providing a rationale for intervention. The locations of EU intervention in the DRC, the CAR and Guinea-Bissau are all countries that are both placed low on the development index and are also regions of lack of development and territories assessed as suffering from political instability and conflict.

Human security imperative. Here the rationale for EU intervention is where the EU has identified the individual, rather the state, as the primary security concern and has consequently intervened for reasons of human security. The EU's Artemis operation is the most dramatic illustration of this imperative at work.

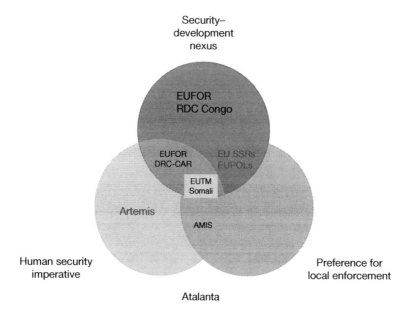

Figure 16.2 CSDP operations, rationale-types.

Preference for local enforcement. The EU has demonstrated a preference for local enforcement in the characteristics of its operations. First, all CSDP operations have been of a set duration, with the EU not seeking a prolonged duration to its commitment. Second, the EU prefer- ence has been to engage in activities to supply know-how to increase indigenous capacity, as through the EUPOL and SSR operations, or to provide support for African peace-keeping capacity through the AMIS operation.

The majority of the EU's sub-Saharan African CSDP operations demonstrate more than one aspect of the EU's SB. The only CSDP operation which cannot be easily located within this threefold schema of the EU's SB is the Atalanta operation. This operation is undertaken under the auspices of a UN mandate as with all other EU CSDP military deployments. As this operation is at an early stage of operation and the most recent of the EU's CSDP sub- Saharan Africa operations it may demonstrate other aspects of SB as it unfolds.

This analysis is a provisional attempt at considering the EU's CSDP operations as a part of a specific exercise in attempting to map the EU's SB. However, there is considerable scope for drawing appropriate comparisons between the EU's activities and those of other actors in future work. A key comparator for the EU's activities in sub-Saharan Africa is that of the United States. There are some potentially interesting comparisons to be drawn here. As Olson has noted it is striking to see how willing the European Union has been to use military forces in Africa in contrast to a greater US reluctance in recent years.[36]

Conclusion

As this chapter is a preliminary undertaking it is also appropriate to reflect upon a number of issues which will require further consideration and examination in the further empirical work needed to refine the analysis.

First, the EU's activities in sub-Saharan Africa raise the question of the extent to which the experiences have been 'downloaded' into the EU's wider SC. To what extent have the EU's policies pursued through the CFSP/CSDP towards sub-Saharan Africa played a key role in impacting both on the direction of development of the totality of the EU's foreign, security and defence policy strategic culture and, crucially, in the forms of military intervention contemplated in the future?

Second, what is the relationship between the EU's SB in sub-Saharan Africa and the strategic cultures of the individual member states? This is particularly significant because decisions as to when and where to undertake CSDP operations have been driven by individual member states. Analysing EU involvement in sub-Saharan Africa in a manner that facilitates the study of the duality of the CSDP structure and involves the SC of individual EU member states as well as EU institutions and EU decision-makers has been previously identified as important by analysts.[37]

Third, where to best seek the evidence for how the EU SC has been generated and so to gauge its characteristics and development? This is a problematic recognized within the general literature on SC:

> Just as all strategy has to be 'done' by operations which consist of tactical behaviour, so all strategic, operational, and tactical behaviour is 'done' by people and organisations that have been encultured supranationally, nationally, or sub-nationally.[38]

It is, however, still possible to draw a number of conclusions from the analysis within this chapter. The case study examination of the EU's foreign security and defence policy engagement with sub-Saharan Africa has allowed for the identification of components of the EU's SB. The use of strategic declarations that the EU has made towards the continent has allowed these to be identified and these have been further validated through examination of the CSDP operational activity that has been undertaken. Using the concepts of SB and SC the chapter tentatively suggests that the EU policy pursued towards sub-Saharan African demonstrates three characteristics to the EU's SB.

Sub-Saharan Africa has proved to be an invaluable case study through which to conduct this examination, as over recent years the continent has become an increasingly significant venue for the EU's foreign, security and defence policy. However, the EU has had a small 'footprint' in the region, confining its activities for the most part to the Great Lakes region, conflicts within Central Africa and a more recent involvement in the Horn of Africa. Consequently it remains to be seen if the EU will expand the scope and range of activities on the African continent and whether the SB identified in this chapter gains greater depth.

Notes

1 Council of the EU (2007f).
2 Council of the EU (2008e: 8).
3 It is, however, noteworthy, how the agenda issues have shifted across time, with South Africa a predominant concern in early phases and with a wider set of agenda issues subsequently. For accounts of the development of the CFSP see: Nuttall (2000: ch. 9); Holland (1997, 2005). For a definitive account of the development of the CSDP see: Howorth (2007).
4 See the 'secondary source' section of note 35.
5 Krause (2003); Sicurelli (2008); Gegout (2005).
6 Johnston (1995a: 34).
7 Johnston (1995a).
8 Meyer (2006); Katzenstein (1996); Hoffmann and Longhurst (1999).

9 Gray (1999b: 50).
10 Gray (1999b: 51).
11 Rynning (2003).
12 Cornish and Edwards (2001, 2005).
13 Cornish and Edwards (2005: 820).
14 Menon (2009); Witney (2008).
15 There have been six Western Balkans CSDP operations to date: Althea; Concordia; EUPM/BiH; EULEX Kosovo; EUPAT/FYROM; Proxima/FYROM.
16 This chapter will largely confine itself to examination of the CSDP, rather than CFSP, strands of the EU's foreign and security policy as it provides the best basis from which to assess strategic behaviour.
17 These are key statements about the EU's intended strategy guiding its relationship with third parties. For a full exploration of the concept see: Whitman (1998: ch. 1); Whitman and Manners (1998). The idea is much refined and presented by Manners as informational diffusion, which is 'the result of strategic communications' (2002: 244).
18 Grilli (1994).
19 Olsen (2009c).
20 See note 17 and Manners (2002) for the notion of informational diffusion.
21 Council of the EU (2003c).
22 Council of the European Union, European Council 12 and 13 December 2003, Presidency Conclusions, 5381/04, Brussels, 5 February 2004.
23 Whitman (2006).
24 Council of the EU (2007f: 2).
25 Council of the EU (2008e).
26 Whitman (2006).
27 Council of the EU (2004e).
28 On the same date as approving the Common Position the Council also adopted conclusions on this subject, stressing that it was committed to assisting the African continent in developing a comprehensive conflict prevention policy with a view to long-term conflict prevention (Bull. 1/2-2004, point 1.6.185).
    On 22 November 2004 the Council approved a peace and security action plan for Africa, focusing on capacity-building, and the disarmament, demobilization and reintegration of combatants (Bull. 11-2004, point 1.6.119).
    On 13 December 2004, it approved guidelines on implementation of support to peace and security in Africa under the European security and defence policy. The guidelines deal with the legal instruments required, budgetary and management aspects, and logistical and operational support (Bull. 12-2004).
    On 2 December, 2004 further to existing Joint Action 2002/589/CFSP on combating the destabilizing accumulation and spread of small arms and light weapons, the Council offered a funding and technical assistance to the Economic Community of West African States (Ecowas) Decision 2004/833/CFSP (OJ L 359, 4.12.2004; Bull. 12-2004).
29 Commission of the European Communities (2005).
30 The four objectives are: (a) peace and security, (b) governance and human rights, (c) trade and regional integration and (d) key development issues.
31 Africa–EU Partnership on Peace and Security, <http://ec.europa.eu/development/icenter/repository/EAS2007_action_plan_peace_security_en.pdf>.
32 Council of the EU (2006c).
33 For a full discussion of the funding arrangement and its support for APSA see: Pirozzi (2009).
34 See 'Secondary source material', note 35.
35 Primary source material: CFSP Joint Actions for each mission; International Institute for Strategic Studies (2005, 2006, 2007, 2008); United Nations Development Programme (2004, 2005, 2006, 2007).
    Secondary source material: Bagayoko (2004); Duke (2008); Faria (2004); Fiott (2008); Hendrickson, Strand and Raney (2007); Hoebeke, Carette and Vlassenroot (2007); Martinelli (2006, 2008); Merlingen and Ostraukaite (2005a); Ulriksen, Gourlay and Mace (2004).
36 Olsen (2009a).
37 Grimm (2003).
38 Gray (1999b).

17

THE EU AND ASIA

Towards proactive engagement?

Eva Gross

The emergence of Asia in economic and in political terms is of increasing global significance – not least because of the rise of China and India, but also because of the increasing range of foreign and security challenges that face the region and the international community as a whole. Asia, including Central Asia,[1] is a diverse and dynamic region. It accounts for more than half of the world's population and a quarter of the global economic wealth. Aside from high-income industrialized countries, countries in the post-Soviet space and emerging economies, Asia is also home to over two-thirds of the world's poor. The EU's traditional focus on trade, development cooperation and humanitarian assistance thus remains an important aspect of involvement.

Over the past decade a set of political and security challenges emanating from Asia have progressively gained prominence. These have challenged the EU not only to formulate interests and objectives towards Asia but also to apply a range of instruments in pursuit of them. In addition to poverty and weak governance, concrete security threats include terrorism, narcotics, nuclear proliferation, organized crime and state weakness and/or failure. Environmental degradation, migration and potential cross-border conflicts further increase the risk of regional instability.

In light of the region's diversity – including as it does established trading partners, rising powers, but also weak and failing states – the EU by necessity pursues a number of foreign policy interests in Asia. These include concerns over the maintenance of a multilateral, rules-based international order in light of ongoing power shifts that favor emerging powers China but also India; strengthening regional cooperation mechanisms; engaging in post-conflict reconstruction in Afghanistan; countering state weakness, nuclear proliferation and the potential for inter-state conflict with India in the case of Pakistan; military conflict, including a nuclear confrontation, between North and South Korea; securing Europe's energy supply in the case of Central Asia; and a cross-cutting concern with strengthening the rule of law, human rights and good governance.

The variety of policy responses required to meet these multi-faceted challenges in a complex region make a concise analysis and evaluation of EU approaches a somewhat challenging endeavor. This is also in light of the fact that the EU's own foreign policy instruments have been continually evolving since the formulation of specific EU rather than European/member state security interests – in Asia and elsewhere – that culminated in the ratification of the Lisbon Treaty and the launch of the European External Action Service (EEAS) in 2010.

The following sections analyze evolving EU interests and its professed strategic objectives vis-à-vis Asia, taking as their baseline the European Security Strategy (ESS) as well as policy documents and statements related to individual engagements that touch on foreign and security policy. The chapter then critically assesses the effectiveness of EU external policies in pursuit of its stated interests. It focuses on four dimensions of EU engagement: the individual strategic partnerships and bilateral relationships with Asian powers; the EU's engagement in, or in support of, regional integration efforts; the EU's attempt to forge bilateral relations with Asian countries in pursuit of particular security interests; and the EU's engagement through individual CSDP missions. Finally, the chapter considers whether the EU has achieved its objectives – and to what extent these objectives have been clearly defined to begin with. It argues that the EU has come a long way in defining and addressing individual policy challenges. However, a comprehensive and proactive approach towards the region as well as to the pursuit of individual EU security objectives that relate to it remains in the making. The chapter concludes by formulating some recommendations on how the EU can strengthen its strategic engagement with Asia as well as its approach towards concrete policy areas as they relate to the EU's foreign and security policy interests.

Defining EU interests and strategic objectives in Asia

The evaluation of the EU's security policy in Asia necessitates an exercise in defining and delineating foreign policy goals. Taking the 2003 European Security Strategy as a guideline, the core of EU interests and objectives in Asia (and elsewhere) can be divided into systemic, regional and individual threat-specific concerns and challenges. The systemic challenge is twofold. First, it concerns the EU's overall objective of working towards 'effective multilateralism' – that is, working with NATO, strengthening the UN system as well as regional organizations such as the OSCE and upholding and developing international law and a rule-based international order. In light of the ongoing global power shifts in favor of China and India – and, more generally, a multi-polar world – there is a concomitant concern over whether these two emerging powers will adopt a multilateral approach, or whether they will pursue individual policy objectives on a bilateral basis. Thus, the EU can only meet its objective if emerging powers that will form part of a multi-polar system subscribe and participate in a multilateral, rule-based international system. Individual bilateral strategic partnerships with individual countries, most of all China but also India, and the EU's existing relationship with Japan and South Korea, will ensure stability in EU foreign relations, including in security but also in trade, but also reinforce the EU's position in favor of multilateralism.

A second set of objectives for the EU is the maintenance of not only systemic but also regional stability. The creation and strengthening of regional cooperation mechanisms thus represents another core security interest for the EU. In Asia, this takes the form of two approaches: forging a regional approach towards Central Asia; and strengthening existing regional cooperation mechanisms in Asia. These include an interregional forum for discussion between Europe and Asia, the Asia–Europe Meeting (ASEM); but also the EU's engagement with regional groupings including the Association of South East Asian Nations (ASEAN), the Asian Regional Forum (ARF) and the South Asian Association for Regional Cooperation (SAARC). In addition, the OSCE, which includes a significant number of Asian countries and thus engages regional actors, also represents an institutional instrument for work towards good governance and democratization that the EU can actively support in its work towards common regional security aims in Asia (Lynch, 2009).

Finally, there are a number of issue-specific security interests that were identified in the ESS and reaffirmed in its 2008 implementation report that affect Asia in particular. These include state failure; regional instability, interstate conflict and nuclear proliferation; terrorism and organized crime; but also humanitarian emergencies; the fight against poverty; and adverse effects of climate change, including migration. In light of the inherent interconnectedness of these challenges, climate change and migration feed into the broader security–development nexus and the EU's emerging peace-building agenda. Energy security, finally, has become a core concern for the EU and its member states, and constitutes one of the underlying motivations behind the adoption of the EU Central Asia strategy in 2007.

The application of CFSP/CSDP instruments in Asia

Placed in the context of the ongoing evolution of EU foreign policy both in terms of available instruments and geographical reach, Asia is a relative latecomer when it comes to the formulation of the EU foreign policy interests and objectives. The EU has engaged in individual Asian countries or conflicts, but a comprehensive view on the continent and its political and security challenges has been slow to develop. This refers both to the process of developing EU rather than member state foreign policy interests as well as filling declarations and documents with policy content.

The European Commission was the first EU-level actor to formulate policy objectives by releasing, in 1994, a Communication on the EU's New Asia Strategy. The creation of the EU CFSP and later CSDP has further led to the formulation of political and strategic interests and objectives, not least through the drafting of the 2003 ESS. The institutional changes as a result of the Lisbon Treaty have further unified EU presence in the field by turning former Commission Delegations into EU Delegations with EU diplomatic representation through the EU External Action Service (EEAS). They have also led to a consolidation of foreign policy instruments at the Brussels level. With respect to policy interest and objectives, growing expectations as to the EU's global role as well as global power shifts have moved the EU's engagement with its strategic partners in Asia further up the political agenda

The EU gradually did become active as political and security actor through CFSP and CSDP policies, particularly in response to increasing expectations as to its response to global security challenges. These include the terrorist attacks on 9/11 and the subsequent appointment of an EUSR to Afghanistan, which reflected the most immediate EU foreign policy reaction on the part of EU member states to a crisis in Asia.

While this signals that these two areas were regarded as politically relevant and meriting special attention on the part of the EU, it also gives some indication that, with regard to the rest of the Asian continent, EU engagement was politically underdeveloped. Confined to economic and developmental cooperation, EU member states also often overshadowed EU activities and prevented the evolution of European interests.

Central Asia occupies a separate policy space from the rest of Asia due to the region's post-Soviet legacy, its relative proximity to the EU and the added security aspects of energy and trafficking. In its regional rather than bilateral focus, the 2007 EU Central Asia strategy explicitly builds on the European Neighborhood Policy (ENP) in an attempt to draw the Central Asian Republics closer to the EU. The strategy cites energy security as a key concern together with border management as well as the mutual commitment to good governance, democracy, rule of law and human rights.[2] To these ends, the EU maintains additional political representation through the post of EU Special Representative (EUSR) to Central Asia that was created in 2005.[3]

In addition, the conflict in neighboring Afghanistan, where the EU and its member states engage in reconstruction activities, also represents a threat to stability – and therefore indirectly also to EU interests – in Central Asia. The EU's engagement in Asian security is most pronounced in Afghanistan, and in the context of an active conflict and concurrent peacebuilding and reconstruction efforts. In Pakistan on the other hand, where the EU is slowly responding to an increasing security rationale, the EU attempts to strengthen its bilateral engagement through humanitarian and development assistance by increasingly focusing on good governance and the rule of law, and on the political aspects of a bilateral EU–Pakistan relationship.

The most concrete manifestation of EU engagement in security policy in Asia remains its CSDP missions, EUMM Aceh Indonesia and the police mission EUPOL Afghanistan. They reflect the EU's multifaceted engagement in Asia, its evolution but also its limitation as a security actor. The Aceh Monitoring Mission (AMM), which lasted for 12 months starting in September 2005, was established to monitor the implementation of the peace agreement between the Government of Indonesia and the Free Aceh Movement signed on 15 August 2005 in Helsinki. The mission provided monitors, together with five contributing countries from ASEAN, Norway and Switzerland. The mission's objective was to contribute to a peaceful, comprehensive and sustainable solution to the conflict in Aceh, including investigating and ruling on complaints and alleged violations of the peace agreement and establishing and maintaining liaison and good cooperation with the parties.[4] EUPOL Afghanistan, in contrast, was launched in June 2007 with the objective of contributing to the establishment of effective and sustainable Afghan civil policing capacities through advising and mentoring the ministry of the interior and through contributing to limited training activities.[5] In a different and ongoing conflict context, the mission's mandate and strength continue to evolve both in response to evolving needs on the ground as well as broader trends in the politics of international intervention – but has also demonstrated the political and operational shortfalls in the EU's crisis management toolbox (House of Lords, 2011).

Evaluating CFSP/CSDP policies in the context of the EU's overall external action in Asia

Since EU foreign and security interests and policy formulation in Asia have evolved gradually over the course of the past decade and a half, policy instruments in pursuit of these interests have been deployed in a gradual rather than systematic and comprehensive manner. At the inception of EU foreign policy activity through CFSP and CSDP, the 'mental map' of EU security interests encompassed the Balkans and Middle East, the Eastern Neighborhood and sub-Saharan Africa. When it came to Asia, supplementing traditional concerns over aid and trade as well as inter-regionalism with security policies and more generally developing a political approach towards the region necessitated a cognitive process of interest formulation on the part of the EU as well as its member states, which frequently pursued bilateral policies in support of national interests. Identifying European objectives, formulating EU-level policies and balancing them against member state bilateral preferences, therefore, has been and remains an ongoing process (Geeraerts and Gross, 2011). Perhaps unsurprisingly, rather than engaging in a systematic stock-taking and formulating a proactive policy towards individual conflicts, the EU has taken a reactive position towards, for instance, Afghanistan, but has also taken advantage of an opportunity to intervene, in the case of the Aceh Monitoring Mission – and has adopted bilateral and regional approaches to underpin these individual policy activities.

The EU, a strategic actor in Asia?

While the EU has come to pursue a number of strategic interests in Asia, it would be an overstatement to say that the EU constitutes a strategic actor in Asia. This is not merely on account of the differing policies applied as well as their objectives. The EU's strategic engagement with Asia often remains overshadowed by US predominance in the region. The influence wielded by individual EU member states with long-standing interests and engagement in individual countries or sub-regions often further eclipses the EU's political standing and visibility. Establishing itself as a political and security actor – rather than an economic actor – in the perception of its Asian partners continues to be a lengthy and to date incomplete process as a result (Holland, 2009). Brussels has recognized this lacuna: the policy instrument of strategic partnership is to enable political engagement and cooperation with partners, including Asian powers. At the same time, there is a clear sense that the EU has not yet exhausted this particular platform – nor has it formulated what specific policy goals it intends to pursue through this instrument, or how those goals identified will and can be pursued (Balfour, 2010).

The EU and regional groupings

The EU's relationship to ASEAN, but also its efforts at strengthening regional cooperation mechanisms and institutions, while in existence, could be explored and strengthened in more detail. When it comes to the EU's emphasis on regional integration and dialogue, a slight shift towards security is detectable. The EU's approach to regional integration such as the annual EU–ASEAN summit focuses on trade and development rather than security concerns: the implicit assumption is that increasing economic integration will lead to a stronger regional identity and peaceful relations as a result.

The EU also holds regular Asia–Europe Meetings (ASEM). The tenth such meeting took place in October 2010. While it focused mainly on global economic governance and sustainable economic development, the summit also addressed global security concerns including piracy, terrorism and organized crime, disaster relief, human security and human rights and democracy and nuclear proliferation – as well as their regional dimension. ASEM as a regional consultation mechanism expands the membership from Asia and Central Asia to (since 2010) also include New Zealand, Australia and Russia, which expands the regional scope of this particular format.

The variable geometry of the countries participating in ASEM and ASEAN as well as SAARC can be read as an asset but also as a liability. These regional groupings enlarge the number of stakeholders; at the same time, they do not necessarily strengthen coherence in developing a common approach towards common challenges.

The EU–Central Asia strategy: a regional approach in the making?

The EU–Central Asia strategy represents an attempt on the part of the EU to put a regional approach into action, although this has not served as a model towards other regional clusters in Asia but rather replicates the policy model adopted through the European

Neighborhood Policy (ENP). It explicitly serves a set of security and integration aims, and is partly driven also by the assumption that the diffusion of European values is a key component of ensuring security. The EU implements its strategy through existing instruments, including Partnership and Cooperation Agreements (PCA) as well as Trade and Cooperation Agreements.

More concretely, EU engagement with Central Asia has included the EU's rapid response to the crisis in Kyrgyzstan in cooperation with the UN and the OSCE; and a strengthened EU presence in the region through the opening of an EU Delegation in Kyrgyzstan and Tajikistan – as well as the entry into force of the PCA with Tajikistan, and the interim agreement of the PCA with Turkmenistan. At the same time, the EU's 2010 strategy progress report noted limited regional cooperation between the five republics, and lack of progress on human rights, rule of law, good governance and democracy.[6]

In the area of governance and the rule of law, the EU and key member states launched a Rule of Law Initiative in 2008. Given that programmes have only recently reached their implementation phase, an analysis of policy effectiveness, particularly with regard to this particular initiative, is premature. At the same time, the 2010 progress report highlighted intensified engagement between the EU and the five republics. This engagement included both bilateral relations and responses to individual policy problems, but also a strengthened overall bilateral engagement in terms of developing political influence in the region. Given the relative youth of the policy and its components it is too soon to draw conclusion over the strategy's impact; however, given the low starting points on governance and human rights coupled with the EU's limited reach in terms of political representation on the ground (the EUSR is Brussels-based) EU activities in Central Asia remain less visible and concentrated than regional approaches closer to the EU's borders.

The CSDP missions: EUMM Aceh and EUPOL Afghanistan

When it comes to CSDP proper, and the manifestation of the EU's security policy, the record is mixed: the EU has launched two small missions in very different theatres of operations. While the Aceh mission is universally judged a success and effective at reaching its core objectives (Braud and Grevi, 2005), the same cannot be said for EUPOL Afghanistan, a mission that has been fighting an uphill battle to assert itself as a credible actor in Kabul. Granted, Aceh profited from a fortunate constellation of events that facilitated EU intervention: a natural disaster that led conflict parties to settle on a peace agreement; EU–member state/Finnish involvement and initiative-taking at realizing a CSDP mission; and a relatively precise and manageable mandate. In the case of EUPOL Afghanistan, on the other hand, ongoing shortfalls in personnel coupled with mobility problems, continuously readjusting mission design and an ongoing and deteriorating conflict setting have negatively impacted EUPOL's effectiveness. At the same time, ongoing institutional improvements as a result of the Lisbon Treaty mission design have had a positive impact on EUPOL and the broader EU presence. Some of this also had to do with a greater transatlantic acceptance of the EU's approach, and the particular conflict setting where the EU acts alongside not only an ongoing military operation through ISAF but also a NATO training mission, NTM-A.

While the EU's priorities as far as the conflict itself is concerned – establishing good governance and the rule of law, as well as a focus on rural development and health – are long-term peace-building measures, they do not directly contribute to the military operations; nor does the EU's particular political presence and decision-making structure lend itself to impact on the international political agenda setting as far as approaches towards the conflict itself are concerned. The overall political direction tends to be set by Washington, and EU member states have in the past prioritized bilateral relationships either to the USA or approaches towards the Afghan government and this has negatively impacted the EU's visibility and also its impact. At the same time, in the current political and security climate the EU's contribution has come to be more valued and the coordination with NATO and US activities has improved (Gross, 2010).

EU policy effectiveness in Asia: sufficiently ambitious, achieving objectives?

The analysis of the effectiveness of the EU's policy in Asia reveals a mismatch between stated aims and ambitions on the one hand, and policy content and resources extended, on the other. The incremental nature of the EU's foreign policy reach has increased the unevenness of policy developments – as have the different policy models employed to reach the EU's aim, which span strategic partnerships, a regional policy, but also individual CSDP missions.

When it comes to taking ownership of certain policy challenges and to increasing the EU's reach beyond specific countries or problem areas, EU policy in Asia is marked by tentativeness. To be fair, the EU's policy evolution in Asia has been complicated by a number of factors that include pre-existing spheres of interests and influence on the part of the United States. In addition, the size and growing influence of China coupled with the EU's profile as a non-traditional foreign and security actor have made the exertion of policy interests and influence difficult. This has been the case also with respect to the EU's relations with India, where similar values and forms of governance have raised expectations of more intensive cooperation than has been achieved to date (Peral, 2010). All too often, therefore, the EU has either not been perceived as a foreign-policy but rather as a trade or development actor; or has had difficulties translating its growing political clout in the pursuit of specific EU interests. Individual member states' ongoing investments in their bilateral relationships with individual Asian powers have further complicated the task of increasing the visibility of the EU's contribution. These factors are reflected in the EU's engagement with individual Asian powers and also with individual policy issues.

The EU's strategic partners: common values and interests?

The EU's strategic partnerships with individual countries but also its engagement with regional associations in principle express the intent to develop and engage in focused dialogue and engagement in pursuit of EU but also joint interests. In reality, however, they are of a sufficiently different nature and of sufficiently different content for the term 'strategic partnership' to mean relatively little; and to create the impression of incoherence given the divergent challenges addressed in each strategic partnership (Renard, 2010a). The EU has not helped matters by remaining vague in its commitments to each partner, even if policy-makers have acknowledged the challenge of missing content and purpose.

Besides the question over policy content, the term 'strategic partnership' is also somewhat contradictory in that it suggests a commonality of interests and values between the EU and its partners. Whereas this might be the case in Japan, China's worldview, value assumptions and resulting policy positions differ considerably from those of the EU. These different assumptions and actions make the pursuit of a joint approach towards common challenges, including those near the top of the EU's policy agenda such as climate change or effective multilateralism, a difficult undertaking. Individual strategic partnerships, particularly with China and India, also suffer from lack of EU–member states cohesion – and the EU position has been frequently shaped but also undermined towards a lowest common denominator position to do justice to the member states' bilateral interests.

Not quite a strategic partner: the EU and Pakistan

Strategic partnerships are of concern for the EU because they allow engagement with stakeholders in maintaining global but also regional order. As a result, the EU is gradually adopting a strategic approach towards other countries in Asia that are crucial for the attainment of regional stability and security. This applies in particular to Pakistan, where EU policy illustrates once more the difficulty facing the EU in forging a policy at the EU level in a country where individual member states either had too much or too little interest to graft a strategy at the European level (Islam, 2010). EU–Pakistan summits have taken place although these have not necessarily focused on the security dimension. Instead, EU engagement with Pakistan has tended to focus on trade and humanitarian and development assistance. The EU has increased its support for civil society and good governance, but more could be done to do justice to the security interests the EU pursues in Pakistan and the wider region. A strategic approach has yet to emerge – towards Pakistan or its broader region, which would include connecting EU interests (and by extension the application of policy instruments) in Pakistan with those in India but also Afghanistan, where the EU and its member states have made significant investments over the past decade.

Non-proliferation

On the issue of non-proliferation in Asia the EU has been relatively subdued. While the EU can look to its engagement with Iran as a record of engagement as well as a case study of policy action – and cooperation with other stakeholders – on this particular issue, this experience has not been replicated in Asia. The EU supports the Six-Party Talks (but without being a party to it) in the case of North Korea – where other EU assistance has been suspended without plans for drawing up a new country strategy paper in the absence of domestic developments. In the case of Pakistan and India, on the other hand, the EU has tended not to raise the issue of non-proliferation in favor of other policy concerns (Quille, 2008b). As a result, despite the EU's overall concern with non-proliferation – after all, the fact is that there has been a personal representative for WMD to first Javier Solana and then Ashton since December 2003 – the EU's engagement in Asia is marked by little visibility but also little engagement with individual countries in the region. This is a manifestation both of the EU's lacking strategic actorness but also of the dominance of external powers as well as individual regional players. And yet, given the prominence the EU attaches to this particular policy field, the lack of engagement on non-proliferation in Asia is striking.

Climate change and energy security

Finally, climate change and energy security represent separate and at the same time two intrinsically linked challenges for the EU: asserting leadership in international climate negotiations on the one hand, and emphasizing energy security on the other. Policy responses, therefore, should focus on the EU's place in the international system and its ability to persuade other stakeholders to work through multilateral means; and on bilateral and regional engagement with countries in possession of energy resources. With respect to Asia, this means bilateral engagement with the EU's strategic partners China and India for shaping policy positions, and strengthening commitments towards a multilateral approach towards climate change. It also includes, however, the exploration of the EU Central Asia strategy for securing energy supplies. EU policy instruments suitable for these aims, namely the strategic partnerships with China, a key stakeholder in climate negotiations, and the EU's Central Asia strategy, however, to date have underexplored these two security challenges.

Conclusion

This chapter has argued that European engagement in Asia is cross-cutting and increasingly comprehensive – but that it lacks overall strategic and political depth when it comes to EU security interests in Asia. Despite the number of policy initiatives launched the degree to which they contribute to effectiveness, and the degree to which the overlap between bilateral and regional approaches mutually reinforce various EU policy interests, remains open for improvement. Over the past five years, the EU has mapped its security interests in Asia and defined its policy objectives and increasingly also the policy instruments to be applied in pursuit of these objectives. Despite some criticism and weaknesses when it comes to implementing policies, as well as in individual instances policy design, this represents a significant improvement to the EU's foray into foreign and security policy as well as into Asia as a security actor.

The history of policy implementation shows, however, that the application of policy instruments in Asia has been uneven both in terms of the resources extended but also in the ratio between security threat and political attention – and the eventual policy instrument extended. Individual threats such as weak and failed states receive a significant level of interest in the case of Afghanistan, but less has been done in the case of Pakistan. And, the strategic engagement with Asian powers and regional organizations is further developed in some instances than in others. There is a sense, therefore, of selectivity and a reactive stance on policy implementation – and in some instances, such as nuclear proliferation, insufficient engagement with particular policy areas as they pertain to Asia. There is thus a need to strengthen the political content of the EU's engagement and the coherence between the EU's individual policy strands. In this regard, the emerging Lisbon structures present an opportunity to strengthen the EU's political presence and to better align EU and member state instruments. Member states, finally, must play their part in strengthening the EU's position in Asia.

Finally, the threat assessment of EU security interest in Asia suggests that the EU's scope of involvement could be expanded to include, for instance, more concrete assistance to improve governance and the rule of law in Pakistan; addressing the conflict in Kashmir; strengthening local capacity; and contributing its significant experience in border management in an attempt to fight organized crime and terrorism. This presupposes, however, that the EU together with its member states engage potential host countries as well as other international and regional actors with stakes in particular conflict or issue areas. This will not only facilitate EU involvement but also make it more effective when it does happen. And, in case the EU does not want to get involved directly – save for the most pressing circumstances – it should nevertheless proactively define its security interests and its approach towards addressing them: either by acting bilaterally or by influencing target states as well as states in the broader region to address specific security challenges. Meeting its security interests in

Asia, at the end of the day, does not have to involve the range of EU instruments in every instance – but the EU should be in a position to influence others to take on particular policy challenges; or to bring about a change in a particular regional political dynamic.

To conclude, pursuing EU security interests in Asia does not and should not necessarily mean that the EU increase the number of its CSDP missions, or that it get involved as a political actor in every conflict context. It does mean, however, that the EU strengthen its political capacity in order to achieve more with the considerable economic, political and security presence it already possesses in Asia. In the end, pursuing EU security interests in Asia is a predominately political challenge: to achieve greater coherence between EU instruments; to balance systemic, regional and issue-specific security interests and activities; and to thus maximize the EU's political impact – and move from a reactive to a proactive engagement in Asia.

Notes

1 To date the EU pursues separate Asia and Central Asia strategies, an approach that honors the different geographical, historical and cultural priorities and circumstances in these two geographical groupings. The two strategies are driven by a diverse and only partially overlapping set of security concerns, to which the EU responds through a different set of policies. In the interest of comprehensiveness, this chapter discusses the two geographical entities jointly.
2 Council of the European Union (2009e).
3 Under their current mandates, Pierre Morel is EUSR in Central Asia, whereas Vygaudas Usackas functions simultaneously as EUSR and Head of EU Delegation.
4 See EU Council Secretariat (2006).
5 See European Union (2010a).
6 See Council of the European Union (2010a).

18

A NEW GEOGRAPHY OF EUROPEAN POWER?

James Rogers

The naval historian and geostrategist Alfred Thayer Mahan understood the utility of military power perhaps better than anyone before or since. In an article called 'The Place of Force in International Relations' – penned two years before his death in 1914 – he claimed: 'Force is never more operative then when it is known to exist but is not brandished' (1912: 31).[1] If Mahan's point was valid then, it is perhaps even more pertinent now. The rise of new powers around the world has contributed to the emergence of an increasingly volatile and multipolar international system. Making the use of force progressively more dangerous and politically challenging, this phenomenon is merging with a new phase in the proliferation of weapons of mass destruction. At the same time, many European governments are increasingly reluctant – perhaps even unable – to intervene militarily in foreign lands. The operations in Afghanistan and Iraq have shown that when armed force is used actively in support of foreign policy, it can go awry; far from reaffirming strength and determination on the part of its beholder, it can actually reveal weakness and a lack of resolve. Half-hearted military operations – of the kind frequently undertaken by democratic European states – tend not to go particularly well, especially when there is little by way of a political strategy or the financial resources needed to support them. A political community's accumulation of a military reputation, which can take decades, if not centuries, can then be rapidly squandered through a series of unsuccessful combat operations, which dent its confidence and give encouragement to its opponents or enemies.[2]

Nevertheless, since the Wars of the Yugoslav Succession in the 1990s, there has been a strong belief that Europeans need to be more willing and able to use armed force. Indeed, the constitution and development of the Common Security and Defence Policy was in many respects a reaction to the Yugoslav bloodbath (Rogers, 2009a; Shepherd, 2009). To this end, the European Security Strategy asserts that the European Union needs a 'strategic culture', which fosters 'early, rapid and when necessary, robust intervention' (European Council, 2003: 11).[3] Brussels has subsequently conducted a series of small and seemingly experimental 'crisis management' operations in a range of countries, whose crowning glory has been the anti-piracy naval operation in the Gulf of Aden, Atalanta. Yet, excepting those in the Western Balkans, almost all of these operations share a common theme: they have been heavily reactive and/or lack geopolitical focus. For example, while Europeans were militarily engaged in distant sub-Saharan Africa during August 2008, a war broke out in the European

211

Neighbourhood in a potential transit corridor for the planned Nabucco gas pipeline – which aims to bypass Russian territory and reduce European gas dependency. Likewise, it took almost two years of rising pirate infestation around Somalia – on the main European–Asian maritime communication line – before Europeans got directly involved. This lack of geopolitical focus is a consequence of an outmoded European geostrategy, which fails to integrate the maritime with the continental component (Rogers, 2009b; Rogers and Simón, 2009). Equally, it is driven by a dearth of European grand strategy, the hardening of which would draw together the European Union's means and wherewithal to overcome foreign threats and challenges, while simultaneously working for the pursuit of common objectives (Biscop, 2009a, 2009b; Venusberg Group, 2007).

The aim of this chapter is to offer an analysis of the geography of European power in the early twenty-first century. It will begin by looking at the sub-components of grand strategy: geopolitics, geostrategy and forward presence. This will be followed by an analysis of the European Union's geopolitical situation, something that is frequently overlooked in contemporary European politics. The improvement and further integration of the European homeland will bolster the European Union as a base of power, which itself could then be exploited à la Mahan to diffuse awe into foreign governments and make them more respectful of European preferences. Most importantly of all, though, the chapter will show why and how the European Union should focus less on disjointed 'crisis management' operations and more on the quiet and covert expansion of its political and economic power into geographic locations of particular significance (see Figure 18.1). The chapter will identify these locations as the proximal belt of surrounding countries, buttressed by overseas maritime zones that are of specific importance to the European economy. Acquiring influence in such regions will necessitate the final completion of the 'comprehensive approach' through the creation of a European 'forward presence': first, to deter foreign powers from meddling in countries in the wider European Neighbourhood and second, to dissuade obstinacy and misbehaviour on the part of local rulers.[4] In other words, a truly comprehensive European grand strategy should be inculcated with a grand design: the constitution of an extended 'Grand Area', a zone where European power would be progressively institutionalized by the dislocation of existing divisions and their reintegration into a new liberal order. By reducing the likelihood of having to use military force reactively, it would better connect with the conception of preventative engagement as outlined in the European Security Strategy (European Council, 2003: 11). And by filling political vacuums with the gradual expansion of European power, conflicts could actually be prevented from breaking out before they start or spiral out of control – thus stifling the potential for dangerous 'vacuum wars'.[5]

Geography, politics and strategy

In recent years, the linkages between geography and politics have been ignored or downplayed. Scholars and analysts have been 'overdosing' on globalization, which became the main framework in the 1990s through which international relations was understood (Gray, 2004: 9). This approach merged with a number of laudable but nevertheless peculiar fantasies, which saw the rise of a multilateral and civilized era in international relations as inevitable, while force and coercion would be progressively and irrevocably abolished. As Toje says: 'These movements were united in the belief that the world could be, or already had been, fundamentally changed by new ideas and new assumptions. This spawned a rejection of national interests, and national identity among intellectual elites' (2008b: 209). United by a Hegelian or teleological reading of History, which was further amplified by the West's own

Current 'crisis management' approach

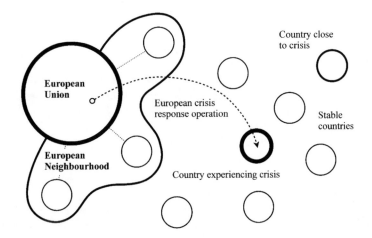

Proposed 'Grand Area' approach

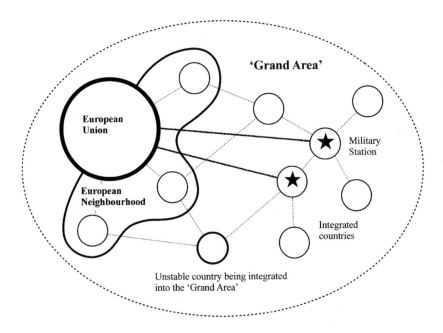

Note: This figure shows the differences between the European Union's present 'crisis management' approach versus the proposed 'Grand Area' approach. The former approach leaves countries adjacent to the European Neighbourhood in a state of permanent flux, where European military forces and civilian services intervene periodically to arrest disorder. However, the 'Grand Area' approach would attempt to integrate those countries into a permanent European-led system, underpinned by military stations, better communication lines and tighter partnerships – a European 'forward presence' – to reduce the need for sporadic intervention.

Figure 18.1 'Crisis management' versus 'Grand Area'.

hegemony after the Cold War, these perspectives came to see geography and geopolitics as outmoded (Fukuyama, 1989).[6] In short, internationalism, openness and globalization had become fashionable, while considerations of geography, power and political interest were seen as archaic, even immoral. The enormous energies and resources poured into protecting liberal civilization, either before or during the Cold War, were forgotten or deliberately downplayed because they did not fit in with the new paradigm (Cooper, 2003; Kagan, 2008). The triumph of the liberal international trade system was no longer seen as the outcome of a European and American geostrategy that devoted the material means and political will necessary to maintain a favourable balance of geopolitical power, but rather as due to the inherent superiority of the liberal order itself.

However, as European and American hegemony has gone into relative decline since its apex in the early years of the first decade of the twenty-first century, the linkages between geography and politics have started to manifest themselves again (Kaplan, 2009b; Rogers, 2009b). Geography is, after all, 'fundamental' and 'pervasive' for it 'impose[s] distinctive constraints and provide[s] distinctive opportunities that have profound implications for policy and strategy' (Gray, 1996: 248). While geography may not determine social and political development, either by giving certain peoples an advantage,[7] it should nevertheless be understood as the material for social and political development (Owens, 1999). Spykman used the analogy of clothes manufacturing to get this point across: 'to admit that the garment must ultimately be cut to fit the cloth is not to say that the cloth determines either the garment's style or its adequacy' (1938a: 30). This is because a piece of land, a river or a mountain range cannot take sides with any particular group of people or force them to accept its presence in any particular way. In Gray's words:

> The point in need of the clearest recognition simply is that all political matters occur within a particular geographical context; in short, they have a geopolitical dimension. ... Of course, physical geography is politically 'neutral.' But the combatant who adapts best to the terms and conditions of life and warfare in the jungle [for example], will count that particular terrain as an ally rather than a 'neutral' geographic stage.
>
> (Gray, 1999b: 173).

A political community like the UK, for example, may be an island nation surrounded by sea, but this inescapable orientation did not force its inhabitants to implement a grand strategy whose objective was to become a maritime superpower with a deep reach into the European mainland, North America, Asia, Africa and Australasia. Japan, also an island nation, located on the edge of a continent, did quite the opposite: it closed itself off from the outside world for many centuries, allowing only nominal trade with the Portuguese and Dutch. The British thus took advantage of their geographical perspective and worked with it to maximize their political and economic leverage, whereas the Japanese did not, consequentially emerging much later and from a position of relative weakness.

This is where geostrategy comes in. At a very rudimentary level, geostrategy accounts for the geographic direction of a political community's foreign policy. As Grygiel notes: 'The geostrategy of a state ... is not necessarily motivated by geographic or geopolitical factors. A state may project power to a location because of ideological reasons, interest groups, or simply the whim of its leader' (2006: 22). Indeed, there is no a priori linkage between strategy and geography; governments have often failed to properly link the two. For example, Simms (2007) has shown how during the second half of the eighteenth century, the rise of powerful ideologies and interest groups in the UK eroded the country's established concentration on the Low Countries and Central Europe and replaced it with a new and near-exclusive maritime geostrategy. Drunk with victory after the Seven Years War, London thought it could hide behind the might of the Royal Navy and focus almost entirely on its new-found and growing worldwide imperium. But this was a profound mistake, for 'Britain's security depended on maintaining her "ramparts" in Europe. It was there, in Germany and Flanders, in the "counterscarp" of England, that Britain's fate would be decided' (Simms, 2007: 684). The test came just over a decade later when Britain's colonies in North America declared their independence. As a succession of European governments pledged support for the rebellion, London was forced to divide its forces to defend itself from direct foreign attack. Britain was punished for failing to maintain a favourable balance of power in its most important zones of geographic and geopolitical interest, consequentially losing its first overseas empire.

Clearly, a failure to adequately connect geography and politics can be very dangerous. Gray puts it succinctly: 'the possible constrains and frictions of space and time must always command the strategist's respect' (1999b: 173). While there has been a tendency to downplay geopolitics in the West over the past two decades, non-European countries – such as China, Russia, India, South Korea and Brazil – have been busily crafting sophisticated and entwined domestic and foreign geostrategies (see: Kaplan, 2009a, 2009b, 2010a, 2010b, 2010c; Rogers, 2009b). Agricultural and energy output has been expanded, in some cases, quite dramatically. New railways, motorways and communication systems have been built to connect various cities and provinces. And stronger and less corrupt forms of government have been implemented to rule over those provinces. Fuelled by rapid economic growth, the Chinese, for example, have built numerous new power stations, hydro-electric systems and tens of thousands of kilometres of new road and railway – with even more planned. This building bonanza was crowned in 2008 by the construction of the monumental Qingzang railway, which links long-isolated Tibet with China's increasingly industrialized and densely populated seaboard. Beijing plans to extend this railway considerably over the next 20 years, greatly amplifying its sovereignty and continental reach over its western provinces and making possible deep demographic changes across the region – which will further entrench Chinese power (Arya, 2008; Lustgarten, 2008). Indeed, so fast has China been investing in its railway system that by 2012, the country will have more high-speed lines than the rest of the world put together (Robinson, 2010). Unsurprisingly, Beijing has felt less constrained and more confident to project its domestic strength and transform it into regional and global clout, not least with plans for a 'New Silk Road' of railways, roads and energy transmission pipelines deep into Central Asia (Follath and Neef, 2010), as well as a sustained effort at naval expansion (see Holmes and Yoshihara, 2009; Rehman, 2009; Scott, 2008; Xu, 2006 [2004]).

But there is nothing necessarily new here: governments have long sought to domesticate and integrate their domestic territory more effectively to provide a springboard for maritime reach and commercial expansion (Spykman, 1939b). From the earliest period in history, political communities were forced to grapple with the extension of technological, logistical and armed power over the natural world – over geography – to 'establish' themselves over territorial space, stake out a homeland, connect it together and push back its borders so as to ensure its longevity and survival (Spykman, 1939a). The existence of physical obstructions to freedom of movement (i.e. the sheer size of a territory, rivers, hills and forests) or dangers (i.e. wild animals, rival tribes and nations and climatic extremes) could spell disaster for the community by dividing it up, or blocking its ability to exploit or take advantage of new food sources or raw materials. Those who could not circumvent geographic obstacles or dangers often died out or were overcome or replaced by those who could. Any political community with the means to master geography and connect it with politics – through good geostrategy – has tended to extend its advantages over its adversaries.

It is well known that Ancient Rome, for example, built a radial system of roads for internal communication and aqueducts for the formation of large urban settlements. More recently, the British developed better agricultural techniques to support a growing population and dug lengthy canals and built railways to connect their inland manufacturing centres to their coastal ports, while the Germans, Americans and Russians utilized railway technology to open up their interiors and make them productive on an industrial scale (W. A. Hay, 2003: 306–7). Indeed, with the commissioning of the trans-Siberian railway, Russia finally linked the two ends of its continental empire together for the first time by a direct and relatively fast land route and extended its sovereignty firmly over Siberia. Alternatively, the United States – an isolationist power for much of the nineteenth century – was trapped within the western hemisphere until it was able to link its eastern and western seaboards by railways and a canal through Central America. The transcontinental railroads and the Panama Canal transformed the United States, amplifying its power by bringing the country geographically together into a cohesive economic unit (Spykman, 2007 [1942]: 51). American ships no longer had to take lengthy and dangerous voyages around Cape Horn, and were consequentially able to move between the eastern and western seaboards more quickly. Equally, American naval ships in the Atlantic and the Pacific theatres could rapidly reinforce one another, effectively doubling overnight the size of the United States naval fleet (Spykman, 1944: 36). The aim of these agricultural and transportation systems was therefore thoroughly strategic: to amplify the economic output of the homeland and bring distant or isolated provinces more closely under sovereign control. And by linking core areas to the outside world, they led to the consolidation of each respective imperial or national power base. Even in the modern and increasingly globalized world, a political community's territory still continues to function as a base of operations, from which it draws material and demographic strength. This power can then be harnessed to protect the territory and its people from hostile forces, whether those forces are domestic or foreign, or natural or human, in form.

A strong base of operations gives a political community the ability to prosecute a grand strategy in the international arena. Foreign geostrategy is predicated on the assumption that it is very difficult to sustain an 'all-directions' or truly global approach, focusing resources and resolve on key regions instead (Grygiel, 2006: 22). Thus, a comprehensive and balanced geostrategy represents a political community's attempt to circumvent its geographical predilection to maximize its security in the pursuit of a series of common goals, or even a grand design. For smaller powers, a Swiss-style deterrence policy might be favourable, especially if a defensive geography (like mountains) is present or if there is a lack of resources for power projection. For larger political communities, however, especially those with access to the sea, geostrategy has tended to be far more expansive and assertive, often following a series of phases: first, the consolidation of the national territory; second, the expansion of leverage into neighbouring zones; third, the control over maritime approaches; and lastly, if possible, the pursuit of influence over particularly important nodes and spaces on the earth's surface and the crafting of a permanent and wide-ranging political presence in the international system (Friedman, 2009: 38–46). Geostrategy therefore aims to enhance the community's power and prosperity by gaining access to certain communication lines like trade routes, as well as geographical bottlenecks like maritime straits, mountain passes, rivers, islands and seas. For the largest powers, it has frequently mandated the creation and maintenance of a far-reaching political presence, backed up with forwardly deployed armed forces. This has often required the opening of military stations, including the construction of warships for deep oceanic power projection (Krepinevich and Work, 2007: ii).

A good foreign geostrategy also requires an extensive network of alliances with key powers whose geographic interests are largely coterminous and who seem willing to assist with the maintenance of a favourable balance of geographic power. But not only the strongest powers are important. Partnerships with smaller 'lynchpin states' or 'geopolitical pivots', which are located in vital regions, are also necessary.[8] Georgia and Azerbaijan, for example, provide the only territorial corridor – bypassing Russian or Iranian territory – between the European Union and the Caspian Sea (and Central Asia); the Falkland Islands provide command over the South Atlantic and Cape Horn; the United Arab Emirates provide control over the Strait of Hormuz; while Singapore provides the same in relation to the Strait of Malacca. A well-considered geostrategy should aim to provide pervasive influence over the key places on the global map, while simultaneously co-opting as many other major powers as possible into the enterprise. Brzezinski puts this very colourfully:

> To put it in a terminology that hearkens back to the more brutal age of ancient empires, the three grand imperatives of imperial geostrategy are to prevent collusion and maintain security dependence among the vassals, to keep tributaries pliant and protected, and to keep the barbarians from coming together.
>
> (Brzezinski, 1997b: 40).

The ultimate aim of geostrategy, then, is to link geography and politics to maximize the power and reach of the domestic territory and to entrench a favourable international order. Such an approach must be backed up by a subtle but formidable military posture, which aims to prevent potential rivals from emerging, encourages a high degree of security dependency on the part of foreign governments and prevents dangerous non-state and state actors from working with one another.

The European Union's geopolitical orientation

The history of the European Community has long been as a 'civilian power', whose aim was to 'domesticate' and 'institutionalize' the relations between its component Member States and prevent them from even considering military action as a possible option in their interactions with one another (Duchêne, 1972, 1973). European integration thus aimed to transcend geopolitics, at least within Europe. It is perhaps for this reason that there has been a tendency for contemporary Europeans to play down the significance of geopolitics. As Hill has noted: 'Students of the European Union have for too long neglected geopolitics, either because they could not see its relevance to a "civilian power" or because they were uneasy with that kind of discourse for normative reasons' (2002: 99).[9] However, as the deepening of the European Union has continued, and as progressively more of the European peninsula has come into its jurisdiction, it has become possible – and necessary – to see European integration through a geopolitical lens (Rogers and Simón, 2009: 5–6). For not only does a geopolitical analysis of the European Union's geographical position provide a better understanding of the constraints and possibilities facing Europeans in the early twenty-first century, it also facilitates better foreign policy prescriptions. In this respect, two geographic factors stick out above all others: first, the European Union remains thoroughly anchored to the northern European plain, a vast and fertile territory stretching across most of the top of the European mainland; second, the European region is not so much a continent as a peninsula, which protrudes out of the Eurasian super-continent into the Atlantic Ocean, thus providing Europeans with a primarily maritime geography (Rogers, 2010). These two factors have given Europeans solid geographic foundations on which they have built their success for over five centuries – and could continue to do so well into the twenty-first century.

With regard to the first factor, the European plain is a vast expanse of fertile territory stretching from the English Midlands and western France through Germany and Poland to the eastern border with Belarus.[10] This territory is criss-crossed by numerous rivers and streams, which contribute to its fertility and provide Europeans with ready access to the oceans and seas. Warmed by the currents of the Gulf Stream, the European plain is ripe for agriculture and it is no surprise that the annual yield is massive: the surplus generated enabled urbanization on a vast scale and the systematic diversification of economic activity. As the cradle of the agricultural and industrial revolutions in the eighteenth century, the European plain and its enormous resources ultimately propelled Europeans to accumulate and maintain the greatest concentration of technology and wealth on earth. Today, this plain supports over 200 million people, who have come to live in dense concentrations, particularly in northern France, western Germany, the Low Countries and southern England. These regions form the European Union's heavily populated 'core area'. Indeed, it was in this central zone that European integration began; equally, it was from this area that European enlargement radiated outwards in a series of phases through the utilization of a traditional continental geostrategy.[11]

The second factor, relating to the geography, but a consequence of European enlargement, means that the European Union has an increasingly maritime disposition. With a contiguous space stretching from the Black Sea to the Atlantic Ocean and the Baltic Sea to the Mediterranean, the European Union has come to cover almost all of the European peninsula. It now shares a relatively short land border – totalling 5,460 km – with only five countries: Russia, Belarus, Ukraine, Moldova and Turkey (Central Intelligence Agency, 2010).[12] However, the European Union is nevertheless surrounded on the other three fronts by sea, with a maritime frontier accounting for almost 66,000 km – over 12 times longer than the land border (Central Intelligence Agency, 2010). This maritime orientation is further compounded by the European Union's position on the global map: it sits on the western tip of the Eurasian landmass, which has been described, due to its location, size and resources, as the 'World Island' or the world's 'axial super-continent' (Mackinder, 1904; Brzezinski, 1997b: 50). Geopolitically, any power dominant in Eurasia would also – by proximity – have command over the Middle East and Africa, as well as the surrounding seas (Brzezinski, 1997a: 50). Given the position of the European peninsula on Eurasia's western promontory, the sea becomes necessary to reach other parts of Eurasia. Indeed, until Europeans developed sailing vessels capable of circumventing Africa, the eastern hemisphere remained largely cut off, isolated and unknown. While aeroplanes, railways and energy transmission pipelines have mitigated this problem to some extent, commercial activity still moves between Europeans and Asians primarily through the maritime domain, making the communication line running from the Suez Canal to the city of Shanghai particularly significant (Rogers, 2009b: 21–30). As Map 18.1 shows, this shipping route passes through almost all of the world's most significant 'strategic choke-points' – such as the Straits of Hormuz and Malacca, depending on destination – and along or by some of the most potentially volatile 'strategic flash points' on earth.

Map 1

The European Union and the 'Grand Area'

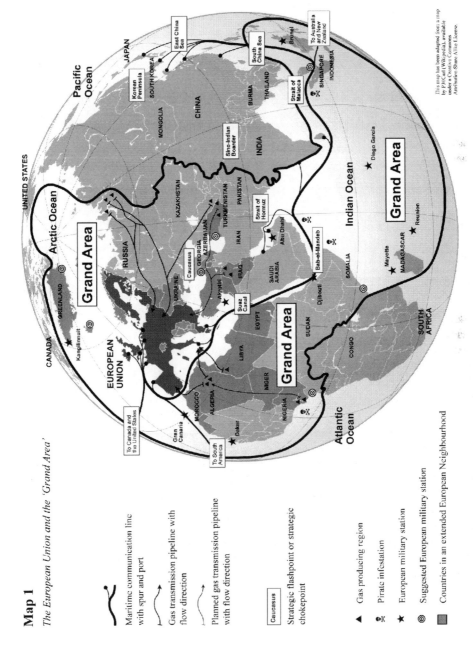

Maritime communication line
with spur and port

Gas transmission pipeline with
flow direction

Planned gas transmission pipeline
with flow direction

Caucasus

Strategic flashpoint or strategic
chokepoint

▲ Gas producing region

⊙✗ Pirate infestation

★ European military station

◎ Suggested European military station

▨ Countries in an extended European Neighbourhood

Map 18.1 The European Union and the Grand Area.

Towards a new geography of European power

Until recently, the European Union has given little consideration to high political matters, at least when they occurred beyond its borders. When issues of foreign and military policy presented themselves, they were dealt with almost exclusively by the Member States or delegated to the Atlantic Alliance. Yet, with the functional and geographic expansion of the European Union over the past decade; the development of the Common Security and Defence Policy; the passage of the Treaty of Lisbon; the 2008 financial crisis; and the ongoing transformation in the global balance of power, the European Union has been both asked and compelled to assume an increasingly active international posture. In recent years, this posture has even begun to assume explicit geopolitical overtones. Three spaces of critical interest came to be identified in the two decades after the end of the Cold War: first, the Western Balkans, including all the states of the former Yugoslavia that have not yet gained accession into the European Union itself; second, the Eastern Neighbourhood, which includes Belarus, Ukraine, Moldova and the Caucasus; and third, the Mediterranean basin, from Turkey to Israel and from Egypt to Morocco. Further, the rise of piracy in the Gulf of Aden has drawn attention to the wider Indian Ocean, while the High North – the so-called 'Northern Dimension' – has also grown in prominence as the countries around the Arctic Circle have realized how further contractions in the ice sheet could have economic and political consequences.

The rapidly changing balance of power in the twenty-first century makes functional integration at the European level, particularly in the realm of foreign and military policy, more important. The rise of large continental powers, which for the first time in history are criss-crossed by increasingly integrated railway, road and telecommunication networks, has finally ended what was once described as the 'Columbian Epoch', a maritime period dominated by the small but extraordinarily powerful West European nation-states (see Mackinder, 1904: 421). While some of the individual European powers are likely to remain in the top rankings of world economic output and military spending well into the current century, the gulf between them and the largest five actors – China, India, the United States, Brazil and Russia – is projected to grow (Renard, 2009; Wilson and Purushothaman, 2003: 9). Moreover, the position and standing of the European powers relative to a ream of smaller powers – such as Turkey, Mexico, Indonesia, Iran, Nigeria, South Africa – is also projected to decline (O'Neill, 2007: 149). These rising powers are giving considerable attention to their political and economic reach over geography: not only their domestic territories, but the world beyond them. As a former Belgian Representative to the European Union Military Committee has pointed out, Europeans cannot therefore continue to play ping-pong while the rest of the world engages in chess (Coelmont, cited in Biscop, 2009b: 12). The time has come for the European Union and its Member States to give far greater attention to the geography of European power, both on the domestic and international planes. Only by working together will Europeans remain influential and retain the means to protect themselves and exert power over other parts of the world, in line with their values and interests.

To be sure, and much like other political communities, the European Union's future success will depend on the homogeneity and integrated capacity of its domestic territory. Europeans will therefore need to think harder about how to 'shrink' geographic space and time across their entire continental homeland – from the border with Belarus to the Atlantic seaboard, and from the Arctic Circle to the Mediterranean – to make their economy progressively more efficient and productive, with an ever-increasing yield. At the very least, a dense lattice of high-speed railways should be planned at the European level to link together the principal cities and manufacturing centres, synthesizing, building on and, wherever possible, accelerating existing programmes in the Member States. Not only will this curtail carbon emissions by reducing the need for intra-European air transport, but it will also make the European economy more dynamic by cutting transportation times and opening up previously isolated regions.[13] High-speed railways should be supplemented with a pan-European motorway network similar in size and scope to the United States' Eisenhower system of interstate and defence highways. Given the existing and intricate networks in many of the Member States, this could be constituted through general motorway reclassification across the continent, allied to the extension of the system to the newer Member States to the east. A common European energy policy will also be necessary, bringing together enhanced energy pipeline and electricity transmission systems, renewable energy sources and centralized research and development funding at the European level. Based on new powers provided by the Treaty of Lisbon, the European Commission has already drawn up an initial strategy with a series of proposals to enhance the autonomy, number of sources and efficiency of European energy supply systems.[14] This will ensure that Europeans cannot be held to ransom by the economic or political whims of a foreign power, particularly Russia.

Increasing the efficacy of the European economic space dovetails with the need to extend European political and economic leverage into the proximal belt of countries that surround this zone. As the economy of the European Union is geared towards the export of high-tech manufactured goods and financial services, Europeans are among the most trade-dependent people in the world, with approximately 90 per cent of imports and exports travelling by water (European Commission, 2006b: 1–2). And due to the 'just-in-time' approach taken by modern container-shipping corporations, Europeans are particularly vulnerable to short-term and long-term seaborne transportation disruption (Willett, 2008). Indeed, Europeans depend on unfettered access to the open oceans – part of the 'global commons' – which have been kept open since World War II by American naval power (Posen, 2003). However, the rise of new economic and political powers over the past decade and their adoption of new geostrategies has opened up a number of new fissures and fault lines across and around much of Eurasia, such as in the Caucasus, the Yellow Sea and the South China Sea. Given that certain powers have sought to take advantage of key regions and entrench themselves – often to the disadvantage of others – the European Union should do more to ascertain the minimal geographic area required to sustain the continued expansion of its own economy. From a geopolitical perspective, this zone would have to meet five criteria. It would have to:

1   hold all the basic resources necessary to fuel European manufacturing needs and future industrial requirements;
2   contain all the key trade routes, especially energy transmission pipelines and maritime shipping routes, from other regions to the European homeland;
3   have the fewest possible geopolitical afflictions that could lead to the area's disintegration and thereby harm future European economic development;
4   show the least likelihood of significant encroachment by powerful foreign actors, relative to its importance to the European economy and geopolitical interests;
5   represent an area the European Union can work towards defending most cost-effectively through the expansion of the Common Security and Defence Policy – in other words, without mandating an excessive and draining defence effort.

In what regions, then, should this new geography of European power be anchored, inculcated and sustained? At the very least, Map 18.1 shows that the European Union depends on unfettered access through a vast adjacent zone that includes the Eastern Neighbourhood and western Russia, the Caucasus and much of Central Asia, the Arctic region, the northern half of Africa, all of the Middle East, as well as the Indian Ocean and South East Asia. This 'Grand Area' contains most of the resources needed by the European economy; all of the key maritime shipping routes from Asia, Australasia, Africa and the Middle East; all of the energy transmission pipelines – current and future – from Russia, Central Asia and North Africa; all of the countries in the Eastern and Southern Neighbourhoods covered by the Eastern Partnership and Mediterranean structures; several of the European Union's outermost regions and a chain of European overseas military installations.[15] Likely to become progressively more important in the coming decades, this zone is the minimal space needed for the assured and effective functioning of the European Union's economy, as well as the maintenance of a geopolitical balance of power that favours democratic interests.

What is clear is that the future success and integration of the 'Grand Area' will depend on intense collaboration between the European Union and the United States. The recalibration of America's geostrategic leverage towards East and Southeast Asia means that a power vacuum may open up in the western half of Eurasia, not only in Europe itself, but also in the Eastern Neighbourhood, the Middle East and the western sector of the Indian Ocean (where the United States has long been dominant) (see Simón and Rogers, 2010). This is the space – coterminous with the 'Grand Area' –which Europeans will be forced and expected to fill with their influence: forced, because their security will depend on it; expected, because the United States will need European aid in maintaining a favourable balance of power in western Eurasia as it is drawn towards stabilizing eastern Eurasia and the Pacific rim. In this respect, the European Union should give far greater attention to its 'strategic partnership' with India, the country best placed, geopolitically and ideologically, to assist with the management of the 'Grand Area'. The European Union should make India a truly strategic priority and provide New Delhi with sufficient investment to intensify the country's economic and industrial modernization. In particular, European expertise and funding should be freed up for India's extensive national highways development project, which aims to integrate the sub-continent more effectively and extend Indian influence over neighbouring countries.[16]

At one and the same time, the European Union should seek to extend and refine its 'strategic partnerships' with smaller powers in the 'Grand Area', especially future energy suppliers and transit nations, such as Georgia, Azerbaijan, Turkmenistan and Iraq, which are likely to feed or host the Nabucco gas pipeline. Countries in geopolitically significant locations along European trade routes or near the 'strategic chokepoints', like Djibouti, the United Arab Emirates, the Maldives and Singapore, warrant a position as European Union 'strategic partners' due to their potential as guardians of their neighbourhoods. And states that are likely to be pressured by larger foreign powers into closer relations with them, particularly if this draws them away from the European Union, should also be given further attention.

Finally, to remain credible, and to prevent the disintegration of their own system, the European Union's Member States will have to integrate, develop and refine their military assets – especially naval capabilities and long-range and unmanned combat aircraft – far more rapidly and effectively over the next two decades than they have over the last. In particular, new overseas military installations may be required, especially in those areas where new energy transmission pipelines from foreign gas fields and commercial distribution routes from distant manufacturing centres are built to supply the European economy. Accordingly, as Map 18.1 shows, new European military stations may be required in the Caucasus and Central Asia, the Arctic region and along the coastlines of the Indian Ocean. The intention behind these installations would be to contribute to a comprehensive 'forward presence':

first, by representing – à la Mahan – a certain determination on the part of the European Union to exercise a latent but permanent power within the 'Grand Area'; second, by exerting a calming influence throughout the zone to encourage expectations of peaceful change on the part of local governments; and finally, to discourage the encroachment of larger external powers into the region, whose intentions may be predatory and/or antithetical to the European agenda and the general peace.[17]

Conclusion

Geography and geopolitics have often been neglected in European foreign and security policy. This is a mistake. The rising powers of the twenty-first century have already begun to integrate their homelands more effectively and chart the regions where their own geographic and geopolitical interests lie. The European Union's future is dependent on the adoption of a truly comprehensive and preventive approach, which fuses together civilian and military assets for permanent power projection into the regions most vital to the maintenance of European prosperity and the democratic way of life. These regions – forming the 'Grand Area' – should be placed at the centre of a new European geostrategy, whose aim should be to lock as many countries in that area under European influence as possible. It should go without saying that this approach should not be a militarist or aggressive strategy, but should rather be subtle, gradual and firm. In so far as European military power is deployed – and it must be – it should be used passively: knowledge of its existence on the part of foreign governments should count for more than its active use. Ultimately, a new European geostrategy should be guided by three simple and overriding objectives: preventing hostile forces from coming together by drawing them all closer to European preferences; encouraging smaller, surrounding countries and those along European maritime and territorial communication lines to work with the European Union to enhance the security of all; and maximizing the dynamic power of the European homeland by investing heavily into communications infrastructure necessary to mitigate geographical impediment and increase economic efficiency. Meeting these objectives should enable the mapping of a new geography of European power, one that contributes to the European Union's economic leverage and political authority, while simultaneously increasing the security and prosperity of the European citizenry.

Notes

1   Others have also expressed a similar sentiment. Best known would be Theodore Roosevelt, former president of the United States, who is credited as having once said: 'Speak softly and carry a big stick'. Likewise, and more recently, Jo Coelmont, the former Belgian Representative to the European Union Military Committee, stated: 'If you want to use military power, flaunt it!' (2008).
2   It has been argued that the British Army's political defeat at the hands of foreign and insurgent Islamists in Basra damaged Britain's martial reputation (see, for example, Cordesman, 2007). Another example might be the well-known 'Vietnam Syndrome' in the United States after the country suffered defeat at the hands of the Vietcong in the early 1970s.
3   For a discussion on the development of a European 'strategic culture', see Cornish and Edwards (2001, 2005).
4   The 'comprehensive approach' is often lauded as a fusion of civilian and military capabilities, except that the latter dimension – along with the grand strategic and geostrategic components – is often sorely lacking (Simón, 2010: 16–17). Bringing the military instrument more firmly in, but in a preventive fashion, would therefore make the so-called 'comprehensive approach' truly comprehensive.
5   A 'vacuum war' is a conflict that starts in a small, weakened country but rapidly sucks in larger powers, potentially leading to a conflagration (see, for a good summary, Grygiel, 2009).

6 Gray shows aptly why geopolitics has become so unpopular: 'Geopolitics treats the world as it is and tends to scepticism over the prospects for progress towards lasting peace. Because much of the academe holds to the liberal illusion that international relations can be transformed benignly, it associates geopolitics, and its generally realist approach to statecraft, with conditions that need to be changed' (2004: 18).

7 Diamond, for example, argues that Western Europeans were aided by a number of geographic and environmental conditions in their rise to dominance. These conditions included the horizontal aspect of the European continent, thus avoiding climatic extremes; domesticable animals, to provide food, transportation, labour and disease; and a maritime perspective, to encourage new technologies (Diamond, 1997a, 1997b).

8 A 'lynchpin state' can be understood as a country, which is not a major power, but nevertheless deserves special attention because of its geopolitical location or position (see Korski, 2010).

9 Biscop (2010) has also argued that European studies needs to engage more actively with strategic studies.

10 For a good roundup of the role played by the European plain in European geopolitics, see Stratfor (2010: esp. 2–4).

11 Spykman provided an excellent analysis of the differences between land and sea powers, especially with regard to the way that each expands: 'Their differing conceptions ... of the conquest of space indicate one of the outstanding differences between land and sea powers. A sea power conquers a large space by leaping lightly from point to point, adjusting itself to existing political relationships wherever possible, and often not establishing its legal control until its factual domination has long been tacitly recognised. An expanding land power moves slowly and methodically forward, forced by the nature of its terrain to establish its control step by step and so preserve the mobility of its forces. Thus a land power thinks in terms of continuous surfaces surrounding a central point of control, whereas a sea power thinks in terms of points and connecting lines dominating an immense territory' (1938b: 224). There can be no doubt that the European Union has adopted the continental approach to enlarge, as opposed to the maritime one.

12 Of course, the European Union also shares land borders with Norway, Switzerland and the former Yugoslav states, but these are also a part geopolitically of the wider European Union's area through their participation in the European Economic Area or their 'enlargement perspective', among other initiatives.

13 For a range of maps and visual indicators showing accessibility to various regions within the European Union and the economic impact of a lack of accessibility, see European Spatial Planning Observation Network (2006: esp. 34–42).

14 The delivery of a common European energy policy could cost in excess of €1 trillion. But, according to the European Commission, a failure to deliver such a policy could be disastrous, especially as competition breaks out for dwindling supplies of oil and gas. As it points out: 'Energy is the lifeblood of our society' (2010e: 2).

15 The concept of a 'Grand Area' was first developed in an American context by the Council on Foreign Relations (1941).

16 India has the ambition of building 20 km of road per day to underpin its economic modernization. At present, due to lack of funds, political inertia and engineering capacity, this goal may not be reached. European input into this project would build up India's economic wealth, bring goodwill and provide Europeans with a more geostrategically capable partner. For a brief overview of the road-building programme, see Upadhyay (2010).

17 For a succinct discussion of the concept of 'forward presence', albeit from an American perspective, see Fullenkamp (1994).

19

THE EU AND COUNTER-TERRORISM

Javier Argomaniz and Wyn Rees

International terrorism has become one of the principal security scourges of the twenty-first century. Terrorism itself is not a new phenomenon for many members of the European Union, who have either experienced it as a domestic problem or suffered it during periods of transition from colonial power status. As a domestic problem for some European Community states from the 1960s onwards, it created an unhappy precedent chiefly because Western European states achieved very little cooperation in countering the problem (Den Boer, 2009: 211). This was because the groups acted primarily within their own borders and there was consequently an absence of shared threat perceptions amongst the major European countries.

The contemporary wave of international terrorism has drastically altered those perceptions. This terrorism, motivated by religious extremism, seeks to conduct mass casualty attacks around the world (Hoffman, 1998). It is perpetrated by loosely affiliated Islamist groups from many different countries, which appear able to move with ease across state boundaries. They strike against targets all around the globe in Western and Muslim countries, thereby deserving the description of a global insurgency. The *modus operandi* of the attacks is usually multiple suicide bombings, and the aim is not to obtain sympathetic media coverage but rather to inflict the maximum amount of destruction. These groups recruit new members either through radical preaching or by spreading their ideology across the Internet. They have developed a global discourse that links the suffering of Muslim peoples around the world, in Chechnya, Palestine and Bosnia, and use it to justify a conflict between religious communities.

The primary danger for EU countries has derived from the radicalization of members of their own societies. Second and third generations of immigrant people, suffering a sense of alienation within their own communities, have been susceptible to radicalization. They have been willing to train abroad in places such as Pakistan and then conduct suicide attacks either on their own societies, such as the London Tube bombings in July 2005, or go to fight in war zones such as Iraq, Afghanistan and Somalia (Neumann, 2006; Wiktorowicz, 2005; Dalgaard-Nielsen, 2010). They present a particularly significant source of danger for three reasons. First, they are drawn from large immigrant populations that reside in Western Europe. Second, their process of radicalization can mean that they have never been brought to the attention of the security services, resulting in these 'clean skins' presenting a sudden and unexpected source of danger. Third, when training abroad they acquire a range of skills and contacts that can be put to deadly use once they have returned home.

The EU has faced the task of fashioning a response to this threat amidst a complex environment. Part of this complexity has related to the fact that the Union is a constrained actor in the field of counter-terrorism. Most of the means to fight terrorism remain at the national level with states reluctant to relinquish additional powers to the EU. For example, the Union does not possess a police force capable of arresting terrorist suspects and it only possesses criminal intelligence that its members are willing to share with it. EU efforts have mainly focused on assisting with the coordination of national responses. This has resulted in a congested institutional architecture with a large number of actors involved in the development of counter-terror policies at the Union and national level. The EU's own competences have, prior to the Lisbon Treaty, been divided across its three pillars: the European Communities, Common Foreign and Security Policy and Justice, Liberty and Security. This has meant that the EU has been required to engage in cross-pillar coordination in order to act purposefully against the threat.

The other part of this complexity has been the EU's attempt to design a comprehensive counter-terrorism response in the face of the US-led War on Terror. The US has put pressure on other Western countries for a robust approach but it has projected its own interpretation of the nature of the threat. US thinking since 9/11 has been shaped by the fear that states opposed to the Western conception of international order could make available to terrorist organizations weapons of mass destruction. This has led the USA in its security strategy to emphasize the need to be proactive in addressing threats a long way from its territory, to be willing to use force and to be prepared to act pre-emptively.[1] This military-driven foreign policy strategy has been complemented by an energetic 'homeland security' policy that seeks to work with allies to minimize the risk of future attacks on the American homeland. Yet European policy-makers have been wary that excesses in US policy could reflect badly on the legitimacy of the EU's actions. American detention of suspects in the legal limbo of Guantanamo Bay, the use of torture techniques such as water-boarding and the outsourcing of interrogations through the practice of Extraordinary Rendition have led to the EU being circumspect about the extent of the cooperation it undertakes with the USA. This was further reinforced by the unpopular invasion of Iraq and has only recently been mitigated by the election of the Obama administration. Pressure from Washington to cooperate has been regarded as a two-edged sword in Brussels.

This chapter seeks to look at the two strands of the EU's counter-terrorism response; the foreign and internal security agendas. It argues that counter-terrorism activity in the field of foreign policy has been modest, whilst the internal security agenda has grown more substantively. EU Member States have accorded a progressively larger role to the EU in combating the internal security dimensions of terrorism, creating a host of institutions and agencies. This has led to a dense institutional framework and has resulted in demanding coordination efforts within the Union.

Counter-terrorism, CSDP and CFSP

External action has been an instrument of secondary importance in the EU's counter-terrorism efforts. The external response of the EU has, in the words of Keohane, 'lag[ged] far behind its internal security reaction in terms of political impetus, resources and ... initiatives' (Keohane, 2008a: 127). This has reflected the fact that the Union has seen the threat from international terrorism primarily in terms of a law enforcement, intelligence and judicial challenge. This was signalled in 2004 by the decision to prioritize a response through the third pillar of Justice and Home Affairs (JHA, later retitled Justice, Liberty and Security). It has been reinforced by the traditional ethos of the EU as a non-military power, thereby according the lead role to civilian agencies. In light of the extensive Muslim communities within Western Europe, this approach has minimized the risk of alienating elements of the domestic population.

In the case of the European Security and Defence Policy (ESDP, subsequently renamed the Common Security and Defence Policy), its contribution to counter-terrorism has been conceived largely in terms of military capabilities that could provide assistance in the aftermath of a terrorist attack. It has not focused on deploying major military forces overseas. Tangible military initiatives have been few: expanding the contents of the military database of assets and capabilities relevant to the protection of civilian populations;[2] chemical, biological, radiological and nuclear (CBRN) exercises involving civil military responders as part of the Community Civil Protection Mechanism;[3] European Defence Agency research projects to enhance the protection of crisis management personnel and infrastructure;[4] and related programmes with tangential impact in counter-terrorism.[5] Member States have remained sceptical about the added value that ESDP/CSDP can offer. EU capabilities in this area continue to be modest and the Union has often struggled to achieve concerted action (Wright, 2006: 294). Moreover ESDP involvement overlaps with NATO, whose capabilities are more considerable, yet still of limited significance in the fight against terrorism.

The Lisbon Treaty offers some innovations in this respect with the inclusion of a Solidarity Clause (Title VII, Article 188) that calls upon countries to 'act jointly in a spirit of solidarity if a Member State is the object of a terrorist attack' and also to mobilize all available instruments including 'military resources' to prevent the 'terrorist threat'. The Clause had already been invoked in the aftermath of the Madrid attacks in the European Council Declaration and it is no more than a political act since it is up to each Member State 'to choose the most appropriate means to comply with this solidarity commitment'.[6] So the Clause represents no legal obligation. Moreover, no terrorist attack in Europe has ever strained a state's capabilities to the extent that it has been forced to request military assistance from other European countries. Complementing the Clause, Article 43 also inserts new actions announced in the European Security Strategy (ESS) of 2003 to join the Petersberg tasks, actions which 'may contribute to the fight against terrorism, including by supporting third countries in combating terrorism in their territories'.[7] Of these, only military advice and assistance hold direct relevance to the external fight against terrorism but their deployment is unlikely due to the political implications and the above-mentioned scepticism amongst European countries regarding the use of military capabilities in this area.

In terms of more general foreign policy activity, particular Member States have close relationships with individual countries but pursue these links at a bilateral level. Hence UK involvement with Pakistan is pursued outside of the confines of the EU, rather than being routed through Brussels, as is French cooperation with Algeria and Spanish cooperation with Morocco (Keohane, 2005; Brady, 2009). The EU does play an active role in supporting the counter-terrorism efforts of the United Nations, believing that multilateral cooperation is the most effective and legitimate way of countering the threat from both terrorist groups and states that may be willing to sponsor them. The Union took an active part in steering through UN Security Council Resolution 1373 in September 2001 that mandates financial reporting by countries designed to prevent funds reaching terrorist groups. It also encourages universal adherence to the 16 UN conventions against terrorism.

Where the EU has made a more substantive contribution in foreign policy terms is by acknowledging the paradox that its own internal security has an external policy dimension. At the special summit at Tampere in October 1999 devoted to JHA, Section D of the Conclusions stated the EU's desire to build 'Stronger External Relations in the Field of JHA'.[8] Recognition of the intimate relationship between internal and external security has led the Union to try to draw its neighbours into patterns of counter-terrorism cooperation that will contribute to its own internal security. This became a priority because the enlargement process has made the Central and East European countries the external frontiers of the Union with the responsibility for keeping out such problems as criminals and illegal migrants (Huysmans, 2006). The main mechanism by which the Union has been able to secure compliance from its neighbours has been the prospect of accession. The principle of conditionality has enabled the EU to impose its own security perceptions upon countries seeking membership.

The EU, consistent with its own ethos, has preferred to offer positive incentives to states to enter into counter-terrorism cooperation. Whereas in the 1990s the USA sought to contain and isolate countries such as Iran and Libya that were accused of state sponsorship of terrorism, the Union sought to critically engage with them. In 1996 the USA brought forward extra-territorial sanctions, the Iran–Libya Sanctions Act, but the EU refused to participate in the action and even threatened to take America to the World Trade Organization if European companies were penalized (Niblett and Mix, 2006). Since 9/11, there has been more evidence of the willingness of the EU to employ its economic strength to put pressure on other countries. Since March 2004 the European Council has committed the Union to include counter-terrorism clauses in all its agreements with third countries. Determining the appropriateness of a trade agreement or the export of arms is regarded as dependent upon that country's policies towards countering terrorism.

EU counter-terrorism policies

The EU responded to the 9/11 attacks in the USA by drawing up a multi-dimensional Action Plan on Counter-terrorism. This *Anti-terrorist Road Map* drew upon a range of measures that had been approved at the 1999 Tampere European Council, and contained over 60 initiatives prioritizing the strengthening of police and judicial cooperation, development of international legal instruments, fighting terrorism financing, improving air security and further cooperation with third countries.[9] Since that time the Union has brought forward a series of initiatives, usually in response to terrorist outrages such as the March 2004 attacks in Madrid and the July 2005 bombings in London. Post-attack periods of intense activity have tended to be followed by slow-down and inertia until the process is reactivated by the next event.[10] As a product of this disjointed expansion, a coherent set of policies has taken time to emerge.

The early institutionalization of counter-terrorism as an EU policy arena was accompanied by the 2002 *Framework Decision on Combating Terrorism*.[11] This legislation marked a milestone in so far as it produced the first common legal definition of terrorism produced by an international organization. Moreover it introduced a list of harmonized terrorist offences and penalties, and in doing so providing a solid framework for the development of further European cooperation. Complementing this basic harmonization, the Council Regulation issuing a *Common List of Terrorist Organizations* also represents a common operational reaction in the form of the freezing of assets of both organizations and individuals suspected of involvement in terrorism.[12]

In parallel to these harmonizing efforts, a *European Arrest Warrant* was approved in 2002 to replace the hugely complex system of the multilateral extradition of suspects. Despite the substantial problems in the national transposition of this instrument, the EAW has become the biggest 'success story' so far in European counter-terror cooperation as it led to the reduction of the average length of time for extradition procedures from more than 9 months to 45 days.[13] For example, one of the July 2005 London bombers fled to Italy after the attacks but was speedily returned to the UK.

In contrast, the 2002 Framework decision on *Joint Investigation Teams*, which permits law enforcement officials and representatives from the judiciary – plus Europol and Eurojust representatives – to work jointly in cross-border judicial investigations,[14] has been far less utilized. These teams have been made to work by countries such as Spain and France, who have engaged in long-standing counter-terrorism cooperation.

Some states have taken long periods of time to implement agreements that have been made at the EU level. Whilst all states have ratification processes that have to be respected, some have only rarely met the Council's implementation deadline for the transposition of EU-wide measures into domestic legislation (Rees, 2006: 89). Both of the Counter-Terrorism Coordinators (CTC) that have been appointed to draw together the work of EU Member States have called attention to the slow domestic implementation of European legislation. Delays for some instruments have reached several years.[15] This implementation gap represents a significant problem because it undermines the added value of the EU and generates significant confusion and frustration amongst national practitioners (Argomaniz, 2010).

It was not until the Madrid attacks that counter-terrorism emerged as a distinctive area of European governance, inspired initially by the political significance of the 25 March 2004 *European Council Declaration on Combating Terrorism*. The Declaration called for reinforced cooperation and faster implementation and offered clear guidelines for action by setting out seven overarching strategic objectives.[16]

More importantly in terms of tangible results, the Road Map was replaced by an updated and greatly expanded *Plan of Action* involving more than 175 individual measures presented in a scoreboard form with clear specific tasks and deadlines. Terrorism financing received additional attention in the form of a separate 2004 EU *Anti-Terrorist Financing Strategy* heavily influenced by the Union's international obligations in the form of the nine Financial Action Task Force (FATF) Recommendations on Terrorism Funding. The Strategy has guided EU efforts along three dimensions: improved cooperation in the exchange of information, enhanced traceability of financial transactions and greater transparency of legal entities. Whilst the initial priority was to generate legislative action, the current emphasis has shifted towards better implementation and improving operational coordination amongst national authorities.[17]

Similarly, the reaction to the July 2005 bombings in London helped to crystallize the formulation of the first *EU Counter-Terrorism Strategy*. An adaptation of the UK's own domestic strategy, the document reflected some important changes in the representation of the threat, highlighting its home-grown dimension and inherent complexity. The seven pre-existing strategic objectives in the Action Plan were reformulated into four pillars of action: Prevent (combating radicalization and recruitment), Protect (the strengthening of the defence of possible terrorist targets), Pursue (disrupting terrorist planning, cutting off funding and apprehending terrorist activists) and Respond (enhancing the EU's crisis management capacities).

The preventive dimension evolved into a major priority for EU action. As a reflection, the Commission set up a network of experts and delivered a Communication that constituted a catalyst for the joint *EU Action Plan* and *Strategy for Combating Radicalisation and Recruitment to Terrorism*.[18] As part of the Strategy, the Council approved a *Media Communication Strategy* aiming to improve the portrayal of EU policies across the world by challenging inaccurate depictions of EU measures.[19] EU efforts have so far focused on mapping out the problem, allocating tasks in terms of 'streams', thematic areas assumed by individual countries, often according to previous national experiences and expertise. This is an innovative approach centred on enhancing transgovernmental learning through the sharing of best practices. Yet at the same time it illustrates that Member States believe that anti-radicalization policies should remain a national competence, in light of the marked differences in experience that defy a harmonized approach.

The lack of any major attack in Europe since 2005 has led to a loss of momentum in EU counter-terrorism, a process that the CTC has described as 'fatigue'.[20] Notwithstanding some high-profile legislative acts, such as the *2008 Amendment on the Framework Decision on Terrorism* criminalizing public provocation, training and recruitment for terrorism,[21] a period of stability has resulted, evidenced by the substantial reduction in the number of initiatives contained in the Action Plan. Far from this being a negative, the absence of public pressure should allow European and national policy-makers a 'breathing space' for gradual and deliberate policy development and an opportunity to gather efforts towards a better implementation of those instruments already approved.

Institutional response

Within efforts to counter terrorism under the third pillar, Member States have shared the right of initiative with the Commission. The latter has become, following the Madrid attacks, an active policy entrepreneur producing a substantial number of initiatives generally channelled through the Justice, Liberty and Security Directorate General (DG JLS)[22] and often also involving a variety of other DGs (Relex, Transport, Energy and others).[23] Yet at the same time, due to the political sensitivity of these policies, the Council has preserved a central strategic role.

At the Working Group level, terrorism issues have been discussed in a wide variety of Working Parties, including those on Visas, Civil Protection, Police Cooperation and particular geographical regions, such as the Maghreb. Specialized discussions have been developed within the Working Group on Terrorism (TWG), where practitioners from Member States' security services work on the internal dimension of the threat and the Committee on Terrorism (COTER) composed of diplomats from foreign ministries and dealing with evaluations of the threat in particular regions and cooperation with third countries and international actors.[24] Both technical bodies produce consolidated terrorism trend analyses and policy recommendations. In addition, the Common Position 931 Working Party (CP 931) meets in the 'Clearing House' format to update the EU's list with the terrorist entities whose assets are to be frozen by national authorities. Whereas the work of COTER, CP 931 and other external WPs is coordinated by the Political and Security Committee (PSC) and discussed at the Foreign Affairs Council (Foraff), TWG outputs are channelled through the Article 36 Committee before it reaches the Justice and Home Affairs Council (JHA).

Partly to alleviate the dysfunction resulting from these separate parallel decision-making channels, the figure of a Counter-Terrorism Coordinator (CTC) was announced in the European Council 25 March 2004 Declaration. Initially placed under the High Representative for CFSP Javier Solana, the former Dutch junior minister of interior Gijs de Vries was appointed to:

coordinate the work of the Council in combating terrorism and with, due regards to the responsibilities of the Commission, maintain an overview of all the instruments at the Union's disposal with a view to regular reporting to the Council and effective follow-up decisions.[25]

Following the decision of de Vries to step down in 2007, he was replaced by the former director of the JHA Directorate within the Council Secretariat, Gilles de Kerchove. In addition to internal and inter-institutional coordination, the current priorities of the post involve evaluating the implementation of the EU Anti-Terrorist Action Plan, suggesting policy and institutional changes and representing the EU in international fora and third countries. However, the CTCs reach and effectiveness has been hampered by the limited formal powers and resources with which the position has been endowed, the CTC office comprising just two secretaries and two national officials (Kerchove and Biolley, 2010: 239).

Currently the CTC works exclusively under the Secretary General of the Council and the European President. As such the post is formally no longer under the High Representative. Nevertheless the post-Lisbon High Representative for Foreign Affairs and Security Policy (HR), Catherine Ashton, is still heavily involved with the EU's external counter-terror relations, supported by a new European External Action Service (EEAS) and the Situation Centre (Sitcen). Sitcen is particularly important in this regard. Integrated in 2010 to the EEAS, analysts seconded to Sitcen work with open sources and assessed (non-operational) intelligence submitted by national security services. Along with Europol, Sitcen is the main producer of threat assessments in the area of counter-terrorism at the EU level and provides reports for the HR, national capitals and relevant Council WP's and ESDP structures such as the Policy Planning and Early Warning Unit (PPEWU) or European Union Military Staff (EUMS) (Müller-Wille, 2004: 29).

Europol, the European law enforcement organization entrusted with providing analytical support to national police forces since starting operations in 1999, is the leading EU agency in the fight against terrorism. As a direct response to the 9/11 attacks, Europol extended its mandate to terrorism-related crimes such as kidnapping and cyber crime and a Counter-Terrorism Unit[26] was established with internal analysts and seconded liaison officers (ELOs). The Unit has been producing Analytical Work Files from 'raw' intelligence (including classified information on suspects, victims and contacts) provided by national police forces.[27] Europol's main analytical database, the Europol Information System, also holds information pertaining to terrorism under the Counterterrorism Support System (Den Boer, 2006: 102). An overview of terrorism attacks and arrests is provided in an annual Terrorism Situation and Threat Report (TE-SAT). Counterterrorism Task Forces, comprising police and intelligence representatives from Member States and Europol officials, were set up in 2001 and 2004 but were subsequently discontinued. This was due to the scarcity of high-quality data provided by domestic agencies, which has been by far the greatest obstacle confronting Europol's activities.

Terrorism data have also been exchanged with third countries through the signing of information-sharing agreements and the exchange of ELOs. The USA has been the leading beneficiary, through the negotiation of data-sharing agreements in December 2001 and 2002. US liaison officers have also been permitted to work inside Europol headquarters in The Hague.

In parallel, Eurojust, the European judicial cooperation body created by a 2002 Council Decision to improve the fight against terrorism, aims to enhance judicial coordination of cross-border and complex terrorism cases. Work on this area is channelled through a specialized Terrorism Team of national members with practical expertise. The Team prepares strategic meetings with national representatives of EU Member States and third countries to nurture networks and the transfer of information. Tactical meetings have also been conducted to discuss specific terrorism cases brought about by national prosecutors (Eurojust, 2007). A Counter-Terrorism Monitor provides national prosecutors with an overview of relevant judgments across Europe (Coolsaet, 2010). Although the steady antiterrorism case workload reflects positively on the organization,[28] Eurojust officials have often deplored the unfulfilled potential of the institution due to the slow implementation by Member States of European legislation that would speed up the vertical exchange of information and the disappointing levels of support provided to some Eurojust national members by their governments (Eurojust, 2006).

In addition to Europol and Eurojust, other European bodies have been drawn into the framework of counter-terrorist activities and have been endowed with competencies. These include the European Border Agency (Frontex), the European Police College (CEPOL), the Police Chiefs Operational Task Force (PCOTF) and networks such as Critical Infrastructure Warning Information Network (CIWIN) or the European Network of Experts on Radicalization (ENER). This illustrates some of the difficulties that the EU has experienced in trying to manage this congested space and take action across the Union's three-pillar structure. The pillars have traditionally hindered efforts at efficient action because they reflect a mix of legal bases as well as different decision-making processes. Measures that have straddled the pillar divide have often advanced slowly or have required parallel legislative acts.

The Lisbon Treaty has sought to overcome some of these coordination problems by dissolving the pillars into the Community structure. This has had the effect of 'communitarizing' police and judicial cooperation in criminal matters. It has created a single, more transparent legal framework and streamlined policy-making by transforming the Commission into the main policy initiator. The future involvement of the European Court of Justice (EJC) introduces, after a five-year transition period, long-overdue judicial oversight into an area that has been severely criticized for the impact of some policies on European citizens' rights. Co-decision powers have been extended to the European Parliament (EP), whose LIBE Committee on Civil Liberties, Justice and Home Affairs has already made confident use of the new powers in high-profile clashes with the Council.[29] The new internal security committee (COSI) has the potential to alleviate coordination weaknesses between EU and national operational bodies. Yet Lisbon does little to bridge the separation between the external and internal dimensions of EU policy, since the Union's CFSP and CSDP remain intergovernmental and preserve a separate structure and decision-making methods. There can be little doubt that Lisbon's 'shadow of the pillars' signify that the internal–external gap in EU counter-terrorism is clearly here to stay.

Conclusion

Counter-terrorism powers within Europe remain divided between the national and the EU level. Union states remain in charge of the lion's share of counter-terror work and hold all of the operational powers. Several countries have proved reluctant to share intelligence and law-enforcement information with agencies such as Europol, in spite of repeated demands for them to do so. Leading countries have even formed ad hoc intergovernmental frameworks within the orbit of the Union in order to cooperate more closely with their neighbours, whilst avoiding the loss of powers to the EU. For instance, the 'Group of 6', comprising France, Germany, the UK, Italy, Spain and Poland coordinate closely and share best practice.

Similarly, the Prum Treaty was an initiative by seven Member States (Belgium, Germany, Spain, France, Luxemburg, the Netherlands and Austria) in 2005 to improve the sharing of law-enforcement data.

Yet the EU has advanced a long way since the 9/11 attacks and has developed into a recognized counter-terror actor. It has developed a strategy, an extensive action plan with periodically updated measures and a constellation of agencies and actors able to contribute to the coordination and the sharing of best practices in the European fight against terrorism.

It remains the case that significant challenges are still to be overcome. The multiplicity of actors within the field of counter-terrorism results in a complex, overlapping institutional framework. The over-population of the decision-making structure results in a diffusion of authority and the need for onerous coordination efforts. The office of the CTC struggles to bring this apparatus together as its formal mandate is restricted to the Council and it can only rely on its own powers of persuasion when liaising with other EU institutions or member states. What is certain, however, is that the challenge presented by international terrorism will continue to evolve. The EU offers its members added value in fighting this menace and its growth in counter-terrorism responsibilities has every prospect of continuing.

Notes

1 United States National Security Strategy (2002).
2 Council of the European Union (2007a: 35).
3 Council of the European Union (2009b: 31).
4 Examples include: CBRN Detection, Identification and Monitoring (MID), CBRN Explosive Ordnance Disposal (EOD), Countering IEDs and Man Portable Air Defence Systems (C–ManPads). See Council of the European Union (2009d: 20).
5 Such as the Future Unmanned Aerial Systems (FUAS) project or the EU-wide Maritime Surveillance Network. Council of the European Union (2009d: 32).
6 European Council (2004a).
7 These are: joint disarmament operations, military advice and assistance, conflict prevention and post-conflict stabilization. See European Council (2007).
8 European Council (1999).
9 Council of the European Union (2001).
10 Argomaniz (2010).
11 Council of the European Union (2002a).
12 Council of the European Union (2003).
13 See European Commission (2005a).
14 Council of the European Union (2002b).
15 Council of the European Union (2009a: 15).
16 These were: deepen international efforts, impede terrorist access to funding and other resources; investigate and prosecute terrorists; protect transport and ensure effective border control; enhance states' consequence management; address support and recruitment into terrorism; and assist third countries in their fight against terrorism.
17 Council of the European Union (2008: 5).
18 The Strategy three pillars are: the disruption of radical networks and individuals activities, the support for mainstream voices over extremism and the promotion of 'security, justice, democracy and opportunity for all'. See Council of the European Union (2005).
19 Council of the European Union (2006b: 5).
20 Council of the European Union (2009c: 2).
21 Council of the European Union (2008c).
22 With the appointment of Barroso's second administration in 2009, DG JLS has been separated into two independent DGs: DG Home Affairs and DG Justice and Fundamental Rights. An individual Unit continues to deal specifically with the fight against terrorism: D.1 in DG JLS, now renamed A.1 within DG Home Affairs.
23 Interviews with Commission officials, DG JLS, January 2006 and April 2008.

24 Council of the European Union (2004b: 3).
25 European Council (2004a).
26 The so-called O 4, previously SC-5.
27 Interview with Europol Officials, Serious Crime Unit and SC-5 Unit, January 2006.
28 In 2009 the number of cases experienced a decrease. See Eurojust (2009: 17).
29 More specifically in the passing of the EU–US Passenger Name Records agreement and the EU–US Bank Data Transfer.

20

THE EU AND NON-PROLIFERATION OF WEAPONS OF MASS DESTRUCTION

Gerrard Quille

This chapter sets out the EU's approach to non-proliferation based upon a cooperative strategy embedded under the Common Foreign and Security Policy (CFSP). The chapter will then look in more detail at the so-called non-proliferation clauses which illustrate how the EU is trying to combine political cooperation with economic incentives to achieve its non-proliferation objectives. The paper argues that the EU has demonstrated a real potential to promote non-proliferation through bilateral economic agreements and promoting universal membership of multilateral non-proliferation regimes. However, for the EU to enhance its effectiveness in this area it will have to take full advantage of the innovations in the Lisbon Treaty and engage with key actors (including through strategic partnerships and multilateral regimes) in pressing ahead with important EU foreign policy matters such as non-proliferation and disarmament.

Finding a place for non-proliferation in the emerging EU foreign policy system

With the Lisbon Treaty expectations are growing for the EU to have a more strategic, coherent and effective approach to EU foreign policy. Other chapters (Whitman, etc.) in this book have set out the new innovations following the Lisbon Treaty that are essentially based around a permanent President of the Council, a new upgraded High Representative for Foreign Affairs and Security Policy, who is at the same time double-hatted as a Vice President of the Commission (i.e. HR/VP), and supported by a new 'foreign ministry' known as the European External Action Service (EEAS). The latter brings together the external relations elements of the former Council and Commission services, which helps to pursue a more integrated use of the EU's external relations instruments and thereby achieve a more coherent approach to key policy areas such as non-proliferation and disarmament.

Not only does the Lisbon Treaty introduce important institutional innovations in the area of EU external action, but it creates a 'once in a generation opportunity' to create a new EU foreign and security policy. This system is built around the new upgraded HR/VP and the

EEAS; a more strategic approach to foreign policy formulation; a more coherent application of EU instruments (including diplomacy, development, trade and CSDP); as well as strengthening the role of EU Member States throughout the policy planning, policy formulation and implementation stages of foreign and security policy.

In the process of creating a new EU foreign policy, one of the earliest and most important developments will be a shift to a more strategic definition of foreign and security policy objectives. Early examples of this approach can be seen in the EEAS-led review of the EU's approach to the Arab Spring; the recent Security and Development Strategy for the Sahel; and the Strategic Framework for the Horn of Africa. In addition, despite an initial setback the EU has achieved enhanced status in the UN General Assembly and the HR/VP continues to lead the international community's response towards Iran and, more recently, in efforts to relaunch the Middle East peace process. The latter will lead to re-establishing an EU Special Representative for the Middle East.

The EEAS will be instrumental in supporting the HR/VP to develop further strategies and (with its network of EU Delegations) to implement these policies. The EEAS will also include actors who previously sat separately in the Council or in the Commission or even in Member States' capitals and who all worked on different documents (for the Council, Commission or Member State) for the same region or thematic policy issue. They will now work together within the EEAS to review the individual (Commission and Council) policy documents as a basis for developing a new comprehensive strategy for these regions. In the area of non-proliferation, the EEAS can build upon the 2003 EU Strategy against the proliferation of materials and weapons of mass destruction and its six-monthly review of the implementation of the strategy in order to support Council Decisions on specific actions or prepare the strategic guidelines for Commission financial instruments to be used (including the Instrument for Stability and the other geographic instruments). Within the EEAS the Managing Director for Global and Multilateral Issues, Maria Marinaki, and her Directorates for Non-proliferation and Disarmament and the Unit for security policy will be providing the key support to the HR/VP. In addition, EU financial resources identified to support the non-proliferation strategy will be managed by a service (for Foreign Policy Instruments) directly attached to the HR/VP. Beyond EU external relations instruments there will also be a need to cooperate closely with other Commission Directorates General that have an important bearing on EU foreign policy objectives in this area, such as *inter alia* DG for Enlargement, DG for EuropeAid and Development Cooperation, DG for Trade, DG Home Affairs, DG health and Consumers and DG energy (Grip, 2011). Finally, the European Parliament will be using its powers across the range of political oversight, budgetary actor and legislator to monitor the implementation of the new strategies and assert its views on the direction that they take.

It will be important for the new High Representative to show that the Union can meet its political and security ambitions and set the agenda in dialogue with important third countries in addition to its traditional economic role. Furthermore, it has been argued that the EU can do more in this area if it deepens its analysis of third countries, in particular the emerging powers and strategic partners, when implementing its non-proliferation strategy (Sauer, 2011).

Finally, the new permanent President of the European Council, Herman Van Rompuy, has also demonstrated the importance of this policy area to the EU. When President Obama convened a Nuclear Security Summit in Washington in April 2010 to reflect on the future of nuclear security and in particular to make new commitment to securing nuclear materials around the world building on and going beyond the G8 Global Partnership, Van Rompuy reiterated the EU's commitment to nuclear security, underlining the importance of a cooperative approach by stating that:

> Nuclear terrorism, with terrorists getting access to nuclear materials or to radioactive sources, represents a most serious threat to international security with potentially devastating consequences to our societies. This is a common threat that requires a common response ... Today's Summit will be the starting point of a joint effort that will require participation on an even broader basis. Reaching out to all players and involving all countries will allow us to advance our shared goal to strengthen nuclear security. Today's meeting sets an ambitious goal of securing all vulnerable nuclear material in four years. We can only achieve it in full co-operation with all UN members. The European Union will extend its co-operation to all members of the international community united in this joint endeavor.
>
> (Van Rompuy, 2010a)

The EU: developing an approach on non-proliferation and disarmament

It was in 2003, that the EU made a breakthrough by becoming a new voice in arms control and entering a policy area previously dominated by its Member States. In that year, the EU's Member States, shaken by their divisions over the Iraq War, decided to overcome their differences through a process that led to the adoption of its first ever strategic document on security, the European Security Strategy (ESS) (Bailes, 2005; Biscop, 2005; Quille, 2004). At the same time and in recognition of the specific differences that were raised over the existence of weapons of mass destruction (WMD) in the prelude to that conflict, a separate strategy was adopted entitled 'EU Strategy against the Proliferation of Materials and Weapons of Mass Destruction' (Meier and Quille, 2005).

Discussion about whether the events following 11 September 2001, including the invasion of Iraq in *pursuit* of WMD, marked a paradigm shift may be contentious conceptually, nevertheless the underlying tensions in balancing non-proliferation and disarmament commitments in the NPT and between EU Member States (which include 2 nuclear weapon states and 25 non-nuclear weapon states) remains, as can be seen in the ongoing negotiations with Iran or in the debate surrounding the USA–India nuclear deal (Kubigg, 2006). It has been argued that the future success of the EU's WMD Strategy is to some extent dependent upon maintaining that balance between its nuclear and non-nuclear weapon states and the consensus in the EU Strategy to reconcile new and old non-proliferation and disarmament objectives.

The EU's strategy is implemented through a range of activities which are set out in detail (including objectives, financial resources and a time frame for implementation) in specific Common Foreign and Security Policy (CFSP) Joint Actions and Common Positions (henceforth, with the adoption of the Lisbon Treaty, all future actions will be called Council Decisions).[1] Initially, the EU has prioritized non-proliferation with a particular commitment to multilateral treaties and bodies that underpin the non-proliferation regimes, e.g. support to the Organisation for the Prohibition of Chemical Weapons, the Comprehensive Test Ban Treaty Organisation, the Biological and Toxins Weapons Convention, the International Atomic Energy Agency and to the implementation of UN Security Council 1540 (Meier,

2008). This approach has been termed one of pursuing *effective multilateralism* in the ESS (Martinelli, 2006; Grevi and de Vasconcelos, 2008).

The Joint Actions, Common Positions, Council Decisions and Action Plans detail the EU contribution to specific activities and programmes. There are also European Commission-funded programmes such as its contribution in recent years to the G8 Global Partnership against the Proliferation of Materials and Weapons of Mass Destruction and emerging proposals under the Instrument for Stability.[2] These activities are reviewed every six months in the form of a 'Progress Report'.[3] This process of drawing up a progress report has contributed to a useful mechanism to benchmark the implementation of the EU WMD Strategy. To some extent the European Security Strategy has suffered because of the absence of such a monitoring mechanism.

The emphasis upon *multilateralism* reflects the inherent nature of the EU, where its own development has depended upon effective and peaceful cooperation amongst its Member States (Nickel and Quille, 2007). The EU is, therefore, developing an approach that emphasizes non-proliferation and disarmament initiatives that pursue *cooperative, consultative and confidence-building strategies*. A strategy based upon these three Cs is bolstered by a fourth 'C', i.e. *commerce*, whereby the EU's longer-standing economic weight is used as leverage to pursue non-proliferation and disarmament objectives such as in the form of *cooperative* non-proliferation clauses or *coercive* sanctions.

The EU's approach to the Iranian nuclear crisis

The first major test for the EU's WMD Strategy followed on from the August 2002 revelation that Iran was secretly constructing uranium-enrichment and heavy-water production facilities. This led to an International Atomic Energy Agency (IAEA) investigation and concerns that Iran might be pursuing nuclear weapons. The resulting IAEA investigation revealed other serious breaches of Iran's safeguards obligations and set in motion a process, led by the EU and encouraged by the UN Security Council, to persuade Iran to provide reassurances on the peaceful intentions of its nuclear programme.[4] The Security Council and the IAEA remain unsatisfied with Iran's cooperation and this process continues today with periodic rounds of negotiations, IAEA Board of Governors assessments, UN Security Council resolutions and the incremental application of sanctions (Kubigg, 2006).

This position was once again reiterated recently by the High Representative for Foreign Affairs and Security Policy, Catherine Ashton, when she stated on 21 September 2011 that:

> [W]e [the P5 + 2] have reaffirmed our determination and commitment to seek a diplomatic solution to this issue ... we noted with grave concern Iran's installation of centrifuges in its facility near Qom as part of plans to increase the capacity to enrich uranium to 20% and the IAEA's increasing concern about the possible military dimension to Iran's nuclear programme ... we remained determined and united in our efforts to work towards a comprehensive, negotiated, long-term solution – involving the full implementation by Iran of UNSC and IAEA Board of Governors Resolutions – which restores international confidence in the exclusively peaceful nature of Iran's nuclear programme, while respecting Iran's legitimate right to the peaceful use of nuclear energy consistent with the NPT. ... We reaffirm our offer of June 2008 and the proposals we made to Iran in Istanbul in January. ... [I]f Iran is prepared to engage more seriously in concrete discussions aimed at resolving

international concerns about its nuclear programme, we would be willing to agree on a next meeting with the Iranian side.[5]

Whilst the Iranian episode highlights the role of EU in first taming initial fears of a broader conflict in the region following the invasion of Iraq in 2003, the process has also raised the visibility of the EU as a security actor committed to pursuing a multilateral path and able to build a diplomatic consensus from the initial EU 3 (France, Germany and the UK) to include the USA (from February 2005), China and Russia, i.e. P5 + 1. Iran's resistance remains problematic, and whether the process will result in a long-term solution of the dispute remains to be seen. Iran still insists it will not give up its capacity for enrichment and reprocessing completely.

The EU non-proliferation clauses

The use of the Union's economic leverage to pursue political objectives in the form of the non-proliferation clauses is very recent and so the jury is still out on their full potential. The initial declaratory intention by the Union is to seek the introduction of such clauses in cooperation with third states (Grevi and de Vasconcelos, 2008). The EU non-proliferation clause was adopted in November 2003 as part of the implementation of the EU WMD Strategy and is designed to mainstream non-proliferation policies into the EU's wider relations with third countries.[6] The clause has two main parts, the first constitutes an 'essential element' that must be included in all third party mixed agreements and specifies that:

> The Parties consider that the proliferation of weapons of mass destruction and their means of delivery, both to state and non-state actors, represents one of the most serious threats to international stability and security. The Parties therefore agree to co-operate and to contribute to countering the proliferation of weapons of mass destruction and their means of delivery through full compliance with and national implementation of their existing obligations under international disarmament and non-proliferation treaties and agreements and other relevant international obligations.[7]

This element of the non-proliferation clause is a *declaratory* commitment by all parties to non-proliferation agreements that they have already entered into, but it does not include any verification procedures or commit a state to sign, ratify and implement through national legislation any additional treaties. Thus, India, Pakistan and Israel, who are de facto nuclear states, would not be obliged to sign and ratify the Nuclear Non-Proliferation Treaty (NPT).

However, the second part of the clause adds additional commitments for a third state to:

- take steps to sign, ratify, or accede to, as appropriate, and fully implement all other relevant international instruments;
- establish an effective system of national export controls, controlling the export as well as transit of WMD related goods, including a WMD end-use control on dual use technologies and containing effective sanctions for breaches of export controls.

The Member States have stated in the clause that these two further elements might be considered as *essential* 'on a case-by-case basis'. but it does not state what criteria would be used for deciding to apply all these additional demands. These elements clearly put additional demands upon the signatories to the agreement, e.g. if such additional elements were part of a clause signed by India, Pakistan and Israel, the implication would be that they would be asked to sign and ratify the NPT. When read in conjunction with the WMD Strategy it is expected that states agreeing to such a clause (i.e. with the further elements in the second part of the clause) would receive support, should they wish, from the European Union to set up export control and end-user licence systems. Such export control technical assistance programmes are being looked at by the European Commission under its community instruments such as the Instrument for Stability.[8]

Towards a non-proliferation clause with India?

On 23 April 2007 the Council approved a mandate for the negotiation of a Free Trade Agreement (FTA) with India, i.e. an agreement that does not require a clause. However, in the same decision the Council requested the Commission to engage with India in exploratory talks for the possible negotiation of a Partnership and Cooperation Agreement (PCA), which would replace the 1994 agreement. Such a PCA would notably include the so-called standard EU political clauses, i.e. require a non-proliferation clause. The exploratory talks were launched on 4 September 2007. However, at the time of writing, although negotiations have stalled, it has become clear that the EU has been unable to convince the Indians on the importance of putting political issues on the table alongside a trade agreement, therefore the option of an FTA-only agreement is being pursued that does not include additional political conditionality (or a 'parallel instrument') (Khandekar, 2011).[9]

The inability of the Union to press for a political agreement with India on non-proliferation highlights a growing challenge for the Union in moving beyond its traditional role as an economic partner and power, to becoming a global power with political (and security) responsibilities. Can the EU be satisfied with an FTA that is not accompanied by a 'parallel instrument' that meets its own declared ambition that 'Non-proliferation of WMD is a major concern for the EU and constitutes a fundamental element for the EU when it considers the decision of entering into negotiations with a third country or assess the advisability if progressing towards a contractual relationship.'[10] With the adoption of the Lisbon Treaty and expectations for a more strategic and coherent EU foreign policy, it will be important for the new High Representative to show that the Union can meet its political and security ambitions and set the agenda in dialogue with important third countries like India in addition to its traditional economic role.

Moreover, the adoption of the new Lisbon Treaty and the establishment of the Union's new external relations instruments and structures provide another opportunity to take stock of the early experience of initiatives such as the non-proliferation clause. Some lessons learned have already been carried out including Syria, Tajikistan and in the revised Cotonou Agreement – although not yet in force – with the African Caribbean and Pacific (ACP) states).[11] Getting the balance right is also an important part of the successful handling of the clause, whereby conditionality on non-proliferation does not become an obstacle to the objectives of achieving development, economic or other political objectives. A regular review of the clause provides an important opportunity to get the balance right and speed up discussions on identifying which states will be subject to the more demanding or weaker clause. Such discussions need to be jointly conducted between the Member States, through the Council's Working Group on Non-Proliferation (CONOP) and the Commission and in full transparency with the European Parliament (Grip, 2009).

Conclusion

The EU's early role in the security policy area has prioritized non-proliferation. But it has also shown a willingness to cooperate with the United States on new initiatives (such as UN Security Council Resolution 1540, G8 Global Partnership against the Proliferation of Materials and Weapons of Destruction and the Proliferation Security Initiative) as well as pursuing its own approach to non-proliferation that commits political and financial support (in specific Joint Actions) to the multilateral disarmament and non-proliferation regimes. The European Parliament has added its support, including budgetary through the CFSP budget and Instrument for Stability, to the development of the EU's approach to tackling materials and weapons of mass destruction. In particular the European Parliament set out is position in a comprehensive resolution adopted in 2005 and a specific resolution ahead of the 2010 NPT Review Conference that endorsed the EU Strategy and encouraged the further strengthening of the multilateral non-proliferation regimes (European Parliament, 2005).

In addition to the incremental development of the EU's strategy on non-proliferation, the EU has played a much more visible political role in leading negotiations on behalf of the UN Security Council with Iran. It has also sought to back up this role with economic and political incentives as well as the application of coercive economic sanctions, although the efficacy of such sanctions is coming under increasing criticism from within Europe and the United States (United States Government Accounting Office, 2007).[12]

To conclude, the EU approach is well suited to cooperation with the USA on strengthening the multilateral regimes and on certain new initiatives that emphasize cooperation, such as the G8 Global Partnership on Materials and Weapons of Mass Destruction. The EU has been less visible in the field of applying military coercive initiatives, i.e. it does not have a policy on counter-proliferation. Having a public debate on counter-proliferation is made more difficult due to the scepticism generated by the use of force in the Iraq War. More fundamentally, the Member States have decided to limit their military cooperation in the framework of the EU to concentrate on crisis management and stabilization missions. This will remain a difficult subject even if language on 'joint disarmament operations' has been introduced with the new Lisbon Treaty (Popielawska and Deuter, 2008; Quille, 2008a).

Finally, the EU will need to reflect on the criticisms raised at the 2005 and 2010 NPT Review Conferences. Although the 2010 meeting proved to be a 'success' in comparison with the 2005 meeting, many countries still looked to the EU for leadership behind its declaratory posture on disarmament. This will remain an issue for the European Union: in focusing upon non-proliferation it has avoided the divisions between its nuclear weapons states and, majority, non-nuclear weapons states. While this approach is holding and the nuclear weapons states make good on their commitment to nuclear reductions and eventually disarmament, the Union's strategy will continue to have success. However, the lack of activity in nuclear disarmament will no doubt be back in the spotlight, especially if the nuclear weapons states are perceived to be back-tracking on their commitments and as the Lisbon Treaty results in raising expectations for a more coherent and visible EU on the world stage, including in the area of disarmament as well as non-proliferation. The perceived success of the 2010 review conference came on the back of a major diplomatic and policy impetus of President Obama (in his 2009 Prague speech, followed by his successful negotiations for nuclear reductions with Russia under START, and by his Nuclear Security Summit in April 2010). The European Union and others will need to think how they can capitalize on the progress inspired by the US president in a period when he will be managing withdrawal from Afghanistan and a weakened mandate in Congress.

Nevertheless, the 2010 review conference is an important benchmark in the process of strengthening 'multilateral' approaches to non-proliferation and disarmament and thereby getting the 'grand bargain' back on track between nuclear states and non-nuclear states (this is very important politically in regional disputes, including the Middle East, Iran, etc.). However, there are possible tensions along the way, not least over Iran, but also arising from the fact that despite President Obama's strong commitments and successful negotiations with Russia on START and a follow-up process, the USA will 'almost certainly' not have ratified the Comprehensive Test Ban Treaty (which Congress rejected in 1999) before 2011. It will therefore be important for the EU, US and like-minded countries to reflect on their strategies to ensure that such tensions are not used by 'spoilers' who want to undermine the significant momentum represented by the above developments in this area.

Notes

1 A Joint Action (Article 14 TEU) provides the legal basis for operational action by the EU and which sets out the objectives, scope and means (financial) to be made available to the Union. As well as defining a common approach to a particular issue, Common Positions (Article 15 TEU) also demand that Member States ensure their national policies are aligned to conform with the approach.
2 For an overview see Walker, 2007, and the CSIS project Strengthening the Global Partnership at <http://www.csis.org/isp/sgp/>.
3 The latest progress report was the ninth in the series. For more information and details on the activities see: <http://consilium.europa.eu/showPage.asp?id=718&lang=en&mode=g#Bookmark>.
4 For the UNSC support to EU-led diplomacy see for instance 1737 (2006); para. 10 UNSC Resolution 1747 (2007); para 16 UNSC Resolution 1803 (2008).
5 Ashton, 2011b
6 Model text is set out in Council of the EU, 2003d. See also Council of the EU, 2003e.
7 Council of the EU, 2003d.
8 The Instrument for Stability was established in 2007 in order to respond across the spectrum of conflict prevention, crisis response and peace-building activities (European Parliament, 2005).
9 Foreign Affairs/Trade Council Conclusions (2011: 9).
10 Council of the EU, 2003d.
11 Statement by Annalisa Giannella at the Sub-Committee on Security and Defence, European Parliament, September 2009.
12 United States Government Accounting Office, 2007.

21

ENERGY SECURITY

A missing link between EU energy and foreign policies

Sami Andoura

A comprehensive European energy policy has to be viewed in a global context not only because of the global dimension of energy issues, but also because countries and industries are interdependent in terms of resources and markets. In the unstable energy landscape of the twenty-first century, the question for the European Union is especially how current developments can deal with the numerous and wide energy issues it faces today and in the future on an unprecedented scale.

Humankind consumes more resources than nature can provide. Europeans, who represent 7 per cent of the world population, use 17 per cent of world natural resources each year. In general, demand for energy should continue to grow markedly over the next 20 years. At a global level, primary energy demand is projected to increase by 1.5 per cent per year between 2007 and 2030 – an overall increase of 40 per cent by 2030. The needs of developing Asian countries alone will account for 87 per cent of this rise, with China and India representing half of this increase (IEA, 2009a). The European Union's consumption will increase by 11 per cent (European Commission, 2010a).

Fossil-fuel energy will continue to dominate the energy mix across the world (77 per cent) (IEA, 2009a) and Europe (78.6 per cent) between 2007 and 2030. At a European level, the dominant fuels in the primary fuel mix for the foreseeable future are oil (36.4 per cent) and natural gas (23.9 per cent), followed by coal (18.3 per cent), nuclear energy (13.4 per cent) and renewable energies (7.8 per cent) (European Commission, 2010b). The complete substitution of fossil energies by alternative sources remains unlikely in the near future, in particular due to delays in developing the necessary new technologies and the persistent difficulty of connecting sources to the electricity network (European Commission, 2010c).

Fossil-fuel resources are also becoming increasingly rare. Given proven resources, current technologies and the coming increase in consumption, the current extrapolated lifetimes are 40 to 50 years for oil, about 60 years for natural gas and about 250 years for coal (IEA, 2009a). The exhaustibility of these resources is evidenced in the European Union, where the production of primary energy has fallen considerably in the last ten years, causing increased reliance on imported energy. One example is the UK, which has become a net importer of primary energy (20.1 per cent in 2007) (European Commission, 2010c). Whereas the Union already imported 53.1 per cent of its energy needs in 2007 (European Commission, 2010c) with a relative 82.6 per cent of its needs in oil and 60.3 per cent in natural gas, its imports will reach 59 per cent in 2030 with 93 per cent for its oil and 83 per cent for its natural gas needs (European Commission, 2010c).

The European Union's dependence on external sources for its energy supply should therefore increase. International competition for these fossil-fuel resources has become a major issue for the years to come. Increased consumption of increasingly rare fossil energy has stoked major international rivalries. Countries supplying fossil energy have understood their interests and are trying to maximize their advantage, not only in economic terms but also on occasion as a political lever vis-à-vis dependent states. The great economic powers, emerging or otherwise (United States, China, India, Russia, EU, etc.), have committed themselves to unprecedented strategies of energy-source diversification. Various competing and controversial projects for oil and gas pipelines along diversified supply routes have emerged (such as Nabucco versus South Stream, Nord Stream, etc.). This competition has a particular impact in Europe, where the increasing vulnerability and dependence of EU member states is causing intra-European rivalries which undermine the solidarity principle at the heart of European integration, as repeatedly illustrated during the gas crises between Ukraine and Russia.

Those international events and crises (energy related, environmental, economic and financial, etc.) have jolted the European Union into debating the development of a comprehensive European Energy Policy with an enhanced external dimension. Several recent developments indeed justify an increased focus on the external aspects of the energy policy: Europe's strong feeling of insecurity has increased tenfold due to the successive gas disputes between Ukraine and Russia directly affecting the EU; the tremendous increase (then fall) of energy prices; the uncertain and controversial state of energy reserves; the disequilibrium between the increase of demand and the contraction of the supply; and finally Europe's increasing energy dependence on chronically unstable energy suppliers, together with a decrease of its indigenous energy production and a limited combined contribution from renewable and nuclear energies.

Against this background, the aim of this chapter is to identify what exactly the EU external energy policy is, whether it builds on both EU energy and foreign policies and to what extent the concept of energy security can serve as a bridge between these two policies, thus enabling the EU to develop its energy relations with its external partners and become a strategic actor in this field. Based on a critical assessment of what the EU has achieved so far, this chapter concludes with some policy recommendations, supporting the development of a European Energy Community with external competence.

The late acknowledgement of energy as a matter of security

Energy security as a new 'bridging' concept

Energy security is a complex issue because a mix of both internal and external policies is necessary to make the EU a leading actor in the field, to equip itself with the capacity to influence the global governance of energy issues and to expand its principles/norms and values at the international level (Youngs, 2007). Completing the EU-wide energy internal market is seen as a prerequisite for a common external energy policy. In this sense, there should be a direct link between internal and external energy goals. However, the Union's energy policy has developed belatedly and without an overall vision bringing together its different dimensions, both internal and external. In particular, this concerns the necessary balance and trade-offs between the three main objectives which the policy must pursue: energy security, competitive access to energy, and sustainable development. Among these three objectives, all effort has long been concentrated on the internal market and free competition, to the detriment of the two others and the coherence of the whole project. While major progress has been achieved since 2005 in developing a common internal energy policy and completing a single common energy market, it has been much more complicated to develop such a common approach for the external dimension of the European energy policy (Chevalier, 2009).

From the end of the 1950s to the beginning of the 1990s, initiatives taken at the EU level regarding the external dimension of energy policy were mainly in the form of soft law, i.e. communications, statements of objectives and declaratory resolutions adopted by the Commission and/or the Council, but without binding commitments (Daintith and Hancher, 1986). The only area in which the Community undertook legislative action is related to security of supply and the issue of crisis management. In reaction to the energy crises that occurred at that time, the EC mainly followed the initiatives taken within the OECD and the IEA, namely setting rules on minimum stocks of oil products and crisis management.

In any case, during the past few years, there has been political momentum regarding the concept of energy security in Europe. However, there is still a need to clearly define the concept of energy security and to address the following questions: what precisely is the EU concept for energy security? What should be the core principles which underpin such a policy? How can the Community and member states better promote diversity of supply for oil and gas? Should the EU develop new partnerships with its neighbours, including Russia, and the other main producer and consumer nations of the world? Consideration must also be given to how best to react to external energy crises in order to ensure greater solidarity between member states.

The concept of energy security has in fact been turned to fit diverging, sometimes conflicting perceptions and positions (Egenhofer *et al.*, 2006). Consumer and producer countries, developed or developing, dependent or not on energy imports, all have different priorities, interests and needs. For some, it is important to secure energy supplies for their markets, while for others, it is more important to secure access to the European market for their energy resources. Some seek to stabilize energy prices at a high level, others at a low level, etc. Among these differing and sometimes competitive approaches to energy security, the European Union is developing its own concept. The energy security concept of the European Union as conceived, aims at 'ensuring the uninterrupted physical availability of energy products on the market at an affordable price for all consumers, whilst respecting environmental concerns and looking towards sustainable development' (European Commission, 2006a).

The European Commission's Green Paper on 'A European Strategy for Sustainable, Competitive and Secure Energy' (European Commission, 2006) contributed to the emergence of a new, more dynamic and ambitious approach to European energy security. To provide a broader framework for that policy, in January 2007, the Commission issued its communication entitled 'An Energy Policy for Europe' (European Commission, 2007b) as the central piece which led to the adoption of the 'Energy and Climate Package' by the Council, designed to establish a comprehensive European energy policy by 2009 (Dehousse and Andoura, 2007). Increasing security and competitiveness of energy supply through solidarity among member states was one of the main pillars and priorities of this new EU energy policy, as well as developing relations with third countries.

An external policy to serve Europe's energy interests

The 'European Security Strategy – A Secure Europe in a Better World', released in December 2003, contained almost nothing with regard to energy security. Besides a short section on the global challenges the EU has to face in the post-Cold War environment, like increasing dependence – and hence vulnerability – no revolutionary ideas have been developed. There are only a few words on the competition for natural resources, aggravated by global warming over the next decades. The strategy calls for more coherence among EU instruments and capabilities, diplomatic efforts, development, trade and environmental policies.

The first real step towards a European external energy policy was a joint paper from the European Commission and High Representative Javier Solana in 2006 (European Commission, High Representative, 2006), which describes the main elements of a real integrated energy policy for Europe with a strong external dimension. This chapter considers how all EU external relations, including Common Foreign and Security Policy, can be used more effectively to enhance the collective external energy security of the Union. It stresses the need to combine internal and external policies. It also tries to set out the criteria for any European external energy policy. According to this chapter, such policy must be coherent (backed up by all Union policies, the member states and industry), strategic (to fully recognize the geopolitical dimensions of energy-related security issues) and focused (geared towards initiatives where action at the EU level can have a clear impact in furthering its interests). The chapter also highlights the need to base external energy policy on a clear prior identification of EU interests and a reliable risk assessment, by endowing the EU with the necessary monitoring capabilities.

Their paper interestingly divides the concept of energy security into two main building blocks: functioning markets and diversification. Through the functioning market approach, the EU should extend its own energy market to its neighbours within a common regulatory area. More widely, the EU should advocate reciprocity in market opening and respect for market rules. And finally, the EU should convince non-EU consumer countries of the benefit of worldwide functioning markets. Through diversification, the EU must give prominence to diversifying energy sources and geographical origin as well as transit routes. Emphasis is also put on the key importance of energy infrastructures.

This common paper from the Commission and High Representative is so far the most interesting concept document dealing with the external dimension of any European energy policy and the objective of security of energy supply. Very short, clear and realistic, it draws the main contours of a future European external energy policy. It also suggests concrete actions to be undertaken. All things considered, the approach is well balanced between the market approach and geopolitical concerns. It underlines the benefits that the EU can achieve when both institutions (the Commission and the Council) work together.

The first European Commission Strategic Review issued in January 2007, which tried to give a broad overview of a meaningful external energy policy, endorsed the vision of a long-term framework for the external energy dimension set out by the Commission and High Representative in their joint paper. The Review covered many important aspects approved by all relevant services of the Commission and received the 'political' mandate of the Council. Accordingly, energy must become a central part of all European external relations. The EU must, therefore, develop effective energy relations with all its international partners (with both developed and developing countries, energy consumers and producers), and broadened in geographical and substantial scope.

Last but not least, the 2008 revision of the European Security Strategy, further urges the development of an energy policy which combines the external and internal dimensions, and calls for the development at EU level of the following policy dimensions: a more unified energy market inside Europe; greater inter-connection with particular attention to the most isolated countries; crisis mechanisms to deal with temporary disruption to supply; greater diversification of fuels, sources of supply, and transit routes, including through Turkey and Ukraine; as well as good governance, respect of rule of law and investment in source countries. These objectives should be supported by greater engagements with the EU's neighbourhood, based on a 'wide-ranged agenda', including energy matters (energy security), especially in the frame of the Union for the Mediterranean and the Eastern Partnership. Partnerships for multilateral cooperation on energy issues are also invoked, with for example Central Asia, the Caucasus and Africa, as well as with Russia. With partners like China, India, Japan and the USA, the EU should further promote renewable energy, low-carbon technologies and energy efficiency, alongside transparent and well-regulated global markets. The new policy should also take into account the danger of the ruthless exploitation of natural resources and the increasing tensions over raw materials which could lead to new conflicts. Options for strengthening the coherence between policies and instruments are again mentioned and the Lisbon Treaty is considered a new framework to achieve this coherence.

However, no clear guidance is provided on how to proceed in that field. The energy dimension is also to be included and developed in the new 'European Security Strategy' to be elaborated in the near future (and to replace the first one, 2003–8). So far, energy is part of the debate but not really instrumentalized in concrete terms.

The development in practice of an EU external energy policy: a fragmented process

In quest of a European energy foreign policy

The Union is still experiencing numerous difficulties in implementing a common energy policy with a strong external dimension. The European Union today constitutes only the sum parts of 27 national energy markets which are liberalized but heterogeneous and fragmented when considering the ambitioned single market for energy (Glachant and Lévêque, 2009). Furthermore, there are still many obstacles preventing the EU from developing a comprehensive external energy policy. The main ones are:

- the persistent national sovereignty regarding the choice of energy resources used (energy mix);
- the preference accorded to bilateral relations with producer countries in the name of national interest;
- the preference given by member states to (non-EU) national and/or international solutions to the late twentieth century's energy crises;
- a certain reluctance of member states to share natural resources with neighbours;
- the absence of a legal basis in the treaties permitting the Union to develop a genuine overarching energy policy;
- the timidity of European institutions in promoting such a policy.

Moreover, member states remain reluctant to see the EC/EU interfering in their areas of national sovereignty, i.e. foreign and security policy, and often prefer international cooperation – instead of European – as the best defence of their national positions. The fact that the EU has not been capable of developing a common foreign policy has reinforced this tendency and remains an obstacle for the realization of a comprehensive common European energy policy. Indeed, the energy policy has an important strategic dimension – mainly the relations with external suppliers – which has been neglected at the EU level and remains the prerogative of the member states. The paradox is that, vice versa, the fact that Europe has not developed such a comprehensive common energy policy is an obstacle to the development of a common foreign policy.

As we could see in the case of the European Security Strategy, there is a growing tendency to include energy issues in discussions of the EU's role as a global power. But, there are still very few opportunities to tackle this potential in concrete terms: to make a direct link between the internal and external dimensions and build an ambitious common external energy policy or strategy. External and internal policy objectives are pursued in parallel, but they often intertwine, and can even compete with each other. There is a damaging lack of a holistic approach in this field and a lot of confusion between the external and the internal aspects of the EU's energy policy. The boundaries and the very nature of the EU's external energy policy are not yet clearly defined.

The progressive inclusion of the energy dimension into the external policies of the EU

Despite the scattered state of the treaties, the European Union has to some extent developed the energy dimension in its external relations with third countries and within international organizations. The EU-wide range of legal instruments (i.e. trade agreements, association treaties, stabilization and association agreements, the energy community with southeastern European countries, enlargement process, European Neighbourhood policy, strategic partnerships and transatlantic relations) already contains some energy purposes. Nevertheless, as recently developed, such an 'embryonic' and 'fragmented' EU external energy policy does not so far cover the full set of foreign policy instruments that could contribute to the development and strengthening of the Union's external relations in the field of energy. Beyond the simple inclusion of energy objectives in foreign relations, the EU needs to achieve a more systematic, structured and coherent use of the legal instruments at its disposal to promote its energy policy goals externally.

The most striking example is EU Trade Policy. Energy chapters are progressively included in trade negotiations with big energy suppliers and transit countries through the Free Trade Agreements (Libya, Ukraine) and WTO accession process (Algeria, Kazakhstan, Russia). Another example is the EU Cooperation and Development Policy, which provides more and more policy space for energy matters (see the development of an EU–Africa Energy Partnership and the recent identification of energy as a priority area of the European Development Fund). Energy aspects should, however, be further integrated into these two policies.

There is scope to make better use of trade policy tools to promote energy goals such as the development of a more secure investment climate and non-discriminatory energy transit regulations. For instance, the EU could press for stronger reference to active WTO rules and principles dealing with energy in its bilateral, regional or multilateral trade initiatives. International bilateral and multilateral trade agreements concluded by the EU with third countries could also further integrate toughened market-based requirements on energy and trade-related energy issues together with provisions on market opening (access to energy resources), transit of energy resources (gas and oil pipelines etc.), investment, regulatory convergence and competition.

Diversification of energy sources and resources

The key dimension of a European External Energy Policy is to guarantee a high level of diversification of supplies both in term of sources and resources. The optimal solution is a highly heterogeneous European energy mix. It is therefore important to diversify energy supplies by supporting and developing other sources than oil and gas. Such a policy is indispensable not only for the EU as a whole, but also for specific member states or regions. The second branch of the diversification policy is to launch various projects ensuring diversity of country of origin and transit of supply for the European Union. The EU is indeed trying to develop partnerships with its neighbours, including Russia, as well as with other main energy producers, transit and/or consumer nations of the world (i.e. EU bilateral, regional and multilateral international relations with producer, transit and consumer countries).

However, the Union suffers from a damaging lack of international credibility in that area (Mandil, 2008). It remains incapable of speaking with a single voice on the international energy scene, either within the relevant forums or, even more so, vis-à-vis producer and transit countries. This prevents it from exerting its full weight, economic, commercial and political, in its relations with interlocutors. Persistent national sovereignty over these sensitive issues explains why it is so difficult to reach an agreement of all 27 member states. Hence, the basic principle – strongly defended in the Council – is that the energy policy in general should fully respect member states' choice of energy mix and sovereignty over primary energy sources. Meanwhile, the unilateral approach of the member states to secure their energy supply remains the rule, and bilateral deals between separate EU states and external energy suppliers continue to prevail over a specific EU approach.

In this context, it is worth mentioning the 'crisis' in the relation between the European Union and Russia as illustrated by the early refusal of the EU, led by Poland and then Lithuania, to launch the negotiation of a new *Partnership and Cooperation Agreement* with Russia, mainly justified by energy concerns (Andoura, 2007). These negotiations finally began at the end of 2008, but very little progress has been achieved so far, especially in the field of energy. The outcome of this comprehensive negotiation will have a particular bearing on the EU's ability to develop a coherent energy policy with a comprehensive external dimension in the future.

If it wants to succeed, the EU needs above all to pursue this process of concluding separate binding international agreements and energy partnerships with producer and transit countries, and other international actors dealing with energy.

Energy crisis management

When confronted with serious disruption of security of energy supplies, the EU hardly responded structurally but rather through voluntary *'solidarités de fait'*. For instance, the recent bilateral oil and gas crises between Russia and Ukraine or Belarus in which the EU could not intervene technically have demonstrated the need for the EU to be capable of reacting quickly and in a fully coordinated manner to such experiences, both internally and in cooperation with its external partners (transit and supply countries and/or companies). Nevertheless, the mechanisms for preventing and managing crises are insufficient to respond effectively to crises on a scale like that of winter 2009 between Russia and Ukraine. In addition, numerous technical obstacles prevent the Union's member states from making practical responses to a rupture of supply to their neighbours, even when they wish to give help. A Russo-Ukrainian crisis can thus hide another crisis – an intra-European one.

The gas crises between Russia and Ukraine (repeated between 2006 and 2009) have shed light on the acute vulnerability of certain member states, essentially in Central and Eastern Europe, as well as the patent lack of European solidarity – both in practice and in law – between members of the Union. To meet the challenge of energy security, these states face a little-diversified range of sources; increased dependence on Russian gas; a lack of necessary infrastructure for the creation of a Europe-wide energy network; limited storage capacities; and persistent technical difficulties (for example, in allowing the direction of pipe flow to be switched between countries when supply is broken) which prevent states from helping neighbours in times of crisis. Is another severe crisis necessary in order for it to become clear that, in this domain as in others, there can be no satisfactory solutions without increased cooperation between member states?

The EU should therefore develop a formal and targeted Community mechanism for rapid and coordinated management of external energy crisis both inside the EU (cohesion) and outside (cooperation). Such mechanisms or instruments should provide for increased collaboration, effective exchange of information, coordination of approach and direct assistance to a country facing difficulties. It should furthermore be permanent, capable of providing early warnings and cover all energy-producing and transit regions linked to the EU.

On the one hand, it is necessary to rethink the European approach to emergency oil and gas stocks by reviewing the corresponding Community legislation. A first step in that direction is the recent revision of Community legislation for the security of gas supply. The new Regulation on the security of gas supply was adopted by the European Parliament and the Council in Autumn 2010 in order to create a genuine EU mechanism for rapid and coordinated management of external energy crises aimed at ensuring the proper and continuous functioning of the internal gas market. This new instrument also provides for a better definition and attribution of responsibilities at the European and national levels. However, the success of this new Regulation as an effective mechanism for responding to external energy crises remains highly dependent on its effective application by EU member states, as well as on the effective coordination of response at the level of the member states and the Union regarding both preventive action and reaction to concrete disruptions of supply.

Short- and long-term approaches to energy security: the potential of the Lisbon Treaty and options beyond

Institutional innovations in foreign policy: towards real European energy diplomacy?

It is important to consider whether the Lisbon Treaty is capable of delivering the framework for realizing the objectives of a new, efficient and credible energy policy with a strengthened external dimension. The inclusion of a new Energy Title in the Lisbon Treaty is a result of a carefully crafted compromise between national sovereignty over natural resources issues and shared Union competence over the rest. In this respect, the Lisbon Treaty does not fundamentally change the existing division of competences between the Union and the member states on energy issues and can be seen as a mere codification of the existing practice in that area.

The Lisbon Treaty also includes important institutional reforms impacting the external action of the Union. It is therefore of interest to address these institutional innovations in foreign policy in the light of the need for a 'multifaceted' European external energy policy

(Kurpas *et al.*, 2007). At the heart of the reforms, the Treaty establishes a High Representative for the Union in Foreign Affairs and Security Policy (HR) responsible for ensuring the consistency of all external action. The HR is to be supported by an External Action Service and will have a separate budget. However, the HR will not have competence over all EU policies with an external dimension, most notably environment or energy. Also, decision-making powers in the international field will not change fundamentally. They continue to rely on intergovernmental cooperation. It follows from this brief overview that the Lisbon Treaty will not fundamentally change the present situation. However, when implementing the above-mentioned institutional innovations, the European Union should push for better coordination of its external action on energy through the new diplomatic service. In this respect, the EEAS should have a clearly defined and strong energy component.

Towards a European energy community with external competence

In light of the structural deficiencies from which the EU energy policy is suffering and of the current situation, national solutions are no longer sufficient to meet the major challenges ahead. It is now crucial to develop a comprehensive common European policy in the field of energy. In this regard, the external challenges faced by the European Union imply its capability to speak and act in unison on the international scene, either in the context of maintaining good foreign relations or when confronting external suppliers. Whatever the internal rules on the division of powers may be, Europe and the European states will only be heard if ranks are closed in terms of foreign policy.

Closed ranks may require that the European Union have the capacity to question commercial deals at the national level, which may be beneficial to the parties to the deal, but not for Europe's security-of-supply as a whole. The European Union should be in a position to question, and/or pre-empt as a last resort, deals concluded by private and/or public undertakings and act (albeit on a temporary basis) as a single buyer when it comes to concluding long-term supply relationships with foreign suppliers, in particular with state-controlled suppliers of authoritarian states. Security of supply is too important an issue to be left only to the discretion of select commercial interests.

This does not mean that competition should be excluded in relation to international purchasing markets. Market forces will continue to play the predominant role when negotiating supply deals with suppliers complying with market rules and market logic. They will also dictate how external supplies will be allocated once they have reached the internal energy market. In other ways, too, where market forces can, should, and will play a role.

Last but not least, the European Union needs to project the reach of the internal market beyond its borders. The possibility of earning a reasonable return on investment in a stable and prosperous environment will continue to attract private investment – both European and foreign investors as well as energy suppliers. Foreign investment, export of new technologies and trade relations create a mutual interdependence that makes Europe less vulnerable to erratic external decision-making.

Conclusion

The urgency of the situation requires public policies reorienting societies to more sustainable, targeted and secure energy uses. Markets alone are not sufficient to deal with the global goals of a *renewed* European comprehensive energy policy; there is a strong need to combine market forces and public policies. As such, this action must be European, energy-specific and result-oriented. Europeans should develop a common answer to common threats that are profoundly relevant to their current state of integration as well as to the future well-being of the global community. In this context, the EU needs to look for new means to reduce its external energy dependence, but above all to develop an enhanced common approach to its energy relations with external partners. A coherent external energy policy would further enable the European Union to play a more effective leading international role with respect to its energy partners worldwide. The future of the external dimension of its energy policy has thus become a major long-term geopolitical, economic, environmental and social concern for Europe.

However, the chief question for the European Union is how current developments can deal with the numerous and wide external energy issues it faces today and in the future on an unprecedented scale. In this respect, it remains difficult to see the European Union as a vast homogeneous consumer and importer bloc, and subsequently as a coherent and major external actor in that field. Until now, the national energy sectors and policies of the 27 European member states reflect high levels of disparity and asymmetry, with different energy cultures, structures and external policies. Moreover, the strategic dimension of the energy policy, i.e. security of supply and the relations with external suppliers and transit countries, has long been neglected at the EU level and remains the prerogative of the member states. At the same time, the fact that Europe has not developed so far a real comprehensive common energy policy is an obstacle to the development of a common foreign policy, and vice versa.

The numerous factors blocking the creation of a genuine common energy policy, together with doubts over the current capacity of the EU and its member states to meet its challenges, lead us to question whether the Union possesses the necessary foundations to conduct such a common energy policy and push forward a policy proposal in order to move towards a real European Energy Community with strong external components.

But all this requires setting collective ambitions at a higher level both in terms of substance and procedure. As in 1952 and 1957, there must be an endeavour to help collective ambitions focus on energy. A unique challenge requires a unique response. In this respect, the solution proposed in order to achieve that ultimate goal is to develop a fully-fledged European Energy Community in the most efficient and democratic manner (Delors *et al.*, 2010). It will require a stronger and more coherent European energy regulatory space governed by credible institutions capable of delivering effective solutions on the basis of democratic legitimacy. This common project offers the European Union, its member states and the industry the opportunity to design an enhanced common energy policy with both concrete internal and external dimensions.

PART IV

Partners

22

NATO AND THE UNITED STATES

Working with the EU to strengthen Euro-Atlantic security

Leo Michel

As the world has become less divided, it has become more interconnected. And we've seen events move faster than our ability to control them – a global economy in crisis, a changing climate, the persistent dangers of old conflicts, new threats and the spread of catastrophic weapons. None of these challenges can be solved quickly or easily. But all of them demand that we listen to one another and work together; that we focus on our common interests, not on occasional differences; and that we reaffirm our shared values, which are stronger than any force that could drive us apart.

President Barack Obama in Prague, 5 April 2009[1]

The maxim 'Nothing avails but perfection' may be spelled 'Paralysis'.

Winston Churchill[2]

For several years after the inception of the EU's European Security and Defense Policy (ESDP), Europeans could be forgiven for asking if Americans *really* supported such an initiative. Since NATO's creation in 1949, Washington had regularly hectored its European Allies to assume a larger share of the burdens of collective defense and – beginning with NATO's involvement in Bosnia in 1995 – crisis management. However, when President Jacques Chirac and Prime Minister Tony Blair agreed in December 1998 that the EU 'must have the capacity for autonomous action, backed up by credible military forces, the means to decide to use them and a readiness to do so, in order to respond to international crises', Washington's initial reaction struck Europeans as distinctly chilly. Secretary of State Madeleine Albright stressed the need for Europeans to avoid 'the Three Ds': 'decoupling' European decision-making

---

These are the author's personal views and do not necessarily reflect the views of the Department of Defense or any other agency of the Federal Government.

from the Alliance; 'duplication' of NATO structures and planning processes; and 'discrimination' against Allies (notably Turkey) who are not EU members (Albright, 1998). Other American officials and experts privately fretted that key consultations and decisions on security matters might migrate over time from NATO, where America's unique political and military strengths ensure it has a preponderant role in shaping Alliance policies and operations, to the EU, where there is no US seat at the table.

In late 2000, Secretary of Defense William Cohen, convinced that perceived US opposition to ESDP was proving counterproductive, proffered a more positive vision of a future NATO–EU relationship – a shift that was warmly received by his European counterparts.[3] But his successor, Donald Rumsfeld, who seemed to waver between skepticism and indifference toward ESDP during 2001–2, shifted to thinly veiled suspicion during 2003–4.[4] By early 2005, Washington began to reverse field and sought to engage the EU as a close partner in the struggle against international terrorism and weapons proliferation and in stabilization efforts involving failed and failing states.[5] But it was not until early 2008 that senior US officials once again embraced, at least in principle, the EU-led defense efforts.[6] (Helpfully, by 2008, European officials had dropped their occasional suggestions that that ESDP would develop into a regional and global 'counterweight' to American influence.)

US worries about 'too little' Europe

Today, the prevailing concern among American officials and experts is not that the EU's activities in the security and defense domains risk sidelining or overshadowing NATO. Instead, most worry that neither NATO nor the EU will be able, separately or together, to respond effectively to the 'persistent dangers' mentioned by President Obama absent reinvigorated strategies, major organizational reforms, adequate and more efficient resourcing, more equitable sharing of operational risks and responsibilities and, of course, the political will needed to implement these objectives.

Several factors explain American nervousness.

NATO is clearly under strain. Backed by strong US military and political commitments, it has been the primary guarantor of Europe's defense from armed attack since 1949. With the end of the Cold War, NATO assumed new roles: building defense and security partnerships with new democracies in Central and Eastern Europe that prepared many for Alliance membership; offering dialogue and cooperation on political-military issues to Russia, Ukraine, and other states of the former Soviet Union; and leading complex military operations in the Balkans, Afghanistan, and Libya. Over more than six decades, NATO also has performed the vital job of promoting intra-European as well as transatlantic collaboration on threat assessments, political-military strategy, defense planning, equipment standards and interoperability, and training and exercises.

Still, with memories of the Cold War fading, many Europeans no longer view the most pressing threats to their security, or the tools needed to address them, as predominantly military. Moreover, while public opinion polls indicate a modest recovery in positive European views of the United States since the Iraq-related nadir of 2003–4, Europeans arguably remain less confident than a decade ago that US interests, strategy, and policies closely match their own.[7]

Europeans are not alone in questioning previous assumptions. When outgoing US Secretary of Defense Robert Gates delivered his valedictory speech on NATO to a prestigious Brussels audience in June 2011, he did not mince words. After acknowledging that NATO, overall, has performed well in Afghanistan and that a few smaller Allies, including

Denmark and Norway, joined the United Kingdom and France in making major contributions to strike operations in Libya, Mr Gates spoke bluntly of his major worries. NATO, he said, was turning into a 'two-tiered alliance' divided between members who specialize in 'soft' tasks (such as humanitarian and development assistance and less risky peacekeeping) and those who conduct the 'hard' combat missions – a development that he called 'unacceptable'. Equally disconcerting, he suggested, was the connection between the 'lack of will' demonstrated by some Allies and their 'lack of resources'. Citing examples of the latter's impact on ongoing operations and future readiness, he warned: 'If current trends in the decline of European defense capabilities are not halted and reversed, future US political leaders ... may not consider the return on America's investment in NATO worth the cost.'[8]

In October 2011, on his first trip to NATO as Secretary of Defense, Leon Panetta broadly echoed Mr Gates' message. He added, as well, a strong reminder that defense resources are under strong pressure on both sides of the Atlantic. 'Many might assume,' he warned, 'that the US defense budget is so large that it can absorb and cover Alliance shortcomings. But make no mistake about it, we (in the United States) are facing dramatic cuts with real implications for Alliance capability.'[9]

Afghanistan challenges

For many Americans, NATO's solidarity and effectiveness will be decided in the caldron of Afghanistan, where European Allies and Partners contribute approximately 37,000 of the 130,000 troops (including some 90,000 Americans) in the International Security Assistance Force (ISAF.)[10] European and American leaders broadly agree that if Afghanistan were to become a failed state, terrorist networks would re-establish themselves there, posing an increased threat to the European and American homelands. But with few exceptions, public support for the Afghanistan mission is generally lower – and eroding faster – in Europe than in the United States.

At the November 2010 NATO Summit in Lisbon, Allies and Partner countries in ISAF expressed support for President Armid Karzai's objective for Afghan forces to lead and conduct security operations in all provinces by the end of 2014. Yet, this does not constitute a pledge by all those countries to stay in Afghanistan until then – much less beyond. The United States has announced plans to progressively withdraw the 33,000 'surge' troops (approved by President Obama in December 2009) by the end of the summer of 2012, and several Allies have announced proportionate reductions in their forces, as well. But as ISAF gradually passes the lead for security operations in selected provinces and districts to Afghan forces, pressure will build within several troop-contributing nations now deployed in those areas (mostly in the north and west) to withdraw their forces entirely rather than shift them to training and mentoring functions, which are not risk-free tasks. The danger is that during the planned transition to an Afghan 'lead' in 2014, the operational burdens and risks might fall even more disproportionately on those US and other Allied forces now deployed in the more volatile southern and eastern regions. Meanwhile, the increasingly precarious situation in Pakistan could heighten friction among the Allies, especially if some conclude that US pressure against extremist sanctuaries is hindering more than helping chances for a regional settlement.

Lessons of Libya

NATO's performance in Libya has drawn mixed reviews within the American defense establishment. On the positive side, NATO proved to be very responsive to the fast-changing situation in Libya: within two weeks of the UN Security Council's approval of Resolution

1973, authorizing member states and regional organizations to take 'all necessary measures' to protect civilians in Libya, NATO took overall command of international military operations to protect civilians from attack or the threat of attack. Its actions arguably saved tens of thousands of civilians in Benghazi and elsewhere threatened by the Qaddafi regime, while causing minimal collateral loss of life. NATO structures were able to adapt quickly to the specific command and control needs of the operation, including the participation of Swedish, Qatari, UAE, and Jordanian military forces. And NATO's consultative mechanisms and consensus-based decision-making helped maintain broad political solidarity on the overall goals of the operation, despite reservations expressed by a small number of Allies.

On the other hand, as Mr Gates noted in his aforementioned speech in Brussels, the Libyan experience demonstrated the Allies' disturbingly high reliance on US 'enablers' – such as tanker aircraft, precision munitions, intelligence, surveillance, and reconnaissance assets, and targeting specialists – in a limited campaign 'against a poorly armed regime in a sparsely populated country'. It also rekindled simmering concerns within NATO over the political and operational impact of decisions by certain Allies to either not participate militarily or to attach caveats to their participation.

Russia and other challenges

While NATO grapples with the demands of expeditionary operations, Russia's behavior in Georgia (especially during the August 2008 armed conflict) and elsewhere in the former Soviet space – combined with menacing statements, such as President Dmitry Medvedev's vow 'to protect of the life and dignity of (Russian) citizens, wherever they are' – has refocused attention on NATO's collective defense role. To be sure, Russia does not represent the type of existential threat posed by the Soviet Union, and no Allied government advocates a return to Cold War models of territorial defense. Indeed, some see Russian actions in Georgia as largely a 'one off' action – an opportunistic show of force to destabilize a weak but impetuous neighbor and prevent further NATO enlargement. Yet, others divine a more deliberate and comprehensive Russian strategy that extends from discouraging investments in southern energy pipelines to intimidating Ukraine and other neighbors in the 'near abroad' with substantial populations of ethnic Russians and, over time, to sowing disagreement within Europe and division between Europe and the United States. Given such differing assessments regarding Moscow's motivations, strategy, and capabilities, it is clear that sorting out relations with Russia will remain a major strategic challenge for the United States and Europe for years to come.

At the Lisbon Summit, NATO and Russia agreed to pursue improved dialogue and practical cooperation to meet common security interests, ranging from counter-terrorism, counter-narcotics, and counter-piracy to non-proliferation of weapons of mass destruction. New arrangements to facilitate transit of non-lethal ISAF goods through Russian territory are a tangible sign of the improved relations between NATO and Russia. Nevertheless, realizing NATO's declared goal of a 'true strategic partnership' with Russia will not be easy. In addition to the Georgian dossier, Russia's suspension (since late 2007) of its CFE Treaty obligations and refusal to address the overall disparity in non-strategic nuclear weapons stoke Allied concerns.

And notwithstanding the more positive tone of Russian statements at Lisbon regarding possible 'cooperation' on missile defense, Russian leaders subsequently charged that the US Phased Adaptive Approach (upon which NATO's missile defense system would be based) would threaten their country's strategic nuclear deterrent. Hence, after suggesting a 'joint system', they have pressed for formal agreements that in effect would give Moscow a direct role in deciding the configuration, capabilities, and employment of NATO's missile defenses.[11] It remains to be seen if Russia's long-term intention is to develop a cooperative architecture that does not interfere with NATO's legitimate and necessary autonomy, including in command and control functions, to defend its territory and population from the growing ballistic missile threat. As NATO Secretary General Anders Fogh Rasmussen has succinctly pointed out: 'NATO cannot outsource to non-members collective defense obligations which bind its members.'[12]

NATO's challenges extend beyond Afghanistan, Libya and Russia. As the Group of Experts on NATO's New Strategic Concept wrote in their May 2010 report:

> Most dramatically, the 9/11 and subsequent attacks demonstrated the deadly connection between technology and terror, triggering a response that has drawn NATO troops far from home, illuminated the need for timely intelligence-sharing, and complicated planning for defense. Further, the global nuclear non-proliferation regime is under increasing stress; incidents of instability along Europe's periphery have revived historic tensions; innovative modes of gathering, sending and storing information have brought with them new vulnerabilities; the security implications of piracy, energy supply risks and environmental neglect have become more evident; and a worldwide economic crisis has spawned widespread budgetary concerns.[13]

NATO and the EU 'sharing the stage'

As so-called 'non-traditional threats' to European security gain more prominence, NATO will increasingly need to share the stage with the EU as a security provider. Indeed, the new Strategic Concept approved by NATO heads of state and government in Lisbon acknowledged that 'the EU is a unique and essential partner for NATO ... NATO recognizes the importance of a stronger and more capable European defense'.[14]

Here rests another explanation for American nervousness: the widely perceived inability of the EU to deliver the promised capabilities and political will that will be necessary to meet its ambitions as a 'global player'. From an American perspective, the record of two dozen ESDP military and civilian operations undertaken to date – virtually all of which have taken place under UN Security Council resolutions approved by the United States – is generally positive, although most of those operations have been modest in size, of limited duration, and relatively low-risk. In recent years the limits of such efforts have become clearer.

For example, the EU's largest military ground operation to date, EUFOR ALTHEA in Bosnia-Herzegovina, has been trimmed from 7,000 troops at the end of 2004 to approximately 1,400 by the fall of 2011. The EU's ongoing maritime mission – a naval and marine patrol aircraft effort to protect vessels off the coast of Somalia – is part of an international anti-piracy effort, including ships from NATO and partners such as China and India. The EU force has captured some pirates and no doubt deterred some attacks, but even EU officials acknowledge that the real solution lies in restoring a measure of security and stability ashore under Somali government authorities – a potentially huge task that the EU (like other international organizations) would prefer to avoid. Elsewhere in Africa, the year-long (2008–9) ESDP operation in Chad and the Central African Republic, which at its highest point involved some 3,700 troops, was arguably successful in meeting its limited mandate, but the effort proved more difficult and expensive than anticipated. Indeed, operational fatigue among EU member states no doubt was an important reason why the French EU Presidency turned down the UN Secretary General's plea in late 2008 to dispatch another EU force to reinforce some 17,000 UN 'blue helmets' in eastern Democratic Republic of Congo.

And while some EU officials dispute the point, many Europeans and Americans voiced disappointment with the EU's skittish attitude regarding any military involvement in the Libyan crisis. Although it agreed in April to a legal and planning framework for a minimalist military operation to 'contribute to the safe movement and evacuation of displaced persons and support humanitarian agencies in their activities in the region', the EU stipulated that the operation could not be launched until specifically requested by the UN Office for the Coordination of Humanitarian Affairs – an office known to be reluctant to invite any military involvement in humanitarian assistance (Michel and Herbst, 2011).

Similarly, the EU's disappointing record in capability development – as catalogued, for example, in a July 2008 report by former EDA Chief Executive Nick Witney (2008) – has not escaped US attention.[15] To be fair, since Witney's report the EDA has tried to play a more active role in supporting bilateral and regional cooperation among EU member states – for example, in third-party logistical support, maritime surveillance, and training of helicopter crews. But even senior officials in key member countries acknowledge privately that the EU's Common Security and Defense Policy (CSDP) – as ESDP was renamed under the Lisbon Treaty – has largely stagnated since 2008. Hence, one of the main novelties of the Lisbon Treaty, the instrument of 'Permanent Structured Cooperation' intended to spur selective cooperation among member states 'with military capabilities fulfilling higher criteria and with more advanced mutual commitments', has yet to be fully defined, much less implemented. Similarly, the EU has faced growing difficulties in getting member states to commit forces to the EU Battlegroups roster, despite the agreement several years ago to maintain two Battlegroups on stand-by (for possible near simultaneous deployment) at any given time.

Increasingly, many EU members look toward their civilian capabilities – including police mentors and experts in justice, corrections, customs, and public administration – as key tools to be deployed in crisis prevention or crisis management operations. These capabilities can be used in conjunction with EU financial and developmental assistance and, in theory, alongside a CSDP military component.[16] But as Witney warned in 2008, persistent shortfalls in civilian capabilities, both at the EU and member state levels, need to be addressed. Recruiting, training, and deploying qualified civilians has not been easy, especially in cases where the EU finds itself, in effect, competing with its member governments.

Logic of NATO–EU cooperation

From an American perspective, the strains evident within NATO and the EU, coupled with persistent international demand for their services, have revived interest in closer cooperation between the two organizations. Globalization has blurred the dividing lines between 'external' and 'internal' (or 'homeland') security. The latter problems of greatest concern to European publics fall under the purview of EU structures; among these are illegal immigration, so-called homegrown extremism, transnational crime, critical civilian infrastructure protection, and environmental security. And while such problems can have serious impact on transatlantic relations, many have limited, if any, direct connection to NATO's core competencies. Still, the argument for NATO–EU cooperation on security and defense matters remains compelling and rests on three pillars of strategy, capabilities, and operations.

- *Strategy.* Twenty-one of the 27 EU member states are NATO Allies (sometimes referred to as the 'EU Allies'), and five of the remaining six (Cyprus is the exception) are members of the Partnership for Peace; the latter are closely associated with NATO in areas such as defense planning, operations, and political-military cooperation. Logically, these 26 governments should not be schizophrenic, adopting different views of their national security interests depending upon whether they are looking through an EU or NATO prism. Indeed, at the strategic level, one detects largely convergent views on challenges to the Euro-Atlantic community. The EU's European Security Strategy (ESS) lists key threats – including terrorism, proliferation of weapons of mass destruction; regional conflict, state failure, and organized crime – that track closely with NATO's April 1999 and November 2010 Strategic Concepts.[17] The ESS emphasizes non-military tools to prevent and defuse crises, but hardly strikes a pacifist stance. And since early 2008, major NATO pronouncements (including the latest Strategic Concept) have recognized, as does the EU, the growing importance of a 'comprehensive political, civilian, and military approach' wherein member states use all their tools for effective crisis management.

- *Capabilities.* Each of the EU Allies and Partners has one set of military forces and, equally important, one defense budget. These must serve their respective national missions as well as those that might be undertaken under NATO, EU, UN or 'coalition of the willing' leadership. Given the current and projected governmental austerity measures affecting most European defense budgets, including those of the United Kingdom, Germany, Italy and France, there is no room for wasteful and unnecessary duplication. And when it comes to doctrine, training, and equipment interoperability, European military commanders understand well that inconsistent practices could increase the inherent risk of military operations.

- *Operations.* Moreover, European forces are increasingly involved in a common set of operations. The formal NATO–EU arrangements known as 'Berlin Plus' were used for the transition from a NATO-led to EU-led security presence in Macedonia in early 2003.[18] A few months later, ISAF transitioned from an ad hoc coalition (with mainly European troops) serving under a UN mandate to a NATO-led force. In late 2004, NATO terminated its nine-year peacekeeping force in Bosnia-Herzegovina and, again using Berlin Plus, transferred its security role to EUFOR ALTHEA. (Many of the European personnel simply switched shoulder patches.) NATO, meanwhile, remained engaged with a modest Sarajevo headquarters to facilitate cooperation with EUFOR ALTHEA and assist Bosnian authorities with defense reform. NATO and EU military forces also have cooperated, to varying degrees, in aiding African peacekeepers in Darfur and in ongoing anti-piracy operations off Somalia.

As military operations are not always so predictable, other scenarios need to be considered. It could happen one day that an operation begun as an 'autonomous' EU military operation might encounter unforeseen contingencies and need to seek assistance from NATO.

Areas of growing NATO–EU cooperation

Thankfully – and despite some lapses and inconsistencies – pragmatic NATO–EU cooperation is more and more a reality, and it occurs in five interrelated 'baskets'.

First, there exist several 'formal' channels for cooperation. This area of cooperation often draws the most attention, in large part due to political sensitivities involving Turkey (an Ally and candidate for EU membership) and Cyprus (an EU member not recognized by Turkey) – a legacy of the decades-old dispute between the Greek Cypriot and Turkish Cypriot communities. Hence, formal agendas for meetings between NATO's North Atlantic Council (NAC) and the EU's Political and Security Committee (PSC), as well as those between each organization's military committee, have been limited to their cooperation in Bosnia, which is less and less relevant to their top priorities. Formal information exchanges between NATO and the EU are difficult, since EU legal experts have ruled that NATO classified and unclassified documents delivered to the EU pursuant to Berlin Plus arrangements will not be distributed to any member states if they cannot be distributed to all.[19]

Still, there are several examples of formal and ongoing NATO–EU cooperation. The NATO–EU Capability group has scored some modest successes by sensitizing their member states to the problems of duplicative and/or conflicting capabilities development efforts and by exploring possibilities for technical cooperation on specific projects.[20] A NATO Permanent Liaison Team works with the EU Military Staff (EUMS), and a counterpart EU Cell works with NATO's Supreme Allied Headquarters Europe (SHAPE), the staff supporting NATO's Supreme Commander for Operations (SACEUR.) These liaison elements attend the majority of daily operational briefings held at their respective headquarters, contributing to greater transparency between NATO and the EU. In addition, NATO and EU senior officials now formally and regularly participate in each other's high level meetings. And the continuing Berlin Plus arrangement for EURFOR ALTHEA, which provided for the designation of NATO's Deputy SACEUR (DSACEUR) as Operational Commander, provides senior EU defense officials with regular access to NATO's second highest military officer in the operational chain of command. This is a valuable conduit through which the entire range of European defense issues can be discussed on a regular basis.

'Informal' channels constitute a second basket for NATO–EU cooperation. Admittedly, not all attempts have gone smoothly; on occasion, informal meetings at NATO or EU headquarters (for example, between the NAC and PSC) have been leaked to the press to serve the political ends of one or more of the participants. But other examples of discussions held outside NATO or EU institutional frameworks – including 'transatlantic dinners' at the level of foreign ministers from NATO and EU member states or meetings of the 'Friends of Kosovo' and 'Friends of Afghanistan' – have proved useful. Non-institutional venues in Brussels – such as the Security and Defence Agenda, German Marshall Fund, European Policy Center, Carnegie Europe and Egmont Institute – also provide excellent opportunities for informal discussions that, over time, weave an ongoing dialogue among NATO and EU officials and national representatives.[21] According to knowledgeable European officials, the usefulness of such informal channels was amply demonstrated during the Libyan crisis.

A third basket involves staff-to-staff interaction, which is vital to ensuring complementarity in, and mutual reinforcement of, NATO and EU activities. Such interaction is inherent in important tasks, such as developing and presenting briefings, de-conflicting schedules and programs, and identifying possible new steps for senior decision-makers. Moreover, the Berlin Plus arrangements authorize and encourage staff-to-staff interaction, to include the appropriate use of classified materials. Representatives of the rotating EU Presidency nation at NATO now give weekly updates on EU activities to the NAC and NATO Military Committee. A senior EU defense policy civilian regularly consults with DSACEUR and NATO Assistant Secretaries General for Operations, Defense Policy and Planning, and Political Affairs and Security Policy. Preparations for the Capability Group fall to the EU Presidency country, the Council General Secretariat, and the office of NATO's Assistant Secretary General for Defense Planning and Policy. The NATO and EU Situation Centers are in regular contact, as are the chairmen of the respective military committees and military staffs.

Within this context, the EU's EDA and NATO's Allied Command Transformation (ACT) have undertaken promising steps to cooperate on capability development. The two organizations already work with each other in the vital areas of countering improvised explosive devices (the greatest single threat to ISAF personnel) and improving medical support for deployed personnel. Other areas of potential pragmatic cooperation, such as protection against chemical, biological, radiological and nuclear threats as well as cyber security, are under active consideration.

A fourth basket covers a range of 'on-the-ground' cooperation. NATO and EU representatives on the scene have considerable experience in sorting out issues that their Brussels-based political masters were unable to resolve. Operational imperatives drove military commanders – in Macedonia in 2003 and in Bosnia-Herzegovina in 2004 – to find practical solutions on matters such as logistics, communications, intelligence sharing, and relations with local authorities where no precedent or actionable political guidance existed.[22] Later, in Kosovo, NATO's Kosovo Force (KFOR) commander and the planning team for the EU's rule of law (EULEX) mission negotiated draft technical agreements to cover mutual physical and operational support and informally agreed to abide by those drafts absent political endorsement from their respective Brussels headquarters. In Afghanistan, after a difficult start, local interaction between the EU Police Training Mission (EUPOL) and the NATO Training Mission-Afghanistan is reported to be very good. (Both NATO and EU sources lament the fact that EU member states have failed to resource adequately the EUPOL mission, particularly in areas of communications, in-theater transportation, and close protection teams for EUPOL trainers and mentors.)

NATO and EU cooperation with third parties represents a fifth and final basket of cooperation. Third parties can be other international organizations – for example, the United Nations, Organization for Security and Cooperation in Europe, European Gendarmerie Force, and African Union. They also can be other countries – for example, China and India – which loosely coordinate their anti-piracy efforts off Somalia with NATO and EU naval and air forces through an informal 'Shared Awareness and De-confliction' network. Paradoxically, perhaps, NATO–EU relations in this area might generally work well because the two organizations are not cooperating with each other directly or exclusively; rather, they are operating 'side-by-side' with – and, in some cases, on behalf of – someone else. Indeed, working with a third party might actually encourage better NATO–EU coordination. In mid-2005, for example, NATO and the EU briefly engaged in an unseemly competition to aid the African Union mission in Darfur only to discover that some African officials were deliberately playing one organization against the other. This realization helped end the worst of the political sniping between the two Brussels-based organizations.

Improvements are possible

There is, without question, room for improvement in all of these facets of NATO–EU cooperation. For example:

• The Capability Group could discuss a prioritization of projects in train within each organization. This could facilitate autonomous decisions by NATO and the EU to agree to priority lists consistent with one another; in this way, national defense planners would not be receiving ambiguous or, worse, contradictory guidance from their NATO and EU delegations. In a related move, NATO and the EU could expand the concept of an EU cell at SHAPE and NATO liaison team at the EU Military Staff by establishing an EDA cell at NATO's ACT with a reciprocal arrangement for ACT liaison within the EDA. Such an arrangement would strengthen confidence in NATO and EU member states that their capabilities development and interoperability efforts maximized efficiencies and synergies. This would be an especially valuable channel as both EDA and ACT are working with member states to identify and facilitate new and/or expanded forms of pooling and sharing capabilities as one response to declining defense budgets.

• 'Staff-to-staff' relations between NATO and the EU, which have been largely confined on the EU side to the Council Secretariat, could be expanded to include European Commission representatives. This would be a particularly timely move as the EU External Action Service includes some of the key Commission offices with which NATO needs to work in implementing an effective 'comprehensive' civil–military approach to crisis prevention and stabilization operations. Moreover, NATO agreed at the Lisbon Summit to create 'an appropriate but modest civilian crisis management capability to interface more effectively with civilian partners … This capability may also be used to plan, employ and coordinate civilian activities until conditions allow for the transfer of those responsibilities and tasks to other actors.' As NATO implements this agreed step, it makes practical and political sense to work closely with the EU in areas including, but not limited to, identifying 'best practices' in the recruitment, training, exercising, and deployment of civilian experts in crisis prevention, crisis response, and stabilization missions.

• An expansion of 'informal' consultations might be useful in dealing with emerging crises. Such consultations would include the NAC and PSC national representatives, plus each organization's senior civilian leaders (e.g., NATO's Secretary General and the EU's High Representative) and military leaders (e.g., NATO's SACEUR and DSACEUR, plus the respective Chairmen of the NATO and EU Military Committees.) They would discuss preliminary assessments of the potential pros and cons of civilian, military, or civil–military options for the crisis at hand; the capabilities that might be required and available; and whether an eventual crisis prevention or crisis response operation might be more appropriately handled under NATO auspices, or as an autonomous EU operation, or as an EU operation with NATO support. This would not be a joint decision-making meeting, but it would allow all parties to reach better-informed national positions and, eventually, NATO and EU decisions. The principle of autonomous decision-making by each organization would be respected. In addition, current informal arrangements could be enhanced to include transatlantic dinners at the defense minister and military chiefs of defense levels, eventually expanding to include NATO and EU permanent representatives and military committee members.

The prospects for such improvements are aided significantly by the reportedly good cooperation between NATO Secretary General Rasmussen and EU High Representative Catherine Ashton. Mr Rasmussen has been an outspoken advocate and behind-the-scenes facilitator of closer NATO–EU cooperation, sometimes ruffling the feathers of one or more Allies.[23] Baroness Ashton has been noticeably less voluble on the subject, but apparently shares many of Rasmussen's concerns.[24]

As such efforts progress, it would be logical to consider an even more ambitious project: establishment of an 'international community planning mechanism', wherein NATO and the EU would play leading roles to develop a coherent, cross-disciplinary and cross-organizational approach toward preparing and implementing a comprehensive approach to crisis prevention and, if necessary, crisis response. Time and time again, from the Balkans to Southwest Asia, the limits and costs of ad hoc approaches have become self-evident. In nearly all crisis management and peacekeeping missions today and tomorrow, the militaries of the

Euro-Atlantic community are not – and will not be – alone in the operational theater. They must work closely with an array of civilian agencies and actors from international, governmental, and non-governmental organizations to prevent conflict or stabilize the situation and begin reconstruction in the post-conflict phase. This is true for operations conducted under NATO or EU or 'coalition of the willing' auspices, even if the precise tools used might vary from case-to-case. If the principles and practices of civil–military cooperation were better understood and accepted by all, this could go a long way toward lowering the obstacles to practical cooperation between NATO and the EU.[25]

Limits of NATO–EU and US–EU cooperation

In discussions regarding NATO–EU cooperation, two questions often arise:

*   Would both organizations, given legitimate concerns for maintaining their distinctive character and decision-making autonomy, be better served by a formal 'division of labor' rather than emphasizing their cooperation?
*   And given the remaining obstacles to such close cooperation – notably, the continuing dispute involving Turkey and Cyprus – would the transatlantic relationship be better served by focusing on an expanded bilateral relationship between the United States and EU rather than dealing with the political morass of NATO–EU relations?

The arguments for a formal 'division of labor' seem weak on several grounds. As most recently demonstrated by the unexpected upheavals in several Arab countries since late 2010, we cannot predict where or how future crises will arise, or know in advance the right combination of military and/or civilian capabilities that are necessary for their prevention or management. EU member states would find it as difficult to agree on a fixed 'ceiling' for CSDP military or civilian operations – in terms of types of missions, force composition and capabilities, and deployment regions – as NATO would find it difficult to set a 'floor' for its involvement. Similarly, neither organization will or should be expected to subordinate its decision-making autonomy to the other; nor should either seek to systematically inject itself into missions under consideration or conducted by the other.

That said, certain notional differences in each organization's level of ambition already exist. For example, as demonstrated in Kosovo, Afghanistan, and Libya, none of the EU members is prepared to engage in large-scale combat operations without the United States, although only the United Kingdom has been willing to state this explicitly. On the other hand, many Europeans believe the EU has a comparative advantage, thanks to its array of developmental and civil–military tools, in crisis prevention and crisis management in parts of Africa. And many US officials and experts acknowledge that even with the 'modest' NATO civilian crisis management capability foreseen by the new Strategic Concept, they would prefer to see the Alliance work closely with the EU in deploying and sustaining an effective comprehensive approach in stabilization operations.[26]

The proposition that US–EU cooperation should somehow supersede NATO–EU cooperation is similarly flawed. In fact, an important and growing bilateral US–EU relationship already exists in areas such as law enforcement, counter-terrorism, counter-narcotics, transportation security, and non-proliferation. With respect to crisis management operations, some 70 American police trainers currently work within the 2,000-person EULEX mission in Kosovo. Moreover, thanks to a US–EU 'framework agreement' signed in May 2011, the door has been opened for future participation by US civilian experts, as decided on a 'case-by-case' basis, in EU crisis management operations.[27] Other areas of cooperation, such as the coordinated delivery of humanitarian assistance, should be developed.

Since the EU increasingly serves as the Europeans' venue for strategic discussions and decision-making on security issues that do not involve military commitments – for example, diplomatic efforts, including economic and financial sanctions, to deal with Iranian nuclear ambitions or the Syrian government's brutal repression of internal dissent – the United States will want to ensure that its views are taken into account before EU policies are set in stone. This, in turn, will periodically pose a difficult policy question for Washington: where does it draw the line between discussing strategic questions at NATO, where there is a US seat at the table, and at the EU, where the United States and 'Europe' sit across the table from one another?

There is no easy answer to that question, but there are clearly inherent limits to bilateral US–EU relations insofar as defense matters are concerned.

One factor is the obvious mismatch of memberships: while 21 of 27 EU members are also NATO Allies, the United States would be loathe to put at risk its long-term military and political relationships with the non-EU Allies (Canada, Turkey, Norway and Iceland) by effectively circumventing the NAC and NATO military structures to consult, plan, and conduct one or more operations with the EU Allies. Any such shift in US policy also would risk encouraging the creation, either formally or informally, of an 'EU caucus' within NATO. This would run counter to NATO's tradition of consensus decision-making by individual, sovereign member states – something that US policymakers and leading Members of Congress are keen to preserve. (Truth be told, many EU Allies would not be happy with an 'EU caucus' in NATO, since it could diminish their national prerogatives in areas of critical importance to their national security.)

A second factor, albeit less obvious, is equally important: NATO's strength and effectiveness derive, in large part, from the multinational and multi-layered nature of its civilian and military structures where Americans, Canadians and Europeans sit side by side to discuss, plan, decide, and implement a broad range of political and military tasks. A bilateral US–EU relationship would not include those structures, and it is hard to see how they could be compatible with the EU's emphasis on 'autonomous' decision-making and capabilities. Moreover, there is no obvious rationale for duplicating such structures, since they already exist and generally function well in NATO.

A third factor goes to the heart of CSDP's *raison d'être*: if the EU is serious about creating new capabilities that it is able to use, in some cases at least, as an 'autonomous actor', it makes little sense to encourage an EU dependency upon US assets and capabilities to accomplish EU operations. Yet, dedicating US military assets to the EU (as the United States does for NATO) would have precisely that effect. This need not close the door to some modest and case-by-case coordination – for example, between the US Africa Command and Europeans who provide concrete and valuable assistance in Africa.[28] Similarly, one could imagine the US European Command working with the EU, on a case-by-case basis, in the areas of humanitarian relief and disaster assistance.

Conclusion

NATO and the EU likely will be joined at the hip in facing a range of future challenges and operations. The practical result of their overlapping interests is that neither organization can afford to fail, or afford to see the other fail. Hence, the NATO–EU relationship should ensure transparency, avoid contradictions in their respective approaches and, more positively, develop new capabilities and bring 'added value' to conflict prevention and crisis management.

Of course, a healthy dose of realism is needed on all sides. Some NATO–EU tensions are inevitable. Despite shared democratic values and many convergent interests, the two organizations are and will remain profoundly different in terms of structure, scope, and procedures. Furthermore, the EU, unlike NATO, aspires to 'political union'. And as the Libyan case demonstrated afresh, different political calculations both within Europe and within the wider Euro-Atlantic relationship will come into play in any specific case.

Still, with better tools in place for cooperation between these central pillars of the Euro-Atlantic community, the chances of mounting effective international efforts to prevent and manage crises will increase – if and when the political will exists to do so. This is an imperfect solution, to be sure, but that's where Sir Winston got it right.

Notes

1 See: <http://www.whitehouse.gov/the_press_office/Remarks-By-President-Barack-Obama-In-Prague-As-Delivered/>.
2 A minute [brief note] to General Ismay, 6 December 1942, on proposed improvements to landing-craft, published in Churchill (1951). The memo is reproduced in Appendix C (which starts on p. 750).
3 In remarks to NATO defense ministers in October 2000, Cohen stated: 'First, we must develop a clearer and, to be blunt, a more positive vision of the future NATO–EU relationship. For my part, I am convinced that a close, coherent, cooperative, and transparent relationship will prove to be in the best interest of Allies and EU members, both current and future, and further our overarching vision for the entire Euro-Atlantic community in all its political, economic, social, and security dimensions. Second, we must ensure that the Alliance and the EU have the necessary military capabilities to perform their respective missions. This means that both organizations must: take a hard look at what they really need in terms of military capabilities, based upon an objective assessment of current and likely future threats; identify those areas where their capabilities fall short; agree together on how to rectify those shortfalls; and find the resources for the task.' See: <http://www.defense.gov/speeches/speech.aspx?speechid=740>.
4 Especially in the aftermath of the September 2001 terrorist attacks, ESDP did not rank very high among the Bush Administration's priorities. Although US efforts were critical to concluding formal arrangements for NATO–EU consultation and cooperation (known as 'Berlin Plus') in early 2003, serious US disagreements with several Allies regarding the war in Iraq spilled over to European defense issues. Later that year, for example, US Permanent Representative to NATO Nicholas Burns called a proposal by several EU members to establish a dedicated EU military operational planning headquarters outside Brussels 'one of the greatest dangers to the transatlantic relationship' (Dempsey, 2003).
5 President George W. Bush highlighted this shift in February 2005 when, following a meeting at NATO headquarters, he traveled downtown and became the first American President to meet with the European Council, Presidency, and President of the Commission at the very seat of the EU.
6 For example, at the February 2008 Munich Security Conference, Secretary of Defense Robert Gates aligned himself with calls by the NATO Secretary General and French defense minister for a pragmatic sharing of roles and 'complementary' relationship between NATO and the EU. Later that month, the US Permanent Representative to NATO, Victoria Nuland, surprised French officials with her forceful and forthcoming statement in Paris: 'We agree with France: Europe needs, the United States needs, NATO needs, the democratic world needs – a stronger, more capable European defense capacity. An ESDP with only soft power is not enough. As we look to the French Presidency of the EU this summer, we hope France will lead an effort to strengthen European defense spending, upgrade European military capabilities with badly needed investment in helicopters, UAVs, special forces, interoperable communications and counterinsurgency trained soldiers and civilians. Because President Sarkozy is right – NATO cannot be everywhere.' See: <http://www.america.gov/st/texttrans-english/2008/February/20080222183349eaifas0.5647394.html>. According to his senior aides, President George Bush struck a similar chord at the NATO Summit in Bucharest in April 2008.
7 'Transatlantic Trends 2011', a comprehensive survey prepared annually by the German Marshall Fund and several European partners, found that President Obama's overall approval remains high

(75 percent) in the 12 EU countries surveyed, despite a slight decline from 2010 (78 percent.) At the same time, the majority of EU respondents (54 percent) 'found it desirable that the United States exert strong leadership in world affairs', compared with 36 percent in 2007–8. See: <http://www.gmfus.org/publications_/TT/TT2011_final_web.pdf>.

8 See: <http://www.defense.gov/speeches/speech.aspx?speechid=1581>.

9 Speech to Carnegie Europe in Brussels, 5 October 2011.

10 Source: NATO figures as of September, 2011. See: <http://www.isaf.nato.int/images/stories/File/Placemats/9%20September%202011%20ISAF%20Placemat%281%29.pdf>.

11 See Russian Foreign Minister Lavrov's remarks to the Munich Security Conference in February 2011. See also: 'Military Chiefs Press Case for Integrated All-Europe Missile Defense', in *Voyenno-Promyshlennyy Kuryer* (online), June 1, 2011.

12 'NATO Rejects Russian Missile Defense Proposal', *Washington Times*, 8 June 2011, p. 10.

13 'NATO 2020: Assured Security; Dynamic Engagement. Analysis and Recommendations of the Group of Experts on a New Strategic Concept for NATO'. See: <http://www.nato.int/strategic-concept/expertsreport.pdf>.

14 'Strategic Concept for the Defense and Security of the Members of the North Atlantic Treaty Organization', approved 19 November 2010. See: <http://www.nato.int/cps/en/natolive/official_texts_68580.htm>.

15 One of his key conclusions reads: 'Nearly two decades after the end of the Cold War, most European armies are still geared towards all-out warfare on the inner-German border rather than keeping the peace in Chad, or supporting security and development in Afghanistan. European defense resources still pay for a total of 10,000 tanks, 2,500 combat aircraft, and nearly two million men and women in uniform – more than half a million more than the US hyper-power. Yet 70 percent of Europe's land forces are simply unable to operate outside national territory, and transport aircraft, communications, surveillance drones and helicopters (not to mention policemen and experts in civil administration) remain in chronic short supply. This failure to modernize means that much of the €200 billion that Europe spends on defense each year is simply wasted.' His assessment remains largely valid today.

16 To date, however, most ESDP military operations have not been accompanied by a significant EU civilian component, in part because such operations have been relatively short.

17 Unlike the ESS, NATO does not specify organized crime among its primary threats.

18 For a brief explanation of 'Berlin Plus' background and arrangements, see the NATO website: www.nato.int. A November 2009 fact sheet prepared by the Assembly of the Western European Union also describes Berlin Plus and notes that the actual text of the agreement has not been made public. See: <http://www.assembly-weu.org/en/documents/Fact%20sheets/14E_Fact_Sheet_Berlin_Plus.pdf?PHPSESSID=ad7ba3060e75d20eca30f2c9c9daaedd>.

19 Cyprus does not have a security agreement with NATO; therefore, it cannot receive NATO classified or unclassified documents.

20 De facto cooperation can take many forms. For example, through the Strategic Airlift Capability Initiative, ten Allies – including nine 'EU Allies' – plus Sweden and Finland operate three C-17 strategic air transporters. The collective approach saves on operating, maintenance and other costs and provides a capability that is available, under agreed provisions, to either organization. A similar approach has been discussed for helicopters.

21 A particularly innovative event took place in February 2010, when the Security and Defence Agenda organized a dozen think-tanks in a five-day online event ('Security Jam') sponsored by NATO and the European Commission. See: <http://www.securitydefenceagenda.org/SecurityJamSession/tabid/967/Default.aspx>.

22 It is noteworthy, in this context, that NATO's small headquarters in Sarajevo is collocated with the EU force headquarters. See: 'NATO and the European Union: Improving Practical Cooperation': Summary of a Transatlantic Workshop organized by the Institute for National Strategic Studies in partnership with the Ministry of Defence of Finland, Washington, DC, 20–21 March 2006.

23 For example, in a news conference (15 September 2010), Rasmussen stated: 'In concrete terms I have suggested that the European Union conclude an arrangement between Turkey and the European Union Defence Agency. I've also suggested that the European Union concludes the annual security agreement with Turkey. And finally I have suggested that the European Union involves non-EU contributors in decision-making when it comes to EU operations like the one in Bosnia. It would be equivalent to how we do it in NATO. We have 19 ISAF partners outside

NATO and we include them in decision-making. I think the European Union should do the same when it comes to EU operations, like the one in Bosnia. By the way, Turkey is the second largest contributor to the EU operation in Bosnia. And then of course, in exchange, all NATO allies should recognize that all EU members participate in such EU–NATO cooperation.'

24 Ashton's comments during a brief joint press conference with Rasmussen in May 2010 summed up her approach: '[T]here is a great strength and willingness across both organizations to try and find pragmatic ways of dealing with issues. I'm a political realist, so we deal with them within the political context in which we operate. But I think, too, the more that we're able to have the dialogue and to ensure that on the ground the best possible collaboration happens, in a practical way, then I think we will have fulfilled what our aspiration is, which is to make this relationship as strong as possible.' See: <http://www.nato.int/cps/en/natolive/opinions_63848.htm>.

25 For a fuller explanation of the International Community Planning Forum concept, see 'NATO and the EU: Achieving Unity of Effort in a Comprehensive Approach', Leo Michel, 21 September, 2010, accessible at: <http://www.equilibri.net/nuovo/sites/default/files/ICTF%20Atlantic%20 Council%20Sep%2010.pdf>.

26 In the 'Lisbon Summit Declaration', Allies agreed that under some circumstances, NATO support may be needed for other actors and organizations having the 'relevant expertise, mandate, and competence' for stabilization and reconstruction activities. The Allies agreed on the following approach: 'To improve NATO's contribution to a comprehensive approach and its ability to contribute, when required, to stabilization and reconstruction, we have agreed to form an appropriate but modest civilian capability to interface more effectively with other actors and conduct appropriate planning in crisis management.' See: <http://www.nato.int/cps/en/natolive/official_ texts_68828.htm>.

27 The text of the Framework Agreement, signed on 17 May 2011, by EU High Representative Catherine Asthon and US Secretary of State Hillary Clinton, is published in the *Official Journal of the European Union*, 31 May 2011.

28 AFRICOM and the EU are engaged in complementary efforts to support African peacekeepers in Somalia and train Somali security forces.

23

THE UN AND EUROPEAN STRATEGY

Richard Gowan

The relationship between the European Union (EU) and United Nations (UN) has been the topic of copious quantities of public relations material from the two organizations, such as a joint campaign proclaiming their 'partnership for a better world', and a reasonable amount of serious analysis.[1] Of the various strategic goals laid down in the 2003 *European Security Strategy*, the call for 'effective multilateralism' with the UN at its core has proved particularly resonant among academics and policy analysts. This is in part a matter of grand strategy. For the think-tankers of the EU Institute for Security Studies, 'making multilateral structures more effective and more legitimate is both a matter of principle and a question of interest for the EU' (de Vasconcelos, 2010: 4). For scholars attempting to measure the EU's global impact, the relationship with the UN is also appealingly quantifiable. The EU pays two-fifths of the UN's peacekeeping costs and covers even higher percentages of its humanitarian and development budgets, while European diplomats hold well over 1,000 coordination meetings in New York alone each year (Wouters, 2007: 4). In some quarters, the level of EU unity within forums such as the UN General Assembly, which has gradually improved since the end of the Cold War, has become a virtual fetish – although this number-crunching has been challenged by authors who note unity does not always convert into impact (see for example Kissack, 2007: Gowan and Brantner, 2008; and Smith, 2010).

For those specifically focused on European security cooperation, interactions between EU and UN peace operations at the field level have also generated large quantities of material to mine for insights. Two-thirds of the EU's civilian and military missions to date have been co-deployed with some sort of UN presence (Gowan, 2009: 117). In cases including the Democratic Republic of Congo (DRC) and Chad, the strategic purpose of the EU's interventions has been to reinforce or pave the way for a UN force. In Bosnia and Herzegovina and Kosovo, by contrast, EU police missions took on duties from the UN. To analyse how the EU performs on the ground it is thus often necessary to take the UN into account.

Although theoretical perspectives on the EU–UN relationship vary, a predictably persistent question is whether the EU demonstrates any distinctively 'European (multilateral) identity and interests' vis-à-vis the UN (Jørgensen, 2009: 1). From this perspective, cases where EU member states act within UN structures (such as the rapid dispatch of thousands of European troops to Lebanon in 2006 to secure a ceasefire between Israel and Hezbollah) matter less than those where the EU is an autonomous actor (such as the slower, smaller deployment of an EU-led force to help the UN in the DRC the same year).

This prioritizes institutional issues over strategic concerns: crisis management is evaluated according to its role in the EU's evolution rather than its actual contribution to security and the alleviation of suffering. The goal of this chapter is to offer an alternative framing device for analyzing EU–UN relations. It emphasizes the extent to which the UN actually implements a security agenda defined by the main European powers and European institutions. Members of the EU have taken a lead role in constructing and financing the UN's systems for dealing with fragile states, humanitarian disasters and the proliferation of weapons of mass destruction. They also play a decisive role in shaping the priorities of the Security Council. The next two sections of this chapter review Europe's role in the UN system, looking first at the Security Council and peacekeeping and then at humanitarian aid and peacebuilding.

The level of European political and financial investment across these fields raises the (deliberately provocative) question of whether we should treat the post-Cold War UN as a distinctively *European* security institution. If that is a stretch, it is less controversial to argue that one by-product of European powers' investment in the UN has been to create a political and operational framework for many of the EU's own security initiatives. The third substantive section of this chapter looks at ways in which EU military and civilian missions have slotted into this framework. The chapter concludes by shifting its focus to EU–UN interactions over nuclear proliferation, in which the UN also provides the basis for EU action.

Some immediate qualifications are necessary. Although European powers made instrumental use of the UN in the Balkans in the early 1990s, the UN has primarily been of service to the EU outside Europe since the end of the Bosnian war, with the exceptions of Cyprus and Kosovo. More specifically, it has mainly been of use in Africa and parts of the Middle East. As the next section of the chapter argues, this partially reflects European decision-making. But for those EU members without strong historical links or cultural exposure to African or Middle Eastern countries, the UN framework is of no great interest. The 2008 Russo-Georgian war – during which Russia blocked any action by the Security Council – underlined that the UN offered extremely little to those whose overriding security concern is a resurgent Moscow. In this context the EU's position vis-à-vis NATO obviously has primacy. But the UN *has* provided part of the framework for both NATO and EU efforts to stabilize Afghanistan through its mission there, and NATO officials have made strenuous efforts to improve their own ties to the UN.

In spite of these qualifications, situating the emergence of an EU security identity within the UN framework lets us see Europe's global security role in a new light. In some senses, it makes the EU's contribution look small: in purely quantitative terms the number of uniformed peacekeepers deployed under the EU's banner has never touched those under UN command, for example. As of late 2010, the UN had some 85,000 military personnel and 14,600 police in the field – the respective numbers for the EU were 4,000 and 1,600, including personnel involved in anti-piracy operations off Somalia.[2] These comparisons fail to capture important differences in the cost and quality of the forces involved, but the difference in scale remains striking. Yet if we view the UN's activities as – in part – a function of European security concerns, we may also re-evaluate Europe's contribution to global security more positively. Taken in isolation, many of the EU's crisis management efforts appear 'heavily reactive' and 'disjointed' (Rogers, 2011: 4). EU-flagged troops and vessels often scurry to and from trouble-spots to achieve limited goals. Yet if we grasp how some EU-flagged missions fit in with European initiatives launched through the UN system, they make more sense – and Europe's strategic role looks more substantial than before.

The Security Council and peacekeeping

Since the end of the Cold War, the UN system's contribution to international security has expanded exponentially. The simplest indicator of this process has been the transformation of the Security Council, often paralyzed or lethargic in the years of East–West confrontation, into a constantly active if inconsistently effective crisis-management body. The Council issued just under 600 resolutions between its foundation in 1945 and the conclusion of the Iran–Iraq War in 1988. Since then it has issued over 1,400. As David Malone has noted, elements of the Council's transformation have included a significant drop in the use of the veto by its five permanent members, a far greater willingness to mandate enforcement actions under Chapter VII of the UN Charter and a particular focus on addressing civil wars (Malone, 2010: 60, 63–6). Although the Council's credibility has rested on America's willingness to work through it – an issue brought into focus over Iraq – a close study of the forum's decision-making suggests that European security priorities have been central to its increased activity.

This is underlined by a recent analysis by the International Peace Institute (IPI) of the Council's turn to focus on civil wars (Cockayne, Mikulaschek and Perry, 2010). Covering the period 1989 to 2006, this identifies some 617 resolutions dealing with civil wars, but highlights that the Council's attention appears skewed to wars in Europe and Africa: 'roughly four in five resolutions on intrastate war adopted during that period address those two regions' (Cockayne, Mikulaschek and Perry, 2010: 21). This is partially but not wholly explained by the fact that there have been more internal conflicts to deal with in these two regions than elsewhere. But IPI's data show that Council has definitely had a selection bias in favor of European and African conflicts, engaging less frequently with civil wars in Asia and the Americas. The researchers suggest that this reflects the fact that European powers have leverage within the Council and can use this to prioritize conflicts in their neighborhood and former African colonies. The EU's members typically account for four members of the 15-seat Council, while France and Britain's permanent seats, vetoes and close coordination with the USA give them additional influence in New York. It is hardly surprising, therefore, that the Council has often followed a European-inspired security agenda.

In the early 1990s, this agenda centered on the Balkans. In the first phase of the Yugoslav wars, France proposed a military intervention under the auspices of the Western European Union (WEU). Deflected by American concerns over the implications for NATO, the French turned to the UN instead. European countries provided the core of the resulting UN Protection Force (UNPROFOR) in Croatia and Bosnia and Herzegovina, and Susan Woodward has argued that the Security Council was reduced to playing 'the handmaiden of European security' while Britain, France and Germany searched for a conclusion to the Bosnian war (Woodward, 2008: 407). UNPROFOR's multiple failures, culminating in the Srebrenica massacre, left many European soldiers deeply suspicious of the UN although the operation's flaws were also attributable to ineffectual European diplomacy. After this catastrophic experience, it appeared likely that European powers would not work through the UN again. Yet the relationship regained vitality from 1999 onwards, as the UN set up interim administrations in Kosovo and East Timor with European support and sent peacekeepers to stabilize a series of ex-colonies in Africa emerging from civil wars, including Burundi, Côte d'Ivoire, the DRC, Sierra Leone and Sudan. The number of UN peacekeepers grew incredibly fast from 1999 to 2007, moving from just over 10,000 military personnel to over 70,000 – in addition to police and civilians – before rising more slowly to the figures for 2010 noted above.

The resurgence of UN peacekeeping from 1999 onwards has multiple explanations. UN Secretary-General Kofi Annan played a significant role in overhauling the UN's operational systems, restoring trust in its ability to manage operations (although the number of new missions put the organization under strain). The readiness of African powers, especially South Africa and Nigeria, to invest in peacekeeping helped legitimize these operations. But the European powers played an instrumental role in advocating these missions in the Security Council while, as previously observed, two-fifths of the UN's rapidly expanding peacekeeping budget. However, this level of political and financial support was not matched by a consistent military contribution. In 2000, the UK deployed troops to help beleaguered UN peacekeepers in Sierra Leone. French units have operated alongside the UN in Côte d'Ivoire since 2004. Yet both permanent Security Council members avoided putting these forces under UN command, a legacy of their experiences in Bosnia. Some EU members, including Denmark, Ireland, the Netherlands and Sweden, did contribute to UN operations in Africa, but all avoided making open-ended commitments.

As we note later in this chapter, the European powers' desire to support UN operations in Africa without deploying large numbers of troops in blue helmets led them to deploy EU missions to work alongside the UN instead, giving the European Security and Defence Policy much of its momentum. Nonetheless, European investment in UN peacekeeping in Africa was mainly an exercise in *indirect* security-building. In a period in which even France, the last European power to maintain significant forces in Africa, was disengaging from ex-colonies, the UN framework offered an alternative way to stabilize the continent.

European powers have utilized the Council less consistently on non-African issues. In 1999, they were willing to bomb Serbia during the Kosovo crisis without a Security Council resolution, but pushed for a UN mission (including a European Commission pillar dealing with economic affairs) after the air campaign. In 2001, the Europeans advocated for a UN presence in post-Taliban Afghanistan. In the run-up to the Iraq War, the pro- and anti-invasion camps within the EU aired their differences in the Council in the false belief that the UN's blessing mattered to the Bush administration. Once the invasion was over, however, Europeans who had been for and against it concurred that they wanted the UN involved in post-conflict reconstruction. EU officials contacted the UN with an offer of gendarmerie for Iraq, but the bombing of the UN's Baghdad offices in August 2003 led it to cut back its mission (Power, 2008: 409).

The UN's importance to the European position in the Arab world would be emphasized by two further episodes: the 2006 Lebanon war and the 2011 Libyan crisis. In the first case, France took the lead in negotiating a ceasefire through the Security Council in tandem with the USA. While the French and other EU members – most notably Italy and Spain – recognized the need for a significant post-conflict peace operation in Lebanon, their initial preference was to send an EU-flagged or ad hoc multi-national force. The Lebanese government rejected this option, and the Europeans deployed under a UN banner instead (Novosseloff and Gowan, 2010). In the Libyan case – which is still ongoing at the time of writing – the main European powers were unable to agree a coherent political response to the civil war that broke out between Colonel Gaddafi and his opponents through either the North Atlantic Council or EU Council. Instead, after much Franco-British pressure and with belated American support, it fell to the Security Council to mandate the use of force to protect civilians in Libya from attacks by forces loyal to Gaddafi. Germany abstained on this resolution, and it is unlikely that those EU members that favored an intervention could have gathered a military coalition without the legitimacy offered by the UN: even after the Security Council mandated force it took NATO some days to agree to take on the mission.

In both the Lebanese and Libyan cases, therefore, the UN offered European powers a mechanism for initiating action at moments when there were diplomatic obstacles to doing so through NATO or the EU.

By contrast, the UN's role in Europe has been slight since the 1990s, with two exceptions. One has been Cyprus, where the UN has remained central to efforts to find a route towards reunification. Although most Europeans may not perceive this as a 'UN issue', it has proved a time-consuming business for successive Secretaries-General. The second, more widely recognized, exception is Kosovo. After taking over administration of the Serbian province in 1999, the UN embarked on a prolonged process of state-building with the – often very explicit – goal of one day handing responsibility to the EU. This project almost broke down in 2007 and 2008, when Serbia rejected a plan to give Kosovo supervised independence and Russia and China threatened to veto any proposals to this effect in the Security Council. After Kosovo unilaterally declared independence in February 2008, the UN and EU went through eight months of agonizing diplomacy to find a *modus vivendi*, complicated by a split within the EU over whether to recognize the self-proclaimed state. In October 2008, the Security Council adopted an interim solution permitting the EU to take over responsibility for most aspects of Kosovo's tutelage – most importantly oversight of policing and justice – while the UN maintains a token political presence.

In both broad terms and individual instances, therefore, it is possible to argue that the Security Council and UN peacekeeping continue to serve European interests – and that the UN has sometimes offered EU members a level of diplomatic flexibility that other organizations, including the EU itself, have not. Without European initiatives, the Security Council could well have been far less active in recent years, and UN peacekeeping would probably never have recovered from the disasters of the 1990s. The UN framework for crisis management consists of more than the Security Council and peacekeepers, however, and the EU's influence has arguably been as great in humanitarian affairs and peacebuilding.

Humanitarian aid and peacebuilding

The international humanitarian aid system, which is dominated by UN agencies and the Red Cross, has not only undergone huge growth since the Cold War but also prioritized war-torn countries. Between 1997 and 2005, the number of humanitarian aid workers worldwide jumped from just over 130,000 to more than 240,000 (Stoddard, Harmer and Haver, 2006: 8). Meanwhile, there was an observable increase in the percentage of humanitarian aid going to conflict-affected states. Lydia Poole calculates that by 2008, nearly three-quarters of all humanitarian by Western donors – including the USA, EU members and the European Commission – was directed towards territories in conflict (Poole, 2010). While these included Palestine, Iraq and Afghanistan, there was also an emphasis on countries where the UN had peacekeepers such as Sudan and the DRC. In the DRC, humanitarian spending rose from $52 million in 1999, when the UN peacekeeping operation to the country began, to $549 million in 2008. While humanitarian aid is ostensibly apolitical, it has clearly become a conflict management device.

Although the USA is the biggest single donor, a number of European states and the Commission have also been significant financiers of humanitarian aid – making combined contributions comparable to the American figure – and have taken the lead in driving reforms in the UN humanitarian system. Abby Stoddard observes that Britain in particular 'has emerged as an undisputed leader of humanitarian reform and champion of multilateral cooperation in the field' (Stoddard, 2010: 259). Other EU members with a major stake in the UN's humanitarian structures include the Netherlands, Nordic countries, Germany and Spain. The EU's humanitarian aid arm, ECHO, has also emerged as a key donor. A report by the European Court of Auditors noted that 'in 2008 ECHO committed a total of 937 million euros of which 404 million euros (43%) was channeled through UN organizations' (European Court of Auditors, 2009: 9). Although this was not all earmarked for conflict-affected states, European officials noted that the UN's ability to access insecure zones was a key argument for a close relationship. While the Court heavily criticized the UN's accountability systems and efficiency, ECHO has continued to be a staunch supporter of UN agencies. While calling for the EU to develop stronger humanitarian mechanisms, the Lisbon Treaty stipulates that its efforts should be 'coordinated and consistent' with those of the UN system.

If European support has been vitally important in shaping the UN's peacekeeping and humanitarian systems, the same is true in the field of post-conflict peacebuilding. Within the UN system, the importance of long-term peacebuilding strategies – involving the use of development aid to revitalize war-damaged economies, building up effective public administration and in many cases security sector reform – has become a commonplace. In 2006, the importance of these concepts was recognized through the creation of an inter-governmental UN Peacebuilding Commission (PBC), a corresponding Peacebuilding Support Office (PBSO) in the UN Secretariat and a new Peacebuilding Fund (PBF). Although these instruments got off to a difficult start due to the UN's internal politics, EU members played a significant role in their start-up phase. Sweden and Germany gave particular attention to the PBC, and 57 per cent of the $334 million committed to the PBF by 2010 came from European governments.[3] The bulk of the PBF's grants in this period went to projects run by UN agencies in African countries.

Most EU members' support for the UN's peacebuilding efforts continues to flow through direct grants to specific funds and agencies, however, and it is difficult to trace and quantify as a result. Catriona Gourlay has undertaken a detailed study of the European Commission's cooperation with the UN in this field, and notes a 2008 Commission report that calculated that it had contributed some €318 million to UN programming 'with direct links to peacebuilding' the previous year, of which two-fifths covered institution-building and nearly a third went on rule of law and human rights issues (Gourlay, 2009: 72). Another study shows that 'total [Commission] spending for peacebuilding increased dramatically from €86 million in 2001 to over €1 billion in 2007, totaling some €5.9 billion from 2001 to 2008' (Gourlay, 2009: 74). Of the total sum disbursed by the Commission in this period, €2.2 billion (37 per cent) was funneled through the UN. The Commission's peacebuilding priorities – including UN and non-UN programming – were the Palestinian Territories, Iraq, Afghanistan, Sudan and the DRC, replicating its humanitarian spending.

The level of Commission funding disbursed through the UN varies significantly by case (this paragraph follows Gourlay, 2009: 78–81). In Iraq the percentage was very high as the Commission and EU member states directed funds through the International Reconstruction Fund Facility for Iraq, which was administered by the World Bank and UN Development Programme (UNDP). By contrast, a large part of Commission aid to Sudan in the 2000s went via its African Peace Facility to support the African Union operation in Darfur, although it also partnered with UNDP on post-conflict reconciliation schemes. EU and UN relations have been most closely intertwined in the case of the DRC. Here, UNDP and the Commission jointly managed preparations for the countries first post-conflict national elections in 2006, and the Commission provided tens of millions of euros for UN-led projects to demobilize combatants and rebuild the justice sector. The EU and UN presences in the DRC expanded and gained in complexity as the 2000s progressed, sometimes creating frictions between them. The DRC also proved to be the primary laboratory for EU–UN cooperation in both military and civilian crisis management operations. We now turn to how EU missions fit in to the peacekeeping and peacebuilding framework supplied by the UN in DRC, and how this was replicated in 2008–9 in Chad and the Central African Republic.

An uneasy fit: EU and UN operations in Africa

In 2003, the UN peacekeeping mission in the DRC (MONUC) faced a major crisis in the northeastern region of Ituri, where it was unable to contain anti-government militias. Since its initial deployment in 1999, MONUC had gradually grown and attempted to restore order throughout the country's east, which had been the epicenter of the country's extremely bloody civil war in the later 1990s. The Ituri crisis, centered on the town of Bunia, threatened to undo the peacekeepers' progress and undermine the mission.

Kofi Annan turned to France for help. The French, looking for ways to revitalize European security cooperation in the wake of the Iraq debates, suggested that the EU mount a mission to assist MONUC. The result was Operation Artemis, which deployed to Bunia for three months and succeeded in quelling the militias. In spite of some hard fighting, the EU force sustained no fatalities, and MONUC went on to mount further anti-militia operations throughout the eastern DRC. Artemis was not quite the straightforward success for EU–UN cooperation it first appeared: coordination between the two organizations' personnel was minimal, and the EU mission's departure was arguably too abrupt. Equally, Artemis consisted almost entirely of French troops – with the important exception of a Swedish contingent that engaged in combat – and its EU identity was more significant politically than operationally. Nonetheless, many analysts saw this episode as a model for future EU–UN cooperation in Africa. While the UN took on long-term, large-scale peacekeeping, the EU could offer a high-end reserve capacity ready to swing into action in a crisis (see Ulriksen, Gourlay and Mace, 2004; Morsut, 2009).

This strategic vision was iterated in an EU–UN joint declaration on crisis management in 2003, and a more narrowly focused paper on military collaboration the following year. Although the latter flagged potential obstacles to future Artemis-type deployments, the operation was clearly the model for the EU's Battle Groups initiative, launched in early 2004 by Britain, France and Germany. The initial Battle Group proposal stipulated that these brigade-sized rapid reaction forces would be particularly useful in support of the UN in Africa. The Ituri crisis thus brought into focus the potential importance of the UN as the provider of a strategic framework in fragile states that the EU could plug into when necessary.

After Artemis, EU officials looked for further ways to slot EU elements into the UN framework in DRC. These extended beyond immediate peacekeeping to aspects of peacebuilding, as the EU deployed a police mission – initially sent to train a Congolese police unit to protect the government in Kinshasa – and a Security Sector Reform (SSR) Mission. The police mission, deployed in 2005 as EUPOL Kinshasa and later relaunched as EUPOL RD Congo with a new mandate to help stabilize the east of the country, did not fit into the UN framework easily, not least because its mandate overlapped with that of MONUC's own police component (Vircoulon, 2009: 228). Turf wars also emerged between the EU and UN over the direction of SSR after the launch of EUSEC RD Congo in 2005 – a situation exacerbated by the presence of numerous other players with influence over the ramshackle Congolese army, ranging from Angola to China. Nonetheless, the head of EUSEC RD Congo and MONUC's chief of staff collaborated on devising an SSR strategy with the Congolese army in 2007, and in 2008 the Security Council directed MONUC to ensure that it coordinated with both EUSEC and EUPOL (Clément, 2009: 251–2). Even if the EU's small civilian missions found it hard to fit in with the UN at the operational level, it should be clear that they have ultimately contributed to a common strategic project to stabilize the DRC.

This project was further advanced in 2006 when the EU responded to a request from the UN for military assistance during the DRC's national elections (which, as we have noted, also involved collaboration between UNDP and the European Commission). EUFOR RD Congo, which deployed to Kinshasa in the last quarter of the year, differed from Artemis in that it involved contingents from a wide range of EU members, with a German general as overall commander. The level of collaboration with MONUC was much better than 2003, although it was still complicated by the EU and UN's very different command and control arrangements (Major, 2008: 27–31). Intelligence and risk assessments were also sources of contention. But EUFOR and MONUC personnel managed to contain significant street violence in Kinshasa, and the EU mission's presence arguably deterred worse trouble during the polls. It was, however, criticized for leaving too soon – sticking rigidly to its schedule – and there were major riots once it had concluded. MONUC had to deal with these alone. Nonetheless, by the end of 2006, it was possible to argue that the EU's mix of financial, military and civilian support to the UN in the DRC represented both a unique level of inter-organizational integration and a real strategic success story.

This optimistic assessment requires some revisions in retrospect. The eastern DRC has remained disorderly, and the UN has struggled to manage the situation – a challenge exacerbated by the need to work with the Congolese army, which has an appalling record of military failures and human rights abuses. In late 2008, MONUC was again thrown into crisis when militia forces launched an offensive around the eastern Congolese town of Goma, driving over 200,000 civilians into flight. In spite of a surge of pressure within the EU for another Artemis-type operation, the EU Council did not meet a request from UN Secretary-General Ban Ki-moon for reinforcements. Although the EU had been happy to plug into the UN framework in the past, its support was very far from unconditional (Balossi-Restelli, 2011).

While the EU failed to intervene in the DRC in 2008, it did deploy a force (EUFOR Tchad/RCA) to Chad and the Central African Republic (CAR) in close cooperation with the UN in the same year. The EU's primary goals were to help secure UN-led humanitarian aid efforts in eastern Chad – where hundreds of thousands of refugees from Darfur were living in camps – and open the way for a UN mission, MINURCAT. MINURCAT was meant to deploy in two stages, getting police on the ground alongside EUFOR and then taking over military duties in 2009. In this case, therefore, the EU was attempting to both reinforce the UN's existing humanitarian framework in Chad – which was well established but endangered by widespread violence – and lay the groundwork for a longer-term UN peacekeeping framework. The European Commission pledged a sizeable package of funding to boost humanitarian aid and reconstruction efforts in EUFOR's area of operation, as well as €10 million to fund a Chadian police force to operate in the refugee camps in tandem with MINURCAT police officers (Helly, 2009a: 343). As in the DRC, EU–UN relations were testy: MINURCAT was very slow to get police on the ground and the UN struggled to identify sufficient non-European troop contributors to take over from EUFOR in 2009. A number of EU member states, including France, Ireland and Poland, agreed to 're-hat' their EUFOR contingents under UN command to fill the gap. Relations between MINURCAT and Chad's government deteriorated after the end of the EU mission, and MINURCAT was closed down at the end of 2010.

In spite of these problems, the EUFOR/MINURCAT combination has been credited with both successfully facilitating the supply of humanitarian aid in eastern Chad and contributing to a gradual increase in stability in the region. Damien Helly concludes that the EU and UN managed to 'agree to disagree' often enough to make the joint operation function, and useful lessons were learned for future cooperation (Helly, 2009a: 348). Although imperfect, the Chadian episode arguably underlines the extent to which the EU has adapted its strategic thinking to fitting in with UN frameworks in Africa. A further, operationally unusual, example of this trend has been EU's anti-piracy operation off Somalia (Atalanta) which is tasked with protecting humanitarian shipments by the World Food Programme. This is a small part of its mission – taking up less than 10 per cent of its efforts – but is an indicator of how cooperation with UN agencies is now a standard part of the EU's African operations (Helly, 2009b: 398).

Turning to EU–UN operational cooperation outside Africa, we find a more mixed picture. We have already noted the uneasy transition in Kosovo in 2008, during which mid-level EU and UN officials often sparred over the procedural aspects of the shift to the EU. In the case of Georgia, there was tentative cooperation between EU and UN observers in the aftermath of the 2008 war, but this came to halt when Russia insisted that the UN mission close down in 2009 (Fischer, 2009: 388). UNDP is also involved in the EU's Border Assistance Mission to Moldova as an 'implementing partner', although this is a technical rather than political relationship and there were only four UN staff working in the mission as of mid-2011.[4] While the European Commission and EU members are essential funders of UN humanitarian activities in the Palestinian Territories (and both the EU and UN are members of the Quartet dealing with Israeli–Palestinian diplomacy, along with the USA and Russia) accounts of the small EU missions deployed to the West Bank and Gaza do not emphasize their cooperation with the UN.

The model of the UN providing a framework for EU-flagged missions that we have laid out is, therefore, rooted in both organizations' commitments to Africa in the 2000s – although we have seen that European powers have found other ways to utilize the Security Council and UN peacekeeping in the Middle East. In recent years, a number of analysts have concluded that the EU is likely to avoid sending further sizeable military crisis management missions to sub-Saharan Africa in the years ahead in light of shifting financial and strategic priorities (Norheim-Martinsen, 2011: 27). It is possible that the foregoing narrative is of historical interest only, as the EU is likely to rely on the UN less in operations outside Africa. There is also growing evidence that financial constraints will place limits on the EU's financial support to the UN's humanitarian and development arms may shrink in the future for budgetary reasons (Vaïsse and Kundnani, 2011: 122 and 127).[5] But it would be unwise to rule out the possibility that future conflicts and humanitarian crises in Africa will compel the EU to re-engage on the continent. And even if it does not, the UN provides a strategic framework for the EU in at least one other field: the struggle to halt the proliferation of nuclear weapons.

The nuclear option: the UN and proliferation

This chapter has shown how European countries have helped build up the UN's peacekeeping, humanitarian and peacebuilding structures and then plugged EU operations into them. If we turn to the architecture for combating nuclear proliferation, a similar pattern emerges. Since 2003, when the EU agreed its first strategy on weapons of mass destruction (distinct from the *European Security Strategy*) its members have prioritized reinforcing the existing UN-centered system for dealing with proliferation, including the Non-Proliferation Treaty (NPT), International Atomic Energy Agency (IAEA) and the Security Council as the primary enforcement mechanism, in addition to the international mechanisms dealing with biological and chemical weapons. Sten Rynning has nicely dubbed the EU a 'force for multilateral conservation' in this field (Rynning, 2007: 272). The EU has prioritized funding for IAEA programmes aimed at securing nuclear materials in the former Soviet Union (Meier, 2008). But the main tests for the EU's strategy have been Iran's nuclear activities and the stagnation of diplomacy around the NPT. The 2005 NPT Review Conference even failed to agree an agenda. There were warnings that the Treaty – and with it much of the architecture for stopping the spread of nuclear weapons – was losing credibility.

France, Germany and the UK have led the EU's efforts to deal with Iran's nuclear ambitions – with EU High Representatives Javier Solana and Catherine Ashton also playing lead negotiating roles – but their goal has been to manage the problem through the UN system. This was a source of strain with the Bush administration while it was still in its most hawkish phase after the Iraq War, although Bush's team gradually moved closer to the European approach during his second term and the Obama administration committed itself to the UN route. Having taken up the file in 2003, the EU initially offered a series of incentives – even including assistance to Iran's tourism industry – to persuade Tehran to suspend its nuclear enrichment activities and work with the IAEA (Gowan, 2007: 57). As relations with Iran deteriorated, the EU proceeded to champion strengthening UN-based sanctions. When the USA and UN secured a Security Council resolution to this effect in May 2010, the EU followed up with an extremely stringent set of sanctions of its own that – coupled with a comparable set of American measures – appeared to throw Iran off balance (Vaïsse and Kundnani, 2011: 124). Although Iran appears to continue its proliferation activities, the EU can take some credit for both sustaining UN-based diplomacy in the period when the USA opposed it and for giving the UN's sanctions teeth.

Yet the EU's members are far from entirely united over nuclear issues, in part because of an inevitable split between the interests of France and Britain as nuclear powers and the Union's other 25 members. The EU's attachment to the NPT and UN-centric non-proliferation regime duly contains many ambiguities, not least concerning the NPT obligations on nuclear powers to disarm. While the EU's members agree that they would like to see the NPT strengthened – through, for example, greater use of intrusive inspections – they have also had to modify their ambitions to maintain a minimum of global consensus over the Treaty's future. At the 2010 NPT Review Conference, the EU had to 'accept compromise language on contentious issues including tactical nuclear weapons, intrusive IAEA inspections of nuclear sites and the cessation of the production of fissile materials' (Vaïsse and Kundnani, 2011: 125). The 2010 conference at least generated more agreement than that in 2005.

Some analysts have seen the EU's reliance on the existing non-proliferation system as reflecting a lack of sufficient strategic clarity to devise more innovative responses to shifting nuclear threats (Rynning, 2007: 283–4). While EU members have participated in both the Bush administration's non-UN-based Proliferation Security Initiative and the Obama administration's 2010 Nuclear Security Summit (a leaders' event similar in style to the G20 summits) they have not yet unveiled comparably creative non-proliferation initiatives of their own. But this fits in with the diagnosis of the EU's engagement with the UN system outlined above: European powers prioritize strengthening multilateral institutions and then launching EU initiatives within these frameworks, rather than attempting to set up rival frameworks.

Conclusion

The EU's attachment to the multilateral system can appear excessively defensive (Vaïsse and Kundnani, 2011: 114). In a period of rapid and fundamental global power shifts, emerging powers are increasingly challenging European powers' privileged place in the international system. China and India have, for example, both attempted to constrain European-backed human rights initiatives at the UN and insisted (with US support) on being given a greater share of voting rights in the international financial institutions (Gowan and Brantner, 2008; Vaïsse and Kundnani, 2011: 117). It is increasingly a commonplace that the EU's members should accept a diminution of their influence in the UN and wider international system if they wish that system to retain its credibility. But this chapter has tried to show why this is so hard: the EU's members have been among the most dedicated architects of global multilateral structures, to the extent that there is often a blurring of the line between EU and UN policies towards important security issues. This is not something that can be easily untangled, however powerful the dynamics in favor of change may appear.

The purpose of this chapter has not, however, been to make a case for or against maintaining the current relations between the EU and the UN. Its more modest goal has been to show how an analysis of the EU's contributions to international security must treat the UN not only as a useful partner but as both a tool of European policy and a strategic framework for the EU's own actions. Greater recognition of how European powers work *through* the UN may help us grasp how and why the EU works *with* the UN in managing specific crises, giving us a more comprehensive picture of Europe's global influence.

Acknowledgements

The author wishes to thank Emily O'Brien for her research support and Catriona Gourlay, Alexandra Novosseloff, Thierry Tardy and Ben Tortolani for many useful conversations on the EU–UN relationship.

Notes

1 For details of the EU–UN 'partnership for a better world', see <http://www.un-eu.org/>.
2 These figures are based on CIC, 2011: 120, 121, 149 and 151.
3 Figures are available at <http://www.unpbf.org/pledges.shtml>.
4 For a profile of the mission see <http://www.eubam.org/en/about/who_we_are>.
5 The author of this chapter researched and drafted the section on multilateral issues for Vaïsse and Kundnani, 2011, which is drawn on here and in the next section.

24

CSDP AND THE OSCE

Time for partnership to reach its full potential?

Oleksandr Pavlyuk

The EU and the Organization for Security and Co-operation in Europe (OSCE) are key multilateral players, whose contribution to security and stability in wider Europe is difficult to overestimate. Their relationship, which traces back to the origins of the 1975 Helsinki Final Act, has had a long history and has been a mixture of positive synergies and unfulfilled promises (Bailes, Haine and Lachowski, 2008).

OSCE–EU cooperation in conflict prevention and resolution and crisis management is a relatively new phenomenon that has largely evolved since 1999, when the European Security and Defense Policy (ESDP) was launched. Today, as conflict settlement and crisis management put an increased demand on international organizations, it is also coming on top of the OSCE–EU cooperation agenda. After the entry into force of the EU Lisbon Treaty and after the OSCE summit in Astana in December 2010, this is a proper political moment to look afresh at mutual experiences and cooperation to date and hopefully embark on a partnership that might bring new dynamics in dealing with conflict prevention and resolution and crisis management.

OSCE–EU cooperation: does it matter?

Since 1999, the OSCE and the EU have gone through notable transformations. Equally, the places occupied by the two organizations in European security have changed as well. Just several years ago, the role of the OSCE had been seriously contested. On the contrary, the EU was emerging as a powerful security actor, as its Common Foreign and Security Policy (CFSP) and ESDP had gradually evolved (Lynch, 2009). Yet both CFSP and ESDP have remained constrained by internal political divisions on some key foreign policy issues, while the Union's newly gained confidence has been seriously shaken by the ongoing financial troubles. The OSCE, in turn, has some new and long due momentum, with the launch of the Corfu process, re-engagement of participating states in an open-ended political dialogue on the future of European security, and the conduct of the first OSCE summit in 11 years. The Astana summit reconfirmed the full adherence of participating states to all OSCE norms,

---

The views expressed in this chapter are those of the author only, who writes in a personal capacity.

principles and commitments, and reaffirmed a vision of a free, democratic, common and indivisible Euro-Atlantic and Eurasian security community stretching from Vancouver to Vladivostok and rooted in agreed principles, shared commitments and common goals. The summit, however, could not agree on a specific Framework for Action that was meant to translate the common vision into concrete practical steps in fulfillment of the objective of a security community.

For the OSCE, the EU is arguably a most important multilateral partner. The two organizations share many objectives, such as maintaining security and stability on the continent, promoting economic development and environmental safety and protecting human rights and fundamental freedoms, while the values of democracy and rule of law enshrined in the 1990 *Charter of Paris for a New Europe* and other OSCE commitments are central to the EU acquis.

The 27-strong EU counts for almost half the 56 OSCE participating states. Within the OSCE the EU speaks with one voice. Together with candidate countries, the Stabilization and Association process countries and potential candidate countries, the European Free Trade Association countries and members of the European Economic Area, as well as with other countries that often align themselves with EU statements, the EU collective position reflects the opinion of up to 42 OSCE participating states. No other group of participating states within the OSCE can claim to be so representative.

Furthermore, EU members provide some three-quarters of the OSCE annual unified budget and over 55 per cent of all extra-budgetary contributions. Close to 70 per cent of OSCE seconded and half of contracted staff in the secretariat, institutions and field operations come from the EU member states. Until 2010, when the OSCE Chairmanship was taken over by Kazakhstan, the OSCE had been led by an EU member state for eight consecutive years. The OSCE Chairmanships in 2011 and 2012 are again EU members, Lithuania and Ireland respectively.

All this gives the EU significant political weight within the OSCE and makes the Union OSCE's indispensable partner. It also provides the EU with a big stake and leverage in contributing to shaping the OSCE's priorities and designing the organization's activities, although arguably the EU could be more active and efficient in pursuing its interests and agenda within the OSCE (Perrin de Brichambaut, 2009).

In sum, the EU has a special role to play within the OSCE as well as vis-à-vis the OSCE as a partner organization.

For the EU, the OSCE matters too and for several reasons. First, the OSCE is a unique platform for advancing CFSP and its goals. In fact, it is within the OSCE's predecessor – the Conference on Security and Co-operation in Europe (CSCE) – that the EU (in those days the European Communities) started to speak with one voice and gradually emerged as a security actor. The negotiations on the Helsinki Final Act and the post-Helsinki process provided the first major opportunity for EC members to coordinate their foreign policy efforts on security and security-related issues (Pijpers, 1990: 125–39). Later, the OSCE became one of the first venues where EU members practiced CFSP.

Second, while almost half of the OSCE participating states are now the EU member states, another half are not. The OSCE therefore remains the most inclusive security forum in its area. As such, it offers the EU a unique venue to engage multilaterally with the USA and Canada, Russia, non-EU European states, among them Norway, Turkey and Ukraine, as well as with states of the South Caucasus and Central Asia. Naturally, the OSCE cannot and will not substitute bilateral channels of communication between the EU and non-EU countries. Nevertheless, the OSCE serves as an important multilateral forum for regular dialogue on a wide range of political and security issues.

Furthermore, the OSCE Corfu process – a series of informal ambassadorial-level meetings in Vienna to discuss the future of European security that were run in the second half of 2009 and throughout 2010 – has reinvigorated the organization's role, which had declined in previous years, as a forum for substantive political dialogue. Through such a dialogue within the OSCE, the EU can strengthen its strategic partnership with Russia and enjoy a greater and more systematic engagement with its Eastern Partners, as well as with countries in Central Asia.

Third, the OSCE has developed, and is a repository for, a wide range of political commitments across three security dimensions – the politico-military, economic and environmental, and human – starting from basic principles guiding relations among states in its area to confidence-building and arms control measures, to human rights, democracy, rule of law and freedom of media. The European Commission regularly requests OSCE contributions when it comes to preparing annual progress reports on the candidate countries and potential candidate countries. Adherence to OSCE values and standards and implementation of OSCE commitments, which have been voluntarily subscribed to by all participating states, are seen as important benchmarks for the Union's bilateral relations with its non–EU neighbors. In some cases, the OSCE standards, e.g. in election observation, are widely recognized as a model. The implementation of OSCE commitments helps to enhance security in the region, which cannot but benefit the EU.

Fourth, the OSCE is also an operational player. It has limited resources, but it is flexible and, in some cases, the only acceptable multilateral actor on the ground. Since the early 1990s, the CSCE/OSCE has become a vehicle for supporting post-communist transition, thereby also facilitating the process of EU accession and enlargement. Through the work of its current 16 field operations, 3 institutions (Office for Democratic Institutions and Human Rights/ODIHR, High Commissioner on National Minorities/HCNM, and Representative on the Freedom of Media) and Vienna-based secretariat, the OSCE assists participating states in implementing their commitments. Democratic institution-building and promotion of the rule of law and good governance have been at the heart of the OSCE's engagement with the post-communist countries, which is very much in line with the EU's policy goals and approaches towards these states. When the OSCE deployed its field operations throughout Southeastern and Eastern Europe, the South Caucasus and Central Asia, in some places those were the first and for a while the only international presences on the ground. In Central Asia, the OSCE remains until today the main vehicle for multilateral international engagement.

Such mutual complementarity, if not dependence, makes it only natural that the OSCE and the EU should coordinate and work closely together to advance their common causes.

Evolution of a general framework for cooperation

Interaction between the then CSCE and the European Communities goes back to the Helsinki process, when the European Commission participated in the preparatory negotiations of the 1975 Helsinki Final Act, with the latter also being signed by the Italian prime minister in his capacity as President of the Council of the European Communities. In 1990 and 1999 respectively, presidents of the European Commission signed two other basic OSCE documents: the *Charter of Paris for a New Europe* and the *Charter for European Security*.

More practical contacts between the CSCE/OSCE and other organizations and institutions, including the European Community, started to develop in the early 1990s. With the end of the Cold War, the CSCE functions expanded from being a forum for political and security dialogue to providing practical assistance to the post-communist states in their democratic transitions, as well as to preventing and resolving conflicts that erupted in Southeastern and Eastern Europe and in the South Caucasus. By the mid-1990s, the CSCE transformed from a conference into a regional security organization – OSCE – with its permanent structures and operational capabilities. Furthermore, this was the time when the wider Europe saw the emergence of a whole series of new regional and sub-regional groupings, each of them looking for its role and place in post-Cold War Europe, while the traditional European institutions – the EU, NATO and the Council of Europe – proved their value to members and were highly attractive to most non-members in the region.

How these various regional actors should interact was a dilemma of both conceptual and practical significance. Should there be one leading organization, a sort of European United Nations, to take the main responsibility for ensuring security and stability on the continent? And if so, could the CSCE/OSCE, being the most inclusive and comprehensive organization in the area and recognized in 1993 by the UN as a Chapter VIII regional arrangement, serve this function? Or should there be rather a horizontal interaction of equals, and in this case what would the principles and modalities of such an interaction be?

The answers were given by the OSCE summit in Istanbul in 1999 when heads of state and government adopted the *Platform for Cooperative Security* as an operational document of the *Charter for European Security*.

The idea of the Platform was put forward by the EU in 1994, in response to a series of Russian proposals on 'enhancing the effectiveness of the CSCE'. Inter alia, the Russian proposals anticipated 'a genuine division of labour' between regional organizations and the 'overriding responsibility' of the CSCE for ensuring security and stability on the continent. In contrast, the EU advocated a concept of 'mutually reinforcing organizations' and a 'cooperative relationship' among them. Organizations 'concerned with the promotion of comprehensive security within the OSCE area' were meant to complement each other in order to avoid duplication of efforts and wasting resources (Pavlyuk, 2009).

As far as the OSCE–EU relationship was concerned, the adoption of the Platform prompted the establishment and development of a broad cooperation framework aimed at the regular exchange of views and information, in line with the cooperation modalities outlined in the Platform. In 2002, a practice was established of holding two OSCE–EU Ministerial and two Ambassadorial meetings per year (under each EU Presidency), and in 2003 these were supplemented with the annual staff-level meeting. The OSCE Secretary General is invited twice a year to brief the EU Political and Security Committee, while various EU representatives address regularly the OSCE Permanent Council in Vienna. Within the OSCE, the EU member states hold a weekly coordination meeting to agree on joint statements.

Such close interaction between headquarters has been further reinforced by consultations and practical cooperation in the field, in particular in those countries that host OSCE field presences and where the EC/EU has established its delegations.

These modalities as well as guiding principles and specific areas of the EU–OSCE cooperation were codified in the Council *Conclusions on EU–OSCE Cooperation in Conflict Prevention, Crisis Management and Post-Conflict Rehabilitation*, adopted on 10 November 2003. Despite their title, the Conclusions addressed broader aspects of the EU–OSCE cooperation. Inter alia, the document recognized the role of the OSCE as 'a valuable instrument for the promotion of peace and comprehensive security in the area from Vancouver to Vladivostok' and as 'an important partner for the EU', and affirmed the EU's determination to continue enhancing its relationship with the OSCE.[1]

In December 2003, the two organizations approved their respective security strategies: the *OSCE Strategy to Address Threats to Security and Stability in the Twenty-First Century*, and the EU's *A Secure Europe in a Better World*. Both displayed similarities in understanding contemporary security threats and challenges and in placing emphasis on cooperation. The OSCE participating states further upheld and developed the provisions of the 1999 Platform and pledged the OSCE to expand its relations with all organizations and institutions that are concerned with the promotion of comprehensive security within the OSCE area.[2] The EU members in the ESS underscored the role of effective multilateralism and recognized a 'particular significance' for the EU of the strength and effectiveness of the OSCE.

Overall, 2003 and 2004 were important years for the OSCE–EU relationship. On 1 May 2004, the EU completed the largest enlargement in its history, when ten new members, the majority being the post-communist states, joined the Union. In parallel, the EU adopted its European Neighbourhood Policy (ENP), covering inter alia the OSCE participating states in Eastern Europe and the South Caucasus. This EU embrace of more OSCE participating states, accompanied also by NATO enlargement, raised some fears as to the erosion of the OSCE's political role and functions (Ghebali, 2005: 18).

This was a particular concern as the OSCE itself entered a difficult period. Due to disagreements among participating states, the organization failed to secure a traditional political declaration at the end-of-year Ministerial Council meetings in Maastricht (2003) and Sophia (2004), which has ushered an unfortunate precedent for a number of years to come. As the EU was on the rise, the OSCE spiraled down into a limbo, when the very relevance of the organization was seriously questioned.

Moreover, democratic transitions came to a halt in some OSCE participating states, while peaceful democratic revolutions in Georgia and Ukraine provoked strong criticism of the OSCE's role in election observation. In both cases (parliamentary elections in Georgia in November 2003, and presidential elections in Ukraine in December 2004), the OSCE/ ODIHR-led international election observation missions concluded that the elections held did not meet a considerable number of OSCE commitments. On 3 July 2004, the informal summit of the Commonwealth of Independent States (CIS) in Moscow issued a *Declaration Regarding the State of Affairs in the OSCE*, and on 15 September 2004 eight CIS countries launched the *Astana Appeal to the OSCE*, both heavily criticizing the OSCE for 'misbalance' in its activities and 'double standards'.

Under such circumstances, the EU position on the OSCE became of special significance. On 14 June 2004, the Council of the European Union adopted conclusions on the *Role of the EU within the OSCE* that stated that 'the OSCE is a valuable instrument for the promotion of security and co-operation' and underlined the EU's interest in enhancing its partnership with the OSCE 'in a comprehensive way'.[3] On 10 December 2004, the Council of the European Union endorsed the *Assessment Report on the EU's Role vis-à-vis the OSCE*. This 27–page report remains the most comprehensive EU document on the OSCE to date. In it, the EU defined its long-term objective as preserving the integral implementation of OSCE values and standards in the Euro-Atlantic area and developed suggestions on strengthening the relationship between the EU and the OSCE, as well as on reinforcing the EU performance in the OSCE.[4]

In the first half of 2006, the EU Austrian Presidency initiated the adoption of a joint declaration on cooperation between the EU and the OSCE, aimed at codifying the existing framework of interaction between the two organizations and at providing impetus to enhanced cooperation. The proposal was welcomed by the OSCE Belgian Chairmanship, but failed to reach consensus among the OSCE participating states. The OSCE–EU relationship has thus remained non-formalized, but nevertheless intensive.

Indeed, as the EU expanded geographically and functionally and engaged deeper with countries and regions where the OSCE had traditionally been in the lead, the increased overlap in membership and areas of responsibility called for closer cooperation and coordination between the two organizations. The adoption of EU policy documents such as the ENP, the Black Sea Synergy (2007), and the Strategy for a New Partnership with Central Asia (2007), as well as the appointment of EU Special Representatives (for Moldova, the South Caucasus, and Central Asia, but also in Bosnia and Herzegovina, the Former Yugoslav Republic of Macedonia, and Kosovo), have not only enlarged the EU's outreach, but also significantly expanded the boundaries and scope for the EU–OSCE cooperation. These EU strategies contained specific references to the OSCE and its values, standards and commitments, while the Strategy for Central Asia stated the EU's intention to seek strengthening cooperation with the OSCE in the region.

In 2009, the OSCE was formally invited for the first time to join on a permanent basis the EU strategic policy initiative – the Eastern Partnership, in particular its multilateral Platform 1 on Democracy, Good Governance and Stability, which was a sign testifying to enhanced EU–OSCE cooperation, as well as recognition by the EU of the OSCE contribution to strengthening democracy, good governance and stability in Eastern Europe and the South Caucasus.

Since 1999, the OSCE and the EU have, therefore, developed a solid political foundation and an extensive framework for regular consultations and exchange of information, although there has hardly been a strategic approach to ensure that efforts are indeed mutually reinforcing.

Cooperation in conflict settlement and crisis management

With armed conflicts breaking out across the area in the early 1990s, their resolution became one of the CSCE/OSCE's primary tasks. CSEC/OSCE was the first body to be called upon for help in crisis situations. This was particularly the case when dealing with conflicts on the territory of the former Soviet Union, where other European organizations were unwilling and unprepared to engage, or even unwelcomed by some parties concerned.

Still a Conference, virtually unprepared operationally and organizationally to deal with conflict settlement, the CSCE, to its credit, put in place rather quickly relevant capacities and structures and deployed a number of field operations with an explicit conflict prevention and/or settlement mandate, such as the CSCE/OSCE Spillover Monitor Mission to Skopje in November 1992, the CSCE/OSCE Mission to Georgia in December 1992, and the CSCE/OSCE Mission to Moldova in February 1993.[5]

Throughout the 1990s, CSCE/OSCE developed a variety of specialized conflict prevention and resolution tools (including special and personal representatives of the Chairperson-in-Office, field operations, HCNM, and the Vienna-based Conflict Prevention Centre, etc.), mechanisms and procedures (Ackerman, 2009). Partly by design and to some extent by default, CSCE/OSCE had to take the lead in dealing with conflicts in the former Soviet Union, including providing political frameworks for negotiations on the peaceful settlement of the Transniestrian, Georgian–Ossetian, and Nagorno-Karabakh conflicts.

It was not by accident that in the 1999 *Charter for European Security* participating states defined the OSCE 'as a primary organization for the peaceful settlement of disputes within its region and as a key instrument for early warning, conflict prevention, crisis management and post-conflict rehabilitation'.[6]

Interaction between the CSCE/OSCE and the EC/EU on conflict prevention and crisis management emerged already in the early 1990s. For example, the decision to establish a

CSCE Monitoring Mission in the Former Yugoslav Republic of Macedonia was taken in mid-1992 in the context of the efforts to extend the European Community Monitoring Mission (ECMM) to neighboring countries of the Federal Republic of Yugoslavia to help avoid the spread of tension to their territories. Since 1995, the OSCE and the EU coordinated closely in implementing the Ohrid General Framework Agreement for Peace in Bosnia and Herzegovina. Until the end of the 1990s, the EU was mainly absorbed with bringing stability to the Western Balkans, while the countries of the former Soviet Union remained beyond its sphere of immediate interest.

As is the case with interaction among international organizations in general, 1999 opened a new page in the OSCE–EU cooperation in conflict prevention and crisis management. The ground was laid as the EU began to develop its civilian and crisis management capabilities with the establishment of the ESDP.

The OSCE 1999 *Platform for Cooperative Security* anticipated cooperation among international organizations and institutions in responding to specific crises. Relevant organizations and institutions were encouraged to 'keep each other informed of what actions they are undertaking or plan to undertake to deal with a particular situation'. The OSCE was offered, as appropriate, 'to serve as a flexible framework for cooperation of the various mutually reinforcing efforts' in responding to specific crises.

Consequently, and as an example, in 2001 the OSCE and the EU successfully coordinated their respective activities in preventive action during the political crisis in the Former Yugoslav Republic of Macedonia, including constant information sharing, regular meetings and the establishment (together with NATO) of a joint operations room. International effort to contain inter-ethnic conflict resulted in a rare memorandum of understanding signed in 2002 between the OSCE and the European Commission, regarding cooperation between the two organizations on the implementation of the Framework agreement related to police development.

The November 2003 *Conclusions of the Council of the European Union on EU–OSCE Co-operation in Conflict Prevention, Crisis Management and Post-Conflict Rehabilitation* further suggested that the enhanced cooperation between the OSCE and the EU should include 'exchange of information and analysis, cooperation on fact finding missions, coordination of diplomatic activity and statements, including consultations between special representatives, training and in-field coordination', and went as far as offering 'possible contribution by the EU to the OSCE's operational efforts in crisis management' and the possibility of 'EU crisis management operations following a request from the OSCE'.[7]

With the adoption of its 2003 *European Security Strategy*, which set the task 'to promote a ring of well governed countries to the east of the European Union', and the strengthening of the latter's civilian and crisis management capabilities as the ESDP continued to develop, the EU has extended its geographic vision and has started to display interest and involvement in conflict settlement in Eastern Europe and the South Caucasus, where the OSCE had traditionally been the main player. This shift was probably partly caused by the OSCE's internal weakness and lack of progress in resolving any of the protracted conflicts, but largely came as a result of the EU's 'big bang' enlargement in May 2004 when the protracted conflicts moved closer to the EU borders.

Subsequently, the EU launched a number of policy initiatives in its 'immediate neighborhood' and beyond. In 2004, the EU member states agreed that the ENP 'should reinforce the EU's contribution to promoting the settlement of regional conflicts',[8] and the EU's 2007 Black Sea Synergy explicitly advocated 'a more active EU role through increased political involvement in ongoing efforts to address the conflicts (Transniestria, Abkhazia, South Ossetia and Nagorno-Karabakh)'.[9]

In line with this policy approach, unresolved conflicts in the South Caucasus and Moldova became the first testing ground for the EU's growing readiness to involve itself in conflict prevention and resolution in its Eastern neighborhood. In October 2005, the EU joined as an observer in the so-called '5+2' negotiation format for the settlement of the Transniestrian conflict where the OSCE is one of the three mediators (together with Russia and Ukraine), and a month later the EU established its Border Assistance Mission in the Republic of Moldova and Ukraine (EUBAM). The mandates of several EU Special Representatives, in particular for the South Caucasus (2003) and Moldova (2007), included a contribution to the resolution of conflicts.

Gradually conflict settlement and crisis management has evolved into a key area for the OSCE–EU cooperation. Protracted conflicts and mutual efforts to address them now comprise a regular item on the agendas of OSCE–EU political and staff-level consultations.

Of 23 ESDP missions and operations deployed to date, 9 were established in the OSCE area, with 5 that continue to operate: the EU Police Mission in Bosnia and Herzegovina/ EUPM (since 2003), EUFOR Althea, also in Bosnia and Herzegovina (2004), EUBAM, the EU Rule of Law Mission in Kosovo/EULEX (2008), and the EU Monitoring Mission in Georgia/EUMM (2008). All of them have developed a degree of cooperation and information-sharing with the OSCE on the ground.[10]

A further remarkable development took place in 2008. The EU effectively took the political lead in brokering the cease-fire agreement between Russia and Georgia, two OSCE participating states and non-EU members. Following the August 2008 war, the 300-strong EUMM was deployed on 1 October 2008 to monitor the implementation of the peace agreements of 12 August and 8 September and to contribute to the stabilization and normalization of the areas affected by the war. Until the end of 2008, the EUMM operated side by side with the OSCE military monitors. Yet the participating states failed to agree on the renewal of the mandate of the OSCE Mission to Georgia and the latter was discontinued in December 2008, once more revealing the difficulty of dealing with conflicts in the former Soviet Union, compared even to the Balkans, where in the same year the OSCE was able to maintain its status-neutral mission in Kosovo. The EUMM has thus remained the only international monitoring presence on the ground that operates along the administrative boundary lines. The EU also appointed its Special Representative for the Crisis in Georgia, who along with counterparts from the OSCE and the UN acts as a Co-Chair of the Geneva Discussions on security and stability in Georgia.

In the spring and summer of 2010, the OSCE coordinated closely with the EU (as well as with the UN) in the effort to reduce tension and stabilize the situation during the violent events in Kyrgyzstan. The contacts that had been built between the two organizations in previous years benefitted their coordinated action, by allowing a quick, smooth opening of the necessary channels of communication at all levels. In practical terms, the OSCE and EU special envoys on the situation in Kyrgyzstan, together with their UN counterpart, were issuing joint statements and delivering coordinated messages to the Kyrgyz authorities. In Bishkek, the weekly coordination meetings were held at the OSCE premises. The resulting regular information exchange proved very helpful for planning relevant activities of the concerned organizations and avoiding overlap and contradiction. Within the OSCE, the EU actively supported the decision on the launch of the OSCE Community Security Initiative in Kyrgyzstan. All in all, the OSCE–EU interaction in responding to the crisis in Kyrgyzstan was a rather promising experience of close coordination and synergy.

The crises in Georgia and Kyrgyzstan have highlighted three points. The first is that violent conflicts in the OSCE area – both inter-state and intra-state – that many hoped had been consigned to the past, are actually a fact of our present. Second, both crises have demonstrated the weakness, if not helplessness, of the international community, including the OSCE and the EU, in preventing the emerging crisis situations. Third, they have marked the emergence of a new reality – a more proactive stance of the EU on conflict settlement and crisis management in the regions where until recently the OSCE had borne the main responsibility.

Conclusion

As unresolved conflicts continue to pose a serious threat to security and stability and as new crisis situations occasionally flare up in the OSCE area, conflict prevention and crisis management are certain to remain among the key tasks of the OSCE and the EU. This will increasingly require the strengthening of their individual capacities and effectiveness, as well as enhanced OSCE–EU cooperation and coordination in resolving the protracted conflicts and in responding to possible new crisis situations.

So far, the two-decade-long efforts by the OSCE to resolve protracted conflicts in its area have not produced a single final settlement, but neither for that matter have those of any other international organization. Yet the OSCE remains a key multilateral instrument for early warning, conflict prevention and resolution, crisis management and post-conflict rehabilitation in its area of responsibility. It is no longer the only, but remains an important and in some cases the main player. The OSCE continues to provide a political framework for the settlement of the Transniestrian and Nagorno-Karabakh conflicts, it co-chairs the Geneva discussions, and it maintains a unique presence and lead in the countries of Central Asia, where potential for instability is high and might further increase after the withdrawal of NATO troops from Afghanistan. Moreover, under the 2010 Kazakh Chairmanship the OSCE's focus naturally shifted to the region of Central Asia. In essence, despite all the existing problems, the OSCE remains a main multilateral instrument for conflict settlement and crisis management in the former Soviet Union.

Prompted by the recent experiences, conflict prevention and resolution and crisis management are back on the top of the OSCE political agenda. Within the framework of the Corfu process, participating states identified issues related to early warning, conflict prevention and resolution, crisis management and post-conflict rehabilitation as core priorities for the organization. The need was widely acknowledged for the OSCE to make full use of the instruments, mechanisms and procedures at the organization's disposal, but also to improve its analytical and operational capabilities, and to strengthen its effectiveness in dealing with all phases of the conflict cycle.

The issue of moving from early warning to early action to ensure a prompt and effective response was the focus of particular attention. Yet while agreeing on the need to strengthen the organization's effectiveness, participating states have expressed different, sometimes conflicting views on how to achieve that. The problem is how to combine the operational needs and the organization's consensus-based working methods. While some states favored strengthening the role of the Chairmanship to empower it to act more quickly in crisis situations, others strongly insisted on the need to preserve the consensus-based decision-making process and the importance of the consent of the parties concerned, and suggested instead developing uniform principles for conflict prevention and crisis management. These discussions have continued under the 2011 Lithuanian Chairmanship within the framework of the so called 'V to V' dialogue and their outcome remains unclear at the time of this writing.

Oleksandr Pavlyuk

Within this debate, the EU countries in particular called upon the OSCE to be a first responder in crisis situations and an initiator of international cooperation in the field of conflict prevention, crisis management and post-conflict rehabilitation. This is a role that was broadly envisaged for the OSCE in the 1999 *Platform for Co-operative Security* – a role that the organization has not been pro-active and persistent enough in carrying out.

The latter call by the EU within the OSCE is an encouraging sign, as the effectiveness of future international efforts in conflict prevention and crisis management in the OSCE area is likely to depend a lot on EU willingness to support the OSCE and the latter's role in this field, as well as on EU interest and ability to further enhance its own engagement and contribution. The OSCE will be able to provide better values for the EU only if the EU keeps its political commitment to strengthen the OSCE and effectively work with it.

The EU has traditionally played a key role in conflict prevention and crisis management in the Balkans and in recent years has gradually emerged as an important contributor to conflict settlement and crisis management in the South Caucasus and in Moldova. The EU's increased involvement has been largely welcomed by the parties in conflict and by the OSCE.

The implementation of the Lisbon Treaty and strengthening of the EU's common institutional framework in the area of CFSP (including the introduction of the post of the High Representative for Foreign Affairs and Security Policy, assisted by the European External Action Service) are expected to increase the Union's effectiveness in the field of conflict prevention and crisis management, as well as to enhance the EU's capability to interact with its partners, including the OSCE. These are promising developments.

At the same time as EU enlargement has taken a break and does not seem to be on the cards for the Union's 'Eastern partners', it is an open question how successful the EU might be in dealing with conflict prevention and crisis management in its Eastern 'neighborhood' without its most powerful leverage, the prospect of accession. Neither the EU's Eastern Partnership initiative nor bilateral agreements in the making on political association and on a deep and comprehensive free trade area are likely to replace the magnetism of the membership option. Furthermore, the current financial and economic crisis is likely to put tough constraints on the EU budgets, including possibly in the conduct of crisis management operations.

Part of a solution lies in ever closer OSCE–EU cooperation and coordination in conflict prevention and crisis management. This should be not only the emerging trend, but a priority for both organizations for the future. The recent experiences in Georgia and Kyrgyzstan have proved that neither the EU nor the OSCE (nor any other organization) can succeed by acting alone, and that results can be achieved better and faster when the OSCE and the EU work together. Furthermore, the OSCE and EU approaches to conflict settlement and crisis management are based on largely overlapping strategies and a comprehensive approach aimed at fostering confidence-building, promoting economic development and encouraging rule of law, good governance and democratic institution-building.

In this regard, it is time for the EU-sponsored concept of 'mutually reinforcing' organizations, enshrined in the OSCE 1999 *Platform for Co-operative Security*, to get a new breath of life and be translated from a principle into an operational tool. In case of the OSCE–EU relationship, with inter-institutional mechanisms of consultations and cooperation well in place and functioning, including regular political dialogue and working-level contacts, and with cooperation experience accumulated in recent years, it is expedient to give some further thought to how the existing framework for cooperation could serve better the purpose of enhanced practical coordination in conflict prevention and resolution, including in the final settlement of the protracted conflicts, and in actual crisis situations. It is often on the eve of and during

290

crises that organizations tend to be less successful in coordinating their efforts. The reality is often too complex and rapidly evolving to leave much time for consultations, especially since it often takes time to shape collective responses within organizations themselves, given the diversity of views and interests of member states.

At the operational level, further practical arrangements could be considered for improving inter-operability on the ground, especially in response to specific crisis situations. At the political level, both the OSCE and the EU should display stronger commitment to making better use of the existing regular cooperation mechanisms for policy coordination, and a stronger will to coordinate approaches and actions in response to crisis situations and in search of the final settlement of the protracted conflicts, by drawing on the respective strengths of the OSCE and the EU. Better synergy between the OSCE and the EU, based on the former's inclusiveness and resulting legitimacy and on the latter's political clout, economic and trade opportunities on offer and financial resources at its disposal, could produce a powerful and attractive instrument in conflict prevention and resolution and crisis management in the OSCE area.

Such an approach will, no doubt, require a degree of trust and commonality of interests and values among OSCE participating states. This is an ambitious goal behind the Astana summit vision of a security community in the Euro–Atlantic and Eurasian region. Whether this vision becomes a reality remains to be seen.

Notes

1 Council of the EU (2003).
2 OSCE (2003: 9–10, paras 52–7).
3 Council of the EU (2004a: 28).
4 Council of the EU (2004c).
5 See OSCE (2009).
6 OSCE (1999: 3, para. 7).
7 See Council of the EU (2003).
8 See European Neighbourhood Policy (2004: 6).
9 European Commission (2007b: 4).
10 For more on the relationship between EULEX and the OSCE Mission in Kosovo, see Czaplinski (2009).

25

THE AFRICAN UNION

A partner for security

Malte Brosig

For decades the African continent has been a conflict-ridden region in which African organizations did relatively little to settle conflicts and sanction war crimes, crimes against humanity and genocide effectively. Indeed it has been argued that membership in the Organization of African Unity (OAU) was primarily a means to ensure international legitimacy by often domestically challenged African leaders (Herbst, 2007). The OAU as an organization with a relatively low degree of institutionalization and weak secretariat could not throughout its existence from 1963 to 2002 develop a meaningful security strategy capable of solving African conflicts. The OAU's coming into being was shaped by ideas of pan-Africanism, anti-colonialism and the attempt to consolidate national borders, often disputed as a result of arbitrary border-drawing during colonialism. Consequently non-intervention in domestic affairs became a core principle of the OAU in a move to prevent external intrusion in young and often politically unstable African states. This, however, led to the often criticized culture of impunity in which domestic human rights violations and ethnic conflicts were not perceived as international issues of urgency. Notorious dictators such as Idi Amin were not punished or sanctioned by the OAU. Only in a small number of cases (Congo, Nigeria, Chad and Sudan) was the OAU engaged in conflict prevention and peace negotiations (Walraven, 2010: 45–7).

It was only in the 1990s that African organizations made a more serious effort in engaging proactively in conflict areas and developing peacekeeping capabilities. In 1993 the OAU developed a Mechanism for Conflict Prevention, Management and Resolution and in 1996 the Southern African Development Community (SADC) approved the Organ on Politics, Defense and Security Co-operation. In 1999, the Economic Community of West African States (ECOWAS) signed the Mechanism for Conflict Prevention, Management, Resolution, Peacekeeping and Security. The impulse for these developments came primarily from ECOWAS, which under the leadership of Nigeria started a number of peacekeeping operations from 1990 in Liberia, Sierra Leone, Côte d'Ivoire and Guinea-Bissau. Indeed, today ECOWAS is still the African organization with the most experience in peacekeeping operations. It provided a leading example for the AU.

The evolving African peace and security architecture

The 1999 summit of the OAU assembly in Sirte, Libya, initialized the transformation of the OAU into the AU and the emergence of the so called African Peace and Security Architecture (APSA). The Constitutive Act (2000) of the AU marks a remarkable step forward in overcoming the OAU's incapability as a serious security actor. The Constitutive Act provides for progressive tools of intervention in cases of severe human rights violations or unconstitutional changes in government (Art. 4p and Art. 30). Article 4h puts forward 'the right of the Union to intervene in a Member State … in respect of grave circumstances, namely: war crimes, genocide and crimes against humanity'. The Constitutive Act ends impunity against severe human rights violations in Article 4o. Additionally the AU in its so-called Ezulwini Consensus of 2005 has acknowledged international norms on the responsibility to protect. At this point it should, however, be mentioned that so far Article 4h has not been invoked. Even for the AU mission in Darfur which is widely perceived as a case of genocide, the AU did not activate this article, nor did it in the case of Libya in 2011.

The APSA is a construct of several institutions of which the AU and Regional Economic Communities (RECs) form a still-emerging and developing security regime (Engel and Porto, 2010). At its heart is the AU Peace and Security Council (PSC), constituting the highest authority in security matters within this system. Under the guidance of the PSC the AU is developing a Continental Early Warning System (CEWS), an African Standby Force (ASF) and an advising council, the Panel of the Wise (POW). The ASF and CEWS especially rely on the ability of RECs to set these structures in place. Force creation for the ASF is only accomplished sub-regionally and there is no AU Standby Force as such. Operationlizing the APSA is further complicated by the diverse number of overlapping and intersecting RECs on the African continent. More than a dozen exist, most of which have not engaged in security policies so far. The AU's division of Africa into five regions (North, East, West, Central and South) does not in all cases lead to a clear allocation of sub-regional responsibilities. Only in the case of Western and Southern Africa can we locate ECOWAS and SADC as sub-regional and capable RECs institutions. In the case of Eastern and Central Africa competences are divided between different organizations and AU relations with Northern Africa are the least developed. Nonetheless, with these four instruments the AU has taken an important step in strengthening African organizations and building up crucial capacities for taking security matters into African hands. It remains, however, clear that even when fully operational the APSA will need to cooperate with external security actors such as the UN and EU. The AU and EU peacekeeping capacities will in the foreseeable future not be able to replace UN peacekeepers (Cilliers, 2008; Cilliers and Pottgieter, 2010). It is clear that its capacity limits and the complex inter-regional governance structure between RECs and the AU pose real challenges for the APSA and its effective implementation. Its dependencies are multi-layered. First, the AU's capacity to act largely depends on the political willingness of its member states to use these institutional structures. Formally, decision-making in the PSC has been designed to avoid deadlock situations and vetoing as it appears to happen in the UN Security Council. If no consensus is found decisions can be made by a two-thirds majority. However, in practice the 15 members of the PSC decide by consensus (Sturman and Hayatou, 2010: 65). While the AU does not have much in common with its predecessor the OAU, the tendency to make decisions by unanimity encourages agreement on the lowest common denominator. Controversial discussions and debates are thus prevented.

Second, the APSA is a cooperative construction of RECs and the AU. This governance structure, on the one hand, results from pure necessity, as the AU does not have any significant executive powers over its member states and Africa is a greatly diverse continent which creates significant dependencies towards sub-regional organizations. Thus the AU occupies a coordinative instead of executive and implementation role. On the other hand, this peculiar security system is increasing complexity and is diversifying political responsibility to such an extent that it might actually undermine its overall efficiency. In an ideal situation RECs function as gatekeepers for the AU which is coordinating internal African and non-African support, as happened in the case of Somalia. If institutional egoism prevails the AU might be sidelined by its African partners. ECOWAS and SADC have so far been rather reluctant in cooperating fully with the AU on issues relating to their own members (see the example of Madagascar).

Third, at the global level the APSA is dependent on cooperation with the UN and EU. The envisioned and so far only partially operational ASF will remain dependent on UN peacekeepers and their experience in conflict management. The ASF which only comprises a maximum of 25,000 troops is hardly able to replace the existing 88,076 UN peacekeepers in Africa in June 2011 (United Nations Peacekeeping Operations, Fact Sheet 30 June 2011). The lack of AU financial resources has led to a near total dependency on the EU and other donors. Through the African Peace Facility (APF) established in 2003 the EU channeled some €700m for capacity-building, peace operations and early response measures.[1] In comparison to this the AU's budget for 2010 was only €197 million.[2]

Not surprisingly these institutional capacity shortages have led to the creation of a multi-actor game in security matters in Africa (Brosig, 2010). Regarding peacekeeping operations we can observe a division of labor between the AU, UN and EU. Although the APSA is not yet fully operational, the AU has embarked on a number of peace operations. The AU has demonstrated a tendency for early intervention under conditions in which the UN and the EU as well declined to take action. In contrast to the UN and EU, it is of course more problematic for the AU to disengage from an emerging crisis in Africa as it is the only pan-African organization which is mandated to promote peace and security on the continent. Examples for such an early intervention can be found in the 2003–4 Burundi operation (ONUB), the 2004–7 mission to Darfur (AMIS) and the Somalia mission (AMISOM), deployed since 2007, and the Comoros (2008). In three of the four cases the AU functioned as early responder and facilitator for the UN and EU. Institutional shortcomings on the side of the AU, however, prevented the organization from engaging in fully comprehensive peacekeeping and post-conflict reconstruction measures. The AU's strengths seem to primarily lie in negotiating peace agreements and initiating early interventions. Here the AU fulfills a bridging role in which external actors have to be integrated in order to leave a sustainable positive footprint. In three operations the AU has either handed over or merged its missions with the UN and has received substantial financial support from the EU. In the case of Somalia, the EU has started to train Somali security personnel in Uganda in May 2010 and was, in the case of Sudan, supporting AMIS with an EU civilian–military action in 2005 (European Union 2005). This mission provided for training, troop transport and technical support until AMIS was merged with a UN mission forming the AU–UN Hybrid Mission to Darfur.

Despite the engagement meanwhile of the EU in ten African crisis management missions throughout the continent and the EU and AU setting up an APSA, the two organizations have so far not directly started a joint peacekeeping operation, nor have they taken or handed over a mission to each other. The reasons for this can be found in the EU's preferences for bridging missions instead of long-term comprehensive operations, its limited military capabilities and the lack of member state support for engagement in long-term comprehensive peacekeeping and post-conflict operations in Africa. The fact that both organizations tend to set up bridging or specialized mission has led to a situation in which they tend to cooperate more closely with the UN instead of seeking direct cooperation with each other.

The EU and peacekeeping in Africa

This section analyzes the EU's engagement in the APSA by following two aims. First, it examines the EU's institutional preferences for engagement in peace operations in Africa and second it scrutinizes the EU's linkages with the AU in the area of capacity-building and institutional support.

The creation of an APSA through the transformation of the OAU into the AU is providing Africa with new and better-adapted tools for shaping the continent's foreign and security policies. European foreign policy has likewise undergone substantial reforms in the last ten years. It has strengthened its foreign policy capacities significantly by launching the European Security and Defence Policy in 1999, the establishment of a High Representative for the EU's Common Foreign and Security Policy from 1999 to 2009, and the drafting of the first European Security Strategy in 2003. Finally through the Lisbon Treaty entering into force the EU now is represented by a High Representative of the Union for Foreign Affairs and Security Policy who is supported by the European External Action Service with several thousand members of staff. Such substantial topping-up of EU institutional capabilities potentially provides the EU with the necessary political clout it needs to match its economic importance in the world. However, so far the High Representative, Catherine Ashton, has disappointed many observers by applying a quiet diplomacy approach instead of actively crafting and guiding EU foreign policy. In fact the EU's role during the Arab Spring and in particular during the civil war in Libya in 2011 was one of a bystander and not a driver. Additionally the EU has worked extensively on a military component of its security and defense policy. The setting up of 15 EU Battle Groups, the establishment of a Defense Agency and civilian–military planning cell in Brussels have given the EU military assets it did not possess previously. As far as Africa is concerned we have also noticed that the EU is becoming the preferred tool through which European countries are multilateralizing their African security policies. How stable this trend turns out to be remains to be seen. In 2011 France acted in the case of Cote d'Ivoire and Libya outside the EU framework.

In 2003 the EU drafted its first ever security strategy in which it laid down its vision of the Union in foreign and security affairs. This document supports 'an international order based on effective multilateralism' (see also Biscop in this volume), of which regional governance structures such as the APSA are one expression. At another point the security strategy speaks about the need 'to develop a strategic culture that fosters early, rapid, and when necessary robust intervention'. In this vein the EU aims at taking global responsibility and wants to be prepared for actively engaging in peacekeeping operations, of which Africa is the world's biggest receiver. However, the document also makes clear that the main responsibility for peace and security lies within the hands of the UN and the Security Council. A similar position is taken by the AU PSC, which does not claim exclusive responsibility for African security but refers to the UN as a central and legitimate provider of international peace and security. At this point it becomes apparent that both the EU and AU do not attempt to monopolize security policies but want and need to cooperate with the UN to accomplish their goals. The EU has underpinned the importance of cooperation with the UN in its own Council Common Positions on conflict prevention in Africa (2004e, Art. 1) and the PSC Protocol makes cooperation with the UN obligatory (Art. 17). Thus while the AU and RECs are developing an APSA and the EU is involved in capacity-building for this African security regime, both organizations refer to the UN as main provider for peace and stability. This in the end supports the emergence of a security regime which is based on a triangle of inter-organizational relations between the AU, EU and UN. Indeed looking at all peacekeeping missions deployed in Africa we find that a security regime is developing between these three actors and that they are dominating this multi-actor game of peacekeeping by forming a variety of different cooperation modes ranging from bridging operations and co-deployment of troops to fully integrated or hybrid missions.

In its joint cooperation declaration with the UN (2003) the EU had outlined the conditions under which it is willing to deploy troops. In essence, the EU is reluctant to take over long-term and comprehensive peace-building operations on its own but is willing to provide for bridging and specialized operations on a short-term basis. The set-up of EU Battle Groups largely follows this concept. As small military units of 1,500 soldiers per Battle Group they are primarily deployable as a bridging force and rapid-reaction tool. The AU is in a similar position – its main competence so far is with negotiating peace agreements and early intervention. It does struggle with setting up long-term comprehensive missions covering the full spectrum from peace negotiations to post-conflict peace-building. For a sustainable positive impact the AU relies on the UN and not the EU to take over its missions. For this reason EU–AU relations are far less developed on the operational military level than on the institutional one. Both organizations are focusing on bridging tasks, which hinders them from engaging in joint peacekeeping operations.

Despite the EU and AU not co-deploying troops in crisis areas, the EU has supported the AU missions to Burundi, Comoros, Darfur and Somalia. This support encompassed financial contributions, troop transport, providing military equipment, delivering logistical support and police training. Thus the EU played an active and substantial part in AU peacekeeping missions, leaving political and military leadership to the AU and its member states and thereby strengthening African ownership. While it is true that the EU is providing much-needed support for the evolving African security structure through supporting AU peacekeeping it has not strengthened regional African structures systematically in its African missions.

The EU missions on the African continent have hardly integrated the AU or RECs enough to allow Africans to claim ownership of their matters (Aning and Danso, 2010: 56). In its peacekeeping missions the EU is largely cooperating with the UN instead. In general the UN and AU are not competing for EU cooperation. EU involvement in peacekeeping in Africa is also a reaction to the limited peacekeeping capabilities of the AU and RECs and is based on a formal invitation of the AU. In situations in which the AU or an REC has taken the lead such as the AU in Darfur or in Somalia, the EU has made important contributions to these missions and in fact strengthened AU institutions. In other situations in which African leadership is less pronounced the EU has tended to support existing UN operations, such as in Congo, or has helped the UN to establish its missions, as for example in Chad and the Central African Republic. In this context it becomes apparent how the EU's involvement in African peacekeeping is shaped by external conditions such as the existence of viable regional institutions adequately equipped with peacekeeping and conflict prevention instruments which also display political leadership.

EU–AU institutional relations

The relationship between Europe and Africa in the post-colonial era has largely been shaped by a number of formal trade agreements (Yaoundé, Lomé, Cotonou). Only in the last ten years have both the EU and AU set up institutions on foreign and security policy providing for an institutional framework for their continents. It is primarily with the emergence of the AU and its plans for the APSA that a more structured EU foreign and security policy can effectively cooperate with the AU. From 2007 onwards AU–EU relations developed very dynamically. The 2007 EU–Africa Summit in Lisbon established the Joint Africa–EU Strategy which today forms the institutional framework through which the EU is channeling its capacity-building efforts for the AU. The Joint Strategy is not to be interpreted as an EU development program in the classical sense but is aiming to overcome 'the traditional donor–recipient relationship', developing a 'partnership of equals' and 'building on common values and goals' (Lisbon Declaration 2007).

The Joint Strategy is made up of eight pillars, of which one is on Peace and Security. Its specific goals have been laid down in two Action Plans, one for 2008–10 and one for 2011–13. These Action Plans emphasize three priorities: first, enhancing AU–EU dialogue on security matters; second, full operationalization of the APSA; third, providing for predictable funding for AU peace operations.

The first priority seeks to develop 'common positions and implement common approaches' in security matters. A number of inter-institutional EU–AU meetings have therefore been set up and make up the core of institutional cooperation between the two organizations. An Africa–EU Summit takes place every three years, the EU Political and Security Committee and the AU PSC and EU Commissions have met regularly, EU–AU ministerial Troika meetings are gathering several times each year. At the heart of AU–EU institutional inter-change are the Joint Africa–EU Expert Groups (JEG), which met for the first time on 18 November 2008 and are supposed to meet biannually (Elowson, 2009: 31). Furthermore, a Joint Africa–EU Task Force (JTF) has been set up and in 2011 members of the AU Military Staff Committee (MSC) and EU Military Committee (EUMC) were scheduled to meet for the first time and establish a regular exchange. In late 2007 the EU appointed an EU Special Representative to the AU who simultaneously heads the European Commission Delegation to the AU. Between the EU and AU a whole network of inter-institutional meetings and working groups at all levels has emerged, at least guaranteeing a steady communication flow (see Figure 25.1).

The second priority in the action plan is far more ambitious and could not be realized within the time frame of the first Action Plan (2008–10). Core elements of the APSA such as the ASF or CEWS are not fully operational. Progress in the implementation of the ASF and CEWS is visible but unevenly distributed across the African continent. Central and Northern African regional organizations have not been able to contribute their share to the building up of the ASF. EU capacity-building should take account of this unequal preparedness.

The EU's capacity-building efforts have taken very concrete steps. In February 2008 General Pierre-Michel Joana was appointed as a Special Advisor for African Peacekeeping Capabilities (Brussels, 29 February 2008, S091/08). In liaison with the EC Delegation to the African Union and the EU Special Representatives (EUSR) the Special Advisor constitutes the EU focal points for capacity-building which are primarily funded by the APF. APF funding automatically excludes financial aid for military equipment, and thus EU support for building up the ASF is largely focusing on civilian and training measures at regional (AU) and sub-regional level (RECs).

So far the APF has provided more than €700m in support of the APSA and its components. The sum of €600m has been spent for AU peacekeeping operations (Darfur and Somalia). Indeed, the APSA does provide for the necessary conflict-resolution and management instru-ments but it does not possess the financial resources to maintain its peacekeeping operations. Therefore, the 2010 APSA Assessment Report has criticized the apparent 'mandate–resource

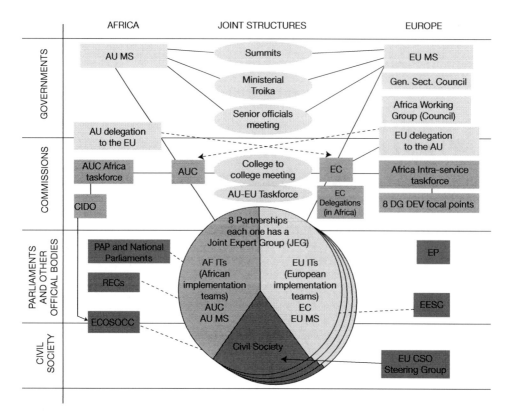

Source: Europeafrica.net: News and Resources on the Joint Africa–EU Strategy. Online. Available
HTTP: http://europafrica.net/jointstrategy/diagram-on-the-jaes/.

Figure 25.1 EU–AU common institutional structures.

Table 25.1 Ninth and tenth EDF for APF 2004–mid-2011

	€m
Peace–support operations	600
Capacity–building APSA	92
Early–response mechanism	15
Total	707

Source: Annual Report: African Peace Facility, 2010. Brussels: European Commission.

gap', pointing to the ability and willingness of the AU/PSC to mandate peacekeeping missions but to the lack of resources to sustain them.

Capacity-building programs received a more modest allocation of €92m. The most important EU initiative is probably the Amani Africa–Euro RECAMP initiative, which in principle aims at 'strengthening the politico-strategic capabilities' (Factsheet EURO RECAMP 2009) of the AU and in particular the AU Peace Support Operations Division (PSOD). The Amani Cycle as it is called consists of a number of training and exercise seminars and workshops between 2008 and 2010 which enable the AU and RECs to operationalize the ASF. The last exercise took place in October 2010 and the readiness of the APSA to respond to a fictional crisis scenario. As a result a number of deficits came to the fore. The ASF has been criticized for over-emphasizing military aspects in comparison with police and civilian functions; the PSOD appeared as not sufficiently resourced to manage several peacekeeping missions concurrently; the logistical and communication infrastructure supporting the ASF is insufficiently developed; and despite the adoption of a memorandum of understanding between the RECs and the AU there is still uncertainty about which legal obligations RECs possess to support the APSA.[3]

In fact, the successful operationalization of the APSA depends to a large extent on effective relations between the AU and RECs. A joint meeting of the EU, AU and RECs in Akosombo (Ghana) in December 2009 has prioritized this issue. One EU strategy is to support the various regional training centers which exist in different African regions and support liaison offices of RECs in Addis Ababa in order to provide for a basic infrastructure for communication. In general, the EU prefers to cooperate with RECs via the AU which is supposed to provide coordinative leadership. Thus the EU has not developed a systematic strategy to support capacity-building for the various RECs active within the APSA but has lent individual support for single organizations.

With the adoption of the 10th European Development Fund (EDF) for the years 2009 to mid-2011, an Early Response Mechanism (ERM) has been established with a budget line of €15m. The ERM has been designed as an ad hoc instrument to support political mediation efforts undertaken by the AU. Funds have already been used in the case of Guinea, Guinea-Bissau, Madagascar, Niger, Somalia and Sudan.[4] As a result ERM funds have reinforced the political role of the AU as a peace-broker in the region.

EU capacity-building and institutional linkages with the AU and RECs now take place in a systematic and institutionalized manner. The framework for effective cooperation is in place. The idea behind capacity-building for the APSA is to provide support for 'African organisations for African-led operations'.[5] This idea, however, may be compromised by a number of conditions.

First, EU–AU dialogue and capacity-building for AU peacekeeping are systematic and institutionalized but operational cooperation in peacekeeping missions is hardly existent. Both the EU and AU at the operational level primarily work together with the UN but have not set up joint operations. The issue of institutional cooperation is at the heart of operationalizing the APSA as most AU peace missions have been taken over by the UN. A crucial node thus exists between the AU and UN which EU–AU relations should address adequately.

Second, member-state support on both sides the EU and AU is often lukewarm, except in the case of some lead nations. Such a tendency is potentially undermining the APSA, which is crucially dependent on sub-regional support from all African regions to become fully functional. Within the EU, initiative rests primarily on France, Belgium and Britain, which in a Union of 27 countries may not suffice to establish capacity-building for the APSA as a long-term political priority despite the existing institutional framework.

Third, EU capacity-building is also reliant on the AU and RECs' ability to absorb external support. The understaffing of the PSOD and the PSC, which both only have a handful of full-time support staff to run these crucial organs, sets clear limits to EU capacity-building efforts. In fact, the unequal power relations between the EU and AU, with the EU commanding over considerably more resources financially and on the administrative side, threaten to challenge African ownership of the process.

Fourth, the concept of African ownership in which capacity-building should be demand-driven is more difficult to realize than is commonly imagined.[6] Ideally the EU's engagement within the APSA, would in large part be responsive to external demands for support. In practice demand for capacity-building is so substantial that the EU's offer for support will generally be welcomed. The concept of African ownership only works if there are actors who expressly want to own the process. However, in some situations the EU would be forced to either generate ownership before engaging in capacity-building or limit its engagement until ownership has grown from below. To a substantial degree the JAES remains rather cosmetically a joint project.

Fifth, the JAES is a politically empty vessel. The JAES established institutional links between decision-making organs in the AU and EU without providing content for a political agenda. The goals and targets of the JAES remain rather technical and abstract. Despite the reference to supposedly common values of human rights and democracy, which are apparently not shared by all countries, the JAES fails to craft a truly common political project expressing a strategic and shared vision for cooperation between Africa and Europe.

Sixth, Africa and Europe do not share the same understanding of concepts of state sovereignty, humanitarian interventionism and issues of international criminal law. This political divide became apparent during the civil war in Libya in 2011. While the AU tried to defer the prosecution of Gaddafi before the International Criminal Court (ICC) and rejected the linkages between regime change and protection of civilians, European countries took a more interventionist position and expressed clear support for the ICC and acceptance for forceful regime change in the case of Gaddafi. European and African security concepts do not always point in the same direction and the JAES has so far not been a place in which differentiating security cultures could be mediated.

In summary, the EU's supporting activities for the APSA are crucial for helping the ambitious AU plans to finally become fully operational, but this process will take longer than foreseen in the Action Plan for the Joint Africa–EU Strategy. Problems, however, will remain even until after the APSA has been set up successfully. Contrasting the planned troop numbers for the ASF with the number of current UN troops deployed it is apparent that the APSA cannot rely on its own capabilities but needs to work closely with the UN and EU. Considering the weak financial resources which the AU and RECs command, there will also be a long-term need for external funding for AU peace operations. If this funding is not provided the whole system of the APSA runs the risk of becoming a bystander to conflicts instead of preventing and solving them.

Conclusion

With the transformation of the OAU into the AU, African states embarked on an ambitious project, the development of the APSA. Despite the APSA not being fully operational today it has given the AU a wide array of valuable instruments with which it can detect potential future violent conflicts through a CEWS, engage in finding diplomatic solutions through the POW, take political leadership through the PSC and set up peacekeeping missions through the ASF. Thus, the AU is becoming a true partner in African security matters for the EU and UN. The institutional framework for solving the most pressing security issues is evolving and depends on the political commitment of AU member states to use these tools and support their further development and implementation.

Alongside the emerging APSA, AU–EU relations have developed dynamically and found an institutional set-up in the Joint Africa–EU Strategy. Institutional linkages between the two organizations exist at all levels including peace and security. The EU has funded all AU peace operations, which would not have been deployed without this financial support. EU capacity-building measures concentrate on the final operationalization of the APSA, for example through Amani Cycle. The extent to which the finally implemented APSA can take ownership of African security politics remains to be seen. Peacekeeping operations on the ground have been conducted as cooperative undertakings between the UN, the EU and the AU. Current trends in peacekeeping in Africa show a division of labor in which the AU takes responsibility for regional peace negations and early troop deployment and the UN takes over these missions at a later point, fulfilling more demanding post–conflict reconstruction tasks. The EU prefers not to engage in long-term comprehensive missions but provides for crucial financial support. Its approach is comparable to the AU's preference for bridging operations.

In sum, any analysis of peacekeeping in Africa must seek to integrate various players, beginning from AU member states, AU institutions, RECs, the UN and EU and their respective member states. Since the APSA is in practice extending beyond the PSC, ASF, CEWS and the POW, this accounts for an increasingly complex security regime which is characterized by inter-organizational cooperation of various IOs and their member states, thus gradually forming an African security regime.

Acknowledgements

I thank Eva Strickmann (visiting researcher at the South African Institute of International Affairs) for her comments on an earlier draft.

Notes

1 <http://ec.europa.eu/europeaid/where/acp/regional-cooperation/peace/index_en.htm>, accessed 15 June 2010.
2 African Union, 2010.
3 AMANI Africa Cycle, 2010.
4 African Peace Facility, 2010: 7–9.
5 Council of the European Union, 2004d.
6 Council of the European Union, 2006c.

26

THE EU AND ITS STRATEGIC PARTNERS

A critical assessment of the EU's strategic partnerships

Thomas Renard

Strategic partnerships have become very fashionable. They are blossoming in the post–Cold War era, partly due to their inherent flexibility and ambiguity, making strategic partnerships a central feature of the early twenty-first century diplomatic discourse. Such grand rhetoric can be misleading, however, as strategic partnerships can mean everything – and thus mean little or nothing. Most governments probably do not even realize how many they have signed. Every government has its own definition, and every partnership is a variant in itself. In this globally accepted confusion, the EU is no exception.

Quite naturally, academics responded to this trend with an equally blossoming literature on strategic partnerships – although with delay as well as with a strong focus on bilateral partnerships rather than on the concept of 'strategic partnership' per se. In this sense, most of the literature on strategic partnerships is a mere recycling of the existing literature, and there is therefore a profound lack of understanding of strategic partnerships as a foreign policy instrument or as a strategy. There are a few exceptions, however, such as Kay (2000) or Nadkarni (2010), for instance. Recently, some literature has developed with a specific focus on the EU's strategic partnerships, not only bilaterally but also historically, conceptually and horizontally – i.e. looking at all the partnerships at the same time, and across all dimensions. Some of the leading work in this field was produced by Bendiek and Kramer (2010); Grevi (2010b); Grevi and de Vasconcelos (2008); Holslag (2010); Renard (2009, 2010a, 2010b, 2011); Sautenet (2007, 2012); and Smith and Xie (2010).

This chapter proposes first a rapid overview of what the literature says on the concept of 'strategic partnership'. Then it looks more specifically at how the EU interprets strategic partnerships and how it uses them in its external action. Finally, this chapter offers a critical assessment of the existing strategic partnerships of the European Union and eventually makes some suggestions to upgrade (some of) them into *true strategic partnerships*.

In search of a meaning

What is a strategic partnership?

There is no common understanding of the meaning of strategic partnerships in international relations[1] – not to mention the absence of a common definition. This is increasingly becoming problematic in light of the proliferation of such partnerships in the post-Cold War system. The nascent literature on the topic has recognized the inherent ambiguity of the concept (Kay, 2000; Ko, 2006; Wilkins, 2008; Nadkarni, 2010). It is therefore possible to read in 'strategic partnerships' any kind of behaviour, from soft balancing to hard balancing, or from bandwaggoning to hedging. As Jonathan Holslag put it: 'A strategic partnership is what states make of it. Because international relations theory provides no transparent definition, its significance is limited to the features that its members, rightfully or not, ascribe to it' (Holslag, 2011: 295).

The literature offers nonetheless some helpful criteria to identify and understand the meaning and purpose of strategic partnerships. First of all, there seems to be a consensus on distinguishing strategic partnerships from alliances (Ko, 2006; Wilkins, 2008; Nadkarni, 2010). Indeed, in comparison to alliances, strategic partnerships are softer arrangements, more flexible and with lower commitment costs. Moreover, strategic partnerships are not necessarily underpinned by shared values, and they are driven by a shared purpose rather than by a common threat.

Various authors have suggested a series of defining elements for strategic partnerships. According to Vidya Nadkarni, for instance, a strategic partnership exhibits the following properties:

> (1) They are formalized in multiple written declarations, statements, agreements, and memoranda of understandings that outline clear policy objectives and attempt to build upon and deepen multifaceted ties; (2) they create formal institutional links at various governmental and non-governmental levels, generating multiple interactive channels at the levels of Track I (official) and Track II (people-to-people) diplomacy; (3) they set up a mechanism for summit meetings between top leaders that are held alternately in the capital cities of the two countries, with more frequent meetings at the sub-ministerial and bureaucratic levels where officials explore common interests or concerns, often in joint task forces established to address specific issues; (4) they work to develop ties between respective military establishments through joint military exercises, having naval vessels make ports of call, and working on confidence building measures; (5) they seek to establish a stronger economic relationship; and finally, (6) they attempt to foster greater awareness of each other's culture through youth exchanges and cultural fairs.
>
> (Nadkarni, 2010: 48–9)

Beyond these technical elements, what makes a partnership truly 'strategic'? First, a strategic partnership must be *comprehensive*, in order to allow linkages and tradeoffs between various policies. Second, it must be built upon *reciprocity*, short of which it cannot be deemed a partnership at all. Third, a strategic partnership has a strong *empathic* dimension, which means that both partners share a common understanding of their mutual values and objectives. Fourth, a strategic partnership must be oriented towards the *long term*, which is to say that it is not put into question by casual disputes. Finally, a strategic partnership must go beyond bilateral issues to tackle (with the potential to solve) *regional and global* challenges, because that is its true *raison d'être*.

Strategic partnerships in this sense go beyond bilateral relations and focus on the instrumentalization of the bilateral relationship for broader ends (i.e. regional or global goals). The bilateral relationship per se is not the core *finalité* of the strategic partnership, although the depth and the quality of the bilateral relationship obviously determine the potential of the strategic partnership, and therefore the former remains crucially important to the latter.

Which EU strategic partnerships?

In previous articles, this author offered a historical overview on the evolution of the EU strategic partnerships, from their origins to this day, based on an analysis of EU documents and on interviews with EU and national officials (Renard, 2010c, 2011). This research concluded that the EU strategic partnerships derived from the Common Strategies – established by the Amsterdam Treaty – and eventually replaced them as the latter disappeared from the Lisbon Treaty. It was not until the European Security Strategy, however, that strategic partnerships were fully acknowledged as an EU instrument of foreign policy 'to pursue our objectives' (Council of the EU, 2003c: 13). Yet, as the ESS is mute on the foreign policy objectives of the European Union (Biscop, 2009) the meaning and purpose(s) of strategic partnerships, as well as the list of potential partners were left unspecified. Following the recommendations from the ESS, nonetheless the EU agreed strategic partnerships with a number of third countries. The 2008 review of the ESS did not bring much clarification on the concept (ESS, 2008e).

In September 2010, taking advantage of the new instruments established by the Lisbon Treaty, the 27 Member States debated the EU's strategic partnerships for the first time ever (Renard, 2011). Although the debate had some institutional purpose – notably to establish firmly the new President of the European Council and the new High Representative vis-à-vis the Member States in terms of relations with important third countries[2] – and some external image purpose – to assert the EU as a global strategic player vis-à-vis emerging powers – it was also a recognition of the need to rethink the long-neglected strategic partnerships. Having such debate was positive in itself, as it forced European leaders to think about the EU's global role and to confront their views with their European counterparts. The 2010 September European Council even took some steps forward in this debate, initiating a transformation of strategic partnerships from a meaningless *concept* into some kind of foreign policy *instrument*, as its conclusions acknowledged that 'the European Union's strategic partnerships with key players in the world provide a useful *instrument* for pursuing European objectives and interests' (European Council, 2010a: 2; my emphasis). It also encouraged the EU to act more 'strategically' and 'assertively' on global stage. Nevertheless, for as long as these 'European objectives and interests' remain undefined, strategic partnerships will be purposeless: there is no point adopting sub-strategies if there is no global strategy to guide them – no grand strategy.

Catherine Ashton, the High Representative of the Union for Foreign Affairs and Security Policy, was subsequently tasked to produce 'progress reports' assessing the current strategic partnerships and offering new guidelines. In December 2010, she presented some preliminary results in which she identified what she sees as the *motto* of this review exercise: fewer priorities, greater coherence and more results (Sopinska, 2011). Most observers would agree with this motto, but they are also eager to notice changes in how the EU is implementing its strategic partnerships – and these changes are slow to materialize.

As the meaning and purpose(s) of EU strategic partnerships have remained undefined since the beginning, it is not surprising that the list of strategic partners of the European Union appears somewhat odd. Today, in 2011, the EU has ten strategic partnerships with third countries: Brazil, Canada, China, India, Japan, Mexico, Russia, South Africa, South Korea and the United States.[3] Yet, as this author has argued before, each strategic partnership has its own rationale: they came into existence for different reasons and followed different patterns. Some became perhaps strategic partners *by accident* (Renard, 2011). Therefore, rather than the 'special ten' (Gratius, 2011), the EU's strategic partners could be deemed the 'accidental ten'.

A critical assessment of the EU's strategic partnerships

The second part of this chapter offers a critical assessment of the ten strategic partnerships from four different perspectives: the strategic nature of each partner; the strategic nature of each relationship, in terms of substance and form; and finally, the strategic nature of the EU itself.

Are all strategic partnerships similar?

In light of the above list, the first argument is that the ten strategic partnerships are neither identical nor equal.

Not all strategic partnerships are identical. Although all these relationships are qualified as a strategic partnership in either formal or informal documents, they did not come into existence in the same way, nor are they at the same stage. On the one hand, the relationships with Canada, Russia, the USA and Japan – the established powers – are regulated by just a few core documents and a continuous political dialogue. The EU considers these long-standing relationships to be inherently 'strategic' for various reasons, and their natural evolution did not require over-formalization. On the other hand, the EU finds it much more complicated to regulate its relations with Brazil, India, China, South Africa, South Korea and Mexico – the emerging powers – because it had to adapt to the rapid emergence of these newcomers on the global stage. As the relationship did not evolve as naturally as with the previous category of countries, and as bilateral agreements with them were blossoming in every direction following their emergence, the EU granted them a new kind of reward to maintain a comprehensive framework for the relationship and ensure their continued commitment.

Not all strategic partnerships are equal. Strategic partners can be categorized as follows. (1) The essential partner: the strategic partnership with the USA seems to be above any other partnership, as the transatlantic relationship is certainly no less important for Europe in today's uncertain global environment than it was in the past. This partnership is essential because little can be done without the support of the American superpower. (2) The pivotal partners: the strategic partnership with Russia and China, and to a certain extent with Brazil and India, is more complex but almost as important to cope with contemporary global challenges and achieve core EU foreign policy objectives. These partnerships are pivotal because they can tip the international balance to the benefit or to the detriment of the EU depending on how they are approached. (3) The natural allies: the strategic partnerships with Canada, Japan and South Korea appear less strategic than those with the USA or the BRIC countries. However, these countries are not negligible as they are like-minded countries with a significant footprint in international affairs (notably through their presence in the G8 and the G20). (4) The regional partners: Mexico and South Africa are dwarfed by the other strategic partners of the EU although they can bring a certain added value at the regional level (probably more obviously in the case of South Africa than that of Mexico).

To a certain extent the many differences among the ten strategic partners are reflected also in the legal status of the relationship. Indeed, strategic partnerships are political statements or can eventually be seen as 'soft law' instruments, but they differ from the legal framework for the bilateral relationship (Sautenet, 2012). A quick overview of the legal frameworks established and under negotiation between the EU and its strategic partners shows a large diversity of frameworks and diverging priorities for each partnership. For instance, whereas all energy is currently directed towards a Partnership and Cooperation Agreement (PCA) with Russia and China, efforts are channelled towards a Free Trade Agreement (FTA) in the case of India.

Are all these partnerships truly strategic?

Following up on the first argument above, particularly on the observation that not every partner is equal and that some might be inherently more strategic than others (e.g. because of their military strength, economic weight or geostrategic position), a second argument can be developed: the cooperation of the EU with its partners on international strategic issues is limited at best. It would be unrealistic to expect the EU to cooperate with all its partners on every single issue, for various reasons, including the fact that most issues are significant to only some partners. Moreover, at times, the EU and its partners might have diverging interests, making cooperation difficult, if not impossible. Nevertheless, there are certain key international strategic issues on which one could reasonably expect the EU and its partners to develop at least a coordinated approach or, better, a cooperative framework. Yet, this does not always seem to be the case.

Three issues illustrate this well. This section focuses on these issues because they are considered particularly important from a European perspective while recognizing that this choice remains somewhat limitative and arbitrary. The three international strategic issues are: the proliferation of Weapons of Mass Destruction (WMD), conflict management and climate change.

WMD proliferation. The EU identified the proliferation of WMD as one of its key security challenges, 'potentially the greatest threat to [Europe's] security' (Council of the EU, 2003c: 3). In principle, the EU shares this priority with all its strategic partners, some of which are strong advocates of a nuclear-free world. This shared concern is often recalled in joint statements on the occasion of bilateral summits, and there even exist established dialogues on these issues with several partners. India appears at first sight the most problematic partner here in the sense that it has refused to sign the Non-Proliferation Treaty (NPT) yet it is widely perceived as a 'natural partner' of the EU in dealing with new security challenges (Wagner, 2008), including proliferation, which is regularly discussed bilaterally through the security dialogue.

The more we move away from the level of principle to a more concrete level, however, the more we notice a lack of cooperation between the EU and its partners – and even at times some form of clash. In the Iranian case, for instance, the positions of China and Russia are particularly ambiguous and raise significant concerns in Europe. Indeed, both countries seem reluctant to condemn the Iranian nuclear programme, mainly for economic reasons (e.g. investment, arms deals or natural resources), whereas Europe is painfully yet unsuccessfully attempting to lead the negotiations. The negative impact of their ambiguous positions on their international image (and what it means for their relationship with Europe) or on long-term regional stability does not seem to have sufficient influence to make them switch positions, and Western negotiators seem clueless as to how to involve them more. In the North Korean case, the EU's involvement is very limited, which in itself might be seen as a problem given the high stakes for the region and for global security, not to mention the fact that half of the EU's strategic partners are involved in the six-party talks.[4] In fact, with the exception of Iran, the EU has little or no impact in most key initiatives related to non-proliferation, such as the New START (Strategic Arms Reduction Treaty), the six-party talks or the Indo-US nuclear deal.

Conflict management. There are a lot of conflicts and crises of all kinds around the globe that need to be solved. Therefore, one could envision a lot of potential for cooperation among strategic partners. Yet, in practice, cooperation remains very limited. Each government sees the world from a different angle and partners can cooperate when they share similar interests, but can also undermine each other's efforts or, worse, face each other across the front line when their interests clash, hence contributing more to the conflict than to its management. In Georgia, for instance, Europeans found themselves in a direct clash with Russia. Such cases are the most challenging to the concept of strategic partnership. In most cases, however, the problem is not so much one of diverging interests but rather of too little cooperation between the EU and its strategic partners. In Afghanistan, for instance, Europeans have been asking for more active support from China, India and Russia, notably in the civilian field of operations, e.g. related to police training or capacity-building. The reasons behind the lack of cooperation can be manifold (including the result of a strategic decision by some partners to engulf the EU and the US in strategic deadlocks while they can themselves focus freely on other strategic interests) but their constant occurrence is surely a sign of the weakness of the strategic partnership. There are finally other cases in which the EU is cooperating success-fully – although to a limited degree – with several of its partners. Yet this cooperation might at times hide another problem, which is that such cooperation can possibly trigger concerns among some *other* partners. In the Gulf of Aden, for instance, the EU is cooperating with several partners (including China, India and Japan) in counter-piracy operations, although an indirect consequence of these operations is the rising concerns in Asia (but also among some in Europe and in the USA) that China is using these operations to develop its blue-water navy, hence destabilizing the regional (and global) security order.

Another way to assess how the EU cooperates with its partners in conflict management is to look at UN peacekeeping operations, where they regularly have the opportunity to work constructively together in the UN framework.[5] In Lebanon, for instance, Europeans (5,050) work alongside Indians (897), South Koreans (369) and Chinese (344) in the UNIFIL mission. Yet the level of involvement with UN peacekeeping operations varies from one partner to another and barely reflects any form of strategic partnership. In terms of staff, for instance, India is the biggest contributor, whereas China and Brazil have significantly increased their contributions in recent years but not yet to similar levels. European Member States contribute a big chunk as well, with over 7,000 men and women. On the other hand, countries like Japan, Mexico, Russia or the USA contribute little to UN peacekeeping opera-tions staff. In terms of financial contributions to the operations, it is a different story. Europe tops the chart, covering over 40 per cent of the total budget, and the USA almost 30 per cent. Japan is another important financial contributor, although its contribution to the total budget in relative terms has diminished by over 35 per cent over the last six years. All the other part-ners are very small contributors, China covering for instance less than 4 per cent of the total budget and India 0.1 per cent. As the EU and all its partners recognize the legitimacy of the UN, one would expect that a true strategic partnership would translate into greater coopera-tion and involvement in peacekeeping operations yet practice shows otherwise.

Climate change. The EU identified climate change as a global challenge and as a 'threat multiplier' (Council of the EU, 2008e: 5). However, the sense of urgency that is very palpable in Europe is not shared by all our partners. Russia, for instance, does not seem particularly concerned with the consequences of climate change (Fischer, 2008). The same could be said about India or China. The Copenhagen conference was a very good illustration of how the EU can be sidelined by its own partners in international negotiations of strategic importance to the EU, as the BASIC countries (Brazil, South Africa, India and China) decided to nego-tiate a separate deal with the USA, keeping the Europeans outside the negotiating room. What was perhaps most remarkable in Copenhagen was that the EU seemed unable to reach out to its strategic partners, despite the fact that – for once – the EU was carrying a single message (Renard, 2010a). This again raises questions regarding the strategic nature of the strategic partnerships.

Are these partnerships designed strategically?

A third argument that needs to be developed here is that the strategic partnership status has little impact on the structural arrangements of the relationship and on the EU institu-tional set-up. In fact, interviews conducted in 2009–10, with staff members of the European Commission revealed that people dealing with the strategic partners were sometimes barely aware that 'their' country was a strategic partner and in most cases had no clear idea of what a strategic partnership is and what it means concretely. Most interviewees also had difficulties to identify significant differences between dealing with a strategic partner or a non-strategic partner country in their daily routine.[6] According to one respondent, however, a strategic partnership introduced more dynamism internally (more dialogue among EU institutions) and bilaterally (more intense and diversified exchanges).[7]

Bilateral structural arrangements. It could reasonably be expected that the establishment of a strategic partnership with a third country would have an impact on the scope and the depth of bilateral structural arrangements. Yet, reality proves otherwise. For instance, the EU has a bilateral summit with all its strategic partners, but this alone does not seem to be a conse-quence of having a strategic partnership, as it had regular summits with South Korea before the relationship was upgraded and as it also has established regular summits with Pakistan and Ukraine which are not (yet) strategic partners. Moreover, whereas the EU holds a summit with each partner, the pace can vary from biannual (Russia) to annual (Brazil, Canada, China, India, Japan, South Africa, South Korea and the US) to biennial (Mexico).

An overview of the political and sectoral dialogues between the EU and its strategic part-ners shows the gap that still exists in the diversity and intensity of dialogues from one partner to another (see Table 26.1). For instance, the EU rightly has more dialogues with the USA and China than with other partners, covering a broad spectrum of issues, whereas the under-development of dialogues with other partners (e.g. Russia) seems less comprehensible. Of course, it is not only the amount and the scope of the dialogues that should be assessed but also their effectiveness, which should guide their future development. However, the under-development of dialogues with some partners raises questions regarding the strategic nature of the partnership.

Furthermore, in a strategic partnership, one would correctly expect that dialogues cover the broad spectrum of bilateral, regional and global issues. However, with various part-ners, some issues remain entirely unaddressed (at least within the framework of established dialogues) or under-addressed. More importantly, several partnerships have no established political and strategic dialogues, whereas there is no sectoral dialogue covering security and

Table 26.1 Overview of the EU summits, political and strategic dialogues and sectoral dialogues with its strategic partners (as of March 2011)

Summit	Political and Strategic Dialogues	SD Agriculture and Fisheries	SD Culture, Education and Media	SD Development and Human Rights	SD Environment, Energy and Nuclear Affairs	SD Health, Social Policies and Migration	SD Science, Technology and Space	SD Security and Defence	SD Trade, Economy and Finance	SD Transport and Tourism	Other Sectoral Dialogues	Total Sectoral Dialogues	Total
Brazil	1	–	3	2	3	2	2	–	4	2	2	20	22
Canada	1	3 (1)	1	1	4 (2)	1	2	15 (1)	4	2	2	35	41
China	1	1	3	3 (2)	5	5	3	2 (2)	14	6	7 (1)	49	56
India	1	2	2	2	3	3	2	2	11 (1)	–	2	29	34
Japan	1	–	1	1	2 (1)	2 (1)	1	–	8 (3)	2	2	19	20
Mexico	0.5 (biennial)	–	2	1	1	–	1	–	–	–	–	5	5.5
Russia	2 (biannual)	2	2	1	2	2	2	–	8	1	1	21	26
South Africa	1	–	1	2	2	3	3	–	1	1	2	15	16
South Korea	1	1	–	–	1	2	3	–	13	–	–	20	21
USA	1	2 (1)	2	4 (1)	7 (3)	9 (1)	2	19 (2)	7 (2)	3	1	56	63

Source: Figures collected by the author.

Note: Figures in brackets = the number of High Level Sectoral Dialogues within the stated number of Dialogues.

defence with most partners (except for the USA, Canada, China, and India). As some scholars have shown, the EU's strategic partnerships are still mainly driven and dominated by the economic dimension, mostly trade (Holslag, 2011; Sautenet, 2012). In these conditions, it is difficult to qualify those partnerships as truly strategic.

Institutional set-up. It is striking so far that the strategic partnerships have had no impact on the institutional organization of the EU, more particularly on the structure and composition of the EEAS. For instance, in the current organization chart,[8] there is no person in charge of strategic partnerships (together or separately). The lack of importance and visibility given to the strategic partnerships in the EEAS organigramme is another sign of the lack of concrete follow-up on the establishment of strategic partnerships. The unfortunate result will likely be continuous problems of coordination and cooperation among different services of the EEAS (e.g. in following a coherent strategy with all partners), among different EU institutions (e.g. ensuring a coordinate approach with relevant Commission DGs, such as DG Trade or DG Dev, and other relevant bodies), and between the EU and its Member States (e.g. a link between the EEAS and the national ministries of foreign affairs), not to mention coordination and cooperation with the partner itself. This absence of coordination mechanisms will only make it harder – if not impossible – to develop a truly strategic approach towards EU partners. To solve this problem partly, Giovanni Grevi (2010b) has proposed the creation of 'focal points' within the EEAS to ensure coordination within the EU, and between the EU and its Member States.

An overview of the EU delegations in strategic partner countries confirms the general absence of logical institutional reform following the establishment of a strategic partnership (see Table 26.2). For instance, all delegations without exception remain critically under-staffed (particularly in comparison to the Member States' local embassies) despite the strategic importance of these countries and the new functions devolved to the delegations following the implementation of the Lisbon Treaty (e.g. the role of coordination and information-sharing among the 27 embassies previously undertaken by the rotating presidency), which would normally require significantly more human and financial resources, whereas delegations have so far maintained their pre-Lisbon size. Even in the current format, there are incomprehensible discrepancies among the 10 delegations, as their size varies from fewer than 20 (South Korea and Canada) to over 100 (Russia and China). Furthermore, being now relabelled 'EU delegations' instead of 'delegations of the European Commission', the composition of these delegations could and should have significantly changed, opening more space for diplomatic and security staff (e.g. a military attaché) in line with the new competences and responsibilities of the delegations (Emerson *et al.*, 2011).

Table 26.2 Staffing of EU delegations in strategic partners (as of March 2011)

	Brazil	Canada	China	India	Japan	Mexico	Russia	South Africa	South Korea	USA
EU staff	21	5	70	44	15	23	65	25	7	36
Local staff	29	13	40	51	35	15	65	40	10	49
Total staff in EU delegation	50	18	110	95	50	38	130	65	17	85

Source: Figures collected by the author.

The half-hearted implementation of the Lisbon Treaty so far has led to the daunting task for EU delegations to do more with the same, unsurprisingly resulting in dissatisfaction from most Member States and from many third countries, including some strategic partners. As a result, foreign capitals increasingly turn directly towards the national embassies, mainly from the big Member States, hence sowing the seeds of more fragmentation, contrary to the initial goal of the Treaty.

Is the EU a strategic partner?

A final argument developed here is that the EU is often perceived as the weak end in the strategic partnerships. Indeed, looking at the world from Washington, Beijing, New Delhi or Moscow, the strategic value of the EU can be questioned in light of its discrete profile on many issues of prime strategic importance, including for Europe (think for instance about the popular uprisings in the Arab world). As a matter of fact, several strategic partners have proven better at dividing Europe than at acting strategically alongside Europe to tackle global challenges (see e.g. Fox and Godement, 2009). To be frank, Europeans have very often rendered their task easy.

Giovanni Grevi lists some of the reasons to explain why the EU is not seen as a strategic partner:

> Strategic partnerships require unity of purpose, focus, sometimes hard bargaining, a flexible negotiating posture and always political authority. It is fair to say that today's pivotal countries, whether established or rising powers, question whether the EU is endowed with these attributes, except on some trade issues.
>
> (Grevi, 2010b: 8)

Digging further into some of these reasons, the lack of coordination between the EU and its Member States is deemed to be one of the biggest constraints on the EU's strategic actorness. Member States, particularly big ones, will maintain for a long time some form of national preferences in terms of foreign policy, but hopefully further developments of a truly *common* CFSP will narrow the gaps and tensions between national interests. One of the key objectives of the EU today is to push the CFSP forward by injecting small doses of rationality, good sense and coordination at the core of European foreign policies, in order to make the EU a more credible and perhaps more powerful actor. An EU speaking with one voice is unrealistic in the short to medium term, at least as a generalized practice, but it remains an ideal Europeans must strive for in the long term. An EU bearing a single message, on the other hand, seems more realistic in the short term and is already a general practice in less sensitive issues. Whether this single message is the right one or not is yet another issue.

Another major reason for the EU not to be considered as a strategic partner by its counterparts is that it is an unpredictable actor due to its lack of grand strategy. If the EU is unable to identify its interests and its values and articulate them coherently in a strategy, then strategic partnerships are simply meaningless and useless to both parties.

In a broader perspective, the challenge for the EU is to be considered as a strategic partner, a notion with clear *realpolitik* resonance, while promoting a Kantian vision of the world through its so-called normative power (Laïdi, 2005). There is an inherent tension within the EU between modernist and postmodernist visions of the world (Cooper, 2003), leading to ambiguous rhetoric and hybrid foreign policy, and always resulting in confusion. This tension in itself is not a problem; the source of the problem lies in the EU's fundamental incapacity to channel this tension into a coherent and constructive global vision.

Towards true strategic partnerships

Strategic partnerships are only strategic in name, for now. A historical overview of documents and debates shows the total absence of strategic rationale behind the elaboration of strategic partnerships since the very beginning, with no definition of the concept or of its fundamental objectives, and an ad hoc selection of partners. In addition, as the previous section of this chapter demonstrated, strategic partnerships are not so strategic when looked at up-close for a variety of reasons, including (1) not every partner is equally strategic; (2) the EU is not cooperating with its partners on most truly strategic issues; (3) the strategic partnership has no structural or institutional impact on the relationship; (4) or, finally, the EU itself is simply not considered a strategic partner in many cases. As other authors have observed: 'The use of the label "strategic partnership" in fact functions as a rhetorical façade which masks the reality that the EU has failed to transform the relations' with other global powers into strategic partnerships (Keukeleire and Bruyninckx, 2011: 389).

Despite this lack of strategic thinking, there were sensible reasons to establish strategic partnerships in the first place. First, the partnerships started to take shape with the 2003 ESS, that is to say after the invasion of Iraq – a jolt to Europeans, who realized that the transatlantic alliance cannot tackle and solve all global challenges, in view of our potential strategic dissensions. In this context, the EU needed to reaffirm the importance of the transatlantic relationship, while opening the possibility of new strategic partnerships with rising powers. Second and related to the first, in the context of rising multipolarity and interdependence, the EU needed to address the emergence of new powers in order to ensure their commitment to solving today's challenges, and to deepen and strengthen partnership today in order to better address tomorrow's challenges. Third, strategic partnerships were a reaction to the failure of the EU's interregional and multilateral approach to international affairs, as well as to the frustrations arising from the stagnation of bilateral relations with emerging powers. The partnerships then appeared as an alternative to reinvigorating European diplomacy in an international context of return to *realpolitik* in which bilateral approaches seem to dominate international relations, even in multilateral forums. Finally, strategic partnerships constitute an attempt to assert the growing importance of the EU over the national diplomacies of the Member States, not least because according to the Lisbon Treaty, the EU now has the tools and legitimacy to act in the name of Europe vis-à-vis third countries.

These four reasons were certainly compelling enough to launch strategic partnerships, and they remain more relevant than ever. Having this in mind, the demise of the concept is simply neither desirable nor recommendable, although strategic partnerships should certainly be reviewed. Herman Van Rompuy understood this and translated it into a catchy yet right-on phrase: 'We have strategic partnerships, now we need a strategy' (Van Rompuy, 2010b). This author would add: we need a grand strategy for the EU to identify its interests and objectives, *and* a (sub-)strategy at the partnership level to pursue them strategically.

In fact, in a purely rational world, any sub-strategy should logically flow from a grand strategy. And the list of strategic partners should only come at the end, as the 'who' should be conditioned by the 'what'. Yet, the European Union operated in reverse order. This fact is inevitably creating confusion for everyone – in Europe and beyond – but it does not necessarily invalidate existing partnerships. Indeed, some reflection on the EU's strategic objectives and interests is already taking place at the informal level. Moreover, the EU has already adopted many topical strategies – on terrorism, WMD proliferation, internal security, neighbourhood or growth – which together form the *building blocks* of a grand strategy. Paradoxically, progressing in reverse order might be a necessary evil for the European Union to move forward, but it has clear limitations as well: through the adoption of these strategies, the EU increases expectations from other global actors, which can thereafter only be disappointed by the lack of European commitment. Nonetheless, these building blocks could become a useful instrument to assess the *relevance* and *effectiveness* of the existing strategic partnerships (Is Country A *a necessary partner* to fulfil the objectives of Strategy Z [relevance]? Is Country B *an effective partner* in the pursuit of the objectives of Strategy Y [effectiveness]?). A broader reflection connecting all these *building blocks* together is, however, still necessary to a more coherent European foreign policy (e.g. how does the ESS support the objectives of the Europe 2020 strategy, and vice versa?). Such reflection should guide future developments of the strategic partnerships.

Working simultaneously on various strategic levels is a daunting task. It is certainly not the best way to proceed, but it is the European one. The existence of strategic *building blocks* renders possible the complementary development of a grand strategy and strategic partnerships. Time has come to get things started. Strategic partnerships are on the table and have created expectations which can only be disappointed at a high cost – that of becoming irrelevant in the twenty-first century multipolar world. The European Council gave a clear mandate to the High Representative to review the strategic partnerships. Yet, after the preparation of three interesting 'progress reports' assessing the partnerships with China, Russia and the USA (European Council 2010b),[10] the review process was abruptly interrupted by other external events – Arab uprisings, Libya – monopolizing the attention of Catherine Ashton and her service. After a (too) long pause, three additional 'progress reports' on India, Brazil and South Africa were eventually discussed during the September 2011 Gymnich in Sopot, Poland. Discussions were substantial, with some very concrete suggestions from various Member States. Yet, some diplomats complain of the lack of 'operationalization' of strategic partnerships.[11] Another complaint relates to the absence of clear indications regarding the next steps to be taken (e.g. what is the purpose of 'progress reports'? Will the EU have 'progress reports' on all ten strategic partners?).

As important as the events in North Africa and the Middle East are, the EU cannot lose sight of its long-term interests. Brussels should naturally be reactive to major events in its neighbourhood or even beyond, but it needs a broader vision to become increasingly proactive and become a significant pole among others in a multipolar world. Jo Coelmont captured this in the following manner: 'while the EU is playing ping-pong, the [other major powers] are playing chess' (quoted in Biscop, 2009: 12). And as George Bernard Shaw once said: 'The possibilities are numerous once we decide to act and not to react' (quoted in Youngs, 2010: 208).

With this proactive purpose in mind, the EU should develop a grand strategy to give a clear direction to its foreign policy, and design true strategic partnerships to pursue it. *True strategic partnerships* should therefore be seen as a sub-strategy, subsumed under a grand strategy, aimed at developing the EU's relationship with some key third countries in accordance with its global objectives and interests.

Notes

1 We specifically refer to international relations here, as the term 'strategic partnership' is commonly used in other fields, such as in the business community.
2 Discussion with EU officials, Brussels, 6 July 2011.
3 The EU also has five strategic partnerships with two regions and three organizations: Latin America and the Caribbean, the Mediterranean and the Middle East (we should note, however, that the strategic partnership with the Mediterranean and the Middle East, agreed in 2004, is no longer the reference document in our relationship with that region since we now have other arrangements, such as the Union for the Mediterranean), the UN, the African Union and NATO. However, the objectives of these partnerships seem different from those with third countries and they should therefore be treated separately. In any case, they will not be addressed here.
4 In addition to North Korea, the other parties are: China, Japan, Russia, South Korea and the USA.
5 All figures are from March 2011. Available at: <http://www.un.org/fr/peacekeeping/>.
6 Interviews with over 30 staff members of the European Commission conducted in Brussels between 4 June 2010 and 7 July 2010.
7 Interview with a staff member of the European Commission, Brussels, 24 June 2010.
8 Official organization chart as of 1 April 2011, <http://www.eeas.europa.eu/background/docs/eeas_organisation_en.pdf>.
9 Interview with a member of the Cabinet of Catherine Ashton, Brussels, 11 February 2011.
10 China, Russia and the USA are arguably considered the three most important partnerships of the EU. The decision to review these partnerships first reinforces this impression.
11 Interview with a European diplomat, Brussels, 21 September 2011.

BIBLIOGRAPHY

Abrahams, F. (1998) *Police Violence in Macedonia: Official Thumbs Up*, Human Rights Watch Report 10, New York: Human Rights Watch.

Acheson, D. (1987) *Present at the Creation*, New York: Norton.

Ackerman, A. (2009) 'OSCE Mechanisms and Procedures Related to Early Warning, Conflict Prevention, and Crisis Management', in Institute for Peace Research and Security Policy at the University of Hamburg (ed.), *OSCE Yearbook*, Baden–Baden: Nomos.

Adler, E. (1997) 'Seizing the Middle Ground: Constructivism in World Politics', *European Journal of International Relations* 3(3): 319–63.

Adler, E. (2008) 'The Spread of Security Communities: Communities of Practice, Self-Restraint, and NATO's Post Cold War Transformation', *European Journal of International Relations* 14(2): 195–230.

Adler, E. and Barnett, M.N. (1998) *Security Communities*, Cambridge: Cambridge University Press.

African Peace and Security Architecture (APSA) (2010) Assessment Study, Addis Ababa.

African Peace Facility (2010) *Annual Report*, Brussels: European Commission.

African Union (2000) *Constitutive Act*, Lomé, Togo, 11 July.

African Union (2002) Protocol Relating to the Establishment of the Peace and Security Council of the African Union, adopted by the 1st Ordinary Session of the Assembly of the African Union, Durban, 9 July.

African Union (2005) *The Common African Position on the Proposed Reform of the United Nations, 'The Ezulwini Consensus'*, Executive Council 7th Extraordinary Session, 7–8 March 2005, Addis Ababa.

African Union (2010) Press Release 30, 14 AU Summit, Decisions of the 14th African Union Summit, Addis Ababa, 4 February.

Aggestam, L. (2004) *A European Foreign Policy? Role Conceptions and the Politics of Identity in Britain, France and Germany*, Stockholm: Stockholm University.

Aggestam, L. (ed.) (2008) *The EU as an Ethical Power, International Affairs* 84: special issue.

Akçakoca, A., Vanhauwaert, T., Whitman, R. and Wolff, S. (2009) *After Georgia: Conflict Resolution in the EU's Eastern Neighbourhood*, EPC Issue Paper 57, April, Brussels: European Policy Centre. Online. Available HTTP: <http://www.epc.eu/documents/uploads/961937412_EPC%20Issue%20Paper%2057%20-%20After%20Georgia.pdf>.

Albright, M. (1998) 'The Right Balance Will Secure NATO's Future', *Financial Times*, December 7.

Aldecoa, F. and Keating, M. (eds) (1999) *Paradiplomacy in Action: The Foreign Relations of Subnational Governments*, London: Routledge.

Allen, D. (1998) 'Who Speaks for Europe? The Search for an Effective and Coherent External Policy', in J. Peterson and H. Sjursen (eds), *A Common Foreign Policy for Europe*, London: Routledge.

Allen, D. and Smith, M. (2004) 'External Policy Developments', *Journal of Common Market Studies* 42 (Annual Review): 95–112.

Allen, D. and Wallace, W. (1977) 'Political Cooperation: Procedure as Substitute for Policy', in H. Wallace, W. Wallace and C. Webb (eds), *Policy-Making in the European Communities*, London: John Wiley and Sons.

Almeida, J.V. de (2010) 'The Evolution of the EU's External Policy and the State of EU/US Relations', speech at the European Institute 2010, Washington, DC, 9 December. Online. Available HTTP: <http://www.eurunion.org/eu/2010-Speeches-and-Press-Conferences/The-Evolution-of-the-EU-s-External-Policy-and-the-State-of-EU-US-Relations-Joao-Vale-de-Almeida-December--9--2010.html>.

AMANI Africa Cycle (2011) Command Post Exercise (CPX). Executive Summary of the Evaluation Report, 3 November 2010. Online. Available HTTP: <http://www.amaniafricacycle.org/spip.php?article79&artsuite=0&lang=en>.

Amin, S. and El Kenz, A. (2005) *Europe and the Arab World: Patterns and Prospects for the New Relationship*, New York: Zed Books.

Ammon, R.J. (2001) *Global Television and the Shaping of World Politics: CNN, Telediplomacy, and Foreign Policy*, Jefferson, NC: McFarland & Co.

Anderson, M.B. (1999) *Do No Harm: How Aid Can Support Peace or War*, Boulder CO: Lynne Rienner.

Andersson, J.J. (2001) *Cold War Dinosaurs or Hi-Tech Arms Providers? The West European Land Armaments Industry at the Turn of the Millennium*, Occasional Paper 23, Paris: European Union Institute for Security Studies. Online. Available HTTP: <http://www.iss.europa.eu/nc/actualites/actualite/select_category/22/article/cold-war-dinosaurs-or-hi-tech-arms-providersbrthe-west-european-land-armaments-industrybrat-the/?tx_ttnews[pS]=978303600&tx_ttnews[pL]=31535999&tx_ttnews[arc]=1&cHash=1e4fdeb71e>.

Andersson, J.J. (2003) *Butter or Guns? Cross-Border Defense Industry Collaboration in Western Europe 1950–2000*, Ann Arbor: UMI.

Andoura, S. (2007) 'Towards a New Agreement between Russia and the European Union?', *VESTNIK ANALITIKI – Foreign Affairs* 29(3) (Moscow: Institute of Strategic Studies and Analysis (ISSA)).

Aning, K. and Danso, K.F. (2010) 'EU and AU Operations in Africa: Lessons Learned and Future Scenarios. An African Perspective', in N. Pirozzi (ed.), *Insuring Peace and Security in Africa: Implementing the New Africa-EU Partnership*, Rome: Instituto Affari Internazionali.

Anten, L. (2009) *Strengthening Governance in Post-Conflict Fragile States*, Clingendael Issues Paper, The Hague: Netherlands Institute of International Relations.

Antonenko, O. and Yurgens, I. (2010) 'Towards a NATO-Russia Strategic Concept', *Survival* 52(6): 5–11.

Aradau, C. and Van Munster, R. (2009) 'Exceptionalism and the "War on Terror"', *British Journal of Criminology* 49: 686–701.

Argomaniz, J. (2010a) 'Post-9/11 Institutionalisation of European Union Counter-Terrorism: Emergence, Acceleration and Inertia', *European Security* 18(2): 151–72.

Argomaniz, J. (2010b) 'Before and after Lisbon: Legal Implementation as the "Achilles Heel" in EU Counter-Terrorism', *European Security* 19(2): 297–316.

Art, R.J. (2007) 'The Four Functions of Force', in R.J. Art and R. Jervis (eds), *International Politics: Enduring Concepts and Contemporary Issues*, New York: Pearson.

Arya, S. (2008) 'The Train to Lhasa', *Journal of Defence Studies* 2(2): 105–24.

ASD (2010) Aerospace and Defence Industries Association. About Us. Online. Available HTTP: <http://www.asd-europe.org/site/index.php?id=2>.

Ashton, C. (2009) Press Conference, 19 November. Online. Available HTTP: <http://news.bbc.co.uk/1/hi/world/europe/8369568.stm>.

Ashton, C. (2010) 'Europe and the World', speech, Athens, 8 July. Online. Available HTTP: <http://europa.eu/rapid/pressReleasesAction.do?reference=SPEECH/10/378&format=HTML&aged=0&language=EN&guiLanguage=en>.

Ashton, C. (2011a) Statement on Behalf of E3+3 Following the Talks with Iran in Istanbul, 21 and 22 January. Online. Available HTTP: <http://www.consilium.europa.eu/uedocs/cms_data/docs/pressdata/EN/foraff/118915.pdf>.

Ashton, C. (2011b) Statement on Behalf of the E3/EU+3, Brussels, 21 September. Online. Available HTTP: <http://www.consilium.europa.eu/uedocs/cms_Data/docs/pressdata/EN/foraff/124694.pdf>.

Avery, G. *et al.* (2007) *The EU Foreign Service: How to Build a More Effective Common Policy*, EPC Working Paper, Brussels: European Policy Centre.

BAE Systems (2010) Key Facts. Online. Available HTTP: <http://www.baesystems.com/AboutUs/FactSheet/index.htm>.

Bagayoko, N. (2004) 'L'opération Artémis, un tournant pour la politique européenne de sécurité et de défense?', *Afrique contemporaine* (Spring): 101–16.

Bagayoko, N. and Gilbert, M.V. (2009) 'The Linkage between Security, Governance and Development: The European Union in Africa', *Journal of Development Studies* 45(5): 789–814.

Bailes, A.J.K. (2005) *The European Security Strategy – An Evolutionary History*, Policy Paper 10, Stockholm: Stockholm International Peace Research Institute.

Bailes, A.J.K., Haine, J.-Y. and Lachowski, Z. (2008) 'Reflections on the OSCE–EU Relationship', in Institute for Peace Research and Security Policy at the University of Hamburg (ed.), *OSCE Yearbook*, Baden-Baden: Nomos.

Balfour, R. (2010) *EU Strategic Partnerships: Are they Worth the Name?*, EPC Commentary, 15 September, Brussels: European Policy Centre.

Balfour, R. and Ojanen, H. (2011) *Does the European External Action Service Represent a Model for the Challenges of Global Diplomacy?*, IAI Working Papers 11, Rome: Istituto Affari Internazionali.

Balossi-Restelli, L.M. (2011) 'Fit for What? Towards Explaining Battlegroup Inaction', *European Security* 20(2): 155–84.

Barkin, J.S. (2010) *Realist Constructivism: Rethinking International Relations Theory*, Cambridge: Cambridge University Press.

Barnett, M.N. and Finnemore, M. (2001) 'The Politics, Power, and Pathologies of International Organizations', in L.M. Martin and B. Simmons (eds), *International Institutions: An International Organization Reader*, Cambridge, MA: MIT Press.

Bátora, J. (2005) 'Does the European Union Transform the Institution of Diplomacy?', *Journal of European Public Policy* 12(1): 44–66.

Bátora, J. (2009) 'Problems of the European Defence Agency', *West European Politics* 32(6): 1075–98.

Bechev, D. and Nicolaïdis, C. (2010) 'From Policy to Polity: Can the EU's Special Relations with Its "Neighbourhood" be Decentred?', *Journal of Common Market Studies* 48(3): 475–500.

Beck, U. (1992) *Risk Society: Towards a New Modernity*, London: Sage.

Beck, U. (1999) *World Risk Society*, Cambridge: Polity Press.

Bendiek, A. and Kramer, H. (2010) 'The EU as a "Strategic" International Actor: Substantial and Analytical Ambiguities', *European Foreign Affairs Review* 15(4): 453–74.

Bengtsson, R. (2010) *The EU and the European Security Order: Interfacing Security Actors*, Abingdon: Routledge.

Behrendt, S. and Hanelt, C.H. (2000) *Bound to Cooperate – Europe and the Middle East*, Gutersloh: Bertelsmann Foundation.

Bertin, T. (2008) 'The EU Military Operation in Bosnia', in M. Merlingen and R. Ostrauskaitė (eds), *European Security and Defence Policy: An Implementation Perspective*, Abingdon: Routledge.

Biava, A. (2011) 'The Emergence of a Strategic Culture within the Common Security and Defence Policy', *European Foreign Affairs Review* 16(1): 41–58.

Bicchi, F. (2006) '"Our Size Fits All": Normative Power Europe and the Mediterranean', *Journal of European Public Policy* 13(2): 286–303.

Bickerton, C. (2011) *EU Foreign Policy: From Effectiveness to Functionality*, Basingstoke: Palgrave Macmillan.

Bigo, D. (1996) *Polices en réseaux. L'expérience européenne*, Paris: Presses de Sciences Po.

Bigo, D. (2002) 'Security and Immigration: Toward a Critique of the Governmentality of Unease', *Alternatives* 27(1): 63–92.

Biscop, S. (2004) 'Able and Willing? Assessing the EU's Capacity for Military Action', *European Foreign Affairs Review* 9: 509–27.

Biscop, S. (2005) *The European Security Strategy: A Global Agenda for Positive Power*, Aldershot: Ashgate.

Biscop, S. (2009a) 'Odd Couple or Dynamic Duo? The EU and Strategy in Times of Crisis', *European Foreign Affairs Review* 14(3): 367–84.

Biscop, S. (ed.) (2009b) *The Value of Power, the Power of Values: A Call for an EU Grand Strategy*, Egmont Paper 33, Brussels: Egmont Institute.

Biscop, S. (2010) 'European Studies Discovers Strategy', *European Geostrategy*. Online. Available HTTP: <http://europeangeostrategy.ideasoneurope.eu/2010/07/19/european-studies-discovers-strategy/>.

Biscop, S. (2011) *Europe Deploys: Towards a Civil–Military Strategy for CSDP*, Egmont Paper 49, Brussels: Egmont Institute.

Biscop, S. and Andersson, J.J. (eds) (2008) *The EU and the European Security Strategy: Forging a Global Europe*, Abingdon: Routledge.

Biscop, S. and Coelmont, J. (2010) *A Strategy for CSDP: Europe's Ambitions as a Global Security Provider*, Egmont Paper 37, Brussels: Royal Institute for International Relations.

Biscop, S., Howorth, J. and Giegerich, B. (2009) *Europe: A Time for Strategy*, Brussels: Academia Press.

Bonvicini, G. (2006) 'The European Neighbourhood Policy and Its Linkage with European Security', in F. Tassinari, P. Joenniemi and U. Jakobsen (eds), *Wider Europe: Nordic and Baltic Lessons to Post-Enlargement Europe*, Copenhagen: Danish Institute of International Studies.

Booth, K. (1991) 'Security and Emancipation', *Review of International Studies* 17(4): 313–26.

Booth, K. (ed.) (2005) *Critical Security Studies and World Politics*, Boulder, CO and London: Lynne Rienner.

Börzel, T. A. (2010) *The Transformative Power of Europe Reloaded: The Limits of External Europeanization*, KFG Working Paper 11, Berlin: Freie Universität. Online. Available HTTP: <http://www.polsoz. fu-berlin.de/en/v/transformeurope/publications/working_paper/WP_11_February_Boerzel1. pdf>.

Bowen, W. and Kidd, J. (2004) 'The Iranian Nuclear Challenge', *International Affairs* 80(2): 257–76.

Brady, H. (2009) *Intelligence, Emergencies and Foreign Policy: The EU's Role in Counter-Terrorism*, London: CER.

Brahimi, L. and Ahmed, S. (2008) *In Pursuit of Sustainable Peace: The Seven Deadly Sins of Mediation*, New York: Center on International Cooperation, New York University.

Braud, A. and Grevi, G. (2005) *The EU Mission in Aceh: Implementing Peace*, Occasional Paper 61, Paris: European Union Institute for Security Studies.

Brosig, M. (2010) 'The Multi-Actor Game of Peacekeeping in Africa', *International Peacekeeping* 17(3): 329–43.

Brown, K.S. (2000) 'In the Realm of the Double-Headed Eagle: Parapolitics in Macedonia, 1994–9', in J.K. Cowan (ed.), *Macedonia: The Politics of Identity and Difference*, London: Pluto Press.

Bruter, M. (1999) 'Diplomacy without a State: The External Delegations of the European Commission', *Journal of European Public Policy* 6(2): 183–205.

Brzezinski, Z. (1997a) 'A Geostrategy for Eurasia', *Foreign Affairs* 76(5): 50–64.

Brzezinski, Z. (1997b) *The Grand Chessboard: American Primacy and Its Geostrategic Imperatives*, New York: Basic Books.

Büger, C. and Vennesson P. (2009) *Security, Development and the EU's Development Policy*, Florence: European University Institute. Online. Available HTTP: <http://erd.eui.eu/media/vennesson2. pdf>.

Bull, H. (1982) 'Civilian Power Europe: A Contradiction in Terms?', *Journal of Common Market Studies* 21(2): 149–82.

Buzan, B. (2004) 'A Reductionist, Idealistic Concept that Adds Little Analytical Value', *Security Dialogue* 35(3): 369–70.

Buzan, B. (2010) 'Culture and International Society', *International Affairs* 86(1): 1–26.

Buzan, B., Wæver, O. and De Wilde, J. (1997) *Security: A New Framework for Analysis*, Boulder CO: Lynne Rienner.

Campbell, David (1998) *Writing Security*, revd edn, Minneapolis, MN: University of Minnesota Press.

Carr, E.H. (2002) *The Twenty Years' Crisis: An Introduction to the Study of International Relations*, 2nd edn, New York: Palgrave.

CASE Collective (2006) 'Critical Approaches to Security in Europe: A Networked Manifesto', *Security Dialogue* 37(4): 443–87.

Castle, S. (2010) 'Aiming to Amplify EU's Global Voice', *International Herald Tribune*, 16 September.

Center on International Cooperation (CIC) (2011) *Annual Review of Global Peace Operations 2011*, Boulder, CO: Lynne Rienner.

Central Intelligence Agency (CIA) (2010) 'European Union'. Online. Available HTTP: <https:// www.cia.gov/library/publications/the-world-factbook/geos/ee.html>.

Chandler, D. (2000) *Bosnia: Faking Democracy after Dayton*, London: Pluto Press.

Chandler, D. (2010) *International Statebuilding: The Rise of Post-Liberal Governance*, Abingdon: Routledge.

Checkel, J. (2001) *'Going Native' in Europe? Theorizing Social Interaction in European Institutions*, Arena Working Paper 01/23. Online. Available HTTP: <www.arena.uio.no/publications/wp01_23.htm>.

Chevalier, J.-M. (ed.) (2009) *The New Energy Crisis: Climate, Economics and Geopolitics*, Basingstoke: Palgrave Macmillan.

Christou, G. (2010) 'European Union Security Logics to the East: The European Neighbourhood Policy and the Eastern Partnership', *European Security* 19(3): 413–30.

Chryssochoou, D. (2001) *Theorizing European Integration*, London: Sage.

Chubin, S. (2006) *Iran's Nuclear Ambitions*, Washington, DC: Carnegie Endowment for International Peace.

Churchill, W.S. (1951) *The Second World War*, vol. IV, *The Hinge of Fate*, London: Cassell.

Churchill, W.S. (1954) *The Second World War*, vol. VI, *Triumph and Tragedy*, London: Cassell.

CIDSE *et al.* (2010) 'Lawyers Reveal Ashton's EEAS Proposal Breaches EU Law, Warn Development NGOs', media release on the European External Action Service, Brussels, 23 April.

Cilliers, J. (2008) *The African Standby Force: An Update on Progress*, Institute for Security Studies Paper 160, Pretoria: Institute for Security Studies.

Cilliers, J. and Pottgieter, J. (2010) 'The African Standby Force', in U. Engel and J.G. Porto (eds), *Africa's New Peace and Security Architecture: Promoting Norms, Institutionalizing Solutions*, Farnham: Ashgate.

Clément, C. (2009) 'EUSEC RD Congo. The EU Mission to Provide Advice and Assistance to Security Sector Reform in the Democratic Republic of Congo', in G. Grevi, D. Helly and D. Keohane (eds), *European Security and Defence Policy: The First Ten Years (1999–2009)*, Paris: European Union Institute for Security Studies.

Cleveland, H. Van B. (1966) *The Atlantic Idea and Its European Rivals*, New York: McGraw-Hill.

Clinton, D. (1994) *The Two Faces of National Interest*, Baton Rouge: Louisiana State University Press.

Cockayne, J., Mikulaschek, C. and Perry, C. (2010) *The United Nations Security Council and Civil War: First Insights from a New Dataset*, New York: International Peace Institute.

Coelmont, J. (2008) Comments made at the Lisbon Treaty and ESDP: Transformation and Integration conference, Brussels, 28–9 April.

Coker, C. (2001) *Humane Warfare*, London: Routledge.

Coker, C. (2002) *Globalisation and Insecurity in the Twenty-First Century: NATO and the Management of Risk*, Adelphi Paper 345, London: International Institute for Strategic Studies.

Collier, P. (2008) *The Bottom Billion: Why the Poorest Countries are Failing and What Can be Done about It*, Oxford: Oxford University Press.

Comelli, M. and Matarazzo, R. (2011) *Rehashed Commission Delegations or Real Embassies? EU Delegations Post-Lisbon*, IAI Working Papers 11/23, Rome: Istituto Affari Internazionale.

Commission of the European Communities (1997) Communication from the Commission to the Council, the European Parliament, the European Economic and Social Committee and the Committee of the Regions. Implementing European Union Strategy on Defence-Related Industries. Brussels, 04.12.1997. COM(97)583.

Commission of the European Communities (2003) Communication from the Commission to the Council, the European Parliament, the European Economic and Social Committee and the Committee of the Regions. European Defence – Industrial and Market Issues. Towards an EU Defence Equipment Policy. Brussels 11.3.2003. COM(2003) 113 final.

Commission of the European Communities (2004) Green Paper, Defence Procurement (presented by the Commission). Brussels, 23.09.2004. COM(2004) 608 final.

Commission of the European Communities (2005) EU Strategy for Africa: Towards a Euro–African Pact to Accelerate Africa's Development. Communication from the Commission to the Council, the European Parliament and the European Economic and Social Committee. Brussels, COM (2005) 489 Development (SEC (2005)1255), 12 October.

Commission of the European Communities (2006) Interpretative Communication on the Application of Article 296 of the Treaty in the Field of Defence Procurement (Presented by the Commission). Brussels, 7.12.2006. COM(2006) 779 final.

Commission of the European Communities and Soges SpA (2008) Support Study in View of the Follow-Up to the 2007 Commission Communication, Council Conclusions and EP Resolution on Situations of Fragility: 'Mapping of Donors, Actors, Financial Instruments and Assessment Tools in Situations of Fragility', Brussels: European Commission

CONCORD and AidWatch (2009) *Lighten the Load: In a Time of Crisis, European Aid has Never been More Important*, Brussels: CONCORD/AidWatch.

CONCORD and AidWatch (2010) *Penalty against Poverty: More and Better EU Aid Can Score Millennium Development Goals*, Brussels: CONCORD/AidWatch.

Constantinou, C.M. and Der Derian, J. (2010) 'Sustaining Global Hope: Sovereignty, Power and the Transformation of Diplomacy', in Constantinou and Der Derian (eds), *Sustainable Diplomacies*, Basingstoke: Palgrave Macmillan.

Cook, D. (1989) *Forging the Alliance: NATO 1945–1950*, London, Secker & Warburg.

Coolsaet, R. (2010) 'EU Counterterrorism Strategy: Value Added or Chimera?', *International Affairs* 86(4): 857–73.

Cooper, C. and Johansen, M. (2003) 'Evaluation of Completed Twinning Projects'. Online. Available: <ec.europa.eu/enlargement/pdf/ ... /phare_ex_post_twining_en.pdf>.

Cooper, R. (2003) *The Breaking of Nations: Order and Chaos in the Twenty-First Century*, London: Atlantic Books.

Copeland, D. (2000) 'The Constructivist Challenge to Structural Realism: A Review Essay', *International Security* 25(2): 187–212.

Cordesman, A.H. (2007) *The British Defeat in the South and the Uncertain Bush 'Strategy' in Iraq: 'Oil Sports', 'Ink Blots', 'White Space' or Pointlessness?*, Washington, DC: Center for Strategic and International Studies.

Cornish, P. and Edwards, G. (2001) 'Beyond the EU/NATO Dichotomy: The Beginnings of a European Strategic Culture', *International Affairs* 77(3): 587–603.

Cornish, P. and Edwards, G. (2005) 'The Strategic Culture of the European Union: A Progress Report', *International Affairs* 81(4): 801–20.

Council of the EU (1999) Presidency Conclusions, Special European Council, Tampere, Finland.

Council of the EU (2001) Anti-Terrorism Roadmap, SN 4019/01, 26 September.

Council of the EU (2002a) Council Framework Decision 2002/584/JHA of 13 June 2002 on the European Arrest Warrant and the Surrender Procedures between Member States, Official Journal of the European Union, L 190, 18 July.

Council of the EU (2002b) Council Framework Decision 2002/465/JHA of 13 June 2002 on Joint Investigation Teams, Official Journal of the European Union, L 162/1, 20 June.

Council of the EU (2003a) Conclusions on EU–OSCE Co-operation in Conflict Prevention, Crisis Management and Post-Conflict Rehabilitation, Brussels, 10 November. Online. Available HTTP: <http://register.consilium.europa.eu/pdf/en/03/st14/st14527-re01.en03.pdf>.

Council of the EU (2003b) Council Decision 2003/48/JHA of 19 December 2002 on the Implementation of Specific Measures for Police and Judicial Cooperation to Combat Terrorism in Accordance with Article 4 of Common Position 2001/931/CFSP, Official Journal of the European Union, L 16, 22 January.

Council of the EU (2003c) *A Secure Europe in a Better World: The European Security Strategy*, Brussels, 13 December. Online. Available HTTP: <http://www.consilium.europa.eu/uedocs/cmsUpload/78367.pdf>.

Council of the EU (2003d) 'Mainstreaming Non-Proliferation Policies into the EU's Wider Relations with Third Countries', Document no. 14997/03, 19 November.

Council of the EU (2003e) 'Fight against the Proliferation of Weapons of Mass Destruction – EU Strategy against Proliferation of Weapons of Mass Destruction', Document no. 15708/03, 10 December.

Council of the EU (2004a) General Affairs and External Relations, 'Role of the EU within the OSCE – Council Conclusions', Luxemburg, 14 June. Online. Available HTTP: <http://www.consilium.europa.eu/uedocs/cms_data/docs/pressdata/en/gena/80951.pdf>.

Council of the EU (2004b) Working Structures in the Council in Terrorism Matters – Options Paper, 9791/04, 2 October.

Council of the EU (2004c) Conclusions on Assessment Report on the EU's Role vis-à-vis the OSCE, Brussels, 10 December. Online. Available HTTP: <http://register.consilium.europa.eu/pdf/en/04/st15/st15387-re01.en04.pdf>.

Council of the EU (2004d) Political and Security Committee, Action Plan for ESDP Support for Peace and Security in Africa, Brussels, 16 November.

Council of the EU (2004e) Council Common Position 2004/85/CFSP of 26 January 2004 Concerning Conflict Prevention, Management and Resolution in Africa and Repealing Common Position 2001/374/CFSP 2004. In Eurlex website, 28 January. Online. Available HTTP: <http://eur-lex.europa.eu/LexUriServ/LexUriServ.do?uri=OJ:L:2004:021:0025:0029:EN:PDF>.

Council of the EU (2004f) Conceptual Framework on the ESDP Dimension of the Fight against Terrorism, 14797/04, 18 November.

Council of the EU (2004g) European Council 12 and 13 December 2003 Presidency Conclusions, 5381/04, Brussels, 5 February.

Council of the EU (2005) The European Union Strategy for Combating Radicalisation and Recruitment to Terrorism, 14781/1/05 REV 1, 24 November.

Council of the EU (2006a) General Affairs and External Relations, 2760th Meeting, Brussels, 13 November.

Council of the EU (2006b) Implementation of the Strategy and Action Plan to Combat Terrorism, 15266/1/06, 24 November.

Council of the EU (2006c) Council Conclusions on Strengthening African Capabilities for the Prevention, Management and Resolution of Conflicts 2006, 2760th Council General Affairs Meeting, Brussels, 13 November. Online. Available HTTP: <http://www.consilium.europa.eu/uedocs/cmsUpload/Capabilities_Africa_20.11.pdf>.

Council of the EU (2007a) EU Action Plan on Combating Terrorism, 7233/07, 9 March.

Council of the EU (2007b) Presidency Conclusions of the European Council 8/9 March 2007, Brussels, 9 March.

Council of the EU (2007c) Council Conclusions on Security and Development, Brussels, 20 November.

Council of the EU (2007d) Council Conclusions on an EU Response to Situations of Fragility, Brussels, 20 November.

Council of the EU (2007e) *Lisbon Declaration* – EU Africa Summit, Lisbon, 8–9 December, 2007.

Council of the EU (2007f) *The Africa–EU Strategic Partnership: A Joint Africa–EU Strategy*, 9 December, Lisbon. Online. Available HTTP: <http://ec.europa.eu/development/icenter/repository/EAS2007_joint_strategy_en.pdf>.

Council of the EU (2008a) Javier Solana, EU High Representative for the CFSP, Appoints General Pierre-Michel Joana as Special Advisor for African Peacekeeping Capabilities, S091/08, Brussels, 29 February.

Council of the EU (2008b) Revised Strategy on Terrorism Financing, 11778/1/08, 17 July.

Council of the EU (2008c) Council Framework Decision 2008/919/JHA of 28 November 2008 Amending Framework Decision 2002/475/JHA on Combating Terrorism, Official Journal of the European Union, L 330/21, 9 December.

Council of the EU (2008d) Declaration by the Presidency on Behalf of the European Union on the Deployment of EULEX, Brussels, 28 November.

Council of the EU (2008e) *Report on the Implementation of the European Security Strategy – Providing Security in a Changing World*, S407/08, Brussels, 11 December.

Council of the EU (2009a) EU Action Plan on Combating Terrorism, 9717/09, 14 May.

Council of the EU (2009b) EU Action Plan on Combating Terrorism, 15358/09, 26 November.

Council of the EU (2009c) EU Counter-Terrorism Strategy – Discussion Paper, 15359/1/09, 26 November.

Council of the EU (2009d) Report on the Implementation of the Strategy and Action Plan to Combat Terrorism, 9715/1/09, 26 November.

Council of the EU (2009e) The European Union and Central Asia: The New Partnership in Action, Brussels, June. Online. Available HTTP: <http://www.consilium.europa.eu/uedocs/cmsUpload/EN_and_RU_EU_and%20CentralAsia.pdf>.

Council of the EU (2010a) Relations with Central Asia – Joint Progress Report by the Council and the European Commission to the European Council on the Implementation of the EU Strategy for Central Asia, Brussels, 28 June. Online. Available HTTP: <http://register.consilium.europa.eu/pdf/en/10/st11/st11402.en10.pdf#page=2>.

Council of the EU (2010b) Council Decision Establishing the Organisation and Functioning of the European External Action Service, Council Decision 2010/427/EC, Brussels, 20 July.

Council of the EU (2011) Overview of the Missions and Operations of the European Union, June. Online. Available HTTP: <http://www.consilium.europa.eu/showPage.aspx?id=268&lang=en>.

Council on Foreign Relations (1941) *The Role of the Grand Area in American Economic Policy*, Studies of American Interests in the War and the Peace, New York: Council on Foreign Relations.

Cox, R.W. (1981) 'Social Forces, States and World Orders', *Millennium: Journal of International Studies* 10(2): 126–55.

Cross, M.K.D. (2007) *The European Diplomatic Corps: Diplomats and International Cooperation from Westphalia to Maastricht*, Basingstoke: Palgrave Macmillan.

Cross, M.K.D. (2010) *Cooperation by Committee: The EU Military Committee and the Committee for Civilian Crisis Management*, Occasional Paper 82, Paris: European Union Institute for Security Studies. Online. Available HTTP: <http://www.iss.europa.eu/uploads/media/op82_CooperationbyCommittee.pdf>.

Cross, M.K.D. (2011) *Security Integration in Europe*, Ann Arbor: University of Michigan Press.

Crowe, B. (2005) *Foreign Minister of Europe*, London: Foreign Policy Centre.

Crowe, B. (2008) *The European External Action Service: Roadmap for Success*, London: RIIA.

Czaplinski, M. (2009) 'The OSCE in the New International Environment in Kosovo', in Institute for Peace Research and Security Policy at the University of Hamburg (ed.), *OSCE Yearbook*, Baden-Baden: Nomos.

Daintith, T. and Hancher, L. (1986) *Energy Strategy in Europe: The Legal Framework*, Berlin: Walter de Gruyter.

Dalgaard-Nielsen, A. (2010) 'Violent Radicalization in Europe: What We Know and What We Do Not Know', *Studies in Conflict and Terrorism* 33: 797–814.

Dannreuther, R. (ed.) (2004) *European Union Foreign and Security Policy: Towards a Neighbourhood Strategy*, London: Routledge.

Dannreuther, R. (2006) 'Developing the Alternative to Enlargement: The European Neighbourhood Policy', *European Foreign Affairs Review* 11(2): 183–201.

De Coning, C. (2010) *Civilian Capacity in United Nations Peacekeeping and Peacebuilding Missions*, NUPI Policy Brief 4, Oslo: Norwegian Institute of International Affairs.

de Gaulle, C. (1959) *Mémoires de guerre. II, Le salut 1944–1946*, Paris: Plon.

de Schouteete, P. (2006) 'The European Council', in J. Peterson and M. Shackleton (eds), *The Institutions of the European Union*, Oxford: Oxford University Press.

de Vasconcelos, A. (ed.) (2010) *A Strategy for EU Foreign Policy*, Report 7, Paris: European Union Institute for Security Studies.

Dehousse F., Andoura, S. *et al.* (2007) 'Towards a Real New Energy Policy for the European Union?', *Studia Diplomatica* 60(2): 11–23.

Deighton, A. (1997) 'Britain and the Creation of Western European Union, 1954', in Deighton (ed.), *Western European Union 1954–1997*, Oxford: University of Oxford European Interdependence Research Unit, St Anthony's College.

Delors J., Andoura, S., Hancher, L. and van der Woudde, M. (2010) *Towards a European Energy Community: A Policy Proposal*, Paris: Notre Europe.

Dempsey, J. (2003) 'NATO Urged to Challenge European Defence Plan', *Financial Times*, 16 October.

Den Boer, M. (2000) 'The Fight against Terrorism in the Second and Third Pillars of the Maastricht Treaty: Complement or Overlap?', in F. Reinares (ed.), *European Democracies against Terrorism: Governmental Policies and Intergovernmental Cooperation*, Onati International Series in Law and Society, Aldershot: Ashgate Dartmouth.

Den Boer, M. (2006) 'Fusing the Fragments: Challenges for EU Internal Security Governance on Terrorism', in D. Mahncke and J. Monar (eds), *International Terrorism: A European Response to a Global Threat?*, Brussels: PIE/Peter Lang.

Denza, E. (2005) 'Non-Proliferation of Nuclear Weapons: The European Union and Iran', *European Foreign Affairs Review* 10(3): 289–311.

Der Derian, J. (1987) *On Diplomacy*, Oxford: Blackwell.

Der Derian, J. (1992) *Antidiplomacy*, Oxford: Blackwell.

Deyermond, R. (2009) 'Matrioshka Hegemony? Multi-levelled Hegemonic Competition and Security in Post-Soviet Central Asia', *Review of International Studies* 35(1): 151–73.

DfID (2009) *Building the State and Securing the Peace*, Emerging Policy Paper, London: Department for International Development.

Diamond, J. (1997a) 'Disunity Is Strength', *Prospect Magazine* 21, July.

Diamond, J. (1997b) *Guns, Germs and Steel: A Short History of Everybody over the Past 10,000 Years*, London: Jonathan Cape.

Diez, T. (2009) 'EU Superpower Temptations and the Beauty of Complexity', speech on the occasion of accepting the Anna Lindh Award, University of Gothenburg, 25 September.

Doelle, P. and de Harven, A.G. (2008) 'Security Sector Reform: A Challenging Concept at the Nexus between Security and Development', in D. Spence and P. Fluri, *The European Union and Security Sector Reform*, London: John Harper Publishing.

Drieskens, E. and van Schaik, L. (eds) (2010) *The European External Action Service: Preparing for Success*, Clingendael Paper 1, The Hague: Netherlands Institute of International Relations.

Duchêne, F. (1972) 'Europe's Role in World Peace', in R. Mayne (ed.), *Europe Tomorrow: Sixteen Europeans Look Ahead*, London: Fontana.

Duchêne, F. (1973) 'The European Community and the Uncertainties of Interdependence', in M. Kohnstamm and W. Hager (eds), *A Nation Writ Large? Foreign Policy Problems before the European Community*, London: Wiley.

Duffield, J. (1996) 'The North Atlantic Treaty Organization: Alliance Theory', in N. Woods (ed.), *Explaining International Relations since 1945*, Oxford: Oxford University Press.

Duffield, M. (2001) *Global Governance and the New Wars: The Merging of Development and Security*, London: Zed Books.

Duke, S. (2005) *The Linchpin COPS: Assessing the Workings and Institutional Relations of the Political and Security Committee*, Working Paper 2005/W/05, Maastricht: European Institute of Public Administration.

Duke, S. (2006) 'Intelligence, Security and Information Flows in CFSP', *Intelligence and National Security* 21(4): 604–30.

Duke, S. (2008) Consensus Building in CSDP: Lessons of Operation Artemis, UCD Dublin European Institute Working Paper 08–7, July, Dublin: UCD.

Duke, S. (2009) 'Providing for European-Level Diplomacy after Lisbon: The Case of the European External Action Service', *The Hague Journal of Diplomacy* 4: 211–33.

Dunne, T. (1995) 'The Social Construction of International Society', *European Journal of International Relations* 1(3): 367–89.

Dura, G. (2009) 'The EU Border Assistance Mission to the Republic of Moldova and Ukraine', in G. Grevi, D. Helly and D. Keohane (eds), *European Security and Defence Policy: The First Ten Years (1999–2009)*, Paris: European Union Institute for Security Studies.

Dwan, R. (2002) *EU Policing for Peace Operations: What Does It Mean?*, Discussion Paper EIRU/023, Oxford: University of Oxford European Interdependence Research Unit, St Anthony's College.

Dwan, R. (2004) 'Civilian Tasks and Capabilities in EU Operations', background paper for the Study Group on Europe's Security Capabilities, Centre for the Study of Global Governance, London School of Economics.

EADS (2010) Our Strategy. Online. Available HTTP: <http://www.eads.com/eads/int/en/our-company/our-strategy.html>.

ECDPM and ODI (2010) *Setting up the European External Action Service: Building a Comprehensive Approach to EU External Action*, London and Maastricht: ODI and ECDPM.

Edwards, G. and Rijks, D. (2008) 'Boundary Problems in EU External Representation', in L. Aggestam, F. Anesi, G. Edwards, C. Hill and D. Rijks, *Institutional Competences in the EU External Action*, Sieps Report 6–7, Stockholm: Swedish Institute for European Policy Studies.

Egenhofer, C., Grigoriev, L., Socor, V., Riley, A. and Heisbourg F. (2006) *European Energy Security: What Should It Mean? What to Do?*, European Security Forum Working Paper 23, October, Brussels, London and Geneva: CEPS, IISS and DCAF.

Elgström, O. and Smith, M. (eds) (2006) *The European Union's Role in International Politics*, Abingdon: Routledge.

Ellner, A. (2008) 'Regional Security in a Global Context: A Critical Appraisal of European Approaches to Security', *European Security* 17(1): 9–31.

Elowson, C. (2009) *The Joint Africa–EU Strategy: A Study of the Peace and Security Partnership*, Stockholm: FOI, Swedish Defence Research Agency.

Emerson, M. (2008) *Making Sense of Sarkozy's Union for the Mediterranean*, CEPS Briefs 155, March, Brussels: CEPS.

Emerson, M., Balfour, R., Courthaut, T., Wouters, J., Kacynski, P. and Renard, T. (2011) *Upgrading the EU's Role as Global Actor: Institutions, Law and the Restructuring of European Diplomacy*, Brussels: CEPS.

Emerson, M., Boonstra, J., Hasanova, N., Laruelle, M. and Peyrouse, S. (2010) *Into EurAsia: Monitoring the EU's Central Asia Strategy. Report of the EUCAM Project*, Brussels and Madrid: CEPS and FRIDE.

Engel, U. and Porto J.G. (eds) (2010) *Africa's New Peace and Security Architecture: Promoting Norms, Institutionalizing Solutions*, Farnham: Ashgate.

EU Council Secretariat (2006) EU Monitoring Mission in Aceh (Indonesia), Factsheet, Brussels, 7 December. Online. Available HTTP: <http://www.consilium.europa.eu/uedocs/cmsUpload/060907AcehCouncilFactsheetREV6.pdf>.

Eurocorps (2009) Eurocorps – A Force for the European Union and the Atlantic Alliance, Strasbourg: Eurocorps Public Affairs Office.

Eurojust (2006) Eurojust 2006 Annual Report, The Hague: Eurojust.

Eurojust (2007) Eurojust 2007 Annual Report, The Hague: Eurojust.

Eurojust (2009) Eurojust 2009 Annual Report, The Hague: Eurojust.

European Commission (2001) Communication on Conflict Prevention, COM (2001) 211 final.

European Commission (2005a) Commission Evaluation Report: The European Arrest Warrant has Broadly Achieved Its Objectives, Memo/05/58, 23 February.

European Commission (2005b) Communication, 'Policy Coherence for Development – Accelerating Progress towards Attaining the Millennium Development Goals', COM (2005) 134 final.

European Commission (2006a) 'A European Strategy for Sustainable, Competitive and Secure Energy', Commission Green Paper, March.

European Commission (2006b) Maritime Transport Policy: Improving the Competitiveness, Safety and Security of European Shipping, Brussels: European Commission.

European Commission (2007a) Communication, 'An Energy Policy for Europe', Brussels, 10 January.

European Commission (2007b) Communication to the Council and the European Parliament, Black Sea Synergy – A New Regional Cooperation Initiative, Brussels, 11 April. Online. Available HTTP: <http://ec.europa.eu/world/enp/pdf/com07_160_en.pdf>.

European Commission (2008a) Energy, Transport and Environment Indicators, Luxemburg: Office for Official Publications of the European Communities.

European Commission (2008b) 'Kosovo (under UNSCR 1244/99) 2008 Progress Report', Brussels, 5 November.

European Commission (2009a) 'Kosovo (under UNSCR 1244/99) 2009 Progress Report', Brussels, 14 October.

European Commission (2009b) Thematic Evaluation of the European Commission Support to Conflict Prevention and Peace Building. Preliminary Study: Scoping and Mapping, Louvain-la-Neuve: EuropeAid Cooperation Office, implemented by Aide à la Décision Economique S.A. (ADE).

European Commission (2009c) Communication, 'Policy Coherence for Development – Establishing the Policy Framework for a Whole-of-the-Union Approach', COM (2009) 458.

European Commission (2009d) Commission Staff Working Paper Accompanying the Communication 'Supporting Developing Countries in Coping with the Crisis', SEC 2009 444.

European Commission (2010a) EU Energy Trends to 2030 – Updated Brussels, 2009, Luxemburg: Publications Office of the European Union, 4 August.

European Commission (2010b) EU Energy and Transport in Figures, Luxemburg: Publications Office of the European Union, June.

European Commission (2010c) Energy Statistics: Supply, Transformation, Consumption – All Products – Annual Data, Brussels, September.

European Commission (2010d) Policy Coherence for Development Work Programme 2010–2013, SEC 2010 421 final.

European Commission (2010e) Energy 2020: A Strategy for Competitive, Sustainable and Secure Energy, Brussels: European Union.

European Commission (2010f) European Neighbourhood Policy: Funding. Online. Available HTTP: <http://ec.europa.eu/world/enp/funding_en.htm>.

European Commission (2011a) Commission Staff Working Paper: 'Kosovo 2011 Progress Report', Brussels, 12 October, SEC 2011 1207.

European Commission (2011b) Commission Staff Working Paper: 'Bosnia and Herzegovina 2011 Progress Report', Brussels, 12 October, SEC 2011 1206.

European Commission (2011c) Commission Staff Working Paper: 'The Former Yugoslav Republic of Macedonia 2011 Progress Report', Brussels, 12 October, SEC 2011 1203.

European Commission, High Representative (2006) An External Policy to Serve Europe's Energy Interests, Paper, Brussels, June.

European Commission and High Representative of the European Union for Foreign Affairs and Security Policy (2011) A New Response to a Changing Neighbourhood, Brussels, 25 May, COM (2011) 303. Online. Available HTTP: <http://ec.europa.eu/world/enp/pdf/com_11_303_en.pdf>.

European Council (1999) Helsinki European Council, Presidency Conclusions, 10–11 December.

European Council (2004a) Declaration on Combating Terrorism, 25 March.

European Council (2004b) Action Plan for Civilian Aspects of ESDP, Doc. 10307/04.

European Council (2005) EU Concept for ESDP Support to Security Sector Reform (SSR), Document no. 12566/4/05 REV 4.

European Council (2006) EU Concept for Support to Disarmament, Demobilisation and Reintegration (DDR), Approved by the European Commission on 14 December and by the Council of the European Union on 11 December.

European Council (2007) Treaty of Lisbon, Official Journal of the European Union, C 306/1, 17 December.

European Council (2008a) Report on the Implementation of the European Security Strategy – Providing Security in a Changing World, Brussels, 11 December.

European Council (2008b) Civilian Headline Goal 2008, Doc. 14823/07.

European Council (2008c) Presidency Conclusions, Brussels, 19–20 June.

European Council (2010a) Conclusions from the European Council of 16 September 2010, EUCO 21 January 2010, Brussels, 12 October.

European Council (2010b) Conclusions from the European Council of 16–17 December 2010, EUCO 30 January 2010, Brussels, 21 January.

European Court of Auditors (2009) EU Assistance Implemented through United Nations Organisations: Decision-Making and Monitoring, Special Report 15, Luxemburg: European Court of Auditors.

European Defence Agency (EDA) (2005) Intergovernmental Regime to Encourage Competition in the European Defence Equipment Market. Defence Ministers Steering Board, Brussels, November.

European Defence Agency (EDA) (2006) *An Initial Long-Term Vision for European Defence Capability and Capacity Needs.* Defence Ministers Steering Board, Levi, Finland, 3 October.

European Defence Agency (EDA) (2007) *A Strategy for the European Defence Technological and Industrial Base*, Brussels, 14 May.

European Defence Agency (EDA) (2008) Intergovernmental Regime to Encourage Competition in the European Defence Equipment Market. Online. Available HTTP: <http://www.eda.europa.eu/genericitem.aspx?id=153>.

European Defence Agency (EDA) (2010a) *Defence Data 2009*, Brussels: European Defence Agency.

European Defence Agency (EDA) (2010b) *European–United States Defence Expenditure in 2009*, Brussels: European Defence Agency.

European Defence Agency (EDA) (2010c) European Defence Agency. Background. Online. Available HTTP: <http://www.eda.europa.eu/genericitem.aspx?area=Background&id=122>.

European Neighbourhood Policy (2004) Strategy Paper. Communication from the Commission, Brussels, 12 May. Online. Available HTTP: <http://ec.europa.eu/world/enp/pdf/strategy/strategy_paper_en.pdf>.

European Parliament (2005) *Resolution on Non-Proliferation of Weapons of Mass Destruction: A Role for the European Parliament* (2005/2139(INI)), Strasbourg, Thursday 17 November.

European Peacebuilding Liaison Office (2006) *Five Years after Göteborg: The EU and Its Conflict Prevention Potential*, Brussels: EPLO.

European Spatial Planning Observation Network (2006) *ESPON Atlas: Mapping the Structure of the European Territory*, Bonn: European Spatial Planning Observation Network.

European Union (2004) Council Common Position 2004/85/CFSP of 26 January Concerning Conflict Prevention, Management and Resolution in Africa, Official Journal of the European Union, 28 January 2004, L 21/25.

European Union (2005) Joint Council Action 2005/557/CFSP of 18 July on the European Union Civilian–Military Supporting Action to the African Union Mission in the Darfur Region of Sudan.

European Union (2006) 'The European Consensus on Development', *Official Journal of the European Union*, 24 February 2006, C46, 1–19.

European Union (2009) EURO RECAMP, AMANI AFRICA (2008–2010), Factsheet, EU Council Secretariat, February.

European Union (2010a) EU Police Mission in Afghanistan (EUPOL Afghanistan), Factsheet, Brussels, November. Online. Available HTTP: <http://www.consilium.europa.eu/uedocs/cms_data/docs/missionPress/files/101123%20FACTSHEET%20EUPOL%20Afghanistan%20-%20version%2022_EN.pdf>.

European Union (2010b) 'A New Step in the Setting-Up of the EEAS: Transfer of Staff on 1 January 2011', press release IP/10/1769, 21 December.

Everts, S. (2004) Engaging Iran: A Test Case for EU Foreign Policy, Working Paper, March, London: Centre for European Reform.

Faria, F. (2004) Crisis Management in Sub-Saharan Africa: The Role of the European Union, Occasional Paper 51, April, Paris: European Union Institute for Security Studies.

Faria, F. and Ferreira, P.M. (2007) *Situations of Fragility: Challenges for a European Response Strategy*, Maastricht: European Centre for Development Policy Management.

Faria, F. and Youngs, R. (2010) European Conflict Resolution Policies: Truncated Peace-Building, Working Paper 94, March, Madrid: FRIDE.

Farrell, T. (2002) 'Constructivist Security Studies: Portrait of a Research Program', *International Studies*

Review 4(1): 49–72.

Farrell, T. (2005) *The Norms of War: Cultural Beliefs and Modern Conflict*, Boulder, CO: Lynne Rienner.

Fierke, K. and Wiener, A. (1999) 'Constructing Institutional Interests: EU and NATO Enlargement', *Journal of European Public Policy* 6(3): 721–42.

Finel, B. (2001) 'Black Box or Pandora's Box: State-Level Variables and Progressivity in Realist Research Programs', *Security Studies* 11(2): 187–227.

Finmeccanica (2010) The Group. Online. Available HTTP: <http://www.finmeccanica.com/Corporate/EN/Corporate/Il_Gruppo/Profilo/index.sdo>.

Finnemore, M. (1996) 'Norms, Culture, and World Politics: Insights from Sociology's Institutionalism', *International Organization* 50(2): 325–47.

Finnemore, M. (2003) *The Purpose of Intervention: Changing Beliefs about the Use of Force*, Ithaca, NY and London: Cornell University Press.

Finnemore, M. and Sikkink, K. (2001) 'Taking Stock: The Constructivist Research Program in International Relations and Comparative Politics', *Annual Review of Political Science* 4: 391–416.

Fiott, D. (2008) 'EU SSR Missions: The Case of Guinea-Bissau', *ISIS Europe: European Security Review* 38: 8–11.

Fischer, S. (2008) 'The EU and Russia: A Contested Partnership', in G. Grevi and A. De Vasconcelos (eds), *Partnerships for Effective Multilateralism: EU Relations with Brazil, China, India and Russia*, Chaillot Paper 109, Paris: European Union Institute for Security Studies.

Fischer, S. (2009) 'The European Union Monitoring Mission in Georgia (EUMM)', in G. Grevi, D. Helly and D. Keohane (eds), *European Security and Defence Policy: The First Ten Years (1999–2009)*, Paris: European Union Institute for Security Studies.

Fitchett, J. (2000) 'In a Cop-Out, Europeans Fail to Supply Promised Police', *International Herald Tribune*, 22 February.

Flessenkemper, T. (2008) 'EUPOL Proxima in Macedonia, 2003–05', in M. Merlingen and R. Ostrauskaitė (eds), *European Security and Defence Policy: An Implementation Perspective*, Abingdon: Routledge.

Follath, E. and Neef, C. (2010) 'The World Powers Court Central Asia', Spiegel Online International. Online. Available HTTP: <http://www.spiegel.de/international/world/0,1518,druck–727171,00.html>.

Foreign Affairs/Trade Council (2011) Conclusions 14620/11 3112th Council Meeting, Brussels, 26 September.

Foreign Policy (2011) 'The Failed States Index 2011'. Online. Available HTTP: <http://www.foreign-policy.com/articles/2011/06/17/2011_failed_states_index_interactive_map_and_rankings>.

Forsberg, T. and Seppo, A. (2011) 'The Russo-Georgian War and EU Mediation', in Roger E. Kanet (ed.), *Russian Foreign Policy in the 21st Century*, Basingstoke and New York: Palgrave Macmillan.

Forster, A. (2006) *Armed Forces and Society in Europe*, Basingstoke: Palgrave Macmillan

Fox, J. and Godement, F. (2009) *A Power Audit of EU–China Relations*, Policy Report, London: European Council on Foreign Relations.

Framework Agreement (2001) *Framework Agreement between France, Germany, Italy, Spain, Sweden and the UK Concerning Measures to Facilitate the Restructuring and Operation of the European Defence Industry*, Treaty Series 2001, 33, Cm 5185, London: Stationery Office Books.

France and the United Kingdom (2010) Declaration on Defence and Security Cooperation, UK–France Summit, 2 December.

Freedman, L. (1980) *Britain and Nuclear Weapons*, London: Macmillan.

Freedman, L. (ed.) (1984) *The Troubled Alliance*, Basingstoke: Palgrave Macmillan.

Freyburg, T. and Richter, S. (2010) 'National Identity Matters: The Limited Impact of EU Political Conditionality in the Western Balkans', *Journal of European Public Policy* 17: 263–81.

Friedman, G. (2009) *The Next 100 Years*, New York: Doubleday.

Fukuyama, F. (1989) 'The End of History?', *National Interest* 16: 3–18.

Fullenkamp, B.H. (1994) *Forward Presence and the Search for Peacetime Influence*, Newport, RI: United States Naval War College.

Furness, M. (2010) The European External Action Service: A New Institutional Framework for EU Development Cooperation, Discussion Paper 15, Bonn: German Development Institute.

Fursdon, E. (1980) *The European Defence Community: A History*, London: Macmillan.

Gaddis, J.L. (2009) What Is Grand Strategy?, Karl Von Der Heyden Distinguished Lecture, Duke

University, 26 February. Online. Available HTTP: <http://www.duke.edu/web/agsp/grandstrat-egypaper.pdf>.

Gänzle, S. (2009) Coping with the 'Security–Development Nexus': The European Community's Instrument for Stability – Rationale and Potential, Bonn: German Development Institute.

Gauri, K. (2011) The EU and India, FRIDE Policy Brief 90, August, Madrid: FRIDE.

Geeraerts, G. and Gross, E. (2011) *Perspectives for a European Security Strategy towards Asia*, Brussels: VUB Press.

Gegout, C. (2005) 'Causes and Consequences of the EU's Military Intervention in the Democratic Republic of Congo: A Realist Explanation', *European Foreign Affairs Review* 10(3): 427–44.

General Dynamics (2010) European Land Systems. Online. Available HTTP: <http://www.gdels.com/index.asp>.

Geuijen, K., Hart, P. and Princen, S. (2008) *The New Eurocrats: National Civil Servants in EU Policy-Making*, Amsterdam: Amsterdam University Press.

Ghaissari, A. and Nasr, V. (2006) *Democracy in Iran: History and the Quest of Liberty*, Oxford: Oxford University Press.

Ghani, A. and Lockhart, C. (2008) *Fixing Failed States*, Oxford: Oxford University Press.

Gharibabadi, K. and Qasempur, A.A. (2009) *The International Atomic Energy Agency and Iran's Right to a Peaceful Nuclear Programme* (in Persian), Tehran: Khane-ye Ketab and Presidential Research Office.

Ghebali, V.-Y. (2005) *The OSCE between Crisis and Reform: Towards a New Lease of Life*, Policy Paper 10, November, Geneva: Geneva Centre for the Democratic Control of Armed Forces.

Gheciu, A. (2005) *NATO in the 'New Europe': The Politics of International Socialization after the Cold War*, Stanford: Stanford University Press.

Giannella, A. (2009) Statement at the Sub-Committee on Security and Defence, European Parliament, September.

Giddens, A. (1999) 'Risk Society: The Context of British Politics', in J. Franklin (ed.), *The Politics of the Risk Society*, Cambridge: Polity Press.

Giegerich, B. (2006) *European Security and Strategic Culture*, Baden-Baden: Nomos.

Giegerich, B. (2010) 'Budget Crunch: Implications for European Defence', *Survival* 52(4): 87–98.

Giegerich, B. and Nicoll, A. (2008) *European Military Capabilities*. IISS Strategic Dossier, London, International Institute of Strategic Studies.

Gilpin, R. (1986) 'The Richness of the Tradition of Political Realism', in R. Keohane (ed.), *Realism and Its Critics*, New York: Columbia University Press.

Glachant, J.-M. and Lévêque, F. (2009) *Electricity Reform in Europe: Towards a Single Energy Market*, Cheltenham: Edward Elgar Publishing.

Glarbo, K. (1999) 'Wide-Awake Diplomacy: Reconstructing the Common Foreign and Security Policy of the European Union', *Journal of European Public Policy* 6(4): 634–51.

Gomez, R. (1998) 'The EU's Mediterranean Policy: Common Foreign Policy by the Back Door?', in J. Peterson and H. Sjursen (eds), *A Common Foreign Policy for Europe? Competing Visions of the CFSP*, London: Routledge.

Gourevitch, P. (1978) 'The Second Image Reversed: International Sources of Domestic Politics', *International Organisation* 32(4): 881–911.

Gourlay, C. (2009) *EU–UN Cooperation in Peacebuilding: Partners in Practice?*, Geneva: UNIDIR.

Gourlay, C. (2010) 'EU–UN Cooperation in Peacebuilding: Natural Partners?', in S. Blockmans, J. Wouters and T. Ruys (eds), *The European Union and Peacebuilding: Policy and Legal Aspects*, The Hague: TMC Asser Press.

Gourlay, C. (2011) *The Politics of EU Civilian Interventions and the Strategic Deficit of CSDP*, Brussels: ISIS-Europe.

Gow, J. (1997) *The Triumph of the Lack of Will. International Diplomacy and the Yugoslav War*, London: Hurst.

Gowan, R. (2007) 'The European Security Strategy's Global Objective: Effective Multilateralism', in S. Biscop and J.J. Andersson (eds), *The EU and the European Security Strategy: Forging a Global Europe*, Abingdon: Routledge.

Gowan, R. (2009) 'ESDP and the United Nations', in G. Grevi, D. Helly and D. Keohane (eds), *European Security and Defence Policy: The First Ten Years (1999–2009)*, Paris: European Union Institute for Security Studies.

Gowan, R. and Brantner, F. (2008) *A Global Force for Human Rights? An Audit of European Power at the UN*, London: European Council on Foreign Relations.

Gowan, R. and Korski, D. (2009) *Can the EU Rebuild Failing States? A Review of Europe's Civilian*

Capacities, Report of the European Council on Foreign Relations, London: European Council on Foreign Relations.

Grachev, A. (2008) *Gorbachev's Gamble: Soviet Foreign Policy and the End of the Cold War*, Cambridge: Polity.

Graham, T. (2010) 'The Sources of Russia's Insecurity', *Survival* 52(1): 55–74.

Gratius, S. (2011) *The EU and the 'Special Ten': Deepening or Widening Strategic Partnerships?*, Policy Brief 76, Madrid: FRIDE.

Graw, A. (2009) 'Europas Selbstverzwergung schockt die USA', *Die Welt*, 21 November.

Gray, C. (1981) 'National Style in Strategy: The American Example', *International Security* 6(2): 21–47.

Gray, C.S. (1996) 'The Continued Primacy of Geography', *Orbis: A Journal of World Affairs* 40(2): 247–59.

Gray, C.S. (1999a) 'Inescapable Geography', *Journal of Strategic Studies* 22(2): 161–77.

Gray, C.S. (1999b) 'Strategic Culture as Context: The First Generation of Theory Strikes Back', *Review of International Studies* 25: 49–69.

Gray, C.S. (2004) 'In Defence of the Heartland: Sir Halford Mackinder and His Critics a Hundred Years On', *Comparative Strategy* 23(9): 9–25.

Gray, C.S. (2009) 'The 21st Century Security Environment and the Future of War', *Parameters* Winter 2008/9: 14–26.

Greathouse, C.B. (2010) 'Examining the Role and Methodology of Strategic Culture', *Risk, Hazards and Crisis in Public Policy* 1(1): 57–85.

Greenwood, S. (1989) 'Return to Dunkirk: The Origins of the Anglo-French Treaty of March 1947', *Journal of Strategic Studies* 6(4): 49–65.

Grevi, G. (2007) *Pioneering Foreign Policy: The EU Special Representatives*, Chaillot Paper 106, Paris: European Union Institute for Security Studies.

Grevi, G. (2009) *The Interpolar World: A New Scenario*, Occasional Paper 79, Paris: European Union Institute for Security Studies.

Grevi, G. (2010a) 'The Interpolar World', *BEPA Monthly Brief* 33: 4–6.

Grevi, G. (2010b) *Making EU Strategic Partnerships Effective*, Working Paper 105, Madrid: FRIDE.

Grevi, G. and de Vasconcelos, A. (eds) (2008) *Partnerships for Effective Multilateralism: EU Relations with Brazil, China, India and Russia*, Chaillot Paper 109, June, Paris: European Union Institute for Security Studies.

Grevi, G., Helley, D. and Keohane, D. (eds) (2009) *European Security and Defence Policy: The First Ten Years (1999–2009)*, Paris: European Union Institute for Security Studies.

Grieco, J.M. (1993a) 'Anarchy and the Limits of Cooperation: A Realist Critique of the Newest Liberal Institutionalism', in D. Baldwin (ed.), *Neorealism and Neoliberalism: The Contemporary Debate*, New York: Columbia University Press.

Grieco, J.M. (1993b) 'Understanding the Problem of International Cooperation: The Limits of Neo-Liberal Institutionalism and the Future of Realist Theory', in D. Baldwin (ed.), *Neorealism and Neoliberalism: The Contemporary Debate*, New York: Columbia University Press.

Grieco, J.M. (1995) 'The Maastricht Treaty, Economic and Monetary Union and the Neo-Realist Research Programme', *Review of International Studies* 21: 21–40.

Grieco, J.M. (1997) 'Realist International Theory and the Study of World Politics', in M. Doyle and J. Ikenberry (eds), *New Thinking in International Relations Theory*, Boulder, CO: Westview.

Grilli, E.R. (1994) *The European Community and the Developing Countries*, Cambridge: Cambridge University Press.

Grimm, S. (2003) *Die Afrikapolitik der Europäischen Union: Europas aussenpolitische Rolle in einer randstän-digen Region*, Hamburg: Institut für Afrika-Kunde.

Grip, L. (2009) The EU Non-Proliferation Clause: A Preliminary Assessment, SIPRI Background Paper, November, Solna: Swedish International Peace Research Institute.

Grip, L. (2011) *Mapping the European Union's Institutional Actors Related to WMD Non-Proliferation*, Non-Proliferation Papers 1, May, EU Non-Proliferation Consortium.

Gros-Verheyde, N. (2010) 'Les ministres de la Défense, à l'heure de la crise, s'engagent à mieux coopérer', Blog Bruxelles-2, 9 December. Online. Available HTTP: <http://www.bruxelles2.eu/defense-ue/defense-ue-droit-doctrine-politique/les-ministres-de-la-defense-a-lheure-de-la-crise-sengagent-a-mieux-cooperer.html>.

Gross, E. (2009) 'Operation Concordia (fYROM)', in G. Grevi, D. Helly and D. Keohane (eds),

European Security and Defence Policy: The First Ten Years (1999–2009), Paris: European Union Institute for Security Studies.

Gross, E. (2010) 'Towards a Comprehensive Approach? The EU's Contribution to Security Sector Reform (SSR) in Afghanistan', *Security and Peace* 28(4): 227–32.

Gross, E. (2011) 'Explaining EU Foreign Policy towards the Western Balkans', in F. Mérand, M. Foucault and B. Irondelle (eds), *European Security since the Fall of the Berlin Wall*, Toronto: University of Toronto Press.

Grygiel, J. (2006) *Great Powers and Geopolitical Change*, Baltimore: Johns Hopkins University Press.

Grygiel, J. (2009) 'Vacuum Wars: The Coming Competition over Failed States', *American Interest* 4(6): 40–5.

Hadfield, A. (2007) 'Janus Advances? An Analysis of EC Development Policy and the 2005 Amended Cotonou Partnership Agreement', *European Foreign Affairs Review* 12(1): 39–66.

Haftendorn, H., Keohane, R.O. and Wallander, C.A. (eds) (1999) *Imperfect Unions: Security Institutions over Time and Space*, Oxford: Oxford University Press.

Hague, W. (2010) *HC Debates* 3 June 2010, c. 600.

Hague, W. (2011) *HC Debates* 11 May 2011, c. 1165–80.

Haine, J.-Y. (2009) 'The European Crisis of Liberal Internationalism', *International Journal* 64(2): 453–79.

Hall, I. (2010) 'The Transformation of Diplomacy: Mysteries, Insurgencies and Public Relations', *International Affairs* 86: 247–56.

Hall, P. and Taylor, R. (1996) 'Political Science and the Three New Institutionalisms', *Political Studies* 44(5): 952–73.

Halliday, F. (1986) *The Making of the Second Cold War*, London: Verso.

Hamilton, K. and Langhorne, R. (1995) *The Practice of Diplomacy*, London: Routledge.

Hansen, L. (2006) *Security as Practice: Discourse Analysis and the Bosnian War*, London and New York: Routledge.

Hartley, K. (2003) 'The Future of European Defence Policy: An Economic Perspective', *Defence and Peace Economics* 4(2): 107–15.

Haukkala, H. (2008) 'The European Union as a Regional Normative Hegemon: The Case of European Neighbourhood Policy', *Europe–Asia Studies* 60(9): 1601–22.

Haukkala, H. (2010) *The EU–Russia Strategic Partnership. The Limits of Post-Sovereignty in International Relations*, Abingdon: Routledge.

Hay, C. (2002) *Political Analysis: A Critical Introduction*, Basingstoke: Palgrave Macmillan.

Hay, W.A. (2003) 'Geopolitics of Europe', *Orbis: A Journal of World Affairs* 47(2): 295–310.

Hayes-Renshaw, F. (2006) 'The Council of Ministers', in J. Peterson and M. Shackleton (eds), *The Institutions of the European Union*, Oxford, Oxford: University Press.

Helly, D. (2008) 'EU's Influence in Its Eastern Neighbourhood: The Case of Crisis Management in the South Caucasus', in L. Delcour and E. Tulmets (eds), *Pioneer Europe? Testing EU Foreign Policy in the Neighbourhood*, Baden-Baden: Nomos.

Helly, D. (2009a) 'EUFOR Tchad/RCA', in G. Grevi, D. Helly and D. Keohane (eds), *European Security and Defence Policy: The First Ten Years (1999–2009)*, Paris: European Union Institute for Security Studies.

Helly, D. (2009b) 'EU NAVFOR Somalia', in G. Grevi, D. Helly and D. Keohane (eds), *European Security and Defence Policy: The First Ten Years (1999–2009)*, Paris: European Union Institute for Security Studies.

Hendrickson, R.C., Strand, J.R. and Raney, K.L. (2007) 'Operation Artemis and Javier Solana: EU Prospects for a Stronger Common Foreign and Security Policy', *Canadian Military Journal* 8(1): 35–42.

Her Majesty's Government (2009) *Pursue, Prevent, Protect, Prepare. Containing the Terrorist Threat: The UK Government's Strategy*, London: Her Majesty's Government.

Herbst, J. (2007) 'Crafting Regional Cooperation in Africa', in A. Charya and A.I. Johnston (eds), *Crafting Cooperation Regional International Institutions in Comparative Perspective*, Cambridge: Cambridge University Press.

Hill, C. (1990) *European Foreign Policy: Power Bloc, Civilian Model – or Flop?*, Boulder, CO: Westview.

Hill, C. (2002) 'The Geopolitical Implications of Enlargement', in J. Zielonka (ed.), *Europe Unbound: Enlarging and Reshaping the Boundaries of the European Union*, London: Routledge.

Hocking, B. (2004) 'Diplomacy', in W. Carlsnaes, H. Sjursen and B. White (eds), *Contemporary European Foreign Policy*, London: Sage.

Hocking, B. (2008) 'Reconfiguring Public Diplomacy: From Competition to Collaboration', in J. Welsh and D. Fearn (eds), *Engagement: Public Diplomacy in a Globalised World*, London: FCO.

Hoebeke, H., Carette, S. and Vlassenroot, K. (2007) *EU Support to the Democratic Republic of Congo*, Paris: Centre d'Analyse Stratégique.

Hoffman, B. (1998) *Inside Terrorism*, New York: Columbia University Press.

Hoffmann, A. and Longhurst, K. (1999) 'German Strategic Culture and the Changing Role of the Bundeswehr', *Welt Trends* 22: 145–62.

Holden, P. (2009) *In Search of Structural Power: EU Aid Policy as a Global Political Instrument*, Aldershot: Ashgate.

Holland, M. (ed.) (1997) *Common Foreign and Security Policy: The Record and Reforms*, London: Pinter.

Holland, M. (ed.) (2005) *Common Foreign and Security Policy: The First Ten Years*, 2nd edn, London: Continuum.

Holland, M. (2009) 'Assuming Superpower Status? Evolving Asian Perceptions of the EU as a Political and Economic Actor', in N. Chaban, M. Holland and P. Ryan, *The EU through the Eyes of Asia*, London: World Scientific Publishing Co.

Holmes, J.R. and Yoshihara, T. (2009) 'A Chinese Turn to Mahan?', *China Brief* 9(13): 8–11.

Holslag, J. (2010) *The Normative Disconnect between Europe and the Emerging Powers*, Asia Paper 5(4), Brussels: Brussels Institute of Contemporary China Studies.

Holslag, J. (2011) 'The Elusive Axis: Assessing the EU–China Strategic Partnership', *Journal of Common Market Studies* 49(2): 293–313.

Hopf, T. (1998) 'The Promise of Constructivism in International Relations Theory', *International Security* 23(1): 171–200.

Horvath, G. (2011) 'CSDP Military Ambitions and Potentials: Do We Know What We Have?', *Studia Diplomatica* 64(1): 55–60.

House of Commons (2009) Foreign Affairs Committee, 'Human Rights Report 2008', 7th Report of Session 2008–9, July, London: House of Commons.

House of Lords (2010) European Union Committee, 'Stars and Dragons: The EU and China', 7th Report of Session 2009–10, March, London: House of Lords.

House of Lords (2011) European Union Committee, 'The EU's Afghan Police Mission', Report with Evidence, 8th Report of Session 2010–11, London: House of Lords.

Hout, W. (2010) 'Between Development and Security: The European Union, Governance and Fragile States', *Third World Quarterly* 31(1): 141–57.

Howorth, J. (2001) 'The "New Faces" of Lisbon: Assessing the Performance of Catherine Ashton and Herman van Rompuy on the Global Stage', *European Foreign Affairs Review* 16(3): 303–23

Howorth, J. (2004) 'Discourse, Ideas, and Epistemic Communities in European Security and Defence Policy', *West European Politics* 27(2): 211–34.

Howorth, J. (2007) *Security and Defence Policy in the European Union*, Basingstoke: Palgrave Macmillan.

Howorth, J. (2009) 'The Case for an EU Grand Strategy', in S. Biscop, J. Howorth and B. Giegerich, *Europe: A Time for Strategy*, Egmont Paper 27, Brussels: Egmont.

Howorth, J. (2010) *The 'Political and Security Committee': A Case Study in 'Supranational Inter-Governmentalism'?*, Cahiers Européens de Sciences Po 1, Paris: Centre d'Études Européennes, Sciences Po. Online. Available HTTP: <http://www.cee.sciences-po.fr/fr/publications/les-cahiers-europeens.html>.

HTSPE Ltd (2008) *RELEX/Studies/IFS/Security and Development 2008. Final Report*, Hemel Hempstead: HTPSE Ltd.

Huysmans, J. (2000) 'The European Union and the Securitization of Migration', *Journal of Common Market Studies* 38(5): 751–77.

Huysmans, J. (2002) 'Defining Social Constructivism in Security Studies: The Normative Dilemma of Writing Security', *Alternatives: Global, Local, Political* 27(1): 41–62.

Huysmans, J. (2006) *The Politics of Insecurity: Fear, Migration and Asylum in the EU*, Abingdon: Routledge.

Huysmans, J. (2007) 'Revisiting Copenhagen: Or, on the Creative Development of a Security Studies Agenda in Europe', *International Security* 4: 43–67.

Hyde-Price, A. (1991) *European Security beyond the Cold War: Four Scenarios for the Year 2010*, London: Sage.

Hyde-Price, A. (2000) *Germany and European Order: Enlarging NATO and the European Union*, Manchester: Manchester University Press

Hyde-Price, A. (2004) 'European Security, Strategic Culture, and the Use of Force', *European Security* 13(4): 323–43.

Hyde-Price, A. (2006) 'Normative Power Europe: A Realist Critique', *Journal of European Public Policy* 13 (2): 217–34.

Hyde-Price, A. (2007) *European Security in the Twenty-First Century: The Challenge of Multipolarity*, Abingdon: Routledge.

Ikenberry, G.J. (2001) *After Victory: Institutions, Strategic Restraint, and the Rebuilding of Order after Major Wars*, Princeton: Princeton University Press.

Ikenberry, G.J. and Moravcsik, A. (2001) 'Liberal Theory and the Politics of Security in Northeast Asia', paper prepared for the Ford Foundation Project on Non-Traditional Security, Seoul, South Korea. Online. Available HTTP: <http://www.princeton.edu/~amoravcs/publications.html>.

Institute for National Strategic Studies (2006) NATO and the EU: Improving Practical Cooperation. Summary of a Transatlantic Workshop Organized by the Institute for National Strategic Studies in Partnership with the Ministry of Defence of Finland, Washington, DC, March 20–21.

International Atomic Energy Agency (IAEA) (2004) Communication Dated 26 November Received from the Permanent Representatives of France, Germany, Islamic Republic of Iran and the United Kingdom Concerning the Agreement Signed in Paris on 15 November 2004 (INFCIRC/637), 26 November. Online. Available HTTP: <http://www.iaea.org/Publications/Documents/Infcircs/2004/infcirc637.pdf>.

International Crisis Group (2010) *The Rule of Law in Independent Kosovo*, Europe Report 204, Brussels: International Crisis Group.

International Energy Agency (IEA) (2009a) *World Energy Outlook*, Paris: IEA.

International Energy Agency (IEA) (2009b) *End User Petroleum Product Prices and Average Crude Oil Import Costs*, Paris: IEA.

International Institute for Strategic Studies (2005) *Strategic Survey 2004/5*, Abingdon: Routledge.

International Institute for Strategic Studies (2006) *Strategic Survey 2005/6*, Abingdon: Routledge.

International Institute for Strategic Studies (2007) *Strategic Survey 2007*, Abingdon: Routledge.

International Institute for Strategic Studies (2008) *Strategic Survey 2008*, Abingdon: Routledge.

Ioannides, I. (2007) 'Police Mission in Macedonia', in M. Emerson and E. Gross (eds), *Evaluating the EU's Crisis Missions in the Balkans*, Brussels: Centre for European Policy Studies.

Islam, S. (2010) 'Pakistan–EU Summit', Dawn.com, 17 April. Online. Available HTTP: <http://www.dawn.com>.

Jackson, R. (2000) *The Global Covenant: Human Conduct in a World of States*, Oxford: Oxford University Press.

Jakobsen, P.V. (2000) 'Focus on the CNN Effect Misses the Point: The Real Media Impact on Conflict Management is Invisible and Indirect', *Journal of Peace Research* 37(2): 131–43.

Jervis, R. (1999) 'Realism, Neoliberalism, and Cooperation: Understanding the Debate', *International Security* 24(1): 42–63.

Johnston, A.I. (1995a) 'Thinking about Strategic Culture', *International Security* 19(4) 33–64.

Johnston, A.I. (1995b) *Cultural Realism: Strategic Culture and Grand Strategy in Ming China*, Princeton: Princeton University Press.

Johnstone, I. (2010) 'Emerging Doctrine for Political Missions', in *2010 Review of Political Missions*, New York: New York Centre on International Cooperation.

Jørgensen, K.E. (ed.) (1997a) *European Approaches to Crisis Management*, The Hague: Kluwer.

Jørgensen, K.E. (ed.) (1997b) *Reflective Approaches to European Governance*, London: Macmillan Press.

Jørgensen, K.E. (2004) 'European Foreign Policy: Conceptualising the Domain', in W. Carlsnaes, H. Sjursen and B. White (eds), *Contemporary European Foreign Policy*, London: Sage.

Jørgensen, K.E. (2009) 'The European Union and International Organizations: A Framework for Analysis', in K.E. Jørgensen (ed.), *The European Union and International Organizations*, Abingdon: Routledge.

Jørgensen, K.E. (2010) *International Relations Theory: A New Introduction*, Basingstoke: Palgrave Macmillan.

Juncos, A.E. (2007) 'Police Mission in Bosnia and Herzegovina', in M. Emerson and E. Gross (eds), *Evaluating the EU's Crisis Missions in the Balkans*, Brussels: Centre for European Policy Studies.

Juncos, A.E. and Pomorska, K. (2006) *Playing the Brussels Game: Strategic Socialisation in CFSP Council Working Groups*, European Integration Online Papers 10(11). Online. Available HTTP: <http://eiop.or.at/eiop/index.php/eiop/article/view/2006_011a>.

Juncos, A.E. and Reynolds, C. (2007) 'The Political Security Committee: Governing in the Shadow', *European Foreign Affairs Review* 12: 127–47.

Juppé, A. (2011) Interview given to *Mondes – Les Cahiers du Quai d'Orsay*, no.7, June. Online. Available HTTP: <http://www.ambafrance-uk.org/Alain-Juppe-s-interview-in-Foreign>.

Kagan, R. (2003) *Paradise and Power: America and Europe in the New World Order*, London: Atlantic Books.

Kagan, R. (2008) *The Return of History and the End of Dreams*, London: Atlantic Books.

Kaldor, M. and Glasius, M. (n.d.) 'EU Security Architecture in Relation to Security and Development'. Online. Available: <www.cercle.lu/wp-content/uploads/imported/doc/dfid_final.pdf>.

Kaldor, M. and Martin, M. (eds) (2009) *Human Security in the European Union: External Interventions and Missions*, Abingdon: Routledge.

Kampfner, J. (2009) *Freedom for Sale*, London: Simon & Schuster.

Kaplan, R. (2009a) 'Centre Stage for the Twenty-First Century: Power Plays in the Indian Ocean', *Foreign Affairs* 88(2): 16–32.

Kaplan, R. (2009b) 'The Revenge of Geography', *Foreign Policy* 172, May/June: 96–105.

Kaplan, R. (2010a) 'The Geography of Chinese Power: How Far Can Beijing Reach on Land and at Sea?', *Foreign Affairs* 89(3): 22–41.

Kaplan, R. (2010b) *Monsoon: The Indian Ocean and the Future of American Power*, New York: Random House.

Kaplan, R. (2010c) *South Asia's Geography of Conflict*, Washington, DC: Centre for a New American Security.

Karacasulu, N. and Uzgören, E. (2007) 'Explaining Social Constructivist Contributions to Security Studies', *Perceptions, Journal of International Affairs* 12: 27–48.

Karaganov, S. (2007) 'A New Epoch of Confrontation', *Russia in Global Affairs* 5(4): 23–36.

Karaganov, S. (2010) 'NATO's Emphasis on Russia', *Russia in Global Affairs*, 25 December. Online. Available HTTP: <http://eng.globalaffairs.ru/pubcol/NATOs-Emphasis-on-Russia-15074>.

Katzenstein, P. (ed.) (1996) *The Culture of National Security: Norms and Identity in World Politics*, New York: Columbia University Press.

Kay, S. (2000) 'What Is a Strategic Partnership?', *Problems of Post-Communism* 47(3): 15–24.

Kelley, J. (2006) 'New Wine in Old Wineskins: Promoting Political Reforms through the New European Neighbourhood Policy', *Journal of Common Market Studies* 44(1): 29–55.

Kelstrup, M. and Williams, M. (2000) *International Relations Theory and the Politics of European Integration: Power, Security and Community*, London: Routledge.

Keohane, D. (2005) *The EU and Counter-Terrorism*, London: CER.

Keohane, D. (2008a) 'The Absent Friend: EU Foreign Policy and Counter-Terrorism', *Journal of Common Market Studies* 46(1): 125–46.

Keohane, D. (ed.) (2008b) *Towards a European Defence Market*, Chaillot Paper 113 (November), Paris: European Union Institute for Security Studies.

Keohane, R.O. (1986) 'Theory of World Politics: Structural Realism and Beyond', in Keohane (ed.), *Realism and Its Critics*, New York: Columbia University Press.

Keohane, R.O. (1989) *International Institutions and State Power: Essays in International Relations Theory*, Boulder, CO: Westview Press.

Keohane, R.O. and Nye, J.S. (1977) *Power and Interdependence: World Politics in Transition*, Boston: Little, Brown.

Keohane, R.O, Nye, J.S. and Hoffmann, S. (eds) (1993) *After the Cold War: International Institutions and State Strategies in Europe, 1989–1991*, Cambridge, MA: Harvard University Press.

Kerchove, G. de and Biolley, S. de (2010) 'The EU Counter-Terrorism Coordinator', in J. Monar (ed.), *The Institutional Dimension of the European Union's Area of Freedom, Security and Justice*, Brussels: PIE/Peter Lang.

Keukeleire, S. (2003) 'The European Union as a Diplomatic Actor: Internal, Traditional, and Structural Diplomacy', *Diplomacy and Statecraft* 14(3): 31–56.

Keukeleire, S. (2004) 'EU Structural Foreign Policy and Structural Conflict Prevention', in V. Kronenberger and J. Wouters (eds), *The European Union and Conflict Prevention: Policy and Legal Aspects*, The Hague: TMC Asser Press.

Keukeleire, S. and Bruyninckx, H. (2011) 'The European Union, the BRICs, and the Emerging New World Order', in C. Hill and M. Smith (eds), *International Relations and the European Union*, Oxford: Oxford University Press.

Khandekar, Gauri (2011) *The EU and India: A Loveless Arranged Marriage*, Policy Brief, Brussels: FRIDE.

Khasson, V., Vasilyan, S. and Vos, H. (2008) '"Everybody Needs Good Neighbours": The EU and Its Neighbourhood', in J. Orbie (ed.), *Europe's Global Role: External Policies of the European Union*, Aldershot: Ashgate.

King, A. (2006) 'Towards a European Military Culture?', *Defence Studies* 6(3): 257–77.

Kirchner, E. and Sperling, J. (2007) *EU Security Governance*, Manchester: Manchester University Press.

Kirchner, E.J. and Sperling, J. (2010) *National Security Cultures: Patterns of Global Governance*, Abingdon: Routledge.

Kissack, R. (2007) *European Union Member State Coordination in the United Nations System: Towards a Methodology for Analysis*, Working Paper 2001/1, London: European Foreign Policy Unit.

Ko, S. (2006) 'Strategic Partnership in a Unipolar System: The Sino–Russian Relationship', *Issues and Studies* 42(3): 203–25.

Koeth, W. (2010) 'State Building without a State: The EU's Dilemma in Defining Its Relations with Kosovo', *European Foreign Affairs Review* 15: 227–47.

Koivula, T. (2009) 'Towards an EU Military Ethos', *European Foreign Affairs Review* 14: 171–90.

König, N. (2011) *The EU and the Libyan Crisis: In Quest of Coherence?*, IAI Working Papers 11/19, Rome: Istituto Affari Internazionale.

Korski, D. (2009) *Shaping Europe's Afghan Surge*, Policy Brief, London: European Council on Foreign Relations.

Korski, D. (2010) 'The Rise of the World's Lynchpin States', European Council on Foreign Relations. Online. Available HTTP: <http://ecfr.eu/content/entry/commentary_europe_and_the_rise_of_the_worlds_lynchpin_states_korski/>.

Kouchner, B. (2010) Statement on the Appointment of Pierre Vimont as Executive Secretary-General of the European External Action Service Paris, 25 October. Online. Available HTTP: <http://www.ambafrance-uk.org/French-diplomat-appointed-EEAS.html>.

Kowert, P. and Legro, J. (1996) 'Norms, Identity, and Their Limits: A Theoretical Reprise', in P.J. Katzenstein (ed.), *The Culture of National Security: Norms and Identity in World Politics*, New York: Columbia University Press.

Krahmann, E. (2003) 'Conceptualizing Security Governance', *Cooperation and Conflict* 38(5): 5–26.

Krahmann, E. (2005) 'Security Governance and Networks: New Theoretical Perspectives in Transatlantic Security', *Cambridge Review of International Affairs* 18: 15–30.

Krahmann, E. (2011) 'Beck and Beyond: Selling Security in the World Risk Society', *Review of International Studies* 37: 1–24.

Krastev, I. and Leonard, M. (2010) *The Spectre of a Multipolar Europe*, London: European Council on Foreign Relations.

Krause, A. (2003) 'The European Union's Africa Policy: The Commission as Policy Entrepreneur in the CFSP', *European Foreign Affairs Review* 8(2): 221–37.

Krause, K. and Williams, M.C. (eds) (1997) *Critical Security Studies: Concepts and Cases*, London: UCL Press.

Krebs, R.R. (1999) 'Perverse Institutionalism: NATO and the Greco-Turkish Conflict', *International Organization* 53(2): 343–77.

Krepinevich, A. and Work, R.O. (2007) *A New Global Defence Posture for the Second Transoceanic Era*, Washington, DC: Center for Strategic and Budgetary Assessments.

Kubigg, B.W. (2006) 'Iran and the Nuclear Non-Proliferation Treaty', Policy Department Briefing Paper, August, European Parliament.

Kurowska, X. (2008) 'More than a Balkan Crisis Manager: The EUJUST Themis in Georgia', in M. Merlingen and R. Ostrauskaité (eds), *European Security and Defence Policy: An Implementation Perspective*, Abingdon: Routledge.

Kurpas, S., Crum, B., de Schoutheete, P., Keller, J., Dehousse, F., Andoura, S., Missiroli, A., Hagemann, S. and Bribosia, H. (2007) *The Treaty of Lisbon: Implementing the Institutional Innovations. Joint Study of CEPS, EGMONT and EPC*, Brussels: Centre for European Policy Studies, Egmont and the European Policy Centre.

Kuzio, T. (2011) 'Political Culture and Democracy: Ukraine as an Immobile State', *East European Politics and Societies* 25(1): 88–113.

Laïdi, Z. (2005) *La norme sans la force: l'énigme de la puissance européenne*, Paris: Presses de Sciences Po.

Lavenex, S. and Schimmelfennig, F. (eds) (2010) *EU External Governance: Projecting EU Rules beyond Membership*, Abingdon: Routledge.

Leander, A. (2005) 'The Power to Construct International Security: On the Significance of Private Military Companies', *Millennium: Journal of International Studies* 22: 803–26.

Lellouche, P. (2010) Speech to the National Assembly Foreign Affairs Committee Paris, 2 October. Online. Available HTTP: <http://www.ambafrance-uk.org/Pierre-Lellouche-in-National>.

Leonard, M. (2005) *Why Europe Will Run the 21st Century*, London: Fortune Books.

Leonard, M. and Popescu, N. (2007) *A Power Audit of EU–Russia Relations*. London: European Council on Foreign Relations. Online. Available HTTP: <http://www.ecfr.eu/content/entry/eu_russia_relations/...>.

Lesser, I., Hoffman, B., Arquilla, J., Ronfeldt, D., Zanini, M. and Jenkins, B. (1999) *Countering the New Terrorism*, Washington, DC: RAND.

Lewis, J. (1998) 'Constructing Interests: The Committee of Permanent Representatives and Decision-Making in the European Union', PhD dissertation, University of Wisconsin-Madison.

Lindley-French, J. (2002) 'In the Shade of Locarno? Why European Defence is Failing', *International Affairs* 78(4): 789–811.

Lindstrom, G. (2011) 'The EU Battlegroups: Options for the Future', *Studia Diplomatica* 64(1): 29–40.

Linklater, A. (2000) 'The Question of the Next Stage in International Relations Theory: A Critical-Theoretical Point of View', in A. Linklater (ed.), *International Relations. Critical Concepts in Political Science*, London: Routledge.

Linklater, A. (2005) 'Political Community and Human Security', in K. Booth (ed.), *Critical Security Studies and World Politics*, Boulder, CO: Lynne Rienner.

Lippert, B.(1993) 'Questions and Scenarios on EC–CIS/Republics Relations – An Outline on the Political Dimension', in H.-G. Ehrhart, A. Kreikemeyer and A.V. Zagorski (eds), *The Former Soviet Union and European Security: Between Integration and Disintegration*, Baden-Baden: Nomos.

Lobell, S., Ripsman, N. and Taliaferro, J. (eds) (2009) *Neoclassical Realism, the State and Foreign Policy*, Cambridge: Cambridge University Press.

Luhmann, N. (1993) *Risk: A Sociological Theory*, trans. R. Barrett, New York: Walter de Gruyter.

Lustgarten, A. (2008) *China's Great Train: Beijing's Drive West and the Campaign to Remake Tibet*, New York: Times Books.

Lutterbeck, D. (2005) 'Blurring the Dividing Line: The Convergence of Internal and External Security in Western Europe', *European Security* 14: 231–53.

Lynch, D. (2005) 'The Security Dimension of the European Neighbourhood Policy', *International Spectator* 40(1): 33–43.

Lynch, D. (2009) 'ESDP and the OSCE', in G. Grevi, D. Helly and D. Keohane (eds), *European Security and Defence Policy: The First Ten Years (1999–2009)*, Paris: European Union Institute for Security Studies.

McCalla, R. (1996) 'NATO's Persistence after the Cold War', *International Organization* 50(3): 445–75.

Mace, C. (2003) 'Operation Concordia: Developing a "European" Approach to Crisis Management?', *International Peacekeeping* 11: 474–90.

McFarlane, S.N. and Khong, Y.F. (2006) *Human Security and the UN: A Critical History*, Bloomington: Indiana University Press.

Machiavelli, N. (1961) *The Prince*, London: Penguin Books.

Mackinder, H.J. (1904) 'The Geographical Pivot of History', *Geographical Journal* 23(4): 421–44.

McSweeney, Bill (1996) 'Identity and Security: Buzan and the Copenhagen School', *Review of International Studies* 22(1): 81–93.

Mahan, A.T. (1912) 'The Place of Force in International Relations', *North American Review* 195(674): 28–39.

Major, C. (2008) *EU–UN Cooperation in Military Crisis Management: The Experience of EUFOR RD Congo in 2006*, Occasional Paper 72, Paris: European Union Institute for Security Studies.

Malone, D. (2010) 'An Evolving Security Council', in B.D. Jones, S. Forman and R. Gowan (eds), *Cooperating for Peace and Security: Evolving Institutions in a Context of Changing U.S. Security Policy*, New York: Cambridge University Press.

Mandil, C. (2008) 'Sécurité énergétique et Union européenne – Propositions pour la Présidence française', Report for the French Prime Minister, April.

Mann, J. (2009) *The Rebellion of Ronald Reagan: A History of the End of the Cold War*, New York: Viking.

Manners, I. (2002) 'Normative Power Europe: A Contradiction in Terms?', *Journal of Common Market Studies* 40(2): 235–58.

Manners, I. (2006a) 'Normative Power Europe Reconsidered: Beyond the Crossroads', *Journal of European Public Policy* 13(2): 182–99.

Manners, I. (2006b) 'European Union "Normative Power" and the Security Challenge', *European Security* 15(4): 405–21.

Manners, I. (2007) 'Another Europe Is Possible: Critical Perspectives on European Union Politics', in K.E. Jørgensen, M. Pollack and B. Rosamond (eds), *The Handbook of European Union Politics*, London: Sage.

Marshall, Sir Peter (2008) Cited in House of Common Foreign Affairs Committee, *Foreign Policy Aspects of the Lisbon Treaty*, London: The Stationery Office.

Martin, L.M. and Simmons, B. (eds) (2001) *International Institutions: An International Organization Reader*, Cambridge, MA: MIT Press.

Martinelli, M. (2006) 'Helping Transition: The EU Police Mission in the DRC (EUPOL Kinshasa) in the Framework of EU Policies in the Great Lakes', *European Foreign Affairs Review*, 11(3): 379–400.

Martinelli, M. (2008) 'Implementing the CSDP in Africa: The Case of the Democratic Republic of Congo', in M. Merlingen and R. Ostrauskaitė (eds), *European Security and Defence Policy: An Implementation Perspective*, Abingdon: Routledge.

Matlary, J.H. (2006) 'When Soft Power Turns Hard: Is an EU Strategic Culture Possible?', *Security Dialogue* 37(1): 105–21.

Maull, H. (1990) 'Germany and Japan: The New Civilian Powers', *Foreign Affairs* 69(5): 91–106.

Maull, H. (1993) 'Civilian Power: The Concept and Its Relevance for Security Issues', in L. Babic and B. Huldt (eds), *Mapping the Unknown: Towards a New World Order*, Stockholm: Swedish Institute of International Affairs.

Maull, H. (1996) 'Zivilmacht Deutschlands: Vierzehn Thesen für eine neue deutsche Aussenpolitik', in D. Senghaas (ed.), *Frieden Machen*, Frankfurt am Main: Suhrkamp.

Maulny, J.-P. (2010) *L'Union européenne et le défi de la réduction des budgets de défense*, Paris: IRIS.

Mearsheimer. J. (1990) 'Back to the Future: Instability in Europe after the Cold War', *International Security* 15(1): 5–56.

Mearsheimer, J. (1995a) 'The False Promise of International Institutions', *International Security* 19(3): 5–49.

Mearsheimer, J. (1995b) 'The False Promise of International Institutions', in M. Brown, S. Lynn-Jones and S. Miller (eds), *The Perils of Anarchy: Contemporary Realism and International Security*, Cambridge, MA: MIT Press.

Mearsheimer, J. (2000) 'A Realist Reply', in M. Brown, O. Cote, S. Lynn-Jones and S. Miller (eds), *Theories of War and Peace*, Cambridge, MA: MIT Press.

Mearsheimer, J. (2001) *The Tragedy of Great Power Politics*, New York: W.W. Norton & Co.

Meier, O. (2008) 'The EU's Nonproliferation Efforts: Limited Success', *Arms Control Today* 38. Online. Available HTTP: <http://www.armscontrol.org/act/2008_05/OliverFeature>.

Meier, O. and Quille, G. (2005) 'Testing Time for EU Non-proliferation Strategy', *Arms Control Today* 35(4). Online. Available HTTP: <http://www.armscontrol.org/act/2005_05/Oliver_Quille>.

Meister, S. (2011) *A New Start for Russian–EU Security Policy? The Weimar Triangle, Russia and the EU's Eastern Neighbourhood*, Genshagener Papers 7 (July), Genshagen: Stiftung Genshagen. Online. Available HTTP: <http://www.robert-schuman.eu/doc/actualites/genshagener-papiere–2011–7-eng.pdf>.

Melvin, N.J. (2007) *The European Union's Strategic Role in Central Asia*, CEPS Policy Brief 128 (March). Online. Available HTTP: <http://www.ceps.eu/ceps/download/1315>.

Menon, A. (2004) 'From Crisis to Catharsis: ESDP after Iraq', *International Affairs* 80(4): 631–48.

Menon, A. (2009) 'Empowering Paradise? The CSDP at Ten', *International Affairs* 85(2): 227–46.

Mérand, F. (2003) 'Dying for the Union?', *European Societies* 5(3): 253–82.

Mérand, F. (2008) *European Defence Policy. Beyond the Nation State*, Oxford: Oxford University Press.

Mérand, F., Foucault, M. and Irondelle, B. (eds) (2011) *European Security since the Fall of the Berlin Wall*, Toronto: University of Toronto Press.

Merlingen, M. (2007) 'Everything is Dangerous: A Critique of "Normative Power Europe"', *Security Dialogue* 38: 435–53.

Merlingen, M. (2009) 'The EU Police Mission in Bosnia and Herzegovina (EUPM)', in G. Grevi, D. Helly and D. Keohane (eds), *European Security and Defence Policy: The First Ten Years (1999–2009)*, Paris: European Union Institute for Security Studies.

Merlingen, M. and Ostrauskaitė, R. (2005a) 'A Dense Policy Space? The Police Aid of the OSCE and the EU', in Institute for Peace Research and Security Policy at the University of Hamburg (ed.), *OSCE Yearbook 2004*, Baden-Baden: Nomos.

Merlingen, M. and Ostrauskaité, R. (2005b) 'CSDP Police Mission: Meaning, Context and Operational Challenges', *European Foreign Affairs Review* 10(2): 215–35.

Merlingen, M. with Ostrauskaité, R. (2006) *European Union Peacebuilding and Policing: Governance and the European Security and Defence Policy*, Abingdon: Routledge.

Meyer, C.O. (2005) 'Convergence towards a European Strategic Culture? A Constructivist Framework for Explaining Changing Norms', *European Journal of International Relations* 11(4): 523–49.

Meyer, C.O. (2006) *The Quest for a European Strategic Culture: Changing Norms on Security and Defence in the European Union*, Basingstoke: Palgrave Macmillan.

Meyer, C.O. (2011) 'The Purpose and Pitfalls of Constructivist Forecasting: Insights from Strategic Culture Research for the European Union's Evolution as a Military Power', *International Studies Quarterly* 55(3): 669–90.

Meyer, C.O. and Strickmann, E. (2011) 'Solidifying Constructivism: How Material and Ideational Factors Interact in European Defence', *Journal of Common Market Studies* 49(1): 61–82.

Mezzera, M., Pavici, M. and Specker, L. (2009) *Governance Components in Peace Agreements: Fundamental Elements of State and Peace Building?*, Clingendael Paper, The Hague: The Netherlands Institute of International Relations.

Michel, L. (2010) *NATO and the EU: Achieving Unity of Effort in a Comprehensive Approach*, Washington, DC: Institute for National Strategic Studies. Online. Available HTTP: <http://www.equilibri.net/nuovo/sites/default/files/ICTF%20Atlantic%20Council%20Sep%2010.pdf>.

Michel, L. and Herbst, J. (2011) 'Why the EU Should Patrol Libya', *European Voice*, 14 July.

Missiroli, A (2001) 'European Security Policy: The Challenge of Coherence', *European Foreign Affairs Review* 6(2): 177–96.

Missiroli, A. (2004) 'The EU and Its Changing Neighbourhood: Stabilization, Integration and Partnership', in R. Dannreuther (ed.), *European Union Foreign and Security Policy: Towards a Neighbourhood Strategy*, London and New York: Routledge.

Missiroli, A. (2010) 'The New EU "Foreign Policy" System after Lisbon: A Work in Progress', *European Foreign Affairs Review* 15: 427–52.

Mitchell, L. (2007) 'Beyond Bombs and Ballots: Dispelling Myths about Democracy Assistance', *National Interest* March/April: 36

Mohammadi, M. (2005) 'Nuclear Case from Beginning to End in Interview with Dr Hasan Ruhani', *Keyhan*, 26 July.

Moravcsik, A. (1998) *The Choice for Europe: Social Purpose and State Power from Messina to Maastricht*, Ithaca, NY: Cornell University Press.

Moravcsik, A. (1999) 'Is Something Rotten in the State of Denmark? Constructivism and European Integration', *Journal of European Public Policy* 6(4): 669–81.

Moravcsik, A. (2001) 'Constructivism and European Integration: A Critique', in T. Christiansen, K.E. Jørgensen and A. Wiener (eds), *The Social Construction of Europe*, London: Sage.

Morgenthau, H. (1993) *Politics among Nations: The Struggle for Power and Peace*, New York: McGraw-Hill.

Morsut, C. (2009) 'Effective Multilateralism? EU–UN Cooperation in the DRC, 2003–2006', *International Peacekeeping* 16(2): 261–72.

Moshes, Arkady (2010) 'Avenue of Independence: Will Russian–Belarusian Relations Take the Ukrainian Path?', *Russia in Global Affairs* 8(2). Online. Available HTTP: <http://eng.globalaffairs.ru/number/Avenue_of_Independence–14895>.

Mounier, G. (2009) 'Civilian Crisis Management and the External Dimension of JHA: Inceptive, Functional and Institutional Similarities', *Journal of European Integration* 31: 45–64.

Mousavian, S.H. (2008) *Iran–Europe Relations. Challenges and Opportunities*, Abingdon: Routledge.

Mowle, T. (2004) *Allies at Odds? The United States and the European Union*, Basingstoke: Palgrave Macmillan.

Mühlmann, T. (2008) 'The Police Mission EUPM in Bosnia, 2003–05', in M. Merlingen and R. Ostrauskaité (eds), *European Security and Defence Policy: An Implementation Perspective*, Abingdon: Routledge.

Müller-Wille, B. (2004) *For Our Eyes Only? Shaping an Intelligence Community within the EU*, Occasional Paper 50, Paris: European Union Institute for Security Studies.

Murphy, J. (2008) 'Foreword', in J. Welsh, and D. Fearn (eds), *Engagement: Public Diplomacy in a Globalised World*, London: FCO. Online. Available HTTP: <http://ics.leeds.ac.uk/papers/pmt/exhibits/3055/pd-engagement-jul–08.pdf>.

Bibliography

Musu, C. (2011) 'European Security and the Middle East Peace Process', in F. Mérand, M. Foucault and B. Irondelle (eds), *European Security since the Fall of the Berlin Wall*, Toronto: University of Toronto Press.

Nadkarni, V. (2010) *Strategic Partnerships in Asia: Balancing without Alliances*, Abingdon: Routledge.

NATO (2010a) 'Strategic Concept for the Defense and Security of the Members of the North Atlantic Treaty Organization', approved November 19. Online. Available HTTP: <http://www.nato.int/cps/en/natolive/official_texts_68580.htm>.

NATO (2010b) *NATO 2020: Assured Security: Dynamic Engagement, Analysis and Recommendations of the Group of Experts on a New Strategic Concept for NATO*, Brussels: NATO Public Policy Division. Online. Available HTTP: <http://www.nato.int/strategic-concept/expertsreport.pdf>.

Nau, H.R. (2002) *At Home Abroad: Identity and Power in American Foreign Policy*, Cornell Studies in Political Economy, Ithaca, NY: Cornell University Press.

Neumann, I. (2005) 'To Be a Diplomat', *International Studies Perspectives* 6: 72–93.

Neumann, P.R. (2006) 'Europe's Jihadist Dilemma', *Survival* 48(2): 71–84.

Niblett, R. and Mix, D. (2006) *Transatlantic Approaches to Sanctions: Principles and Recommendations for Action*, CSIS Europe Program Report, 10 October, Washington, DC: Center for Strategic and International Studies.

Nickel, D. and Quille, G. (2007) *In the Shadow of the Constitution: Common Foreign and Security Policy – European Security and Defence Policy Adapting to a Changing External Environment*, Jean Monnet Working Paper 2/07, New York: Jean Monnet Center for International and Regional Economic Law and Justice, New York University School of Law.

Nicolaidis, K. (2004) 'The Power of the Superpowerless', in T. Lindberg (ed.), *Beyond Paradise and Power: Europe, America, and the Future of a Troubled Partnership*, Abingdon: Routledge.

Nicolson, H. (1953) *The Evolution of Diplomatic Method*, Westport, CT: Greenwood Press.

Niebuhr, R. (2005) [1932] *Moral Man and Immoral Society*, London: Continuum.

Norheim-Martinsen, P.M. (2011) 'Our Work Here is Done: European Union Peacekeeping in Africa', *African Security Review* 20(2): 17–28

North, D.C., Wallis, J.J. and Weingast, B.R. (2009) *Violence and Social Orders. A Conceptual Framework for Interpreting Recorded Human History*, Cambridge: Cambridge University Press.

Noutcheva, G. (2009) 'Fake, Partial and Imposed Compliance: The Limits of the EU's Normative Power in the Western Balkans', *Journal of European Public Policy* 16: 1065–84.

Novosseloff, A. and Gowan, R. (2010) 'Le renforcement de la force intérimaire des Nations Unies au Liban', *Annuaire Français de Relations Internationales* 11: 45–67.

Nuttall, S. (1992) *European Political Cooperation*, Oxford: Oxford University Press.

Nuttall, S. (2000) *European Foreign Policy*, Oxford: Oxford University Press.

Oakeshott, M. (1991) *Rationalism in Politics and Other Essays*, Indianapolis: Liberty Press.

OCCAR (2010) OCCAR at a Glance. Online. Available HTTP: <http://www.occar-ea.org/1>.

ODI and Netherlands Ministry of Foreign Affairs (2010) 'Development, Security and Transitions in Fragile States', Meeting Report, February.

OECD (1998) *European Community Development Co-operation Review Series*, 30, Paris: OECD-DAC.

OECD (2002) *European Community Development Assistance Committee (DAC), Peer Review*, Paris: OECD-DAC.

OECD (2007a) *Principles for Good International Engagement in Fragile States and Situations*, Paris: OECD-DAC.

OECD (2007b) Reporting Directives for the Creditor Reporting System. Online. Available HTTP: <http://www.oecd.org/dataoecd/16/53/1948102.pdf>.

OECD (2007c) *European Community Development Assistance Committee (DAC), Peer Review*, Paris: OECD-DAC.

OECD (2008) 'Is It ODA', Factsheet, November 2008. Online. Available HTTP: <http://www.oecd.org/dataoecd/21/21/34086975.pdf>.

OECD (2010) *Report on Multilateral Aid*, Paris: OECD-DAC.

OECD (2011) *Supporting State-Building in Situations of Conflict and Fragility*, Paris: OECD-DAC.

Olsen, G.R. (2004) 'Changing European Concerns: Security and Complex Political Emergencies instead of Development', in K. Arts and A.K. Dickson (eds), *European Development Co-operation: From Model to Symbol*, Manchester: Manchester University Press.

Olsen, G.R. (2009a) 'Conflict Management in Africa: American and European Union Policies Compared', paper presented at ISA 50th Annual Convention, New York, 15–18 February.

Olsen, G.R. (2009b) 'The Missing Link: EPAs, Security and Development Interventions in Africa', in G. Faber and J. Orbie (eds), *Beyond Market Access for Economic Development: EU–Africa Relations in Transition*, Abingdon: Routledge.

Olsen, G.R. (2009c) 'Africa: Still a Secondary Security Challenge to the European Union', in T. Tardy (ed.), *European Security in a Global Context: Internal and External Dynamics*, Abingdon: Routledge.

O'Neill, J. (2007) *BRICs and Beyond*, New York: Goldman Sachs.

Onuf, N. (2001) 'The Politics of Constructivism', in K. Fierke and K.E. Jørgensen (eds), *Constructing International Relations: The Next Generation*, Armonk, NY: M.E. Sharpe.

Orbie, J. and Versluys, H. (2008) 'The European Union's International Development Policy: Leading and Benevolent?', in J. Orbie (ed.), *Europe's Global Role: External Policies of the European Union*, Aldershot: Ashgate.

Organization for Security and Co-operation in Europe (OSCE) (1999) *Charter for European Security*, Istanbul, November. Online. Available HTTP: <http://www.unece.org/trans/osce/osceunece/istachart99e.pdf>.

Organization for Security and Co-operation in Europe (OSCE) (2003) 'Strategy to Address Threats to Security and Stability in the Twenty-First Century'. Online. Available HTTP: <http://www.osce.org/documents/mcs/2003/12/17499_en.pdf>.

Organization for Security and Co-operation in Europe (OSCE) (2008) 'Background Report – Human Rights, Ethnic Relations and Democracy in Kosovo (Summer 2007 – Summer 2008)', Pristina, 5 September.

Organization for Security and Co-operation in Europe (OSCE) (2009) 'Survey of OSCE Field Operations', SEC.GAL/165/09, 9 October, OSCE Secretariat, Conflict Prevention Centre. Online. Available HTTP: <http://www.osce.org/documents/cpc/2008/10/3242_en.pdf>.

Owens, M.T. (1999) 'In Defence of Classical Geopolitics', *Naval War College Review* 52(4): 59–76.

Paris, R. (2004) 'Human Security Paradigm Shift or Hot Air?', in M. Brown, O. Coté, S. Lynn-Jones and S. Miller (eds), *New Global Dangers: Changing Dimensions of International Security*, Cambridge, MA: MIT Press.

Parker, G. (2009) 'Supremacy of the Nation State Wins Out', *Financial Times*, 19 November.

Parmentier, F. (2008) 'The ENP Facing a *de facto* State: Lessons from the Transnistrian Question', in L. Delcour and E. Tulmets (eds), *Pioneer Europe? Testing EU Foreign Policy in the Neighbourhood*, Baden-Baden: Nomos.

Parrein, P.-J. (2010) *Some Ideas for European Defence Cooperation from the Case Study of the Belgian–Dutch Naval Cooperation*, Focus Paper 25, Brussels: Royal High Institute for Defence.

Pavlyuk, O. (2009) 'The Platform for Co-operative Security: Ten Years of Co-operation', in Institute for Peace Research and Security Policy at the University of Hamburg (ed.), *OSCE Yearbook*, Baden-Baden: Nomos.

Pedersen, T. (1998) *Germany, France and the Integration of Europe. A Realist Interpretation*, London: Pinter.

Pelkmans, J. and Murphy, A. (1991) 'Catapulted into Leadership: The Community's Trade and Aid Policies vis-à-vis Eastern Europe', *Journal of European Integration* 14(2/3): 125–51.

Peoples, C. and Vaughan-Williams, N. (2009) *Critical Security Studies: An Introduction*, Abingdon: Routledge.

Peral, L. (2010) *EU–India Relations: In Search of a Paradigm: Report and Policy Options*, Paris: European Union Institute for Security Studies.

Perrin de Brichambaut, M. (2009) 'It's Time the EU Stopped Undermining the OSCE', *Europe's World*, Autumn. Online. Available HTTP: <http://www.europesworld.org/NewEnglish/Home_old/Article/tabid/191/ArticleType/articleview/ArticleID/21473/language/en-US/Default.aspx>.

Perthes, V. (2000) 'The Advantages of Complementarity: US and European Policies towards the Middle East Peace Process', *International Spectator* 33(2): 41–56.

Pijpers, A. (1990) *The Vicissitudes of European Political Cooperation: Towards a Realist Interpretation of the EC's Collective Diplomacy*, Leiden: Leiden University Press.

Pilegaard, J. (2009) '… and Never the Twain Shall Meet? An Institutionalist Perspective of EU Trade and Development Policies in the Context of the EPA Negotiations', in J. Orbie and G. Faber (eds), *Beyond Market Access for Development: EU–Africa Relations in Transition*, Abingdon: Routledge.

Pirozzi, N. (2009) *EU Support to African Security Architecture: Funding and Training Components*, Occasional Paper 76 (February), Paris: European Union Institute for Security Studies.

Pirozzi, N. and Sandawi, S. (2009) *Military and Civilian ESDP Missions: Ever Growing and Effective?* Documenti IAI 09/29 (November), Rome: Istituto Affari Internazionali. Online. Available HTTP: <http://www.iai.it/pdf/DocIAI/iai0929.pdf>.

Poole, L. (2010) 'Humanitarian Aid in Conflicts: More Money, More Problems?', 8 July. Online. Available HTTP: <www.globalhumanitarianassistance.org>.

Popescu, N. and Wilson, A. (2009) *The Limits of Enlargement-Lite: European and Russian Power in the Troubled Neighbourhood*, London: European Council on Foreign Relations. Online. Available HTTP: <http://ecfr.eu/content/entry/ecfr_eastern_neighbourhood_wilson_popescu/>.

Popielawska, J. and Deuter, J.M. (2008) Workshop Summary. The Impact of the Lisbon Treaty on ESDP, 11 February. Brussels: European Parliament.

Posch, W. (ed.) (2006) *Iranian Challenges*, Chaillot Paper 89, Paris: European Union Institute for Security Studies

Posch, W. (2011) 'Foreign Minister Mottaki Sacked, Salehi Installed', *SWP-Comments* C02, Berlin, January.

Posen, B.R. (2003) 'Command of the Commons: The Military Foundation of US Hegemony', *International Security* 28(1): 5–46.

Posen, B. (2004a) 'ESDP and the Structure of World Power', *International Spectator* 39(1): 5–17.

Posen, B. (2004b) 'The European Security Strategy: Practical Implications', *Oxford Journal on Good Governance* 1(1): 33–8.

Power, S. (2008) *Chasing the Flame: Sergio Vieira de Mello and the Fight to Save the World*, New York: Penguin Press.

Price, R. and Reus-Smith, C. (1998) 'Dangerous Liaisons? Critical International Theory and Constructivism', *European Journal of International Relations* 4(3): 259–94.

Prodi, R. (2000) '2000–2005: Shaping the New Europe', speech to the European Parliament, Strasbourg, 15 February, Speech/00/41.

Quille, G. (2004) 'The European Security Strategy (ESS): A Framework for European Union Security Interests?', *Journal of International Peacekeeping* 11(3): 1–16.

Quille, G. (2008a) 'The EU's Approach to Tackling the Proliferation of Materials and Weapons of Mass Destruction and Prospects for Cooperation in the Event of a New US Administration', Working Paper, Brussels: European Parliament Directorate General External Policies of the Union.

Quille, G. (2008b) 'The Lisbon Treaty and Its Implications for CFSP/ESDP', Policy Department, European Parliament (PE 388.943), April.

Quille, G. and Keane, R. (2005) 'The EU and Iran: Towards a New Political Security Dialogue', in S.N. Kile (ed.), *Europe and Iran Perspectives on Non-Proliferation*, SIPRI Research Report 21, Oxford: Oxford University Press.

Rasmussen, M.V. (2001) 'Reflexive Security: NATO and International Risk Society', *Millennium: Journal of International Studies* 30(2): 285–309.

Rasmussen, M.V. (2006) *The Risk Society at War: Terror, Technology and Strategy in the Twenty-First Century,* Cambridge: Cambridge University Press.

Rees, W. (2006) *Transatlantic Counter-Terrorism Cooperation: The New Imperative*, Abingdon: Routledge.

Rehman, I. (2009) 'Keeping the Dragon at Bay: India's Counter-Containment of China in Asia', *Asian Security* 5(2): 114–43.

Reissner, J. (2004) 'Europas Beziehungen zum Iran', *Aus Politik und Zeitgeschichte* 9(23): 48–54.

Renard, T. (2009) *A BRIC in the World: Emerging Powers, Europe, and the Coming Order*, Egmont Paper 31, Brussels: Egmont.

Renard, T. (2010a) *Strategy Wanted: The European Union and Strategic Partnerships*, Security Policy Brief 13 (September), Brussels: Egmont.

Renard, T. (2010b) 'Le Syndrome de Copenhague', *Revue Défense Nationale* 731 (June): 155–61.

Renard, T. (2010c) 'EU Strategic Partnerships: Evolution of a Concept, from Amsterdam to Lisbon', *EU–China Observer* 5 (October): 16–22.

Renard, T. (2011) *The Treachery of Strategies: A Call for True EU Strategic Partnerships*, Egmont Paper 45, Brussels: Egmont.

Renard, T. and Biscop, S. (2009) 'The EU's Strategic Partnerships with the BRIC: Where's the Strategy?', *BEPA Monthly Brief* 29 (September): 6–8.

Risse-Kappen, T. (1995) 'Democratic Peace – Warlike Democracies? A Social Constructivist Interpretation of the Liberal Argument', *European Journal of International Relations* 1(4): 491–517.

Risse-Kappen, T. (1996) 'Collective Identity in a Democratic Community: The Case of NATO', in P. Katzenstein (ed.), *The Culture of National Security: Norms and Identity in World Politics*, New York: Columbia University Press.

Robinson, M. (2010) 'China's New Industrial Revolution', BBC News. Online. Available HTTP: <http://www.bbc.co.uk/news/business–10792465>.

Rogers, J. (2009a) 'From "Civilian Power" to "Global Power": Explicating the European Union's "Grand Strategy" through the Articulation of Discourse Theory', *Journal of Common Market Studies* 47(4): 831–62.

Rogers, J. (2009b) *From Suez to Shanghai: The European Union and Eurasian Maritime Security*, Occasional Paper 77, Paris: European Union Institute for Security Studies.

Rogers, J. (2010) *To Rule the Waves: Why a Maritime Geostrategy Is Needed to Sustain European Union*, Brussels: Egmont.

Rogers, J. (2011) *A New Geography of European Power?*, Brussels: Egmont.

Rogers, J. and Simón, L. (2009) *The Status and Location of the Military Installations of the Member States of the European Union and Their Potential Role for the European Security and Defence Policy*, Brussels: European Parliament.

Rose, G. (1998) 'Neoclassical Realism and Theories of Foreign Policy', *World Politics* 51(1): 144–72.

Rutten, M. (ed.) (2001) *From Saint-Malo to Nice. European Defence: Core Documents*, Chaillot Paper 47, Paris, WEU-ISS. Online. Available HTTP: <http://www.iss.europa.eu/uploads/media/cp047e.pdf>.

Rynning, S. (2003) 'The European Union: Towards a Strategic Culture?', *Security Dialogue* 34(4): 479–96.

Rynning, S. (2007) 'Peripheral or Powerful? The European Union's Strategy to Combat the Proliferation of Nuclear Weapons', *European Security* 16(3/4): 267–88.

Salman, A. and Lakhdar, B. (2008) 'In Pursuit of Sustainable Peace: The Seven Deadly Sins of Mediation', in *Annual Review of Global Peace Operations 2008*, New York: Center on International Cooperation.

Santiso, C. (2002) 'Reforming Foreign Aid: Development Cooperation as an Element of Foreign Policy', *European Foreign Affairs Review* 7(4): 401–22.

Saryusz-Wolski, J. (2011) European Parliament Plenary Session, 11 May. Online. Available HTTP: <http://www.europarl.europa.eu/wps-europarl-internet/frd/vod/player;jsessionid=B9C113608A 5BD25192A1ABBA9E987659?language=en&menusearchfrom=bymep&pageby=unit&idmep=28 297&discussionId=0&page=0&category=0&format=wmv&askedDiscussionNumber=3>.

Sasnal, P. (2009) *The Czech Presidency and the Challenge of Gaza Strip Crisis – Conclusions for Poland*, Warsaw: Polish Institute of International Affairs (PISM). Online. Available HTTP: <http://www.pism.pl/files/?id_plik=2972>.

Sasse, G. (2008) 'The European Neighbourhood Policy: Conditionality Revisited for the EU's Eastern Neighbours', *Europe–Asia Studies* 60(2): 295–316.

Sauer, T. (2011) *The Emerging Powers and the Nuclear Non-Proliferation and Disarmament Regime*, Security Policy Brief 27, Brussels: Egmont.

Sautenet, A. (2007) 'The Current Status and Prospects of the "Strategic Partnership" between the EU and China: Towards the Conclusion of a Partnership and Cooperation Agreement', *European Law Journal* 13(6): 699–731.

Sautenet, A. (2012) 'The EU's Strategic Partnerships with Emerging Powers – Institutional, Legal, Economic and Political Perspectives', in T. Renard and S. Biscop (eds), *The European Union and Emerging Powers: How Europe Can Shape a New World Order*, Aldershot: Ashgate.

Schelling, T. (1966) *Arms and Influence*, New Haven: Yale University Press.

Scheye, E. (2009) *Pragmatic Realism in Justice and Security Development: Supporting Improvement in the Performance of Non-State/Local Justice and Security Networks*, Clingendael Paper, The Hague: The Netherlands Institute of International Relations.

Schimmelfennig, F. and Sedelmeier, U. (2004) 'Governance by Conditionality: EU Rule Transfer to the Candidate Countries of Central and Eastern Europe', *Journal of European Public Policy* 11: 661–79.

Schmidt, G. (2001) 'Getting the Balance Right: NATO and the Evolution of EC/EU Integration, Security and Defence Policy', in G. Schmidt (ed.), *A History of NATO: The First Fifty Years*, vol. 2, Basingstoke: Palgrave Macmillan.

Schmidt, V. (2010) 'Taking Ideas *and* Discourse Seriously: Explaining Change through Discursive Institutionalism as the Fourth New Institutionalism', *European Political Science Review* 2(1): 1–25.

Schmitt, B. (2000) *From Cooperation to Integration: Defence and Aerospace Industries in Europe*, Chaillot Paper 40 (July), Brussels: WEU Institute for Security Studies.

Scott, D. (2008) 'The Great Power "Great Game" between India and China: "The Logic of Geography"', *Geopolitics* 13(1): 1–26.

Searle, J. (1995) *The Construction of Social Reality*, New York: The Free Press.

Sen, A. (2000) 'Why Human Security?', text of presentation at the International Symposium on Human Security, Tokyo, 28 July.

Sergounin, A. (2006) 'Russian Views on the Wider Europe Concept', in F. Tassinari, P. Joenniemi and U. Jakobsen (eds), *Wider Europe: Nordic and Baltic Lessons to Post-Enlargement Europe*, Copenhagen: Danish Institute of International Studies.

Sharp, P. (1998) 'Who Needs Diplomats? The Problem of Diplomatic Representation', in J. Kurbalija (ed.), *Modern Diplomacy*, Gaza: Academic Training Institute. Online. Available: <www.ati. usacademy.info>.

Sharp, P. (2009) *Diplomatic Theory of International Relations*, Cambridge: Cambridge University Press.

Shaw, M. (2005) *The New Western Way of War: Risk-Transfer War and Its Crisis in Iraq*, Cambridge: Polity.

Shearman, D. and Smith, J.W. (2007) *The Climate Change Challenge and the Failure of Democracy*, Westport, CT: Praeger Publishers.

Shepherd, A.J.K. (2009)'"A Milestone in the History of the EU": Kosovo and the EU's International Role', *International Affairs* 85(3): 513–30.

Sheriff, A. (2007) 'Security Sector Reform and EU Norm Implementation', in D.M. Law (ed.), *Intergovernmental Approaches to Security Sector Reform*, Geneva: Democratic Control of the Armed Forces and Lit Verlag.

Sicurelli, D. (2008) 'Framing Security and Development in the EU Pillar Structure: How the Views of the European Commission Affect EU Africa Policy', *European Integration* 30(2): 217–34.

Sil, R. and Katzenstein, P. (2010) *Beyond Paradigms: Analytic Eclecticism in the Study of World Politics*, Basingstoke: Palgrave Macmillan.

Simms, B. (2007) *Three Victories and a Defeat: The Rise and Fall of the First British Empire, 1714–1783*, London: Allen Lane.

Simón, L. (2010) *Command and Control? Planning for EU Military Operations*, Occasional Paper 81, Paris: European Union Institute for Security Studies.

Simón, L. and Rogers, J. (2010) 'The Return of European Geopolitics: All Roads Lead through London', *RUSI Journal* 155(3): 58–64.

SIPRI (2010) 'The SIPRI Top 100 Arms-Producing Companies, 2008'. Online. Available HTTP: <http://www.sipri.org/research/armaments/production/Top100/data/copy2_of_top1002008>.

Sjursen, H. (2005) 'The EU as a Normative Power: How Can This Be?', *Journal of European Public Policy* 6(4): 235–51.

Small, A. (2010) 'Beijing is Worth a Missed Dinner – Lady Ashton Goes to China', *GMF Commentary*, 2 September. Online. Available HTTP: <http://blog.gmfus.org/2010/09/02/beijing-is-worth-a-missed-dinner%e2%80%94lady-ashton-goes-to-china/>.

Smith, K.E. (1998) 'The Use of Political Conditionality in the EU's Relations with Third Countries: How Effective?', *European Foreign Affairs Review* 3(2): 185–203.

Smith, K.E. (1999) *The Making of EU Foreign Policy: The Case of Eastern Europe*, Basingstoke: Macmillan.

Smith, K.E. (2005) 'The Outsiders: The European Neighbourhood Policy', *International Affairs* 81(4): 757–73.

Smith, K.E. (2006) 'The European Union, Human Rights and the United Nations', in K. Verlin Laaitainen and K.E. Smith (eds), *The European Union at the United Nations*, Basingstoke: Palgrave Macmillan.

Smith, K.E. (2010) 'The European Union at the Human Rights Council: Speaking with One Voice but Having Little Influence', *Journal of European Public Policy* 17(2): 224–41.

Smith, M.E. (1998) 'Rules, Transgovernmentalism and the Expansion of European Political Cooperation', in W. Sandholtz and A.S. Sweet (eds), *European Integration and Supranational Governance*, Oxford: Oxford University Press.

Smith, M.H. and Xie, H. (2010) 'The European Union and China: The Logics of "Strategic Partnership"', *Journal of Contemporary European Research* 6(4): 432–48.

Snyder, J. (1977) *The Soviet Strategic Culture: Implications for Limited Nuclear Operations*, R–2154-AF, Santa Monica: RAND Publications.

Solana, J. (1999) Remarks to the Press, 18 October. Online. Available HTTP: <http://www.consilium.europa.eu/uedocs/cms_data/docs/pressdata/EN/discours/04500-R3.EN9.html>.

Solana, J. (2000) 'Reflections on a Year in Office', speech to the Swedish Institute for International Affairs 27 October. Online. Available HTTP: <http://www.consilium.europa.eu/uedocs/cms_data/docs/pressdata/EN/discours/001026%20Stockholm.htm>.

Sopinska, J. (2011) 'Leaders Briefly Discuss Relations with Strategic Partners', *Europolitics*, 28 February. Online. Available HTTP: <http://www.europolitics.info/leaders-briefly-discuss-relations-with-strategic-partners-art290662-46.html>.

Sørensen, G. (2008) 'The Case for Combining Material Forces and Ideas in the Study of IR', *European Journal of International Relations* 14(5): 5–32.

Sperling, J.A. (2009) 'Introduction: Security Governance in a Westphalian World', in C. Wagnsson, J.A. Sperling and J. Hallenberg (eds), *European Security Governance: The European Union in a Westphalian World*, Abingdon: Routledge.

Spykman, N. (1938a) 'Geography and Foreign Policy I', *American Political Science Review* 32(1): 28–50.

Spykman, N. (1938b) 'Geography and Foreign Policy II', *American Political Science Review* 32(2): 213–36.

Spykman, N. (1939a) 'Geographic Objectives in Foreign Policy I', *American Political Science Review* 33(3): 391–410.

Spykman, N. (1939b) 'Geographic Objectives in Foreign Policy II', *American Political Science Review* 33(4): 591–614.

Spykman, N. (1944) *The Geography of the Peace*, New York: Harcourt, Brace and Company.

Spykman, N. (2007 [1942]) *America's Strategy in World Politics: The United States and the Balance of Power*, New Brunswick: Transaction Publishers.

Stahl, B., Boekle, H., Nadoll, J. and Johannesdottir, A. (2004) 'Understanding the Atlanticist–European Divide in the CFSP: Comparing Denmark, France, Germany and the Netherlands', *European Foreign Affairs Review* 9(3): 417–42.

Steele, B.J. (2007) 'Liberal-Idealism: A Constructivist Critique', *International Studies Review* 9(1): 23–52.

Stephens, P. (2010) 'Capital E', *E!Sharp*, September–October. Online. Available HTTP: <http://esharp2.tttp.eu/issue/2011-2/Capital-E>.

Stewart, F. (2004) *Development and Security*, CRISE Working Paper 3, Oxford: University of Oxford Centre for Research on Inequality, Human Security and Ethnicity (CRISE).

Stoddard, A. (2010) 'International Humanitarian Cooperation: Aiding War's Victims in a Shifting Strategic Environment', in B.D. Jones, S. Forman and R. Gowan (eds), *Cooperating for Peace and Security: Evolving Institutions in a Context of Changing U.S. Security Policy*, New York: Cambridge University Press.

Stoddard, A., Harmer, A. and Haver, K. (2006) *Providing Aid in Insecure Environments: Trends in Policy and Operations*, London: Overseas Development Institute and Center on International Cooperation.

Stratfor (2010) *The Geopolitics of France: Maintaining Its Influence in a Changing Europe*, Geopolitical Monographs 14, Austin, TX: Stratfor.

Strobel, W.P. (1996) 'The CNN Effect', *American Journalism Review* May. Online. Available HTTP: <http://www.ajr.org/article.asp?id=3572>.

Strobel, W.P. (1997) *Late-Breaking Foreign Policy: The News Media's Influence on Peace Operations*, Washington, DC: USIP Press.

Sturman, K. and Hayatou, A. (2010) 'The Peace and Security Council of the African Union: From Design to Reality', in U. Engel and J.G. Porto (eds), *Africa's New Peace and Security Architecture: Promoting Norms, Institutionalizing Solutions*, Farnham: Ashgate.

Suganami, H. (2003) 'British Institutionalists, or the English School, 20 Years On', *International Relations* 17(3): 253–71.

Tadjbakhsh, S. and Chenoy, A.M. (2006) *Human Security: Concepts and Implications*, Abingdon: Routledge.

Tannenwald, N. (1999) 'The Nuclear Taboo: The United States and the Normative Basis of Nuclear Non-Use', *International Organization* 53(3): 433–68.

Teuten, R. and Korski, D. (2010) *Preparing for Peace: Britain's Contribution and Capabilities*, RUSI Whitehall Paper 74, London: Royal United Services Institute.

Thales (2010) About Us. Online. Available HTTP: <http://www.thalesgroup.com/AboutUs.aspx>.

Tocci, N. (2008) 'The EU and Conflict Resolution in Turkey and Georgia: Hindering EU Potential through the Political Management of Contractual Relations', *Journal of Common Market Studies* 46(4): 875–97.

Toje, A. (2008a) 'The Consensus–Expectations Gap: Explaining Europe's Ineffective Foreign Policy', *Security Dialogue* 39: 121–41.

Toje, A. (2008b) 'The European Union as a Small Power, or Conceptualising Europe's Strategic Actorness', *Journal of European Integration* 30(2): 199–215

Torbakov, I. (2010) 'The "Southern Vector": Russia's Strategic Interests in Central and South Asia', in R. Dossani, D.C. Sneider and V. Sood (eds), *Does South Asia Exist? Prospects for Regional Integration*, Washington, DC: Brookings Institution Press.

Trauner, F. (2009) 'From Membership Conditionality to Policy Conditionality: EU External Governance in South Eastern Europe', *Journal of European Public Policy* 16: 774–90.

Traynor, I. (2011) 'On the Lady's Service', *E!Sharp*, January–February. Online. Available HTTP: <http://esharp2.tttp.eu/issue/2011-1/On-the-Lady-s-Service>.

Treacher, A. (2004) 'From Civilian Power to Military Actor: The EU's Resistable Transformation?', *European Foreign Affairs Review* 9(1): 49–66.

Trenin, D. (2009) 'Russia's Spheres of *Interest*, not *Influence*', *Washington Quarterly* 32(4): 3–22.

Trybus, M. (2006) 'The New European Defence Agency: A Contribution to the Common European Defence Policy and a Challenge to the Community Acquis?', *Common Market Law Review* 43(3): 667–703.

Tschirgi, N. (2006) 'Security and Development Policies: Untangling the Relationship', in S. Klingebiel (ed.), *New Interfaces between Security and Development: Changing Concepts and Approaches,* Bonn: German Development Institute.

Tschirgi, N., Lund, M.S. and Mancini F. (eds) (2010) *Security and Development: Searching for Critical Connections,* Boulder, CO: Lynne Rienner.

Tsygankov, A.P. (2006) 'If Not by Tanks, then by Banks? The Role of Soft Power in Putin's Foreign Policy', *Europe–Asia Studies* 58(7): 1070–99.

Tywuschik, V. and Sherriff, A. (2009) *Beyond Structures? Reflections on the Implementation of the Joint Africa–EU Strategy*, ECDPM Discussion Paper 87, Maastricht: ECDPM.

Ulriksen, S., Gourlay, C. and Mace, C. (2004) 'Operation Artemis: The Shape of Things to Come?', in G. Bono and S. Ulriksen (eds), *The EU, Crisis Management and Peace Support Operations, International Peacekeeping* 11(3), special issue: 508–25.

Ulusoy, H. (2003) 'Revisiting Security Communities after the Cold War: The Constructivist Perspective', *Perceptions, Journal of International Affairs* 8: 161–96.

United Kingdom (2005) United Kingdom Statement at the IAEA Board of Governors, on behalf of the European Union, Vienna, 9 August 2005. Online. Available HTTP: <http://www.iaea.org/NewsCenter/Focus/IaeaIran/bog092005_statement-eu.pdf>.

United Nations (1945) *Charter of the United Nations*, San Francisco, 26 June.

United Nations (2003) Joint Declaration on UN–EU Co-operation in Crisis Management, New York, 24 September.

United Nations (2009) *A New Partnership Agenda Charting a New Horizon for UN Peacekeeping*, Department of Peacekeeping Operations and Department of Field Support New York, July.

United Nations Development Programme (1994) *Human Development Report 1994. New Dimensions of Human Security*, New York: UNDP.

United Nations Development Programme (2001) *Human Development Report 2001: Making New Technologies Work for Human Development*, New York: Oxford University Press.

United Nations Development Programme (2004) *Human Development Report 2004*, New York: UNDP.

United Nations Development Programme (2005) *Human Development Report 2005*, New York: UNDP.

United Nations Development Programme (2006) *Human Development Report 2006*, New York: UNDP.

United Nations Development Programme (2007) *Human Development Report 2007/2008*, New York: UNDP.

United Nations Security Council (2008) 'Report of the Secretary-General on the United Nations Interim Administration Mission in Kosovo', New York, June.

United States Government Accounting Office (2007) 'Iran Sanctions: Impact in Furthering US Objectives is Unclear and Should be Reviewed', Report to the Ranking Member, Subcommittee on National Security and Foreign Affairs, House Committee on Oversight and Government Reform, December.

United States Strategy for Homeland Security (2002) Washington, DC: The White House.

Upadhyay, B. (2010) 'Will India's Highway Project be a Path to Growth?', BBC News. Online. Available HTTP: <http://news.bbc.co.uk/1/hi/business/8635419.stm>.

Uz Zaman, R. (2009) 'Strategic Culture: A "Cultural" Understanding of War', *Comparative Strategy* 28(1): 68–88.

Vahl, M. (2001) *Just Good Friends? The EU–Russian 'Strategic Partnership' and the Northern Dimension*, CEPS Working Documents 166, Brussels: Centre for European Policy Studies.

Vahl, M. (2005) 'Lessons from the North for the EU's "Near Abroad"', in Christopher S. Browning (ed.), *Remaking Europe in the Margins: Northern Europe after the Enlargements*, Aldershot: Ashgate.

Vaïsse, M., Mélandri, P. and Bozo, F. (eds) (1996) *La France et l'OTAN 1949–1996*, Brussels: Complexe.

Vaïsse, J. and Kundnani, H. (eds) (2011) *European Foreign Policy Scorecard 2010*, London: European Council on Foreign Relations.

Van Munster, R. (2004) 'The War on Terrorism: When the Exception Becomes the Rule', *International Journal for the Semiotics of Law* 17(2): 141–53.

Van Munster, R. (2007) 'Review Essay. Security on a Shoestring: A Hitchhiker's Guide to Critical Schools of Security in Europe', *Cooperation and Conflict* 42(2): 235–43.

Van Munster, R. (2009) *Securitizing Immigration: The Politics of Risk in the EU*, Basingstoke: Palgrave Macmillan.

Van Rompuy, H. (2010a) 'Statement on Behalf of the European Union at the Nuclear Security Summit in Washington', Washington, DC, 12 April.

Van Rompuy, H. (2010b) 'We Have Strategic Partnerships, Now We Need a Strategy', video message from Herman Van Rompuy, 14 September. Online. Available HTTP: <http://vloghvr.consilium. europa.eu/?p=2377>.

Vaquer, J. (2010) *Focusing Back on European Security Again: The Medvedev Proposal as an Opportunity*, CIDOB Documents 6 (July), Barcelona: CIDOB.

Vasquez, J. (1998) *The Power of Power Politics: From Classical Realism to Neorealism*, Cambridge: Cambridge University Press.

Venusberg Group (2007) *Beyond 2010: European Grand Strategy in a Global Age*, Gütersloh: Bertelsmann Stiftung.

Vircoulon, T. (2009) 'EUPOL Kinshasa and EUPOL RD Congo', in G. Grevi, D. Helly and D. Keohane (eds), *European Security and Defence Policy: The First Ten Years (1999–2009)*, Paris: European Union Institute for Security Studies.

Wagner, C. (2008) 'The EU and India: A Deepening Partnership', in G. Grevi and A. De Vasconcelos (eds), *Partnerships for Effective Multilateralism: EU Relations with Brazil, China, India and Russia*, Chaillot Paper 109, Paris: European Union Institute for Security Studies.

Wagner, W. (2003) 'Why the EU's Common Foreign and Security Policy Will Remain Intergovernmental: A Rational Choice Analysis of European Crisis Management Policy', *Journal of European Public Policy* 10(4): 576–95.

Walker, P.F. (2007) 'Looking Back: Kananaskis at Five. Assessing the Global Partnership', *Arms Control Today*, September. Online. Available HTTP: <http://www.armscontrol.org/oct/2007_9/ Lookingback>.

Wallace, H. *et al.* (1999) 'Review Section Symposium: The Choice for Europe: Social Purpose and State Power from Messina to Maastricht', *Journal of European Public Policy* 6(1): 155–79.

Wallander, C. (2000) 'Institutional Assets and Adaptability, NATO after the Cold War', *International Organization* 54(4): 705–35.

Walraven, K. van (2010) 'Heritage and Transformation: From the Organization of African Unity to the African Union', in U. Engel and J.G. Porto (eds), *Africa's New Peace and Security Architecture: Promoting Norms, Institutionalizing Solutions*, Farnham: Ashgate.

Waltz, K. (1959) *Man, the State and War: A Theoretical Analysis*, New York: Columbia University Press.

Waltz, K. (1979) *Theory of International Politics*, New York: McGraw-Hill.

Waltz, K. (1986) 'Reflections on *Theory of International Politics*: A Response to My Critics', in R. Keohane (ed.), *Realism and Its Critics*, New York: Columbia University Press.

Waltz, K. (1995) 'Realist Thought and Neorealist Theory', in Charles Kegley (ed.), *Controversies in International Relations Theory. Realism and the Neoliberal Challenge*, New York: St. Martin's Press.

Waltz, K. (2000) 'Structural Realism after the Cold War', *International Security* 25(1): 5–41.

WEAG (2005a) Western European Armaments Group. History and Objectives. Online. Available HTTP: <http://www.weu.int/weag/index.html>.

WEAG (2005b) Western European Armaments Group. European Armaments Agency. Online. Available HTTP: <http://www.weu.int/weag/index.html>.

WEAO (2006) Western European Armaments Organisation. Our Mission. Online. Available HTTP: <http://www.weao.weu.int/site/frameset.htm>.

Webber, M. (2007) *Inclusion, Exclusion and the Governance of European Security*, Manchester: Manchester University Press.

Webber, M., Croft, S., Howorth, J., Terriff, T. and Krahmann, E. (2004) 'The Governance of European Security', *Review of International Studies* 30: 3–26.

Wendt, A. (1992) 'Anarchy is What States Make of It: The Social Construction of Power Politics', *International Organization* 46(2): 391–425.

Wendt, A. (1999) *Social Theory of International Politics*, Cambridge: Cambridge University Press.

Werthes, S. and Debiel, T. (eds) (2006) *Human Security on Foreign Policy Agendas: Changes, Concepts and Cases*, Duisburg: Institute for Development and Peace, University of Duisburg-Essen.

Werts, J. (2008) *The European Council*, London: Harper.

Western European Union (1988) *The Reactivation of WEU: Statements and Communiqués, 1984–1987*, Brussels: WEU.

Westerwelle, G. (2011) 'Europe Asserts Itself in a Globalized World', speech to the Munich Security Conference, 4 February. Online. Available HTTP: <http://www.auswaertiges-amt.de/EN/Infoservice/Presse/Interview/2011/110204_BM_SiKo.html>.

Wheeler, N. (2007) 'The Kosovo Bombing Campaign', in C. Reus-Smith (ed.), *The Politics of International Law*, Cambridge: Cambridge University Press.

White, B. (2004) 'Foreign Policy Analysis and the New Europe', in W. Carlsnaes, H. Sjursen and B. White (eds), *Contemporary European Foreign Policy*, London: Sage.

Whitehead, L. (2009) 'Losing "the Force"? The "Dark Side" of Democratization after Iraq', *Democratization* 16(2): 215–42.

Whitman, R.G. (1998) *From Civilian Power to Superpower? The International Identity of the EU*, Basingstoke: Macmillan.

Whitman, R.G. (2006) 'Road Map for a Route March? (De-)civilianizing through the EU's Security Strategy', *European Foreign Affairs Review* 11: 1–15.

Whitman, R.G. and Juncos, A. (2009) 'The Lisbon Treaty and the Foreign, Security and Defence Policy: Reforms, Implementation and Consequences of (non-)Ratification', *European Foreign Affairs Review* 14: 25–46.

Whitman, R.G. and Manners, I. (1998) 'Towards Identifying the International Identity of the European Union: A Framework for the Analysis of the EU's Network of Relationships', *Journal of European Integration* 21: 231–49.

Whitman, R.G. and Wolff, S. (2010) 'The EU as a Conflict Manager? The Case of Georgia and Its Implications', *International Affairs* 86(1): 87–107.

Wiktorowicz, Q. (2005) *Radical Islam Rising: Muslim Extremism in the West*, London: Rowman & Littlefield.

Wilkins, T.S. (2008) 'Russo-Chinese Strategic Partnership: A New Form of Security Cooperation?', *Contemporary Security Policy* 29(2): 358–83.

Willett, L. (2008) *British Defence and Security Policy: The Maritime Contribution*, RUSI Occasional Paper, London: Royal United Services Institute.

Williams, M.J. (2008) *NATO, Security and Risk Management: From Kosovo to Kandahar*, Abingdon: Routledge.

Williams, M.J. and Neumann, I.B. (2000) 'From Alliance to Security Community: NATO, Russia and the Power of Identity', *Millennium: Journal of International Studies* 29(2): 357–87.

Williams, P. (2004) 'Critical Security Studies', in A.J. Bellamy (ed.), *International Society and Its Critics*, Oxford: Oxford University Press.

Wilson, A. (2010) 'Eastern Europe's Balancing Act', *Current History* October: 295–300.

Wilson, D. and Purushothaman, R. (2003) *Dreaming with BRICs: The Path to 2050*, Global Economics Paper 99, New York: Goldman Sachs.

Witney, N. (2008) *Re-energising Europe's Security and Defence Policy*, European Council on Foreign Relations, 29 July. Online. Available: <www.ecfr.eu/content/entry/european_security_and_defence_policy>.

Wolfers, A. (1962) *Discord and Collaboration: Essays in International Politics*, Baltimore: Johns Hopkins University Press.

Woods, N. (2005) 'The Shifting Politics of Foreign Aid', *International Affairs* 81(2): 393–409.

Woodward, S. (2008) 'The Security Council and the Wars in the Former Yugoslavia', in V. Lowe, A. Roberts, J. Welsh and D. Zaum (eds), *The United Nations Security Council and War*, Oxford: Oxford University Press.

World Bank. (2011) *World Development Report 2011: Conflict, Security and Development*, Washington, DC: World Bank.

Wouters, J. (2007) *The United Nations and the European Union: Partners in Multilateralism*, Working Paper 1, Leuven: Leuven Centre for Global Governance Studies.

Wright, J. (2006) 'The Importance of Europe in the Global Campaign against Terrorism', *Terrorism and Political Violence* 18: 281–99.

Wyn Jones, R. (2005) 'On Emancipation: Necessity, Capacity, and Concrete Utopias', in K. Booth (ed.), *Critical Security Studies and World Politics*, Boulder, CO: Lynne Rienner.

Xu, Q. (2006 [2004]) 'Maritime Geostrategy and the Development of the Chinese Navy in the Early Twenty-First Century', *Naval War College Review* 59(4): 47–67.

Young, J.W. (1984) *Britain, France and the Unity of Europe*, Leicester: Leicester University Press.

Youngs, R. (2007) *Europe's External Energy Policy: Between Geopolitics and the Market*, CEPS Working Document 278 (November), Brussels: Centre for European Policy Studies.

Youngs, R. (2008) 'Fusing Security and Development: Just Another Euro-Platitude', *Journal of European Integration* 30(3): 419–37.

Youngs, R. (2009) *Energy Security: Europe's New Foreign Policy Challenge*, Abingdon: Routledge.

Youngs, R. (2010) *Europe's Decline and Fall: The Struggle against Global Irrelevance*, London: Profile Books.

Zagorski, A. (2009) 'The Limits of a Global Consensus on Security: The Case of Russia', in L. Peral (ed.), *Global Security in a Multipolar World*, Chaillot Paper 118 (October), Paris: European Union Institute for Security Studies.

Zandee, D. (2011) 'European Capability Development: A Must!', *Studia Diplomatica* 64(1): 61–70.

INDEX

Printed in Great Britain
by Amazon